GROUP BEHAVIOUR AND DEVELOPMENT

QUEEN ELIZABETH HOUSE, INTERNATIONAL DEVELOPMENT CENTRE, UNIVERSITY OF OXFORD (QEH)

is the Centre for Development Studies in Oxford University, encompassing anthropology, economics, history, law, politics, and sociology. It is also the focus of a worldwide network of scholars and practitioners in developing countries, many of whom come to QEH as academic visitors. QEH comprises a core of established academic staff, junior researchers, and about a hundred graduate students.

Development Studies is an interdisciplinary and multidisciplinary enquiry into change and transformation. We seek to challenge narrow theoretical and policy approaches derived from a single model of development. Our aim is to encourage innovative and critical approaches to research and development, always maintaining rigorous standards.

UNU WORLD INSTITUTE FOR DEVELOPMENT ECONOMICS RESEARCH (UNU/WIDER)

was established by the United Nations University as its first research and training centre and started work in Helsinki, Finland in 1985. The purpose of the Institute is to undertake applied research and policy analysis on structural changes affecting the developing and transitional economies, to provide a forum for the advocacy of policies leading to robust, equitable, and environmentally sustainable growth, and to promote capacity strengthening and training in the field of economic and social policy-making. Its work is carried out by staff researchers and visiting scholars in Helsinki and through networks of collaborating scholars and institutions around the world.

Group Behaviour and Development

Is the Market Destroying Cooperation?

Edited by

JUDITH HEYER, FRANCES STEWART,
AND ROSEMARY THORP

A study prepared for Queen Elizabeth House, International Development Centre, University of Oxford (QEH) and the World Institute for Development Economics Research of the United Nations University (UNU/WIDER)

OXFORD
UNIVERSITY PRESS

OXFORD
UNIVERSITY PRESS

Great Clarendon Street, Oxford OX2 6DP

Oxford University Press is a department of the University of Oxford.
It furthers the University's objective of excellence in research, scholarship,
and education by publishing worldwide in

Oxford New York

Auckland Bangkok Buenos Aires Cape Town Chennai
Dar es Salaam Delhi Hong Kong Istanbul Karachi Kolkata
Kuala Lumpur Madrid Melbourne Mexico City Mumbai Nairobi
São Paulo Shanghai Taipei Tokyo Toronto

Oxford is a registered trade mark of Oxford University Press
in the UK and in certain other countries

Published in the United States
by Oxford University Press Inc., New York

World Institute for Development Economics Research
of the United Nations University (UNU/WIDER)
Katajanokanlaituri 6B, 00160 Helsinki, Finland

The moral rights of the authors have been asserted
Database right Oxford University Press (maker)

First published 2002

British Library Cataloguing in Publication Data

Data available

Library of Congress Cataloging in Publication Data

Group behaviour and development: is the market destroying cooperation?/edited by
Judith Heyer, Frances Stewart, and Rosemary Thorp

p. cm. – (Queen Elizabeth House series in development studies)

"A study prepared for Queen Elizabeth House, International Development Centre,
University of Oxford (QEH) and the World Institute for Development Economics Research
of the United Nations University (UNU/WIDER)."

Includes Index.

1. Organizational behaviour. 2. Organizational behaviour—Developing countries. 3. Associations,
institutions, etc. 4. Associations, institutions, etc.—Developing countries. 5. Economic development.
6. Developing countries—Economic conditions.

I. Heyer, Judith. II. Stewart, Frances, 1940 III. Thorp, Rosemary. IV. Series.

HD58.7 G76 2002   302.3'5–dc21   2002066228

ISBN 0-19-925691-8 (hbk.)
ISBN 0-19-925692-6 (pbk.)

1 3 5 7 9 10 8 6 4 2

Typeset by Newgen Imaging Systems (P) Ltd., Chennai, India
Printed in Great Britain
on acid-free paper by
Biddles Ltd., Guildford and King's Lynn

Foreword

Institutions, such as firms, families, contracts, rules, regulations, values and social norms, are fundamental for economic development. They influence both the level and the distribution of economic growth, which, in itself, can and frequently does trigger institutional change. Institutions can neither be ignored, nor taken as a given, as in much of standard modern economics with its assumptions of individualistic behaviour of rational economic man.

While dominant, the 'rational economic man' approach leaves much unexplained in terms of economic growth, income distribution and success in overcoming the problems of externalities as well as in individual behaviours. Differences in growth rates are usually explained on the basis of variations in inputs of labour, capital and technology, but values and social norms that influence economic behaviour and economic performance are extremely important. Moreover, the dominant approach cannot explain many group activities, including cooperative production and NGO activities, or how social norms and individual motivations evolve. An understanding of the ways in which these motivations and institutions evolve is essential to understand how developing countries can break out of poverty.

Thus, it is crucial to understand how different types of motivations develop, especially with reference to key areas such as good governance, the behaviour of firms, solutions to the problems of the commons, rural development and so on, and how they may be reinforced by policy action. The focus on group behaviour is therefore an exciting and important area in the study of development. Yet the analysis of group functioning has not received enough attention, particularly among economists.

This book co-edited by Judith Heyer, Frances Stewart, and Rosemary Thorp, which explores group behaviour analytically, and through eleven case studies drawn from all over the world, makes an important contribution to our understanding in this area. It focuses on group behaviour in developing countries and it includes studies of producer and community organizations, NGOs and some public sector groups.

The book argues that cooperative within-group behaviour is essential for efficiency as well as equity. Yet this is being undermined by the current dominance of a market model of development. Thinkers and policymakers need to learn from this, and to provide systematic support for cooperative modes of behaviour.

This book also explores why some groups function well in terms of equity, efficiency and wellbeing, while others do not. It covers groups that perform three types of function: overcoming market failures (e.g. producer organizations); improving the position of their members (e.g. trade unions), and distributing resources to the less well-off (e.g. NGOs and the public sector). It contrasts three modes of group behaviour: power and control; co-operation; and the use of material incentives. It explores what determines modes of behaviour of groups, and the consequences for efficiency, equity and wellbeing.

The book's eleven case studies include producers' associations in Brazil, farmers' organizations in Korea and Taiwan, community forestry groups in South Asia, organizations of sex-workers in Calcutta, and health NGOs in Uganda. Claims groups tended to be the most cooperative, cooperation fostering empowerment and self-esteem. Distributive or *pro bono* groups mostly operated according to power and control, while market failure groups often combined all three modes.

The studies show the strong impact of norms in society as a whole on group behaviour. The recent shift towards a stronger role for market incentives has exerted powerful pressures on groups to use more material incentives, undermining the cooperation essential to sustain efficiency and equity. The universal presumption in favour of monetary incentives needs to be abandoned. Non-market behaviour needs to be valued and protected as well.

In reflecting upon the worldwide change in paradigm that we are witnessing today—towards emphasis on the market and individual incentives and away from Keynesian policies and a strong role for the state in economic activities—this book provides an invaluable reminder of the importance of cooperative action in groups for efficient as well as equitable solutions. I strongly commend this book to the academic community with an interest in development economics. The volume would also be of enormous value to practitioners, whether official policymakers or NGOs and to observers, whether individuals or institutions, concerned with the way economies are run.

Giovanni Andrea Cornia
University of Florence, and
former director of WIDER

Preface

This publication is the outcome of a WIDER project on Institutions and Development. The project was mainly supported by a generous financial contribution from the Royal Ministry of Foreign Affairs, Denmark. The government of Sweden (Swedish International Development Cooperation Agency – Sida) also made a contribution. WIDER gratefully acknowledges the cooperation and support it receives from the development cooperation agencies of the Nordic countries.

The authors would like to thank the World Institute for Development Economics Research (WIDER) for supporting this project, and in particular, the then Director, Andrea Cornia, for his enthusiastic interest and help. We have also received very useful ideas and comments both at seminars specifically on the project (in Oxford and Helsinki) and in other venues where some of the ideas have been discussed. We are particularly grateful to Herb Gintis, Gillian Hart, and Judith Tendler for their stimulating and useful comments on the project. Abigail Barr, Paolo De Renzio, Tom Hewitt, Alejandro Ramirez, Sam Wangwe, and David Wield all generously shared their work with us and made very useful contributions at an earlier stage of the project. The administrative personnel in WIDER, especially Lorraine Telfer-Taivainen and Barbara Fagerman, have been unfailingly helpful; and, as always, we have received outstanding support from the staff at Queen Elizabeth House, especially from Denise Watt and Wendy Grist who have sorted out any problems with their usual commitment and friendliness. We also thank Michael Wang for editorial assistance.

Judith Heyer, Frances Stewart, and Rosemary Thorp
January 2002

Contents

Notes on Contributors

BINA AGARWAL is Professor of Economics at the Institute of Economic Growth, University of Delhi. She has written extensively on the political economy of gender; environment and development; poverty and inequality; property rights, land and livelihood; and agriculture, technology and rural transformation. Her last book was *A Field of One's Own: Gender and Land Rights in South Asia*, winner of the Edgar Graham Book Prize (UK), the A.K. Coomaraswamy Book Prize (USA) and the K.H. Bhateja Award (India). She has held distinguished positions at Harvard, Princeton, Columbia, and Sussex. She is also on the Executive Committee of the *International Economic Association*; on the Board of the *Global Development Network* (Washington DC); has been on the expert committees of international organizations, NGOs, and the Indian Planning Commission; has served on the editorial advisory boards *of World Development; International Labour Review; Oxford Development Studies*, and others; and is Associate Editor for *Feminist Economics* and *Signs*.

SABINA ALKIRE is a senior research fellow at the Von Hugel Institute at the University of Cambridge, and is currently the Research Writer for the Commission on Human Security chaired by Sadako Ogata and Amartya Sen. She did a DPhil in economics at Queen Elizabeth House, University of Oxford. Her book *Valuing Freedoms: Sen's Capability Approach and Poverty Reduction* is published by OUP. She coordinated the Dutch-funded Culture and Poverty learning and research program at the World Bank.

TITO BIANCHI is a doctoral candidate in the Department of Urban Studies and Planning at MIT. His research and publications analyse the conditions under which organizations of small-scale producers prove sustainable and promote the economic development of depressed areas. His dissertation compares the Italian agrarian reform of the 1950s with international experience of redistributive rural development programmes in the 1960s and 1970s.

LARRY L. BURMEISTER is Associate Professor of Sociology at the University of Kentucky, USA. His published work on South Korean and East Asian agricultural and rural development issues has appeared in a number of journals, including *World Development, Economic Development and Cultural Change, Asian Survey, Development and Change*, and *The Journal of Developing Areas*. He is presently doing research on local responses to the globalization of the agri-food system in the US and on the emergence of land leasing and custom farming institutions in East Asian production agriculture.

CHRISTY CANNON LORGEN completed her DPhil at Nuffield College, Oxford, in 1998. Her research, on which her chapter in this book is based, concerned the relationships between NGOs, donors, and the government in Uganda's health sector. Since 1999, she has been working for Kroll Associates, a risk mitigation consulting firm. As a director in Kroll's Africa Practice, she has managed projects for both governments and private sector clients in several African countries.

SÉVERINE DENEULIN is a doctoral student at Queen Elizabeth House and St Antony's College, University of Oxford. Her research interests lie in the intersections of political philosophy and economics. She is currently working on the assessment and implementation of development policies according to Sen's capability approach.

FREDERIC GASPART is a member of the Groupe de Recherche en Economie du Bien-Etre (GREBE) and of the Centre de Recherche en Economie du Developpement (CRED) at the University of Namur. In 1994, he wrote a PhD dissertation on social choice theory. His research interests include the axiomatic approach to resource allocation problems (e.g. fairness and implementation), game theory applied to market-related institutions, and the empirical analysis of collective action.

LUCY GILSON is a health economist. She holds a joint position as Associate Professor in the Centre for Health Policy, University of Witwatersrand, South Africa and Senior Lecturer in the Health Policy Unit of the London School of Hygiene and Tropical Medicine, UK. Her research interests include health care financing, user fee systems and exemption mechanisms, health system organization and the promotion of equity through health systems. She is specifically interested in understanding the formal and informal institutions embedded within health systems, and how they affect health system performance. She has worked extensively in Southern and Eastern Africa, and in her current position in South Africa she is involved in research, policy analysis, and capacity development activities.

NANDINI GOOPTU is University Lecturer in South Asian Studies and Fellow of St Antony's College, Oxford. She is a faculty member of Queen Elizabeth House, International Development Centre, Oxford. She is the author of *The Politics of the Urban Poor in Early Twentieth-Century India* (CUP 2001). Her research interests include the comparative history and politics of poverty, labour and class relations, urban social history, ethnic and sectarian conflicts, religious and nationalist movements.

JUDITH HEYER is University Lecturer in Economics and Fellow and Tutor in Economics at Somerville College, Oxford. She is also a Senior Research Associate at Queen Elizabeth House. Prior to coming to Oxford in 1975, she was a member of the Economics Department at the University of Nairobi. She has written on agricultural and rural development in Kenya, and on different aspects of rural development in South India. Her current interests include environmental and institutional aspects of rural development in sub-Saharan Africa, and the economic impact of caste and class in rural South India.

MAUREEN MACKINTOSH is Professor of Economics at the Open University, UK. She is currently working on reform and regulation in health care, including joint research with Paula Tibandebage on the Tanzanian health care system. She is also coordinator of an UNRISD project on globalization, privatization, and welfare. She has a longstanding research interest in the economics of non-market relationships in market-dominated social sectors. Recent publications include *Economic Decentralisation and Public Management Reform*, edited with Rathin Roy (Edward Elgar, 1999).

SIMEEN MAHMUD studied Statistics at the Dhaka University and Medical Demography at the London School of Hygiene and Tropical Medicine. She joined the Bangladesh Institute of Development Studies after completing her Masters and is currently Senior Research Fellow in the Population Studies Division. She was a MacArthur Fellow at the Harvard Centre for Population and Development in 1993. Her past research has been on demographic estimation, the relationship between women's work, status and fertility, and demographic transition under poverty. Currently, she is working on empowerment and development, citizenship and collective action, and social policy and exclusion.

JEAN-PHILIPPE PLATTEAU is Professor of Economics at the University of Namur (Belgium). His scientific works encompass a wide array of topics dealing with rural institutions, markets, and determinants of collective action. Recent books are *Institutions, Social Norms, and Economic Development* (Routledge, 2000), and *Halting Degradation of Natural Resources—Is There a Role for Rural Communities?*, co-authored with Jean-Marie Baland (Clarendon Press, 1996). He has also written numerous articles in international academic journals.

GUSTAV RANIS is the Frank Altschul Professor of International Economics at Yale University and the Henry R. Luce Director of the Yale Center for International and Area Studies. He was Assistant Administrator for Program and Policy for the Agency for International Development/Department of State, 1965–67, Director of the Economic Growth Center at Yale, 1967–75, and Director of the Pakistan Institute of Development Economics, 1958–61. He received an Honorary Degree from Brandeis University in 1982. His publications include more than 20 books and 200 articles in professional journals. His main research interest concerns models of the dual economy and the transition to modern economic growth.

J. MOHAN RAO is Professor of Economics at the University of Massachusetts, Amherst. He was educated at Bombay, Ahmedabad, and Harvard, and has previously taught at Harvard, Boston, and Rome Universities. His current research interests include the political economy of the state and the impact of globalization on development, inequality, and poverty. His work combines theoretical, empirical, and historical analyses. He has published widely on structuralist macroeconomics, agriculture–industry interactions, microeconomics of agrarian institutions, and government interventions in agriculture. He has also made numerous contributions on the Indian economy, both historical and contemporary.

DAVID SNEATH is Director of the Mongolia and Inner Asia Studies Unit, Lecturer in the Department of Social Anthropology, and Fellow at Corpus Christi College, Cambridge. Most of his research has concerned Inner Asian pastoralism, particularly in Mongolia and Inner Mongolia. His most recent books are *Changing Inner Mongolia: Pastoral*

Mongolian Society and the Chinese State (OUP 2000), and *The End of Nomadism? Society, State and the Environment in Inner Asia*, with C. Humphrey (Duke University Press, 1999). Current research interests include pastoralism, land-use and the environment, decollectivization and post-socialist social transformations, political culture and economic institutions in Inner Asia, and the anthropology of development. He is co-editor of the journal *Inner Asia*.

FRANCES STEWART is Professor of Development Economics, and Director of the International Development Centre, Queen Elizabeth House, University of Oxford. She has written widely on development issues. Her books include *Technology and Underdevelopment* (Macmillan 1977), *Adjustment with a Human Face*, with G. A. Cornia and R. Jolly (OUP 1987); and *War and Underdevelopment*, with Valpy FitzGerald and Associates (OUP 2001). Her current research interests include global influences on conflict; and analysing horizontal inequalities in developing countries.

ROSEMARY THORP is University Reader in the Economics of Latin America and Fellow of St. Antony's College, Oxford. She is a member of Queen Elizabeth House and for 2001–02 its Acting Director. She is also a member of the Latin American Centre and has been its Director for two periods. She is the Chair of Oxfam's Board of Trustees. Recent books include *Progress, Poverty and Exclusion: An Economic History of Latin America in the Twentieth Century, Decentralising Development* (with Alan Angell and Pam Lowden), and a three-volume edited series, *An Economic History of Twentieth Century Latin America* (with Enrique Cardenas and José Antonio Ocampo).

PAULA TIBANDEBAGE is a former Senior Research Fellow at the Economic and Social Research Foundation, a not-for-profit, non-government policy research institute in Tanzania. She currently works as a research associate for the Foundation. She is a political economist specializing in social policy issues. Her most recent research work has been in the areas of managing and regulating health care in a liberalized environment and on the employment situation and job security in enterprises. She is co-author of 'Inclusion by Design? Rethinking health care market regulation in the Tanzanian context' (forthcoming) in the *Journal of Development Studies*.

MICHAEL WANG is a former researcher at Queen Elizabeth House, University of Oxford, and the Economic Growth Centre at Yale University. His research interests include the economic and social costs of conflict, and the distributional impact of trade liberalization. He has degrees from Yale, Cambridge, and Oxford Universities.

List of Figures

The publisher has made every effort to contact copyright-holders for permission to use previously published material, and will be happy to rectify any omissions in future printings of this book.

List of Tables

1

Group Behaviour and Development

JUDITH HEYER, J. MOHAN RAO, FRANCES STEWART,
AND ROSEMARY THORP

1.1. INTRODUCTION

Most economic decisions are taken by people acting within, and very often on behalf of, groups. As consumers, individuals are members of families; as producers, they operate within firms. Moreover, there are a variety of less formal groups, such as neighbourhood or community associations and networks of producers, which play an important role in influencing behaviour and outcomes. Yet much of economics puts individuals at the centre of analysis. In the basic neoclassical framework individual consumers are assumed to maximize their own utility, while firms—which are treated as cohesive units, that is, as quasi-individuals—are assumed to maximize profits. Inter-action between the two is deemed to underlie resource allocation, and, in certain rather restrictive conditions, result in a welfare optimum. Even governments are mostly treated as if each were an individual with unitary objectives. Important departures from the utilitarian approach led by Sen, arguing that development consists of the expansion of capabilities or freedoms, continue to take an individualistic stance—the objective in question being expansion of *individual* capabilities or freedoms (Sen 1999).

This study focuses explicitly on group behaviour in the context of development. There is abundant, if casual, evidence that some groups function well, from the per-spective of equity, efficiency, and well-being, while others function poorly according to one or more of these criteria. This book explores why this is so. In other words we are primarily concerned with analysing the determinants of *group* capabilities. In this chapter we present a framework for analysing group behaviour. To develop the framework we draw on the case studies which form the body of the book.[1] In the con-cluding chapter we review in detail the way in which the case studies give substance to our argument. The aim is to identify major factors influencing group behaviour, in order to improve our understanding of group functioning, with a particular focus on the effects on equity and well-being. The pervasiveness of groups and their effects constitute the crucial reason for being concerned with their functioning. Overarching changes in policy regimes must, then, be evaluated not just in terms of conventional

---

[1] References without dates indicate chapters in this book.

criteria but also in terms of their consequences, perhaps subtle, for the existence and functioning of various types of groups. It is particularly important to understand the mechanisms that determine group behaviour when there are major paradigm changes, as currently with the shift to market liberalism. Our project aims to elucidate some of these mechanisms, so as to help predict some of the consequences of the paradigm shifts and identify means of influencing their effects.

Economic interactions involving groups can be divided into within-group and between-group activities, where groups encompass organizations (formal or informal) in which individuals come together to undertake joint activities. Groups include firms (large and small), governments (central and local), community and voluntary organizations, and families. Some groups operate in the context of market production and exchange (firms, cartels, producer associations, unions, informal interest groups within firms, etc.); other groups operate largely outside markets (families, NGOs); and some are, in a sense, above markets (states).

In quantitative terms, within-group transactions certainly exceed between-group transactions. Within-group behaviour is therefore of enormous importance in determining the equity and efficiency of resource allocation. Not only does it affect efficiency and resource distribution within the group, but it also influences the nature of group interactions with others. Between-group relationships are generally arm's length, but they can be mediated by groups which evolve to facilitate such interactions, for example, networks, alliances of firms, etc. Hence, it is not always possible to draw a clear dividing line between within-group and between-group activities.

Group behaviour is influenced both by the external environment in which the group operates and by internal modes of operation, with interactions between the two. We examine how these two sets of influences affect group behaviour, through theoretical analysis and empirical case studies. In the empirical part of this book, our aim is to cover groups which are particularly relevant to improving the well-being of the poor and less privileged. For this reason, and also to put limits on a potentially vast field of enquiry, we focus on producer and community organizations.[2] Two types of causality are explored: how society influences group behaviour, and how the mode of operation of groups influences outcomes. The outcomes on which we focus here are the efficiency of group operations; equity within the group and outside it; and general well-being within and outside the group.

The study draws on two alternative theoretical perspectives on the study of groups. One is firmly in the tradition of economists, focusing on individual maximizing behaviour to explain behaviour within groups. As we shall see, a range of assumptions about motivation and behaviour has been explored within this tradition, from short-term maximization of self-interested individuals whose preferences are exogenously determined, to more long-term, altruistic or community focused behaviour with preferences heavily influenced by the social and economic context. The second theoretical perspective gives a more central role to the group and social influences, and sees

---

[2] One reason for this choice is the fact that there already exists a large literature on large firms and on families, categories which we have chosen to exclude.

individual behaviour less as a building block and more as an outcome of these influences. In this approach the group is perceived as being more than the sum of individual actions, with an independent existence, though of course this existence is constructed from individual actions. This perspective is in the tradition of sociological enquiry. At their extremes, the two approaches produce very different results, but when the first approach assumes that preferences are socially embedded, and when individual agency is recognized as a central feature of group behaviour in the second approach, the conclusions of the two perspectives become very similar. Below we attempt to use both to understand the connections between individuals, groups, and norms. The individual case studies adopt different theoretical perspectives, some much more in the economists' maximizing tradition; and others with more focus on collective identities, putting less emphasis on individual agency and on exchange.

The rest of this chapter outlines the framework of analysis used in this study. The discussion is organized as follows. Section 1.2 puts more flesh on the way in which the concept of groups is used here, illuminating their diversity and drawing on the case studies; section 1.3 provides a classification of alternative modes of operation of groups to be adopted in the study; section 1.4 contrasts the different approaches to the analysis of groups, noted above, with the aim of drawing on both to encompass the major influences on group behaviour; section 1.5 concludes by pointing to the important questions raised, on which the case studies that follow will help shed light.

1.2. GROUPS AND GROUP FUNCTIONS

Groups are defined in this study as collections of individuals who come together to undertake joint activities. They evolve historically, being formed sometimes for social reasons, sometimes to fight common causes, sometimes to produce (or consume) goods collectively.[3] Many groups have primarily non-economic functions, for example, sports clubs, religious organizations. The focus in this study is on groups with economic functions, defining 'economic' to include both production of goods and services (marketed and non-marketed), and activities directed at securing control over resources. It must be noted, however, that the distinction between groups with economic and non-economic functions is not clear cut. Not only can most group functions (including social ones) be counted as producing some economic 'output', but also many groups which come together for non-economic reasons acquire economic functions (Gooptu's study in this volume of the association of sex workers in Calcutta provides an example). Economic groups often spawn 'non-economic' activities too.

In the modern economy intra-group activities greatly exceed inter-group. Intra-firm transactions of multinational corporations account for as much as a quarter of manufacturing trade,[4] while many major corporations have alliances with others, substantially extending the sphere of influence of the group as a whole; the public sector often accounts for a third or more of national income; and within-family activities perhaps

---

[3] See Granovetter in Etzioni and Lawrence (1991) *et al*. Also Gooptu, Mahmud, Bianchi, and others in this volume.   [4] United Nations 1992.

the equivalent of over half measured national income.[5] Intra-group activities account for the major proportion of economic activity even in the more market-oriented economies. In such successful 'market economies' as Japan and Korea, companies grouped into *zaibatsu* (pre-Second World War Japan) and *keiretsu* (post-Second World War Japan) or *chaebol* (Korea) account for the dominant portion of industrial production. Elsewhere (e.g. Taiwan) family groups play an equivalent role.

The extent to which individual members of a group share the interests of the group as a whole varies. In some groups, for example, producer associations, unions, cartels and some families, shared interests predominate and conflicts of interest are rare. But in others, there are conflicting interests among members, for example, in firms, in some community and voluntary organizations, and some families. In many cases (including private firms), all members may have a shared interest in the successful outcome of the group activities, but have conflicting interests in how the benefits are shared among members. Some groups that are often thought of as having interests in common in fact only enjoy broadly shared interests, for example, those producer associations which include both rich and poor producers. Nor is the unity of interests fixed over time: a family may fly apart or come together depending on the occasion or its past history.

Groups range from the hierarchical and unequal to the democratic and egalitarian. In some groups members take decisions together. In others, decisions are taken by a subset of members. Objectives may be defined by the majority, or by dominant individuals or subsets of individuals, or implicitly in the practice of the group. Goals may be wholly shared by all members or only partly or contingently shared and only by a subset of members. Group goals may be defined internally by group members or externally, for example, by the state or by an NGO (usually in the hope that they will be internalized over time). Moreover, group goals may be defined differently by different individuals or collections of individuals within and outside the group, and these definitions may change over time, for example, differences within Ugandan NGOs between founder members operating 'as a family' and more recent members supporting more professionalism (Lorgen). The extent to which individual members agree or disagree with objectives is likely to affect their behaviour. Groups in which subsets of members take decisions and define goals may find it difficult to get the commitment of members who are not part of the subset, for example. Thus Agarwal (Chapter 9 this volume) shows that in some Indian forest groups in which women have less 'voice', women's contributions to group goals are significantly reduced.

Most individuals participate in a number of different groups; for example, the family, their work, and social organizations. This can give rise to conflicting loyalties, but it may also generate complementarities. Larger groups (e.g. governments) contain subgroups which form decision-making units in certain domains (e.g. ministries).

---

[5] UNDP (1995) estimates women's unpaid work as equivalent to 48% of measured income and men's unpaid work as another 22%.

1.2.1. *Groups and Markets*

Groups and markets represent alternatives in some of the activities they perform. In some functions markets may generally succeed better than groups, for example, for certain types of commodity production and distribution. In others, non-market groups are likely to be more successful, for example, the management of common pool resources, or the provision of certain types of health care, and for certain types of co-ordination (Williamson 1975). Where markets and groups are alternatives, they may compete: the market growing at the expense of groups or vice versa, for example, private property taking over from common property.

In other areas, in contrast, groups and markets complement each other. The market may succeed only because groups succeed, for example, families and governments help to sustain capitalism (Hirschman 1977), or particular groups may succeed because the market succeeds, for example, new revenue bases make possible new sorts of collective action. There may also be more 'dialectical' possibilities, for example, market successes may make possible the welfare state even as market failures may make it necessary; similarly with trade unions. Markets and groups may also be parasitic on each other. The market may benefit from groups and yet also undermine them: for example, the market benefits from social capital built up by groups but can weaken that capital by undermining communities.

In many areas the relationships between groups and markets are multi-facetted. It is not enough to look at groups simply as alternatives to markets. The relationship is more complex.

1.2.2. *Group Functions*

We may categorize group functions into three main types, recognizing that particular groups may perform more than one function at a time.

Overcoming Market Failures
One important function for groups, and a major reason why they have evolved, is to overcome a variety of market failures, in the economists' sense.[6] Groups overcoming market failure may help increase efficiency in both the technical and allocative senses. For shorthand we shall describe groups whose prime function is overcoming market failure as 'market failure' groups.

In many cases groups emerge as substitutes for missing markets or solutions to market imperfections. Major market imperfections leading to the formation of groups include:

- Indivisibilities and imperfect information leading to high transactions costs.[7] Given indivisibilities of production or consumption and high transactions costs, individuals

---

[6] 'Market failures' according to economists are defined specifically as ways in which the unregulated market may fail to reach a Pareto optimal resource allocation. Of course, the popular connotation of market failure goes much beyond this to include issues of the distribution of income and poverty, recession and unemployment, and how the market affects the quality of life more generally.

[7] See e.g. Nugent (1986).

cannot produce certain goods and services efficiently for themselves. Hence groups are formed to produce goods (this is the case for firms); or to provide common marketing for small-scale producers, for example, the associations of Brazilian sisal and cashew producers (Bianchi), the Colombian Coffee Federation (Thorp), and Mongolian Collectives (Sneath); or to provide communal facilities, for example, communal kitchens such as those that developed in Peru during the adjustment crisis in the 1980s.[8]

- Imperfect and asymmetric information giving rise to risk and uncertainty. Groups are formed for risk-pooling, as a type of collective insurance, for example, some credit groups.

- Externalities associated with non-excludability so that group or collective action is needed to produce public goods. Groups formed to manage common pool resources are examples, for example, Senegalese fishing groups (Gaspart and Platteau), or Indian and Nepalese forest associations (Agarwal).

Groups whose primary functions are to overcome market failures include both private sector groups (e.g. firms or networks of firms), and groups in the public sector or the community. Analysis of these groups, how and when they form, and their probable outcomes, has been the central focus of New Institutional Economics (NIE), which generally adopts an individual maximizing approach.

Claims Functions
The second important category of group functions is 'claims' functions. These arise where one of the purposes of the group is to advance the claims of its members to power and/or resources. This is the major explicit role of such organizations as associations of the landless, trade unions, cartels, and other interest groups, and is also one of the functions of private monopolies. The claims may be advanced against other members of society, for example, poor rural women seeking to advance claims for higher wages in Bangladesh (Mahmud), or sex workers seeking to advance claims against landlords in Calcutta (Gooptu); or the claims may be advanced against the government, for example, the Sarvodaya Shramadana in Sri Lanka campaigns for a variety of services to be provided by the government (Hulme and Montgomery 1994). Or claims may be advanced in international markets, for example, through pressure for international commodity agreements (Thorp). Groups with claims functions may not only advance new claims but may aim to enforce legally recognized rights, for example, helping to ensure that land reforms are fairly implemented.[9]

Individuals' willingness to engage in collective action in support of group claims has also been analysed from an individual maximizing perspective (cf. Olson 1965; Ostrom 1990; Taylor 1987; Hechter 1987; Elster 1989). These groups, however, are particularly suitable for analysis from a social perspective, with an emphasis on group identity and group loyalty (see below).

---

[8] Graham (1994: 109–10).

[9] Montgomery suggests that land reform has been more effective where group enforcement of this kind occurred (Montgomery 1988).

Pro Bono Functions

The third type of group function we term *pro bono* functions. Like groups peforming claims functions, groups performing pro bono functions also seek to alter the distribution of benefits within society, but they differ from groups performing claims functions in that they are directed mainly towards individuals *outside* the group, in contrast to claims groups in which functions are pursued by groups on behalf of group members. Pro bono functions are performed by groups in the public sector or NGOs, and are typically associated with such service provision as health, education, microcredit, etc.

These groups can be analysed from both theoretical perspectives, though to date theorizing of such groups has been somewhat rare (but see Titmuss 1970).

Many groups perform more than one of the categories of functions delineated. For example, many local organizations both engage in joint production activities (overcoming market failures, improving efficiency, and sometimes equity) and act as pressure groups for their members advancing their claims and their power, for example, rural women's groups in Bangladesh. Hirschman found that 'certain cooperative activities, originally undertaken strictly to improve the private economic position of members (sewing lessons . . . .), were seen to lead to constructive involvement in public affairs and to public advocacy' (Hirschman 1984: 59). Private firms, or associations of firms, also perform more than one category of function at a time, as Barr (2000) shows in an analysis of networks of small firms in Ghana.[10] Goods and services provided under the service umbrella are often also associated with overcoming market failures, for example, externalities, indivisibilities, or lack of information: this is illustrated in the health services by Tibandebage and Mackintosh, and in the provision of microcredit by Mahmud.

1.3. GROUP FUNCTIONING AND MODES OF OPERATION

Groups consist of collections of individuals—in some cases collections of very large numbers of individuals (e.g. governments or large multinational firms may employ tens of thousands of people); in others, such as small firms or the family, membership is very small. As noted above, group objectives may not always be shared by every individual in the group. One of the critical aspects of group functioning is how individual action within the group is kept in line with group objectives (Arrow 1963).

Where individual action is not kept in line groups become ineffective; for example, if individuals working for a firm shirk, pilfer, recommend rival products, or sabotage operations, the firm is not likely to be successful. Similarly, cooperatives or public sector institutions may be used by members/workers to serve their private interests and as a consequence fail to meet the group objectives. There is a spectrum ranging from situations where members devote their energies exclusively to serving group interests to those where they serve their own interests exclusively. Ways in which individual action is (or is not) reconciled with group objectives is thus a vital aspect of group functioning.

[10] See also Esman and Uphoff (1984).

The problem of securing individual action in line with group aims can be termed 'the consistency problem'. Achieving consistency is a problem even if the individuals that make up the group have formulated the objectives together, because individuals might still benefit by shirking themselves, or by pursuing their own private objectives, leaving others to realize group objectives. But where the individuals who form the group share the group objectives, and take part in making decisions over group objectives and ways of achieving them—for example, some producer cooperatives—consistency is likely to be achieved more easily than where they do not—for example, employees in profit-maximizing firms. In the latter cases, especially, therefore, there is likely to be a need for special mechanisms to ensure consistency (e.g. incentive systems).

An overview of group functioning suggests some important differences in the ways in which individual action is kept in line with group objectives. We distinguish alternative modes of operation below.

1.3.1. *Modes of Operation of Groups*

Modes of operation define broad types of behaviour and motivation within groups. We categorize modes of operation into three types. In practice, the functioning or mode of operation of particular groups rarely falls neatly into any one of the categories but shares features of each. However, in most cases one mode of operation tends to be more influential than others.

Power/control in Hierarchical Relations with Intra-group Bargaining Playing an Important Role (P/C)
In this mode—analysed, for example, in some of the works of Bowles and Gintis—one or a group of dominant actors determine what the rest will do, normally reflecting the interests of those with most power. The dominant group gets the rest to do what it wants by using threats and sanctions of various types. These may be backed up by norms reducing the need to use such threats and sanctions. Both the basis of unequal power and the type of threat vary with the institution.[11] The motivations behind the exercise of unequal power also vary. The operation of a modern army is a classic example of P/C. Williamson has argued that firms tend to be organized on hierarchical lines, via a P/C relationship, although empirical research indicates that many firms do not operate in this way.[12] Some of the work on gender points to P/C relationships within households too.[13] P/C relations may require considerable supervision and monitoring to ensure consistency, which can be costly.

Mackintosh and Gilson (this volume) distinguish operations in which dominant individuals or groups have benevolent motivation (P/C1) from those in which their motivation is self-serving (P/C2). The case of an army, for example, is one of P/C that is not normally self-serving. Some health facilities are examples of P/C that is benevolent, although often containing self-serving elements (Mackintosh *et al.* 1995,

---

[11] The basis of unequal power in the health sector is explored by Mackintosh and Gilson.
[12] Williamson (1975); Denison (1990).   [13] Kandiyoti (1988); Sen (1990), for example.

Le Grand 1997), as are some families or households. Firms are good examples of P/C that is almost always self-serving (P/C2).

Almost all groups contain some element of P/C. P/C can contribute to the efficiency of group operations to the extent that it is associated with reduced transactions costs. If individuals are sufficiently intimidated by, or accepting of, the power of those in control, they may do what is required without much monitoring or use of sanctions. P/C can even sometimes be attractive to those being controlled in that it relieves them of unwanted duties and responsibilities. The disadvantages of P/C are that it can be oppressive and exploitative, contributing to within-group alienation and inequality. As a minor element in a mixed mode, P/C may be desirable, if not essential, from an efficiency point of view. In certain circumstances it may also be effective or necessary in the pro bono role (see Mackintosh and Gilson for example).

It seems probable that P/C will be associated with considerable within-group inequality, as the more powerful retain a disproportionate share of the group income or benefits. However, in some societies (notably communist ones) a P/C mode of operation both within and between groups has been accompanied by a strongly egalitarian philosophy, limiting inequality. A similar philosophy informs some pro bono groups.

Both the way in which P/C operates, and whether it is dominant or not, is influenced by what is happening in the society in which it is situated. Like other behaviour, it is socially embedded. P/C tends to be more dominant and extreme (although not necessarily overt) in societies that are unequal and authoritarian, in which there is a history of P/C, and an ideology that supports it. The extent of P/C is subject to legal restrictions (e.g. the outlawing of slavery, an extreme form of P/C), and social and political pressures. It is also influenced by the society's values, beliefs, and traditions, and the history of the society and of the group.

*The Use of Material Incentives, Quasi-Market Operations (*M*)*
Material incentives provide the dominant incentive and support the dominant mode of operation (M) in arm's length transactions among and between individuals and firms in a market economy. They are also used within some groups in which a quasi-market is formed, as people are rewarded (and penalized) in material terms according to their contribution to group objectives. While markets are generally pervasive for between-group transactions, quasi-markets are rarely the dominant mode of operation within groups, since groups are frequently formed precisely because of the high transactions costs of market exchange; nevertheless, elements of material incentives are often present within organizations (e.g. all wages and salaries, piece rates for workers, and financial penalties for disobeying group rules). Firms, the public sector, and even families usually contain elements of quasi-markets in their operations. Recent public sector reform in some countries (e.g. Chile and the UK) has been directed towards giving a greater role to quasi-market modes of operation, while paradoxically many private sector firms are turning away from this type of functioning.[14] With M, monitoring and

---

[14] On the health service in the UK, see Le Grand (1997); Mackintosh (1999); on the private sector see Kay (1998); Che and Yoo (2001).

supervision requirements are always present and can be severe, to the extent that each actor is intent on maximizing private rewards and minimizing effort. Since the mode of operation rests on an assumption of individual self-interested maximizing behaviour, it tends to encourage this behaviour requiring large supervisory/monitoring inputs, crowding out the many valuable unreciprocated contributions that individuals make.

The use of material incentives in groups is widespread, though M is not universally present as is the case with the other modes. It is normally justified by the efficiency bene- fits it is expected to confer. For example, principal-agent theory has drawn attention to situations in which M is expected to be superior to P/C, because of monitoring costs of P/C in the presence of asymmetric information. However, principal-agent theory has also pointed to the limitations of M in conditions in which complete contracts are difficult to write. If M becomes dominant in situations in which implicit contracts or openendedness are advantageous, M can erode the goodwill which is essential to make these contracts work, reducing individuals' willingness to act cooperatively or to make unreciprocated contributions. Che and Yoo (2001) have explored conditions in which monetary incentives discourage a cooperative work morale and encourage employees to adopt restrictive work practices. An example of this is the British National Health Service which was first developed on the assumption that people were 'knights', that is, that 'people are predominantly public-spirited or altruistic'; when the system changed to a quasi-market system based on the assumption that people were 'knaves', that is, motivated primarily by self-interest, cooperative behaviour and good will are believed to have been severely reduced.[15]

The extent of inequality associated with M depends on the distribution of assets (including human capital), and their relative scarcity. Inequality can be severe within and between groups where M dominates, though this is not a necessary feature of the mode.

Cooperation Among Members to Achieve Group Objectives (COOP[16])
In this mode individuals act voluntarily in the group's interest even when not mainly motivated by material rewards (M) or reprisals (P/C). There are a number of reasons why they may do so. Individuals may take action voluntarily in the group interest first because it coincides with their individual interests; and second, because they believe that doing so will be in their long-term interests as they expect reciprocity over the long-term. In these cases COOP behaviour can be seen as motivated by a form of self-interest. Third, individuals may take action in the group interest because they value the well-being of others in the group; that is, their values and motives include Aristotle's *philia*[17] or Sen's sympathy; or their self-image is that of altruistic or

---

[15] Quotations and terminology from Le Grand (1997); see also Glennerster (1995); Mackintosh (1999). See also the labour economics literature on intrinsic vs extrinsic motivation (Kreps 1997; Alkire and Deneulin).

[16] We call this mode COOP as a shorthand for cooperation. We should note that we are using the term as used in everyday life, and not in the narrow sense used in economic models, like the Prisoner's Dilemma.

[17] *Philia* which has been translated as friendship, but which actually means something like affiliation, is the core virtue of living together in society (Deneulin 1999).

cooperative people (Hargreaves Heap 1989). All these cases can be fitted into a utility maximizing model—see below.

Other ways of looking at individuals taking action voluntarily in group interests do not fit within an individual utility maximizing model. For example, individuals may take such action in the spirit of Mauss's 'free gift', neither expecting nor getting anything in return. They may take action from a sense of duty, or commitment, or because they enjoy the activity itself, that is, through *intrinsic* motivation (Alkire and Deneulin). Another possibility, which again does not fit easily within a transactional model, is that individuals identify so strongly with the group—for ideological or other reasons—that group interests override individual interests. An extreme example of actions taken in group rather than individual interests is that of people sacrificing their lives in the interests of others. There are many other cases that involve the subordination of individual to group interest in which individuals make lesser sacrifices in the interests of the group. The actions of people involved in political activism, or trade union activity, provide good examples. People may also act voluntarily in the group interest driven by force of habit, custom, or tradition.

Mackintosh and Gilson differentiate between COOP1, where individuals take action because they expect something in return (*extrinsic* motivation), from COOP2 where action is taken without any expectation of return and cannot be viewed as a form of exchange (*intrinsic* motivation). We include the whole range of motivation noted above within our COOP mode, distinguishing different types within this. We also recognize that different types of COOP may be involved in any one instance.

There are invariably elements of COOP in all group operations. Even in groups that operate primarily in P/C or M modes some COOP is needed to make other modes of operation work—since monitoring and supervision can never be sufficient to ensure that everyone is working in the group interests even in a group which is primarily P/C or M.[18] Moreover, there can be different modes of operation at different levels within groups, so that relationships among managers, for example, are on a COOP basis, but relationships between managers and workers operate according to P/C and M.

While some element of COOP is invariably present, it is less often the dominant mode of operation in a group: moreover, if it dominates, it is not easy to sustain. COOP can be strongly reinforced by social relationships within and outside the group, so it is easier for COOP to dominate in groups that are small, with continuous personal relationships, than in large groups. It may also be more likely to be dominant in the operation of groups in societies that are relatively egalitarian, societies in which there is a history of COOP, and societies with norms and values conducive to COOP. However, COOP also dominates in some groups in societies that have the opposite characteristics, that is, societies which are inegalitarian, have no strong history of COOP, or norms or values conducive to COOP (cf. Gooptu). Such groups are usually claims groups

---

[18] As Smith (1759) and Hirschman (1977), have pointed out, no matter how intensive the monitoring of group members, no matter how dire the sanctions against individual malfeasance, there are almost always opportunities in groups not to do what one is supposed to do. The degree to which members misbehave varies, but if people do not cooperate, at least some of the time, the group cannot operate.

which are specifically and deliberately challenging the dominant societal characteristics (Bianchi, Gooptu).

COOP can contribute to efficiency because it requires less monitoring and supervision than other modes. Moreover, COOP groups can develop and reinforce socially desirable characteristics in individuals and bring about socially desirable consequences. For example, it can contribute to empowerment, self-confidence, individual responsibility and within-group equity. But COOP may sometimes be used as a veil for unequal relationships, as for example, when small producers contribute to cooperative marketing arrangements through which the wealthy obtain disproportionate benefits (Thorp). COOP can be undemocratic, using social pressure to ensure compliance with processes and actions that are associated with inequality and exploitation (Agarwal, Thorp).

Whether equity and empowerment is better in COOP groups than in alternative modes (P/C or M), as well as the comparative efficiency of the three modes, is an empirical issue on which the case studies in this volume throw some light.

Our three-fold classification of group behaviour overlaps with classifications adopted previously. Polanyi's classification of decision-making in a non-market (planned) economy also identified three types of behaviour, reciprocity, redistribution, and exchange (see Polanyi 1957). These are similar to the three types noted above, although our P/C mode covers a wider realm of decisions than redistribution alone while our COOP goes beyond reciprocity. In some of the business literature, the behaviour of firms is divided into bureaucracies, markets, and clans which also has strong similarities to the classifications of modes proposed here (Wilkins and Ouchi 1983: 471).

1.4. THEORETICAL APPROACHES TO THE ANALYSIS OF GROUPS

We noted above that the contributors to this book draw on two different theoretical perspectives, the individual maximizing approach—which we shall term REM (standing for Rational Economic Man), following Folbre; and the more sociological approach, which does not adopt a maximizing perspective and gives primacy to the group as such, although it still recognizes the importance of individual agency—we shall call this SAP (Socially Acting Perspective). In this section we briefly consider some of the theoretical analysis in the two traditions, aiming to identify the ways in which society, groups, and individuals interact.

1.4.1. *The REM Approach: Exchange or Transactions Approaches Assuming Individual Maximizing Behaviour*

The starting point of this approach is that group behaviour derives from the behaviour of the individuals who form the group; and individuals are motivated to maximize the realization of their goals which are derived from individual preferences. Essentially, the approach aims to explain the operation of groups in terms of the benefits that individuals within the group derive *as individuals* from their participation in a collective.

There is a range of assumptions about motivation that informs this approach. At one extreme, individuals are viewed as short-term, self-interested utility maximizers,[19] and the rationale for groups is considered in this light. The assumption of 'rational' individuals whose motive is to maximize their own utility generally forms the basis of the NIE analysis of groups, except within the family as Folbre[20] stresses. Becker extends the analysis to the family too, claiming that: 'All human behaviour can be viewed as involving participants who maximize their utility from a stable set of preferences' (Becker 1976: 14).

In general, REM assumptions support the view that markets operating in an M mode produce efficient outcomes—the Walrasian system has no role for groups. Nonetheless, economists working with REM assumptions have identified a valuable role for groups. Important examples are the work of Coase and Williamson who have used this framework to explore the reasons for the existence of firms; and Olson, Axelrod and others who have identified the conditions in which (mainly non-profit-making) groups evolve to overcome externalities.

Coase (1937) and Williamson (1975, 1985) have suggested that firms develop to reduce the heavy transactions costs involved in arm's length transactions in the presence of imperfect information. Because of the lack of perfect information, there are heavy costs of monitoring, supervision and sanctions if an M mode is adopted for all activity within the firm. Consequently, there are benefits of openendedness and flexibility, and M or P/C modes need to be supported by group loyalty and goodwill (i.e. COOP).

Olson (1965), Axelrod (1984), Taylor (1987), and others, have shown that even where individuals do not communicate, have no relationship with each other, and have no motive other than self-interest, groups can nonetheless emerge and operate successfully on a COOP basis. Such groups are more likely to be successful where the relationship among the individuals is long-lived and small numbers of individuals are involved, so that the benefits to each member are perceptible. Small numbers also make it less likely that members can remain anonymous: shirking becomes noticeable and identifiable (Olson 1965). Such groups are also more likely to emerge where individuals have low time preferences (Axelrod 1984).

The sustainability of groups in this type of model also depends on the technology involved. This is partly because it is easier to sustain COOP when there are large economic benefits to be derived, and also because there may be technological reasons for activities being more or less easy to monitor and enforce (Bianchi, Gaspart and Platteau, Baland and Platteau 1996). Some types of coordinated action are relatively easy to monitor because they necessarily involve individuals operating at close quarters to each other. Platteau and Seki (2001) point to the example of Japanese fishing groups in which individuals fish close to each other, sometimes from the same boat. In contrast, many agricultural activities, for example, the quality of planting and weeding, are difficult to monitor and this is a reason for having individual family farms. Some joint or coordinated actions do not need monitoring or sanctions at all because they

---

[19] Alkire and Deneulin's *homo œconomicus* model.   [20] Folbre (1986, 1994).

are self-enforcing, for example, agreeing on a particular market day or driving on a particular side of the road (Sugden 1986).

Unequal stakes in the formation of the group do not necessarily prevent 'market failure' groups from forming. In fact a few dominant actors may be helpful (Bianchi, Thorp), but extreme inequality among members can impede group formation. Heterogeneity in terms of complementary skills, hierarchies, and leadership is an important feature of the successful functioning of many groups, while modelling collective action has suggested that it works best in situations in which there is a moderate degree of inequality in asset ownership (Olson 1965; Ostrom 1990; Baland and Platteau 1995, 1999; see also Wade 1988).

These approaches explain the emergence of a fairly narrow set of groups, which tend to be rather fragile, depending on the existence of large gains and continued relationships for their sustained existence. Indeed, Gaspart and Platteau show how dependent the fishing groups they analyse in Senegal were on the gains emanating from a particular technology, where self-interest was the dominant motive of participants.

Extending motivation to encompass other-regarding considerations, such as philia and altruism, greatly increases the possibilities of COOP groups and their sustainability.[21] Intrinsic valuation[22]—that is, where people engage in action because they value the activity itself, for example, where people get satisfaction from team work of high quality—can be an important reason for the formation and continuation of groups in which individual advantages are small. For example, members of women's groups in rural Bangladesh value their weekly meetings more for themselves than for anything tangible that they get out of them (Mahmud). After reviewing grass roots organizations in Latin America, Hirschman concluded that 'the formation of a cooperative is one of those human activities that bring their own reward.' (Hirschman 1984: 59). Mackintosh and Gilson, however, argue that 'ethical commitment' (which can be regarded as including altruism) is an important but fragile element of some types of cooperative behaviour within groups, which needs to be nurtured if such cooperative behaviour is to survive for any length of time. Hence, their statement that ' "Free gifts" are hard to sustain on the basis of ethical commitment alone, and are robust only when embedded in other non-market relationships.' (p. 257)

Most of the models considered so far take preferences as being exogenous, which means that group behaviour is independent of the nature of the society in which groups are located (apart from its influence on technical possibilities). Yet it is clear from all the studies in this book, and much other empirical work, that the ways in which groups operate—in particular, their dominant mode of operation, whether P/C, M or COOP—are greatly influenced by the prevailing society, especially its norms and social relationships; that is, groups are embedded in the communities and societies[23]

---

[21] Becker (1996) and Taylor (1987) claim that altruism increases the possibilities of cooperation enormously. Taylor (1987) maintains that introducing altruism makes it too easy to explain cooperative behaviour, arguing that it would be difficult to explain why there is not more collective action than there is if altruism were widespread.   [22] See Alkire and Deneulin on this.

[23] 'Community' refers here to immediate neighbours, geographically or sometimes metaphorically, while society refers to a broader social environment.

of which they are a part, and analysis and understanding of group behaviour group must incorporate considerations of group/society relationships.[24]

The community and society within which groups operate are likely to affect them in many different ways. Economic and social relationships in society provide the backdrop against which groups are formed and operate, affecting the power of different group members and the power, opportunities, and constraints of the group. Individual motivation and preferences are influenced by the community and society within which the individual is situated, property and employment relations, class and ethnic strife, the position of the actor within these, and so on.[25] While each group has its own culture, the institutions and relationships prevalent in the society as a whole are an important influence on group behaviour—sometimes supporting groups, sometimes undermining them.

One of the ways in which the community and society influences group behaviour is through norms, as already noted in the discussion of the three modes of operation, each of which, we argued, is more likely to be prevalent if supported by societal norms. Norms can be seen as influences over behaviour arising from the customs, traditions, values, and way of life of a particular society or group, whose transgression sometimes leads to social sanctions.[26] As Tibandebage and Mackintosh put it, norms can be seen as 'patterns of behaviour that are widespread, are generally tolerated or accepted as proper, are reinforced by responses of others, and are quite hard for individuals to resist even if they run against what is felt to be right' (pp 271–2).[27]

Norms greatly influence how individuals behave in groups. All individuals are subject to a variety of norms pertaining to the various groups and the wider society to which they belong, starting with the family, then extending to the local community, to the education system, and to particular groups with which the individual is associated.[28] The norms of the community affect the norms the members bring with them to the group. Some of the norms that influence group behaviour are specific to the group in question, although usually heavily influenced by those of society as a whole; some emerge from and are shared by the society in which the group is located. Societal and group norms may play an important role supporting group coherence and group behaviour, although because they are historically formed and sometimes change slowly, they can become obsolete or even dysfunctional from this point of view. Below we refer to the norms pertaining to the society as a whole as the *macro*-norms. The *macro-environment*

---

[24] This view is strongly represented in the work of Etzioni and Lawrence 1991; and Granovetter 1991.

[25] This was of course recognized by classical economists such as Smith and Marx.

[26] Norms are used here in much the same way as North's definition of 'institutions': i.e. 'The rules of the game in a society or more formally ... the humanly devised constraints that shape human interaction' (North 1990: 3).

[27] Elster (1989) defines norms in a more restrictive way as 'the propensity to feel shame and to anticipate sanction by others at the thought of behaving in a certain, forbidden way'. He continues 'This propensity becomes a social norm to the extent that it is shared with other people'.

[28] The different attitudes towards redistribution of income in Sweden and the US provide an example of differences in societal norms, which has implications for policies and incentives throughout society—see Coughlin (1991).

includes these macro-norms and policies, organizations and incentives which form the context in which particular groups operate.

There is an important process of cumulative causation in determining individual and group behaviour which works through norms. For example, where COOP is dominant throughout society, it will be likely to be pervasive and effective within groups because of its influence on norms affecting individual behaviour. Conversely if P/C or M dominates the societal norms, it may be more difficult to adopt COOP effectively as the mode of operation of a particular group. One reason for this is that societal norms affect individuals' motivations. It has been argued, for example, that intrinsic motivation may be crowded out by extrinsic motivation. Titmuss was one of the first to draw attention to this in relation to blood donors.[29] Others have looked at ways in which changes in extrinsic motivation in the form of greater use of monetary incentives can destroy intrinsic motivation in employment practices (e.g. Kreps 1997). Another way in which societal norms affect behaviour within groups is through social sanctions supporting one or other type of behaviour which may constrain people from adopting alternative modes—for example, people may be deterred from demanding monetary payment in a context where the norm is to undertake certain functions freely and disapproval and other social sanctions follow when individuals break this norm.

The causation also works the other way. Societal norms are the outcome of many individual and group actions and beliefs, and they change when these change, although societal norms normally change only slowly and as a result of a great number of individual developments.[30] Individuals can reflect upon, react against, and change the norms that govern social life (Lawson 1997). A change in dominant beliefs and mode of operation within a group spreads out to the rest of society through its members' activities, and if many groups and individuals are affected, then societal norms and modes in other groups may change. Stewart shows how changes in norms occurred historically through an iterative process, filtering down through society, with changes in thinking at global and national levels having an important impact on what occurs at the level of individual groups. She explores a dialectical process in which societal norms influence the possibilities of group formation and their norms, while the new identities that arise from group formation in turn affect societal identities and norms. As groups with one mode of operation expand, they contribute to a change in societal norms. For example, as groups switch from P/C to M modes, the use of financial incentives as a mechanism for influencing action becomes accepted in realms in which this might previously have been thought of as unthinkable.

---

[29] He pointed out that while people might be intrinsically motivated to give large amounts of blood, the introduction of some extrinsic motivation in the form of payment might destroy this intrinsic motivation, and end up with less blood being given overall (Titmuss 1970).

[30] Durkheim emphasises the relatively immutability of 'concepts' (or norms in our terminology), arguing that they develop as a result of 'an immense cooperation' of individuals 'which stretches out not only into space but also into time; to make them, a multitude of minds have associated, united and combined their ideas and sentiments'; (Durkheim 1976, pp 16 [quoted in Bhargava 1992: 218]) 'Concepts then . . . are the social work of individuals. This is what lends them their stability and authority. They force themselves on us, resist us, and are therefore not easily manipulable.' (Bhargava 1992: 218–9).

The social embeddedness of groups, which, of course, incorporates the influence of norms, can be analysed within the extended REM approach, via the influence of norms on preferences. Norms may be understood to affect individual preferences directly so that preferences are endogenous, or to act as constraints on what individuals can do, given exogenously determined preferences.[31] While many economists work within the Walrasian approach and assume that human motivation is exogenous (or innate), others within the individual utility maximizing tradition, including Akerlof, North, and Becker, have explored how preferences are shaped by social and economic relationships, and by norms.[32]

The influence of society on individual preferences is incorporated into an individual utility maximizing model by Becker (1996) through the stock of personal and social capital, which include a range of personal and social experiences, and enter as arguments in the utility function.[33] Preferences are only loosely endogenous for Becker, however, as there is no feedback within his model between actions or outcomes, on the one hand, and the personal and social capital that shape preferences, on the other. An alternative approach is adopted by Akerlof (1983) with the concept of 'loyalty filters', defined as follows: 'When people go through experiences, frequently their loyalties, or their values change. I call these value-changing experiences "loyalty filters".' Akerlof illustrates this process by the way that Quakers, elite schools, and elite academies, among others, cultivate values and behaviours that are non-self-interested in the short term and thus change the behaviour and further the long-term interests of their members.

Another way that community and social influences have been introduced into individual utility maximizing models is through the concept of identity (Akerlof and Kranton (2000)). A person's sense of identity, made up of their view of themselves as belonging to a particular gender, community, ethnicity, social class, nationality, or as supporting particular values (e.g. environmentalism), is a powerful influence over behaviour. Introducing identity into the utility function enables Akerlof and Kranton to explain behaviour that bolsters the sense of self, leading to the claim that the choice of identity may be the most important 'economic' decision people make. But the model does not explain at all fully how people come to choose (or recognize themselves as belonging to) a particular identity. This choice itself is the outcome of individual and group actions, norms and influences, in what is often termed the 'social construction' of identity.

---

[31] Bowles and Gintis (1993).

[32] Bargaining models of group behaviour represent a different way of looking at social influences on individual and group behaviour, within the individual maximizing framework. See McElroy and Horney (1981) where it is assumed that individuals maximize utility functions constrained by what they call extra-environmental parameters which include social influences. In Sen's (1990) bargaining model the distribution of resources within the family depends on individual threat points which are determined by factors outside the family as well as within. In these models, preferences remain exogenous and societal influences act as constraints.

[33] 'Personal capital, P, includes the relevant past consumption and other personal experiences that affect current and future utilities. Social capital, S, incorporates the influence of past actions by peers and others in an individual's social network and control system.' (Becker 1996: 4) Alkire and Deneulin discuss Becker's model.

Using repeated games, the social determination of norms and preferences has been endogenized more formally. Thus, Aoki endogenizes the formation of community norms: 'through repeated interactions they [agents] may autonomously generate implicit rules regulating their individual choices and thus internalize their welfare. We may refer to such endogenous rules as community norms.' (Aoki 2001: 97) Aoki goes on to propose an economic transactions domain embedded in a social exchange domain. Games played in the two domains are linked and players coordinate their strategies in the two. A community norm, such as the degree of cooperative behaviour, supported by credible beliefs of the occurrence of ostracism in the event of deviant behaviour, is the endogenous outcome of linked games in this analysis.

The individual maximizing framework thus has much to contribute to our understanding of group behaviour. The REM model in its narrow interpretation explains the development of certain groups in a rather restricted range of circumstances, mainly those designed to overcome market failure, though it can be extended to include some claims groups. The narrow individual utility maximizing approach, however, has trouble in explaining why groups sometimes continue for considerable periods of time despite the fact that economic advantages are small or non-existent (for example, those reported on by Mahmud and Bianchi). Once one incorporates a broader range of preferences, including altruism and intrinsic motivation, it is possible to explain a much wider range of groups, and also to show why COOP modes persist. Yet this type of motivation is fragile if unsupported by societal influences. A more robust and realistic attempt to explain group formation, and mode of operation, needs to recognize the social embeddedness of groups, and in particular the influence of norms over the formation of individual and group behaviour. We have shown that this type of embeddedness can be analysed within an extended REM framework, though once one extends the model in this way there is a danger that the approach loses its explanatory power and becomes tautological, explaining everything and nothing. An alternative approach is to start with the collective, abandoning the individual maximizing perspective. We look at this next.

1.4.2. *The SAP View: The Social as an Independent Objective and Influence*

A different approach to the analysis of groups is suggested by Gooptu's question: 'Is it not possible that individuals cohere in a group from a genuine belief in the normative superiority of the collectivity even when little direct or immediate benefit accrues to the individual from participating in such a collectivity?' (Gooptu 2000: 3). This leads us to approaches that explain action by collective entities such as group loyalty and group identity, in which individual self-interest is secondary. The emphasis shifts to a primary focus on the influence of collective entities on individual behaviour rather than the reverse.

Many sociologists, anthropologists, and political theorists adopt a collectivist approach to understanding groups in the sense that they put the main emphasis on the collective, but they generally do not deny the role of individual agency, indeed some maintain a strong belief in individual agency. However, the weight of their attention and analysis is at the group rather than the individual level. Generally, they do not think that the individual maximizing model is a good representation of individual behaviour, or a useful basis for understanding individual or group behaviour. Furthermore, they believe that using the REM approach may detract from the important role of the collectivity: 'methodological individualism prevents us from engaging with the central issue of collective or group identity in group dynamics, and thus undermines the ways in which group action and behaviour can be effectively conceptualised' (Gooptu 2000: 44–5). Moreover, 'If we try to understand group dynamics only in terms of what individuals bring to and gain from groups, then we undermine the determining influence of groups themselves on individual action and motivation.' (Gooptu 2000: 47).

From this perspective, being a member of a group is seen as largely determining individual behaviour—individuals act the way they do because they are members of the group, because they identify with the group and its objectives, out of loyalty to it. Being a member of a group may lead individuals to subordinate their interests to those of the group. The group can change individual self-awareness, self-confidence, self-esteem, identities, ideologies and perceptions of what is right, or acceptable (Gooptu, Agarwal). Individual action may also be influenced by other collective entities, including societal norms, including established patterns of behaviour. Thus: 'In addition to explanations rooted in individual incentives, we therefore also treat norms and established patterns of behaviour as having explanatory power, not as themselves requiring explanation from individualist premises' (Mackintosh and Gilson p 255). Norms are seen as changing behaviour through changing perceived possibilities and constraints, as well as through changing preferences or goals.

Many using a SAP, non-exchange, approach reject what Bhargava calls 'the causal view of action', viz. that '(all) action can be analysed as composed of three different elements: behaviour, intentional states, and the relation of causality that binds them.' (Bhargava 1992: 209). While those subscribing to the individual utility maximizing model also recognize cognitive problems, they assume that they are marginal and unavoidable. Here, on the other hand, they are regarded as central, and avoidable by adopting a non-maximizing approach.

In this book, Gooptu provides an example of a SAP approach. She focuses on political and social activism in which changing perceptions and ideas are the key to behaviour. In her analysis the process of collective action leads to the construction of a collective identity ('we' rather than 'I') and this sustains collective action. She treats the prevailing group ideas about what is possible and beneficial as having an important influence on the way group members see themselves (their self-awareness and self-confidence), and on the way group members think about their capacity as individuals and as groups. She puts the emphasis on what being a member of a group does to individuals not what individual behaviour does to the group. 'Here we see how individuals find meaning in and identify themselves with the group, and how the group defines their identity, and shapes their goals and patterns of behaviour.' (Gooptu p 27). It is the construction of the group identity and the way it structures individual motivation, and the perception of opportunities and constraints, that explains the success of group action in Gooptu's study of sex workers. It follows that an important task of groups is the formation (and sustaining) of group identities and loyalties.

Agarwal argues, in a similar vein, that changes in state, community, and family ideologies with respect to gender change what can be (and is) done to strengthen the position of women. Whereas Gooptu focuses on changes occurring at the local level through group action at that level, Agarwal considers the influence of changes in ideologies occurring outside the group. Thus, feminist discourse enhanced the possibilities of women getting together and organizing themselves in groups (Agarwal 1994, 1997*b*).

Also adopting a SAP approach, Mackintosh and Gilson draw on the concepts of social anthropology,[34] arguing that both social relations and social understandings are important influences on group behaviour. Social understandings arise from everyday practice, in the context of social relations. Social (or power) relations are determined by extra- as well as intra-group relationships. Thus Mackintosh and Gilson show how health facility workers' behaviour towards patients is directly related to the unequal social status of people in the two groups. Social relations also influence the formation and development of shared understandings. This is a reason why P/C relationships in society are likely to be reproduced within groups, as argued earlier.

There are marked differences between Gooptu and Agarwal, on the one hand, and Mackintosh and Gilson, on the other: first, the former emphasize changes in perceptions and practice brought about *intentionally* by the group, while Macintosh and Gilson focus on social understandings that are the *unintended* consequences of everyday practice; and second, Mackintosh and Gilson emphasize social relations outside the group determining group activities. One reason for these differences is the functions of the groups studied. Gooptu and Agarwal both examine claims groups, while Mackintosh and Gilson look at pro bono groups. It seems plausible that claims groups will be more activist, better able to inspire and change the membership than pro bono groups, and more interested in doing so.

The SAP approach has important contributions to make to our understanding of groups, which is either not captured, or given little emphasis, in the REM approach. In the first place, it draws attention to the role of group formation in changing identities, goals, and actions of group members; second, it emphasizes how these can contribute to the formation of norms within and outside the group; and third, it recognizes the importance of social relations outside the group in influencing relationships within it. The SAP approach—in particular the emphasis on the importance of the group in changing identities—is especially appropriate for examining claims groups, whose intention is to challenge societal distribution of power and resources. But the insights also form an important complement to REM models in understanding market failure groups. As noted earlier, pro bono groups have rarely been discussed in theoretical terms. Mackintosh and Gilson make an important contribution in this area. REM

---

[34] Especially Douglas 1987; see Mackintosh and Gilson p 255.

appears to be able to contribute rather little to the understanding of this type of group.

1.5. CONCLUSION

This introduction has argued that group activity is hugely important in economic and social development. Consequently, investigation of influences on the efficiency and equity of development processes must include a study of within-group functioning. It has also argued clear that to understand group formation, functioning, and outcomes, different types of analysis are relevant and useful. In particular, we have noted that both individual transactional analysis and a social perspective make important contributions to understanding group behaviour.

One important conclusion of this introductory discussion is that the existence and behaviour of groups should not be looked at in isolation, since the behaviour of groups is strongly influenced by the society in which they are embedded, in particular by the prevalent norms and the socio-economic structures which they face. Indeed, exploring norms and socio-economic structures is crucial for understanding group behaviour. Moreover, group behaviour also contributes to the formation of societal norms.

We have argued that analysis of groups must differentiate between groups performing different functions, in particular overcoming market failure, and performing claims and pro bono functions, as their behaviour often differs. We have also argued that analysis of groups needs to differentiate among them according to the dominant mode of behaviour, categorized as P/C, M, and COOP, although we recognize that every group contains elements of more than one mode.

There appears to be an important interaction between societal norms, group norms, and mode of behaviour. The majority of individual groups are likely to adopt the mode of operation that reflects the dominant values of the society. Hence as market values become more pervasive in society generally, particular groups are likely to adopt an M mode, displacing P/C and COOP. Moreover, the more they do so, the stronger the market values in society generally become, and the more groups are liable to shift to an M mode. Yet not all groups are passive reflectors of societal values: they can deliberately challenge them, as emphasized in the SAP approach, in which it is argued that groups create identities and values which then affect the wider society.

A key issue is how far and for what reasons changes in mode of operation matter. One reason they may matter is that the existence and sustainability of some groups depends on individual motivation moving beyond short-term maximizing towards longer term and more other-regarding objectives. The values in society and the mode of operation of particular groups are a major influence in individual motivation in particular groups; there is evidence that the increasing prevalence of an M mode can shift motivation towards the short term and undermine some valuable types of voluntary collective action (see Conclusions).

A second set of reasons why mode of operation may matter is because of the implications for the efficiency of group operations. It is often presumed that an M mode will secure a more efficient use of resources than P/C or COOP—indeed this is a major reason why it is introduced into group operations. Yet, as Williamson and others have pointed out, M within groups may *not* be efficient because of the supervision and monitoring required, given the absence of perfect information. Some COOP is essential for group efficiency. The question then is whether, as is sometimes claimed, adopting an M mode reduces COOP to such an extent that the net effect on efficiency is negative.

A third set of reasons why mode of operation may matter is because of the implications for equity. There is a general presumption that both within groups, and between groups, equity would be better with COOP than P/C and probably than M too. Some evidence for this at a societal level is the increasing inequality that has accompanied the advance of market values in the majority of countries. But as noted earlier, COOP dominated groups can be unequal, so more evidence is needed on this.

All of this is important because groups are crucial for individual and collective well-being. Not only does collective action overcome externalities and help empower the weak, but the dominant mode of behaviour within and between groups is an important aspect of how we relate to one another as human beings. When large changes sweep across society, they inevitably influence group behaviour. The fact that the present era is one of major economic and social change—towards a greater role for markets and quasi-markets in most economies including developing ones—makes it particularly important not to lose sight of groups and to explore the implications of these changes for group behaviour and the policies which might help to improve the efficiency and equity of group functioning.

2

Dynamic Interactions Between the Macro-environment, Development Thinking and Group Behaviour

FRANCES STEWART

The social morality that has served as an understructure for economic individualism has been a legacy of the precapitalist and preindustrial past. This legacy has diminished with time and with the corrosive contact of the active capitalist values. . . As individual behaviour has been increasingly directed to individual advantage, habits and instincts based on communal attitudes and objectives have lost out. The weakening of traditional social values has made predominantly capitalist economies more difficult to manage.

(Hirsch 1976: 117–118.)

2.1. INTRODUCTION

An important hypothesis arising from the analysis in Chapter 1 is that groups' behaviour is greatly influenced by the societal environment in which they operate. This environment encompasses societal institutions or norms, the structure of the economy, and the resulting distribution of incomes and assets. This chapter aims to explore these macro–micro interactions in a dynamic context—examining how societal norms changed over the twentieth century as well as the structure of the economy, and how these in turn have altered the context of group behaviour. This is a very ambitious undertaking, and not one to which it will be possible to do full justice. Yet it is critically important to the central topic of this book. In so far as the macro-environment is a major influence on group behaviour, it is essential to understand how this operates, if we are to understand and influence group behaviour.

A major focus will be on prevailing paradigms of development at a macro-level, which is one aspect of societal norms. The reason for this is that these paradigms have been an important influence over policy and economic structures over these years. Development thinking enters the picture at several stages. First, it has a direct influence on how economies operate (including their incentive and ownership structures)

I am grateful for very helpful comments on a previous draft of this paper from Judith Heyer, Rosemary Thorp, participants at the Helsinki meeting and an anonymous referee.

via its effects on policy—which also affects the incentives individuals face, and therefore how they operate in groups; second, in a more indirect way it influences the
general culture of behaviour which in turn influences individuals' behaviour when in
groups. But development paradigms are not autonomous, coming uninfluenced from
scholars' investigations; they are themselves heavily affected by events in society and
the economy. Hence we have a quite complex process of cumulative causation, in
which development thinking is both an independent force, and part of the chain of
developments influencing group behaviour.

In recent history we have seen some major changes in development paradigms which
have substantially affected not only societal norms but also income and asset distribution. We can categorize these into three eras. First, colonialism and neocolonialism,
in which primary production for exports dominated the formal economy; the second
consists of state-directed planning and production; and the third, the era of the market and laissez-faire. Each has affected the structure of the economy and has had a
markedly different influence on group behaviour. This chapter examines these developments, analysing how the changes in development paradigms influenced policy and
outcomes, and how these in turn affected group behaviour. For this purpose, group
behaviour will be categorized in the ways discussed in Chapter 1: that is, differentiating
group functions into three types—overcoming market failures, claims, and pro bono;
and group behaviour into the three modes—power and control (P/C), cooperation
(COOP), and behaviour according to market-incentives (M). While in Chapter 1 these
modes are applied to the micro-behaviour of groups, in this chapter we use the same
terminology also to describe the macro-environment, that is, the ideology, policies,
and incentives prevalent at a macro-level. This, of course, includes government policy,
but it goes beyond it, informing attitudes, norms, and incentives throughout society.

The chapter is organized as follows. The next section will explore further why the
macro-context matters for group behaviour at a general level. The subsequent section
will discuss the interactions between development thought, policy formation, and
real world developments at a general level. This is followed, in Section 4, by a more
detailed analysis of actual changes in the macro-environment over the last century.
Stages in the changing macro-environment will be described and the implications for
group behaviour explored, illustrating the discussion with specific examples from the
organization of medical services.

2.2. THE MACRO-CONTEXT AND GROUP BEHAVIOUR: DOES IT MATTER?

The theory of social capital has emphasized how the extent of people's membership of
groups and the nature of the groups to which they belong influence the economy and the
functioning of government. Thus Putnam argues—in a hypothesis that has received
wide support—that extensive 'horizontal' group membership, involving reciprocal
ties of trust (i.e. broadly COOP groups and networks) is likely to support efficient
government (Putnam 1993). Others have taken this further and argued that such a
situation (described as 'high' levels of social capital) is also likely to be conducive to

economic efficiency. This has been supported by a variety of empirical studies, some predating the widespread acceptance of the 'social capital' concept. For example, a study by Uphoff of sixteen countries in Asia found that those countries with the best network of local institutions linking rural communities and the central government had the best agricultural performance and also the largest improvements in social indicators. He suggests this arose as the strength of the 'third' sector complemented the state or market, and put pressure on both to maintain efficiency (Uphoff 1993; see also e.g. Grootaert 1997). From this perspective then, group behaviour is a significant input into both government and private sector efficiency with more COOP group behaviour supporting more efficiency.

This chapter, however, is not primarily concerned with this direction of causation—from group behaviour to the wider economy—although we will return to it briefly at the end—but with the reverse connection, *from* development paradigms, policy, and events *to* group behaviour.

There are several reasons for expecting some connections in this direction. First, the norms of a society influence people's expectations and behaviour. For example, where the dominant societal norms are strongly hierarchical, people assume and expect such norms in other walks of life and only exceptionally adopt different (e.g. COOP) norms as group members. The connection is not watertight or inviolable: strongly dominant norms can provoke a reaction as people challenge them. Nonetheless, it is generally likely to be strong, overturned only by deliberate and sometimes costly efforts. Second, the prevalent societal incentive systems may influence groups' mode of behaviour. Since group members are often the same individuals as interact in other relationships outside the group (e.g. family members, members of the same firm), behaviour within the group that deviates from that outside the group (e.g. challenging hierarchies) may be punished by action taken outside the group. Or strong financial incentives for outside group work may prevent group members performing cooperatively and lead them to demand financial incentives in order to work properly within the group (as e.g. among doctors who can earn a lot by private consultancy). Third, groups which are part of or relate to the government—for example, via subcontracting relationships—may be *required* to behave according to the norms to which the government adheres. Fourth, societal norms and norms within the group are likely to be influenced by the structure of the economy, including the prevailing motivation for economic activity (e.g. whether it is predominantly a 'command' economy, an economy of 'affection', or a market economy).

Much empirical material supports the hypothesis of a link between societal and group norms: for example, the difference in behaviour between local government in Bangladesh (dominated by the elite) and Karnataka (where more COOP relations prevailed) was attributed to differences in the environment in which they operated by Crook and Manor (Heyer *et al.* 1999); Village Councils in South India which successfully overcame market failures adopted modes of behaviour broadly consonant with the norms of the villages in which they were located, with elements of hierarchy, incentives, and cooperation (Wade 1988). The 'failure' of some local organizations has been attributed to conflict with societal norms: examples include women's organizations in

Korea that challenged male hierarchies and land reform organizations that opposed powerful landlords (Esman and Uphoff 1984). The organizer of a mothers' club in Korea was beaten, with the justification that 'misfortune will fall upon the house where the hen crows like a rooster' (quoted in Esman and Uphoff 1984: 187), while twenty one prominent members of the Farmers' Federation of Thailand were murdered and the organization collapsed (Morell and Samudavanija 1981). Other groups failed because they challenged prevailing bureaucratic norms: 'the bureaucracy has tried to muzzle, if not curtail self-help organizations because the entire self-help process threatens the bureaucracy's managerial functions, its ideology and ultimately its means of survival' (Holmquist 1979: 137, referring to organizations in East Africa).

There is a general presumption that group mode of operation will be affected by societal norms. Groups which exploit existing relationships (e.g. hierarchies) are more likely to succeed than those which challenge them. Yet many groups are developed in order to challenge existing relationships. These can survive, and with popular support and good organization, they can flourish. When extensive enough, they serve to change dominant societal modes. Many *claims* groups, in particular, have challenged prevailing norms: for example, trade unions which developed in the hierarchical environment of the nineteenth century; popular organizations supporting land reform in countries with highly unequal land distribution; many women's groups. However, as noted above, claims groups which are organized in a way that is contrary to prevalent norms often meet powerful opposition.

The connection between macro-environment and group behaviour will be further explored, with empirical examples drawn from the medical sector, in the remainder of this chapter.

2.3. THE CHANGING MACRO-ENVIRONMENT: A SUMMARY

The macro-environment encompasses the norms and the political economy prevalent in a society; that is it includes the manifold influences—economic, political, and social—to which individuals and groups are subject by the environment in which they operate. Since the world is a complex and heterogeneous place, it is often difficult to identify a unique macro-environment as prevalent, to categorize changes over time, and even more difficult to generalize across societies. Yet, despite the many qualifications, in this chapter I argue that there have been some mega-changes in norms and political economy over the last century or so each of which has greatly influenced group behaviour.

These mega-changes in macro-environment are partly a response to political developments (e.g. to the advent and then the demise of colonialism), and, partly, to a complex, organic, and cumulative process involving an interaction between the prevailing political economy, development thinking, and policy making. The macro-environment influencing group behaviour is the outcome of this process. This environment consists in the nexus of norms and political economy which have both direct and indirect effects on group behaviour.

Changes in the macro-environment in developing countries are strongly influenced by what is happening to norms in the developed countries. Although this influence was most clear and direct under Colonialism, in the post-colonial period, the norms prevalent in developed countries have continued to have a very important influence on those in developing countries, partly as a result of the activities of the international institutions. Of course, in developing countries, as elsewhere, there is rarely or never a unique view of development, universally held; given a multitude of views what is the dominant view at any particular time may often be a matter of controversy. Moreover, differences among developing countries in political economy, stage of development and so on influence the pace and nature of paradigmatic changes in their macro-environment. Views also vary according to the perspective of the observer with Southern thinkers often taking a different view from Northern ones. The views espoused by the development aid community, typically led by the World Bank, are particularly influential in development thinking however because of the considerable resources devoted to disseminating their message, and because they can use conditionality to enforce it.

Despite these caveats, very broadly, we can identify three historical phases of political economy and development thinking in the twentieth century, each associated with a distinct macro-environment for group behaviour. First, the Colonial or neocolonial period, roughly occurring from the late nineteenth century to the Second World War in Africa and Asia—for most of Latin America the Colonial period started and ended at a much earlier date, but the economic aspects of colonialism, associated with the dominance of primary product exports to serve developed country markets, continued there over broadly the same period as in the other regions.[1] The second phase consists of the dominance of a strongly interventionist statist view of economic policy-making, which occurred approximately over the first three decades after the Second World War, though it started in a mild way in the 1930s in Latin America. This era coincided with Keynesianism in Western developed countries and the apparent success of the socialist model in the Soviet Union and Eastern Europe. The third phase encompasses the liberal reaction against statist policies, favouring monetarism and laissez-faire which took place from the early 1980s; this was accompanied by a strong opening to the global economy, or what has been termed 'globalization'. Table 2.1 reviews the historical phases.

Although these prevailing development paradigms were developed internationally and were a common influence on thinking and policy-making, individual countries went through these phases at different times in accordance with their own political and economic developments. For example, as noted countries in Latin America acquired political independence much earlier than other regions, although they adopted broadly similar patterns of development for much of the time. Some countries accepted the paradigms much more wholeheartedly and comprehensively than others: for example, Bolivia and Peru appear to have been fully converted to the laissez-faire paradigm, while many Asian countries maintained more selectivity, combining elements of 'opening up' with elements of protection and state intervention. By the end of the twentieth century

---

[1] See Thorp 1998. We have termed this the 'neocolonial' period.

Table 2.1. *Changing themes in development thinking*

Eras	Dominant strands in developed country thinking	Dominant themes in development economics	Policy implications	Implication for group behaviour
Colonial period				
1850–1950	Considerable variation; free trade and protection; mainly laissez-faire; mainly monetarist	Enclave development by European paternalistic policies. Colonialism as exploitative imperialism	Limited investment in infrastructure. Primary production developed under colonial control	Largely P/C. Traditional society mixture of COOP, P/C and limited M
Post-independence economic planning				
1950s–1960s	Keynesianism in macro-policies Neoclassical trade theory	Growth, planning, and industrialization	Interventionist; protectionist State ownership	P/C with COOP elements. M limited
1970s	A. Keynesianism	Employment; redistribution with growth;	As above but with more focus on employment and poverty reduction	
	B. Marxism	Basic needs Dependency	Limit multinational company access	
	C. Neo-classical revival	The role of prices and the market in resource allocation		
Liberalization and globalization				
1980s	Monetarism and Neoclassical econ. Rational expectations	Pro-market and anti-state; monetarism in macro-policy; New political economy	Role back state; increased role of market	Much greater role for M
Late 1980s–mid-1990s	New theories of growth and trade; informational asymmetries; alternative motivations; institutions	New focus on poverty; human development Role of the state as complementary to the market; role of NGOS and communities	Globalization; further opening to trade and MNC; extend property rights Human resource focus Non-state actors encouraged	

other countries had made almost no moves into the liberalizing, globalizing era (e.g. Laos and Burma). Nonetheless, at an international level the change in paradigms undoubtedly occurred, with important consequences for political economy, for norms, and for group behaviour. The next section of this chapter will explore how the changes came about, their nature, and implications for group functioning.

2.4. CHANGING PARADIGMS: WHY THEY OCCURRED AND THEIR IMPLICATIONS

2.4.1. *The Colonial and Neo-Colonial Period*

In general, one needs to distinguish between the philosophy and behaviour prevalent in the areas directly influenced by Colonial rule, and those where local arrangements dominate. There is, of course, no unique 'Colonial model'. The political systems and philosophies of the Colonial powers themselves differed, as did the political and economic structures and resource base of the colonized areas (Young 1994). In some areas settler communities were numerous and powerful, while elsewhere they were relatively small. However, the dominant and universally shared motive of Colonial policy was to secure economic benefits for the Colonial powers—usually, to provide raw materials for Europe's growing needs and, in some situations, to generate markets for European manufactured goods.[2] The European settlers (and landowners) in Latin America shared the objectives espoused by the Colonial powers elsewhere. To achieve these goals required some infrastructural development, and limited investments in local health and education. There were major differences in policy, however, according to the nature of the commodity to be extracted; in countries where physically concentrated mineral production was the main Colonial product, there was little need to extend infrastructure or development beyond a small enclave—even workers were often imported; in contrast where production of the commodity was spread widely geographically (e.g. coffee, rice), there was more extensive development of the country. Where the climate was propitious for European settlers, production was organized into plantations which they owned, depriving local people of land and opportunities other than that of near or actual slave labour on the plantations. In less salubrious climes, production was left to peasants who thereby acquired some cash opportunities, retained their land, and were provided with necessary education and services.

There were variations in the structure of Colonial government, notably between direct and indirect rule. But throughout in the Colonial enclaves, P/C was the overwhelmingly predominant mode of operation and prevalent philosophy. A French Governor in 1908 stated that 'What must be put in place above all is the undebatable principle of our authority'. (Governor Gabriel Angoulvant of the Cote D'Ivoire, quoted in Young 1994: 101). The Indian Administrative system was 'imposed ready

---

[2] Furnivall (1948) argues that a good deal of the difference in colonial structures was accounted for by whether it was a desire to increase raw material supplies or to generate markets that was the prime Colonial motive.

made from above' (Harvey 1925: 563). Burma's structure of government was typical, with a hierarchy which went from the Chief Commissioner to the deputy Chief Commissioner to subdivisional and township officers in urban areas and local headmen in the rural areas.

The system of indirect rule—that is, reliance on local 'traditional' chiefs for administration in rural areas—also involved a hierarchical mode of operation. This was the system adopted in Burma in the rural areas, with traditional Circle Headmen transformed into appointed officials, and also in much of Sub-Saharan Africa, where traditional chiefs were allocated responsibility for most rural administration. But these chiefs were appointed by the Colonial government, and could be dismissed if they failed to carry out Colonial policy. The Governor-General of Afrique Occidentale Française made this abundantly clear in a statement in 1908: 'Alone the Cercle Commandant [the French official] commands: alone he is responsible. The indigenous chief is only an instrument, an auxiliary' (quoted in Young 1994: 108). Revocations, public whippings, and imprisonment of chiefs for failing to fulfill their duties were common, especially in the early period (Young 1994: 129). The chiefs themselves became mini-despots, 'judge, police chief, military commander, prison superintendent, tax collector, chief medical officer' (Fugelstad 1983: 81). Prior checks on their power, via popular assemblies or customary law were abolished. 'To the peasant the person of the chief signifies power that is total and absolute, unchecked and unrestrained' (Mamdani 1996: 54). '... the Colonial state really liberated administrative staff from all institutional constraints' (Mamdani 1996: 43). In French colonies, summary punishment was authorized for acts which might 'undermine respect owing to French authority or its European representatives, or to injure the exercise of this authority' (Young 1994: 116).

After political independence in the nineteenth century, Latin American countries were ruled by expatriate settlers in an authoritarian fashion, similar to that of Colonialism. The ruling class continued to have strong links with the former Colonial powers. Like other Colonial territories, Latin American economies were dominated by primary production for export to the metropolitan economies. Norms were largely P/C with elements of M and COOP, much the same as in the Colonies elsewhere. The COOP mode of behaviour of the indigenous Indian economy was forcibly displaced by P/C modes. Indian land was expropriated and Indian labour forced to work on settler plantations (Thorp 1998: chapters 2 and 3).

The Colonial and neocolonial era represented one of the strongest examples of a macro-environment organized along P/C lines that one can find, although obviously there were elements of M and COOP. Labour was procured for infrastructure and to work on plantations or in the mines by force, direct or indirect (including imposing head or hut taxes which could only be paid by labouring). Financial incentives, however, played some part in procuring peasant production. Much of the previous 'traditional' system, which had relied on a combination of P/C and COOP was undermined by Colonial practices—for example, customary law was set aside where it conflicted with Colonial needs or values, and autonomous village structures were weakened or destroyed (Mamdani 1996; Furnivall 1948).

While the Colonial and neocolonial environment was a P/C one, there remained many activities outside the influence of Colonial policy, where society continued to operate along pre-colonial indigenous lines. There is a huge anthropological literature on how such societies operated. From this it is apparent that (i) there were large variations in behaviour; (ii) kinship was an important aspect of production relations with much production and many transactions occurring within kinship groups or local communities, often described as a 'domestic mode of production' (see e.g. Sahlins 1972); (iii) within kinship groups and local communities, relationships appear to exhibit a combination of all three of our modes of behaviour, with the balance varying within and across societies. Clearly, COOP was an important element, as might be expected of groups who live in long-term relationships with each other, with reproductive, productive, and consumption relationships and activities intermingled. P/C also played an important part (Polanyi 1957), as exemplified by traditional leaders. Traditional leaders, however, 'were regarded as trustees whose influence was circumscribed both in customary law and religion' (Mboya 1963 in *African Socialism*, quoted in Cowen and Shenton 1996: 326). COOP relationships, like those observed today, covered a range of behaviour, including pooling of labour and output, 'gifts', and more overtly reciprocal activity, although neither the timing nor the nature of reciprocation was neatly defined. In addition, short-term exchange relationships of a utilitarian nature were present (i.e. M as defined above), though they were rarely quantitatively important. (iv) Much production and consumption occurred within groups (in the so-called 'domestic' mode of production). Between group behaviour was largely COOP in recurring relationships, backed up by elements of P/C and M.

According to Sahlins (1972), the mode of behaviour altered with the distance of the social relationship. Pooling (COOP with elements of within family P/C) was the exclusive mode within tightly defined families; as kinship or community ties lessened, explicit reciprocity became more important, moving towards M modes for trade with strangers. Polanyi (1957) makes a similar point when he states that market relationships only arose in association with long distance trade.

In many cases behaviour does not fit into a single mode, but encompasses a range of motives and behaviours. Thus what appear as 'gifts' may in fact involve reciprocity, while exchange is firmly embedded in social relationships. While some combination of COOP and P/C best represents most behaviour—and short-term utilitarian exchange is rare—longer-term interests are often clearly served by the behaviour. This ambiguity is in fact equally true of current COOP relationships, as is apparent from other chapters in this book. But one aspect which differentiates relationships in small communities from those of the modern market economy is the recurrent social relationship between those conducting the transactions. 'A material transaction is usually a momentary episode in a continuous social relation' (Sahlins 1972: 186). In contrast, the opposite could be said in many late-twentieth century market transactions—that is, many social relations are a momentary episode resulting from material transactions. This is a key difference in terms of the conditions favourable for different modes of behaviour; recurrent social relations tend to support COOP, while M may be a more natural method of transaction between strangers in the night.

A study of the Malle in southwest Ethiopia illustrates some of these points.[3] Production was primarily organized on a household basis, with household decisions apparently determined by the head of the household in a P/C manner. In addition there were important elements of cooperation among households which included redistribution of output to households in need and cooperative work arrangements. Among the latter, one type was strictly reciprocal with a short time horizon as households worked in rotation on others' fields; a second type of work cooperation took the form of 'festive work groups', when one household requested work assistance and provided food and drink, while others sent younger members of their household to work for the household. In these activities, there was no exact reciprocity, and no accounting of labour allocation, but 'a long-term, global relationship of mutual social assistance' (Donham 1981: 534).

The Environment for Group Behaviour
In the Colonial era, the macro-environment influencing group behaviour was thus largely P/C, with elements of COOP and M, in areas directly affected by Colonial authority; and a combination of COOP and P/C, with a minor role for M, in 'traditional' activities. The way in which these influences translated into group behaviour is illustrated by a brief examination of medical practices.

Colonial Medicine
Most accounts indicate a strong similarity of medical Colonial systems in different parts of the world (Manderson 1999). Initially Colonial medical policy was almost entirely devoted to protecting the health of Europeans through urban hospitals. Subsequently efforts were made to reduce epidemics among the local population which might threaten the health of Europeans and also adversely affect labour supply (see e.g. Lyons 1994). Missionary medicine was more concerned with improving the health of the local population.

By all accounts the organization of Colonial medicine systematically reflected the P/C nature of Colonial society. For example, in the French Colonial system, medical services were initially actually an arm of the armed forces; even in 1965, military doctors represented more than 90% of the French medical personnel overseas (Patton 1996). In India, medical boards were established in the eighteenth century, consisting of the most senior surgeons, to control appointments and discipline. Appointments were generally made according to seniority (Jeffery 1988: 61). A British Colonial Medical Service was established in 1901, which laid down a strict hierarchy ranging from the principal Colonial surgeon, to the senior Colonial surgeon, Colonial surgeon, and assistant Colonial surgeon. Administration was to be carried out by an inspector general. Although the nomenclature varied over the years, the hierarchical system remained. The role of local personnel was strictly limited, and often entirely excluded especially in Africa; accounts of training of local personnel indicate that a major element was that of imparting unquestioning obedience to superior personnel (Patton 1996; Iliffe 1998).

[3] Taken from Donham (1981) in a study in 1974–75 (i.e. in the post-colonial era), but the particular group appears to have been untouched by the Western economic system.

Most curative services were confined to the elite (mainly expatriates) with services for the mass of the population limited to treating and preventing epidemics (Jeffery 1988). The latter were conducted like military campaigns, and interventions were dictatorial and bureaucratic (Manderson 1999; Vaughan 1991). 'When it came to practice . . . the military campaign was the only model available in the Colonial context . . . the Medical Officer became indistinguishable from the administrator in the eyes of the African community' (Vaughan 1991: 43). For example, in Nyasaland, 'small pox police' were employed to enforce vaccination. There was prison-like isolation of those with sleeping sickness in the Belgian Congo; Africans were forbidden from washing, collecting water, fishing or travelling on waterways that were deemed unsafe (Lyons 1994). House burnings and detention camps were used by Americans against cholera in the Philippines (Manderson 1999). The treatment of yaws in Eastern Nigeria involved compulsory stripping, investigation and treatment, carried out with militaristic precision. Vaughan describes these procedures as 'perfect examples of the most repressive and objectifying of colonial practices. Colonial subjects are here being codified and numbered, deprived of clothing and of any individual choice, they are herded into an enclosure where various agents of the state make a direct assault on their bodies' (Vaughan 1991: 52). The organization of leprosy camps similarly indicates how the P/C nature of Colonial society was reproduced in smaller groups. After describing such organization in some detail, Vaughan concludes that they 'reflected the larger Colonial society, and stood as microcosms of the "British Colony"' (Vaughan 1991: 88).

Initially Missionaries also provided little medical support for Africans, believing that 'faith and prayer were sufficient to ensure native health' (quotation from McCord in Good 1991: p 1). But Missionary provision of medical facilities for local people soon followed. The Missionaries in general were organs and facilitators of the Colonial administration, albeit in the context of their evangelical mission. The latter led to a focus on cultural conversion as an end in itself, an emphasis on the connection between spiritual and bodily issues, and to somewhat greater recognition of their patients as individuals (Vaughan 1991; Good 1991). These differences appear to have lead to a slightly more COOP and less P/C approach. A more voluntary approach was adopted, for example, to the use of childbirth and welfare facilities. Over time distinctions between Missionary and official facilities diminished with the Missionary ones becoming 'more impersonal' (Vaughan 1991: 74). Nonetheless, a common perception remained that 'African populations everywhere almost invariably seem to believe that health workers employed in the Church-related health services provide care that is superior to their Ministry of Health counterparts because they are trained to understand the connection between body and soul and to show greater compassion for human suffering' (Good 1991: 2; see also the evidence in Tibandebage and Mackintosh, Chapter 13 this volume). The price of this more compassionate attitude was that Missionary medicine was more culturally intrusive, generally regarding traditional healers as enemies (though there were exceptions to this—see Vaughan 1991).

Colonial medicine thus exhibited strong P/C features: COOP elements were small; they were present in the treatment of Europeans in the official medical service, and more comprehensively in Missionary hospitals. Those performing medical services did, of course, receive financial rewards, but these were related to a person's hierarchical position and colour, not to performance (Patton 1996).

Traditional healing practices continued alongside the activities of European medicine. These covered a wide range of activities including well structured associations, and diviners, and lay healers working individually. In India, for example, there were two parallel, complex, and sophisticated systems, the Ayurvedic and Unani. These systems mainly adopted a more holistic approach than Colonial medicine, attributing some cases of sickness to spirits, some to sorcery, and some to physiological problems (Feierman 1985; Vaughan 1994; Curto de Casas 1994). In most parts of the world, the role of traditional healers continued into the post-colonial era, for example, the *curanderos* in Latin America. It is not possible to be confident about the mode of operation of these systems without more research, but from limited investigation it seems that they combined elements of each of the three modes; while in many cases hierarchy and control was a major element, there were also COOP elements (probably more so than in Colonial medicine), and payment (either in kind or cash) was also important in securing some services. In fact, Iliffe describes indigenous healers in East Africa as 'entrepreneurial, competitive, and often mercenary', with many refusing to do anything without an initial payment (Iliffe 1998: 11), while in India, the indigenous medical practitioners mainly worked for payment, many making substantial sums (Jeffery 1988: 55).

2.4.2. *Interventionism from the 1950s to the 1970s*

Most countries of the developing world acquired political independence between 1945 and 1960, though, of course, in Latin America it was much earlier. In the developed countries a quite strongly interventionist economic philosophy prevailed then, due to successful planning in the Second World War and the Keynesian revolution in economic thought. This was also the era of apparently thriving socialism in the Soviet empire. The interventionist philosophy resonated with the objectives, politics, and philosophy of the newly independent countries, and of Latin American governments which had already started to initiate active industrial policies in reaction to the fall in commodity prices in the 1930s.

For most developing countries at the beginning of the 1950s the overriding reality was underdevelopment, characterized by low incomes, a predominantly agrarian structure with a large subsistence subsector, and heavy dependence on the industrialized countries for all modern inputs. Developing countries had two related economic objectives: to become economically as well as politically independent and to raise their incomes to the levels of the developed countries. Developed countries, too, recognized the need for a new approach to the former Colonial territories. Indeed, already in 1937, the governor of Nigeria announced that 'The exploitation theory is dead . . . and the development theory has come to take its place' (quoted in Cowen and Shenton 1996: 7). In a famous statement President Truman declared that

We must embark on a bold new program for making the benefits of our scientific advances and industrial progress available for the improvement and growth of underdeveloped areas. The old imperialism is dead—exploitation for foreign profit has no place in our plans. What we must envisage is a program of development based on the concepts of democratic fair dealing. (Inaugural address, 20 January 1949).

Policies in the 1950s and 1960s

The desirability of development planning was widely accepted—by developed country observers[4] as well as developing country theoreticians and practitioners. Development Plans were introduced by Mahalanobis in India, Prebisch in Latin America and visiting economists in many African economies (Killick 1976). The state was given a major role in determining economic priorities via price and import controls, investment planning and sometimes as a producer, with the adoption of a strategy of import-substituting industrialization.

In most countries, the state, continued to be organized in a P/C mode—adapting rather than transforming the Colonial state. As Young puts it: 'Although we commonly described the independent polities as "new states", in reality they were successors to the colonial regime, inheriting its structures, its quotidian routines and practices, and its more normative theories of governance . . . . In short, what Mbembe terms a *principe autoritaire* informed the inner ethos of the postcolonial state'. (Young 1994: 285, 287). One party states were common, and democracy rare: 'development became a top-down agenda enforced on the peasantry' (Mamdani 1996: 288). Extreme examples include the Tanzanian villagization project and the centralized despotism of Mobutu's Congo. In Senegal 'the state aims more and more at direct administrative, ideological and political control over the dominated masses, be they urban or rural' (Copans 1980: 248). A fairly authoritarian approach was adopted, even in the more democratic countries—for example, India and the West Indies.

In line with the prevailing economic philosophy and the nature of the state, economic policies were designed largely in a P/C mode, with planning centrally directed, despite much COOP rhetoric; financial incentives were also used to help bring about the desired developments, although these incentives were not those emanating from an unregulated market, but mainly the product of deliberate state intervention. In general, there was an expansion of private sector activity—as a complement to or in parallel with that of the state—which operated according to M mode, usually heavily circumscribed by state-imposed restrictions.

The policies adopted were in some ways remarkably successful. Savings and investment rates rose dramatically from the mid-1950s and growth accelerated in most countries, while some, notably in East Asia, experienced spectacular growth rates. Social indicators, such as infant mortality and literacy rates, also improved. But other developments were less welcome. Population growth accelerated, and growth in employment lagged behind output. Un- and underemployment emerged as serious problems, and the absolute numbers of people falling below the poverty line increased. A dualistic pattern of development continued, with a small relatively privileged modern sector leaving

---

[4] For example, although the policy prescriptions advocated by Fei and Ranis were not as strongly interventionist as many of the writings of the time, they accepted that 'The need for development planning is well recognised' (Fei and Ranis 1964: 199).

the rest of the economy with low incomes and investment. The ILO summarized the position: '. . . it has become increasingly evident . . . that rapid growth at the national level does not automatically reduce poverty or inequality or provide sufficient productive employment' (ILO 1976: 15). Moreover, the economic independence sought was elusive, as dependence on developed countries for capital and technology increased.

Thinking in the Late 1960s and 1970s
The events of the 1950s and 1960s led to new thinking about development. Three distinct strands may be detected, each a reaction to different aspects of the development experience over the previous twenty years.

First, some became concerned with the lack of economic independence achieved. These formed the dependency school of thought, which included both Marxists and structuralists, largely from the South, such as Frank (1969), Furtado (1967) and Amin (1974) (see Palma 1978). They mostly advocated reduced links between rich and poor countries, although there were important differences within the dependency school.[5] The dependency school did not directly challenge P/C norms but argued that power and control should be located in the South, not the North. The school was dominated by scholars from the South, and their views were in no way shared by the aid community.

A second reaction was to the rising poverty and unemployment that had become evident in the 1960s. It was argued that countries had been pursuing the wrong objective (Seers 1971). Candidates for replacing GNP as the main economic objective were successively employment, redistribution with growth, and the fulfilment of basic needs (BN). This reaction came primarily from the developed countries and the aid community, eventually penetrating the World Bank. It was treated with some hostility by developing country governments. Some of the alternatives advocated involved P/C norms, but differently directed—for example, BN approaches can be highly paternalistic. Others included important COOP elements—some of the BN approaches, for example, advocated participation as an essential basic need (e.g. Streeten *et al.* 1981; ILO 1976).

The third strand of thought initiated in the 1970s, which became dominant in the 1980s, was to advocate a predominantly M mode of behaviour across the economy and a substantially reduced role of government. This stemmed from an interpretation of the differential economic performance across countries; it was argued that the rapid and fairly egalitarian growth experienced in East Asia in contrast to the capital-intensive and elite dominated pattern of growth observed elsewhere was due to a lesser role of government and more use of market mechanisms in many places (see e.g. Little *et al.* 1970; Balassa 1971; Krueger 1974).[6] This criticism of the interventionist model

---

[5] Some believed that the North–South relationship could be controlled by active policies; some that this was impossible because of the political consequences of dependency (e.g. Leys 1975); while some thought that the North–South connection was ultimately progressive and would lead eventually to the emergence of a proletariat and revolution (Warren 1980).

[6] Deeper analysis of the East Asian experience suggested this was an incorrect interpretation, and that they too had intervened heavily in the economy, but in a more efficient way (see e.g. Amsden 1989; Wade 1990).

came almost entirely from Western trained economists, sponsored by major Western institutions—for example, the OECD, the World Bank, and the US government.

Policies in the 1970s
Over the 1970s, the *dependencia* approach was most effective in terms of changing policies, though its effects were short-lived. The underlying belief of the dependency school was of unfairness in the world's economic relations: this formed the background to OPEC and its successful efforts to raise oil-prices and the New International Economic Order (NIEO) put forward by the G-77 in 1974. Other manifestations of the dependency approach were the restrictions on direct foreign investment and controls over technology transfer, introduced most comprehensively by the Andean Pact countries and India. As far as general economic policies were concerned, most countries sustained the previous inward-looking macroeconomic and interventionism policies, in many cases supported by heavy borrowing from abroad.

The BN approach had a strong influence on donor philosophy, for example, on the ILO, the World Bank under MacNamara, major bilateral aid agencies, and the United Nations special agencies. However, few developing countries put BN at the centre of their development strategy, or pursued serious redistributive policies. Progress in meeting BN continued over these years, but there was no evidence of any acceleration. The dependency school had a much more significant impact. In the sellers' market created by high world demand, the belligerent attitude of the oil producers, partly inspired by this school, led to the oil price rise of 1972–73, creating massive imbalances in the world economy and inflationary pressures in developed countries. Most oil-importing developing countries borrowed to finance the resulting trade deficits. Consequently, there was a massive accumulation of debt as well as rising budgetary and trade imbalances, made worse by a further increase in oil prices in 1978–79. In developed countries, inflation rates accelerated. These changes were largely responsible for a major turnaround in thinking in both developed and developing countries in the early 1980s.

In general, P/C style policies continued to dominate in the 1970s, with neither the COOP policies associated with some of the BN and redistributive approaches, nor the M, favoured by the 'get the prices right' school, making substantial headway. Politically, norms continued to be of a P/C type in most countries. Indeed, the tendency towards one party states and suppression of dissent increased and there was a rise in the number of military dictatorships in Latin America and Africa.

The Environment for Group Behaviour 1950s to 1970s
Centralized planning to promote development undoubtedly resulted in a P/C macro-environment, despite the fact that some of the language of the Keynesian-cum-Fabian philosophy of development philanthropists was COOP in intention. Moreover, the socialist model, emulated by many countries, also involved top-down rather than participatory planning. The role of the market was restricted everywhere, most severely in the countries adopting the socialist model. As noted, a P/C mode was in tune with the prevalent political systems. Nonetheless, there was a greater role for COOP relations

than in the preceding era, even within government, and to a much greater extent in the burgeoning non-governmental, non-market sector, while pre-colonial societies, which continued to be important in many places, retained some strong COOP elements.

The size of government increased dramatically in most developing countries, giving rise to extensive areas of non-market relationships. Many institutions, including the public sector, government-supported cooperatives and NGOs, faced only 'soft' budget constraints. Within the public sector, this led to decision-making by 'bureaucratic' man (James 1989), as well as rent-seeking behaviour (Krueger 1974); in the social sectors, public service was emphasized with a combination of P/C and COOP relations practiced. In the emerging popular organizations and NGOs, rhetoric strongly favoured COOP but practice exhibited a combination of P/C and COOP.

Although there was more acceptance of COOP norms than before, some of the structural changes were less supportive of COOP motivation. The mass migration to cities associated with industrialization weakened traditional cooperative arrangements. While new communities developed, they were generally more unstable, with fewer kinship ties. But other circumstances favoured the development of new-style COOP groups—for example, in the form of Trade Unions among those in employment in the formal sector. New community organizations also developed, often with redistributive functions—for example, the Harambee movement in Kenya. Informal efficiency-supporting groups also emerged among low-income producers (rural and urban) to overcome indivisibilities and externalities often organized primarily along COOP lines (see e.g. Baland and Platteau 1998).

M behaviour was officially given a relatively minor role, with restrictions on the role of market incentives even within the private sector. However, in practice (and increasingly over time), parallel activities developed in which market incentives prevailed. The expansion of rent seeking and parallel markets was particularly marked where official prices diverged widely from competitive ones—one reason advanced for a more overt switch to monetary incentives.

In sum, there was a mixed picture. The government, which became increasingly dominant in the formal sector, was largely P/C, but encouraged a greater role for COOP relations than in the Colonial era. In a formal way M relations were downgraded (both for transactions within the public sector and for the private sector), although they played an increasingly important role, especially informally in the form of parallel markets and rent seeking.

Medicine in the Planning Era
At the beginning of this era, the formal medical system was organized on strictly P/C lines, dominated by expatriates and largely devoted to their needs. Government objectives with respect to medicine were similar to the wider societal aims—to indigenize the provision of medicine, especially in the higher echelons, and to provide the standards and type of medicine enjoyed in the West for the whole population: 'Kenya must copy the British model of medical services and nothing else' stated Mungai, the Kenyan Minister of Health in 1963 (quoted in Iliffe 1998: 131). To this end new hospitals and medical schools were established, and students were sent abroad

for training. Medical services were to be provided primarily by the state, generally free of charge. As with the wider political system, these changes involved indigenizing services but not transforming them. Consequently, the basic P/C mode was maintained—although Russian-trained doctors adopted a more collective approach (Patton 1996), while local domination of the service and the professional associations increased solidarity among doctors (Iliffe 1998). In practice, patients sometimes made illicit payments to secure high quality treatment, thereby introducing a stronger element of M (Jeffery 1988: 261–2). COOP also played a role—with medical personnel being motivated by the desire to serve and to do a good job, as well as because they were ordered or paid to do so. For example, a Cuban doctor, operating in a highly P/C system, stated: 'Medicine is a call to services, my business is seeing the patient get well, not the size of my salary' (*Economist* 8 May 1999). In some areas, community health workers, selected from the local community, provided a more COOP model (e.g. in the State of Mahashtra). In general, however, doctors were determined to maintain a hierarchy which they dominated. In Uganda, for example, they rejected proposals to develop a cadre of assistant doctors, while proposals to introduce community health workers in India were postponed for decades (Iliffe 1998: 121; Jeffery 1988).

The inappropriateness of the model gradually became apparent—in particular, the financial impossibility of providing Western standards for all, and the need for priority for preventative health care. Consequently, there was a switch to emphasis on primary health care and immunization in the 1970s, led by WHO and UNICEF, broadly following the BN approach to development. The new approach was more effective, being much lower cost and reaching larger numbers, but it was no more participatory than before. However, when it became impossible for most people to secure the medicines they believed they needed from the public health system, there was a switch to traditional practitioners and self-medication. In East Africa, 'needle men' and drug sellers became increasingly prevalent, despite the practices being outlawed, as indicated by the spate of prosecutions against them (Iliffe 1998). These alternatives, as well as NGO-supported efforts, tended to be COOP and/or M, in mode of operation.

2.4.3. *Liberalization and Globalization*

The neo-liberal reaction to the post-independence interventionism started in the early 1970s. But it had little effect until the 1980s when it received a powerful boost both from the policies adopted in the UK and US and from the debt crisis which enabled the International Financial Institutions (IFIs) to impose pro-market and laissez-faire policies on borrowing countries. Globalization and liberalization are closely intertwined—liberalization provided an impetus to globalization, and globalization contributed to forcing liberalization on recalcitrant governments. The 1990s also saw some reaction to the liberal revolution of the 1980s, both theoretically—with powerful criticisms of the underlying model—and in policy focus, with renewed emphasis on human objectives, especially poverty reduction. But policy response to this reaction has been quite severely constrained by globalization.

The Liberal Revolution of the 1980s and 1990s
The first and most important revolution occurred in developed countries, Thatcher (from 1979) and Reagan (from 1981) espousing monetary policies, in principle, if not always in practice. This imparted a new monetarist, anti-government, pro-market, laissez-faire philosophy which permeated the IFIs, bilateral aid administrations, educational establishments in developed countries and eventually the 'technocrats' in developing countries who had been educated in these establishments.

The view that in developing countries the state had overreached itself had already been powerfully propounded in the early 1970s by a succession of pro-market observers—as noted above. Essentially, they pointed to the inefficiencies associated with government interventions in most areas of policy, including trade, prices, and production, arguing for a smaller role for governments and a greatly enhanced role for the market. Discrediting of what came to be termed *dirigisme*, with the view that government failures almost invariably outweighed market failures, was carried further in the early 1980s (Lal 1983; Bhagwati 1982; Little 1982). This view was reinforced by the 'new political economy' which argued that the actions of self-seeking individuals (bureaucrats and politicians), led to individual rent seeking, group short-termism and state predations, concluding that a minimalist state would do least damage to social welfare.[7] This replaced 'the image of the benign state with its mirror opposite, the negative state' (Grindle 1991: 43).

Policies
By 1980, the anti-state, pro-market philosophy had been adopted by the World Bank, whose power over policy-making in developing countries greatly increased with the onset of the acute debt crisis in the early 1980s and the initiation of structural adjustment loans. While the World Bank emphasized deregulation, reduced price controls, subsidies, tariffs, and the elimination of restrictions against direct foreign investment, the IMF promoted a monetarist view—that the prime objective of macroeconomic policy should be to stabilize the economy through tight control over the budget and money supply.[8] Considerations of poverty reduction or BN virtually disappeared from the policy views of these institutions. Throughout the developing world there were massive policy switches in the 1980s in accordance with the IFI agenda.[9] The policies were intended to bring about a change of behaviour from P/C and COOP to M, all premised on the supposed greater efficiency of M modes of behaviour.

For the regions most subject to Washington tutelage—Africa and Latin America— the stabilization and adjustment policies were accompanied by falling GDP per capita for much of the 1980s, falling real per capita expenditure on the social services and rising poverty. Social indicators worsened in a number of countries and investment rates fell, although it does not appear that economic performance was systematically

---

[7] e.g. Lal 1984; Conybeare 1982; Bhagwati 1982; Bates 1981; drawing on the work of Buchanan *et al.* 1980.

[8] Williamson 1990, conveniently labelled this set of policies as representing the 'Washington consensus'.

[9] e.g. Williamson (ed.) 1990; World Bank and UNDP 1989; Dean *et al.* 1994, for evidence of the advance of these policies in Latin America and Africa.

worse in 'adjusting' than 'non-adjusting' countries—and may have been marginally better.[10] However, some assessments of the social impact—on poverty rates and other social indicators—suggest a slight negative impact.[11] Moreover, the widespread rise in poverty in adjusting countries led many to question the apparent elimination of human concerns from the development agenda.

Table 2.2. *Changing income distribution, 1980s to 1990s*

	No. of countries with rising inequality	No. of countries with falling inequality	No. of countries with no change in distribution
OECD	15	1	2
Eastern Europe and CIS	11	0	0
Latin America	8	3	2
Asia	7	3	0
Africa	3	3	1

Source: UNDP, *Human Development Report 1999* (New York: OUP); Stewart and Berry 1999; Morley 1995.

Implications of Liberalization and Globalization for Group Behaviour

Liberalization has introduced a strong market ethos into norms of behaviour across the world. Numerous enterprises have been moved from the public into the private sector. For those that remained in the public sector, the soft budgets that previously permitted satisfying behaviour became unusual. Increasingly, the public sector was required to compete with the private sector, to contract out to it, and to adopt market incentives in its own transactions. In numerous ways, the culture of reforming societies became oriented towards M behaviour, replacing both P/C and COOP. This change was reinforced by rising inequalities within most economies (see Table 2.2. and Cornia 1999; Stewart and Berry 1999). Rising wage differentials—which occurred in most countries—increased potential private sector earnings for the professional classes, while as maximizing individual earnings became an accepted way of behaving, pressures grew for non-market groups to provide similar differentials. In many societies provision for the poorest weakened. Large numbers of people were marginalized, in both developed and developing countries. Many became homeless and resorted to begging—a phenomenon which it had been thought had been eliminated by welfare states in developed countries after the Second World War. Others resorted to violence (Fukuyama 1999).

Evidence for reduced levels of trust during the 1980s has been documented for developed countries, along with rising levels of crime. (See Figs 2.1 and 2.2 taken from

---

[10] There have been numerous studies of the macro-effects of stabilization and adjustment policies, both by the IFIs themselves and by academics. The assessments of the IMF tend to suggest somewhat negative effects on growth, while those of World Bank slight positive effects compared with an estimated 'counterfactual'. Effects on investment were generally negative. See, e.g. Khan and Knight 1985; Khan 1990; Killick *et al.* 1991; World Bank 1990; Mosley *et al.* 1991; Elbadawi 1992. Most studies have been unable to find significant positive effects in Africa. [11] Easterly 2000; Kakwani 1995.

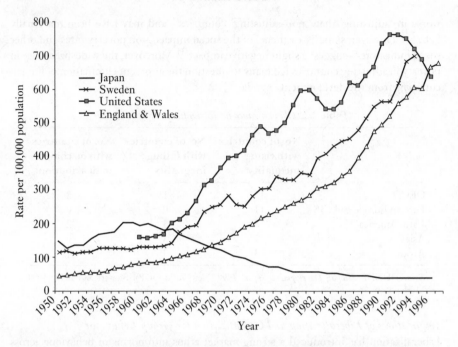

Figure 2.1. *Total violent crime rates, 1950–96*

Source: Fukuyama (1999).

Fukuyama 1999.) There is not such systematic evidence on 'trust' across countries. However, the sharpest increases in crime appear to have occurred in the societies most affected by the transition to market values and forms of organization—viz. in the UK, New Zealand, Canada, and the US—while there was a decline in violent crime in Japan and very little increase in Korea, Ireland, France, the Netherlands, and Finland, countries which appear to have had less strong changes towards market domination of culture and the economy. Of course, figures for crime can be unreliable, depending on reporting rates; policing policies can also alter incidence and reporting of crime, while drug usage is an important and, perhaps, independent cause of rising violence. Data for trust are somewhat subjective, depending on surveys of perceptions. Moreover, the change in dominant economic philosophy was associated with rising inequality and it may be this, rather than the prevalent norms, which accounts for the rise in crime and reduction in trust.

A specific example of how the switch in economic norms affected society is provided by New Zealand, which experienced a radical switch from Keynesian state-centred policies to market orientation, from the mid-1970s. The macroeconomic consequences were small, with growth rising or falling according to the exact dates selected. However, unemployment rose and real wages fell, while inflation seems to have accelerated (data from Dalziel and Lattimore 1996). A major reason for the disappointing macro-response was the huge rise in transaction costs, as the reduced role of COOP

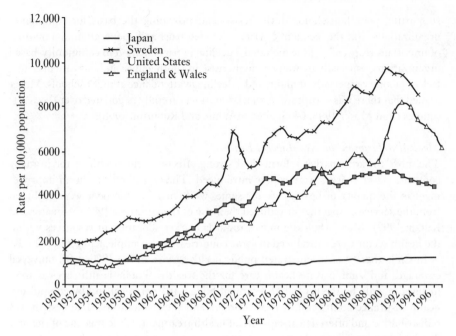

Figure 2.2. *Total theft crime rates, 1950–96*

Source: Fukuyama (1999).

required greatly increased monitoring. The ratio of transactions workers to 'transform-ation' workers rose from 0.49 in 1976 to 0.96 in 1996, with the sharpest increase arising in the decade of radical market reforms.[12] Income distribution worsened markedly (Hazledine 1998).

We had, in the New Zealand of a generation ago, a system based on high-wage full employment sustained by the general observance of *an unwritten but well-understood contract between workers, employers and the state*. It was indeed a market economy, but one in which trust and forbearance, based on empathy and sympathy, did not just temper the excesses of the market but actually allowed them to function with a remarkable lack of fuss, in terms of all those monitoring, managing, guarding and accounting activities required to excess in a more opportunistic society. It was extremely efficient in terms of exchange efficiency . . . if supposedly lacking in . . . allocative efficiency . . .   (Hazledine 1998: 217, my italics).

In developing countries, a study of four poor urban communities in Zambia, Hungary, Ecuador, and the Philippines during economic adjustments of the 1980s showed the importance of COOP relations among and within households for

---

[12] Transactions workers include all workers in industries devoted to providing transactions services 'finance, insurance, real estate, legal, and other business services, guards central administration—plus those workers in other industries in transaction occupations' plus unemployed transactions' workers. The methodology adopted by Hazledine follows that of Wallis and North (1986).

supporting poor households during crisis and providing the basis for community organizations. But the 'economic crisis . . . eroded trust and cooperation in a number of important respects'. These included a decline in participation in community-based organizations, especially by women; an increase in youth gangs; and increase in crime; lack of mobility especially at night; and a decline in attendance at night schools. Moser argued that there was a 'rupture of a social contract carefully negotiated over the years' (quotes from Moser 1996: 64–5, cited in White and Robinson 1998).

Medical Reforms in the Neo-Liberal Era

The move towards market reforms had strong effects on the health sector in many countries. User charges were widely introduced. The typical result was an improvement in the quality of health care for some, while many of the poor were excluded from the services altogether or reduced their use of them (Creese 1991; Nyonator and Kutzin 1999). More wholesale moves towards market allocation of resources within the health sector were introduced in some countries—for example, Chile and the UK.

In Chile there was an integrated public health service in the 1970s with universal coverage, and some private health care for the wealthy. Public health services were financed mainly by the central government budget (65 per cent) and by compulsory health insurance contributions from workers and their employers. The system was redistributive and offered near-equality of health treatment. Chile was one of the first developing countries to adopt market reforms in the economy as a whole under the dictatorship of Pinochet. Market reforms were soon also introduced into the health services, in two stages. In the mid-1970s, there was a reduction in central government finance which was compensated for by direct user payments and by an increase in the compulsory insurance contribution. Reforms of the mid-1980s abolished the National Health Service as such, favouring private intermediary institutions to which workers could assign their compulsory health contributions in exchange for health insurance plans.

The reforms also involved greater decentralization of the public health system. In both periods there was a severe reduction in public funding for health services. The 1981 reforms led to a major opt out from the public health system among the middle classes, leading to a further squeeze on public funding and a loss of medical personnel to the private sector where rewards were higher. The result was rising inequality in health care, and diminished public service. Both infant and maternal mortality rates worsened during the acute public expenditure cuts. There was a sharp reduction in staff per person in the public sector (Montoya-Aguilar and Marchant-Cavieres 1994). Health care expenditure per capita in the mid-1990s was 2.5 times higher for the privately insured than for those receiving public health care. 'The 1981 reforms may be therefore be regarded as a major setback to the establishment of a more equal society' (World Bank 1997*b*, annexe 5: 174).

The medical reforms in Chile were associated with a change in the dominant mode of behaviour. The public system of the early 1970s combined P/C and COOP behaviour. While there were both P/C and COOP elements in staff behaviour, it is claimed that patients were generally treated in a P/C way, paternalistically and harshly: 'In the ward, the patient was isolated . . . and subject to authoritarian discipline . . . they rarely saw [the health staff] . . . who treated them with disdain' (Trumper and Phillips 1996: 41). Nonetheless, the universal coverage led to high standards of health care, as indicated by infant mortality and life expectancy rates. In the small private sector, the staff were mainly motivated by M, the wealthy private sector patients were much better informed about their treatment and generally treated with respect. The reforms increased the proportion of health care facilities operating primarily in an M mode, not only directly in the growing profit-motivated private sector, but also extending into the public sector partly in response to the incentives offered medical staff to switch to the private sector.

The UK was also a pioneer in introducing market reforms in the economy, under Thatcher's leadership, and like Chile this was soon followed by health sector reforms. In this case, the reforms consisted in introducing a quasi-market in the allocation of health care *within* the system. The net effect was to enhance M motivation, while greatly increasing the proportion of administrative staff: as Le Grand pointed out the assumption of 'knightly' behaviour (COOP) was replaced by that of 'knave' like behaviour, and this changed the motivation of medical staff in the same direction, reducing COOP behaviour. It appears that the efficiency of resource allocation increased, but this was offset by greatly increased administrative costs (see Le Grand 1997; Glennerster 1995).

These are two examples of a general trend. They were followed, for example, in Colombia, Argentina, Nicaragua, and Canada, often supported by the World Bank and the Inter-American Development Bank. These changes illustrate the close connection between the macro-environment for group behaviour and changing mode of behaviour in particular groups. However, at the same time there were examples of the introduction of more participatory community-based health services. For example, an integrated health project in the poor areas of Salvador in Brazil, involved the three levels of government and 'the total and complete participation of the future beneficiaries', although, the organizer noted 'Cooperation is not part of our culture; it is a relatively new phenomenon. Institutions and departments are not used to working together' (quoted in IDRC 1995: 19). This too reflects changes at the macro-level. As indicated above, while, on the one hand, marketization has greatly increased at all levels, on the other hand, and partly in reaction to this, there has been increasing emphasis on the need for greater participation, accompanied by greater decentralization of government and a larger role for NGOs.

The 1990s: Reactions to the Neo-Liberal Agenda, and the New Consciousness of Globalization

The liberalization and globalization agenda has been criticized from several perspectives—for failures with respect to poverty, inequality, and the environment; and for the simplistic economic (and political) model that underlay the agenda.

Concern with the rising poverty associated with the policies, was initiated by UNICEF and rapidly gained support (Cornia *et al.* 1987). Poverty reduction became a central objective of the World Bank. By 1990, the President of the World Bank declared that 'poverty is the benchmark against which we must be judged'. The IMF also began to be concerned with poverty: in 1990 Camdessus, Managing Director of the IMF, recognized 'that macroeconomic policies can have strong effects on the distribution of income and on social equity and welfare. A responsible adjustment programme must take these effects into account, particularly as they impinge on the most vulnerable or disadvantaged groups in society' (Speech to US Chamber of Commerce, 26 March 1990). The UNDP's *Human Development Report* first published in 1990 widened the development agenda beyond the market system, focusing on the human dimensions of development. 'People are the real wealth of a nation. The basic objective of development is to create an enabling environment for people to live long, healthy and creative lives' (UNDP 1990: 9). The quality of human lives, both as the central objective of development and as a critical development resource, has been a central theme of development thinking in the 1990s.

The market model was also criticized from an environmental perspective, since by its nature market motivation is ill-suited to take into account externalities, while the long-term future is heavily discounted as a result of positive real rates of interest (Bojo 1990; Pearce 1990). A further criticism (see Chambers 1994) was the lack of popular participation in either Keynesian or market models; the desirability of a more participatory model, as an objective in itself and also to improve efficiency and equity, gained wide acceptance in the aid community, and among some developing country governments.

At the same time, the economic model underlying the adjustment philosophy was critically reviewed. Theoretical critiques of the neoclassical model questioned the view of economic agents as exclusively and unavoidably short-term maximizers, reflecting the finding that trust is an important part of an exchange economy which is economically costly to replace. In the private sector too large firms increasingly emphasized the need for cooperative behaviour for efficient performance.[13] The model's assumptions about individual motivation[14] and about information[15] were shown to be deficient; while new developments in growth and trade theories focused on the importance of learning, economies of scale, oligopoly, and externalities.[16] Such work is, of course, ongoing. Together these criticisms amount to a significant attack on the M model from the perspective of *efficiency*, in addition to its failures with respect to equity and participation.

One alternative proposed was to incorporate COOP behaviour into theoretical models, as a corrective to the myopic view of the 'rational' person as being a short-term egotistic maximizer—see Chapter 3. The recognition of trust and COOP as an essential aspect of efficient *market* relations, even before considering non-market ones, has led to emphasis on the need for more COOP, as exemplified, for example, in the work of Putnam. There is increasingly wide agreement that 'social capital' is an important

---

[13] Some empirical evidence suggests that 'participation, communication, creativity and decentralisation' within the firm is positively correlated with growth in sales and profits (Denison 1993: 266). See also Kay (1998).

[14] See Sen (1977); Bowles and Gintis (1993) and socio-economists such as Etzioni (1993).

[15] In a series of important articles on the implications of asymmetric information by Stiglitz and Weiss (1981) and others.   [16] e.g. Lucas 1988; Roemer 1986; Krugman 1990 and others.

aspect of economic development. The irony is that by assuming, incorrectly, that 'rational' short-term maximizers constitute the basic economic agents, the profession has introduced policies—the neo-liberal package—which come near to making this true and in so doing actually undermine the efficiency of the system they are intending to enhance. Hence Putnam's dismay that 'social capital' is declining in the US, pithily summarized in the title of his book *Bowling Alone* (Putnam 2000).

There were also organizational and political reactions to the adoption of a pure market model. One such reaction has come from the huge expansion in the number of NGOs, both international and local. Some of these new NGOs are groups basically fulfilling efficiency functions, which undertake activities previously conducted by the state, and whose mode of operation is greatly influenced by general government philosophy. But others have developed in reaction to events—performing claims functions. These include popular and campaigning organizations demanding resources or improved services from the state or private sector. For example, national and international NGOs have campaigned effectively for specific market constraints (e.g. against the proposed Multilateral Agreement on Investment; in favour of debt relief; in favour of modifying intellectual property rights). Another reaction has come in the form of *legal* challenges to market outcomes often organized by COOP style groups, for example, towards the tobacco industry, mobile phones, drug prices, and so on. A third reaction was the election of social democratic governments, with the explicit platform of moderating market excesses, although global forces have restricted the ability of such governments to adopt market-restraining policies.

In sum, the view that the pro-market stance of the liberalizers was 'A reaction too far'[17] came to be widely shared. But this reaction has had only limited impact on policy, partly because of the constraints imposed by globalization, partly because the dominant philosophy in the most powerful institutions remains basically pro-market and pro-globalization.[18]

2.5. CONCLUSIONS

This chapter has explored how norms and economic structures at a macro-level shifted quite dramatically over the twentieth century, and how this affected the environment in which groups operate. It was argued that in the Colonial and neo-colonial era, the environment favoured P/C in most formal sector organizations, with combinations of P/C and COOP relationships in local non-colonial activities. During the first post-colonial phase, the Keynesian state-centred paradigm continued to be mainly P/C, but with a somewhat greater role for COOP behaviour. The chapter traces how this paradigm gave way to a strong market orientation, where societal norms and institutions pushed group behaviour towards M-type motivation. Reaction to the domination of the market model has led to pressure for greater participation and COOP modes of

---

[17] A term used by Killick 1988.

[18] Indicated, for example, by the resignations from the World Bank of Stiglitz and Kanbur who had questioned some aspects of the philosophy and practice.

behaviour, which has been taken up to some extent even in such dominant market-oriented institutions as the World Bank.

The impact of these macro-changes in norms on group behaviour was illustrated by examining changing modes of behaviour in the health sector. The dominant P/C orientation of the Colonial and neo-colonial period continued in the subsequent period, combined to a greater extent than before with elements of COOP and M. This gave way to a much larger role for M in the health sector when the macro-environment favoured M. Although the chapter explored changes in the health sector as an example, the influence of the macro-environment extends to all non-market groups. The health case indicates that the connection between macro-environment and individual groups' mode of behaviour is not a watertight one—it is apparent that groups can operate in a way counter to the prevailing ethos. For example, popular grass roots organizations frequently adopt a COOP approach in macro-environments which are predominantly P/C or M. But these cover only a minority of activities. Hence the formation of norms of behaviour at the macro-level is of critical importance for conditioning group behaviour.

The argument presented has parallels with earlier debates about the development of nineteenth-century capitalism. Initially, it was believed that trade would increase 'civility': 'it is almost a general rule that wherever manners are gentle (*moeurs douces*) there is commerce; and wherever, there is commerce, manners are gentle' (Montesquieu 1748 Vol. 2: 8, quoted by Hirschman 1982: 1464); 'through commerce, man learns to be prudent and reserved, in both talk and action' (Ricard 1781: 463, quoted by Hirschman 1982: 1465). But the reverse was also strongly argued: Adam Smith himself predicted that the division of labour would lead to a situation where 'all the nobler parts of human character may be in great measure obliterated and extinguished in the great body of people' (Smith 1937: 736). According to Robert Owen 'The general diffusion of manufactures throughout a country generates a new character in its inhabitants; and as this character is formed upon a principle quite unfavourable to individual or general happiness, it will produce the most lamentable and permanent evils, *unless its tendency be counteracted by legislative interference and direction*' (Owen 1817: 121—my italics). Polanyi pointed to 'the dislocation caused by such devices [the market system] must disjoint man's relationships and threaten his natural habitat with annihilation' (Polanyi 1957: 42). It involves the 'liquidation of every and cultural institution in an organic society' (Polanyi 1957: 159).

The end of the nineteenth century and the first half of the twentieth century saw strong reactions to the consequences of an unregulated market, embodied in economic interventions and social legislation. So strong were these reactions that in the 1940s Polanyi wrote: 'In retrospect our age will be credited with having seen the end of the self-regulating market' (p. 142). He wrote this in the Keynesian era. Since then many of the moderating interventions have been unravelled, while attempts to preserve or increase them are increasingly constrained by global forces.

Yet there are reactions to the renewed dominance of individualistic maximizing norms, ranging from developments in economic theory to the growth of NGOs, and including emphasis on more COOP norms even within the private sector. These reactions are occurring partly because there are efficiency costs arising from reduced levels of trust, in addition to the adverse social and environmental consequences. More COOP modes are needed for efficiency as well as equity. This chapter has argued that only a shift in the macro–paradigm will permit alternative modes to become dominant. The critical question that then arises is how such a shift can be brought about—indeed whether it can happen in the context of global competition, which provides incentives for modes of behaviour which maximize short-term competitiveness.[19] Continuing to advance the market model in most areas, while simultaneously arguing for more social capital and more social safety nets—the present stance of most prominent development institutions such as the World Bank and major aid donors, for example—will not bring about any such shift since the advance of the market in most areas will ensure that the dominant paradigm for group behaviour remains M. There is an inherent inconsistency between giving an overriding role to a market model of development, based on individual maximizing behaviour, and the adoption of more socially oriented norms.

In the nineteenth and early twentieth century, popular struggles combined with democratic structures permitted governments to gain some control over capitalist forces, and guide society in a more COOP and welfarist direction. The same sort of struggle is needed (and to some extent is happening) both within countries and at a global level if another shift of norms is to be achieved in the twenty-first century. Group behaviour itself will contribute to this struggle, with groups which challenge the dominant norms weighed against those that are influenced by and sustain them.

---

[19] Marx raised the same question in the nineteenth century: 'Modern bourgeois society has conjured up such gigantic means of production and exchange it is like a sorcerer who is no longer able to control the powers of the underworld that he has called up by his spells' (Marx and Engels 1968: 66–7).

3

Individual Motivation, its Nature, Determinants, and Consequences for Within-group Behaviour

SABINA ALKIRE AND SÉVERINE DENEULIN

Early in the history of modern physics objection was raised to use of the concept of force, on the double ground that it is never open to direct observation and that it is not objective but animistic or anthropomorphic. It was (and is) pointed out that we observe or measure only the effects of forces and contended that it would be simpler and more candid to talk only about effects, i.e., equations of motion . . . The place of motive in economic choice presents a closely parallel problem.[1]

People vote in presidential elections. They give anonymously to public television stations and private charities. They donate bone marrow to strangers with leukemia. They endure great trouble and expense to see justice done, even when it will not undo the original injury. At great risk to themselves, they pull people from burning buildings, and jump into icy rivers to rescue people who are about to drown. Soldiers throw their bodies atop live grenades to save their comrades. Seen through the lens of the self-interest theory emphasized in current microeconomics textbooks, such behavior is the human equivalent of planets traveling in square orbits.[2]

3.1. INTRODUCTION: HOW TO APPROACH *HOMO ŒCONOMICUS*

To complain about *homo œconomicus*[3] is no novel undertaking. Many cast aspersions on the truthfulness of his skeletal assumptions, his ability to mime human behaviour. After all, one would not buy a new car if its crash tests enlisted an inflated plastic dummy—for the dummy's ability to 'bounce back' is unlikely to be a good predictor of a human's response to a similar circumstance! So too, these groups argue, *homo œconomicus* is not very realistic: he excludes the complex of motivations that people have—from cooperation to self-interest to altruism to attention-getting playfulness. He

We are grateful to Michel De Vroey, Herbert Gintis, Judith Heyer, Jean-Philippe Plattau, Frances Stewart, and Rosemary Thorp and participants at the WIDER conference for helpful comments on a preliminary draft.

[1] Knight (1944) quoted in Lewin (1996: 1312–13).   [2] Frank (1991: xxiii).

[3] *Homo œconomicus* is seen as someone who maximizes his satisfaction by satisfying his preferences, which does not necessarily entail that he is self-interested. We will discuss later the link between self-interest and preference satisfaction.

has no spouse or family or community or culture. For that matter, he has no emotions, no spontaneous impulses, no freedom, no intellectual fallibility and no weakness of will. So how can one trust an economic policy in which our behaviour is predicted to follow in the footprints of this solitary shadowy skeleton?

In bringing evidence to bear on the complexity and richness of human motivations, many have argued that *homo œconomicus* should be coloured in—made more realistic, more intuitively plausible. In light of these repeated criticisms, the persistence of *homo œconomicus* among economists seems baffling. As Josh Billings put it, 'It ain't so much what folks don't know as what they know that ain't so.' The situation is made all the less satisfactory when eminent economists glibly disown their pet skeleton, admit his implausibility and his defects, yet still employ him. *Homo œconomicus* lives on, and his constituent assumptions must be reviewed carefully as they continue to form the basis of much of modern economics and its policy prescriptions.

This chapter intends to evaluate the adequacy of the assumption that people are self-interested insofar as they are motivated solely to maximize their own utility in economic transactions, and in particular to assess how this assumption affects within-group behaviour. Our argument will not merely be that the self-interested assumptions of individual motivation are incomplete—a position to which Smith, Mill, Ricardo, Friedman, and others would have assented.[4] Nor will we argue that self-interest does not account for a good deal of behaviour. Rather, our argument will be a bit more direct: the assumption that motivation is exogenous and can be assumed to be self-interested can be actively detrimental to economic activity. Policy and incentive structures based on the assumption of exogenous and self-interested motivation can undermine other sources of motivation and have negative effects both on cooperative behaviour and also on economic efficiency. Our argument is thus not what 'is the case' about human nature—but rather about what is awry with the assumption of self-interest. In this chapter we do not propose an alternative model of human motivation, but we do try to provide a constructive background about the variety of human motivations.

Groups refer here to 'collections of individuals who come together to undertake joint activities' (Chapter 1, this volume). *Group behaviour* refers to individual behaviour which is reconciled with and furthers group objectives.

Motivation is that which tends to move people to act. This definition is broad and can encompass actions undertaken to realize goals, actions undertaken on the basis of personal principles or social norms, actions undertaken out of emotion or out of self-expression or to please one's colleagues. Yet the definition touches upon the reason that motivation is of interest to economists: they need to be able to predict how people will act;[5] and in certain cases they need to know how to create incentives so that people

---

[4] 'The relevant question to ask about the assumptions of the theory is not whether they are descriptively realistic, for they never are, but whether they are sufficiently good approximations for the purpose in hand. And this question can be answered only by seeing whether the theory works, which means whether it yields sufficiently accurate predictions.' (Friedman 1994: 188).

[5] For example, predicting the economic consequences of a land reform involves predicting what people will do in the face of new opportunities. With a better understanding of their values, of their customs, of what motivates them, the direction of response might be better predicted.

will act in the desired way. An accurate understanding of motivation will help on both counts.

When we say that motivation is assumed to be *exogenous* we mean that the determinants of motivation lie outside of and are not affected by the social or economic context and transactions. In contrast, if individual motivation itself can be affected by economic behaviour, then it is *endogenous*.

This chapter proceeds in three stages. We begin by sketching the motivational assumption of *homo œconomicus*: in the classical formulation, in rational choice theory, and in Becker's later work which introduces personal and social capital into the individual utility function. Using a form of argument that bears in mind the epistemological status of this model, we challenge the position that *homo œconomicus* contains an adequate characterization of human motivation for within-group behaviour. We introduce alternative motivations: *philia* and altruism, identity and self-expression, moral rules, social norms, the motivation to please others, and long-term self-interest. We discuss some empirical studies and some evidence of the interaction between the various motivations. Finally, we consider the implications of moving towards an assumption of endogenous motivation, focusing on group behaviour and policy advice.

This focus on the relationship between motivation and within-group behaviour excludes many interesting things. For example, different patterns of human motivation such as cooperation, rule-following, or altruism may be valuable for various reasons. They may be intrinsically valuable for the agent, as the 'altruistic person' may find direct fulfilment from expressions of generosity and kindness. They may also be intrinsically valuable to others, as the altruists' co-workers may also value the workplace relationships that develop and the excellence of work that they produce together. Non-self-interested motivations may be instrumentally valuable to individual ends. For example, a cooperative person may be promoted more quickly than another who is harder working or cleverer, but uncooperative. These motivations may be instrumentally valuable to group ends, as cooperative or rule-following behaviours may reduce transactions and enforcement costs, increase production, and help develop better processes. A cooperative work environment may encourage employees to generate suggestions for improving production processes. They may also be instrumentally valuable to ends of a different group: the cooperation among local pineapple pickers on a business owned by a multinational not only generates revenue for the producer, but also may carry on a cultural tradition or identity. While we recognize that these many facets of motivation exist—and some of the literature we will discuss does indeed study these different roles of individual motivation in society—we will focus only upon the relationship between assumptions regarding individual motivation, and the resulting within-group behaviour.

3.2. THE MOTIVATION OF *HOMO ŒCONOMICUS*

The figure of *homo œconomicus* has been ascribed a motivation of self-interest, whose definition has several elements. Certain elements might be associated more strongly

54   *Sabina Alkire and Séverine Deneulin*

with one historical period than another, and we describe them in sequence, although earlier concepts recur in later periods.

3.2.1. *Self-interest*

Self-interest as a factor explaining economic phenomena was mentioned in Adam Smith's *Wealth of Nations*, where Smith identified self-interest as the motivation governing a large number of market exchange transactions between strangers.[6]

Oakley argues convincingly that Smith did not propose the model of classical economic man, in which all economic decisions were consequences of a perfectly egoistic and maximizing self-interested individual. Smith clearly presumed that other moral sentiments were operative such as prudence and sympathy.[7] Rather, that model was constructed in the nineteenth century by writers who endeavoured 'to promote political economy as a science in the definite sense that applied to the physical sciences.'[8]

One of those who systematized self-interest as being a necessary and sufficient assumption of economic motivation was John Stuart Mill. Mill emphasized that economics 'is concerned with [the human agent] solely as a being who desires to possess wealth, and who is capable of judging of the comparative efficacy of means for obtaining that end. It predicts only such of the phenomena of the social state as take place in consequence of the pursuit of wealth.' Mill focused the assumption of human motivation on self-interest so as to abstract from 'every other human passion or motive' with the exception of 'antagonizing principles to the desire of wealth, namely, aversion to labor, and desire of the present enjoyment of costly indulgences.'[9] The assumption of self-interest is equivalent to the assumption that every human action is undertaken in pursuit of wealth: 'there is, perhaps, no action of a man's life in which he is neither under the immediate nor under the remote influence of any impulse but the mere desire of wealth.'[10] Mill introduced this principle as part of his wider project of re-establishing political economy on scientific grounds,[11] which required the use of simplifying assumptions.

[6] 'It is not from the benevolence of the butcher, the brewer, or the baker that we expect our dinner, but from their regard to their own interest. We address ourselves not to their humanity but to their self love.' Smith (1776: Book I, Chapter II). See Oakley (1994: Preface and 56f); Sen (1987).

[7] On the misinterpretations of Smith's invisible hand, see Oostendorp (1995); Werhane (1991). They argue that the well-known butcher passage should be read in the sense of the impartial nature of market relationships. Smith did not see the market as a mechanism driven by self-interest and profit, but a fair cooperation mechanism, which, through its impartiality, did not favour one exchange partner. Sen (1994a, 1997a) also argues that economics does not deal with exchange alone but also with production. Moreover, the process of production, as Smith already pointed out, requires a team spirit and collaborative work. See also Ostrom (1998).

[8] Oakley (1994: 123); see Ch. 6 (Human agency and Smith's methodology) and Ch. 7 (Economic man and the formation of classical methodology).

[9] 'On the definition of political economy; and on the method of investigation proper to it' Mill (1967: 321–2), quoted in Oakley (1994: 153).   [10] Mill (1967: 322), quoted in Oakley (1994: 153).

[11] Mill's definition of political economy at an early stage was: 'the science which treats of the production and distribution of wealth, so far as they depend upon the laws of human nature' Mill (1967: 318), quoted in Oakley (1994: 150).

Yet accompanying Mill's pencil sketches of motivation was an awareness that his assumptions were proposed and sustained not because they build a true account of human nature but rather because they are useful for analysing human behaviour in the particular territory covered by economics. Mill wrote of the self-interest assumption that no economist should be 'so absurd as to suppose that mankind are really thus constituted.'[12]

This assumption was used subsequently by utilitarians such as Bentham, Jevons, Edgeworth, Walras, and Cournot, for whom the maximand became utility not wealth. In principle, the switch to utility might have involved a major change, since utility can be interpreted to include many elements, including the well-being of others. In practice, the change was more one of nomenclature than of substance.

These sketches came to inform the study of economic facts. First, *homo œconomicus* was constructed on the basis of real elements of human nature, as a 'double'—much as a sketch of a skeleton does depict real elements of the human body. Then economists came to use *homo œconomicus* independently, and in this way breathed an autonomous existence into this abstract set of assumptions.[13] This construction procedure is problematic not because of the abstraction so operated but because 'the *homo œconomicus*, which was constructed as an abstraction for laboratory use as a partial copy of the real person, comes back as the integral copy of the true human nature.'[14] We will return to that point presently.

What are the characteristics of the classical model of individual motivation? First, the assumption that *homo œconomicus* is motivated by self-interest in his economic actions presumes that motivation is exogenous to economic exchange—that is, it is not affected by the exchange. Second, self-interested motivation was initially considered as modal behaviour, that is, one could assume that most of the time people really did transact economic exchanges in a way that would maximize their own gain. Third, 'utility' was assumed to be what *homo œconomicus* maximized, considered variously as a psychological unit of pleasure (Bentham, for whom maximizing pleasure and avoiding pain was assumed to be the guiding principle of human nature) and as wealth (Mill, for whom wealth was assumed to be the only component of utility).[15]

3.2.2. *Revealed Preferences and Rational Choice Theory*

One problem with utilitarian theory as it developed was the assumption that people had a complete utility map. This clearly unrealistic assumption was addressed by

---

[12] Mill (1967: 322), quoted in Oakley (1994: 153). In fact, Mill wrote that 'human actions are never ruled by any one motive with such an absolute sway that there is no room for the influence of any other', *Ibid*.

[13] Demeulenaere (1996). He argues that this method was initiated by Pareto: 'A physical material consists of chemical material, the mechanical material, the geometric material, and so on; the real human being consists of the *homo œconomicus, homo ethicus, homo religiosus*, and so on. In sum, the consideration of those different materials, those different humans, amounts to the consideration of the distinctive properties of a real material, of that real human, and this only tends to cut into pieces the material to study.' Pareto, quoted in Demeulenaere (1996: 175).   [14] Dembinski (1998: 240).

[15] This seems strangely similar to the contemporary pursuit of economic growth and income maximization as a major proxy for policy objectives.

Samuelson, who in 1938 proposed that the 'interests' of economic man be recognized not by introspection or discussion but rather by observing preferences.[16] *Homo œconomicus* now maximizes preference satisfaction. While this appears much more acceptable than maximizing based on an introspective calculation, two serious problems remain. First, revealed preference theory continues to assume exogeneity of preferences, a problem which also applied, of course, to the earlier approach. Second, it assumes that when people make choices they exhibit their own individualistic preferences and are not behaving as social people, that is, making choices in part to please, offend, or cooperate with others.

The culmination of *homo œconomicus* is expressed in rational choice theory, as, for example, presented by Becker. According to this theory individuals behave in such a way that they 'maximize their utility from a stable set of preferences and accumulate an optimal amount of information and other inputs in a variety of markets.'[17] Hence, they are always rational.

But how meaningful is this account of human behaviour? One can well question whether it is more than a tautology, and whether the assumption of self-interest has survived in any meaningful form in modern rational choice theory. Clearly the restatement of agents' motivation was designed to avoid restricting human motivation to self-interest, if we mean by self-interest concern only for one's own well-being narrowly conceived.[18] Becker, like Smith and Mill before him, recognizes that people have multiple motives. So he articulates the broad consensus of rational choice theorists when he argues (in both early and current work) that the omnivorous assumption of self-interest can cover actions undertaken on the basis of any motivation at all: 'The economic approach I refer to does not assume that individuals are motivated solely by selfishness or material gain. It is a method of analysis, not an assumption about particular motivation. Behavior is driven by a much richer set of values and preferences than narrow self-interest.[. . .] The analysis assumes that individuals maximize welfare as they conceive it, whether they be selfish, altruistic, loyal, spiteful, or masochistic'.[19]

Perhaps it would seem that the 'self-interest' contribution to the *homo œconomicus* skeleton has become non-controversial because it no more implies 'self-interest' than Smith did. However, closer scrutiny of the *method* of rational choice theory shows that this is not the case; the updated assumption of self-interest can only incorporate a subset of human motivations.[20] Let us examine this.

Rational choice theory views rationality as 'intelligently maximizing a payoff function (the pay-off function being a real-valued representation of the person's preferences

---

[16] Samuelson is a convenient marker but was by no means the first or only person to propose this. Lewin points out, for example, that 'Pareto implies [that] economics [can] be studied leaving aside the concept of motives.' Lewin (1996:1309).

[17] Becker (1976:14). See also Sen (1994*b*); Hogarth and Reder (1987).

[18] 'A self-interested person will never prefer x to y if he or she believes that y is better for himself or herself. If nothing but self-interest affects his or her preferences then he or she prefers x to y if and only if he or she believes that x is strictly better for himself or herself than is y.' Hausman and McPherson (1994: 260).

[19] Becker (1993: 385). For applications of that approach, see for example Becker (1976, 1981).

[20] For other criticisms see Nussbaum (1997); Sen (1973, 1993); Hogarth and Reder (1987); Goldstein and Hogarth (1997); Lewin (1996).

over the outcomes), using all the available instruments, subject to feasibility'.[21] So, at first glance, the account can indeed go along with any actual motivations.[22] It has evaded the earlier problematic assumption that self-interest was a modal behaviour in economic exchange, for example. Yet it does not follow that *homo œconomicus Jr.* is agnostic about human behaviour. Rather there are manifold assumptions such as: that people solely act to fulfil their preferences (welfarism), that their preferences are exogenous, and that people value outcomes in any time period insofar as these outcomes have consequences on the present value of their utility (consequentialism). Those outcomes can also refer to others' well-being, but only insofar as they impinge on the chooser's own utility. A particularly critical and contentious assumption is that preference-based choice is internally consistent. Internal consistency of choice 'refers to relations of apparent "agreement" or "coherence" that are required to hold between what are chosen from different sets, that is, different parts of the choice function'.[23] Sen has convincingly illustrated that these assumptions lead to inaccurate explanations of actual human behaviour—such as interpreting choices *per se*, without considering the context of the choice menu.[24]

Each component assumption of *homo œconomicus* has come under scrutiny and discussion. For example, the central term 'preference ordering' represents too many different things: 'A person is given one preference ordering, which is supposed to reflect his interests, to represent his welfare, to summarize his idea of what should be done, to describe his actual choices and behaviour. Can one preference ordering do all these things?'.[25] A substantial set of arguments query the relationship between revealed preferences and individual interest—for example, a young man working on a family farm may have chosen to work at home because he did not know that there is work he would prefer two farms away; he may prefer instead to go to school but have to work in order to contribute to the family income; he may have wanted to work on the farm several years ago and has since changed his mind because new opportunities arose, so is biding his time until he can move on; he may have been entirely indifferent between working at home and going to the city, but having to choose one, randomly stayed home.[26] As these simple scenarios show, to defend each of these different scenarios in terms of the young man's self-interest requires rather elaborate and constantly shifting accounts of what his self-interest actually is. The response to this has often been to lapse into defining self-interest in simple dollar terms, or in terms of a limited subset of variables.

---

[21] Sen (1994*b*: 384).

[22] 'If you are observed to choose x rejecting y, you are declared to have revealed a preference for x over y ... With this set of definitions, you can hardly escape maximizing your own utility, except through inconsistency.[. . .] But if you are consistent, no matter whether you are an egoist, or an altruistic, or a class-conscious militant, you will appear to be maximizing your own utility in this enchanted world of definition.' Sen (1982: 88–9).   [23] Sen (1993: 20). See also, Sen (1995).

[24] Sen (1973, 1993, 1997*b*).   [25] Sen (1982: 99).

[26] Sen gives a balanced evaluation of 'Individual Preference as the Basis of Social Choice' in Arrow, Sen, and Suzumura (1997: 15 ff). On the link between individual preferences and well-being, see Sen (1982). The difficulties in observing preferences has been long recognized, see Houthakker (1961).

But a body of empirical and psychological studies have tested whether an individual does in fact choose what would be 'rational' for him or her to choose if he or she were concerned to maximize material well-being under a budget constraint, and have found that the assumption does not have consistent predictive value.[27]

In sum, the motivational assumption of revealed preference theory can be interpreted as tautological.[28] But when interpreted non-tautologically, serious problems arise. Empirically, it seems that self-interest cannot explain many actions. Nor is the assumption of consistency borne out empirically. Moreover, fundamental problems arise because of the assumption of exogeneity of preferences and the isolation of individual choice, so that each person is treated as a maximizing island and not a social being.

3.2.3. *Endogenous Preferences and Social Capital*

Homo œconomicus had a growing spurt when its artists partially endogenized preferences. Two leading design artists were Coleman and Becker at the University of Chicago. Coleman proposed a concept of social capital in which individuals with access to higher levels of social capital were better able to attain their goals (i.e. to maximize their preferences).[29] According to Coleman, while preferences remain individualistic and exogenously determined, the outcomes from any set of actions are partly dependent on the richness of social capital. Social capital refers to concrete personal relations and networks of relations generating trust, creating and enforcing norms. It is seen as something that 'facilitates certain actions of individuals who are within a social structure.[. . .], and that makes possible the achievement of certain ends that would not be attainable in its absence.'[30] That is, it is a source of productivity, contributing to something that neither markets or states can do—and is in this sense capital—although it cannot be aggregated with other forms of capital.

Becker's 1996 book *Accounting for Tastes* extends the revealed preference approach to deal with 'the *effects* of experiences and social forces' that is, 'to include endogenous preferences'.[31] He does this by incorporating personal and social capital in the individual utility function. At time t, utility is a function of these stocks as well as of goods:

$$U = U(x_t, y_t, z_t, P_t, S_t) \tag{3.1}$$

where U = utility, x, y, z = goods, P = personal capital stocks, S = social capital stocks.

Personal capital is defined to include the individual's past and personal history. It refers to cumulative life experiences which help to determine current preferences,

---

[27] See Tversky and Kahneman (1981); Frank (1991); Hargreaves-Heap (1989); Hogarth and Reder (1987); Thaler (1980).

[28] 'The consumer is said to maximize utility, and utility is defined as that which the consumer attempts to maximize. The statement that individuals maximize their utility is anything but a truism.' Wiggins (1980: 260).

[29] The concept of social capital has many different interpretations. For a review of the different interpretations in the economics and sociology literature, see Fine (1999*a,b*); Harris and De Renzio (1997); De Renzio (1997).   [30] Coleman (1990: 302).

[31] Becker (1996: 4).

including education and experience. For example, if in her childhood, the individual was forced to eat something every day, she might have developed a positive, or negative, preference towards that food. Becker believes that 'habitual behavior permeates most aspects of life.'[32]

In contrast to personal capital, *social capital* cannot be unilaterally built up by an individual but rather 'incorporates the influence of past actions by peers and others in an individual's social network and control system.'[33] It includes peer pressure, and guidelines for achieving social acceptance and recognition. Becker defines social capital as '$S^i_{t+1} = X_i + (1 - d_s)S^i t$ where d_s is the depreciation rate of social capital and $X_i(= \sum X_j)$ is the effect of choices by the j members of i's network on his social capital.'[34] Becker points out that while individual influence on social capital is very small (if j is large), people can to some extent choose social networks that raise their utility. Also, Becker argues that social capital can change much more rapidly than culture if all members of a network face the same exogenous change. For example, after a rise in petrol prices, people might tend to prefer public transportation to their private car. If the upper class begins to take public transportation or do car-pooling, they might have a mimetic influence on their peers. Such a change in social capital can happen more quickly than a change towards a more environmentally-friendly culture in general.

In Becker's explanation of these personal and social capital stocks, it becomes apparent that these include patterns of human interaction and choice-making which in other models would be referred to as human motivation. Motivation as such is not analysed by Becker, who 'retains the assumption that individuals behave so as to maximize utility'.[35] He describes norms of reciprocity, trust, loyalty, and cooperation either as habitual behaviour that individuals cultivate as part of their personal capital and which influences their utility, or as behaviour which increases one's social capital. In both cases, P and S act as 'constraints that operate through preferences' but do not independently influence behaviour.[36] That is, in contrast to psychologists who emphasize the cognitive limitations to rationality,[37] Becker still assumes that individuals 'make forward-looking, maximizing and consistent choices'.[38]

Although Becker's schema provides a useful way of classifying influences over individual choices, by adding personal and social capital to preferences, and increases the explanatory power for phenomena such as violence and addiction, it still 'values' these contingently through their effects on the individual's utility function. The preference function, determining the nature of the individual's utility function, remains exogenous and individualistic, even though social and personal capital are now included.

Moreover, the approach ignores the dynamic interaction between different motivations. Becker's work cannot, for example, predict that a child who mows the lawn might cease to do it freely once his parents start paying him. This is what Frey calls the 'crowding out effect': (monetary) incentives that appeal to self-interest may crowd

---

[32] Becker (1996: 9).   [33] Ibid. (1996: 12).   [34] Ibid. (1996: 12).
[35] Ibid. (1996: 4).   [36] Ibid. (1996: 22).   [37] Simon (1982).   [38] Becker (1996: 23).

out intrinsic motivation, or the motivation to do something for its own sake.[39] We will come back to the issue in Section 3.4. It also does not address the human experience of conflict or even sacrifice. If the partner of a man with a debilitating long-term condition cares for him faithfully, foregoing exciting moves and career possibilities, and foregoing her own needs for friendship and support as the disease progresses, Becker's schema would recognize that her utility function had a large weighting for the personal capital value of 'loyalty'. So in calm and even terms, the rational choice theorist would conclude that during the twenty years of nursing, the woman had maximized her utility. It does not allow for counter-preferential choice, when, as in the present case, perhaps, the agent acts on principle *to the detriment* of her own utility and self-interest. Becker's formulation still does not allow the individual to 'sacrifice' her utility or, as in the case of addictions, to make a mistake about how best to maximize long-term utility.

The first section argued that the assumption of self-interest, and its downstream assumptions of maximizing behaviour in various forms of rational choice theory, not only do not produce a *homo œconomicus* that encompasses or explains the range of actual behaviour—a claim that nobody would refute by the very definition of the construction of *homo œconomicus*, but, also, they do not yield adequate predictions regarding human behaviour. Can a consideration of alternative patterns of human motivation take us any further? We will argue that it can, because on the one hand there are significant motivations that Becker's model cannot take into account, and, on the other hand, there are interactions among these motivations.

3.3. SYMPATHY, COMMITMENT, AND INTRINSIC MOTIVATION

Before launching into a discussion of alternative accounts of human motivation let us consider the issue from a bit upstream, at the junction between motivational assumptions and rational choice theory. In a seminal paper entitled 'Rational Fools', Sen sets out to inquire how neoclassical theory could manage if people were not concerned uniquely with their own self-interest narrowly defined. He defines two grounds of action in which consideration for others' welfare enters: sympathy and commitment.

In *sympathy*, concern for others directly affects one's own welfare. Hence it may be conceived of as a certain type of egoism, because if the other person's pain is reduced, the agent's own welfare is improved. Whereas in earlier forms of revealed preference, sympathy-based behaviour was considered an externality, Sen showed that it could be incorporated into the present models without much difficulty, as Gary Becker's work has indeed done.[40]

A *commitment* does not necessarily affect one's own welfare at all, but it does affect one's subsequent action. One's choice may or may not in fact increase one's own welfare,

---

[39] Frey (1997). See also Frey and Oberholzer-Gee (1997). Their study shows that the willingness to accept a socially desirable but locally unwanted project (namely the acceptance of a nuclear waste repository) declines greatly after monetary compensation is offered.

[40] Becker (1976, 1981, 1993, 1996). A well-known example of how, under certain conditions, preferences of the altruist and the selfish might converge is the 'rotten kid theorem'.

but in either case the choice is not *motivated* by own-welfare considerations at all. It may be motivated by altruism, such as when one's concern for an elderly neighbour means that one buys vegetables for her every week even when the money spent sometimes deprives one's own family. Or, one acts out of one's convictions (justice, honesty), or even a thirst for revenge (non-self-interested motivations need not be benign).[41] Commitment is a counter-preferential choice, 'destroying the crucial assumption that a chosen alternative must be better than (or at least as good as) the others for the person choosing it'.[42] Because it 'drives a wedge between personal choice and personal welfare, and much of traditional economic theory relies on the identity of the two',[43] a reformulation of models would be required in order to incorporate commitment-based behaviour.

Sen argues, in 'Rational Fools', and subsequently, that commitment is significant for several reasons. First, while it may be exhibited only rarely in certain types of economic interaction, such as market exchange, it may be of considerable importance in achieving good welfare outcomes relating, for example, to public goods (roads, street lights, parks, military), and to free-rider problems. Clearly some forms of commitment are highly valued in the labour market for economic reasons because it decreases monitoring and enforcement costs and increases output (hence the surge in business strategies for increasing worker morale, company ethos, and so on).[44] There are also human reasons for appreciating alternative motivations—fulfilling work, relationships, status, and creative expression have strong correlations with human happiness and life satisfaction.[45] Yet the traditional structure of the utilitarian view of economic behaviour cannot coherently incorporate these motivations.

Sen is not unique in separating calculating from non-calculating motivations and it can be fruitful to join his work to a roughly parallel avenue of inquiry. Psychologists as well as economists interested in behavioural motives have studied the motivations that come *from within* a person. One 'is said to be *intrinsically motivated* to perform an activity when one receives no apparent reward except the activity itself.'[46] Intrinsically motivated activities are those 'that are spontaneously initiated and that people subjectively experience as enjoyable'.[47] For example, the activity of gardening is said to be intrinsically motivated if the motivation is the enjoyment of the activity itself, without regard for the neighbour's compliments or the anticipated personal pleasure in contemplating a beautiful garden or the ensuing vegetables.[48] Though an important source of economic behaviour, intrinsic motivation can also be fragile, because it is likely to be undermined by financial incentives, as we will later discuss.[49]

---

[41] Sen (1997*a*).　　[42] Ibid. (1982: 92).　　[43] Ibid. (1982: 94).

[44] See Kaufman (1999), for a review of the psychological basis of rational choice in labour economics.

[45] Lane (1991); Frey and Stutzer (1999). See also the November 1997 issue of the *Economic Journal* (107) which discussed the controversy about Economics and Happiness.

[46] Deci (1971: 105 (italic are ours)) cited in Frey (1997: 13).　　[47] Enzle *et al.* (1991: 468).

[48] Intrinsic motivation has received a lot of attention in labour economics, where it has been recognized that a worker performed her job not as much as for wage as for doing the job for its own sake. See for example Kaufmann (1999); Lane (1991); Frey (1997); Frank (1991); Csikszentmihalyi (1997).

[49] Kohn (1998); Deci and Ryan (1985); Frey (1997).

In contrast, extrinsically motivated activity is undertaken instrumentally, for the sake of some other reward or satisfaction. *Homo œconomicus*, in all forms, is assumed to act on the basis of 'calculations' of how activities affect his utility function. This utterly extrinsic account of behaviour excludes the possibility of acting simply for the sake of acting—because the act itself is valuable.

Motivations can be classified into commitments (that is motivations that can support counterpreferential choices and be independent of one's own welfare considerations), intrinsic motivations, for example, 'intrinsic motivations that people have to perform well in a task,'[50] and motivations governed by external incentives, such as, 'explicit rewards, such as money, that depend on performance'.[51]

The next sections describe several kinds of commitments in which *something else* besides one's own welfare motivates the action—be it *philia* or justice or doing a good job. The different kinds of motivation refer to the different reasons—the different *something elses*—that can motivate action. The goal of these sections is not merely to suggest that human beings in fact have multiple motives but to suggest that considering these motivations will bring into focus the problem with the self-interest assumption for behaviour within groups.

3.3.1. Philia *and Altruism*

One may be motivated to act because of one's relationship or affiliation with another person. Affiliation—from the Greek *philia*—refers to the ability to communicate with others, to form associations and to organize politically. In Aristotle's political thought, *philia* is the core of living together in society. *Philia* connotes any sense of affection, of belonging to others, of communication with others, whether spontaneous or reflected, due to circumstances or to free choice. It can mean friendship, love, benevolence, regard, charity, or philanthropy. *Philia* is the social bond that maintains unity among citizens of the same city, among companions of a group, among associates in a business.[52] Aristotle argues that affiliation, or the capacity human beings have to associate with one another, and to form ties, is intrinsically valuable, and a part of human fulfilment or welfare broadly conceived. He argues that it is also the precondition for group existence. Upon this is founded *koinônia*—any community undertaking action or pursuing a common interest together; and upon both *philia* and *koinônia* is founded the supreme form of political life, the *polis*, whose function consists in providing its citizens the opportunities for them to live a good life.

Philia can be a motive of economic action. One paradigmatic example of this is altruism,[53] when an action is done 'for the good of the other' independently of concern

---

[50] For a review of different forms of intrinsic motivation, see Deci and Ryan (1985).

[51] Goldstein and Hogarth (1997: 244).   [52] Aristotle (1994: 380).

[53] However, *philia* need not be associated with altruism. In Aristotlean ethics, *philia* means a natural inclination every human being expresses towards one another. That natural inclination can take three forms, or have three ends: advantage, pleasure, and 'the person for her own sake'. The only virtuous *philia* was the one that had the person for her own sake as an end, what we would qualify today as 'altruism'. Yet, what is common to all three forms, is that the relationship is characterized by mutual standards of obligations.

for the impact that action will have, positively or negatively, on one's own well-being. Perhaps in a cycle shop a kind elderly man raised the seat of one's bicycle for no charge. The shopkeeper may have done so out of good will—never asking if the visitor lived around there and might frequent his shop again.

While this may sound quite an esoteric motivation it need not be. For example, studies of intrinsic motivation in employment situations find that one source of motivation on the job is the relationships with co-workers, not in the sense of wanting to please them but in the sense of working together as a team, and relating well to one another.[54] *Philia* may also be one facet of cooperative behaviour that is also in one's self-interest. So, regard for other people, taken as ends in themselves, may motivate or partially motivate a range of economic actions.

3.3.2. *Identity or Self-Expression*

Communal identity may also be a powerful drive behind individual behaviour. Actions are undertaken to express group-identity, to express membership in a particular community. For example, what motivates the singing of a national anthem or the raising of a national flag may be the expression of a national identity, of belongingness to a common group, a common nation: 'Community, nationality, class, race, sex, union membership, revolutionary solidarity, all provide identities that can be, depending on the context, crucial to our view of ourselves, and thus to the way we view our welfare, goals, or behavioral obligations.'[55] Identity, as the reflection of a person's character traits (personal dispositions such as friendliness or integrity, or social role identity as being a professor or the daughter of someone, or socially defined group identity such as ethnicity or gender), affect actions in many ways. It affects what is salient to an agent; it directs the formation of habits; it affects beliefs (for example, a person's group or role identity can often provide the best explanation of her holding certain beliefs, and acting in consequence).[56] Identity is a central aspect of human behaviour in the sense that our actions express things about ourselves and the groups to whom we belong.[57] Behaviour is communicative and is often an expression of identity. Our behaviour and actions 'express our ideas about what is worthy in our selves, and by extension the

---

Even the advantage *philia*, in contrast to self-interest, includes something that is beyond individuals and that influences them, namely the norms of reciprocity that arose from the relationship.

[54] Lane (1991); Kreps (1997). Considerations of fairness regarding the wage of others—which may in part reflect the affiliation between workers and employers, and in part norms of reciprocity and fairness—might be very influential even in competitive markets, see Fehr *et al.* (1998: 326).

[55] Sen (1985: 348). See also Sen (1999). Of course, the same action can be undertaken for different motives. A government official may order the singing of an anthem because it *will* serve her self-interest, by reminding people of their national allegiance and so preparing them to listen receptively to her call for increased taxes.   [56] See Flanagan and Rorty (1990).

[57] Monroe (1996) cites the example of choice between using Word, e-mail or chess on the computer: she will choose Word as a writer, e-mail as an academic who wants to communicate with other scholars, and chess as a mother who plays with her children. See also Badhwar (1993), on how altruistic behaviour can be an expression of a self-affirming motivation.

sense which we make of the world. Action is no longer a means to a given end, but is more an activity which is its own end'.[58]

Identity is not to be associated with socially constructed rules that determine how different types of people should behave. Identity cannot be reduced to prescriptions or norms guiding what actions are appropriate or not, because identity-driven behaviour does not solely arise from a fear of sanction as norm-guided behaviour does.[59] Following a set of prescriptions, though it can *reinforce* identity-driven behaviour, is not the initial motivation of such behaviour. For example, prescriptions with regard to what constitutes good table manners may build up an aristocratic image among one's table companions and so might be done out of a motive of conformity or pleasing others. But if the aristocrat continues to use good table manners while travelling alone with servants in the Indian desert, she acts out of the motive of identity that cannot be accounted for in terms of prescriptions. Again, she is not driven by the fear of sanction of what should or should not be done (who will know), but is driven by the desire to express what she is.

Identity may also be quite an important factor in consumption patterns—an insight used far more often in the advertising industry than by economists. Consumers consume to express their identity (or to express a desire to be associated with a particular group identity, which explains responses to some advertisements). This pattern is not limited to consumer societies: Kurien relates that the consumption behaviour of migrants in three distinct Indian villages is guided by the culture and symbolic dimension of their society.[60] Such behaviour has been noted in other anthropological studies. Di Maggio observes that 'economic goods are consumed for what they say about their consumers to themselves and to others as inputs into the production of social relations and identities.'[61]

3.3.3. *Moral Rules and Virtues*

A person's motivation may also reflect none other than his or her inclination to 'do the right thing.' There are different ethical models one can use—evaluating the consequences of an action, awaiting the voice of God, acting upon emotions so as to maintain an inner equilibrium, or acting in accordance with rules or virtues (which can also be thought of as habits built up by following rules such as to act justly or kindly or with gentleness). We discuss only the last.

Persons who learn and choose to follow rules do not evaluate their actions on a case by case basis, but rather compare alternative behavioural patterns and select rules upon which future actions will be based. The central concept of rule-following behaviour is that 'actors do not respond to particular situations as unique events but form categories of situation which they perceive as similar.'[62] Insofar as rule-following is an intrinsic behaviour, however, these rules will again be adhered to independently of their effect

---

[58] Hargreaves-Heap (1989: 5).
[59] See Akerlof and Kranton (1998), for a conception of identity associated with prescriptions following.
[60] Kurien (1994). For the link between culture and economy, see Di Maggio (1994).
[61] Di Maggio (1991: 133), quoted in Kurien (1994).   [62] Maki *et al.* (1993: 176).

on an individual's own interest. For example, in a certain context there may be social pressures to take bribes; it may be necessary in order to bring income levels up to subsistence; honest behaviour may be viewed with suspicion, and not rewarded with job promotions; and yet a doggedly honest person may still refuse to take bribes, at considerable personal and professional cost.

This is not to say that *all* rule-following behaviour is even partially morally motivated. Rule-following is a matter of behaving similarly in similar circumstances. There is no necessary motivational assumption behind it,[63] and persons might choose rules in accordance with self-interest (rule-consequentialism) or even with morality perceived as an efficient strategy rather than as an intrinsically valuable one. Vanberg argues that behaviour (which reflects motivations) is a product of formal, informal, and internal (conscience-led) incentives and sanctions, but also of 'intangible intrapersonal determinants of choice' as societies enforce one or another norm.[64] However, there are some instances in which moral or ethical rules are followed for their own sake, and this comprises a distinct category of intrinsic motivation. Rules also cannot be reduced to norm-guided behaviour because rules do not involve the fear of sanction that characterizes breaking a norm, as we will see in the next subsection.

3.3.4. *Social Norms and the Motivation to Please Others*

There is one other significant factor which 'tends to move people to act', which is as dear to sociologists as utility is to economists, and this is motivation to be well-regarded, to have a good name, to fit into society. Its passive form is merely the impression society leaves on a person's behaviour; at other times it may take the form of an active motivation, in which an action is done for an extrinsic reason, namely to please others or avoid social sanctions (she waters her garden in order to be well regarded by her neighbours).

Durkheim, pioneered a line of objection to rational choice theory which continues to this day. He complained that the individualist, maximizing characterization of individuals in economics is an inaccurate description of human motivation as it ignores societal influences: 'According to [economists] there is nothing real in society but the individual . . . they ignored all circumstances of time, place, and country in order to conceive of man's abstract type in general . . . nothing is left but the sad portrait of an isolated egoist'.[65] Durkheim and others[66] argue that economic action is embedded in ongoing networks of relationships rather than carried out by atomized actors outside

---

[63] Vanberg (1994: 30).

[64] Persons choose rules in accordance with a morality perceived as an efficient strategy, that depends on the community allocation of rewards for moral conduct and punishments for rule violation. Vanberg, (1994: 58), assimilates morality to social capital, in the sense that 'the current level of morality in a community always reflects past enforcement of moral rules, and it will only be maintained by ongoing enforcement. The level of morality can, in this sense be viewed as *social capital* that, in the absence of sufficient reinvestment, will depreciate over time.'   [65] Durkheim (1978: 49).

[66] For the main works in sociological economics see Granovetter (1985); Swedberg and Granovetter (1992).

a social context, and cannot be explained by individual motives alone independent of the social and cultural context.

For economists, since Friedman at least, the above quotation would hardly be relevant, because, as clarified above, the assumption of utility maximization does not require that human beings actually act for this motive, but rather that the assumption be adequate to its purposes of predicting action. Yet an increasing core of literature, both empirical and theoretical, indicates that the embeddedness of human action may often be of considerable economic significance through its influence on economic behaviour.[67] Societies and cultures may introduce habits—for example, towards working hours and holidays, or may enforce behaviour patterns—such as providing appropriate hospitality for professional colleagues, with social sanctions. Societies may have behaviours that confer identity—children of successful parents go to private schools, or that influence people's moral sensibilities of justice and fairness on issues such as whether there are death-deserving crimes, how tolerable is bribery, or to what extent one aims for fulfilment in an afterlife or future lives, rather than focusing on fulfilment in this life.

Following this line of argument, communitarians argue that individual behaviour cannot be characterized independently of the social settings or community (i.e. the set of institutions and practices) in which that behaviour takes place. It is this setting which makes human actions intelligible.[68] According to the communitarians, individuals are constituted by the community of which they are part, or by the network of social relationships in which they grow and live. The individual is not a social atom, rather her identity as an individual is constituted and defined by her social relationships and community ties. Community is pre-existent to individuals in the sense that community is what gives meaning to the life of its members and gives them identity. Just as goals and values individuals pursue cannot be separated from the community in which those goals and values are shaped, the only way to understand human behaviour is to contextualize individuals in their social, cultural, and historical context.

The community imposes a set of norms upon individual actions. Those norms are defined as 'the propensity to feel shame and to anticipate sanction by others at the thought of behaving in a certain, forbidden way. This propensity becomes a social norm when and to the extent that it is shared with other people.'[69] Norms are patterns

---

[67] See for example Akerlof (1997); Fershtman and Weiss (1998); Piketty (1998); Clark and Oswald (1998); Cole *et al.* (1998); Bisin and Verdier (1998).

[68] Communitarian philosophers (MacIntyre, Sandel, Walzer, and Taylor in a more moderate way) have had a strong influence on political philosophy. They oppose the liberal view (Rawls, Nozick, Dworkin) which sees society as a cooperative venture for the pursuit of individual advantage, an essentially private association formed by individuals whose interests are defined independently of the community of which they are members. For an introduction to the communitarian/liberal debate, see Mulhall and Swift (1992); Avineri and De-Shalit (1992).

[69] Elster (1989a: 105). In contrast to sociologists, economists have tended to speak about social norms in a rather instrumental way. Economists regard those norms as institutions that are 'the rules of the game in society, or the humanly devised constraints that shape human interaction. Institutions structure incentives in human exchange.' (North 1990: 3). Social norms have a specific function: they reduce uncertainty and provide a social structure for exchange. Section 3.6 deals with institutions in economic theory.

of behaviour that reflect the customs, traditions, values, or way of life of a particular society or group, whose transgression leads to social sanctions. There are numerous examples of norms, such as those of cooperation (division of labor, tax compliance), those regulating the use of money (for example norms against buying someone's place in a queue), norms of reciprocity (to return favours done to us by others), norms of retribution (to return harms done to us by others, revenge), work norms (equal pay for equal work), consumption norms (manners of dress, table), norms of distribution (regulate what is seen as a fair allocation of income), and moral norms (regarding, e.g. killing, honesty, hospitality).[70] Insofar as the transgression of norms leads to social sanctions (such as ostracism), norms are partly able to explain group behaviour—how people act in groups.[71] One has to note that norms cannot always be explained by the efficiency of their outcome. People would sometimes be better off without norms, and sometimes better off with norms. For example, in a country where there is no respect for arriving on time, a norm that would put a sanction on those arriving late would make everybody better off, avoiding long useless waiting time. Or on a hot summer day, when businessmen would feel more comfortable without wearing a suit and a tie; the social norms make them worse off.

Norms and social structures—from so-called Asian Values to traditionalism—have been considered in a deterministic way, as if they exist independently of the individuals in society, leaving individuals no freedom to alter or ignore them. But many argue that there is a dialectic relationship between social structure and individual agency.[72] Agents are constituted by and constitute norms. Agents act according to norms, since individual actions reproduce norms in their daily lives. But norms have no existence without individual actions. The relationship between norms and motivation, or more generally between institutions and motivation, can also be characterized as partly endogenous (there seem to be some rigidities), because humans can reflect upon, react against and change the norms that govern social life.[73] The agent (individual or group), its sources of motivation, and its norms for evaluation, decision, and action are always, by the social nature of human beings, embedded in a socio-cultural context. Actors are not guided by an individual rationality, but a rationality that is itself contained in the nature of the social relationship. A person's ways of valuing things are structured through social roles, practices, and relationships.

This line of discussion links motivation with the moral aspects of people's relationships with others.[74] Economic action is embedded in ongoing networks of personal relations rather than carried out by atomized actors outside a social context.[75] Moreover, social norms, and the desire for status, can create alternative structures of

---

[70] Elster (1989*a,b*).

[71] Rotating credit is an example of how norms sustain group behaviour. For other examples, see Hechter (1987).

[72] For the interaction between social structures and individual agency see Giddens (1984); Etzioni and Lawrence (1991). See also the notion of *habitus*, i.e. a structure internalized by an agent, in Bourdieu (1977).

[73] Lawson (1997).   [74] See the notion of social game theory in Burns (1994).

[75] It can hardly be argued that culture has *no* influence upon the characteristic patterns of action and even motivations for action within different groups. But a simplistic reduction of human motivation to ethnic or cultural affiliation would similarly overlook many things—from the diversity of people, to their

incentives that appeal to the 'motivation to please others'[76] rather than the motivation of self-interest.

This section has reviewed some of the alternative motivations that may be relevant for within-group behaviour. This is of course not a complete account of the range of motivations—those things that tend to cause us to act; things like vengeance, or a desire to manipulate, or simple curiosity, may also motivate.[77] Also, between the motivation and the action driven by that motivation, there is a distance, what philosophers have called 'practical inference', where factors other than the initial motivation can intervene. For example there is *akrasia*, or a weak will: when, although one is motivated to be patient or thrifty or rational, one encounters oneself being the opposite. Another intervening factor is cognitive failure or simple individual fallibility,[78] in which a person's or group's limited capacity to process information means that their actions only imperfectly achieve their aims. There are also the emotions—anger, compassion, indignation—that strengthen or dampen other motivations and may cause action themselves. All are required in a full account of human action. However, not all are required in order to make the case that an assumption of endogenous motivation would be superior to *homo œconomicus*, and it is to that case that we now turn.

3.3.5. *Long-Term Self-interest?*

A reader who is familiar with *homo œconomicus* will now have rehearsed in her mind, at least several times during the descriptions of commitments and intrinsic motivations above, the shadowy objection which would be raised by those who adhere to revealed preference theory: that all of these observations of human behaviour can be incorporated into the utility model if one takes a long enough time horizon. As discussed earlier (3.2.2) one difficulty with this is the assumption of internal consistency of choice which is needed to derive economic choices from preferences. However, the remainder of this chapter develops another objection, namely that rational choice theory would not take into account the interaction among motivations, hence could generate policies that undermine group behaviour. In order to develop this objection we need to consider groups and motivational assumptions.

3.4. WHY MOTIVATION MATTERS FOR POLICY

Section 3.2.1 argued that if acting upon self-interest were taken as the exclusive mode of human behaviour in economic transactions, this would be a mistake, because people's economic behaviour regularly and predictably seems to exhibit different motivations.

Section 3.2.2 argued further that interpreting choices as preference maximization left serious problems because revealed choices do not necessarily represent people's

---

multiple identities, to the dynamics of cultural change, to the fact that any macro unit will be composed of heterogeneous groups. See Sen (1997a); Di Maggio (1994).

[76] See Fershtman and Weiss (1998); Cole *et al.* (1998).

[77] These are remarkably strong motivations, and, as Bowles and Gintis (1998a,b) argue, underpin norms such as fairness. Unfortunately, we cannot attend to these issues within the bounds of this chapter.

[78] Stiglitz (1991).

self-interested choice, but are the outcome of a complex combination of influences, including social norms, commitment to others, etc. Moreover, connected to these points, the theory assumes exogeneity of preferences.

Section 3.2.3 argued that even Becker's revisionist account of rational choice, which attempts to endogenize some preferences by introducing personal and social capital, retains individualistic exogenously determined preferences as the fundamental building block. Maximizing individualistic behaviour is only one of the multiple motivations that people may have, and individual preferences are largely socially determined. Acting as if maximizing individualistic behaviour were the only type may actually change motivation, by 'crowding out' other motivations, some of which are reviewed in Section 3.3.

To the extent that individualistic maximizing behaviour increases efficiency, crowding out alternative motivations might be regarded as desirable. But there is increasing evidence—shown for example in the social capital literature[79]—that in many cases short-term maximization actually reduces efficiency by increasing transactions costs.

The point we now face is that if there is some competition between different motivations—maximization of own utility, *philia*, work performance, social compliance—and if the other motivations also have direct or indirect effects on economic behaviour which can be efficiency-creating and can enhance well-being, then creating incentives that promote a certain type of behaviour—utility maximization—to the detriment of all others may not consistently lead to optimal outcomes and processes. To give an example: 'providing extrinsic incentives for workers can be counterproductive, because it may destroy the workers' intrinsic motivation, leading to lessened levels of quality-weighted effort and lower net profits for the employer.'[80]

An increasing body of evidence suggests that economists are mistaken when they understate or ignore intrinsic motivation, and when they understate or ignore the fact that motivation is embedded in a social context. Not only is intrinsic motivation necessary for economic activity, but also, a systematic relationship often exists between extrinsic and intrinsic motivation, which neoclassical economists fail to take into account. One aspect of this relationship is what Bruno Frey has called the crowding-out effect. There is also a 'crowding-in effect', according to which intrinsic motivation can be enhanced by some external intervention. Yet, economic theory has generally taken *only* extrinsic motivation to be relevant for behaviour. The economic model of human behaviour, based on incentives applied from outside the person considered, has swept under the carpet the fact that 'people change (motivations for) their actions because they are induced to do so by an external intervention.'[81] By ignoring the link between

---

[79] See for example Narayan and Pritchett (1996); Putnam (1993); World Bank (1997).

[80] Kreps (1997: 360). He makes the point that even though the empirical evidence has somehow been controverted, he assumes there is something to the stylized fact, since 'abundant smoke signifies a fire, and the assertion is too strongly rooted in folk wisdom to be entirely hot air.' (p. 360). Intrinsic motivation appears to be linked with cooperation. For example, Hom *et al.* (1994), investigate the effects of cooperative versus individualistic rewards on students' intrinsic motivation, and find that cooperative rewards generated higher levels of intrinsic motivation.   [81] Frey (1997: 13).

extrinsic and intrinsic motivation, specific policies may crowd out intrinsic motivation, giving rise to the phenomenon of 'hidden costs of rewards'.[82] The following section examines, in more detail, the latter phenomenon.

3.5. INTERACTION BETWEEN MOTIVATIONS

Clearly economics must build a theory of choice. But if there is no one sufficient assumption of individual motivation, if self-interest only works sometimes (how much of the time is a crucial question), then what follows? If self-interest is taken to be an insufficient assumption of human motivation, then one possible response would be to model the more complex bundle of motivations that people have, including altruism and norms. The problem with this approach is that it would ignore the influence that social setting may have on the kind and relative strength of different motivations in different groups and societies. It would assume that motivations are exogenous: we (all people, in all cultures, on average) are, by virtue of our nature, composed of three parts of self-interest, five parts of conformity, and one-fourth part *philia*, work motivation, revenge, and identity-expression. Yet motivations are different across cultures and they respond to changes in external environments.

Consider developments in the health services in Britain when the prevalent mode of motivation changed.[83] Objectively, the English health system reforms in the 1980s developed quasi-markets in welfare provision. Yet, behind this was a shift in understanding: the people who financed, operated, and used the welfare state were no longer assumed to be either public spirited altruists (knights) or passive recipients of state largesse (pawns), but were all considered to be somehow self-interested (knaves). Le Grand argues that in a situation of ignorance concerning human motivation, it would be safest to adopt public policies based on the knaves strategy. A knaves strategy will do little harm if people are actually knights; but a knights strategy could be disastrous if people are actually knaves.[84] However, 'the introduction of a knave-direct strategy may make the knights behave more knavishly.'[85] Since some evidence shows that when people behave altruistically, policies designed on the assumption of their being knaves make them knaves, the considerations about the motivation on which policies are based are not neutral.[86] This leads to the question: Is there some possibility of making people actually behave more like knights?

---

[82] Kreps (1997); Fehr *et al.* (1998); Lindbeck (1997); Enzle (1991); Goldstein and Hogarth (1997); Hogarth and Reder (1987); Hom *et al.* (1994); Sen (1994*a*, 1997*a*); Thill *et al.* (1998); Frey and Oberholzer-Gee (1997). See in particular Lepper and Greene (1978). Their experiment shows that when an activity is undertaken under pure intrinsic motivation (i.e. because people enjoy it), and when a material incentive is then offered and withdrawn, the activity ceases or is performed only in a restricted way.

[83] Le Grand (1997). Stewart (this volume) also discusses this example.

[84] 'High rewards and harsh penalties can activate self-interested deliberation on the part of agents who would otherwise be guided by non-egocentric considerations.' Pettit, 1996, p. 82.

[85] Le Grand (1997: 161). See also Peters and Marshall (1996), who show how the changes in New-Zealand welfare policies (based on individualist instead of communal assumptions) have increased social inequalities, marginalization, and social exclusion.

[86] Titmuss (1970), has demonstrated that when people give blood for altruistic reasons, introducing a payment system would reduce or stop voluntary giving.

Another indication of the influence of the environment on motivation concerns economics students.[87] A well-known study shows that economics students appear to be less cooperative than other students. Academic economists were more than twice as likely as the members of any other discipline surveyed to report that they give no money at all to any private charity. The study also found that economics majors were more than twice as likely as non-majors to defect when playing one-shot prisoner's dilemmas with strangers, the difference in defection rates growing larger the longer a student had studied economics. Is it because students are taught a certain pattern of human behaviour that they end up behaving in that way (or is it because only maximizing types choose to become economists!)?

A rich body of empirical studies suggests that cooperation can indeed be fostered by providing the right incentives (as it can be destroyed by providing the wrong incentives). A laboratory experiment[88] showed that under anonymous conditions, only a tenth of a group was prepared to act cooperatively in a 4-person strict prisoners' dilemma game, while more than three-quarters of the group behaved in a cooperative way when they were allowed to talk to each other before the game, and to establish an atmosphere of higher confidence. Another experiment[89] showed that the level of cooperation could be increased by explicit instruction to adopt a cooperative rather than a competitive or individualistic orientation (e.g. instruction to act as partners, to have regard to the common welfare), by a higher degree of communication and social interaction between players, by the extent to which the players share group membership, and by the experience of sharing a common fate. What seems to matter for cooperation is the presence of variables that produce a mutually cooperative relationship, a kind of 'we-awareness'. Another study[90] in the same line argues that people who hold a value commitment to benefit the collective, are, on average, more likely to engage in behaviours that address collective needs.

Those experiments and many others[91] show that motivation is malleable. Evoking group identity, or raising the awareness of social interests (or attention to collective goals) can make the individual restrict personal gain to preserve a collective good, and can foster cooperation for greater individual and collective welfare. Our final question, then, is: Given that motivations are plural and malleable, how can one encourage those behaviours which are more knightly and not necessarily associated with, or only with, self-interest—in particular, cooperative behaviour?

3.6. INDIVIDUAL MOTIVATION WITHIN GROUPS

COOP is one of the three major modes of within-group behaviour referred to in Chapter 1 of this book.[92] It can enhance efficiency by lowering transaction costs. It also helps to solve problems of externalities and acts as an insurance mechanism coping

---

[87] Frank *et al.* (1993).   [88] Bohnet and Frey (1994).   [89] Turner (1987).

[90] Funk (1998).

[91] See especially the detailed work done by Bowles and Gintis (1993, 1995, 1996, 1998*a,b*).

[92] COOP is defined as 'cooperation among members to achieve group objectives' in Chapter 1 in this volume.

with uncertainties.[93] Institutional economists[94] argue that a prime reason institutions exist is because they reduce uncertainty[95] and provide a structure for exchange. In this and other ways, COOP norms may produce an efficiency gain over short-term self interest. Moreover, COOP may be associated with more equitable outcomes.[96]

COOP is not uniquely associated with any particular motivation. For example, Kreps identifies four possible motivations for acting on a norm (he defines a norm as 'a somewhat general rule of voluntary behavior'—from reciprocity to tipping 15 per cent to facing the front of the elevator). Adherence to a norm may be justified (1) in terms of one's self-interest (because it is 'costless relative to violation') or it may be (2) 'immediately personally beneficial because it permits coordination (e.g. bear to the right in a crowded walkway).' On the other hand, (3) adherence may be better in the long term because it builds up one's reputation in repeated games. (4) Finally, adherence to some norms may be 'desirable *per se*' and may be adhered to out of one or another form of intrinsic motivation.[97] In addition one might want to add that COOP can be fostered by the mere weight of social habit described above—which may account, for example, for elevator etiquette.

So the menu of motivations that might be supportive of COOP includes:

- long-term reciprocity, where self-interest is interpreted over the long term
- *philia* and altruism, where others' welfare is important to the individual
- communitarian motivation where 'we' is important as well as 'I'
- identities where COOP is a significant element of the person's identity
- social norms which favour COOP
- ethical convictions enhancing COOP.

It is easy to say which type of motivation will usually frustrate COOP. The prime candidate is short-term self-interest maximization (unless short-term self-interest happens to coincide with that of the group). Apart from that, certain types of identity might be inimicable to COOP—for example, the person who regards being competitive as a key part of his identity, or being a loner, or a member of a secret society which does not include others in the group.

Both theoretical reasoning and empirical evidence suggest that many of these motivations are liable to be stronger determinants of action (a) where groups are stable and long-lived so that long-term reciprocity makes sense or social norms are binding; (b) where the size of the group is relatively small so that social interactions and their

[93] Hechter (1987); Fershtman and Weiss (1998). See, e.g. Kervyn (1989), who shows how the communal economy of a peasant Andean society is a 'rational' strategy that acts as a means to internalize the externalities and as a way of benefiting from the economies of scale that characterize Andean agriculture.

[94] See the institutional economics literature, North (1990); Dugger (1994); Williamson (1985); Sikkink (1991); North (1989); Nabli and Nugent (1989); Ruttan (1989); Bardhan (1989); Morris and Adelman (1989); Coase (1960); Stiglitz (1989); Sah and Stiglitz (1985); Esman and Uphoff (1984); Wade (1988); Ensminger (1992).

[95] Keynes argued that agents confronted by uncertainty relied on conventions, common practices and everyday life habits, in order to make savings and investment decisions. See Gerrard (1993).

[96] Stewart (1996). As underlined in Section 3.3.4, social norms, as economists understand them, include the notion of efficiency-raising, which the sociological understanding does not.   [97] Kreps (1997: 359).

effects are perceptible; (c) where there are not large personal trade-offs with behaviour favouring personal maximization; (d) where there are not large group trade-offs, in terms of group efficiency, with alternative motivation.[98]

3.7. IMPLICATIONS

In an article reflecting on business and moral principles, and their challenge to the principle of self-interest, Sen argues that one needs a wider conception of motivation rather than a new single principle: 'it would be, I would argue, a great mistake to try to replace the hypothesis of universal profit maximization with another hypothesis of similar, unconditional uniformity (such as ubiquitous altruism, or universal human sympathy, or some other form of non-contingent high-mindedness). The connections are dependent on many social, cultural, and interactive considerations, and the resulting behavioral principles would tend to be complex as well as variable with respect to time, place and group.'[99] In this paper we have argued similarly that motivations are complex and multiple; a single assumption of utility maximization is insufficient for policy purposes. As the individual is always a social being, how she behaves will be dependent on the social context in which she is acting: self-interest in the market, altruism in the family, and reciprocity in community or neighbourhood relationships.

Moreover, much theory, including revealed preference, takes motivation to be exogenously determined. Evidence suggests that this is not the case: the relative importance of extrinsic motivation (such as responding to economic incentives) is not fixed, but rather varies in comparison with the importance of other motivations described in this paper, which include a complex set of factors encompassing among others, societal norms and incentive systems. The assumption should rather be that motivations are partially endogenous to the social and economic context, as well as to peculiar features of a situation. The relative importance of different motivations can and does change over time. Furthermore, the direction of these changes may be partly predicted by knowledge of the incentive structures and beliefs of a society.

If motivations are at least partially endogenous, and if under certain conditions maximizing motivation displaces cooperation, altruism, and even rule-following, then these indirect effects, and their long-term consequences for efficiency and equity, should be taken into account when policies are aimed at fostering certain types of behaviour. In particular, this consideration may refashion the discussion of the use of economic incentives as a way of changing behaviour. The issue is not *only* whether incentives will work to affect the desired behaviour change, but *also* whether in addition to changing behaviour directly, an economic incentive may also change the way people tend to act more generally.

---

[98] Kameda *et al.* (1992), found that the motivation to cooperate between members of a group was an inverted U-shaped function of subgroup size.   [99] Sen (1997*a*: 6).

4

Collective Action for Local-level Effort Regulation: An Assessment of Recent Experiences in Senegalese Small-scale Fisheries

FREDERIC GASPART AND JEAN-PHILIPPE PLATTEAU

The success or failure of collective action depends on two sets of factors which we have identified on the basis of our previous research. The first are the characteristics of the people concerned, such as the size of the group they are forming, the extent of their heterogeneity, and the social capital at their disposal, that is, their tradition of cooperation in other areas. Heterogeneity may result from a variety of sources, such as differences in exit opportunities, time horizons, resource use or techniques adopted, and differences in skill levels or capital endowments. The second are the characteristics of the technical, economic, and political environment that affect the enforcement costs of a collective scheme. Technical aspects may refer to the physical attributes of a common-pool resource such as its location, its degree of compactness, and the frequency and predictability of its produce flows; or to the features of the technique used to extract these flows or to build up a public good. Among economic aspects, we note in particular the market conditions for inputs and outputs of the collective activity concerned. Finally, political aspects mainly refer to the role played by state institutions.

This study would not have been possible without the financial support of the Fondation Universitaire pour la Coopération Internationale au Développement (FUCID) and the Centre de Recherche en Economie du Développement (CRED), both at the University of Namur. We also gratefully acknowledge the collaboration of partner institutions in Senegal, the Centre de Recherche et de Développement de Technologies Intermédiaires pour la Pêche (CREDETIP) and the Collectif National des Pêcheurs Sénégalais (CNPS). Ousseynou Dieng, researcher at the CREDETIP, was a key performer at the level of data collection and coding. He was responsible for the direct supervision of the team of field investigators during the household survey and was continuously present on the field sites from the beginning of the data-collection process. As director of CREDETIP, Aliou Sall assumed on-the-spot responsibility for the administration of the project. François Migeotte and Catherine Mélard, both from CRED, were direct collaborators of Ousseynou Dieng and made an important contribution at the level of collection, coding, and processing data as well as writing insightful field notes and preliminary reports. Finally, the Centre de Recherche Océanographique de Dakar-Thiaroye (CRODT) provided us with data.

Collective management of fish resources can be considered especially problematic: fish move over wide areas, appear with low levels of predictability, and are caught by a large variety of harvesting techniques (see Baland and Platteau 1996: chap. 10). The fact that during the 1990s several important fishing communities along the Senegalese coastline adopted effort-restraining schemes on their own initiative deserves attention as such attempts are a rare occurrence in fisheries. There are four central questions to be investigated:

1. Were these schemes motivated by market power or by resource management considerations? By colluding in order to limit supply, fishermen may want to exercise market power to increase prices. Alternatively, they may wish to stop the dissipation of the resource rent and the depletion of the resource stock by putting an end to an open-access mode of operation.
2. Are the schemes effectively run and have they proved sustainable?
3. What types of fishermen appear to be most supportive of effort-limiting measures, and is it possible to understand their characteristics in the light of economic theory?
4. What are the reasons behind the varying success of such measures in different places on the Senegalese coastline and regarding different techniques or species of fish?

The analytical framework used throughout most of this study is inspired by transaction-cost economics, focusing on monitoring and enforcement costs. With the help of the tools of transaction economics combined with conventional market power considerations, the relative fortunes of different groups of fishermen can be accounted for in terms of techniques and site of operation.

The outline is as follows. In Section 4.1, background information regarding Senegalese small-scale maritime fisheries is provided and the methodology of the study is described. Section 4.2 presents a historical sketch of recent effort-limiting schemes attempted along the Senegalese coast. The methods used to limit fishing efforts are discussed with a view to understanding their rationale. In Section 4.3, question (2) above is addressed by looking at the incidence of rule violations as perceived by the fishermen themselves. Question (1) is also probed by considering fishermen's statements and relating these statements to their perceptions about rule-breaking. Finally, question (3) is tackled by applying the multinomial logit approach to our survey data. Section 4.4 is devoted to question (4) and the results of fitting a time-series econometric model to price and output data. Section 4.5 summarizes the main results of the study.

4.1. THE CONTEXT AND METHODOLOGY OF THE STUDY

4.1.1. *Background Information on Senegalese Maritime Fisheries*

Fishing forms a vital sector of the Senegalese economy, particularly because, with oilseeds, fish is the most important export. About 50,000 artisan fishermen work in this sector, with perhaps three times as many people engaged in fish processing and marketing in the informal fish economy. While the small-scale fishing subsector accounts for more than 60 per cent of the landings destined for export markets (and processed by specialized export companies), its share in total fish output exceeds

75 per cent. Almost 85 per cent of artisan fishermen operate in the areas covered by our study—the Grande Côte (comprising Kayar and Saint-Louis), the Petite Côte (comprising Mbour and Joal), and the Cap Vert (corresponding to the Dakar area). The number of pirogues increased by 42 per cent between 1994 and 1997. Given such a rapid increase of the capital stock, it is not surprising that there was growing pressure on fish resources, particularly on bottom-dwelling species living in coastal waters which are considered to be over-exploited (Barry-Gérard *et al*. 1992*a,b*). Biologists of the Centre de Recherche Oceanographique de Dakar-Thiaroye (CRODT) believe that coastal pelagic species are rapidly nearing optimum exploitation. Evidence of this rising pressure is the tendency of small-scale fishermen to adopt mixed techniques and to go to more distant fishing sites (a strategy that has been made possible by the introduction of pirogues equipped with iceboxes), and also the increasing incidence of conflicts between fishermen's groups using different techniques as well as growing tensions between artisan and industrial operators. The artisanal fishing sector has undergone rapid transformation during the last decades, particularly under the impact of the shift from cotton to nylon nets, the motorization of pirogues, the introduction of large purse seines and the fitting of iceboxes to pirogues designed for hook-and-line fishing. As a result, the productivity of boats and fishing gear in the small-scale sector has increased enormously, compounding the effect of their increase in numbers.

4.1.2. *Methodological Considerations*

Fieldwork took place in two steps. First, an appraisal of fishing sites in the Petite Côte, the Grande Côte, and the Cap Vert area was undertaken with a view to identifying possible schemes of effort control. Hann, Mbour, Joal, Mouette, Tassinaire, Pilote Bar, Kayar, Saint-Louis, Yoff, and Soumbedioune were visited in 1996. Only in the last four sites was evidence found of genuine past or present experimentation with such schemes (short-lived in Soumbedioune). Among the main centres of artisan fishing in Senegal, Mbour, Joal, and Hann have had no organization to limit fish landings while Kayar, Saint-Louis, and Soumbedioune have attempted to create arrangements to do so (Yoff is a port of lesser importance). Second, in sites where regulatory schemes had been tried, we administered household questionnaires addressed to fishermen and fish merchants to determine the level of belief in these schemes among fishermen as well as to examine whether some groups are more supportive than others and why. We also selected a fishing village where no regulation has ever taken place (Hann near Dakar), with the hope of understanding the reasons underlying the absence of regulatory measures. It should be noted that not all fisheries in the ports targeted for this study have been brought under a regulatory scheme, thereby adding observations which we can use to detect circumstances adverse to effort limitation. The household survey was conducted between April and July 1997.

A stratified random sampling method was applied to ensure adequate representation of different fishing techniques in each site and to distinguish between owners and crew within each technique and, when necessary, between resident and immigrant

Frederic Gaspart and Jean-Philippe Platteau

Table 4.1. *The structure of the sample by fishing site, technique, and ownership status*

Fishing site	Purse seine		Line fishing		Line with ice		Bottom-set nets		Beach seine		Total	
	Own	Crew	Own	Crew	Own	Crew	Own	Crew	Own	Crew	Own	Crew
Kayar	19*	17	15°	12	—	—	11°°	6	—	—	45	35
Saint-Louis	19	21	14	8	—	—	10	7	—	—	43	36
Soumbedio.	—	—	13	12	11	14	—	—	—	—	24	26
Yoff	11**	11	10	14	1	0	—	—	5	10	27	35
Hann	7	8	6	8	10	10	—	—	—	—	23	26
Total	56	57	58	54	22	24	21	13	5	10	162	158

*11 residents, 6 immigrants native of Saint-Louis and 2 immigrants from Fass Boye.
**7 residents and 4 immigrants from Saint-Louis.
°8 residents and 7 from Saint-Louis.
°°All native to Saint-Louis.

owners.[1] (It should be noted that many crew come from outside the fishing site, including from the rural hinterland, particularly in the purse seine fishery where unskilled and inexperienced fishermen are more easily accommodated provided that they are suitably supervised by a core of expert crew). Table 4.1 gives the characteristics of the sample for each of the five fishing sites.

A random selection of households within each subsample was made.[2] Unfortunately, difficulties in holding long interviews with household heads were more serious than foreseen, as a consequence of which the actual sample size was significantly smaller than initially envisaged, especially with respect to crew. This was due not only to pressure on their time but also to the reluctance of their employers to let them speak unobserved. Eventually, crew came to form about half the total sample of 320 households interviewed in good conditions.[3]

The sample contains data on the attitudes of two categories of fishermen: those who have gone through a (sustained) experience of effort control and those who have not. Adopting a restrictive definition of what constitutes a regulatory experience, we include 127 fishermen in the former category—corresponding to the sum total of owners and crew operating purse seines in Kayar and Saint-Louis, and lines (without ice) in Kayar and Yoff (figures in bold characters in Table 4.1)—and 193 in the latter. If a broader definition is retained and practitioners of line fishing in Soumbedioune

---

[1] To define the criteria for sample stratification in each fishing site, we consulted agents of the fishing department, enumerators working for the CRODT, local knowledgeable people, and officials of fishermen's organizations or local associations of various types (such as mosque committees).

[2] The random sample was selected by choosing a central physical point in the fishing site and letting enumerators move in different directions and include every house up to a fixed number (which varied according to the site concerned) until the predetermined size of each subsample was reached (the so-called random walk technique).

[3] In Kayar, for example, we could interview only seventeen crew operating purse seines while the initial intent was to include thirty in the sample. In Saint-Louis, the eventual sample of crew fishing with lines is only eight instead of the fifteen initially scheduled. The worst case is that of crew operating bottom-set nets in the same site (seven interviewed instead of the twenty planned).

are considered as having experienced regulation in spite of its short-lived character, the division between the two categories is 152–168 instead of 127–193.

4.2. COLLECTIVE MANAGEMENT OF SEA RESOURCES IN SENEGALESE COASTAL COMMUNITIES

4.2.1. *A Brief Historical Sketch of Effort-limiting Schemes*

The first attempt by small-scale fishermen to regulate their harvesting efforts occurred in 1992 in Kayar. Interestingly, this initiative was launched by the *Comité de Solidarité Kayar-Guet Ndar* which the fishermen established in 1990 with the support of various public sector actors in order to bring to an end the bitter conflicts that set resident fishermen from Kayar against immigrant fishermen from Saint-Louis. In the wake of this emerging collective action movement, it was decided that canoes equipped with purse seines might make a single trip per day during the season. A special committee named *Comité des sennes tournantes* (committee for purse seines) was created to enforce the rule, which was apparently motivated by the desire to increase producer prices for the pelagic species targeted by purse seines and to reduce the market power wielded by local fish merchants. The scheme was still operating at the time of writing, in 1999.

Two years after the creation of the *Comité des sennes tournantes*, the so-called *Comité des pêches* (committee of the fisheries) was set up by fishermen of Kayar to extend the experience of purse seines to line fishing which targets demersal species destined for export markets. This step was taken soon after the devaluation of the CFA when fishermen feared a contraction of their profit margins owing to a rapid rise in production costs. Output prices did not in the event rise significantly, either because the species concerned were not of an exportable variety or because fish intermediaries succeeded in pre-empting a large share of the gains from devaluation.

The latter explanation was confirmed in the course of interviews with managers of fish-processing factories in Dakar. According to them, commission agents in charge of purchasing raw fish at the landing sites on behalf of export companies colluded to prevent producer prices from increasing after the devaluation. In reaction to a glaring manipulation of market prices, fishermen started to demonstrate, first in Yoff and thereafter in Kayar where the protest movement took the form of a three-day strike during which fish merchants were starved of fish. When merchants refused to raise their prices substantially after fishermen returned to fishing, the latter tried to sell the fish to the factories themselves by renting refrigerated vans. This was a temporary solution, soon superseded by an attempt to limit catches of demersal species through the fixing of a maximum number of boxes that a canoe can unload. The scheme was still in force at the time of writing, in 1999, attesting to its viability compared with lockout movements—which are unsustainable given the lack of inter-temporal markets to smooth temporary disruptions of economic activity—and with direct sales of fish to export companies, which are costly for fishermen due to their lack of marketing experience and skills.

The above institutional innovation spread to Saint-Louis through migrant fishermen. To regulate fishing trips by canoes operating purse seines as well as to achieve other collective ends (particularly, to encourage mutual help groups for sea rescue operations and insurance against damage to nets, engines, and canoes), a special organization known as the *Union des Professionnels de la Pêche Artisanale de Guet-Ndar* (UPPAG) was created in November 1992. A first attempt to limit trips by purse seine fishermen was made in October 1993 when fifty-five canoes participated in a scheme allowing only one trip every two days. In order to implement the rotating scheme, the canoes concerned were divided into two groups according to the quarter of residence of their owners. However, in 1995, the scheme was brought to an end due to internal tensions leading to many violations. There was never any attempt to regulate fishing effort among line fishermen in Saint-Louis.

Yoff was the site of the initial experiment with line-fishing quotas. A special committee was in charge of monitoring the regulatory measure. Subsequently, however, serious tensions appeared in the village leading to the discontinuance of the scheme (in February 1997). Opposition to the measures by an important leader eager to recoup considerable investment expenditures is frequently mentioned as the trigger of the crisis, though we also encountered a widespread belief that the members of the committee were not up to their task. Personal antagonisms and leadership rivalries may have contributed to diminishing the authority of the committee.

In trying to emulate their colleagues from Yoff, fishermen of Soumbedioune were much less successful than those of Kayar. In August 1994, they decided to set up a committee to enforce limits on landings of export species. After barely three months, the experience ended amid disillusionment.

The enforcement of regulatory measures is supported by sanctions. In Kayar, when a canoe equipped with a purse seine is found exceeding the limit of one fishing trip per day, a fine of 100,000 CFA is imposed on the owner. If he refuses to comply, the canoe and the net are confiscated until he pays the fine, and they can be sold if default is prolonged. The same system applies to canoes equipped with lines. Payment is exacted under the threat of seizure of equipment. The time allowed for paying the fine can extend to 10–15 days if the rule-breaker is a well-known fisherman with solvency problems. According to several informants, flexibility in meting out punishment was gradually introduced as the rigid procedures that were initially devised aroused too much resistance.

4.2.2. *Measures Aimed at the Allocation of Fishing Space*

In a few cases, measures are aimed at allocating fishing space rather than limiting fishing effort. Thus, in Yoff, there is a prohibition that forbids canoes with purse seines to operate within a certain distance of the beach during the February–May period, in order to reserve inshore waters for beach seines, bell-shaped nets operated directly from the beach.[4]

---

[4] This gear has the advantage of creating a lot of employment (the hauling in of a beach seine needs between 30 and 100 fishermen, including many unskilled workers).

In Kayar, competition for access to in-shore waters has been a constant source of tension between migrant fishermen (from Saint-Louis) operating bottom-set nets and resident fishermen. Such tension may easily erupt into physical violence, even deaths. The conflict is especially severe because it takes on an ethnic dimension. It sets fishermen using passive gear (the bottom-set nets used by fishermen from Saint-Louis) against those using active gear (such as the lines and purse seines used in this case by resident fishermen). It must be borne in mind that fishermen from Saint-Louis have a long tradition of mobility along the West African coast.[5] As a consequence of deep-rooted migration habits, the Saint-Louisiens consider the sea an open access resource, while people from Kayar, originally an agricultural community, are inclined to view the adjacent water as their own territory, much as they see their agricultural land.

In February 1986, the government of Senegal set up a special commission charged with the task of defining and monitoring an exclusive fishing zone, in which bottom-set nets were prohibited from operating. However, illegal encroachments are frequent, and in most cases they are not dealt with by the commission for lack of monitoring equipment. In these circumstances, fishermen who consider that their rights have been infringed tend to punish the alleged culprits without informing the commission (typically, bottom-set nets are seized and re-sold by resident fishermen without the intervention of the commission), thereby creating an atmosphere where reference to justice may well conceal less worthy motives and obscure settlement of private accounts.

4.2.3. *The Rationale of the Methods Used to Limit Fishing Effort*

As pointed out above, technology affects the type of scheme attempted. For purse seine fishermen, reduction of fishing effort is achieved through limitation of the number of sea trips allowed, while for line fishermen, catches per canoe may not exceed a certain number of boxes. From the viewpoint of efficiency, neither method is ideal. The former method encourages fishermen to make up for the limitation of fishing trips by increasing the productivity of each permitted trip, through the lengthening of fishing time or the introduction of technical innovations. Conversely, the latter method induces fishermen to multiply their fishing trips. Waste of capital and labour tends to result. Moreover, new entrants are not prevented from operating, as attested by the rapid increase in the number of artisan boats.

What can explain the selection of different systems of effort regulation, both apparently imperfect, depending on the fishing technique employed? First, the characteristics of purse seine fishing make catch quotas unfeasible. In this type of fishing, huge schools may be caught with a single sweep of the net handled from one or two motorized canoes. There are two reasons why purse seine fishermen resist having to throw excess produce back in the sea. First, forgoing a catch actually achieved entails a much higher subjective cost than forgoing a potential catch. This explains why the punishment imposed on line fishermen who do not comply with quotas takes the form

---

[5] A result of the fact that the fishing zone of Guet-Ndar is not sheltered from the strong winds of the Atlantic Ocean and is therefore accessible only during a limited part of the year.

of a lumpsum fine, not the confiscation of the excess.[6] The second reason has to do with insurance. Since catches vary widely, imposing a ceiling means that fishermen would have to forgo a windfall catch on a 'lucky' trip, while under poor natural conditions their average catch is smaller than the authorized maximum. In the case of purse seine fishing, therefore, limitation of fishing trips with no catch quotas is a second-best solution imposed by technological and ecological constraints.

On the other hand, since catching fish with hooks and lines can be discontinued almost at will, fixing catch quotas per trip is a practical proposition for line fishing canoes. Furthermore, imposing limits on the number of fishing trips per day does not appear to be necessary because (i) the average length of a sea trip for these canoes is close to nine hours due to the distance of the fishing grounds, and (ii) landing sites are not lit, forcing boats to return before markets close at dusk. The system of catch quotas applied to line fishing thus conforms to the prediction of economic theory. As for canoes equipped with iceboxes, they can undertake much longer voyages. Given the high fixed cost of their long journey, it is doubtful that the fishermen concerned would accept a restriction on their catches.

From the standpoint of equity, it is notable that all reported regulatory measures impose an equal amount of catch reduction on each unit. There exists a total consensus about this manner of sharing the burden as revealed by our household survey. All the fishermen interviewed consider it would be unfair to impose identical quotas on all owners, regardless of the size of their capital stock. With identical quotas, large owners would see an abrupt reduction in the profitability of their fishing assets. In addition, crew working on boats prohibited from operating would become unemployed unless some employment-sharing mechanism were agreed upon within the fishing community. Such outcomes appear unacceptable not only to the big owners and the crew but also to the smaller owners. Equally interesting to note is the fact that Senegalese small-scale fishermen consider that it would be unfair to award larger quotas to better skilled operators. We know from economic theory that when quotas are set in a uniform manner there is likely to be opposition from the better skilled or better endowed (Johnson and Libecap 1982; Libecap and Wiggins 1984; Libecap 1990; Baland and Platteau 1998, 1999). We would thus predict that the rules laid down in the groups considered here are likely to be resisted by the best performing members. Unfortunately, we are unable to test this hypothesis since we have no reliable indicator of relative skill levels. In the interviews, many of the Senegalese small-scale fishermen denied that significant skill differentials exist in their community and they took pains to explain that better performances on the part of some fishermen are only transient phenomena likely to be reversed as soon as luck favours other fishing units. The prevalence of this view has no doubt influenced the selection of effort-reducing methods in the villages surveyed: quotas or rules regarding fishing trips are set independently

---

[6] This is an interesting application of the prospect theory of Kahneman and Tversky (1979) according to which subjects tend to evaluate prospects in terms of gains and losses relative to some reference point, rather than hypothetical final states (wealth positions) as assumed by expected utility theory. The so-called value function depicted by these authors captures the idea of loss aversion (the function is steeper for losses than gains).

Table 4.2. *Frequencies of fishermen considering that rule violations are frequent, by village and fishing technique*

Technique/site	Low incidence of rule violations (%)	High incidence of rule violations (%)	Total number in group
Line fishing Kayar	44.4	55.6	27
Line fishing Yoff	45.8	54.2	24
Purse seine Kayar	75.0	25.0	36
Purse seine Saint-Louis	60.0	40.0	40
Total	58.3	41.7	127

of the skill levels of those subject to regulation. Skill differentials are no doubt difficult to measure in an impartial manner, though we do not doubt that fishermen are aware of skill rankings within their community but do not want to disclose them in public.

4.3. RESULTS FROM THE CROSS-SECTION ANALYSIS OF HOUSEHOLD SURVEY DATA

4.3.1. *Perceived Incidence of Rule Infractions*

An obvious way of assessing whether a collective scheme works well is by determining the rate of infraction of the rules adopted. Since no objective measure of this indicator is available, we have to rely on the subjective assessments of the people concerned. In fact, fishermen's beliefs regarding the prevailing extent of rule violations are an important yardstick of the scheme's effectiveness: they tell us whether sufficient trust exists to make the scheme viable in the medium or long run.[7] Table 4.2 summarizes such beliefs as inferred from the household survey.

Several interesting features emerge. First, more than 40 per cent of the sample consider that there are many rule violations under the effort-limiting schemes. As conversations with fishermen revealed, a high perceived rate of infraction points to a belief that too many operators violate the limits without sanctions, with all the attendant consequences in terms of demotivation of participants. Such a conclusion runs counter to the views of many leaders of the effort-limiting schemes: according to them, rules are well enforced and punishment is rarely meted out because there are few rule-breakers. It seems from Table 4.2, however, that fishermen are frequently tempted to freeride on others' efforts.

Second, there are significant variations in the perceived incidence of rule-breaking. The incidence is large among line fishermen, whether in Kayar or in Yoff, and it is significantly larger than that obtaining for purse seine fishermen (in Kayar and

[7] Note that we also asked fishermen whether they themselves violated the rules, but the answers were unconvincing (only 9 out of 127 fishermen in the restricted sample confessed to have done so).

Saint-Louis).[8] The fact that cheating is easier with lines than with purse seines largely accounts for this. It is easier to conceal a box of fish, and to dispose of it secretly, than to make an illegal sea trip without being noticed (here, mutual monitoring is typically sufficient to detect violations). The fact that sales may take place at sea or on the beach amidst crowds of people greatly facilitates the discreet disposal of excess catches. We are now in a position to qualify an earlier statement (see Section 4.2) according to which schemes based on catch quotas are more efficient than those based on limitations of fishing trips: since the former is fraught with more supervision problems than the latter, it may well be more efficient to limit sea trips than landings.

Third, the perceived incidence of rule-breaking among purse seine fishermen is larger in Saint-Louis than in Kayar. This relates directly to the failure of the scheme in the former. To recall, while purse seines may be operated once a day in Kayar, the rule is only once every two days in Saint-Louis. However, fishermen are eager to work every day because ecological conditions may vary significantly. Frustration is especially great when the sea is too rough to fish on their day, since they then consider that they have been robbed of effective fishing time.

Moreover, well-to-do fishermen from Saint-Louis are accustomed to lending their fishing equipment to poorer relatives or friends. However, such loans may only take place on days on which the fishing unit concerned is allowed to operate. This is deemed unfair by both lenders and borrowers. Being permitted to go out only once every two days, well-to-do fishermen feel less inclined to be generous. The previous beneficiaries resent the new situation which the well-to-do blame on the regulatory scheme.

In addition, there is in Saint-Louis a strong tradition of so-called 'special sea trips' (*ndiaylou*) whereby different members of an extended family join together to earn incomes required for a collective purpose, say, financing a wedding, a baptism, or help-ing a relative who has suffered from an accident or illness. These trips fall under the scope of the effort-limiting scheme. Fishermen resist complying with such a require-ment since they do not privately benefit from the income thus earned. Hence a practice has developed of eschewing the commission's approval for these special trips. With this, there is suspicion that some fishermen use the pretext of a *ndiaylou* to increase their fishing time.

4.3.2. *Identification of Fishermen with Positive and Negative Assessments of Rule Abidance*

We estimated a logit model to see if we could say something about the characteristics of the fishermen who believe that the incidence of rule-breaking is large. The results are shown in Appendix A, Table 4.A1. The independent variables included were ownership, wealth (proxied by number of wives—the number of wives is strongly correlated with fishing assets owned), migrant status, age, education, and relationships between fishermen and fish merchants. There is no significant association between

---

[8] According to the Fisher test, the difference between line and purse seine fishermen is statistically significant at the 2 per cent level of confidence.

Table 4.3. *Assessment of extent of rule-breaking according to age and marriage characteristics, all villages (Kayar, Yoff, Saint-Louis) and Kayar only (in brackets)*

Age and marriage characteristics	Proportion of fishermen identifying a large incidence of rule-breaking (%)
a. Aged between 24–35 years and unmarried	57 (64)
b. Aged between 24–35 years and married	32 (15)
c. More than 35 years old and married but excluding people of category (e) below	50 (44)
d. More than 35 years old and married	43 (31)
e. More than 47 years and three wives	21 (10)
f. Total average	42 (38)

fishermen's beliefs about the incidence of rule-breaking and ownership, migration, and age. The other five independent variables are all significant.

Evasion of effort-limiting prescriptions is perceived to be lower by those operating purse seines than by those operating lines (this effect is statistically significant at the 95 per cent level). Moreover, other things being equal, rule-breaking is believed to be more pervasive in comparatively educated fishermen, that is, those with more than six years of Koranic schooling, or six years of primary school in French (significant only at the 90 per cent level). Given that we do not measure actual rates of rule-breaking, it is difficult to interpret this result.

Fishermen involved in exclusive sales agreements with particular merchants in exchange for loans[9] have a tendency to perceive a higher incidence of rule violations, perhaps because they themselves are more prone to evading catch limitations. Indeed, since rules apply to all fishermen irrespective of whether they have exclusive sale agreements with merchants (at least in Kayar), it is easy to understand why those involved in sales-tying will be subject to more pressures (from their creditor-merchants) to land as much fish as possible. After all, this is the objective pursued by fish merchants when they give loans to fishermen.

Finally, controlling for age, fishermen with more wives tend to perceive lower incidences of rule violation. The number of wives is strongly correlated with ownership of fishing assets so wives can be regarded as a proxy for wealth. We explore this further in Table 4.3. This shows that a relatively small proportion of those over forty-seven with three wives (i.e. wealthy) perceive rule-breaking to be serious. Such influential persons play a leadership role in many collective initiatives (cleaning of the beach, construction and maintenance of the village mosque, assistance in the event of sea accidents, etc.). They may have special difficulties in seeing the dysfunctionings of an undertaking with which they are strongly identified. Or, it may be that they are more confident of its ability to succeed eventually in spite of what they perceive as minor problems. The figures

---

[9] Merchants do not insist that the fishermen repay the principal of the loans if they are satisfied with the catch (interest on the loans is paid in the form of lower fish prices offered by the merchant acting as a monopsonist).

in brackets in Table 4.3 show that the leadership phenomenon is even more marked in Kayar. This result reflects the fact that in Kayar there exists a well-established power structure based on ascriptive criteria combined with wealth. The agricultural origin of the village, where even today cultivation (of vegetables) remains an important activity for many fishermen's families, largely accounts for this.

Table 4.3 also shows that fishermen under thirty-six who have one or several wives have a lower propensity to identify high rates of rule-breaking than unmarried fishermen, belonging to the same age class, or older married fishermen. Again, this relationship is stronger for Kayar.

Why is it that married fishermen who are relatively young tend to be optimistic in their statements about rule-breaking, and more so in Kayar than in Saint-Louis or Yoff? A plausible hypothesis might depict the following scenario. Before reaching their thirties, fishermen are typically bachelors working and living with their fathers whose opinions about the effectiveness of the effort-limiting scheme influence their own perceptions. When they marry, they form their own households and become more independent of their fathers (though they may well continue to operate their fathers' boats and nets). At that stage, they usually play an active role in various organizations which are particularly active in Kayar. Participation in these collective ventures has the effect of making them hopeful that organizational dysfunctionings are minimal.

After a few years of experience, however, fishermen come to a more realistic assessment of the schemes' effectiveness. In this, they exhibit more flexibility than the old elite. In Yoff and Saint-Louis, such a turnaround in beliefs is not observed, presumably because there are fewer local organizations through which young married people can have their own direct experience of collective action.

We estimated a more refined logit model to explore this further. The results are shown in Appendix A, Table 4.A2. We introduced a variable *ymarkay* which takes on the value of one when the fisherman is a (relatively) young married person (between twenty-four and thirty-five years) working in Kayar, and the value of zero otherwise. This is significant at the 95 per cent confidence level. We also introduced a variable *leadkay* that takes on the value one when the fisherman is more than forty-seven years old, has three wives and works in Kayar, and is zero otherwise; this is not significant even at the 90 per cent confidence level. However, when variables that are strongly correlated with *leadkay* are removed, it becomes significant.

4.3.3. *Proportion and Identification of Fishermen Holding Various Beliefs About the Effects of Regulatory Measures (Kayar, Saint-Louis, Yoff)*

Fishermen were asked whether effort-limiting measures have the intended effects on economic and environmental levels. The first question is whether limitation of supply has the effect of increasing fish prices (economic effect). The second question is whether it can prevent the fish stock from decreasing (biological effect). The idea is that beliefs about the likely effects of effort-restricting measures influence the actual behaviour of fishermen. Table 4.4 shows, for Kayar, Yoff, and Saint-Louis, the frequencies

Table 4.4. *Frequencies (absolute and relative) of fishermen and perceptions of rule-breaking according to beliefs in effects of effort-limiting measures*

	Biological effect is denied	Biological effect is signalled	Total
Economic effect is denied	20	29	49
	15.8%	22.8%	38.6%
	(20.0%)	(75.9%)	(53.1%)
Economic effect is signalled	23	55	78
	18.1%	43.3%	61.4%
	(21.7%)	(40.0%)	(34.6%)
Total	43	84	127
	33.9%	66.1%	100.0%
	(20.9%)	(52.3%)	(41.7%)

and proportions of fishermen associated with each of the four possible combinations of beliefs. In addition, it shows in brackets the corresponding proportions of fishermen who believe that rule violations are frequent.

Three facts stand out. First, in those villages where prolonged attempts have been made to control fishing effort, more than 43 per cent of the fishermen reckon that controls produce both biological and economic effects, whereas only 16 per cent deny both effects. Second, there are slightly more fishermen signalling the biological effect (about two-thirds) than fishermen signalling the economic effect (about 61 per cent), while we would have expected the opposite given the more direct visibility of the latter effect. However, and third, there is a definite relationship between beliefs in the effects of effort-limiting measures and beliefs regarding the extent of rule-breaking.

One interpretation of this finding is the following: while the presence of even a few rule transgressors may be sufficient to destroy the price effect of effort restriction—a marginal free rider on a cartel may seriously undermine its effectiveness—biological depletion of the fish stock may be reduced even though rule violations occur on a significant scale. This said, initiation of collective efforts to limit fish landings has clearly been motivated by the desire to counter the market power of fish merchants and not by concern about resource degradation. It is also revealing that leaders often express the view that output regulation for economic purposes can be a crucial step towards bringing awareness among fishermen of the need for resource conservation.

Given these facts, we believe that biological concerns are often voiced in a rather perfunctory manner: most of the time fishermen do not seriously consider the possibility of their own responsibility for overfishing and, therefore, the idea that they could combat environmental degradation by restricting their own effort is alien to most of them. Revealingly, there is a clear tendency among Senegalese fishermen to externalize the problem by blaming industrial fishing vessels for the destruction of fish resources.

Table 4.5. *Frequencies (absolute and relative) of fishermen according to beliefs in effects of effort-limiting measures (fishermen believing in low incidence of rule violations only)*

	Biological effect is denied	Biological effect is signalled	Total
Economic effect is denied	16 (21.6%)	7 (9.5%)	23 (31.1%)
Economic effect is signalled	18 (24.3%)	33 (44.6%)	51 (68.9%)
Total	34 (45.9%)	40 (54.1%)	74 (100.0%)

When we consider only those fishermen who believe in a low incidence of rule violations, we obtain the distribution presented in Table 4.5. Figures are now much more congruent with our expectation. Indeed, almost 70 per cent of the fishermen signal the economic effect while only 54 per cent mention the biological effect. Moreover, the probability of fishermen believing in the biological effect also mentioning the economic effect increases noticeably to 0.83 while the reverse probability goes down to 0.65.

To explore this further, we ran multinomial logit regressions to estimate the determinants of the various beliefs held by the fishermen of Kayar, Yoff, and Saint-Louis regarding the likely effects of effort-limiting measures. We took fishermen who did not mention either effect as the reference group and aimed at identifying factors explaining assignments to the following three groups: those who mentioned the economic and not the biological effect (regression 1), those who mentioned the biological and not the economic effect (regression 2), and those who mentioned both the economic and the biological effect (regression 3). We added two further independent variables, one indicating whether fishermen explicitly mentioned the existence of collusive practices among fish merchants, and the other indicating whether there were alternative possible income sources within the household.

The results of the three regressions are shown in Appendix A, Table 4.A3. The first regression was not very successful, the only significant coefficient being associated with the migration variable and that only at the 90 per cent level. The other two regressions were more successful. The coefficient of the education variable is significant at the 99 per cent level of confidence in the second regression and at the 95 per cent level in the third. Fishermen who are relatively educated (i.e. they have more than six years of French or Koranic school) tend to mention the simultaneous presence of biological and economic effects more often (regression 3), or the presence of the biological effect alone as against the alternative of not mentioning any effect at all (regression 2). The fact that environmental problems are nowadays a widely publicized issue, in the media, at school, and in the meetings of various fishermen's organizations (more particularly, in the CNPS and the Federation of GIE) probably explains why many relatively educated fishermen refer to the biological dimension of fish resource management. Furthermore, a general effect of education is to combat fatalistic attitudes and to instil confidence in people's ability to influence their living conditions through various forms of purposeful collective action. This applies not only to environmental but also to social, political, and economic problems. In particular, educated people may appreciate that producers can sometimes change market conditions through organizing collectively.

A second major result is that inter-community tensions tend to reduce people's propensity to organize collectively. The coefficient of the migration variable is significant at (close to) a 100 per cent level of confidence in both regressions 2 and 3. Migrant fishermen native to Saint-Louis and operating in Kayar have a marked tendency to deny the existence of economic and biological effects. Their sceptical attitude seems to be determined by a traumatic experience of tense inter-community relations and what they consider to be an unsatisfactory solution to conflicts. The result is maintained if we group together permanent residents of Kayar who are native to Saint-Louis and temporary migrants from Saint-Louis. This suggests that the problem is more a problem of inter-community relations than one of migrant–resident opposition.

In both regressions 2 and 3 the coefficient of the *leadkay* variable is significant, and large. If the alternative sources of income variable with which the *leadkay* variable is strongly correlated is removed from the equation, the level of significance of the coefficient associated with the *leadkay* variable improves perceptibly. This reinforces our earlier result that Kayar leaders tend to minimize enforcement problems.

Let us now say a few words about factors that apparently fail to influence fishermen's beliefs. The regression results suggest that such beliefs are not significantly influenced by the fishing technology used. While the mode of restricting effort with line-operating canoes gives rise to more monitoring difficulties than the mode used for purse seines, the effects of the former are not reckoned to be weaker than the effects of the latter. Moreover, there is no difference of opinion between owners and crew. (Bear in mind that crew also benefit from effort-restraining schemes if successful, since labour incomes are calculated as a fixed percentage of the catch proceeds.) In addition, belief in the economic effect of the measures considered does not seem to be affected by awareness of collusive practices among fish merchants. Likewise, involvement of fishermen in exclusive sales ties with merchants does not appear to prompt them to mention the economic effect of effort-restraining rules.

Finally, the availability of alternative income sources within the household does not make fishermen more likely to mention the positive effects of such rules. Yet it must be borne in mind that the alternative income variable is strongly correlated with the *leadkay* variable (see above). The effect of alternative income seems to be dominated by that of *leadkay*.[10] There is thus not much support in favour of the following hypothesis: when they can rely on complementary sources of income, fishermen are more prone to favour effort regulation because they are better able to endure the loss of fishing incomes in the short or medium term so as to benefit from higher incomes in the long term, whether through gaining increased market power or ensuring conservation of

[10] If the *leadkay* variable is removed from the second regression, the coefficient of the alternative income sources variable becomes statistically significant.

fish resources. The reason is that there is a contrary effect: fishermen with greater alternative income opportunities depend less on their fishing incomes and may feel less ready to incur sacrifices to make them grow. This is all the more so if alternative incomes originate in fish marketing, since gains accruing to fishermen in the form of increased unit prices must then be weighed against the losses suffered by fish traders in the household.

4.3.4. *Fishermen's Opinions Regarding the Likely Effects of Effort Regulation (All Villages and All Fisheries)*

We now repeat the multinomial logit regression estimation exercise for the whole sample of villages and fisheries, whether they have substantial experience of effort-limiting measures or not. This might enable us to identify factors that explain why some villages (represented here by Han and Soumbedioune) or some fisheries (represented by bottom-set nets in Kayar, lines in Saint-Louis, and purse and beach seines in Yoff) have failed to adopt such measures.

A number of interesting things emerge from the exercise the results of which are reported in Appendix A Table 4.A4. All three regressions produce interesting results this time. The interesting things that emerge are, first, a prolonged, relatively positive experience with effort regulation has the clear effect of prompting beliefs in its economic and biological impact (the coefficient of the variable representing such experience is significant at the 99 per cent level in all three regressions). Second, fishermen who target exportable species and travel longer distances than before in order to reach them have a tendency to stress the effects of effort regulation (the coefficient representing this is again significant at the 99 per cent level in all three regressions).[11] In other words, progressive fishermen eager to seize on new economic opportunities and bent on catching valuable species stress the importance and effectiveness of regulation.[12] This may follow directly from the fact that profitability of effort control resulting in increases of unit producer prices is likely to increase with the initial level of these prices.

Some other results confirm previously reported findings, such as the negative influence of community divisions in Kayar[13] (again, the result holds if all fishermen from

---

[11] This variable could not be used in the previous regressions because too few fishermen in the restricted sample were involved. The majority of those who mentioned it are line fishermen in Hann and Soumbedioune in the Dakar area. While their overall proportion is 11% in the whole sample, they form more than one-third of line fishermen operating canoes equipped with iceboxes in Hann and Soumbedioune; about one-fifth of line fishermen operating simple canoes in Kayar, Hann, and Soumbedioune; and one-fifth of purse seine fishermen in Hann. The proportions of fishermen who mentioned in a general way that they have to go farther out to sea are much higher than these proportions and reflect the increasing perception of resource scarcity in the Senegalese waters.

[12] It bears emphasis that progressivity is measured with respect to the fishing technique and, even more, to the site concerned. Thus, a line fisherman of Hann who has stated that he goes farther and farther out to sea to target species of high exportable value is not necessarily more progressive than a line fisherman from Saint-Louis, where opportunities are less favourable.

[13] Note, however, that the coefficient of the variable representing migration is no longer significant in the first regression.

Saint-Louis are grouped together whether they are permanent residents or tempor-ary migrants). The positive influence of education on ecological awareness is also confirmed (see the second and third regressions).

Contrary to the results of the estimation for those with experience of regulatory schemes only, the variable representing exclusive sales tying has a significant coefficient (at the 95 per cent level) in the first regression, yet continues to perform very badly in the other two regressions. The first regression suggests that fishermen involved in sales-tying relationships are more aware of the economic advantage of effort regulation. This is not surprising given that they usually get lower prices for the fish they are committed to sell through their lender-merchant. They are, therefore, more sensitive to the potential gains of collective organization. On the other hand, since there is no reason why such fishermen should be more alert to the environmental benefits of collective action, the absence of significant relationships between sales tying and either a belief in the biological effects of effort limitation or both (see the second and third regressions) is understandable.

Table 4.6 shows the proportions of fishermen engaged in exclusive sales relationships with merchants according to fishing techniques and sites. It shows that some categories of fishermen in some villages have a higher propensity to accept exclusive agreements with merchants than others. While about one-fourth of the sample of Senegalese fishermen are in this situation, the proportion shoots up for operators of bottom-set nets (59 per cent in Kayar and 76 per cent in Saint-Louis), and for line fishermen in Hann (71 per cent) and Saint-Louis (41 per cent). This finding is a powerful factor accounting for the lack of effort-restraining mechanisms in these fisheries, since it is hard to see how such collective mechanisms could take root when so many fishermen are entangled in exclusive tying relationships with merchants. The fact that in Kayar and Yoff, where effort regulation has occurred, only 22 and 17 per cent, respectively, of the fishermen are engaged in such relationships deserves strong emphasis. The presence of an endogeneity bias—exclusive relationships with merchant-creditors tend to disappear when effort regulation is adopted—is rather unlikely as owners of fishing assets cannot easily terminate such relationships.

Returning to the results of the multinomial logit regression exercise reported in Appendix A, Table 4.A4, the two technological dummies figuring in the third

Table 4.6. *Proportions of fishermen engaged in exclusive sales relationships with merchants, according to fishing techniques and sites (%)*

Technique/Site	Kayar	Saint-Louis	Yoff	Hann	Soumbedi.	Total
Line	22.2	40.9	16.7	71.4	24.0	31.2
Line + icebox	—	—	0.0	15.0	24.0	19.6
Purse seine	13.9	15.0	0.0	26.7	—	13.3
Beach seine	—	—	0.0	—	—	0.0
Bottom-set net	58.8	76.5	—	—	—	67.6
Total	26.3	35.4	6.4	34.7	24.0	25.6

regression have a significant influence on the dependent variable: they suggest that simple line fishermen have a higher propensity to identify both the economic and biological advantages of effort regulation. Also, in the first regression the coefficient of the variable representing line fishermen operating canoes with iceboxes (*icebox*) becomes significant at the 95 per cent level when the exclusive sales-tying variable with which it is correlated is left out. The most solid result regarding the role of technology is that line fishermen operating canoes equipped with iceboxes are comparatively reluctant to recognize the economic effect of effort limitation (whether in conjunction with the biological effort or not). This probably reflects the fact that these fishermen operate in conditions (long journeys out at sea) that make a collective scheme of effort regulation especially hard to put into practice (see Section 4.2).

Finally, migrants from Saint-Louis operating in Soumbedioune exhibit a stronger tendency than residents to identify the economic and biological effects of effort regulation (95 per cent significance in the third regression). Moreover, they never mention either effect exclusively (migration from Saint-Louis operating in Soumbedioune is a perfect predictor in the first and second equations). The coefficient of migration from Saint-Louis in the third regression ceases to be significant if we group together migrants from Saint-Louis and permanent residents who are natives of Saint-Louis, pointing to different opinions among migrants and residents. Unlike in Kayar, here, the migrant–resident difference seems to be more relevant than the ethnic dimension.

Since the belief in high incidences of rule violation significantly and positively influences the biological effects only variable (see the second regression), we repeated the econometric experiment carried out above, estimating a standard logit model in which the dependent variable was a binary dummy representing economic effects. The main findings of this more condensed estimate (not reported here) are the following. (i) As expected, the role of education vanishes. (ii) A prolonged and serious experience positively influences expectations regarding the economic impact of effort regulation (this effect is significant at the 99 per cent confidence level). (iii) Migrant fishermen in Kayar are sceptical about this impact (this effect is significant at the 95 per cent level), yet do not behave in a specific manner in Soumbedioune.[14] (iv) Understandably, a high perceived rate of rule violation tends to destroy the belief that limiting effort is likely to cause an increase in fish prices (this effect is significant at almost the 100 per cent level). (v) Fishing technology has a decisive bearing upon the latter belief: line fishermen working with simple canoes are the most prone to trust economic regulation. (vi) Dynamic fishermen targetting exportable species are confident that the economic effect can materialize (this effect is significant at almost a 100 per cent confidence level). (vii) The impact of leadership in Kayar vanishes,[15] not surprisingly given that what mostly characterizes leaders from Kayar is their strong proclivity to mention both the economic and the biological effects of regulation. (viii) The effect of exclusive sales-tying relationships disappears in favour of a less well-established

---

[14] This is due to the fact that, if migrant fishermen in Soumbedioune have a strong proclivity to mention the economic effect together with the biological effect, they never mention it alone.

[15] In this case, removing the alternative income sources variable does not help establish a significant relationship between *leadkay* and mention of the economic effect.

effect (at only a 90 per cent confidence level) of concerns about collusive practices among fish merchants. The vanishing of the sales-tying effect is not surprising since an exclusive sales relationship with a fish merchant affects the prices obtained for landings but not the biology of fish resources. We may expect that fishermen entangled in such exclusive relationships hold particularly strong views regarding the price effect of output regulation yet do not mention that effect in combination with biological impacts.

4.3.5. *Support for Effort Regulation Among Line Fishermen Without Relevant Experience*

Line fishermen without experience of effort regulation were asked if it was a good idea to limit the number of boxes landed by each canoe. This enabled us to attempt to identify the characteristics of these fishermen that may explain their attitude to the imposition of landing quotas. For lack of space, we do not report the findings of the regression we ran: in summary, they confirm our expectation that line fishermen operating canoes with iceboxes have a strong tendency to believe that catch quotas are detrimental to their interests. They also reveal that progressive line fishermen (those who go far into the sea in order to catch the most valuable species) are more supportive of effort-limiting measures. This confirms previous findings for which an explanation has been advanced: profitability of effort control is likely to be higher for this category. Second, those fishermen who have alternative income opportunities also seem more in favour of catch quotas, even though we did not previously find evidence of their greater awareness of the potential advantages of regulation.

4.4. RESULTS FROM TIME-SERIES ANALYSIS OF PRICE AND OUTPUT DATA

So far, we have implicitly assumed that effort regulation is effective in achieving its economic objective of increasing producer prices. This is not necessarily the case, however. In order to assess the fishermen's ability to exert market power in a sustainable way, we must establish whether demand elasticity is greater or lower than -1 for every regulated product. A value below -1 for demand elasticity would ensure that a monopoly can find a positive level of output that maximizes profit and, therefore, that the fishermen's cartel can define the target level of output.

Estimating demand elasticity is usually a tricky operation because prices and quantities are simultaneously determined by supply and demand. Fishing is nevertheless a special activity in this regard: when sellers meet buyers on the shore, it is too late to adjust the quantity. However, the possibility of conserving fish in freezing facilities enables speculation. Expected prices must enter the determinants of demand if this effect is to be taken seriously. This reintroduces a simultaneity problem in the demand curve, in so far as future prices may be a function of current prices. Fortunately, past prices and seasonal dummies provide good exogenous variables to instrument for expected prices. In addition to quantity and expected future prices, prices of substitute goods also affect demand. These are of course endogenous (since a good is a substitute of its substitutes) and can be instrumented for on the basis of past values and seasonal dummies as well.

On the basis of the above, we assume that market data are generated by a three-step process. First, fishermen form an expectation of the day-price on the basis of past prices and season. Second, quantities are determined by the joint effect of the fishermen's willingness-to-sell at the expected price and of a random shock. And, third, actual prices are fixed by the demand curve. Two points need to be made at this stage. First, we have no special hypothesis to test concerning step 2—indeed, supply curves may well be positively sloped or backward bending since they involve choices between labour and leisure that are known to exhibit a wide variety of patterns. On the other hand, besides our main hypothesis that demand curves have an elasticity less than -1, we want to test whether expectations may be formed with a high degree of accuracy in step 1. This is a condition for an efficient computation of the target level of aggregate output: if prices are not correctly anticipated, a cartel is bound to fail because, on average, day-to-day losses are not likely to be compensated by gains if fishermen are not perfectly patient.

If fishermen are right in reporting price effects wherever fishing effort is controlled, these effects ought to appear in our estimated demand curves. It is evident that in markets where prices are insensitive to quantities supplied it cannot be directly profitable to regulate fishing effort, even though in this case it may make sense to prevent over-exploitation in order to keep cost levels down. We should, therefore, not expect a one-to-one correspondence between low elasticity of demand and the existence of catch quotas. This said, a significant result of our household survey is that fishermen who believe that regulation has a desirable effect on conservation also tend to expect a beneficial price impact, except when they also report high rates of rule violation. Since it is unlikely that regulation is adopted for its biological effect only, there is a strong case for the a priori claim that regulation should be attempted only where demand is relatively inelastic.

We were able to estimate inverse demand functions for a restricted number of fish species at three fishing sites—Kayar, Saint-Louis, and Hann in the years prior to devaluation in 1994.[16] The results for two types of sardines are presented in Table 4.B1 in Appendix B. These results show that inverse demand elasticities are only significantly different from zero for flat sardines in Kayar and Saint-Louis. For round sardines in the three sites and for flat sardines in Hann, we cannot reject the hypothesis of perfectly elastic demand, which should preclude any regulation effort causing an increase in prices. These results are not surprising in the light of the following circumstances. First, in Kayar and Saint-Louis, sardines are not refrigerated but sold immediately to artisan fish processors for local consumption. Second, Hann is a suburb of Dakar and freezing sardines for other markets (such as cities in the hinterland) is much more common there. Moreover, Dakar forms a large integrated market with export outlets,

---

[16] Unfortunately, due to logistical problems, we could only obtain monthly price and landing data for the years prior to devaluation (1994).

contrary to Kayar and Saint-Louis. Third, round sardines are bigger than flat, and therefore more convenient for refrigeration.

It is probably not chance that purse seines, which target only pelagic species among which flat sardines are important, are regulated in Kayar and Saint-Louis but not in Hann and Yoff (bearing in mind that, like Hann, Yoff is located close to Dakar). Still, even where demand is perfectly elastic, regulation can be profitable if marginal costs are (locally) steeply increasing. This condition may be fulfilled if scarcity of fish is sufficiently acute to compel fishermen to attempt more distant fishing grounds. Finally, it may be noted that, as expected, all substitution effects are positive, indicating substitutability not complementarity between species.

As far as demersal species caught by hooks and lines (or bottom-set nets) are concerned, estimations of inverse demand functions show that Kayar is the most suitable location for effective attempts at effort regulation. It is confirmed that demersal species for which demand is not perfectly elastic are the *thiof* in Kayar (but not in Saint-Louis and Hann); the *capitaine* in Kayar; the rose sea bream in Kayar; and the *pagre* in Saint-Louis and Hann.

4.5. CONCLUSIONS

For local-level effort regulation to succeed, it is obviously important that market conditions are such that fish prices respond to supply variations. If demand is perfectly elastic with respect to prices, as happens in well-integrated markets approximating perfect competition, restriction of landings will not cause any price increase. However, we cannot rule out the possibility that effort limitation has the effect of reducing harvesting costs since scarcity may determine steeply increasing cost functions. Data did not permit us to test for the latter, but, to a limited extent, they allowed us to assess market conditions. The main conclusion is that significantly negative price–effort elasticities are not systematically observed and, when observed, they mainly concern the village of Kayar. (Unfortunately, price and output data are only available for the pre-devaluation period (before 1994) and it is quite possible that market conditions have changed in the meantime.) It is revealing that fishermen of Kayar have recently confessed to us that the impact of their effort-limiting measures seems to have decreased. We can, however, assert with confidence that, historically, market conditions have favoured effort regulation in Kayar compared with the other sites. The fact that this village has been the most successful in its regulation efforts is probably not coincidental.

Assuming away incentive problems, we know that imposing catch quotas is theoretically the best way of controlling effort in order to enhance producers' market power or to conserve the resource. Once labour incentive problems are taken into account, while the adoption of catch quotas appears optimal for line fishermen, limitation of fishing trips seems to be more feasible for purse seine fishermen. Further, when problems arising from the monitoring of effort restraint are taken into account, the system of catch quotas applied by the former category seems less efficient than limitations of fishing trips chosen by the latter category. This goes a long way towards explaining why the extent of rule-breaking is perceived to be larger with respect to catch quotas.

In a second-best world pervaded by incentive problems, restriction of effort seems to have a better chance of succeeding in the case of purse seines than in line fishing.

Reviewing what makes schemes likely or unlikely, line fishermen operating canoes equipped with iceboxes and used to making long journeys out to sea emerge as the category which it is especially difficult to bring under any effort-limiting scheme, due to incentive problems. It is thus not surprising that nowhere along the Senegalese coast did we find any sign of attempts at regulating such fishing. Direct competition from this type of sophisticated fishermen (they target the same fish species) may account for the fact that regulation has not been adopted by simple line fishermen in Hann and Soumbedioune where iceboxes are found, yet cannot explain why it could work with simple line fishermen in Kayar but not in Saint-Louis, since in both places no iceboxes are used. The presence of more favourable market conditions for demersal species in Kayar than in Saint-Louis (and Yoff where the regulatory scheme has been discontinued) constitutes an important advantage for Kayar's line fishermen. Another advantage in favour of the latter is the existence of a strong traditional leadership structure. Unfortunately, we are unable to disentangle the respective effects of these two favourable factors.

What we may, nevertheless, note is that Kayar's leadership, rooted in the hierarchical socio-political structure of what was originally an agricultural village, has been able to impose a relatively good measure of discipline and sense of common purpose on people well known for their inveterate tendencies towards individualism. This factor is all the more important as Kayar suffers from severe inter-community tensions. It is noteworthy that the division is not simply a classical opposition between migrants and residents since permanent residents who were born in Saint-Louis do not seem to think and behave differently from temporary migrants from the same area.

Inter-community tensions in Kayar have their origin in grave conflicts between operators of bottom-set nets (exclusively people from Saint-Louis) and users of other fishing techniques, especially if they are native to Kayar. Despite repeated efforts, the problem of how to allocate the limited fishing space available close to shore has never been solved in a satisfactory way. Furthermore, bottom-set net operators have always refused to adopt an effort-limiting scheme even though they target valuable species also harvested by line fishermen (in more distant fishing grounds). A ready explanation for this non-cooperative attitude lies in the fact that many bottom-set net operators are in debt to fish merchants with whom they have exclusive sales relationships. Revealingly, the same phenomenon obtains in Saint-Louis. In the latter site as in Hann, pervasive sales-tying agreements also characterize relations between simple line fishermen and fish merchants, which may again account for the absence of regulation for this fishing technique, as against Kayar where sales tying is less widespread.

Lastly, the most dynamic line fishermen—those who declare that they are going further out to sea to catch valuable species—have a strong proclivity to support effort regulation, presumably because their expected gains are larger owing to the high value of the species targetted.

Many of the above results point to the importance of homogeneity of users as a condition for successful collective action. The fact that regulatory schemes are devised on the basis of a particular fishing technique—with regulating methods varying between line fishing and purse seining—shows that fishermen consciously avoided this kind of heterogeneity. Yet some dimensions of user heterogeneity are not easily reducible, and do matter according to our estimates, namely the presence of fishing canoes with iceboxes, the pervasive existence of fishermen–fish merchant exclusive links in the case of some techniques, the coexistence of different ethnic communities using the same harvesting technique and targetting the same species, and the availability of alternative income opportunities for some but not for others.

One form of heterogeneity turned out not to be significant: support for decentralized measures of effort regulation does not vary as between asset owners and crew. This is not surprising given that the share system of payment used makes them equally interested in better prices. By contrast, the crew are opposed to marketing organizations run by fishermen, presumably because under the same system of payment there would be ample scope for cheating (mainly through under-reporting of sale proceeds) by asset owners.

As the above conclusions show, our study has to a large extent succeeded in explaining variations in both the incidence and continuity of effort-limiting schemes in communities of Senegalese small-scale fishermen. It is noteworthy that many of the significant factors are structural in character, namely, market conditions, features of fishing techniques, which bear upon the enforcement costs of a collective scheme, the nature of relationships between fishermen and fish merchants, and historically-determined patterns of authority and leadership. Overlooking such critical parameters might mean setting up short-lived effort control measures. Moreover, it must be borne in mind that the parameters may evolve and, as a result, measures that worked rather well in a given period may subsequently prove difficult to sustain. This dynamic aspect of reality, as we realized in the course of field interviews, is probably the most difficult to accept for leaders who have played a major role in the initiation and enforcement of local-level regulation.

Further, policy design also matters. Poor design of regulation mechanisms can obviously impair their viability and effectiveness. This is illustrated in our study by the rotation scheme for purse seines in Saint-Louis which has given rise to serious incentive problems by ignoring important income-smoothing considerations.

Bearing in mind that effort-limiting schemes have run into difficulties in Saint-Louis and Yoff and that they have not been started in Hann and Soumbedioune, it appears that most of the conditions mentioned above must be satisfied simultaneously for decentralized regulation schemes to succeed. The market structure must be such that fishermen can influence prices; monitoring costs as determined both by technological or marketing conditions and by the design mechanism adopted must not be too high; most fishermen should be free of exclusive relationships with fish merchants acting as sources of credit; good leaders should be available; heterogeneity of resource users must not be too high (hence the need to devise technique-specific schemes). Note that the first of these conditions must be fulfilled only if effort regulation is motivated by market power rather than by resource management considerations, as has been shown to be the case among these Senegalese coastal fishermen.

Finally, the difficulty of satisfying all these conditions at once suggests that the view expressed in various interviews, that relying on regulatory schemes aimed at increasing fish prices may build up conservation awareness, may be too optimistic. Indeed, market and/or structural conditions may not be suitable for a cartel operation and, as a result, prices may fail to increase following control of fishing effort. Fishermen may then be discouraged and drop out of the scheme before they come to understand the need to manage resources for conservation purposes.

Appendix A

Variable Definitions

infrac a dummy that takes on the value one when the incidence of rule violations is deemed to be large, and zero when it is deemed to be low;

owner a dummy that takes on the value one when the fisherman owns equipment, and zero when he is a crew labourer;

migrkay a dummy that takes on the value one when the fisherman is a migrant from Saint-Louis operating in Kayar, and zero otherwise;

educ a dummy that takes on the value one when the fisherman has more than six years of Koranic schooling or six years of primary school in French, and zero otherwise;

age fisherman's age in years;

wives number of wives, a proxy for wealth;

pursese a dummy that takes on the value one when the fisherman operates a purse seine, and zero when he works with hooks and lines;

exclus a dummy that takes on the value one when the fisherman has an exclusive sale agreement with a particular fish merchant, and zero if he does not;

leadkay a dummy that takes on the value one when the fisherman is a local leader in Kayar, that is, when he is more than forty-seven years old, has three wives and works in Kayar, and the value zero otherwise;

ymarkay a dummy that takes on the value one when the fisherman is a (relatively) young married person (between twenty-four and thirty-five years old) working in Kayar, and the value zero otherwise;

altinc a dummy that takes on the value one when there is in the household at least one member earning income from an activity other than fishing, and/or when the household owns some agricultural land, or more than one house, and zero in all other cases;

collus a dummy that takes on the value one when the fisherman has explicitly mentioned the existence of collusive practices among fish merchants, and zero otherwise;

exper a dummy that takes on the value of one if the fisherman has gone through a prolonged experience of regulation (lines in Kayar and Yoff; purse seines in Kayar and Saint-Louis), and zero otherwise;

icebox a dummy that takes on the value one for line-operating canoes equipped with iceboxes, and zero otherwise. (When *icebox* and *pursese* are both zero, the technique used by the fisherman is simple lines, bottom-set nets, or a beach seine—(fishermen using the latter two techniques are not numerous enough to make up a separate category.)

dist a dummy that takes on the value one if the fisherman has stated that he goes farther and farther into the sea to target species of high exportable value (such as the rose sea bream known as the *dentex*), and zero otherwise;

migrsou a dummy that takes on the value of one when the fisherman is a migrant from Saint-Louis operating in Soumbedioune, and zero otherwise.

Table 4.A1. *Logit estimate of the determinants of fishermen's beliefs regarding the extent of rule-breaking*

infrac	Coef.	Std. Err.	z	$P>\|z\|$	[95% Conf. Interval]	
owner	−0.1421856	0.5423711	−0.262	0.793	−1.205213	0.9208421
migrkay	−0.4854577	0.6086912	−0.798	0.425	−1.67847	0.7075551
educ	0.7311907	0.4189728	1.745	0.081	−0.0899809	1.552362
age	0.0269207	0.0195801	1.375	0.169	−0.0114556	0.0652971
wives	−0.6393262	0.3257245	−1.963	0.050	−1.277735	−0.0009178
pursese	−0.8468396	0.4076245	−2.077	0.038	−1.645769	−0.0479103
exclus	0.9533989	0.5235918	1.821	0.069	−0.0728222	1.97962
cons	−0.5938881	0.6224267	−0.954	0.340	−1.813822	0.6260458

Log likelihood = −76.883164; number of obs = 127; chi2(7) =18.80; Prob > chi2 = 0.0088; Pseudo R2 = 0.1090.

Table 4.A2. *Adjusted logit estimate of the determinants of fishermen's beliefs regarding the extent of rule-breaking*

infrac	Coef.	Std. Err.	z	$P>\|z\|$	[95% Conf. Interval]	
owner	−0.4069745	0.414509	−0.982	0.326	−1.219397	0.4054481
migrkay	−0.3085531	0.60945	−0.506	0.613	−1.503053	0.8859469
educ	0.6617543	0.4264266	1.552	0.121	−0.1740264	1.497535
leadkay	−1.686125	1.131319	−1.490	0.136	−3.90347	0.5312191
ymarkay	−1.696	0.8687579	−1.952	0.051	−3.398734	0.0067345
pursese	−1.025698	0.4266358	−2.404	0.016	−1.861889	−0.189507
exclus	1.002479	0.5381882	1.863	0.063	−0.0523505	2.057309
cons	0.1627518	0.4070024	0.400	0.689	−0.6349582	0.9604618

Log likelihood = −75.335438; number of observations = 127; chi2(7) = 21.90; Prob > chi2 = 0.0026; Pseudo R2 = 0.1269.

Table 4.A3. *Multinomial logit estimates of the determinants of fishermen's beliefs in economic and biological effects of effort-limiting measures (Kayar, Saint-Louis, Yoff)*

	Coef.	Std. Err.	z	$P>\|z\|$	[95% Conf. Interval]	
1. econly						
owner	0.9183656	0.7140784	1.286	0.198	−0.4812023	2.317934
educ	0.5887418	0.7142158	0.824	0.410	−0.8110955	1.988579
migrkay	−1.533036	0.8734431	−1.755	0.079	−3.244953	0.1788813
infrac	0.3324081	0.8381308	0.397	0.692	−1.310298	1.975114
leadkay	(dropped)					
ymarkay	−0.7885451	1.306074	−0.604	0.546	−3.348402	1.771312
techn	0.308619	0.736175	0.419	0.675	−1.134257	1.751495
altinc	−1.904582	1.401945	−1.359	0.174	−4.652345	0.8431798
exclus	−0.3325192	0.705728	−0.471	0.638	−1.715721	1.050682

Table 4.A3. *Contd*

	Coef.	Std. Err.	z	$P>|z|$	[95% Conf. Interval]	
collus	0.198917	0.6799186	0.293	0.770	−1.133699	1.531533
cons	−0.1472421	0.7656247	−0.192	0.847	−1.647839	1.353355
2. bionly						
owner	0.0810431	0.7996471	0.101	0.919	−1.486236	1.648323
educ	2.396745	0.8109191	2.956	0.003	0.8073726	3.986117
migrkay	−3.112952	1.100201	−2.829	0.005	−5.269305	−0.9565982
infrac	3.063997	0.8696592	3.523	0.000	1.359497	4.768498
leadkay	4.460675	1.873074	2.381	0.017	0.7895171	8.131833
ymarkay	0.1101003	1.51558	0.073	0.942	−2.860382	3.080583
techn	0.5525091	0.7777238	0.710	0.477	−0.9718015	2.07682
altinc	−2.14038	1.375992	−1.556	0.120	−4.837275	0.5565149
exclus	0.0700108	0.391456	0.179	0.858	−0.6972289	0.8372504
collus	−0.4294194	0.7370731	−0.583	0.560	−1.874056	1.015217
cons	−1.809203	0.9301536	−1.945	0.052	−3.63227	0.0138646
3. ecobio						
owner	0.3948633	0.707286	0.558	0.577	−0.9913919	1.781118
educ	1.495693	0.6878276	2.175	0.030	0.1475759	2.84381
migrkay	−3.992373	1.079191	−3.699	0.000	−6.107549	−1.877197
infrac	1.639492	0.7831023	2.094	0.036	0.1046398	3.174344
leadkay	2.715988	1.671438	1.625	0.104	−0.5599707	5.991946
ymarkay	1.367391	1.102267	1.241	0.215	−0.7930125	3.527796
techn	0.8664236	0.6955223	1.246	0.213	−0.4967752	2.229622
altinc	−0.459705	1.054752	−0.436	0.663	−2.526981	1.607571
exclus	0.0662535	0.2802763	0.236	0.813	−0.4830781	0.615585
collus	−0.4073856	0.6486115	−0.628	0.530	−1.678641	0.8638695
cons	−0.2237685	0.7441414	−0.301	0.764	−1.682259	1.234722

Log likelihood = −128.13811; number of obs = 127; chi2(29) = 73.98; Prob > chi2 = 0.0000; Pseudo R2 = 0.2240.

Table 4.A4. *Multinomial logit estimates of the determinants of fishermen's beliefs in economic and biological effects of effort regulation (all villages and all fisheries)*

	Coef.	Std. Err.	z	$P>|z|$	[95% Conf. Interval]	
1. econly						
exper	1.299116	0.5075321	2.560	0.010	0.3043711	2.29386
educ	0.0890896	0.3457277	0.258	0.797	−0.5885242	0.7667034
migrkay	−0.4880116	0.5631902	−0.867	0.386	−1.591844	0.615821
infrac	−0.9087412	0.6939173	−1.310	0.190	−2.268794	0.4513118
pursese	−0.4855144	0.4437077	−1.094	0.274	−1.355166	0.3841367
icebox	−0.7735517	0.5019008	−1.541	0.123	−1.757259	0.2101558
altinc	−1.831245	0.7990108	−2.292	0.022	−3.397278	−0.2652129

Table 4.A4. *Contd*

	Coef.	Std. Err.	z	$P>\|z\|$	[95% Conf. Interval]	
dist	2.543566	0.8186858	3.107	0.002	0.9389717	4.148161
owner	0.1301621	0.3495983	0.372	0.710	−0.555038	0.8153623
leadkay	(dropped)					
ymarkay	−1.541686	1.302236	−1.184	0.236	−4.094023	1.01065
exclus	0.7595049	0.3990512	1.903	0.057	−0.0226211	1.541631
collus	0.518986	0.3608229	1.438	0.150	−0.1882139	1.226186
migrsou	(dropped)					
cons	−0.6354918	0.3918712	−1.622	0.105	−1.403545	0.1325617
2. bionly						
exper	1.682911	0.6473854	2.600	0.009	0.4140589	2.951763
educ	0.9996363	0.4638075	2.155	0.031	0.0905903	1.908682
migrkay	−2.082995	0.9093227	−2.291	0.022	−3.865234	−0.3007547
infrac	2.068237	0.6436474	3.213	0.001	0.8067109	3.329762
pursese	−0.0235833	0.5196588	−0.045	0.964	−1.042096	0.9949293
icebox	−0.0041546	0.787993	−0.005	0.996	−1.548593	1.540283
altinc	−0.1295586	0.6558398	−0.198	0.843	−1.414981	1.155864
dist	2.576811	0.9921724	2.597	0.009	0.6321889	4.521433
owner	0.0689103	0.4613471	0.149	0.881	−0.8353133	0.9731339
leadkay	2.066681	1.603032	1.289	0.197	−1.075203	5.208565
ymarkay	−0.2230906	1.442717	−0.155	0.877	−3.050764	2.604583
exclus	−0.0020832	0.5459322	−0.004	0.997	−1.072091	1.067924
collus	0.1698155	0.4563487	0.372	0.710	−0.7246116	1.064243
migrsou	(dropped)					
cons	−2.699395	0.59787	−4.515	0.000	−3.871199	−1.527591
3. ecobio						
exper	1.633759	0.4713625	3.466	0.001	0.7099051	2.557612
educ	0.7111716	0.3374699	2.107	0.035	0.0497427	1.372601
migrkay	−3.07171	0.8960977	−3.428	0.001	−4.82803	−1.315391
infrac	0.4000893	0.5747974	0.696	0.486	−0.7264929	1.526671
pursese	−0.755428	0.4028428	−1.875	0.061	−1.544985	0.0341294
icebox	−1.741813	0.5801645	−3.002	0.003	−2.878914	−0.6047114
altinc	0.0006823	0.4556902	0.001	0.999	−0.892454	0.8938186
dist	2.943645	0.8348808	3.526	0.000	1.307309	4.579981
owner	0.1595337	0.3440594	0.464	0.643	−0.5148104	0.8338777
leadkay	2.096566	1.376379	1.523	0.128	−0.6010878	4.79422
ymarkay	0.392324	1.08429	0.362	0.717	−1.732845	2.517494
exclus	−0.0562446	0.4087139	−0.138	0.891	−0.8573092	0.7448199
collus	0.3771833	0.3467788	1.088	0.277	−0.3024908	1.056857
migrsou	1.727549	0.8214984	2.103	0.035	0.1174419	3.337656
cons	−0.6191525	0.3774321	−1.640	0.101	−1.358906	0.1206007

Log likelihood = −348.58337; number of obs = 320; chi2(39) = 154.48; Prob > chi2 = 0.0000; Pseudo R2 = 0.1814.

Appendix B. **Demand Estimation**

We estimated the following system of equations:

(expectations) $P_t = \alpha + \beta * s + \gamma * B(P) + u_t$, with $P_t^e = P_t - u_t$,

(supply) $\log Q_t = \delta + \varepsilon * \log P_t^e + v_t$,

(inverse demand) $\log P_t = \phi + \rho * \log Q_t + \sigma * \log P_{t+1}^e + \theta * \log P_t^{\text{subst}} + w_t$,

where P_t is the price at time t, s is a vector of eleven dummy variables representing the month of the year, $B(P)$ is a vector of lagged prices (the number of lags is chosen through a standard ARIMA procedure, that is, by inspecting correlograms; typically, zero or one lag is used), Q_t is the quantity at time t; u, v, and w are normally distributed residuals (with seasonal heteroscedasticity); parameters to be estimated include β and γ, which are real vectors, and α, δ, ε, ϕ, and ρ, which are real numbers.

An inverse demand curve is estimated because observation errors occur frequently in prices and rather infrequently in quantities; it is safer to let those errors appear in the residuals of an inverse demand function than to estimate a demand curve with a stochastic regressor (NB. expected prices and prices of substitute goods are replaced by an instrumental variable in this equation).

Table 4.B1. *Econometric estimates of inverse demand functions for sardines (based on price and output data pertaining to the years 1991–93))*

Inverse demand estimations: $\ln P_t = \alpha + \beta \ln Q_t + \gamma \ln P_{\text{subst}} + \delta \ln P_{t+1}^*$

Site	Sub-species (sardines)	Inverse demand elasticity (β)	Substitution effect (γ)	Speculation effect (δ)
Kayar	Round	−0.01	0.46**	—
	Flat	−0.20**	0.97**	—
Saint-Louis	Round	−0.07	−0.00	—
	Flat	−0.11**	1.20**	—
Hann	Round	−0.03	0.36**	0.60*
	Flat	−0.08	0.40*	0.19

**indicates significance at the 95 per cent confidence level while * indicates significance at the 90 per cent level.

5

Leaders and Intermediaries as Economic Development Agents in Producers' Associations

5.1. INTRODUCTION: PRODUCER GROUPS, PARTICIPATION, AND DEVELOPMENT

The development field is currently dominated by two powerful and interconnected ideas: the idea of participation, and the idea of a bottom-up approach. The idea of participation emphasizes the process of development, and claims that development is more likely to be successful if as many as possible of its beneficiaries are actively involved in improving their own conditions. The bottom-up approach—which has a parallel in fiscal decentralization in public finance—maintains that the beneficiaries should choose democratically the means and objectives of the development strategies that concern them.

The ideas or principles that inform current policy appear so intuitively reasonable today that it is difficult to find their origins in the work of any particular scholar, or any single policy experience. Rather they can be considered the historical response to an earlier generation of policies and theories that presented development as a mere transfer of technology and habits from the advanced to the backward regions of the world.[1] The predominant view of those policies today is that they have performed poorly precisely because they have not taken into account the specificity of the problems and needs of the people that they were intended to help, and they have not involved those people enough in their own improvement.

I am grateful to the Bank of the Northeast of Brazil for sponsoring the field research for this project, and to the WIDER project on Group Behaviour and Development. For the Italian part of this research I have to thank Regina Abagnale, Nicola Cacace, Dora Cuomo, Luca Meldolesi, and Antonio Minguzzi for generously offering help, useful contacts, and constructive advice. Sabrina De Carlo, Judith Heyer, Anu Joshi, Hubert Schmitz, Judith Tendler and Rosemary Thorp have given me constructive feedback on earlier versions of this paper.

[1] A non-dogmatic presentation of the two dominant development perspectives is offered in Picciotto (1992), and Peters (ed) 2000.

The proliferation of programmes to help small-scale producers through associations in recent years represents a clear application of these 'new principles' of development policy. Producers' associations are the ultimate expression of a shift of balance from government and donors to organized beneficiaries, as the engine of the development process.

Participatory decision-making within producer groups is valuable in itself, and can be considered part of what development is, or one of the goals of development programmes. The same can be said of shifting decision-making on development issues to the grass roots level, or allowing the voices of all persons involved to be heard in a democratic fashion. But, if one looks at the economic performance of producers' associations, and at the wealth that they are able to create for backward regions, a number of questions arise. Are those principles really conducive to the best outcomes? Do the most successful producers' associations operate according to those principles? What influences the economic results obtained by such groups?

One part of the literature, mostly interested in the sustainability of producers' associations, claims that participation, or a mode of interaction based on trust and reciprocity, is crucial. According to this view many collective initiatives have failed either because they have superimposed western models of interaction on local communities (Attwood and Baviskar 1985), or because they have been dominated by local élites. Most of the problems would be avoided if all members were able to participate more actively in collective organizations. Participation is also valuable because it is an antidote to cultural and political dependency on outsiders. Development theory has stressed the difference between the organizations of producers in which members understand and consciously pursue their collective interest, and those that are superimposed on communities from the outside (Bennett 1983). 'Indigenous' forms of cooperation are said to have much better chances of surviving in the long run.

This finding, however, becomes more controversial when one considers strictly economic outcomes separately from organizational development. Several classic studies of producer associations have stressed the predominant role played by the largest producers or local élites in their economic success (Attwood and Baviskar 1987; Tendler 1983). The problem of democracy in the economic development of cooperatives has sometimes been specified in the form of a trade-off between managerial efficiency and members' empowerment. This view implies that organizational democracy may be valuable in itself, but comes at the cost of reducing decision-making flexibility and effectiveness (de Janvry *et al.* 1993: 568; Wells 1981: 244).

Besides internal modes of interaction, what makes producer associations succeed or fail? Social scientists have recently become interested in this question and increasingly consider the economic incentives to cooperation as one of the critical variables. The cross-disciplinary field which is specifically interested in this is called New Institutionalism and pays particular attention to the material aspects of collective action: costs, rewards, and penalties. According to this view, groups can successfully pursue economic development goals if they devise institutional arrangements that correctly structure the incentives faced by individual group members, and equitably distribute the costs (Kenworthy 1997).

This chapter uses three cases of successful economic development extracted from two larger studies of producers' associations, to test some generalizations about conditions that are conducive to their economic success. This empirical material confirms the claim that groups engaged in economic activities characterized by high economic returns are more likely to be successful on all dimensions of group development (Wade 1985). All of the groups analysed here owe part of their unusually successful economic results to the super-profits they are able to extract from situations of marketing advantage. The body of the chapter is an attempt to understand the most important factors that allowed these producers to find (in some cases), or to construct (in others), high profit product niches.

Members' participation was not one of them. Advantageous marketing positions were not the immediate result of a struggle for better terms of trade by all group members, as the fashionable image of the 'participant' development process would lead us to expect. Marketing intermediaries and other agents external to the groups played a fundamental role in opening up opportunities for commercial success. In some cases outsiders offered access to preferential market channels to groups that had no knowledge of these. In the cases in which producers themselves played an active part in their own commercial success, the initiative for such developments came from a minority within the group.

Does this mean that an asymmetric distribution of power and resources within groups is necessary for their development? The findings of this paper are not so clear cut. Homogeneity of economic interests and values within groups of producers was also found to be an important contributor to fruitful collective action. Instead of being mutually exclusive, homogeneity, and leaders' autonomy coexisted in the best-performing cases.

The ability of groups to leverage the capacities and connections of their leaders was a key to their economic success. While decision-making structures that allow too much participation by members can impair the ability of leaders to pursue high-profit strategies, the most ambitious and educated individuals within groups— those who are more likely to understand trends in distant and modern markets and open contacts with key intermediaries—are attracted to organizations that allow them adequate autonomy of management. At the same time, it is crucial that factors contributing to social and economic homogeneity, such as the clear identification of the group with a particular product or a particular social struggle, help them stick together when the strictly economic rewards of cooperation temporarily disappear.

The homogeneity of group interests, which helps group members to stay together in hard times, and to make sacrifices in the interests of their common goals, is not an innate feature of groups. It is a variable that the Brazilian associations intentionally pursued by means of a 'closed shop' strategy aimed at excluding producers representing different values and interests. The homogeneity of social position and values seemed to add cohesion to groups independently of the sharing of economic interests. The two most successful producer groups in northeast Brazil were the end product of a decades-long process of political consciousness-raising. This common ideological background is at the root of the strategy they pursued to exclude the rich and powerful, who were seen as adversaries in their collective struggle.

The paper draws on research conducted among groups of producers processing and marketing agricultural products collectively in southern Italy and in northeast Brazil.[2] The two regions have in common the fact of being underdeveloped subsections of more advanced countries. They also share the common reputation of being areas in which economic agents have very little traditional propensity to cooperate. Social scientists have argued with respect to both cases that the limited effectiveness of the many economic development programmes targeted at these regions has depended, among other things, on the local anti-cooperative attitude, and on a traditional vertical structure of economic and social relations (Putnam 1993; Almy 1988).

The research looked at groups of producers in the two regions, to try to understand why some of them were able to achieve economic results through collective action, while others were not (Bianchi 1998, 1999*a*). In southern Italy buffalo milk mozzarella cheese producers created a consortium in 1993 to protect and promote their product. The consortium contributed substantially to the reputation and profitability of the industry. Tomato processing firms, in contrast, facing a set of incentives that appeared similar, failed to realize the potential advantages of collective action. The northeast Brazil study analysed six of the longest lived producer associations in four different states in the region, asking why some have been more successful than others in promoting local economic development.

The chapter only uses the material from the three most successful cases in the two studies: the case of mozzarella producers in Italy, and the two best-performing producer associations in Brazil. The findings are derived from a comparison with the other cases not discussed here.

The next section lays out the basic facts about the producer associations which qualify them as exceptionally successful relative to other similar groups, focusing on the issue of protected market niches that is at the heart of their economic development. The following section illustrates the role of marketing intermediaries and group leaders, by way of explaining how high-profit marketing niches were constructed or accessed by the groups. Section 5.4 takes this process of reverse explanation one step further by looking at the role of other groups characteristics: member homogeneity, antagonistic ideology, and exclusionary policies. The concluding section contrasts the generalizations advanced with those found in the economic development literature.

5.2. DEVELOPMENT THROUGH MARKETING

At first sight, all that the successful cases in the two studies seemed to have in common was uniqueness, especially with respect to the nature of the product. The two successful Brazilian associations and the Italian consortium of buffalo mozzarella producers were

---

[2] The Italian field research was conducted for a period of three months in the summers of 1997 and 1998. The Brazilian work took place over two-and-a-half months in the spring of 1998. Both projects involved the collection of data, visits to small-scale enterprises, interviews with entrepreneurs, managers and employees of cooperative institutions, public sector workers and specialists in the sectors in question.

able to take advantage of special, preferential terms of trade that shielded them from the harshness of open market competition. In the Italian case the advantageous market position had to do with the 'genuine' character of the buffalo mozzarella product, which was certified by a collective label of origin. In the two most successful Brazilian cases the advantage consisted in special characteristics of the products that commanded market premia: their 'natural' character, and the fact of being 'fairly traded'.

Instead of making the comparison unfeasible, this uniqueness was the one explanation for their marketing success that was common to all. All the prominent cases of success enjoyed super-profits obtained through a position of market advantage. The resulting super-profits, relative to standardized commodities, explain why these groups, and not the many others that tried to compete on open markets, were able to attack the many obstacles that simultaneously constrained their growth.

5.2.1. *The Consortium of Buffalo Mozzarella Producers in Southern Italy*

The Italian producers of buffalo mozzarella cheese have created a market advantage which consists in positioning their product in a high profit niche. Buffalo mozzarella enjoys today the reputation of a high quality artisan product, for which consumers are willing to pay a high price. Hence, the buffalo mozzarella industry now enjoys much higher profit margins and a much faster growth of sales than, for example, the canned tomato industry, the sector that in terms of size, location, and number of firms, comes closest to it.[3]

The market advantages of buffalo mozzarella producers relative to other Italian food producers are not inherent in the product, but have been constructed through collective action. Southern Italian producers have taken the initiative to promote product quality and protect their monopoly over the supply of buffalo milk, the key ingredient of mozzarella. In fact, they needed to protect their product niche against two threats: one external, the other internal to the group.

The external threat is the *threat of imitation* by larger and more experienced firms. Some large manufacturers from the north have repeatedly tried to enter the buffalo segment of the mozzarella market. To do this they have to get access to a sizeable and reliable source of buffalo milk. They also have to decouple the image of buffalo mozzarella from the south of Italy, to convince consumers that buffalo mozzarella can have a different origin from the one they know.

The internal threat is the *possible decay of the reputation for quality*. There is a strong incentive for producers of mozzarella to adulterate buffalo with cows' milk. In the past this practice was common, and created a bad reputation for the product. The incentives to cheat on the composition of the product originate from the scarcity (and high cost) of buffalo milk. This is particularly acute in the summer months, when less buffaloes produce milk, at a time when demand for the product is particularly

---

[3] Buffalo mozzarella profit rates sometimes reach 25%, compared to 3.5% for canned tomatoes. The 5% a year growth of buffalo mozzarella sales quantity (8% in value terms), is much higher than that of the canned tomato producers whose market is basically static, except for a few innovative product niches.

high. Adding a limited quantity of cows' milk in the production of buffalo mozzarella guarantees a 5–10 per cent reduction in the cost of a product almost two-thirds of whose cost is represented by the milk input. Even more importantly, the adulteration of buffalo milk allows firms to increase production when mozzarella is scarce, and its price is high. What makes cheating very tempting is the fact that a product made with up to 30–40 per cent of cows' milk is also good: even very sophisticated consumers can hardly recognize the difference. However, this practice destroys the image of buffalo mozzarella as a product distinct from the cow equivalent, blurring the boundaries between the two. Customers will not identify buffalo mozzarella as a different product and agree to pay a premium price for it, if they know that the difference between the two is only a matter of percentage buffalo milk content. Moreover, it lowers the entry barriers in the sector, potentially allowing large manufacturers of cheese located outside the south where buffaloes are kept, to enter this profitable market niche. This would increase price competition and lower the overall reputation of the product, bringing down the profit margins for producers in the south. This conflict between individual and industry-level incentives created the rationale for collective action. The creation of a consortium has been an effective way to protect and promote the collective interests of the estimated 250 or so firms producing buffalo mozzarella in southern Italy.

In 1981, four firms operating in both buffalo ranching and cheese production created a consortium, a voluntary association aimed at protecting and promoting buffalo mozzarella. Initially the consortium had little appeal to the majority of producers and few joined it. It gradually increased its appeal, playing a major role in the sector, and changing the discipline of production standards through its lobbying efforts at the central government level.

In 1989 the consortium applied for a 'Denominazione di Origine Controllata' (DOC), a collective label that could only be used for products manufactured within a well-specified geographical area of the south (Campania region plus two or three surrounding provinces), and produced by a certified production technique. Four years later, in 1993, the government accorded the DOC 'Mozzarella di Bufala Campana' to mozzarella cheese produced in this area, assigning to the consortium[4] quasi-governmental responsibility for setting up and enforcing production controls, and suing those who used the label illegally.

After the decree was passed the membership of the consortium increased from fifteen to ninety-five. In 1996 protection was also granted to the product within the European Union. Mozzarella is the only dairy product in southern Italy that has obtained this kind of protection from the state. All the thirteen other types of Italian cheese protected by a DOC are from the north.

The consortium has been effective both in terms of the economic benefits it has delivered to the industry, and in distributing the costs of cooperation among members. The degree of participation and the scope of cooperation in the consortium increased substantially following the award of the DOC label. Firms could join the consortium

---

[4] Consorzio Tutela Mozzarella di Bufala Campana DOC.

Table 5.1. *Consorzio Mozzarella di Bufala Campana: membership trends 1994–98*

Year	1994	1995	1996	1997	1998
Members	—	29	28	26	45
Users	—	66	69	75	54
All	40	95	97	101	99

Source: Consorzio Mozzarella di Bufala Campana.

as 'members', or as 'users' of the DOC name and logo.[5] Table 5.1 summarizes the evolution of membership from 1994–98, showing that firms increasingly chose the status of 'members', shifting towards a higher degree of participation.

The consortium has been a success in terms of the economic results it has produced for member firms. The DOC label helps in the process of entering the larger northern Italian and foreign markets. Consumers all over Italy have started to recognize the mozzarella with the DOC 'Mozzarella di Bufala Campana' label as the 'true' buffalo mozzarella. The largest firms need this system of product certification most, because they do not interact directly with the market, through personal face-to-face relationships with final customers, but sell mostly through anonymous wholesale and supermarket channels. However, all the firms located in the area benefit from an institutional arrangement that has built up a reputation for quality, and sustains price by increasing demand in distant markets. These benefits are retained within the area of production, limiting production increases to those allowed by the local availability of buffalo milk.

Joining this system does not necessarily mean complying with it in practice. Firms can join the consortium and use its name and symbol, and then adulterate the product to increase their volume of sales. This way, 'free-riders' enjoy the advantage of using the reputation created by all the firms who cooperate, and increase their own sales and profits as well.

To prevent this type of behaviour the consortium introduced sanctions for those caught adulterating the product. Besides denouncing illegal behaviour to the judicial system (a weak threat given how slowly it moves), at their first sign of misconduct firms are fined approximately $6000, at their second twice that sum, and if they are found adulterating the product a third time they are expelled from the consortium and denied the use of the DOC.

The consortium appears to have been successful in securing compliance with production rules. Data published by the consortium on the results of its controls, reported in Table 5.2, suggest that the incidence of adulteration has decreased

---

[5] 'Members' pay a higher membership fee of about $4250, and administer the organization through the thirteen-unit steering committee they elect. 'Users' pay a fixed fee of $1820 per year in exchange for the right to use the DOC for their products. In addition, all 'users' and 'members' pay a variable fee of 1.2 cents per kilo of mozzarella sold with the DOC label.

Table 5.2. *Consorzio Mozzarella di Bufala Campana:*
samples collected and analysed, and expulsions

Year	1993	1994	1995	1996	1997
No. of samples analysed		165	194	214	199
Positive results, %	23	15	10	11	7
Expulsions	—	—	2	6	2

Source: Consorzio Mozzarella di Bufala Campana.

substantially.[6] The results delivered by the high reputation strategy of the consortium, complemented by a well devised system of sanctions, single out this case of increasing producer cooperation in a supposedly individualistic society. Not all producer groups for which there are clear potential advantages from cooperation realize these. We come back to the question of how successful cooperation came about in this case in Section 5.3.

5.2.2. *Successful Producer Groups in Northeast Brazil*

In this section I shall describe the successful commercial performance of two groups of small-scale producers in poverty-stricken northeast Brazil. Despite the much lower absolute level of economic development in this region, what distinguishes successful groups from average performers in northeast Brazil appears similar to what distinguishes the successful group in the food-processing sector in southern Italy. The best-performing cases all process and trade relatively high-value products characterized by price premia.

The most prominent case of success among the six cases studied in the Brazil research is APAEB,[7] an association of farmers who have collectively invested in the marketing and processing of sisal fibre.[8] In the course of a struggle to enter the international market for this commodity, with the help of NGOs, which lasted almost twenty years, APAEB first became a major exporter of raw fibre, and more recently invested in a factory manufacturing sisal carpets. APAEB is located in the semi-arid interior of the northeastern state of Bahia, a region characterized by a very high incidence of poverty.[9]

APAEB has obtained impressive economic results in large part thanks to the recent shift in the preferences of advanced countries' consumers in the direction of natural

[6] Three independent investigations of buffalo mozzarella products from different firms conducted by consumers' associations in 1987, 1991, and 1993, reported respectively that 40, 33, and 60% of the samples were adulterated with cows' milk (Bianchi 1999).

[7] Associacão dos Pequenos Agricultores do Municipio de Valente, the small farmers' association of the city of Valente.

[8] Sisal (or agave) is a cactus that grows in the semi-arid region of the state. This plant comes originally from Yucatan in Mexico, where it is used, among other things, to produce the well known Tequila liquor. It was introduced in Brazil around 1903, where it is now mainly used for the vegetable fibre that can be obtained through a process of simple machine processing and sun drying. The fibre is then further cleaned from impurities, selected, dyed, and used to produce rope or simple artefacts like carpets, seat covers, bags, etc.

[9] Sixty-five per cent in 1991 according to the APAEB Annual Report 1997 which takes the 1991 population census figure.

anti-allergic materials in home furniture. This consumer trend has made sisal a valued alternative to synthetic carpeting in the European and North American markets, and has revitalized the demand for a raw material that used to be employed mainly in the manufacture of low value products like rope. APAEB chose to invest in carpet manufacturing after market research performed by hired consultants indicated that sisal carpets represented a potentially growing market.

The new identity of sisal as a 'natural' product has helped the collective enterprise of farmers to attract wealth to a poor dry region, and to distribute benefits to a large number of people. Through its consultants, who have *de facto* become the managers of its sisal activities, APAEB has not just benefited passively from the favourable international trends, but has actively worked to exploit their full economic potential.

APAEB's dynamic export performance first in raw sisal, and more recently in manufactured carpets, has produced positive spill-over effects in a region in which about one million people are estimated to derive part of their livelihood from sisal. Although APAEB promotes the development of the region in several different ways, the strongest positive effects of the association consist in increasing employment, and raising the price of fibre at the local level.

Before APAEB entered the business, buyers at the local level used to pay $0.20 per kg of unprocessed fibre (1990 figure). After APAEB entered the market and started to process and export sisal directly, the price went up to $0.25 per kg, in 1992. Finally, with the industrialization of the product in the collective carpet factory, the price rose to an average of $0.33 per kg, in 1996. Even though APAEB buys and processes only about 5 per cent of the overall production of sisal in the state of Bahia, this quantity has been large enough to influence the sisal price in the region, contributing to an increase of 65 per cent in nominal terms.[10]

Parallel to its core sisal business, APAEB also runs several other programmes. It acts as a financial intermediary collecting farmers' deposits, and funds from foreign NGOs and from the Development Bank of the Northeast (BNB), and lending to more than 600 farmers for production improvements. It is involved in a multitude of social activities in large part financed by foreign NGO funds. It runs a technical boarding school teaching modern farming techniques to seventy-five children in the grades 5–8. It owns and operates a general store. It has installed a radio station, and will soon also operate a TV station, to reach rural villagers with information and educational programmes. In 1995–98, as part of a reforestation programme, APAEB distributed 20,000 drought-resistant fruit and fodder plants to its members free of cost each year.

The association is also very active in the field of research and dissemination of agricultural practices appropriate for the semi-arid region. The two most important of these practices are goat herding and the related use of solar energy-powered

---

[10] In real terms the increase has been between 35 and 40%. A nominal increase of this magnitude compares very well with the average of other primary products. According to IMF data the price of Agricultural Raw Materials increased by only 27.7% between 1990 and 1996, and the more general category of Non-fuel primary Commodities by only 15%. The comparison with these benchmark categories confirms the view of sisal as a particularly dynamic commodity in terms of price and demand.

fences.[11] Finally, APAEB collaborates with the local rural workers' union and provides some material support for the landless movement in its struggle for land redistribution in the region.

The second of our Brazilian groups also benefits from access to a marketing advantage. It has been able to access a premium-price niche in an otherwise standardized market, thanks to the activity of an international non-profit trader of products from developing countries. COOMAP[12] was created in 1993 by a group of small farmers belonging to several community organizations in the region of Picos, in the northeastern state of Piauí, to improve the terms of trade of their products through collective marketing. Different community groups came together in COOMAP under the institutional umbrella of the local Catholic Church. COOMAP specialized in the marketing of one particular product: cashew nuts. A year after its creation, COOMAP exported its first cashew nuts to Europe, contracting the processing[13] out to a local firm. In 1997 COOMAP invested in its own processing plant, today employing twenty-five people. The project was financed mainly by grants.[14]

The success of COOMAP depends on the special, non-competitive market in which it operates. COOMAP sells more than 90 per cent of its production, and all of its exports, to CTM (Cooperazione Terzo Mondo), an Italian NGO which contacted COOMAP through the local Catholic Church. CTM is part of a network of non-profit intermediaries promoting 'Fair Trade' or 'Equal Exchange'. They select cooperatives and similar grass roots organizations in developing countries, pursuing social goals and guaranteeing non-exploitative working conditions to their workers, and use them as suppliers. They pay higher prices than the market to these organizations, and advance payments before delivery to help members to free themselves from what they consider unjust economic relations with intermediaries and moneylenders.

[11] Solar energy may be the most innovative of these techniques. It allows farmers to take advantage of one of the few natural resources of this region, the sun, to power their homes. When it is used to electrify the wires delimiting the farmers' property, this technology also allows them to raise goats—the most appropriate livestock for the region's agriculture—saving up to 70% on the cost of fencing. Goats are more appropriate than the more traditional cows in a dry and variable climate, because they are more efficient in the use of the scarce natural pastures, and allow farmers to break up their assets more, but the cost of fencing is higher.

APAEB works as an extension agent for the installation of solar energy systems in remote farms of the region that are not reached by conventional electrification. One hundred and eighty-six of these systems have been installed in ten surrounding municipalities in the last four years with the advice of the technicians of APAEB, and financed by the credit cooperative. Seventy-three more solar systems have been sold by ABAEB without any accompanying credit.

[12] Cooperativa Mista Agropecuaria dos Pequenos Produtores Rurais, the mixed agricultural cooperative of small-scale producers.

[13] With the help of a simple, hand-operated machine, the nut has to be separated from its external peel. In order to do this, it has to be cooked in two rounds in a large oven, and classified according to its size. The nuts that are broken in the process have to be separated from the others and sold at a much lower price, from 20% to 40% of that of the first quality. The productivity of the factory depends to a considerable extent on the ability of the operators of the cutting machines to reduce the percentage of broken product.

[14] An Italian governmental organization donated $40,000 to buy the machinery for the factory. The World Bank-funded rural development programme of the state of Piauí provided $24,000 more, which covered part of the costs of construction. In total, the grants covered almost 90% of the total costs of the investment.

The products are then sold in the industrialized western countries accompanied by information indicating how the price paid by the final consumer is distributed between the different phases of production and distribution. Consumers know in what ways they are helping producers in developing countries, and what kind of difference they are making by buying 'fairly traded' instead of conventionally traded products. Fair Trade is not dissimilar from a certificate of origin like the DOC. They are both labelling systems certifying that products possess certain characteristics—origin and production technique in the case of the DOC, social promotion and better working conditions in the case of COOMAP—for which consumers are willing to pay a price premium.

CTM bought 7–8 tons of cashew nuts per year from COOMAP between 1995 and 1998. It offered $7.5 per kg instead of the approximately $6 per kg which competitive international markets would have paid (25 per cent more), and paid 50 per cent of the value of the shipment *before* delivery, at the time the order was confirmed. Despite the small size of the order, the product was then sold in Italy under the branded name of COOMAP.

The above-market rent guaranteed to COOMAP by the 'Fair Trade' network might have encouraged the cooperative to develop a 'relaxed' attitude towards productivity, but this did not occur. Apart from introducing collective processing of cashew nuts, COOMAP has also proved successful as a financial intermediary. It stands out from other cooperative groups for its 100 per cent repayment record and has thus obtained repeated loans from the BNB, many of which have been passed on to its farmer-members, contributing to their capitalization.

The cooperative has been able to use its reputation for creditworthiness, to launch new investments. The BNB has recently approved another loan, financing 88 of the 110 active members of COOMAP individually to enlarge their cashew plantations and to buy sheep and goats. Ten percent of the loan ($60,000) will finance two community-level food industries, processing the fruit of the cashew, a separate part from the nut, which is currently wasted or used for animal feed.

With strong external support from international NGOs, COOMAP has made great advances in its first five years of existence. The positive results of collective action are increasing the scope for cooperation, through collective investments. Other positive aspects of this group include (i) the willingness of members to learn, and improve themselves through training, and (ii) its democratic internal decision-making (on which more is given below).

5.3. HOW DID IT ALL START?

The preceding section should have convinced most readers that connecting up with protected and profitable market niches can make a real difference for producers located in regions that lack many of the resources necessary to be competitive in manufacturing. The first question I ask in this section is how groups of producers can identify, create, and access such market niches. How have the successful groups been able to do it?

Perhaps the most important point about protected trading channels is that discovering or creating them is often beyond ordinary groups of producers in poor and marginal regions. Producers often lack information on market trends, and, more specifically, lack an understanding of the culture of more advanced consumer markets, that would help them identify those niches. They cannot be expected to come up by themselves with marketing solutions of the kinds presented above that would create a real discontinuity with their current state of poverty.

The producers I analyse in this paper have been able to enter highly profitable and relatively protected market niches thanks to the initiatives of outsiders. In some cases, atypical marketing intermediaries like NGOs have provided the link with the profitable niches. In others, the most ambitious and forward-looking group members have devised this marketing strategy with the support of outsiders.

5.3.1. *Marketing Intermediaries*

In the northeast Brazilian cases marketing intermediaries were the key to the economic success of the producers. The success of the cashew producers of COOMAP comes from a marketing system that springs out of a developed world movement, whose altruistic methods and goals the cashew producers could not understand in full. It was agents external to the group, the Catholic Church and the Italian NGO CTM, which introduced them to this protected and subsidized market niche. The higher profits and better terms of trade guaranteed by CTM gave local producers a chance to accumulate and invest in collective productive capacity that was not available on the open competitive market for cashew nuts.[15] By themselves, the producers would never have been able to discover or access this NGO network: they lacked the necessary information and contacts.

COOMAP's encounter with the Fair Trade intermediary CTM was brokered by the Catholic Church, whose leadership at the local level is committed to the social and economic problems of the poor. The local church can be seen as an important external development agent in the region; one that, because of its international linkages, has opened up the unique possibilities of the Fair Trade network.

COOMAP is an example of a group that has taken advantage of an opportunity presented to it by intermediaries. APAEB, the older cooperative trading sisal carpets is different in that it has played a more active role in constructing its marketing channels. It gives us a more optimistic picture of the possibilities open to producer groups for actively pursuing commercial success. However, APAEB also benefited from the services of external marketing agents. Its case, therefore, reinforces the idea that groups need external help with collective marketing. One could probably argue that the real cause of APAEB's success was its ability to enlist these intermediaries in the cause of its economic development.

---

[15] In the international market, buyers require that suppliers sell at least fifteen tons of nut (a full container) for which they pay at delivery the full value of about $90,000. The working capital necessary to buy from farmers enough raw product to meet such a big order, and the cost of labour to process it, would be prohibitive for a small organization without access to cheap and efficient sources of financing, or the capacity to conduct delicate financial operations. CTM has helped enormously with the 50% advance on payments, the higher price, and the smaller size of its orders.

External marketing agents provided a critical input for the development process of APAEB, but only at the end of a long struggle by the producers. Created in 1980, the association started to market its members' sisal collectively in the mid-eighties, but the prices it was able to obtain on the local markets were insufficient to start a process of accumulation and development. After a long bureaucratic struggle to obtain the necessary permits, APAEB made its first direct exports in the late 1980s, but it was not content with being a simple exporter of raw material. The contacts it had developed with international donors, and with the local development bank, suggested to the leader of APAEB a new, more ambitious project to industrialize sisal locally. The leader of APAEB was a member of a relatively well-off local family who has been very much involved in local NGOs.

The turning point in the group's history is represented by the moment the leader of APAEB came across an international trading firm based in the state capital, Salvador, which ended up working as APAEB's marketing office. This firm provided the necessary bridge between the world of NGOs and rural development organizations, of which APAEB is a part, and the world of profit-seeking international business. Upon visiting APAEB, the trading firm was persuaded of the viability of the initiative by the enthusiasm of its members, and probably also by the knowledge it had of the growing demand for sisal products. The traders thus started working for APAEB as consultants.

After brief market research, the consultants decided to recommend sisal carpets, which promised potentially valuable market developments in the light of international trends towards the use of natural fabrics in home furniture. At the end of 1993, with the help of the consultants, APAEB submitted a proposal to the BNB for a 1.5 million dollar loan to build a sisal carpet factory. After factory production began in 1996, it immediately became clear that the capacity installed was too low to satisfy the demand. By this time the trading firm had become so involved in the project that it offered part of its property (worth about $270,000) as a guarantee for a second BNB loan, of $1.6 million. Today, the firm has become indistinguishable from APAEB, although it is still formally a separate enterprise. APAEB has permanently hired it on a salary basis and uses it as a sales office, technical advisor, and management agency.

One can see from this story that APAEB, through a more tortuous process, has created for itself what COOMAP found from its start: a developmental intermediary, that is, one that has an interest in the growth of its suppliers, and provides them with opportunities usually unavailable on open commodity markets. Despite their very different economic nature, the two types of intermediaries ended up performing very similar functions. It is the role played by the intermediaries that stands out as a large part of the reason why these cases were so successful relative to other producer associations in northeast Brazil.

5.3.2. *Leveraging the Leaders*

The case of the buffalo mozzarella cheese producers is slightly different. The economic success of this group did not depend on the role of a marketing intermediary, but on the reputation for product quality that the consortium acted to protect, and exclusively

associate with a well-defined geographical area of production. Buffalo mozzarella producers sell their produce individually through a conventional chain of wholesalers,
department stores, and the like. The interesting question arising from this case is
why this group of producers was able to devise such an astute collective development
strategy. Why were they not constrained by the limited imaginative capacity that often
characterizes groups of producers in less developed areas? If we focus our attention on
how the consortium was created, the dissimilarity with the two other producer groups
analysed above becomes less.

The modernizing economic agents in the mozzarella production chain were the most
prominent members of the group of buffalo ranchers, helped by a livestock expert, a
university professor at the local University of Naples. The strong linkages he developed
with the buffalo ranchers at the local level, a fortunate exception by Italian standards,
could be in part explained by the fact that his family owned buffalo land in earlier
generations.

The university professor started by offering free technical assistance to the largest
enterprises, in exchange for the possibility of using their farms to conduct experiments.
The Extension Service of the University of Naples, currently headed by the professor's
main pupil, still works on the basis of the same informal arrangement. This collaboration between public university and private firms resulted in significant productivity
increases.[16]

The university professor chaired the World Association of Buffalo Farmers for many
years and in this role developed international connections with world experts in the
subject. He is the person who took the first initiative to create the consortium for the
Promotion of Buffalo Mozzarella in 1982, 'with ten of the largest and more modern
farmers'.[17]

Among the founders of the consortium was the most innovative buffalo mozzarella
farmer—who was the first to introduce mechanical milking of buffaloes in the 1970s.
Another of the modernizing pioneers of the consortium was very active in politics at the
national level. He supported the industry when he became the Minister of Agriculture,
and then the leader of the National Association of Farmers. As Minister, his signature
appears under the 1993 decree assigning buffalo mozzarella the DOC.

What comes out of this account of the modernization of the mozzarella industry
is the picture of a developmental élite composed of the largest farmers and a few
prominent outsiders. Only a handful of large-scale commercial farmers perceived
the necessity to protect and promote mozzarella in the early 1980s, with the help of

---

[16] The most important of these innovations involves the management of pregnancies. This addresses the
problem created by the seasonal variability of milk production: left to themselves buffaloes give birth in the
autumn, and therefore concentrate milk production in the winter months, when the demand for mozzarella
cheese is low. This creates an insufficient supply in the summer when the demand for the product is high.
As a result of more than twenty years of experimentation and extension, about 70% of the farmers today
adopt a technique that spreads the supply of buffalo milk more evenly across the year. The more constant
availability of milk, in its turn, reduces the incentives for product adulteration, and the use of improper
inputs like frozen buffalo milk that would significantly reduce the quality of mozzarella.

[17] Interview with Prof. De Franciscis.

a well-informed and educated outsider in the person of the university professor. The majority of small-scale buffalo ranchers and dairy firms were initially very skeptical about the consortium. Differences in social status among the producers, and the nature of the relationship between them, eventually helped many small farmers and dairy firms to accept the idea of a collective institution that was devised by a few large landowners.

The few larger farmers responsible for the creation of the consortium consider themselves higher in status than the majority of the buffalo ranchers. They are also better connected to the professional and public sector milieu, where they promote their interests and voice their claims without any sense of inferiority. The smaller farmers, before the consortium was launched, had already had the chance to experiment on their farms with the cattle-raising techniques developed by the few largest ranches. For this reason, and because of their deference towards the larger farmers, they were open to initiatives taken by the ranching élite as something that could also be in their interest. Somewhat paradoxically, the disparity in social status between buffalo ranchers facilitated the adoption of the new product development strategy, giving larger farmers the self-confidence to take the initiative in the interests of the entire group, and giving smaller farmers a certain degree of trust in the initiative.

The simultaneous reading of the three cases presented above leaves us with a more general finding about the construction of market advantage. Ordinary groups of uninformed producers in underdeveloped areas cannot be expected to discover and occupy profitable market niches unless they receive some sort of external help. The economic agents who have proved to be capable of starting such strategies of product differentiation or niche marketing are usually not rooted in local production systems of less-developed areas. They are either total outsiders to groups, as in the case of the autonomous marketing intermediaries described above, or the most powerful and well-informed members of groups, who possess the necessary connections with different social milieu.

One likely sequence of product upgrading, seen at work in the cases of mozzarella and sisal, requires the participation of both the educated and modernizing leadership of the groups, *and* well-connected external agents or intermediaries. Group leaders are most likely to take the initiative in the interests of other group members, or to ally themselves with external agents who can give them access to product upgrading and/or high-price niche strategies. In the case of the Italian mozzarella producers the professor, an outsider who understands the culture of the ranchers because of his family background, used the contacts he had with the richest and most advanced producers, to introduce improvements in production technique and group organization that benefited the entire category of producers.

A similar alliance also took place in the case of the Brazilian cooperative manufacturing sisal carpets, whose successful strategy of looking for allies among international traders did not come from the membership base, but was the initiative of a particularly dynamic and motivated leader. The partnership with a trading firm, which was fundamental to this export success, required overcoming the hostility against marketing intermediaries that characterized members of APAEB as much as the members of other grass roots organizations that originally got together to give themselves an alternative to the stranglehold of local level traders. Most members would probably have disagreed with this choice if it had been thoroughly and democratically discussed, because they tend to believe that marketing intermediaries are the *cause* of their state of dependency, and not the solution.

5.4. HOMOGENEITY OF INTERESTS, EXCLUSIONARY POLICIES, ANTAGONISTIC IDEOLOGY

The development sequence of these groups, as we have seen, is one that acknowledges, and in a certain sense takes advantage of, the differences in economic and cultural levels of the members. This raises the question of whether internal group equality is bad for producer organizations. It is clear that some degree of homogeneity of interests and values among group members is necessary to keep the producers' organizations united. Shared economic interests among members facilitate the task of managing the groups by reducing the number of conflicting goals that the organizations pursue. However, it may also be valuable to have an organization that frees up the creative energies of the leaders from the constraining check of the rank and file. Homogeneity of certain kinds is not entirely in conflict with this unequal distribution of power, and may allow groups to safely transfer management responsibilities to group leaders, because it makes the task of monitoring the results of their activity easier.

Homogeneity of interests, of socio-economic status, of values, among members should not be seen as unchangeable features of groups that give advantage to some organizations over others. They should be seen instead as variables on which groups *can act* to increase the coherence of their activity and the effectiveness of their management. Two of the associations in our sample have pursued member homogeneity in the course of their history along at least two very different dimensions: (i) the economic activity of their members, and (ii) their members' social and economic conditions.

5.4.1. *Product Homogeneity*

The product specialization of the two better performing associations of producers in northeast Brazil has simplified their economic objectives. The same can be said of the Italian consortium of mozzarella producers, which exists because the members all produce exactly the same thing.[18]

The strongest evidence in favour of product homogeneity comes from the transition towards product specialization in the two Brazilian farmers' associations COOMAP and APAEB. In both cases, there was no one single predominant crop among those cultivated by the founders. In the case of APAEB, producers from five different villages of the region got together initially in the association, and only in the local economy of two of them was sisal dominant. The same was true for COOMAP: while certain

---

[18] I don't mean to say that product-specialization is sufficient to guarantee the economic viability of collective initiatives. The experience of other cases not discussed here indicates that comparable collective initiatives of producers organized along industry lines can also fall prey to internal divisions and conflicts of interest (Bianchi 1998).

producers in the original organization were relatively specialized in growing cashew nuts, others concentrated on more traditional products like beans, corn, or livestock.

In the course of their history, both COOMAP and APAEB transformed themselves into product-specific trading organizations. After COOMAP found a channel for marketing cashews profitably, it focused on their processing and marketing. At that point, most of the members who did not produce cashews felt neglected, criticized the association for doing little for them, and eventually left the association, creating other groups. APAEB underwent an even clearer process of product specialization that illustrates the tight relationship between homogeneity and leadership autonomy.

In the early 1990s, the association suffered from the inability to take even the easiest decisions because of conflicts within its administrative council between the representatives of different municipalities which specialized in different crops. The conflict of material interests of the producers from the different municipalities was amplified by a decision-making structure that allowed for continuous discussion and participation in the ordinary management of the association. External consultants contacted for the purpose of addressing this problem recommended the break up of APAEB into five municipal-level organizations, more homogeneous internally, and therefore more manageable. It was only after this organizational restructuring that one of the five resulting organizations, the APAEB, focusing on one particularly dynamic crop, sisal, experienced an economic take-off.

In the case of APAEB there is clear evidence not only that homogeneity of interest within the group has facilitated the work of the leaders, but also that it has helped attract dynamic and ambitious leadership. The current leader of APAEB, who had guided the effort to export sisal, left the administration of the association when it was paralyzed by conflicts of interest between different producers, and plagued by endless debates between different municipal representatives. He came back to APAEB to lead the new effort to industrialize sisal after it had isolated itself from the groups of the other municipalities, and become a more flexible institution in which he could put his ideas into practice. Although he takes most of the important decisions in the group, he is not elected to the administrative council. He invented the role of external consultant for himself, in order to retain more decision-making autonomy.

5.4.2. *Homogeneity of Socio-economic Status and Values*

There is another form of group homogeneity that characterized the membership of APAEB and COOMAP from the start—homogeneity of socio-economic status. Both groups admit only small farmers (as defined by the maximum land holding required to take part in rural workers' unions) who depend on agricultural work for the bulk of their income. COOMAP also requires prospective members to be affiliated to village associations or rural workers' unions. These provisions are clearly intended to exclude the large commercial landowners, who do not live on the land but could potentially come to control the associations, and use them in their interest. The extent to which they are socially and economically homogeneous could be debated. However, these organizations still employ the discourse of class struggle, and describe their activity at least in part as the struggle of the poor and marginal against the rich and powerful. To the extent that homogeneity of class or socio-economic status is achieved, it is the result of a political culture that aims at class solidarity and cultivates antagonism against the rich.

Both organizations have their roots in the political education that groups of poor rural workers have received from the progressive wing of the Catholic Church (sometimes labelled 'Liberation Theology'). They are the product of a strategy used by the church in the 1970s and 1980s, and subsequently adopted by the state and by other development agents, to empower the rural poor by organizing them into groups. The teachings of the progressive clergy, legitimized under the Brazilian dictatorship by their association with religion, taught poor rural workers that the political and economic situation in which they lived was unjust, that their religious beliefs were incompatible with such a situation, and that they had both a moral responsibility and a concrete opportunity to act collectively to reverse this state of affairs.

One effect of this political legacy has been to make the organizations more homogeneous in terms of the economic interests of their members, by means of a membership policy that restricts access. A separate legacy is to give homogeneity to the *ideas* of the members, and consequently to the objectives that the organizations pursue. Besides excluding *ab origine* the rich, who could have co-opted the organizations, this background of political and ideological training has produced beneficial effects in the course of the life of these groups as well, as they have embraced economic and commercial objectives. In the case of the APAEB especially, the antagonistic culture strengthened the internal cohesion of the group and helped it to face many difficulties by presenting the economic development of the group as an uphill battle, as an 'us against them' situation in which 'we' are on the right side.

Both forms of internal homogeneity—the product and the class/ideological—contribute to making the groups more manageable instruments of change in the hands of dynamic leaders. On top of that, the ideology probably adds an additional element of strength: by equating economic development to class struggle it builds a hard shell for the organizations, anticipating the difficulties of the task, and preparing for inevitable setbacks.

Thus the principle of group equality is not entirely in conflict with the observation that the most successful groups are firmly in the hands of their most educated and skillful members. Homogeneity of interest makes it easier to pursue the interests of all members and reduces the need for continuous control and participation for all of them.

5.5. CONCLUSIONS

Generalizing on the basis of the experience of two successful northeast Brazilian associations and one consortium of producers in southern Italy, this chapter has tried to identify some of the factors that allow groups of producers to function as economic development tools for lagging regions, as theory predicts. The major reason for the success of these cases, compared to other similar groups in the two regions, was the discovery of relatively high-profit market niches, characterized by limited competition.

In the presence of super-profits, these groups have been able to overcome the many constraints to their economic development, among which is the problem of establishing and enforcing cooperation.

Most members in such groups are not likely to be in a position to identify profitable market niches, because they are embedded in culturally isolated economic systems, they lack resources or education, or they are otherwise limited in their strategic horizon. For this reason, there is a key role to be played by marketing intermediaries and development agents external to the groups in connecting producers with lucrative market segments, that would otherwise be out of their reach.

In one of the cases examined, a marketing intermediary provided a linkage with a profitable market niche to a group of producers who would not otherwise have been aware of this possibility for expanding their revenues.[19] In the other two cases the market niche characterized by relatively high-profit margins and low competition was accessed, or created, by the group itself, through a process of active product upgrading. In these cases the producers also took advantage of the services of external marketing intermediaries, and of other external experts. But, unlike in the first case, in these cases a few producers also played a leading role in upgrading members' production.

The main lessons from these stories are that certain types of intermediaries can provide groups of producers in underdeveloped areas with opportunities for super-profits that can help them exit from the poverty impasse in which they would otherwise be stuck. The most inventive and ambitious group members, by making contact with developmental agents outside the group, can also start up high-profit commercial strategies to the advantage of all the other producers.

This evidence seems to challenge a widely shared idea that influences thinking about economic development and the policies to promote it. This is the idea that participatory democracy within grass-roots organizations, besides being an important goal, is an important ingredient of the development process. This view conceives the development process as something originating fundamentally from within groups, when the demands of community members are democratically expressed.

The emphasis on participatory democracy at the grass-roots level is fully justified by the well-documented experience of past failures. Associations and other local institutions too often fall captive to local community leaders, who use them for their own purposes. The associations which become the prey of such entrenched leaderships cease to represent the interests of the majority of their members (Fox 1992). This is particularly true in developing areas like northeast Brazil where the tradition of social relations privileges 'vertical' forms of interaction between the powerful few and the dispossessed many (Almy 1988). Superimplanted on these social norms, associations often end up being dominated by local oligarchies. The risk is that those oligarchies, as long as they are in control of the cooperatives, will reproduce the unequal distribution of power, knowledge, and resources. For this reason active member participation

---

[19] The Brazilian research included a second group of producers which provides evidence in support of this same point, but could not be included in this chapter for reasons of space. It is the case of the Association of Furniture-makers of Itinga (Bianchi 1998).

has often been recommended as an important ingredient of successful cooperatives, especially in developing countries (Attwood *et al.* 1985).

The evidence in this chapter suggests that the view of development as something coming fundamentally 'from within', should not be taken too far. The groups reviewed here found successful marketing solutions that triggered a process of broader economic and social development by leveraging the knowledge and resources of group leaders and outsiders. Such solutions are very different from those to which a faithful expression of the will and aspirations of the majority of members would have led. In order to free up the energies of their most educated and ambitious members and thus create a real discontinuity with their original state of underdevelopment, these groups needed to sacrifice at least in part members' participation to the group's administration.

The reason for presenting this view of collective economic development based on leadership autonomy and developmental intermediaries is not to suggest that it should entirely replace the prevalent view according to which group members have to take direct responsibility for their own destiny. As has been repeatedly stressed in the development literature, leadership autonomy can be exercised against the interest of group members. The goals of participation and effective management should both be pursued to the extent that is possible. A decision-making structure which possesses elements of a P/C mode may be useful to the extent that it allows groups to utilize to the fullest extent one of the scarcest resources at the local level: entrepreneurial skills. One question which remains open, and is left for further research, is how to increase the likelihood that socially concerned leaders will exercise this autonomy, instead of the self-interested types that the development historiography knows very well.

The evidence presented in this chapter suggests that certain types of groups may have better chances of attracting the right kind of leaders. The groups reviewed here are all characterized by social and economic homogeneity between members. The Brazilian ones in particular pursued economic homogeneity intentionally, as a result of the ideology of class antagonism, whose influence marked their creation and first years of existence. All associations exclude from membership producers with different economic interests, cherish their internal homogeneity, and see their collective advancement as happening at the expense of other economic agents. This homogeneity need not result in a 'participant' mode of group operation, which reduces management to the least common cultural denominator. The coherence of material interests and cultural values within groups, by clarifying group goals, may make possible an autonomous but democratically controlled group administration. It allows members to transfer autonomy of management to ambitious group leaders, by facilitating the task of monitoring the results of their activity against the shared objectives.

6

Group Behaviour and Development: A Comparison of Farmers' Organizations in South Korea and Taiwan

LARRY BURMEISTER, GUSTAV RANIS, AND MICHAEL WANG

6.1. INTRODUCTION

In response to prevailing agro–ecological and agrarian structural conditions, a variety of rural organizations has arisen throughout East Asia to link small producers to broad national development objectives. Farmers' organizations (FOs) have been critical components of this organizational infrastructure, providing marketing, input supply, technical information, and credit services to farmer-members. In some countries, such FOs have played quite a significant role as institutional vehicles for promoting agricultural development, while in others they have been less effective (see Jones 1971; Lele 1981; Illy 1983). In this paper, we examine two FOs, the Farmers' Association (FA) in Taiwan and the National Agricultural Cooperative Federation (NACF) in South Korea (hereafter Korea), in order to assess the extent to which such organizations permit us to understand better the role of group behaviour in affecting development outcomes.

The post-colonial regimes in Taiwan and Korea faced similar agricultural development problems. With land reform and the demise of the landlord class, the mobilization and coordination of a fragmented smallholder agricultural sector became essential for economic development and political consolidation in both countries. The FA and the NACF, built upon the foundations of predecessor organizations in the Japanese colonial period, were established by state initiatives in the postwar period to perform agro–input supply, marketing support, credit, and technology diffusion functions. While official publications describe these FOs as agricultural cooperatives, farmer-members did not establish them as a result of grass roots collective action. Central government ministries, the Ministry of Agriculture and Forestry (MAF) in Korea and the Provincial Department of Agriculture and Forestry (PDAF) in Taiwan, exercised administrative oversight over the FOs, making them extensions of the state in very important respects. Administrative units in both FOs paralleled the governmental administrative

Our thanks for the able research assistance of Nicola Mrazek. We also thank the editors of the volume for their highly constructive comments and suggestions.

hierarchy (national, provincial, county, township), thus making it easy for the state to engage the FA and the NACF in the service of strategic national development objectives.

Due to their parastatal origins, the organizational structures and operational norms of the FA and the NACF were weighted towards the hierarchical power/control (P/C) 'mode of operation' outlined in Chapter 1. P/C organizational patterns were, however, modified by linkages to local-level groups, both within and outside the formal FO structure. Such groups (e.g. village associations) were comprised of farm households with relatively egalitarian resource bases and social status, a result of significant social levelling brought about by post-Second World War land reforms in both countries. Moreover, these groups often had histories of institutionalized cooperative labour arrangements to deal with the onerous seasonal labour demand and irrigation system maintenance requirements of wet rice cultivation (Bray 1986; Oshima 1986).

This socio-economic environment fostered cooperative norms within villages, inter-jecting important elements of a COOP behavioural mode into the FOs, especially at the lower levels in the organizational hierarchy where routine interactions between farmer-members and FO staff occurred. Thus, the FA and the NACF organizational cultures combined P/C and COOP modes of operation. This combination of group behavioural characteristics helped the FA and the NACF to achieve a level of opera-tional effectiveness that has been evaluated favourably in cross-national comparisons of similar organizations that provide essential services to agricultural producers (Desai and Mellor 1993; Esman and Uphoff 1984: 315–17). The relative success of FOs in Taiwan and Korea illustrate what Evans (1996) and others have conceptualized as synergistic 'co-production' relationships between the state and groups organized to achieve development goals.

While there are significant similarities in the FA's and the NACF's organizational structure and operations, we argue that some differences in agricultural sector per-formance in Taiwan and Korea during the period under review (1950–80) may have been due in part to the different levels of organizational effectiveness of these two FOs. The literature on the role of FOs in East Asia has largely been silent on the implica-tions of group behaviour for their operational efficiency, mostly focusing on the role of FOs in the context of an old-fashioned agricultural production function. For example, Kwoh (1966) and Kuo and Lee (1982) have analysed the ways in which various opera-tions in Taiwan's FA contributed to increasing production without addressing the key question of just why they were able to render their services so effectively.

In this study we examine intra-group behavioural dynamics within FOs as another variable affecting agricultural sector performance. We limit our examination to the 1950–80 period, given the decline in the relative quantitative importance of agriculture from the late 1970s onwards in both Korea and Taiwan, which accordingly reduced the importance of farmers' groups as development agents in both countries in recent years. However, our findings remain relevant for countries still at an earlier stage of development.

In what follows we first briefly set the stage by comparing the role of agriculture in the overall development of the Korean and Taiwanese economies in Section 6.2.

In Section 6.3, we examine the political economy norms affecting the organizational development of FOs in both countries, and briefly review FO organizational histories and structures. We then examine internal organizational differences in more detail in Section 6.4, focusing on institutional variables (e.g. organizational structure, process, and norms) that affected the behaviour of both FO staff and farmer-members. In Section 6.5, the implications of such differences in group behaviour for organizational performance are discussed. We conclude, in Section 6.6, by putting the 'modes of group operation' model into a broader theoretical context that helps explain differences in parastatal FO performance in Taiwan and Korea.

6.2. COMPARING AGRICULTURAL SECTOR PERFORMANCES

Following the Second World War, agriculture initially dominated the Korean and Taiwanese economies, with well over half of the labour force employed and slightly less than half of gross domestic product generated in the sector. The sector was mostly composed of single-family households who engaged in full-time farming and owned the land they cultivated. Tenant farmers were relatively few and the average size of landholdings small and strikingly homogeneous, due to the land reforms of the early postwar period. This initially gave rise to substantial uniformity of production conditions and organization. Rice was at first the dominant crop, supplying nearly half of total agricultural income in both countries (see Ban 1979; Ho 1978).

Over time, the economic importance of agriculture declined in both countries (although more rapidly in Taiwan which had a more robust rural development experience), providing only 7 per cent of GNP in Taiwan and only 18 per cent in Korea by 1981 (Moore 1988: 121). The structure of agriculture also changed gradually, with a shift in production away from grains to livestock; an increase in the commercialization and mechanization of production; and an increase in the share of non-farm activities in rural household incomes (see Ban 1979; Lee and Chen 1979).

From an international perspective, agricultural performance in both countries has been impressive. Average rice yields in Korea and Taiwan during the 1952–70 period were more than double those of South and Southeast Asia, almost matching those of Japan. Agricultural output growth was also comparable to that of Asian neighbours over the same period, and higher than the world average and that of more land-abundant nations in Africa and Latin America (see Table 6.1). Taiwan's agricultural output initially expanded more rapidly than Korea's because of less wartime disruption, a higher initial level of income, and better macroeconomic and structural policies (see Fei and Ranis 1975; Oshima 1987: 149–52). By the mid-1970s, however, agricultural growth in Korea had accelerated, surpassing Taiwan's.

Despite their broadly similar records, the agricultural sector in the two countries played rather different roles in their overall development. As a catalyst for growth and industrialization, the agricultural sector in Taiwan was important, contributing substantial net capital outflows to the development of non-agricultural activities (Oshima 1987; Lee and Culver 1985; Lee and Chen 1979). Agricultural savings

Table 6.1. *International comparison of
agricultural output growth*

	1952/61	1961/71	1952/71
Korea	3.1[a]	3.7	3.5
Taiwan	4.1	3.9	4.0
Thailand	5.2	3.6	4.4
North America	1.1	2.1	1.6
Latin America	3.5	2.4	2.9
Africa	2.8	2.9	2.9
Asia	4.2	2.6	3.4
India	3.6	2.2	2.9
Japan	2.4	2.0	2.2
World	2.8	2.6	2.7

[a] 1954–61.

Source: Ban *et al.* (1980), table 3, reproduced here by
kind permission of Harvard University Press.

in Korea contributed only 9 per cent of total capital formation on average during
the post-1952–70 period, in contrast to 21 per cent in the case of Taiwan (Fei and
Ranis 1975).

Moreover, Taiwan's agricultural households contributed substantial labour inputs
to the development process through a remarkable shift in rural household labour from
agricultural to rural non-agricultural activities, with off-farm labour participation
rising from 29 per cent of total rural employment in 1956 to 67 per cent in 1980
(Ranis 1995). This helped to produce a decentralized pattern of industrialization that,
in contrast to Korea and most other developing countries, was primarily rurally based.
Although Korea's farm sector also supplied labour inputs to the non-farm sectors, it
was less extensive, with a larger share of the labour force retained in lower productivity
agricultural activities in 1980 (Oshima 1987: 160). Lack of rural industrialization in the
Korean countryside limited the extent of the agricultural to non-agricultural labour
transfer that characterized the Taiwanese rural development experience (Ho 1982),
and resulted in less income equality in rural areas and less convergence between rural
and urban household incomes.

Thus, although agricultural development was successful in both countries, agricultural labour productivity in Taiwan rose somewhat faster[1] and total factor productivity
grew much faster in 1952–80, by 2.2 per cent per annum in Taiwan, compared with a
fall of 0.2 per cent per annum in Korea (Oshima 1986, table 1), and there were substantially higher savings from the sector in Taiwan. This was partly due to differences

[1] See *Agricultural Development in China, Japan and Korea*, Chi-Ming Hou, Tzong-Shian Yu (eds),
Academia Sinica, Taipei, 1982, especially the chapter on Korea 'The Growth of Agricultural Output and
Productivity in Korea, 1918–78', by Sung-Hwan Ban and the chapter on Taiwan 'Secular Trends of Output,
Inputs and Productivity' by Yueh-eh Chen and You-tsao Weng. The data indicate a 3.9% annual growth of
agricultural labour productivity in Korea from 1946–77 while Taiwan's increased by 4.3% annually from
1951–77.

in initial endowments, such as Taiwan's more favourable rice-cultivating and multiple-cropping climate, and differences in government policies, such as Taiwan's higher rate of agricultural sector investment, less bias against agriculture in the inter-sectoral terms of trade (Ho 1978; Ranis 1989), and a more favourable climate for rural industrialization. But, we believe, another component was the more effective role of rural institutions in Taiwan, specifically the FA, which appears to have been instrumental in increasing agricultural productivity through its input, marketing, and extension functions. As a result, Taiwan's agriculture was able to supply more resource transfers through savings and consumption to support the national development project. In Sections 6.4 and 6.5, we examine the reasons for the favourable performance of FOs in both countries, exploring the differences between FOs in Taiwan and Korea, focusing on both the internal and external environments that influenced FO group dynamics. But first, we need to review the historical and political economy contexts of FO creation and development in Korea and Taiwan.

6.3. ORGANIZATIONAL HISTORIES AND OVERVIEW

6.3.1. *The Political Economy of FO Development Dynamics*

Important differences in the politics of regime consolidation in the two countries affected FO structure and procedures, as did the broader macro-norms operating in the political economies of both countries.

After Taiwan reverted to the Republic of China (ROC), following the Japanese surrender, the indigenous Taiwanese reacted strongly against perceived Kuomintang (KMT) misrule on the island. Social unrest led to a purge of the Taiwanese elite by the ROC authorities, that is, the infamous 28 February 1947 (2/28) 'Incident' (see Gold 1986: 47–55). This early assault on the indigenous Taiwanese made Chiang Kai-shek's withdrawal to Taiwan from the mainland, following the KMT's defeat in the Chinese Civil War, a potentially explosive political issue, as the mainlanders filled top positions in the state apparatus and the military. In order to mitigate tensions generated by the KMT's withdrawal to Taiwan, the regime had to cede some political and economic space to the indigenous Taiwanese. In the political sphere, a degree of local autonomy was institutionalized through the election of local government executives and the establishment of local legislative assemblies. While the KMT did retain control of larger scale strategic, state-owned enterprises, most of the economy, that is, agriculture and medium- and small-scale industry, remained open to indigenous Taiwanese entrepreneurship.

The need for political legitimization, together with strong pressure from the Joint Commission on Rural Reconstruction (JCRR) (Shen 1970), led to a modicum of self-rule within the FA system. The JCRR, a rural development agency largely supported by US foreign aid funds and staffed by American advisors who worked in concert with Chinese counterparts, pushed for democratic procedures in FA operations. The JCRR's unique influence in the KMT regime encouraged FA development in line with agricultural cooperative ideals of grass roots ties between staff and farmer-members and participatory organizational governance, quite at odds with the one-party, bureaucratic–authoritarian structure of the overall ROC state apparatus. As we shall see, this led to procedures that included an element of farmer-member participation in FA governance through FA assembly elections (see Section 6.4).

Postwar political dynamics in Korea provided less political space than in Taiwan for the institutionalization of formal democratic processes at the local level. During the US military occupation (1945–48), rural social discontent over the slow pace of land reform and the retention of much of the colonial administrative ruling apparatus (lower ranking government officials and police who were viewed as Japanese collaborators) erupted into violent uprisings against the authorities in the countryside in the autumn of 1946 (Cumings 1981; Shin 1996). In the initial stages of the Korean War, territory in the South passed back and forth from Communist to Republic of Korea (ROK) rule, leaving lingering questions about village political loyalties in some regions (Brandt 1971: 189). Threats of anti-regime political agitation and communist infiltration seemed uppermost in government thinking about the consequences of open politics in the countryside. While local level officials were elected during the Rhee regime (1948–60), local autonomy was completely abrogated by the military government of General Park Chung Hee, who came to power in a 1961 coup.

The NACF was established shortly after the Park military coup. It was organized as a centralized, top–down bureaucracy. During the NACF's formative period many of the top administrative officials were either active or retired high-ranking military officers. Unlike the Taiwanese case, there was no external body like the JCRR arguing for farmer-member participation in NACF governance.

It also appears that the different trajectories in regime consolidation produced some differences in modes of behaviour at the macro level. While both countries had P/C as the dominant mode, the system appears to have been less hierarchical in Taiwan, with more independent, or quasi-independent, bodies influencing policy and a greater role for the market. For example, Korean economic policy-making was centralized, the Prime Minister chairing the Central Economic Committee and the Deputy Prime Minister the Economic Planning Board. In Taiwan central planning agencies were more decentralized and generally fell outside formal bureaucratic structures (Cheng *et al*. 1996; Scitovsky 1985; Patrick 1994).

Overall, while P/C elements dominated in both countries, Korea's macro-policy-making appears to have been more centralized and interventionist, while in Taiwan a more decentralized approach was in evidence, with greater elements of COOP motivation. These differences in the political economy context were reflected in differences in the behavioural dynamics of the FA and the NACF. The structures and operational norms of the FOs are examined next.

6.3.2. *Overview of Organizational Structures*

As formal organizations, both the Korean and Taiwanese FOs had similar historical antecedents in the colonial period. FOs became official entities during the Japanese occupation when rural self-help groups that had been established among the

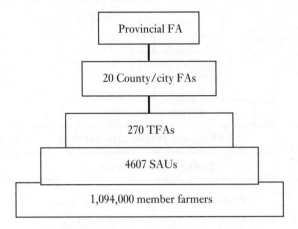

Figure 6.1. *Taiwan FA organizational structure*
Source: Kwoh (1966) and Mao and Schive (1995).

land-owning elite were made part of the colonial administrative apparatus. During the Japanese colonial period, these groups helped to mobilize local resources for the increased production of agricultural commodities as part of overall policies that incorporated the Taiwanese and Korean rural economies into the infamous Greater East Asian Co-Prosperity Sphere (see Kwoh 1966; Jong 1991).

Following the Second World War, between 1946 and 1953, the Taiwanese FA underwent a substantial reorganization. A critical player in these decisions was the JCRR. Based upon the JCRR's recommendations, the FA developed into its present three-tier, vertically organized structure, comprising FA units at the township, county/city, and provincial levels (see Fig. 6.1).

By the 1980s, there were 291 FAs in existence, made up of 1 at the provincial, 20 at the county/city, and 270 at the township levels. Their membership totalled 1,094,000, including over 90 per cent of all farm households. Under the township FAs (hereafter TFAs), there were 4607 small agricultural units (SAUs), one in each village on average, acting as a bridge between the TFA staff and farmer-members, and serving as the basic unit for election purposes (see Lee and Chen 1979: 43). Agencies within the PDAF provided overall supervision of FA operations. A similar, but proportionally smaller, organizational structure existed in the earlier period.

In Korea, the functions and structures of FOs linked to the colonial era administration also underwent reorganization between 1946 and 1961, resulting in a similar three-tier, vertically linked NACF organization.[2] By the 1980s, there were more than two million member farm households in 1545 primary and 140 special cooperatives, supervised by nine provincial offices under the control of the central NACF bureau.

---

[2] In 1981, the system underwent further reorganization, becoming a two-tier organization comprising only national and local-levels, with county-level units merged with provincial units into the federation (national) level and the PACs (township units) as the primary local-level NACF agencies.

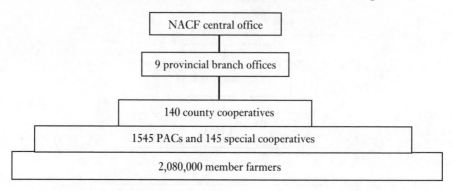

Figure 6.2. *NACF organizational structure*

Source: adapted from Lee *et al.* 1977.

More than 90 per cent of farm households were members of primary agricultural cooperatives (PACs), with the average PAC unit containing about 1200 members (see Fig. 6.2).

No JCRR equivalent existed in Korea, which received US aid in a more traditional fashion, that is, via line ministry allocations coming through the Economic Planning Board. Instead, the highly centralized Korean bureaucracy directed organizational policy changes as well as resource allocations to the NACF. As a consequence, compared to Taiwan, the macro and micro policy environment in Korea was less flexible and accommodating of organizational changes which might have strengthened COOP horizontal linkages between staff and farmer-members.

6.3.3. *Group Behaviour and FO Effectiveness*

Unlike irrigation and other natural resource systems or public goods, the provision of FO services does not fall neatly into the category of a common-pool resource (CPR) problem (see Ostrom *et al.* 1990). Although some of the benefits deriving from FO services share the common feature with CPRs of being costly to exclude beneficiaries, one member's usage does not necessarily subtract from the amount available to others. 'Free-rider' problems are, therefore, not as debilitating as with CPRs. Moreover, because of their parastatal character, collective action problems involved in organizing FO services are also not as relevant because government agencies ultimately ensure provision.

It is, however, with the quality of FO services that collective action and effective group functioning factor in. The effectiveness of FO services depends to a large degree on the interdependent efforts of both officials and members, something referred to in the literature as 'co-production' (Ostrom 1996). For example, FO marketing services require not only technical knowledge related to storage and transportation on the part of staff, but also the time-specific and place-specific local knowledge of the commodities to be marketed that only farmer-members possess. With regard to extension and credit services, the scientific information and administrative skills of FO staff are clearly key, but so is the utilization of such services by farmer-members, to generate efficiency gains through economies of scale.

Working together as a group is, thus, important for FO performance, and inputs from both sets of actors are necessary. In order for group efforts to succeed, incentives must be in place that motivate actors to work collectively towards similar goals. The collective action problem, therefore, is less one of ensuring individual contributions of effort, as in irrigation groups, than one of ensuring that efforts are focused on increasing collective rural welfare. Such group dynamics are not intrinsic to the FO setting, but are conditioned by group relationships within the organization, as well as interactions with the external environment in which the group operates. Organizational variables are particularly important because they help to define the parameters within which interactions between staff and farmer-members take place. Different organizational structures and processes foster different rule- and norm-based relationships, generating principal/agent relationships of varying degrees of effectiveness.

6.4. INTERNAL ORGANIZATIONAL DIFFERENCES AFFECTING GROUP BEHAVIOUR

As we have seen, on the surface the NACF and the FA had similar formal organizational structures, but there were variations in internal structure and process, affecting group behaviour, leading to differences in organizational performance.

6.4.1. *Degree of Operational and Financial Autonomy*

The FOs in both Korea and Taiwan were far from being autonomous grass roots organizations. Rather, they were more akin to parastatals (Mengistu 1993), operating with a heavy dose of central government control and carrying out a number of activities on behalf of the government, such as rice collection and fertilizer distribution. In both countries, village-level FO affairs were strongly regulated by county offices, which, in turn, were directly supervised by the FO provincial and/or national bureaux and ultimately central government ministries. It was not uncommon to have extensive interaction between central government and FO officials at all levels (Aqua 1974).

On closer examination, however, there appear to have been variations in the degree of autonomy under which the two systems operated. The key difference was that, at the local level, Taiwan's FO had relatively more autonomy over the operation of day-to-day activities than Korea's, even though in both cases higher level supervisory bodies often made important organizational decisions. This difference stemmed in part from the strength of Taiwan's TFAs (the lowest organizational level in direct contact with farmer-members) relative to local-level NACF units (PACs) during the first decade of organizational development. Self-financing possibilities for local activities depended on these TFA's capacities to generate funds through the development of local banking operations. This occurred from the outset within the FA system through the TFAs, while PAC (township level) banking operations were only consolidated during the 1970s in the NACF system.

The TFAs had to live with a more binding budget constraint based on locally generated funds than did their Korean counterparts, which were more dependent on central transfers. From the outset of FA establishment, TFAs were expected to operate more or less as self-sustaining economic enterprises (Davison 1993: 198). FA staff members in Taiwan were, therefore, more dependent on the success of local services provided under their supervision, which often generated revenues that supported other FA activities. Moreover, because a greater share of operational funds was generated locally, Taiwan's TFAs also had more operational latitude in making decisions about the allocation of local expenditures.

Degree of Member Participation in Local Decision-making

Again, as a result of their institutional history as parastatals, both the FA and the NACF had limited participatory structures for members. In Korea, only after the 1989 NACF reforms (see Burmeister 1999), were members able to elect PAC presidents, and, for the first time, have some institutionalized voice in organizational governance.

In Taiwan, farmer-members, meeting in small units comprised of members of the same village, voted once every four years for representatives to the TFA assembly, whose main functions were to approve or disapprove TFA activity plans and elect a board of directors and a board of supervisors (Kwoh 1966: 2). The board of directors met every two months and was charged with the policy-making functions of township associations, the most important of which was the selection of a general manager in charge of the TFA's daily functioning and policy implementation. The board of supervisors, on the other hand, dealt only with the auditing of accounts. This process was repeated at both the county and provincial levels (see Fig. 6.3).

Although Taiwanese farmers, thus, had more formal channels through which to participate in FA affairs, the extent to which this actually resulted in greater accountability and responsiveness on the part of FA officials was limited, mainly because they had a direct participatory role at only the most basic level, that is, in electing township assemblies, while for those township bodies actually charged with policy-making powers, that is, the board of directors, farmer-member input was often indirect at best. Especially further up in the organizational hierarchy, the impact of farmer participation became more diluted, as the provincial board of directors was selected by representatives three times removed from direct election by farmer-members (see Fig. 6.3) (see de Lasson 1976: 226–30).

Moreover, the election for FA township representatives was a heavily politicized matter, with intense political competition (de Lasson 1976: 173–84) which might involve vote-buying and the use of patron–client, friendship, and kinship ties to solicit votes (Stavis 1974: 100). The selection process was, therefore, often dominated by concerns which were independent of professional qualifications or farmer preferences.

Even though the election system may have been subject to corrupt practices and was judged to be of limited effectiveness in institutionalizing democratic principles of representation, this flawed election process was, it appears, important for group motivation

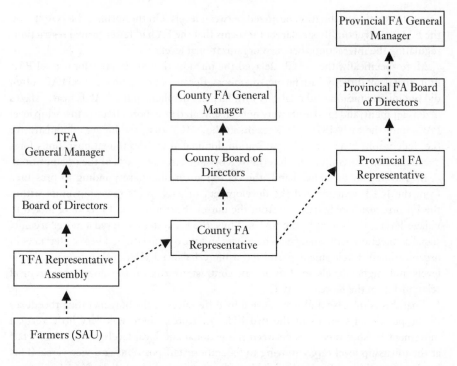

Figure 6.3. *Election system in Taiwan's FAs (◀ ----- = Direction of Elections)*

Source: Stavis (1982: 219).

in Taiwan. From a sample of farmer-members drawn from different TFAs, de Lasson (1976: 219) found that over 65 per cent perceived the FA as belonging to members, and that 49.5 per cent believed that this was because members 'controlled' the FA.

Rather than formal mechanisms, however, informal channels may have been the more important means for members to affect decision-making processes. Although in neither case did interactions between farmer-members and FO decision-making staff occur on a frequent basis, it appears that Taiwanese farmers had much more access. Wade (1982: 84) reported, for example, that in the case of Korean irrigation associations (which he took to be similar to NACF operational modes in important ways), face-to-face communication by farmers with directors was rare. In contrast, de Lasson (1976: 202) reported that, in a sample of 337 FA members, nearly 30 per cent talked with the TFA General Manager at least once during the season, and over 70 per cent at least once during the year, and that communication with the chiefs of the village-level SAUs, charged with conveying concerns to FA officials, was even more frequent.

6.4.2. *Hierarchical Relations within the FOs*

The extent of hierarchy in organizational relationships also affected group behaviour by influencing the degree to which local concerns were transmitted vertically and the extent to which coordination occurred between levels. On the surface, the NACF and the FA were structurally similar, but it seems that the FA had fewer formal restrictions regulating the interactions between organizational levels.

More specifically, the NACF delayed the introduction of effective local-level PAC units that dealt directly with farmer-members. Because of this, village-level PACs often did not initiate meaningful relations with farmer-members in the NACF's early stages of development; and local units were not consolidated into more effective township level PACs until the early 1970s. As a result, in the NACF case, the higher administrative (i.e. federation) levels of the organization dominated organizational operations for a decade before township (local-level) PACs became effective parts of the organization.

In Taiwan, on the other hand, the central government, responding to pressures from the JCRR, encouraged the development of grass roots township units within the FA organizational structure from the outset. Furthermore, TFAs were linked to village-level groups, that is, the SAUs. Thus, the FA system fostered a more 'organic' social connection between farmer-members and the organization. These differences in organizational development permitted a more balanced relationship between local-levels and higher levels in Taiwan, in contrast to a more top-down, hierarchical relationship in the Korean NACF.

That this is the case is also suggested by differences in the bureaucratic procedures in the personnel systems of the two FOs. In Korea, there was very little vertical movement by staff members between the national and local levels, with NACF staff at the township level rarely moving to federation staff positions and vice versa. This hindered the ability of federation field staff to acquire local knowledge or to familiarize themselves with membership interests particular to specific localities. In fact, the NACF personnel system was effectively separated into a higher status federation level subsystem and a lower status PAC level subsystem, with different recruitment practices and career ladders within these subsystems (Wade, personal communication). This strong bureaucratic separation within the organization fostered a hierarchical divide between the federation and the PAC levels of the NACF that attenuated information flows between the levels and may have accentuated the influence of central government directives and reduced that of farmer-member preferences.

In Taiwan, on the other hand, there seemed to be more opportunities for staff to move between organizational levels. Hierarchical relations in Taiwan were mitigated by the system linking upper and lower level FA directorates. The chairs of the boards of directors at the lower level FAs acted as representatives to higher level FA assemblies, thereby serving as institutionalized links between upper and lower levels of the organization. This connection helped to promote more flexible intra-organizational personnel movements (Davison 1993: 194).

Furthermore, the mainlander-Taiwanese ethnic divide manifested itself in the FA hierarchy in a way that may have made higher level FA units more responsive to farmer-member entreaties. de Lasson (1976: 245) reports that FA staff at the TFA level was entirely Taiwanese in ethnic composition, whereas mainlanders comprised 40 per cent of staff in the provincial FA offices. TFA officials were, in a sense, representing a unified ethnic bloc, which, as we have said earlier, resented mainlander domination, which may have made them keener to represent farmer-members in decision-making.

6.4.3. *Personnel Policies*

The FO hiring and promotion practices also affected group action by influencing the incentives facing FO officials in their provision of services. In both countries, practices favoured a commitment to local development initiatives, compared with elsewhere (Wade 1982). For the most part, FO offices in township-level FOs in both Korea and Taiwan were staffed locally, with the majority of staff born in the locality in which they served. Furthermore, FO staff members in both the FA and the NACF were not greatly differentiated from their farmer membership in terms of education or income levels. In fact, many of them were farmers themselves, with a prime motivation for working in rural areas being the ability to be near their farms (de Lasson 1976: 140). The local affiliation of the staff in both organizations was important because it meant that workers had a vested interest in the area of the township FOs. Moreover, the 'embeddedness' of local staff in the local community contributed to a sense of shared mutual obligations and experiences that enhanced staff accountability. In both countries, higher ranking staff at the township level tended to remain in the same position for long durations, often 15 years or more in Taiwan (Stavis 1982: 96). This practice contributed to group motivation, as interaction with the same group of farmers over a long period necessarily encouraged the development of good relations between staff and farmer-members.

6.4.4. *Identity Formation*

In Taiwan, membership in the FA involved two different levels—a category of full members who received more than half of their income from farming and a category of associate members who were rural residents not engaged in full-time farming. Although full and associate members had access to all FA services, only full members could vote for FA representatives. This dual membership system helped strengthen the role of farmer-members in the organization, instituting a sense that the FA was truly a vehicle for serving mainly collective farming interests. Furthermore, the village-level SAUs, as sites of FA activities that brought neighbours together in their status as farmer-members, undoubtedly contributed to feelings of collective identity.

By contrast, identity formation within the NACF seemed much less strong. This was brought home to one of the authors (Burmeister) in fieldwork settings, when farmers, talking about the NACF as an organization and its activities, used the term 'government' interchangeably with 'agricultural cooperative.' The bureaucratic distance we have described earlier that characterized NACF inter-unit relationships, and the fact that it took time for viable PAC units to develop, generated a greater feeling of NACF remoteness among farmers.

6.4.5. *Organizational Differences and Modes of Group Behaviour*

In terms of the theoretical framework laid out in Chapter 1, the combination of organizational differences between the FA and the NACF outlined above led to some differences in group behaviour between the two organizations. Both were largely P/C, but in the FA system, elements of COOP relationships between FA staff and farmer-members were institutionalized as a result of a combination of greater farmer-member participation in organizational governance and a heightened sense of group identity among farmer-members. Moreover, the greater operational and financial autonomy of the TFAs, combined with a more binding budget constraint, which linked profitability to performance, created more M behavioural norms. Further evidence of how these differences affected organizational performance is presented in the next section.

6.5. COMPARATIVE FO PERFORMANCE

Both the FAs and the NACF were organized as multipurpose organizations, providing a variety of services. These included the marketing of farm products, the sale of agricultural inputs such as fertilizer and the provision of agricultural extension services, although this latter function was much more prominent in the FA system than in the NACF. In addition, both organizations provided credit, insurance, and food processing services, which will not be examined here.

In comparative cross-national assessments of FO performance, both the FA and the NACF do rather well. Esman and Uphoff (1984: 315–17) judged FA performance as 'outstanding' in comparison with other Asian FOs engaged in similar activities. Favourable comparisons have also been made between Korean rural organizations (including the NACF) and South Asian counterparts (see Wade 1982). Positive attributes that distinguish them from other FOs in this comparative literature include ubiquitous local branch offices, which makes their services easily accessible to members; the relative homogeneity of membership which makes identification of relevant services easier for FO officials; and the social accessibility of FA and NACF staff to the membership, that is, local staff were often natives of the areas in which they worked and had similar social status as their farmer-member clientele. The well-functioning nature of both the FA and the NACF was in part responsible for the relatively good agricultural performance in both countries. Nevertheless, organizational differences illuminated in the preceding section did lead to some differences between the FA and the NACF in the effectiveness of service provision, a subject to which we now turn.

Due to the nature of the organizations in both cases, organizational goals were multiple and at times contradictory. Given their parastatal nature, government goals for agricultural sector performance, for example, increasing agricultural productivity, fostering strategic intersectoral linkages, maximizing foreign exchange earnings, or generating domestic savings, were given high priority within the respective FO bureaucracies. But the FA and the NACF were also membership organizations, at least in their legal charters and self-descriptions. As a result, farmer-member concerns with respect to reasonably priced services and their timely provision were considered, if not always honoured, in decision-making.

6.5.1. *Agro-input Supply and Product Marketing*

These two functions are treated together because government-'entrusted' business comprised the major component of FA and NACF activities in these areas. Both governments used the FA and the NACF to achieve strategic policy objectives related to food systems. Tight government controls were placed on the staple foodgrain economy (especially rice) in order to stabilize prices for this politically sensitive commodity. Hyperinflation fuelled by staple food scarcities had been experienced by the KMT on the mainland and during the initial stages of US military government rule in post-liberation Korea. These memories help explain why government intervention in the staple foodgrain sub-sector was so pronounced. Moreover, rice had to be provided at below market prices for the military in both countries. On the agro-input side, fertilizer was in chronic short supply in the early postwar period. As a result, both governments invested substantial resources in the establishment of domestic fertilizer industries as part of import substitution industrialization strategies that created backward inter-sectoral linkages (see Burmeister 1990: 211–13). Farmers were then 'conscripted' to purchase the output of this new industry as soon as production came onstream to ensure economic viability. Both the FA and the NACF were merely collection and distribution agents for these strategic 'entrusted' businesses, with rice marketing and fertilizer supply by far the most important in terms of the value of products and of agro-inputs handled. The FA and the NACF received a set commission for handling rice and fertilizer, with government agencies determining amounts marketed and prices at different stages in the marketing chain.

In terms of aggregate contributions to agricultural development objectives, the fertilizer distribution to farmers increased substantially between the 1960s and the mid-1970s. As a result, Taiwanese and Korean farmers enjoyed some of the highest application rates of fertilizer per unit area in the world. Through FA and NACF channels, farmers thus received inputs that contributed substantially to aggregate productivity increases and promoted staple foodgrain self-sufficiency, important government policy goals during this period. The high level of fertilizer use is indicative of the effectiveness of FOs in both countries.

Where organizational differences show up is in the precise way in which fertilizer distribution was handled. Whereas government agencies determined how much fertilizer the FA and the NACF were to distribute in the aggregate, the FA farmer distribution procedure involved more individual farmer input in determining the amount consumed. The procedure for obtaining fertilizer in Taiwan required a formal application by farmers to TFA units, detailing the area of cultivation, the type of crops to be planted, and an estimate of the amount of fertilizer needed. The TFAs then passed on the application to higher level FA offices who delivered the requisite amounts to the township offices for sale (Lee and Chen 1979: 41). In Korea, this distribution was more centrally directed and involved less farmer input, with the NACF deciding on the requisite amounts of fertilizer, based on overall cadastral and crop information provided by the MAF, as well as on the production estimates coming from the state-controlled fertilizer plants. This amount was then distributed to county and township NACF units for sale to farmer-members (Yang 1979: 112). Field investigations by Aqua (1974: 63), Sorensen (1989: 86), and Reed (1979: 99) attest to the top-down, inflexible nature of the NACF distribution process from a farmer-member perspective. The bulk of NACF distribution was handled by geographically remote county level offices prior to the 1970s, before many township units had become viable operations. By contrast, in Taiwan, the distribution was handled by local TFAs, thus providing further evidence for our earlier claim that differences in the historical development of the organizational structure of the two FOs led to more 'bottom-up' information flows and more effective demand satisfaction there than in the 'top-down' NACF mode of operation.

Another important performance difference between the FA and the NACF input service was in the fertilizer/rice terms of trade established during the period under review. It is widely acknowledged in the literature that both the Taiwanese and Korean governments sold fertilizer to farmers at prices above the world market level. That said, terms of trade for fertilizer improved over time in Taiwan. Ho (1978: 153) reported that '. . . the fertilizer/rice barter ratio for aluminium sulphate, the most widely used fertilizer in Taiwan, fell from 1.5 kg of rice per kg of ammonium sulphate in 1949 to 0.9 kg in 1960 and 0.53 in 1972.' While fertilizer was provided by the NACF to Korean farmers at prices below domestic fertilizer production costs during the period under review, the data do not reveal a comparable downward farm-gate price trend as noted for Taiwan. Rather, Moon (1984: 75–6) concluded that '. . . Korean farmers . . . have paid high fertilizer consumption taxes . . .' In effect, Korean farmers helped to subsidize the domestic fertilizer industry which was the starting point for the petrochemical component of Korea's heavy industrialization drive in the 1970s.

The more favourable terms of trade for fertilizer in Taiwan may be indicative of relatively more effective FA articulation of farmer interests within the government bureaucracy. de Lasson (1976: 245–6), for example, attributes this positive outcome from the farmer-members' perspective to greater FA ability to make 'suggestions' to government about policy changes that farmers favoured.

In terms of marketing services, neither the FA nor the NACF had stellar records with regard to self-initiated marketing activities. Evaluation studies (de Lasson 1976: 268, 339; Brake *et al.* undated: 31, 36), completed in the 1970s, indicated farmer dissatisfaction with FO performance in developing stable market outlets for cash crops. This was one of the most glaring weaknesses of FA and NACF operations, as both FOs had difficulty establishing cooperative marketing outlets that facilitated farm household diversification into higher value commodity production.

In the NACF case, government attempts to use the NACF to encourage crop diversification had negative consequences for organizational legitimacy among farmer-members. A particularly painful example was the infamous 'sweet potato' incident in 1965 (Hans *et al.* undated: 33). As part of a government attempt to promote the local production of sweet potato inputs for industrial alcohol manufacturers, the NACF was ordered to allocate production quotas to farmer-members in traditional sweet potato production areas with promises of favourable producer purchase prices. Due to budgetary shortfalls, the government failed to honour its purchase commitment to the NACF. There were several unruly protest demonstrations at NACF offices in affected regions, generating widespread negative publicity for the NACF and damaging farmer-member confidence in the organization. In Taiwan, however, this type of crop promotional activity, orchestrated by the FA, seems to have been more successful. Stavis (1974: 83–4), for example, cites successes in FA involvement with high-value mushroom and asparagus export production, which provided significant income increases for farmer-members.

6.5.2. *Extension Services*

While extension departments were important components of both the FA and the NACF organizational structures, extension outreach activities were quite different in each FO. In Taiwan, the central government placed responsibility for agricultural research with the provincial research department. This department developed new technologies and passed them on to the FA for testing and diffusion. In Korea, by contrast, primary responsibility for both research and extension was housed in a separate agency, the Office of Rural Development (now the Rural Development Administration), administered by the MAF. This meant that the FA in Taiwan was actively engaged in a variety of agricultural technology improvement projects, whereas the NACF's role was much more limited in terms of technology promotion and diffusion. In describing what the NACF 'guidance bureaux' (the extension department) did, the Korean Agricultural Sector Study (KASS) evaluation reported that 'NACF field personnel tend to be generalists and guidance activities are concentrated on developing annual plans and on implementing the lending program and collecting loans.' (Brake *et al.* undated: 36). By contrast, in Taiwan, extension agents were conduits for strategic technical components of improved farming practices such as better seed varieties and livestock reproduction techniques. Stavis' analysis (1974: 81–5) of FA extension activities affirmed patterns of easy communication between extension agents and farmer-members, facilitated by the fact that many extension agents were themselves farmers.

Brandt's (in Ban *et al.* 1980: 270) observations on typical Korean communication patterns in extension work are illustrative of important procedural differences in the two countries. He reported that village heads were often summoned to township offices to meet rural guidance (extension) officers. The officers relayed advice to the village leader who then went back to his village and imparted this advice to farmers. By contrast, FA extension agent procedure was often to go to SAU meetings of FA farmer-members in the villages. This procedure reveals not only the more participatory nature of extension programme communication patterns in Taiwan, but also that this pattern of small-group FA social interaction about farming matters of common concern, undoubtedly, increased farmer-member identification with the FA as 'their' association and enhanced elements of COOP behaviour.

This responsiveness was organizationally reinforced by the way in which extension activities were funded. Township level units were responsible for funding part of local-level extension activities out of FA operating profits. Kwoh (1966: 11) reported that in 1962 total expenditures for FA extension services were funded from the following sources: 14.6 per cent from membership dues and contributions; 31.7 per cent from extension service fees; 13.2 per cent from the net profits of FA business operations; 8.1 per cent from other sources; and only 32.4 per cent from government subsidies. This substantial degree of internal financing meant that local TFAs had some voice in what kind of extension activities were supported and that TFA officials could be held accountable by the membership for services performed, enhancing the incentives for efficiency. de Lasson's report (1976: 255) indicates that this autonomy resulted in rural development initiatives in both farming and non-farming activities.

The ability of local-level TFAs to become involved in a range of non-agricultural development activities (see Ranis and Stewart 1993) was absent in the NACF system. In fact, to the extent that the NACF guidance bureaux were involved at all in rural development promotion, they were enlisted by the MAF and the Ministry of Home Affairs to help implement high profile national projects such as the Tongil high yield variety diffusion effort (see Burmeister 1988), and various village improvement schemes implemented as part of the later vintage Saemaul rural development initiative (see Brandt and Lee 1979), both of which were unpopular with many farmer-members. NACF's participation as an implementation agent in these national mobilization campaigns indeed damaged its credibility as a farmer-member-oriented organization responsive to member needs and preferences.

6.6. CONCLUSIONS

We should start by emphasizing that both countries had very good agricultural performances, and in both countries one reason for this was the effectiveness of their FOs. However, Taiwanese agricultural performance was somewhat better than that of Korea, and its rural development appears to have been more equitable. While both FOs were primarily organized in a hierarchical P/C fashion, in this chapter we have pointed to a number of organizational and other differences that led to the Taiwanese FA having more COOP elements than the Korean NACF. This, along with other differences, may account for the better performance of Taiwanese agriculture and also contributed to the undoubted greater success of Taiwan's rural non-agricultural activities.

The co-production literature (see Evans 1996) provides ideas that help us theorize about linkages between group behaviour, parastatal organizational structures, and organizational performance. The external macro-political environment in post-Second World War Korea and Taiwan, coupled with the ability to build on the rural organizational infrastructure left over from the Japanese colonial period, elicited a parastatal organizational response to agricultural service needs in the two countries. This political economy environment systematically infused the P/C mode of group operation into the FA and the NACF systems, especially with regard to strategic business activities 'entrusted' to the FOs by the two central governments. A co-production synergy was established between the state, the FOs, and their farmer-members, as state agents had the power to mobilize resources that enhanced FO organizational effectiveness; for example, the state was able to secure supplies of needed agro-inputs and credit valued by FO farmer-members, while the FOs had the dense organizational infrastructure needed to deliver these strategic inputs to millions of minifarm households, many of which had been economically empowered by the postwar land reforms. This relationship was based on resource complementarities between state agencies and the FOs. The P/C mode of operation was instrumental in establishing this complementarity through vertical coordination relations between state agencies and the FO delivery system.

But complementarity is only one half of the co-production synergy equation conceptualized by Evans (1996). The other essential component is social embeddedness. That is, co-production synergy also requires notions of shared projects between parastatal (or other state-fostered) organizations and a recipient clientele or membership group. In the context of FO operations, to the extent that FO staff and farmer-members seem to be part of the same local society, are perceived as social equals, and feel comfortable working together to achieve common goals, we can speak of socially embedded relations between them. Embeddedness promotes more efficient service provision by facilitating horizontal information flows within the organization, by providing a degree of voice to the membership or clientele, and by promoting ideas among the membership about their right to monitor performance.

The major difference between FA and NACF organizational effectiveness resided in the greater degree of embeddedness that characterized the FA system, making the FA's co-production synergy relationships more robust than those of the NACF. In group behavioural terms, greater embeddedness within the FA system elicited stronger COOP modes of group operation and greater efficiency. This meant that the operational rigidities associated with P/C organizational attributes were modified in more flexible and responsive directions. As indicated earlier, both the macro-political economy environment and the external policy environment were responsible for this organizational difference.

As a cautionary postlude, we must reiterate that our study encompasses an earlier period (1960–80) of FA and NACF institutional history, focusing largely on an era when agriculture was still the dominant sector in both economies. Given the different problems agriculture now faces in both countries (see Bain 1993; Burmeister 1992; Davison 1993), it might be argued that neither FO has been especially effective in facilitating farmer-member adjustment to the drastic decline in the relative role of the agricultural sector, to rapid domestic development, and to a globalizing world economy. Bain (1993) and Davison (1993) describe a mostly negative FA metamorphosis, characterized by increased factional politicization and rent-seeking, as agriculture is increasingly subsidized instead of taxed. Burmeister (1999) sees positive changes afoot in the contemporary NACF, with an increasingly responsive organization sensitive to farmer-member concerns about the future of Korean agriculture. The assessment of how the Taiwanese and Korean FOs have dealt with agricultural adjustment issues in the 1980s and 1990s requires another analysis. Our comparative study remains, we believe, however, highly relevant to developing countries at earlier stages of development.

7

Has the Coffee Federation become Redundant? Collective Action and the Market in Colombian Development

ROSEMARY THORP

7.1. INTRODUCTION

This paper considers the role and *modus operandi* of a remarkable and controversial group: the National Coffee Federation of Colombia. Over time, the Federation has been both respected and criticized, often fiercely. Today its role is being challenged as inappropriate to the new commitment, in Latin America, and specifically in Colombia, to a free market economy, and as an obstacle to a 'level playing field'. To evaluate both the past and the contemporary challenge, we need to explore the origins and historical role of the Federation, over its seventy years of existence, to provide a basis for an attempt at imagining Colombia without its Federation, and by that means for evaluating what its true role is today.

The paper first considers the puzzle of the Federation's birth and continued survival. As Mancur Olson remarked in a conference in Bogotá, based on his own theory of collective action, the Coffee Federation of Colombia should not exist.[1] Free rider problems consistently lead to the break up of rural producer associations with large numbers of small producers. Yet the Federation is in its eighth decade of existence. Olson finds that the answer lies in the compulsory tax imposed on the coffee sector; Robert Bates, who shares Olson's surprise and his view of the importance of the tax, emphasizes in addition that it was politicians, not producers who took the decision to create and continue the Federation.[2]

While we share in the view of the importance of the compulsory tax, we consider that it still remains to be explained how this was sustained through time. We are not happy with the view which ascribes an overriding importance to the politicians' role. This paper seeks to tease out a fuller story of the institutional, political, and economic

I thank Judith Heyer, Frances Stewart, and Pam Lowden for their helpful comments on an earlier draft. I also thank the Coffee Federation of Colombia for their collaboration and assistance with this study. Financial support was provided by WIDER.

[1] Olson (1997), paper presented in Bogotá on the occasion of the 70th anniversary of the Federation.
[2] Bates (1997: 60).

complexities behind the Federation. We hope this will lead to a clearer assessment of its role in the development and the macro stability of the Colombian economy, the latter being something which has long intrigued observers.

The necessary background to the discussion is the particular nature of the Colombian coffee economy and its political economy. These are described in the first section. The second section analyses the political economy of the formation and early years of the Federation. The third considers the institutional consequences of the rupture represented by the Second World War and the consequent evolution of the role of the Federation in the postwar period. The fourth considers the Federation as coffee declined in importance in the Colombian economy and as the Federation is increasingly seen as an institutional anomaly in a neo-liberal world.

7.2. THE COLOMBIAN COFFEE SECTOR

The best-known and fundamental facts about Colombian coffee are first its potentially very high quality, and second the absence of economies of scale in planting and harvesting. The best coffee is grown at an altitude where only steep slopes prevail. Machinery is unusable because of the terrain and because quality responds to individual picking of berries ripening unevenly. The need for discipline in picking and in cleaning the ground produces a principal agent problem, more important with recent disease problems,[3] to which the traditional and effective solution has been family labour. With appropriate discipline, both high productivity and high quality can be obtained on plots under one hectare in size.[4] Even the first stage in processing, the *beneficio*, which removes the pulp, can be economically performed at a very small scale, since the coffee can be dried in the sun, which with limited electric power is often economical. The bottleneck is the large amount of water required (though recent technological improvements have drastically reduced this[5]). The possibility of interplanting food with coffee, useful as shade for the coffee, provides a subsistence base for the family which makes it resilient to bad times. In all these numerous ways, the small family farm has appeared as something worth conserving in coffee growing. Large estates have played their part, especially in Cundinamarca and Tolima, but their role has decreased with time.[6]

The problem is that economies of scale exist, in threshing, warehousing, roasting and subsequent transporting, and marketing high quality coffee, with the attendant needs for brands, quality control, guarantees, and publicity. Here lie the collective action problems, made all the more significant by the fact that the quality of coffee is very sensitive to the exact area in which it is grown, and to its treatment at all stages.

---

[3] The broca, an insect imported from Africa and very damaging to productivity, can best be controlled at the moment by removing every last ripe berry from the tree, so depriving the insects of food, and by assiduous removal of infected fruit from the ground, though insecticides and the use of parasites which eat the grub are being worked on at CENICAFE (interview, Director of Cenicafe, Manizales 1998).

[4] To secure an *income* above the poverty line, however, more than one hectare is typically required.

[5] By a factor of 40! And with a simple and easily accessible technology and beneficial recovery of by-products.

[6] The structure of property changed greatly between the 1920s and the 1960s, both with estates being divided and with expansion occurring in the areas typified by small farms.

Both factors imply a need for control and monitoring. Productivity also responds to the provision of a number of public goods—roads, health, and education being chief among them.

Two further characteristics of the Colombian coffee sector which have consequences for collective action should be noted. The first is the regional concentration of small-scale production, which has facilitated organization.[7] The second concerns the political economy of the Colombian coffee sector: there are wealthy coffee producers and wealthy coffee families, but often (though not always) they own only a modest *finca*, or farm. The bulk of their wealth typically comes from coffee trading, financial activities, commerce, in general, and real estate—activities often derived from coffee, but not from large-scale production of coffee. In more recent years, of course, wealth has come from industry as well. In addition, the labour intensive nature of coffee production has limited the potential for reinvestment of the surplus back in coffee. Thus, in the decades we consider first, the 1920s and 1930s, when the Federation was born, many well-known politicians came from coffee families, and might well have had a direct interest in a coffee farm, though they could hardly be described first and foremost as coffee producers. They were typically looking elsewhere for profitable opportunities to invest the money made, directly or indirectly, from coffee. This striking characteristic has had three major consequences over time. First, those with organizational capacity and resources have formed an elite within the sector, even though they may have been small producers of coffee. Second, the various politicians who over the decades have fought the Federation have very often shared an underlying common *interest* with the coffee sector.[8] Third, the coffee elite has been interested in investment opportunities elsewhere in the economy. These facts modify any sectoral clashes of interest.[9] Battles might be fought over the manner of organization of the sector, or exactly how to promote coffee abroad—but never over the fundamental role of coffee and the Federation as its key international agent.

7.3. THE EARLY YEARS

For the first thirty years of the twentieth century, Colombia conformed to the general tendency: efforts to form a producers' association failed.[10] In 1920, under pressure of market collapse, the efforts even rose to the height of calling the first Coffee Congress and constituting a *Junta Delegataria* to defend Colombian coffee in the international market. The organization subsequently disappeared without trace.[11] The collapse of boom into bust in the 1920s left the sector vulnerable, as big traders collapsed

---

[7] Montenegro (1996) and (1999) elaborate on the significance of this point.

[8] A classic and extreme example might be President Alfonso Lopez Pumarejo himself, who in his first government (1936–40) fought various battles with the Federation (e.g. over whether it should be taken more fully into the public sector, and over output restrictions) while himself belonging to one of the biggest coffee families of Colombia.

[9] For a brilliant and subtle description of the politics of coffee, see Palacios (1980), especially chapter 10.

[10] The early efforts are described with full documentation in Junguito and Pizano (1997), the definitive history of coffee institutions, and above all the Federation, and a key source for all that follows.

[11] Junguito and Pizano (1997: 2).

and/or abandoned Colombia. By 1927 the price was weakening. Impending economic crisis again forced action: this time traders and producers persuaded the Government of Antioquia to convoke a further Congress, in Medellin in June. Here the Coffee Federation was born. Its functions were assigned to be:[12]

- to adopt and get adopted by official bodies effective measures to ensure the development and defence of the sector
- to oversee the effective application of legal provisions affecting coffee
- to get cost-reducing measures adopted
- to get the best possible conditions of transport for coffee
- to direct publicity efforts inside Colombia and abroad.

A proposal for a tax on coffee arose at this first congress, to be rejected after much debate. It appears to have come from the representatives of government—specifically the Ministry of Industry.[13] The government presumably saw an opening to achieve what had hitherto been unthinkable—a tax on coffee sales—if the proceeds were handed over almost in their entirety and under contract to the coffee sector—namely to the Federation. The Congress, however, concluded with a robust recommendation, that apart from the already existing tax on river transport, the sector should bear no tax whatsoever at any level.[14] The next year, however, the National Committee, constituted by the Congress as the permanent body of the Federation, with full authority when Congress was not in session, returned to the subject and accepted the idea, despite the depressed international price. The revenues were to come to the Federation under a contract which governed the use of the resources, to last for an initial period of ten years.

This was a historic breakthrough, without which the initiative of the Federation would probably have gone the way of previous efforts. The breakthrough was a product of crisis, and was consolidated by the crisis which now worsened. As the coffee price declined, coffee producers and traders fell increasingly into debt. The need to agree action with and through the state became increasingly apparent. Ways of cutting costs became of supreme importance. The 1929 Congress adopted the final version of the statutes of the new Federation, which was to be financed by a tax on the export of coffee, and in 1934 the Congress proposed an increase in the tax to provide additional resources to the coffee sector. The breakthrough was institutionalized, aided, beyond doubt, by a political and economic crisis that '... allowed the coffee bourgeoisie to weld its class interests to the state in a form as indissoluble as a traditional Catholic marriage ...'.[15]

There was nothing in the prevailing orthodoxy of the time to stand in the way of such a development. Intervention in markets was, if anything, the orthodoxy. Civil society organizations could facilitate the role of the state, by making taxation easier,

---

[12] Quoted in Junguito and Pizano (1997: 7). They discuss the various versions and texts.

[13] Junguito and Pizano, (1997: 6 fn 26).   [14] Acuerdo II, cited in Juguito and Pizano (1997: 6).

[15] Palacios 1980: 211. Palacios documents how in the crucial years between 1929 and 1934 the self-concept and internal organization of the new-born Federation *evolved* towards a strongly centrally controlled group with a key political role.

by assuming certain functions which might otherwise have been performed by the state such as monitoring and control of quality, and marketing. It was only much later that the Federation would be perceived as an obstacle to a 'level playing field', in so far as it both set the rules and entered the market as a player.

In its early days, the Federation was small and elite in nature, its power coming from the overwhelming weight of coffee in the economy, the severity of the economic crisis, the public profile and political connections of leading coffee figures, and the urgency, as perceived by the government as well as the coffee sector, of solving collective action problems to improve the marketing and bargaining power of coffee internationally. Its influence was enhanced by the far-sighted perception of its founding members that it needed to be kept above and apart from the political party strife which dogged Colombian politics and was for decades the source of a high level of violence.[16] The web of services which would in due course—principally in the 1950s and 1960s— create a mass base, was to take time to build. In the early years of the 1930s, coffee moving through the Federation's warehouses amounted to only 10 per cent of the crop. By 1938–39 the Federation was only purchasing 6 per cent of the crop. Its role in exports was even smaller, at 3 per cent.[17] But even from the beginning, the Federation was pursuing the interests of small producers. One of its earliest actions was to purchase coffee in the regions of small producers, where the producer price was a lower proportion of the external price than in regions of large estates, and by so doing raise the price.[18]

The Federation was also beginning to work for the defence of the coffee sector as a whole: in 1931 a share issue was authorized to create the *Caja Agraria*, which began to provide some relief from debt, and in 1932 a premium on the rate of exchange was secured to compensate in part for the weak external market.[19] Other activities included the establishment of warehouses in 1929. But the principal focus of activity was international. Colombian coffee needed representation abroad and an international image. Offices were opened in New York in 1930. The key collective action problem which needed solving to improve the quality of international marketing was that of branding. In 1932, the officers of the Federation, already building the central control which was to mark its history, secured the insertion of a clause into its contract with the government, establishing a registry of marks of origin. They also secured a Presidential decree 'making it illegal to ship coffee from one region under the mark established for another and authorizing the creation of a network of inspectors to enforce the decree'. As Bates comments, 'The members of the national committee then served as a virtual court of law'.[20] This was surely as important as access to tax receipts.

Central management was already showing its ability to perceive the long-run interest of the sector, to deliver, and execute what the government also saw as indispensable, and to retain the trust of the members even while individually they fought to maximize

---

[16] This was emphasized in interviews with Jorge Cardenas, General Manager of the Federation today, Gilberto Arango Londoño, and Diego Pizano, September 1999, Bogotá.

[17] Junguito and Pizano (1997: tables VII-1–VII-4).

[18] Ocampo (1989: 249). The number of members was 4000 in 1930, and already 50,000 in 1934 (p. 248).

[19] Junguito and Pizano (1997: 16).   [20] Bates (1997: 63).

their own short-term interest. From an early date, leading members of the Federation appear to have perceived the value of establishing trust and credibility, both at the macro level of government policy-making and at the micro level of individual small producers. Thus, they worked to establish, with successive governments, their technical authority and integrity, in a way which drew them step by step into the heart of policy-making at the national level. The policy-making concerned coffee, but also went wider, since the elite of the Federation understood how far their own fortunes were knit into both the successful support of coffee and the diversification away from coffee. Thus, from the 1930s successive leaders sought to reinforce an ethos which established the Federation as a highly professional organization, with standards of austerity and discipline that were to become a byword. Many interviewed confirmed the role of the General Manager from 1937 to 1958, Manuel Mejía Jaramillo, in developing a culture of austerity and probity. This was continued by subsequent managers.[21] The key elite members persisted in their policy of keeping the Federation 'above' party politics. This strategy is perceived by many observers today as the key in preserving the 'ethic' of the group relatively free from corruption.[22] The element of professional competence is summed up by Palacios: 'By 1935 it was clear that the coffee group in the FNCC were better able to understand and act in the international market, than the changing Ministers of the Exchequer.'[23]

This culture colours our interpretation of the political struggles between the Federation and the Government. These battles were real. The Government began to work towards a pact with Brazil, allocating export quotas; however, the regional producers making up the National Committee did not favour this, preferring to free ride. The government achieved its end, only to have the pact broken by producers in 1937.[24] Simultaneously, the renegotiation of the Federation's contract with the government in 1935 increased the representation of government in the National Committee from one to six, an event treated by some commentators as a significant swing towards government control. The extent to which this measure was a curtailment of the power of the Federation, however, is debatable. Central management could see that having government representatives present in the key debating chamber increased the value of that chamber as a means to concert coffee policy, and certainly placed the Federation at the heart of policy-making.[25] It also increased the management's authority and ability to negotiate solutions in the long-run interest of the sector, against the instinctive short-termism of individual producers. Battles with the government were the necessary stuff of politics: the tax increases on the sector that followed in a steady stream through the 1940s and 1950s ended up in the coffers of the coffee fund which was controlled by the Federation, as we shall see, but it was important for the national government that they could present the result, to *other* sectors of the economy, as the outcome of a battle. Politicians and central management did not exactly orchestrate

---

[21] For example, Mejía was renowned for refusing to use official cars of the Federation. Arturo Gomez, who succeeded Mejía, confirmed this and that he himself continued such practices. (Interview, Buenos Aires, August 1999.)   [22] Interviews cited in fn. 17 above.

[23] Palacios (1980: 309, Endnote 79).   [24] Ocampo (1989), Bates (1997).

[25] *Informes del Gerente*, annual reports to the annual Coffee Congress.

this battle, but there was an underlying perception of its inevitable nature, and trust in the outcome.

7.4. THE COFFEE FUND AND THE POSTWAR FEDERATION

With the Second World War, we come to the second point of rupture. With the abrupt loss of European markets, it was seen as essential by the producing nations of Latin America to share the US market among themselves in an orderly fashion, and to deal with the internal consequences of the resulting quotas. The International Coffee Agreement (ICA) was signed in Washington in November 1940. The government of Colombia decided to create a fund, the *Fondo Nacional del Café*, to buy and sell coffee stocks. This fund was constituted as an account of the National Exchequer, but its management was assigned to the Federation.[26] The General Manager of the Federation was accredited by the Government with powers to represent Colombia abroad and to approve accords on Colombia's behalf. The innovation represented a decisive step in the acceptance of a culture of quotas, as opposed to the previous practice of free-riding on Brazil—a step from which there would now be no turning back.

The enormity of this break was only made apparent once the War was over, and the decision was taken to keep the Fund in existence, and to allow it to invest in 'coffee activity'.[27] The key institutional development now occurred gradually, as the concept of the Fund was broadened to incorporate activities which allowed the coffee sector opportunities to diversify, which could include any income-generating activity. The key instruments here were the various Regional Finance Corporations, created by the Fund as enterprises of the Fund, in the 1960s and 1970s. By this means, the fact that coffee required little direct reinvestment could be turned to advantage, and the need for other channels for investment accommodated, as the coffee surplus was re-allocated, either by the direct investments of those farmers with enough production to have a surplus, or via the investments of the Coffee Fund.

The expansion of functions, to include activities in sectors other than coffee, was made possible by the increase in income. New or increased taxes, or implicit taxes via differential exchange rates, were declared in 1948, 1951, 1958, and 1959. Usually after a debate, the revenue from the tax would be assigned largely to the Fund. The functions of the Fund were broadened to include credit operations designed to broaden coffee market opportunities (1959) and in the 1960s the Fund's role in setting and stabilizing prices was greatly extended. It was given the obligation to act as residual buyer for the entire coffee crop. The Fund developed the marketing of inputs to the sector and increased technical services. Gradually, it became the regulating body of the whole coffee sector, implementing the decisions of the National Committee.[28]

By these means the gradual decline in the importance of coffee in the economy, shown in Table 7.1, could be accommodated without its wealthier producers experiencing

---

[26] Junguito and Pizano (1997: 77). See also Ocampo (1989) for an authoritative account of this period.

[27] Decision of the fifteenth Congress in 1945. See Junguito and Pizano (1997: 16). The investments of the Fund are described on pp. 172ff.

[28] The detail is given in Junguito and Pizano (1997: ch. 2) and in Palacios (1980: 248ff).

Rosemary Thorp

Table 7.1. *Share of coffee in GDP and in agricultural production, 1950–94.*[a] *Five-year averages, in per cent*

Year	GDP (%)	Agricultural value added (%)
1950–54	10.1	25.9[b]
1955–59	10.0	25.6
1960–64	8.2	25.9
1965–69	6.4	22.4
1970–74	2.8	12.1
1975–79	3.5	15.7
1980–84	2.6	15.1
1985–89	2.4	14.4
1990–94		

[a] Excludes products based on coffee.
[b] 1950, 1953, and 1954 only.

Source: adapted from Junguito and Pizano (1991: 43–4)

disadvantages, and without losing its economic influence. Successive government economic teams found it exceptionally useful that restructuring could thus happen harmoniously.

Of course, this diversification happened within the strategy of inward-looking development current at that time. A full evaluation of the developmental significance of the role of the Coffee Fund would require an evaluation of its diverse investments. From the perspective of the 1990s, some were clearly not viable in the longer run, but how far this was a product of too rapid an imposition of an open economy model is a question to be researched. (Certainly the Federation opposed *apertura* in the 1990s.) For our argument here, we wish simply to describe what happened. Its wide role in the economy made the Federation valuable and gave it elements of authority and power, even while coffee as such appeared to be losing its central role.

In fact, the Federation *extended* its influence, by contributing to and participating in *new* organs of government—notably the *Consejo de Política Económica y Social* (CONPES), created in 1967. It is remarkable that of all of civil society, *only* the Federation participates in this crucial Council of Ministers. Its other particularly crucial presence is in the Junta of the *Banco de la República*; it has been present here since the creation of the bank. Other private sector bodies are also present, but the Federation's voice is typically considered to be the one that is crucial.

Thus through the postwar decades the voice of coffee continued to be significant in the key organs of the government. As a result, the Federation was able to ensure that the exchange rate was managed in its own interests. When coffee prices fluctuated, instead of the typical Dutch-Disease-type problems experienced by other primary product producers, Colombia achieved relative stability in macroeconomic terms, and steady management through boom and bust, that contributed to this relative stability.[29]

[29] Montenegro (1996, 1999); Thorp (1991).

For the Federation to have this kind of weight at the level of macroeconomic policy, continued development of the role of the Federation at the micro level was crucial. Above all, the Federation needed to be a major and effective player on the national and international coffee scene. It therefore needed loyal producers committed to selling to it a substantial part of their coffee crop. One obvious route to create loyalty would have been through a substantial margin in the price paid to members. But the Federation knew that the resulting stimulus to production would have undermined the working of the international quota system. So an alternative solution had to be found. This took the form of investment in developing a support structure to small producers and promoting a culture of loyalty. The same micro-level strategy also served to create political support for the Federation's contract for the administration of coffee taxes.

The micro-level role of the Federation developed slowly, though it was there incipiently even in the 1930s. It was seen as important even by the early leaders that to achieve its macro role the organization needed to be a credible mass organization, and further that incorporating more producers would gradually facilitate the solution of collective action problems of monitoring and control. For mass membership to develop, individual producers, small and large, had to learn to trust the Federation and see it as 'their' organization. Services had to be offered so that goodwill and loyalty could be built up. Departmental and Municipal Committees were created in the original design so that producers might develop a sense of ownership. In the 1960s ownership was made explicit through a *Cedula Cafetera*, or membership card, and certain services were only made available to those with *cedulas*. This included technical services and some credit. Arturo Gómez, General Manager of the Federation from 1957, extended the practice of electing Committee members and gave local committees the responsibility for managing the public works carried out by the Federation, which he considers markedly improved the quality and appropriateness of the works carried out.[30] Early data are not available, but by the 1980s Departmental Committees were spending 55 per cent of their funds on public works and services to the community (much of this through the Municipal committees), and about half of the resources of the Federation were being channelled to these Committees.[31] An early measure was a health campaign against malaria. This was a powerful public good in people's perceptions.[32] It was important here that in coffee areas, the fate of the whole community was so tightly tied to coffee, and coffee was so dominant in economic activity, that local expenditure on public works organized by a coffee committee was seen as an expenditure on coffee.

The culture was strongly hierarchical, in a P/C mode. This applied to the position of the General Manager, from the 1930s always a person of considerable influence and power both within and (increasingly) without the Federation. It applied to the National Coffee Committee, comprising the most notable regional coffee figures, skilfully managed by the General Manager but wielding the undeniable power of their regions. It applied to the relations between national, regional, and local committees, and to the

---

[30] Arturo Gómez, interview, Buenos Aires August 1999. He sees the resulting confidence in central management as a great strength in the international negotiations they were conducting in the 1960s.

[31] Data from Junguito and Pizano (1997: 41, 47).

[32] Interview, German Uribe, deputy manager of the Federation, Bogotá, March 1999.

Table 7.2. *The Federation's share of coffee purchases and of exports*[a]

Year	Purchased by the Federation (%)	Federation as % of total coffee exports
1930–34[b]	6.0	1.1[b]
1935–39	10.6	2.4
1940–44	21.0	5.1
1945–49	19.5	3.7
1950–54	12.8	6.7[c]
1955–59	11.5[d]	14.0
1960–64	—	28.2
Almacafe created		
1965–69	58.8	35.5
1970–74	48.7	40.4
1975–79	40.0	49.9
1980–84	57.6	65.6
1985–89	48.0	56.2
1990–94	46.6	44.5
1995–99		

[a] 1932–57: data for 'coffee years'. 1940 is the 1939–40 harvest.
[b] Data 1933–34 only.
[c] No data for 1951.
[d] Data for 1955–57 only.

Source: adapted from Junguito and Pizano (1997: 328–31).

relations of small producers to their local committees. At the local level, cooperatives were gradually formed.[33] It is, however, apparent that these never included many elements of COOP as defined in this project: small producers could attend meetings and propose Committee members, but decision-making processes were never notable for their degree of consultation.

As Table 7.2 shows, by the early 1960s the Federation's purchases represented over 25 per cent of exports. With the creation of a central warehousing facility, *Almacafe*, in 1965, purchases and export sales rose, to an average of over 60 per cent of production purchased and over 40 per cent of exports by the end of the decade.[34] The figures fluctuate greatly with price variations and the growing role of private exporters who could offer a better price in good years, but the share of the harvest bought by the Federation stayed around the same level on average and the share of exports rose into the 1980s.

By all these means, and little by little, a culture was developed, cementing on the part of important sections of the population the sense that the Federation was 'their' creature. What we now know—namely that *government* spending on education and

---

[33] Junguito and Pizano (1997: 58–9). By the 1990s, 59 cooperatives existed, with 120,850 members managing 609 purchasing sites.

[34] *Almacafe* developed also into the branding and grading service of the Federation.

health was *reduced* in coffee areas compared with the rest—was not perceived.[35] The culture was never in practice participatory as it is understood today, but the Federation effectively developed a local presence as 'our' organization, spending 'our' money for 'our' good. The sense of ownership resulted in effective monitoring of local committees by the grass roots.[36]

Producers thus related to the Federation in a range of ways, which we can summarize as M underpinned by COOP and P/C. The principal relationship was the sale of coffee, a monetary transaction in which a below-free-market price was accepted in good times because of the perceived benefits arising from the wide range of other relationships with the Federation, namely price support in bad times, access to technical help and credit, and the value perceived by the more aware members in the Federation's macro claims functions, both nationally and internationally. These elements of reciprocity supported the acceptability of the underlying P/C mode (peasants were more content with their impoverished lot, there were lesser levels of violence and less penetration of guerrillas).

The recent research finding on the extent to which the Federation was substituting for the state in social spending gives us an important clue to the value of the Federation to the government: if the Federation was indeed using tax money for public purposes, in schools, roads, health and so on, then this was a useful delegation. As the Federation developed its professional skills and ethos, it performed many roles useful to the state, given the stake of Colombia in coffee—not least the successful positioning of Colombia in the international market and in international negotiations.[37]

The most serious threat to the whole system over the postwar period was the private exporters' ability to purchase at a better price than the Federation in good times, and effectively free ride on the Federation's provision of marketing, brand development, and publicity. The finances of the Federation depended crucially on the management of the internal price in such a way that it was not only stabilized, but at a level that allowed a margin which represented a useful income for the Coffee Fund, in addition to the coffee tax. By the 1980s the amount raised by this means was roughly equivalent to the value of services to the producer members.[38] Had private exporters taken too much of the market during boom periods, then the system could have been undermined. That this did not happen, owes much to the fact that by the 1960s the culture of the Federation was well developed, though the membership of the Federation never

[35] CRECE (1997). The fact seems to have come as a surprise to many at all levels of the Federation and the general public. The reduction in state spending did not fully compensate for the extra spending by the Federation, but was quite significant.

[36] This was emphasized in the interview with Gilberto Arango Londoño, Bogotá, September 1999. He could not recall a committee member being taken to court: the monitoring was effective at an early stage.

[37] Interviews in the early 1980s, in the course of a previous project, with a number of members of the national Committee, past and present, confirmed how far continuity, and professionalism led to the Colombian delegation outshining all others over the years in the coffee negotiations of the postwar period.

[38] Data for 1986–94 show a total income from this source of US$1092 million, calculating the difference between the producer price paid in Colombia and in other exporting countries. (DOC 012-93, Asesores Nacionales en Asuntos Cafeteros, Bogotá, June 1993.) The value of services to the producer was calculated to be about the same.

exceeded 70 per cent of producers. Loyalty to the Federation and trust in the management of the local cooperative, and the structure above it, was an important asset for the Federation, and a principal institutional characteristic. Trust and loyalty were built up slowly but were clearly evident by the fourth decade of the Federation's existence. One bad experience of being cheated by a non-Federation purchaser was usually enough to confirm producers in a culture that 'they could trust their Federation'.[39]

Membership was not the original source of coffee's power, or of the Federation's political weight. It became important with time, because it provided a defence against free riding. This importance was always in a sense indirect, as a component of the Federation's legitimacy and authority at the national level, rather than the direct delivery of votes or dominance among coffee producers. But it partly explains why many observers agree that the Federation's influence has not contracted as the weight of the sector both in GDP and exports has fallen.[40] As concern about rural violence and drugs has grown, so the mass base of the Federation and the relative peace of coffee areas have become more valued by successive governments. So too has the Coffee Fund's ability and willingness to collaborate in diversification—through the use of the coffee surplus for investment elsewhere rather than through any direct stimulus to producers to collaborate in diversification away from coffee production, where the results so far have not been good.[41]

7.5. THE CHANGING ROLE OF THE FEDERATION: THE 1980s AND 1990s

From the middle of the 1980s and the ending of the most recent coffee bonanza, the role of the Federation has changed. With low coffee prices and the collapse of the ICA in 1988, the Federation has continued to play its role at macro and micro levels only at the expense of the assets of the Fund.[42] At the same time the potential for influence at the grass roots level has grown, as a result of the direct election of mayors starting in 1988 and increased transfers of state funds to the municipal level. The lack of adequate institutions to help channel increased funds results in the coffee committees being able to play an increased role, where they exist. The way this influence is exerted in practice varies, since the Municipal Coffee Committees of the Coffee Federation relate in varying ways to the municipality, given that the departmental Committees have autonomy to set up what rules they like. In Caldas, for example, the Federation's Departmental Committee requires 50–50 funding for public works, and requires the municipal coffee committee to go out and seek this. This gives them leverage with the municipality. If the local mayor does not want to collaborate,

---

[39] Based on interviews with peasant producers in Caldas. The trust expressed by some had its counterweight in vociferous criticisms on other sides. Groups such as the Unidad Cafetera have been fierce critics.

[40] The other reason being the continued wider role the Federation has played.

[41] A classic failure has been citrus fruits. The problem is that the Federation is not well placed to develop markets for non-coffee products.

[42] This is the conclusion of a document prepared for the government representatives in the Comite Nacional de Cafeteros by their assessors, Bogotá, 3 June 1993.

local producers are encouraged to lobby the mayor. The Federation enforces strict controls on contracting and spending in such joint projects, and monitoring is carried out, largely spontaneously, by local groups such as *Grupos de Amistad* and *Clubes de Madres*.[43] Even the severest critics of the Federation (see below) consider that at this level it has on balance improved the effectiveness of the use of resources.[44]

These collective roles, of lobbying and monitoring, depend on a whole culture, developed over decades, which gives the Federation legitimacy, effectiveness, and convocatory power at the local level. The same legitimacy enables it to work alongside peasant producers to control *broca* and introduce '*café tecnificada*' and the associated new culture of production.[45]

At the same time, at the macro level the Federation has come increasingly under fire, as an irrelevance, and impediment, in a neo-liberal world. The fire has intensified with the collapse of the ICA, which has deprived the Federation of a major and prestigious international role. Many would have the Fund abolished and the Federation reduced to a 'mere' professional association. Internationally, the World Bank has been a powerful lobbying force for such an outcome. Nationally, the focus of opposition has come from private exporters, who view the Federation as unfair competition. In the new context of neo-liberal thinking, the Federation is seen as an impediment to the operation of a 'level playing field', since it both sets the rules and participates as a player in the market. What were seen as important functions in the earlier phase—the collective action aspects we have emphasized—are now taken for granted. Producers will continue to cooperate because it is in their interests to do so. The macro roles we have described are ignored, disapproved of, or not fully understood, while the Federation's non-coffee interests are seen as part of a now-discredited ISI model.[46]

To reflect on the challenge, and to evaluate the present-day public good (or bad) role of the Federation, requires that we attempt a difficult exercise of counter-factual analysis, with all the arbitrariness inherent in this.[47] We need to imagine Colombia today without the Federation in the form in which it currently exists, as a product of its specific history.[48]

The first point to make is that the ICA would never have survived as an unusually successful commodity agreement, without Colombia's major role throughout its history, and Colombia would never have developed the web of international offices marketing

---

[43] Based on interviews with members of the departmental Committee and a Municipal Committee in Caldas and on field visits, Caldas, March 1999.

[44] Interview, Oscar Marulanda, Bogotá, March 1999.

[45] Trees are cut right back to a stump after four years and left to regrow, with interplanting of other crops meanwhile, rather than being left untouched for their natural life of 15–20 years.

[46] Oscar Marulanda, interview, Bogotá, March 1999.

[47] A subsequent research effort which could make the counter-factual more solid would be a detailed historical comparison with Costa Rica, where coffee is also produced by small farmers and no entity with the authority of the Federation has developed with the years.

[48] To highlight what Colombia might lose today, by radically reducing the role of the Federation, it does not seem relevant to consider options which are based in a *stronger* interventionist mode, since the pressures for abolishing the Federation come from the opposite quarter. Thus we do not discuss the possibilities opened by for example the rather successful Kenyan Coffee Marketing Board.

coffee and the huge organization monitoring and controlling quality. Colombian coffee today would not have its brand name and its consumer following. None of this would develop spontaneously today either, given the weakness of the coffee market and the propensity to free riding still inherent in small-scale coffee.

The counter-factual therefore needs to be one where coffee income has grown more slowly over the years, and the aggregate wealth of the coffee sector is far less, cumulatively over time. In distributional terms, Colombia would have lost vis-à-vis the world. It might be argued that more diversification would have happened and that this would have been positive. This is doubtful, however, since we have argued that the elite of the coffee sector always had an interest in diversifying. It could even be argued that Colombia actually managed somewhat better than the average medium or large Latin American economy to finesse the relation between its main export crop and the rest of the economy, and that this has at least something to do with the skill and interest of the coffee elite in collaborating in this diversification.[49] Within the sector, coffee wages and small producer incomes were always the outcome of the market. Over time the producer price was not artificially sustained internally, but coffee did benefit from the one outstandingly successful ICA over many years and in that the Federation played a huge role. Coffee incomes in general over the long run would have suffered in that sense from the absence of the Federation—and most importantly, would have fluctuated more. If stability is a good—and we would hypothesize that it is, for the poor—then this is a genuine gain. However, the reality of very low incomes and great poverty at the bottom of the coffee sector is a fact—although it would have been even worse without what has been achieved with coffee. It has also now been made clear, as mentioned above, that poverty was not in fact much reduced by above-average social expenditure in coffee regions, since government expenditure was reduced compared to other regions, in partial compensation for the spending of the Federation.

The counter-factual might well contain a modest producer association, with no resources, no instruments for P/C, more based on COOP. Such an organization would of course play none of the macro roles we have identified—and probably very few of the micro roles. The present loyalty given to the Federation by small producers, the access its extension workers have, the confidence they inspire, would all be lacking. The picture would be one of coffee produced and poorly managed by large numbers of very poor peasant producers. Although we have argued that historically the Federation never solved the problem of low incomes in the coffee sector, it has increased productivity from tiny plots. This would be much reduced as an effect in our counter-factual, and the instruments would be absent for the future. This analysis also provokes a further reflection, starting from the fact that violence and guerrilla penetration is less in coffee areas than in other departments of Colombia.[50] In our counter-factual we must contemplate the possibility that the anarchy and violence characterizing many Colombian departments today might be even worse—a sobering thought. Further,

[49] See Thorp (1998: ch. 3).
[50] Interview, Emilio Echeverrí, Coffee Federation, Bogotá, September 1999.

today the local coffee committees and their networks constitute instruments of access to poor producers; even if they have not been used in a major way in the past to attack low incomes, they represent an institutional instrument available for the future.

A further level to the reflection is the role of local coffee committees relative to local government. Coffee committees effectively channel pressures to make local government spending more effective—and to direct it to the public works the population sees as important.[51] Rural local government is nowhere very effective in Colombia, but it would almost certainly be worse in coffee departments in our counter-factual.

All of this adds up to saying that there are public goods attributable to the existence of the Federation in its present form today. Some of these goods depend heavily on a long, slow process of institution building (particularly of authority, credibility, confidence, etc.). The argument might be made that these elements would not disappear overnight were the Federation to be stripped of its wider roles and reduced to a 'mere' producer association. But it must be seriously questioned how long the institution would survive the consequences of loss of resources, prestige, and authority. The micro role we have described is surely dependent on the culture of legitimacy, professionalism, and authority built up over the years.[52] This is a matter both of political weight and of ethos. Young professionals today choose to work in the core management of the Federation precisely because they understand that it plays a significant social role at many levels, equivalent to a public service post but without the complications of a public sector career, where ethos, continuity, and high standards are concerned.[53]

In Colombia as elsewhere in Latin America, but aggravated by decades of rural violence, there is a notable lack of effective rural development institutions. A culture which monitors and demands responses from the state is to be valued. So is an organization such as the Federation which is well placed to deliver community participation in, say, education or public works, and thus improve the quality of state investment. What the Federation cannot itself deliver are adequate alternatives to coffee, because it does not manage their marketing, or the kind of investment in education that can eliminate poverty among small coffee producers.[54] Here it is the macro level influence of the Federation which is crucial, to lobby for and facilitate state action to provide marketing infrastructure, and to make provision for adequate expenditure on education.

7.6. CONCLUSION

We have argued that it is impossible to understand the history or present-day functioning of the Colombian economy without taking into account the existence and *modus operandi* of the large and complex group—and groups within the group—that

---

[51] Based on interviews in Manizales and in the Department of Caldas, but needing much more work.

[52] This requires research on the reasons why the Federation has influence with small producers. No such study has yet been done.

[53] This is the analysis of Diego Pizano, advisor to the Federation; the idea encountered much resonance in other interviews.

[54] The recent study by CRECE (1997) shows how productivity correlates with education, but not (generally) with size.

is the Federation. We have also argued that the Federation has performed extremely important efficiency and claims functions over time, and that both functions have had outcomes that have improved growth. The efficiency functions involve monitoring and control above all, and the building of an international reputation on that basis. They also involve the purveying of services to small producers. More intangibly, the efficiency function at a macro and meso level has involved a subtle finessing of inter-sectoral relations and adapting of a mono-export economy to a different international climate.

The claims function is clear in regard to Colombia's international position. In regard to other sectors, it is strongly qualified by our analysis of the intersectoral interests of the major actors. The claims function in relation to the mass of producers is complex: the international and national claims functions have given small producers more and more stable income than they would have received under the counter-factual of no Federation—but it has not been concerned with redistribution within the sector or vis-à-vis other sectors.

In relation to modes of operation, we have argued that P/C runs throughout the organization, while M modified by COOP in members' long-run economic interests constitutes the basis of day-to-day relations. The Introduction to this volume posits a 'romantic' hypothesis—a relation between COOP and equity. This is not in evidence in this case. The elements of COOP that exist, do so despite and are embedded in a context of P/C and extreme inequality.[55]

---

[55] Colombia has one of the above-average degrees of income inequality in Latin America. See Thorp (1991).

8

Producer Groups and the Decollectivization of the Mongolian Pastoral Economy

DAVID SNEATH

8.1. INTRODUCTION

This chapter examines the decollectivization of Mongolian pastoralism, and analyses the types of groups and institutional frames within which economic activity was conducted in the collective, pre-collective and post-collective eras. The self-provisioning domestic group with small numbers of livestock is contrasted with large-scale pastoral institutions, two institutional settings that have been symbiotically related in the past. It is argued that while large-scale pastoralist operations can provide a number of benefits and economies of scale, institutions capable of providing these to the majority of pastoral households in the current climate are unlikely to emerge through the operation of market forces alone. It falls to policy makers to establish a climate that can support larger scale pastoral operations, or other institutions capable of providing equivalent benefits.

The first part of the chapter is historical and outlines the role of large-scale pastoral operations of the past. It describes the pastoral household and encampment, and the results of the policies by which pastoralists were incorporated into rural collectives during the state socialist era. There follows a description of the economic reforms launched in the 1990s, the decollectivization of the pastoral sector, and its effects. One of the results of reform was to expand the pastoral economies of individual domestic units at the expense of large-scale institutions. In the atomized pastoral sector that has emerged, establishing larger economic formations without material and institutional support from the state has been beset with difficulties. The next section examines the case of the *horshoo* (producers cooperatives) most of which have collapsed in recent years. The only large livestock holdings that appear to be expanding at present are those of wealthy households. The following section briefly describes the operation of one of the richest of these, and examines current trends in the distribution of herd-wealth between households. The conclusion reviews the contrasting fortunes of the cooperatives and the rich herd owner, and argues that both the household and historically successful large-scale pastoral operations relied upon a series of non-market institutions for their viability. It is argued that without this 'institutional depth' (stable social and political relations outside the narrowly economic), new formations that support efficient large-scale pastoralist activities are unlikely to emerge.

8.2. HISTORICAL PATTERNS OF PASTORALISM

Pastoralism has been practised on the grasslands of Mongolia since ancient times. Much of the land is poorly suited to agriculture, but is used as grazing by pastoralists, most of whom are still mobile and move to different seasonal pastures as part of an annual cycle. The principal domesticated animals are horses, cattle (including yaks in highland regions), sheep, goats, and camels.

In the Manchu period, from the late seventeenth century until the twentieth, Mongolian society can be described as neo-feudal, composed of a ruling aristocracy and subordinate classes that roughly correspond to 'commoners', 'freemen', and a category of personal servants.[1] The Buddhist Church was a vast establishment with enormous wealth, ruling a number of districts and commanding its own servants and subjects. The principal administrative district was the *hoshuu* ('*banner*') ruled by the *Zasag*—the aristocratic prince of a secular *hoshuu*, or the *Hubilgan* (reincarnate senior lama) of an ecclesiastic one. Within the *hoshuu*, the herdsmen were assigned to sub-units called *sum*, and within these to smaller units called *bag*.[2] Each of these units had officials responsible for them, and the herdsmen were usually required to use pastures allocated to these subunits.

Large numbers of the animals of a district were owned by the nobles or monasteries, and herded for them by their subjects.[3] Most of the commoners also owned their own livestock, although the poorest households had few or none and worked for wealthier families to make a living. Although most households owned a range of livestock breeds, there were also specialists who would look after large herds of certain breeds (such as horses) for their noble or monastic masters. Large and small herds were commonly 'leased out' to a herding family who undertook their management in return for a proportion of the animal produce and offspring. The term used for these arrangements was *süreg tavih* (to 'place a herd'). This created a spectrum of pastoral activities, from the immense operations of the wealthy lords and monasteries, through a range of intermediate scale operations managed by more or less wealthy households, to the tiny herds of the poorest subjects. The smaller operations typically formed part of the larger systems. The poor tended to be attached to the better equipped households who were in turn part of the wider economy of the *hoshuu*, either actually herding livestock for the great estates, or simply as subjects of the local authorities who managed land use throughout the district.

---

[1] The English terms are rough translations: the *albat* or *sumyn ard* correspond roughly with 'commoners', *darhad* with 'freemen', and *hamjilga* and *shabi* with 'personal servants'. There were also some slaves (*bool*).

[2] The *bag* was the usual secular subdivision, the subunit used in the ecclesiastical districts had a different term—*otog*.

[3] The pre-revolutionary monasteries, for example, could own more than 60% of the total livestock in a district. Lattimore (1940: 97, fn. 50).

There are a number of reasons for cooperation and coordination in pastoralism on the Mongolian steppe. There is relatively little forage available on much of the arid and semi-arid land on which yields are low.[4] Historically large numbers of livestock could be successfully raised by moving them to different seasonal pastures to make use of the various ecological and climatic conditions that make them more or less suitable in a given season. Conditions are highly variable, so that being able to move livestock in response to changing climatic conditions is a key method of avoiding livestock losses. Pastoralism in Mongolia has, therefore, been based on institutional arrangements that permit flexible use of pastures over large areas.

A reconstruction of the pastoral system of an ecclesiastical *hoshuu* in what is now Bayanhongor *aimag* (province) shows that the pre-revolutionary elites were able to organize highly sophisticated systems of pastoralism. The subjects of the monastery were divided into groups depending on the monastic livestock allocated to them. The groups were assigned different seasonal movement routes to make best use of pastures and conditions throughout the district. The camel herders, for example, made some of the longest movements, spending winter and spring on the slopes of Altan mountain in the Gobi, and summer 150 km north in the foothills of the Hangai range. The horse and sheep herders also summered in the Hangai, but used winter and spring pastures by the southerly Bogd mountain range, and spent autumn by Lake Orog. The cattle herders confined their movements to the valleys of the Hangai, near the monastery to which they supplied milk products. Specified amounts of livestock and produce were delivered to monastery officials every year. Other monastic subjects were assigned the task of raising crops in the more fertile areas, so the *hoshuu* also had its own supply of grain.

All pastoralists are not equally able to make use of high-mobility techniques. Poor households without transportation or draft animals have difficulty moving without assistance. In the past the amount of movement in which a household engaged depended on its wealth, and the institutional frames within which it worked. Poor households incorporated into the establishments of wealthier neighbours moved with them. Those herding large numbers of camels and horses for monastic or noble masters appear to have moved most (see Sneath 1999).

Livestock are separated into single-species herds (except in the case of sheep and goats which are herded together). In most conditions one or two herders can look after several hundred livestock as well as they can a few dozen, so pooling livestock into reasonably large herds can save labour. The most difficult time for pastoralists is generally the winter and spring, when the availability of natural fodder is at its lowest and the stress on livestock is greatest. This 'bottleneck' is eased by the supply of fodder, typically hay, although this did not become widespread until the collective period.

8.2.1. *The Household and Encampment*

In some respects the pastoral household has remained relatively unchanged since the Manchu period. In particular its division of labour and its organization of domestic

---

[4] Average pasture yields are about 1–3 centners per hectare in Gobi regions, 3–4 in steppe regions, and 5–8 in mountain pastures. (A centner is a unit of 100 kg). See Purev in FAO (1991: 43).

space have altered very little. The principal property owning domestic group was and still generally is the *öröh* (family or household), with a head who has formal authority over its assets.[5] The composition of this unit varies widely, but today it often consists of a nuclear or virilocal stem family (a couple, their unmarried children, and the nuclear families of their married sons).

One or more households camping together form an encampment known as the *ail*, *hot*, or *hot-ail*. The households composing an *ail* capture some economies of scale by herding their livestock jointly, and members help each other in numerous everyday tasks. Most pastoral encampments are composed of a number of nuclear and stem families, related in various ways. These may change from year to year, in line with changing interpersonal relations of the members, and in many cases they vary from season to season, so that the membership of an encampment at the summer pastures is often different from that at the autumn, winter, or spring pastures. In some regions, such as the Gobi, *ails* tend to be small, and are usually composed of a single family.

The large encampment cannot be considered a stable producer group. Often it is only the component parts (generally nuclear or stem families) that remain constant units throughout the pastoral year.[6] The encampment might be better conceived of as the manifestation of social relations in a residential form. These relations form a fluid and flexible network, based largely on kinship, but also on friendship, and sometimes employer–employee or patron–client relations. This pattern seems to date from the Manchu period, if not before. The pre-collective encampment described by Simukov in 1933 shows the same characteristics. It is the constituent households and the process by which these come together to form encampments that are persistent institutions, not each encampment itself.[7]

8.2.2. *Collectivization*

In 1911 the Manchu Qing dynasty collapsed, and Outer Mongolia declared its independence under the head of the Buddhist Church, the Bogd Khan—'Holy King.'

[5] The *öröh* is generally the unit of livestock ownership, and the head of the family is only 'in charge' of them. However, the head (*tergüülegch*, or *ezen*) is still much more personally associated with property than other members. Junior family members generally talk of the household and it assets as 'ours' (*manai*), but when talking about some other family's encampment or property they usually use the name of the household head (i.e. 'Damdin's horses' or 'Sodnom's *ail*').

[6] Of 100 *ails* that I studied in Ih Tamir *sum* (district), Ar Hangai *aimag* (province), less than half retained constant composition throughout the year. This is not untypical. In the two pastoral districts (*sums*) of Hanh and Renchinlhümbe, Hövsgöl *aimag*, about half the thirty-four encampments I studied in 1996 changed their composition during the year.

[7] Simukov uses the term *hoton* which was more usual than the term *ail* or *hot-ail* (Simukov 1933: 22–3). He studied 100 hotons in what is now Ih Tamir *sum*, Ar Hangai *aimag*, and classifies them thus: 'the *hotons* with constant composition 45%, the *hotons* of mixed character 25%, the *hotons* with inconstant composition 30%.' In 1996, I made a study of 100 *ails* in the district where Simukov worked in 1932. The detailed results of this comparison will, I hope, appear in print elsewhere. Flexible and fluid though they may be, *hot-ails* are still clearly groups. However, property, income, and autonomy in decision-making are vested in the household, and where encampments are stable this is a reflection of underlying social relations (e.g. kinship), rather than the nature of the *hot-ail* itself as an institution.

The social order remained relatively unchanged until the 1920s, when a Soviet-backed Revolutionary Party took power, and began to dismantle the neo-feudal structures.

The new regime attempted to collectivize pastoralism in the late 1920s and early 1930s, but the policies proved to be so unpopular they had to be abandoned. In order to prevent further damage to the pastoral economy the regime had to allow the monasteries to continue to manage their livestock holdings (*jas*), although these had been reduced in size. By the end of the 1930s, however, the Church and nobility had been largely stripped of their wealth, and much of their livestock holdings distributed to poor households. The Mongolian state simultaneously increased its direct control of the pastoral economy, introducing compulsory state delivery quotas in 1941. In the late 1940s and 1950s collectivization was attempted again, using more gradual and less coercive methods and this time it was carried through successfully.

At the end of the collectivization process about 250 rural districts (*sum*) supported a single collective farm (*negdel*) which raised livestock in accordance with state planning. The pastoral *sum* generally consisted of a central settlement of a few hundred households and a large area of grassland in which something like the same number of pastoral households kept livestock, most of them living in mobile felt yurts. These pastoral families were organized into production brigades.

The collective not only owned most of the livestock of the district, it also controlled land-use. Although the new *sum* districts were generally smaller than the earlier *hoshuu* (banners), and in some regions there was some reduction in the distance of seasonal movements, in general the pastoralists remained highly mobile, moving to seasonal pastures throughout the year, and making additional movements if necessary. The collectives owned and maintained machinery for transportation and hay-cutting services that were used to support pastoralism. Herding households were generally moved by collective trucks on the longest legs of the annual migration, and hay was delivered to help feed livestock during the difficult months of winter and early spring.

Herding became highly specialized in the collectives. A given *suur* would be allocated collective livestock of a single species (except for sheep and goats, which were virtually always herded together), and often of a particular age or sex—such as mares, or one- and two-year-old lambs and kids.[8] Alongside these collective livestock each *suur* herded a number of personal livestock (each household being allowed up to fifty, or seventy-five in some cases). These were generally of several different species so that they could supply families with meat, milk, and other products for domestic consumption. Brigades generally assigned seasonal pastures and movement routes to the *suurs* depending on the collective livestock they had been allocated.

The collectives were designed to produce raw materials for indigenous manufacturing industry and export. Each *negdel* was set a five-year plan by the state, with a quota of products to be delivered at fixed prices. Much higher prices were paid, up to 50 per cent more, for production over the plan. About half the income of the collective was paid as wages to its employees, the rest being used for building programmes, maintaining water resources, and the purchase of hay, fuel, and other inputs.

[8] Humphrey (1978: 142–52).

In terms of pastoral management, the collectives can be compared with the large-scale pastoral institutions of the past. They regulated access to pasture in a way that was comparable to the role of the pre-revolutionary banner authorities. They took ownership of almost all the livestock of the district, but allocated these to households to herd in a way that was not entirely dissimilar to older practices of *süreg tavih*. They also organized specialist herding of large, single-species herds, and extra pastoral movement, as had rich herd-owning agencies of the past; indeed the collectives developed an even greater degree of specialization. They can be seen as the most centralized and monopolistic form that such large-scale institutions have taken in the history of Mongolian pastoralism.

8.2.3. *Macroeconomic Reform and Mongolia's 'Age of the Market'*

The political changes that swept through the Soviet Union and its satellite states in the early 1990s thrust Mongolia into an era of economic reform. The government launched a series of policies designed to create a market economy based on private property. The economic advice that former Soviet-block nations received resembled the stabilization and structural reform packages recommended for poor countries by the IMF and the World Bank in the 1970s and 1980s (Nolan 1995: 75). It included price liberalization, cuts in state subsidies and expenditure, currency convertibility, privatization of public assets and the rapid introduction of markets.

These policy recommendations were based on the notion of a 'transition' from what was seen as an inefficient and moribund centrally planned economy to the presumed efficiency and dynamism of the free market. The aim of reform was to 'emancipate' the economy from the political structure, by introducing private property and the market. A bright economic future was predicted for Mongolia at that time—the government talked of the country becoming the fifth Asian Tiger within five years.[9] In 1991 Mongolia began a huge programme to privatize state and collective enterprises through the issue of share coupons (*tasalbar*).[10] In rural districts the reforms included the dissolution of the collectives (*negdel*) and later most of the state farms (*sangiin aj ahui*) which managed the bulk of pastoral and agricultural production.

The 'Age of the Market' (*zah zeeliin üye*) as Mongolians called the post-socialist period, saw Mongolia plunged into economic crisis. The worst disruption occurred in the early 1990s when incomes plummeted. The World Bank estimated that real wages halved between 1990 and 1992, and then declined by a further third in 1993.[11] Official figures showed that income-poverty increased from almost zero in 1989 to 27 per cent in 1994,[12] and a 1998 survey of living standards suggested that over 33 per cent

---

[9] Odgaard (1996: 113).   [10] Asian Development Bank (1992: 86–8); World Bank (1994: 9).

[11] See World Bank (1994: 19); Griffin (1995: viii) estimates the decline in average incomes at around 30% over that period. IMF data suggest a smaller decline in average incomes of about 25%, see Griffin (1995: 5). UNDP and Asian Development Bank estimates suggested a decline of 34% in GNP per capita from 1989–92, see Griffin (1995: 25).   [12] See Griffin (1995: 31–3); and World Bank (1994: 35).

of Mongolians were living below the poverty line.[13] Social services were cut; real expenditure on health services decreased by 43 per cent from 1990 to 1992, and the education budget was cut by 56 per cent.[14] Further reductions followed and social service spending has remained low since. The official figures for unemployment increased rapidly in the early 1990s, and actual unemployment was estimated at 15 per cent in 1997.[15] The rate of inflation shot up and stayed in triple figures from 1991 to 1993, only falling gradually thereafter.

In part this economic crisis was the result of the loss of Soviet aid (some estimates suggest this amounted to as much as a third of GDP or more)[16] which was reduced in 1989 and stopped altogether in 1991. The Soviet trading block, the Council for Mutual Economic Assistance also collapsed at this time, and Mongolian trade fell dramatically (exports declining from 832 million USD in 1989 to 370 million in 1991). However, the place of Russia as aid donor was taken over, to some extent, by western nations, Japan, and international financial institutions. Between them these donors provided support equivalent to about 15 per cent of GDP in 1991 and 1992.[17] By 1996 this had risen to 25 per cent of GDP.[18] Thus, the loss of Soviet aid can only be held partially responsible for Mongolia's crisis. As Griffin argues, one of the reasons for the severity of the economic collapse was the nature of the reform policies carried out at the time—in particular the rapid privatization programme.[19]

The situation stabilized to some extent in the mid-1990s, with GDP seeing some positive growth in 1994 and 1995, but stalling in 1996 when the prices of copper and cashmere (Mongolia's main exports) fell. A newly elected government embarked on an aggressive programme of economic 'shock treatment' to remove the last vestiges of the centrally planned economy, including liberalizing fuel prices and a campaign to privatize housing.[20] GDP growth was estimated at 2.4 per cent in 1996, and 4 and 3.5 per cent in 1997 and 1998.[21]

The Mongolian economy has become increasingly reliant on pastoralism, which in 1998 accounted for 88 per cent of the total output of agriculture. The relative importance of the agricultural sector increased as GDP as a whole declined and other sectors of the economy collapsed. In 1989 agriculture contributed just 16 per cent of total GDP, for example. By 1998 this had risen to 33 per cent.

---

[13] The United Nations Systems in Mongolia (1999: 5).   [14] World Bank (1994: 41).

[15] The CIA World Factbook 1998 entry on Mongolia. (http://www.odci.gov/cia/publications/factbook/mg.html). Official figures show unemployment increase from 10,300 in 1989 to reach 80,000 in 1996, but an article in the Mongolian daily *Ardyn Erh* suggested that the true unemployment total approached 90,000. (*Ardyn Erh*, No 193 (1411), 27 September 1996).

[16] Bruun and Odgaard (1996: 26) give the estimate of 30%, while some estimates are even higher; the United Nations Systems in Mongolia (1999: 6) estimates that this assistance represented, on average, 37% of annual GDP.   [17] Griffin (1995: 6).

[18] Bruun and Odgaard (1996: 26).   [19] Griffin (1995: 12–13).

[20] United States Embassy (1999).

[21] National Statistical Office of Mongolia (1999: 56). *The Mongol Messenger* (No. 28(313), 9 July 1997).

8.2.4. *The Decollectivization of Pastoralism*

The dissolution of the collectives began in 1991 and was complete by 1993. The bulk of the livestock and other assets was divided between the members, and became their private property. What remained of the collectives were often redesignated joint stock companies (*kompani*), or cooperatives (*horshoo*).

The pastoral sector has emerged from the reforms composed of vast numbers of households engaged in small-scale pastoral production. Decollectivization eliminated the jobs of most of the workers in the *sum* centres. They were given a share of the collective's assets, in most cases livestock, with which to make their living, so that the number of people relying directly on pastoralism increased dramatically.[22] The number of registered herders more than trebled in the 9 years from 1989 to 1998, from 135,420 to 414,433, from less than 18 per cent to 50 per cent of the working population.[23] This change appears to be an enduring aspect of reform. There is little prospect of growth in employment in other sectors of the economy. The number of jobs in manufacturing, industry, construction, transport, and communication have all declined by around 25–50 per cent since 1990. The only sector of the economy, other than pastoralism, in which employment has increased is trade and commerce. This sector remains small, accounting for 9.2 per cent of the national workforce in 1998.[24]

The increase in numbers of pastoral households is affecting the patterns of pastoral land-use as many of these 'new herders' still have dwellings at the *sum* centre and tend to be much less mobile that the established herding households who were part of specialized herding brigades in the collectives. Some can place their livestock with friends or relatives among the remaining mobile households on a long-term basis, but other 'new herders' pasture their livestock relatively near to the settlement for some or all of the year. The effects of these changes on grassland ecosystems have yet to be seen, but recent research from Inner Mongolia and other regions where pastoralism has become sedentary suggests that lower livestock mobility is damaging to pasture land.[25]

The dissolution of the old system has meant the loss of a number of important benefits that the collectives had supplied. Under the collectives, pastoralists were provided with a secure income with which they could buy basic consumer goods that were supplied to collective centres and to distant encampments by truck. The collectives also provided secure basic food supplies and flour was kept cheap and readily available. Since decollectivization the price of flour and other staple foods has increased much more quickly than the prices paid to pastoralists for their products (wool, meat, and milk) and supplies are often unreliable. This is of central importance

---

[22] In Renchinlhümbe *sum*, north Mongolia, for example, about half the working population were employed in non-pastoral occupations in the collective period. When the collective closed most of the residents became directly dependent on livestock for their subsistence—over 70% of the population were officially classed as herders in 1996, and over 20% were classed as unemployed. Only 6.5% of the *sum* population were employed in non-pastoral sectors.

[23] National Statistical Office of Mongolia (1999: 95, 45); Statistical Office of Mongolia (1993: 6).

[24] Statistical Office of Mongolia (1993: 7); National Statistical Office of Mongolia (1999: 45)

[25] Tserendash and Erdenebaatar (1993: 9–15); Humphrey and Sneath (1995: 8–13); Williams (1996: 307–3).

to pastoral households, who have to have carbohydrates to balance their meat-rich diet, and who have few alternatives to flour. Mongolia used to be almost self-sufficient in grain production, but the grain harvest has declined dramatically since reforms began, from 718 thousand tons in 1990 to 195 thousand tons in 1998.[26] The shortfall has had to be filled with imported flour, and prices have risen accordingly.

In the past the cheap fuel that the Soviet Union supplied to Mongolia meant that mechanical transport, a key factor in such a huge and thinly populated country, was affordable and widely available. This was particularly important for pastoralists. As the price of petrol increased in the nineties, transportation became increasingly expensive and medical and veterinary treatment less accessible.

The collectives used to cut hay mechanically, and then distribute it by truck to pastoral households for use as winter fodder. Since decollectivization individual households have had to cut hay by hand, and transport it themselves—often using animal carts. This is physically demanding work, and households without active adult members or the money to buy hay find it difficult or impossible to gain sufficient winter fodder for their animals.

In the collective period pastoralists were often moved on the longest legs of their annual migration by collective truck, which greatly eased the difficulty of these distant movements. The dissolution of the collective motor pools and the increase in fuel costs have made seasonal movement much more difficult for most pastoral families, who have increasingly had to rely on animal transport. This is one of the reasons for a general decline in pastoral movement. There has also been a reduction in the regulation of access to pasture, which had been overseen by collective and state farm officials. Many herding families have become less inclined to make arduous, long distance moves between seasonal pastures for fear that their best pastures may be used by others if they vacate them. In addition to the regular movements between established seasonal pastures, the collectives also organized extra pastoral movement excursions called *otor*—a traditional technique by which livestock are repeatedly and flexibly moved over distant and lesser-used pastures at times of fodder shortage, as a method of intensively feeding them. This was usually done by a team of experienced herders living in tents away from the main encampments. *Otor* has now become less common since many households have neither the labour-power nor the inclination to organize their own *otor* trips, and may or may not be able to place their livestock with herds that are still being taken on them.

8.2.5. *Pastoral Production and Terms of Trade*

Livestock numbers have risen since decollectivization as many rural households have come to rely upon their herds for their subsistence and seek the security of larger herds. As Fig. 8.1 shows, from 1990 to 1998 the national herd increased by over 20 per cent from 25.9 to 31.9 million head.[27] Goat numbers increased particularly rapidly, indeed

---

[26] *The Mongol Messenger* (No. 37(271) 18 September 1996) and The Ministry of Agriculture and Industry of Mongolia (1998) and United States Embassy (1999).

[27] National Statistical Office of Mongolia (1999: 83–4).

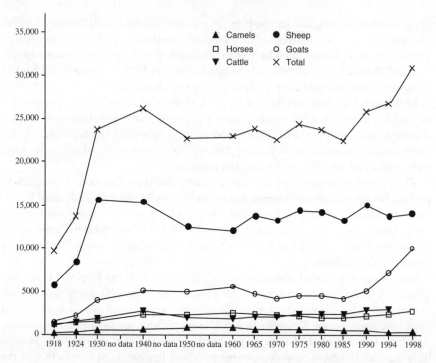

Figure 8.1. *Livestock population of Mongolia, 1918–98*

Sources: Statistical Office of Mongolia (1981: 178); Sheehy (1996: 46); Mongolian Ministry of Agriculture (1998).

goats alone account for most of the increase. This reflects the continued demand for cashmere, and the fact that pastoralists can increase their cashmere sales without slaughtering livestock.

Survival rates of offspring have fallen by around 10 per cent since decollectivization. However, the numbers of livestock consumed and marketed has declined even more dramatically (by about 20 per cent), so livestock totals rose nevertheless. But the new pastoral sector has proved to be more vulnerable to climatic variation than the relatively well supplied and coordinated collective system. Over 6 million livestock were lost in the harsh winters between 1999–2002, and the end of year livestock total had sunk to around 26 million in 2001—little more than the 1990 level. These trends have accompanied a decrease in the associated manufacturing and processing industries. From 1993 to 1998 carpet production fell by 64 per cent, felt production by 31 per cent, camel wool blankets by 46 per cent, and felt boots by 19 per cent. Leather goods have been particularly badly affected, leather shoe, coat, and jacket production falling to a tiny fraction of their earlier levels.[28] Only cashmere sales have increased. Much of this is now being exported for processing in China.

[28] Leather shoe, coat and jacket production showed a 24, 33, and a 160-fold decrease respectively. Sheep skin processing also declined by fifty-five times and processed goat skin by fourteen times. Source—The Ministry of Agriculture and Industry of Mongolia (1998).

Unit: 1000 tons

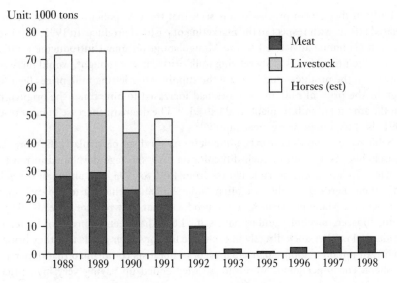

Figure 8.2. *Mongolian meat and livestock*

Note: Data for 1994 are unavailable.

Sources: Statistical Office of Mongolia (1993: 78–79); National Statistical Office of Mongolia (1998: 140); WB (1994: table 5.1).

In part the rapid contraction of these industries was a result of the dissolution of the Soviet trading block which led to a decline in demand for Mongolian finished goods. The surviving industries complain about the difficulties of obtaining sufficient supplies of animal products at prices that are competitive.[29] Although prices have fallen, the difficulties have also been the result of the collapse of the state procurement system including the state farms and collectives that used to supply particular factories directly. The collectives organized vast livestock drives which moved animals along designated corridors to the slaughterhouses in the capital. These operations disappeared with the collectives and livestock is now commonly purchased by relatively small-scale traders, often using a single truck.

Since decollectivization the pastoral sector has become much less able to supply produce for foreign markets. In the collective era Mongolia exported between 25–40,000 tons of meat, 25–30,000 tons of livestock, and over 60,000 head of horses each year. These exports declined in 1991, when the Soviet trading block stopped functioning, and almost collapsed entirely in 1992 when decollectivization was completed. Meat exports in 1998 amounted to only 7500 tons. Livestock and horse exports have become insignificant.[30] This is disappointing, particularly in view of Mongolia's rail links with China, as well as Russia, both of which represent huge markets for meat.

[29] N. Davaa writes 'Despite producing 30% of the world's cashmere Mongolia still suffers shortage'. *The Mongol Messenger* (30 June 1999, p. 5).   [30] National Statistical Office of Mongolia (1999: 144).

Early in the reform process it was seen that the new policies were not having the desired effects with respect to the marketing of pastoral produce. In 1991, for example, western economic advice led to the Mongolian government introducing a policy of freeing the price of milk. Liberalizing milk prices, it was thought, would increase the rewards to the producer and increase the supply. After letting milk prices float for six months the price of milk in the cities had increased to nine times the original price, but the amount of milk available had halved.[31] The dramatic increase in meat prices in 1991 also failed to improve meat supply.[32]

Selling animal products can be difficult for pastoralists, particularly the more remote households. As a result of such difficulties a cash shortage developed in most rural districts. Inflation was in triple figures from 1991 to 1993, and although it has fallen since then, herding families are often understandably reluctant to use cash for their transactions. Many prefer to have the products that they require instead—flour, tea, cloth, tobacco, alcohol, candles, and salt. There has been a spread of barter trade, (traders taking livestock directly in exchange for consumer goods that they bring with them). In remote regions such as Hövsgöl pastoralists complained that opportunities to obtain consumer goods were rare so they ended up paying very high prices (in livestock) for traded goods.

It is difficult to calculate the changing 'terms of trade' for pastoralists because in the collective era pastoralists were paid salaries rather than relying on private sales. However, it is clear that changing prices have reduced the buying power of pastoral households with respect to subsistence items. The most essential foodstuff that pastoralists must purchase is flour. In 1990 the cost of flour was 1 *tögrög* (the Mongolian unit of currency) per kilo, while meat cost 5.9 *tögrög*.[33] In 1998 the cost of flour averaged around 300 *tögrög* per kilo, while mutton averaged around 500.[34] Meat was worth less than a third of its former value in terms of flour.

This is reflected in the budgets of pastoral households. My estimate of the average agricultural household's income in 1990 is 10,990 *tögrög*, which was then the equivalent of about 11 tons of flour.[35] In 1998 the average annual income of rural households was 1,009,660 *tögrög*. This could buy about 3.365 tons of flour.[36] It should be noted that these calculations are based on prices found in the *aimag* centre. Terms of trade are generally even more unfavourable in pastoral districts where transportation costs are usually higher. Indeed, in some remote regions flour may not be for sale at all. Families have to make their own arrangements to have it brought to them from elsewhere.

There seems to be little sign of the relative price of livestock products improving in the near future. A lowering of transportation and marketing costs would require

---

[31] Campi (1994: 240–1).   [32] Asian Development Bank (1992: 103).

[33] Asian Development Bank (1992: 55).

[34] National Statistical Office of Mongolia (1999: 161, 163). These prices varied by as much as 30% around the mean.

[35] This was calculated for a household of five (the average rural household size in 1998) using 1990 national averages for the numbers of workers (1.8) and pensioners (0.4); and the average agricultural income (5400 T) and pension (2448 T). I have also included the allowances given by the state to mothers of five or more children, which represent another 159 T per household on average. National Statistical Office of Mongolia (1993: 9, 95).   [36] National Statistical Office of Mongolia (1999: 159–61).

investment in vehicles and trading facilities. The level of investment in rural districts is low and has declined steadily in recent years. The percentage of all bank loans granted to borrowers outside the capital city of Ulaanbaatar has fallen each year throughout the nineties, from 46 per cent in 1993 to 11 per cent in 1998.[37]

There has been an increase in the activities of Chinese traders, and it is possible that increased competition between buyers will eventually begin to drive up the prices of pastoral products. However, the Mongolian pastoral sector has to compete with that of Inner Mongolia, which is a huge producer of identical pastoral products, much closer and better-connected to major markets in China. Another long-term possibility is that Russian demand might improve.

The thinking behind the decollectivization programme seems to have been that privatization would improve the efficiency and initiative of herdsmen and release the state from the burden of subsidizing collective and state farms. The effect has been to create an atomized pastoral economy, composed of thousands of scattered households oriented primarily towards subsistence production, only a fraction in a position to supply their produce to the urban markets. The reform policies dismantled the state procurement system and the institutions oriented towards providing livestock produce for the cities and export. Without the transportation arrangements of the official procurement system, selling milk and meat represents a good deal of effort for hard-pressed pastoral families who are no longer under any official obligation to sell.

The difficulties faced by the pastoral sector raise the question whether the dissolution of the collectives was an inevitable consequence of changing economic conditions, or whether, in a modified form, the collectives could have survived the withdrawal of Soviet aid.[38]

8.2.6. *Group Functions in the Pastoral Sector*

It is difficult to separate 'internal' and 'external' factors that affect the operation of pastoral producer groups, particularly in the state socialist era when collectives formed part of an integrated national economy. (The terms of trade for the pastoral sector were relatively good, for example, because produce was directed to state factories and ring-fenced CMEA markets). Some of the key 'internal' factors that affect the functioning of pastoral producers, however, are rights to land-use, rights to livestock and other property, the ability to command labour, and the capacity to acquire and

---

[37] National Statistical Office of Mongolia (1999: 69).

[38] World Bank (1994: table 9.5) As the collectives operated as part of the centrally-planned economy it is difficult to estimate the true level of subsidy that the state provided. The Asian Development Bank (1992: 54–6) calculates total subsidies amounted to 637 million *tögrög* in 1990, about 10% of total government spending, whereas the World Bank (1994: table 9.3) gives a much higher estimate 1746 million *tögrög*—26% of government expenditure. Using the higher World Bank estimates, the 1990 total for subsidies on energy, exports, agriculture, fodder transport, veterinary services, and the meat and milk subsidies that benefited consumers came to 964 million *tögrög*, about 14% of government spending. This figure represents the principal subsidies given to industry, agriculture, and pastoralism and amounts to about 9% of GDP, a little more than the 8% spent on social security. If subsidies on wood, coal, glass, felt, and bread are included the total is a little higher at 1049 million *tögrög*, 10% of GDP. See World Bank (1994: tables 9.5 and 9.3).

operate machinery. Different combinations of these determinants allow a greater or lesser amount of herd specialization, labour economies, and optimal use of forage resources in different ecological settings.

An examination of the recent history of Mongolian pastoralism suggests that the possible efficiency gains associated with groups involved in large-scale operations cannot be treated as functions that are somehow independent of their social settings. This is particularly clear with respect to the ability of a group to command labour and investment, and orient management strategies towards its continued existence. These are directly connected with the institutional context of the group in question, be it a household or a large official agency.

Historically, large-scale pastoral institutions combined rights to the flexible use of pasture, often widely dispersed; ownership of large numbers of livestock; and the ability to command labour. When working well they were able to capture considerable economies of scale, optimize land-use and supply large amounts of produce for sale. They were also able to take advantage of economies of scale in marketing pastoral produce and acquiring consumer goods. This was particularly true of the collective period when pastoral production was directed towards state industries and the collectives were large enough to be able to organize activities tailored to particular types of demand—such as the rearing of specialist breeds, large dairies, and livestock drives to slaughterhouses.

It is likely that reform of the collectives would have served Mongolia better than their dissolution, despite the unavoidable changes in the macroeconomic climate. A recent ODI study compared the pastoral sectors of Turkmenistan, where collectives were reformed, and Kazakhstan, where they were disbanded. The findings suggest that the conditions for pastoral households in Turkmenistan, although difficult, are still better than in Kazakhstan, which faces some of the same sorts of problem of atomization as Mongolia.[39] The principal reasons for the dissolution of the collectives in Mongolia seem to have been political. In 1990 an FAO workshop on Mongolian pastoralism concluded 'there is no reason why they [the collectives] should not survive an economic liberalisation programme, although probably with modified functions.'[40]

8.2.7. *The Institutional Frames for Pastoralism*

Looking at the history of pastoralism in Mongolia one can identify two categories of economic groups, and their associated institutional frames. The first is the household; the focus of subsistence activities oriented towards satisfying domestic requirements. In the collective period this was represented by each pastoral family being allowed relatively small numbers of their own livestock (50 head in most regions). As these were the personal livestock of the family, not herded for others under contractual obligation, their products were used by the working household itself.

At the other end of the spectrum stood the large-scale pastoral operations organized by agencies with a large number of animals—usually a noble family, ecclesiastical

---

[39] Kerven (1998: 10). She notes that international experts and donors could learn from this contrast.
[40] FAO (1991: 7).

institution, local government office, rich commoner, or (later) collective farm. These were characterized by the owning agency having herds cared for by other pastoral households, and often involved the specialized herding of large single-species herds. If the owning agency had the authority to do so, these operations might also rotate large single-species herds between widely separated seasonal pastures chosen for being particularly well suited for that species. In such arrangements the subordinate herders generally had contractual obligations to supply a certain quota of produce and retained only the surplus for themselves. Between the theoretical extremes of the vast holdings of a wealthy monastery or lord, and the tiny herd of a poor subject, there was a range of intermediate-scale pastoral operations conducted by more or less wealthy households.

These various economic formations not only differed in scale; the ends of this continuum represented institutional frames with quite different primary objectives. The domestic group's priority was the security, subsistence and provisioning of its members, while the large-scale specialist pastoral and herd-placing operations were undertaken to generate and supply a surplus of livestock and products to the owning agency.[41] These two orientations were symbiotically related—large-scale operations depended on the subsistence of domestic groups, and domestic groups often also depended on large-scale operations to produce their subsistence reliably.

Subsistence pastoralists and wealthy surplus-oriented herd-owners did not necessarily have conflicting interests. The existence of specialist herding seems to have allowed smaller producers to place some of their stock with these larger herds, so benefiting from economies of scale. Wealthy commoners often attracted the labour of poorer households because they could offer such benefits.[42] Furthermore, there were also benefits from participation in the wider politico-economic order of the district. In the neo-feudal period district authorities organized specialist activities of benefit to the whole community, such as the cultivation of wheat. Such activities were often an assigned feudal duty for specialist households.[43]

One of the most important priorities for subsistence-oriented pastoralists is long-term food security, this frequently means they reduce offtake to a minimum so as to build-up livestock numbers in their herd. Figure 8.1 shows that the post-collective increase in livestock numbers is not unprecedented. A comparable increase occurred throughout the 1920s and 1930s, at a time when the large-scale pastoral operations of the aristocracy and monasteries were being dismantled by the new revolutionary government. Confiscated aristocratic and monastery livestock were redistributed among herding households. The surplus animals that would have been extracted by the old

---

[41] By the nineteenth century most of the Mongolian elite was in debt to Chinese merchant firms. Much of the produce of the districts ruled by the princes and senior lamas was expended on servicing this debt (see Sanjdorj 1980: 80). The orientation of such herd-owners was towards the Chinese market, mediated by their debts to merchants, and rich herd-owners had every reason to extract the maximum surplus from the livestock economy.

[42] Simukov noted that wealthy households preferred to have two or three poor households in their *hoton*, and that grouping in *hotons* on the basis of property equality was very uncommon. Simukov (1933: 29).

[43] Simukov (1936: 55–6) describes grain production organized by a monastery.

elite were now accumulated by pastoralists. Total numbers of livestock increased from 10 million in 1918 to over 25 million in 1940.

With the introduction of compulsory state delivery quotas in 1941 and collectivization in the 1950s, herd offtake increased and livestock numbers fell a little and stabilized. Both neo-feudal and collective systems managed to export large amounts of livestock. By the end of the nineteenth century Outer Mongolia was probably exporting at least one million sheep units of livestock to China each year—about 5 per cent of the total national herd.[44] In the collective era the Mongolian state was also able to procure and export large numbers of animals. State procurement in 1985, for example, was almost 207 thousand tons (live weight) of meat and livestock, and 87.4 thousand head of horses. Of this 63.1 thousand horses and 61.5 thousand tons of livestock and meat were exported—4.7 per cent of the national herd, by my estimate, which is rather close to the pre-revolutionary figure above.[45]

8.3. COOPERATIVES (*HORSHOO*)

It was recognized at the time that the dismantling of the state procurement structures in the early 1990s would create a vacuum in the system for marketing pastoral produce. It was hoped that a number of different institutions would fill the gap. In many districts the former *negdel*, now reclassified as a Joint Stock Company, continued for a while to operate as the principal marketing organization. Alongside these some individual traders emerged to buy and sell pastoral produce, often to relatively small numbers of households. The large distances between pastoral households makes transportation a key feature of any such marketing operation, and a household's opportunity to trade with a given agent generally depends on whether or not it makes economic, social, or geographic sense for him to visit it. The personal networks of traders, their kin, and friends, means that most households can expect periodic visits and opportunities to market their produce in this way.

The government made provision for the formation of enterprises termed 'cooperatives' (*horshoo*) to be formed by members pooling their shares of the collective to gain joint ownership of some section of the old *negdel*. Some of these were medium-sized productive operations based on a former collective resource, such as a vegetable-growing or hay-cutting operation, or a small dairy. Most of these

---

[44] Sanjdorj (1980: 91) notes that in the late nineteenth century Chinese traders were taking 25,000 horses, 10,000 cows, and 250,000 sheep from the area of Ih H ree alone every year. This represents about 0.45 million sheep units. Considering that Uliastai and Hovd would have probably been engaged in comparable but smaller amounts of export trade and southerly regions are unlikely to have traded with China via Ih H ree, I think it is safe to assume that the total export was more than twice that of the Ih H ree figure. In 1917 the total herd wealth of Outer Mongolia was just over 20 million sheep units.

[45] I estimate the total exports as equivalent to 2.1 million sheep units out of a total national herd of 45 million sheep units. See State Statistical Office of Mongolia (1993: 45, 82). I estimate the total state procurement to be 6.3 million sheep units using the average live weight of each species of livestock procured by the state in 1980 (see State Statistical Office of the MPR 1981: 221). Using the same average ratio between tons of meat and sheep units I estimate that 1985 exports represented 1.72 million sheep units of cattle, sheep, and goats; adding the 0.38 million sheep units for the exported horses gives the 2.1 million figure.

were classified as 'limited liability companies', 'limited liability cooperatives' or just 'cooperatives'.[46]

An example of such a post-collective enterprise was the Bayan Tsagaan *horshoo* in Bayantumen *sum*, Dornod. Founded in April 1993, it was a relatively small organization composed of ten families, all of whom were kin. The cooperative was formed around a set of former collective assets: some vehicles, a large winter animal enclosure, some haymaking and potato fields. Membership was based upon the kin network of the man who was central to its formation, rather than any residential or neighbourhood group. Several members had come from some distance to join the cooperative that their kinsman had founded. Although all ten member households helped make hay together in the summer, most of them lived in different places for the rest of the year. The *horshoo* was described as a temporary and experimental formation, which might be disbanded if it was not seen to be working well.

By 1996 the Bayan Tsagaan had been disbanded. Indeed the majority of productive enterprises of this type have gone bankrupt or ceased trading, and the average number of staff and livestock holdings of the surviving enterprises has declined. Of the 370 that had been established throughout the country by 1992, less than half (173) still existed in 1998. Of these only 109 owned livestock, the average holding being a modest 1780 head.[47]

A second type of rural cooperative also emerged immediately after privatization. These were small-scale voluntary associations of pastoral households, set-up to act as marketing organizations to sell their produce and deliver consumer goods in return. Several of these were established in almost every district in Mongolia, often one in each *bag* subdistrict. Virtually all of them collapsed within two or three years of their foundation. In two pastoral districts in Hövsgöl province, Renchinlhümbe and Hanh, for example, none of the *horshoo* that had been formed were still operating by 1996. In Hanh the privatization of the local collective began in 1990. Three cooperatives were formed, named Zul ('Lamp'), Bayan Uul ('Rich Mountain'), and Jimst ('Fruitful').[48] By 1994 they had all become bankrupt or had ceased to trade, although they retained a nominal existence in local government records.

The membership of the cooperatives coincided with administrative divisions, so that the clientele of the cooperative were generally the members of a given production

---

[46] The term for limited liability company is—*Büren Bus Hariutslagatai Kompani* (BBHK), or *Hyazgaar-lagdmal Hariutslagatai Kompani* (HHK). Although they called themselves 'companies' these enterprises were generally owned by the members who had pooled shares of the former collective, rather than external shareholders. There was no legal framework in place for the operation of Joint Stock Companies, so these enterprises were registered as cooperatives or limited companies. The term for limited liability cooperatives is *Büren Bus Hariutslagatai Horshoo* (BBHH).

[47] Hödöö Aj Ahyin Horshoologchdyn Ündesnii Holboo (National Association of Agricultural Cooperative Members) Statistical Department, Personal Communication, July 1999. Interestingly, very few *horshoo* were established in the immediate vicinity of Ulaanbaatar; the market being sufficiently close for many herders to have personal access to consumer goods and marketing opportunities—often through their personal networks.

[48] This is a loose translation of a Mongolian term which is generally translated as 'fruit-bearing' or simply 'fruit'.

brigade of the old *negdel*, now renamed *bag*. The Bayan Uul *horshoo* was formed in 1992 by a retired military officer named Batsuur. As a respected senior figure it was felt that Batsuur was someone whom local pastoral families could trust. Around thirty-five households were members of the cooperative, about half the total number of households in the subdistrict (*bag*). For two years the cooperative bought livestock products from member households and marketed it, bringing consumer goods that the households required in exchange. But in 1994 the cooperative went bankrupt and ceased to operate. The main problem, Batsuur explained, was a lack of capital.

There were a number of immediate causes of the failure of Bayan Uul. Produce had to be transported to the provincial centre of Mörön and consumer goods purchased there. At first it had been assumed that the *horshoo* could use the *usan zam* ('water road')—a regular ferry service that had run the length of Lake Hövsgöl from Hanh to Hatgal. However this service became increasingly expensive and unreliable, and instead the passage had to be made using the long and very poor road down the lake edge.

As a result of the increased costs, the *horshoo* soon found that its trading capital was exhausted. The prices paid to the member families for pastoral products in the first year of operation were disappointing. Moreover, the membership proved increasingly unwilling to supply produce on credit as required. They were themselves faced with a cash shortage, and many preferred to trust what produce they had with relatives or friends. The number of families prepared to market their produce through the *horshoo* dwindled to a group largely composed of Batsuur's family and friends.

Some of the other former members of the *horshoo* explained that it had begun to seem better to them to make use of personal contacts, family, and friends to sell and procure goods. They were obliged to see their close kin and friends anyway, and could trust them to bring back consumer goods if any could be found. Households in the *sum* centre villages, towns and cities typically stock up on *idesh* (food supplies) in early winter by visiting pastoral members of their networks to get meat and milk products. It has become very common for households to rely on their own networks of friends and relatives to procure commodities they need in this way, and as an outlet for livestock produce such as wool and cashmere.

It became increasingly difficult to persuade people to give up their time to administer and work on the *horshoo* operation, and there was no available money to pay them. In 1994 Batsuur declared the Bayan Uul bankrupt (*dampuursan*). All its assets had apparently been expended in its last year of trading. The experience of Bayan Uul *horshoo* was not unusual. Both Jimst and Zul, the other cooperatives in the *sum*, had also ceased trading by this time.

Staff at the National Association of Agricultural Cooperative Members in the capital, Ulaanbaatar, explained that the principal reasons for the failure of the *horshoo* were: (a) High interest rates, which rose to 15–20 per cent per month as the government tried to control inflation. Although interest rates have declined since then, they still varied from about 30–70 per cent per annum in 1998, when inflation was around 6 per cent.[49] (b) Increased transportation costs, as both fuel and spare parts became rapidly more

---

[49] National Statistical Office of Mongolia (1999: 68).

expensive. (c) The membership had alternative channels through which to market their produce. (d) It became impossible to raise trading capital. The banking sector as a whole was quickly accumulating a huge amount of bad debt and soon stopped providing much by way of credit to small enterprises.

Although the immediate causes of the failure of most *horshoo* was undoubtedly the adverse economic climate, this raises the question of the underlying ability of these organizations to weather financial storms or raise further investment from their membership or other sources. Their voluntary membership did not support the cooperatives with further investment or labour. Even in the case of the Bayan Tsagaan *horshoo*, rather than the cooperative having a firm institutional basis in its own right, the membership's commitment to it was mediated by their obligations towards their own immediate family and close kin. Members would withdraw from the cooperative if this ever seemed to be in the best interests of their household, family, and friends.

It might seem strange, at first glance, that both producer and marketing cooperatives have not been more successful, as there are undoubtedly economies of scale to be gained in a pastoral economy composed of so many distantly scattered producer households. However, examining the institutional frames of the various pastoral institutions that have operated successfully in Mongolian history, it is striking that they were all socio-political institutions, as well as economic. It was not simply the narrowly economic functions that the old collectives or their predecessors supplied that guaranteed their continued existence. Their depth (i.e. durability and significance) in social and political dimensions provided them with the stability and the command over labour that they needed. Unlike the cooperatives, membership was not conditional on short-term benefits.

8.3.1. *Medium-Scale, Household-Based Pastoralism*

Historically there have been two solutions to the problem of gaining sufficient labour to herd large numbers of livestock. One involved engaging additional labour under the direct management of the owner, often by expanding the household itself. A rich family might adopt children or include a son-in-law for this reason. Additional labour could also be attached to the family through the extension of the encampment. In the pre-communist period there were neo-feudal retainers or servants, (*har'yat* or *hamjlaga*) attached to noble families, and rich commoners might employ servants (*zarts*) in an analogous way. Another common form was for a wealthy family to attract poorer 'client' households who could be invited to join their *hot-ail* and pool their livestock with the larger herds. Since the work of herding was shared between households this allowed richer families to draw upon the greater amount of labour they needed to care for their large herds, while poor households gained access to carts, draft animals and other benefits that the rich had.[50] The other type of arrangement was *süreg tavih*—the 'leasing out' of livestock to poorer households who herded them for the owner in return for a certain portion of the produce.

[50] See Sneath (2000) and Simukov (1933: 29).

Since decollectivization some pastoral households have accumulated large herds of livestock, establishing larger pastoral operations and reaping the benefits of economies of scale and extensive systems of pastoral movement. In 1992 there were reported to be seven households with more than 1000 head of livestock. By 1998 this number had risen to 955, of which thirty-three had more than 2000 animals.[51] The household with the most livestock in the country in 1996 was that of a man named Henmedeh who had 2358 animals at the end of 1995, and over 2800 in 1999.[52]

The reasons for Henmedeh's success, apart from his undoubted herding know-how, can be traced to his position in the collective. He used to manage the horse-herding brigade, breeding and training horses that were entered in the national horse-races. Well-connected, and with responsibility for these valuable assets, Henmedeh had managed to accumulate 1008 head of livestock by 1992, and by 1994 he had more than doubled this to 2045. Henmedeh also owned both a truck and a jeep, and he sold his own produce directly to buyers in Ulaanbaatar. Another of the key factors was Henmedeh's location. He lives only a hundred kilometres or so from Ulaanbaatar and its huge urban markets. This allows him to get relatively good prices for his products and to buy the spare parts and fuel needed to keep his vehicles running.

In 1996 Henmedeh employed four herdsmen, and by 1999 had expanded his operation to include seven herders, in addition to his two sons, who worked for him under contractual arrangements very similar to the historical *süreg tavih* relations.[53] He has been able to accumulate livestock because he has a lower relative rate of consumption and sale than his poorer neighbours. In 1995 the forty households of Henmedeh's subdistrict (*bag*) recorded average internal consumption of 5 per cent of their livestock. Henmedeh's consumption amounted to 4.3 per cent, including food supplies (*idesh*) given to his kin. In the *bag* as a whole, households sold an average of 13 per cent of their livestock in 1995, whereas Henmedeh sold only 7.7 per cent. (This district is so close to the Ulaanbaatar market that the average level of sales was considerably higher than that in more distant pastoral districts.[54]

---

[51] *Zasagyn Gazar Medeel* No. 2 (63) 1992; *Zasagyn Gazar Medeel*, I sar, II doloo honog, 1996.

[52] These are end of year totals, the summer figures are higher. When I stayed with Henmedeh in August 1996, for example, he had over 3000 animals, including newly-born lambs, kids, foals, and calves. Most of these were sheep (2502), but he also owned 332 horses, 240 cows, and 39 goats. Some 500 of these animals were sold and slaughtered that autumn and winter.

[53] In 1996 two employee households herded about 700 'leased' sheep and lambs each. They kept the milk from these flocks and were paid 240,000 *tögrög* (436 USD) per year (about three times the now-miserable state pension). The wool and offspring went to Henmedeh. These families herded their own smaller holdings of livestock—about 60–70 sheep and goats, and 5–10 cattle. Since then Henmedeh has moved to a contract by which client households supply a quota of fifty newborn animals per 100 breeding females, and are allowed to keep additional livestock and all animal produce. In 1995 Henmedeh sold 300 sheep, 10 cattle, around 1500 kg of wool, the proceeds of which were about 6.3 million *tögrög* (11,450 USD), 30–40 times the average per capita income.

[54] In remote Hanh, for example, among the 102 households in *bag* number 2, sales amounted to 10.7% and consumption 8.0%. The overall off-take, in both cases, being around 18%. In both cases households were selling more livestock than they were eating themselves, but most remained primarily concerned with subsistence production. They rely heavily on dairy products, and a large proportion of their livestock sales is to obtain flour. Figures were calculated from local government statistics which still record the number of

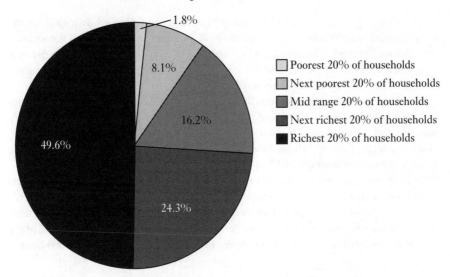

Figure 8.3. *Proportion of total livestock owned by sections of the population of* bag *2* Hanh sum, *(sheep units per household)*

It has been argued that pastoralism has an innate tendency towards an equality of livestock holdings between households, on account of the increasing marginal difficulty of caring for large herds, and in some cases the tendency for richer households to consume more than poor.[55] This argument never appeared convincing when applied to Inner Asian pastoralism, particularly in view of the long history of very wealthy herd-owners and the ancient practice of 'placing herds' with other households. Henmedeh's case also suggested that the wealthy could sell and consume a smaller proportion of their herd than their poorer neighbours. If this is a general trend we can expect to see the emergence of a stratum of wealthy herd-owners who make use of employee or client labour as poorer households fall below the minimum herd-size needed for subsistence. This already appears to be happening as the number of households with more than 1000 livestock has increased from 305 in 1995 to 955 in 1998.[56]

An indication of the wealth differences that have emerged can be seen from the situation of one pastoral sub-district (*bag*) of Hanh *sum*, Hövsgöl. Figure 8.3 shows that the richest 20 per cent of the ninety-nine households in *bag* 2 of Hanh *sum* own almost half the livestock of the subdistrict. The richest five households in the *bag* have between 500 and 850 sheep equivalent units of livestock, which is still a relatively small holding in comparison with Henmedeh who had over 4500 sheep equivalent units at the end of 1995.

animals sold and consumed by each household using the Mongolian sheep equivalent units (counting sheep as 1, horses as 6, cattle as 5, goats as 0.9, camels as 7).

[55] See Dahl (1979: 279). Barth (1964: 76) in his analysis of pastoral Basseri society sites the 'differential consumption rates' of rich and poor as a check to the accumulation of livestock, among other factors.

[56] National Statistical Office of Mongolia (1999: 96).

This distribution appeared to be fairly typical; data from a *bag* subdistrict in nearby Renchinlhümbe *sum* show a similar distribution, and both are in line with the national statistics for livestock distribution, which indicate that in 1996 the poorest 25 per cent of pastoral households owned less than 7 per cent of the national herd, whereas the richest 20 per cent owned more than half the total.[57]

The hypothesis that large pastoral operators tend to have the incentive and ability to retain relatively wide systems of pastoral movement is borne out in Henmedeh's case. He and his employees move with their herds more than most other pastoralists, moving a total of about 110 km in a year, whereas the five other, poorer, *ails* in the vicinity, moved between about 30 and 70 km.

In time rich pastoral households may be able to expand their herds and pastoral operations sufficiently to reintroduce the economies of scale reaped by large herd-owning institutions in the past. However, it may take a long time for such operations to become common enough to encompass the bulk of the pastoral sector. In 1998 of the 275,000 households owning livestock, fewer than 1000 owned more than 1000 head.

8.4. CONCLUSION

The decollectivization of pastoralism has seen a retreat to subsistence for many pastoral families, a reduction in the export and processing of their produce, the development of inequalities of wealth, and a loss of mechanization. Pastoralists, faced with economic crisis, have had to depend on networks of family and friends. The large-scale pastoralism of the collectives formed part of a politico-economic structure that supported manufacturing and processing industries. These declined together, leaving pastoral households to fall back on longstanding domestic systems of self-provisioning and subsistence. The privatization policies were inspired by the notion of a latent but highly productive market economy that could be rapidly emancipated from a restrictive politico-economic system. However, dismantling the large-scale pastoral institutions simply led to the collapse of district-wide operations, and expanded the domestic subsistence operations of individual families that were poorly adapted to supply livestock products to manufacturing industry and commerce.

The pastoral economy to emerge from decollectivization presents something of a paradox. Many of the most obvious problems that pastoralists now face result from the loss of the economies of scale generated by collectives, both in production and marketing, particularly in mechanization and transportation. However, the numerous attempts to establish cooperatives to recapture some economies of scale have tended to fail. This paradox becomes comprehensible when one examines the nature of the institutional frames within which different economic groups existed.

Historically the spectrum of economic activities within Mongolian pastoralism has stretched from the smallest domestic subsistence activities of a poor household with a few dozen sheep, through to the largest collective or pre-revolutionary noble or monastery, managing tens of thousands of animals over a whole district. In the case

---

[57] This is shown by analysis of figures given by National Statistical Office of Mongolia, (1999: 45).

of the household, domestic roles and norms provided the motivational underpinnings for the cooperation of its members. At the district level, the coordination of labour depended upon notions of duty and legal sanctions underpinning the conventional obligations attached to the status of common herdsman or collective farm member. Intermediate-scale operations were typically managed by wealthy families coordinating the labour of some clients or servants, and were founded on the household as an institution. They tended to make use of the morality of family and friendship (in the case of clients) and/or socio-political obligation (in the case of neo-feudal retainers).

The ephemeral nature of the *horshoo* cooperatives contrasts with the durability of the pastoral household and former large-scale pastoral operations and illustrates the importance of institutional settings for economic groupings and their viability. As the essential unit for pastoral residence and reproduction, the stability of the household and the commitment of its members to its economic success, was never in doubt. Similarly, the large-scale public pastoral operations supported by local authorities had a firm institutional setting, and a membership subject to the same authorities. In both cases the group's continued existence was beyond question, its economic activities being only one aspect of the wider social and political functions of the institution. Groups and individuals could assume, with a high degree of confidence, that members of these domestic and official institutions would fulfil their obligations.

The *horshoo* cooperatives, by contrast, had little by way of 'institutional depth', a voluntary and changeable membership, and very limited organizational precedent. Without any political authority to compel or guarantee the actions of others, the *horshoo* proved unable to draw on the resources or labour of member households, and were easily ruined by difficult economic conditions. Households could, and did, simply withdraw and use their own networks to provision themselves and market produce—using kinship and friendship relations that had a strong social component and permanence beyond the purely instrumental. Pastoralists often agreed that the services that the cooperatives could supply were theoretically desirable, but saw little reason to risk the assets belonging to the groups they considered to be really fundamental—their households.

High interest rates and transportation costs played a central role in the failure of the cooperatives. More favourable conditions for credit and infrastructural investment in the national transportation system would have facilitated trade and eased the difficulties faced by pastoralists in marketing their produce and obtaining consumer goods. However, remote districts such as Hanh *sum* need marketing operations accessible to scattered pastoral households to be provided as a service. The marketing cooperatives attempted to provide this sort of inclusive service, but this placed them in a poor position to compete with private traders able to cherry-pick the most profitable customers and commodities, or with kin trusted with the sale of produce. In the short term at least, it is difficult to see how these conditions could be changed without legal or social sanctions to channel sales through the cooperative, or financial support such as low-interest credit or targeted investment for private trade.

Two of the conditions necessary for viable large-scale pastoral production operations are ownership of large numbers of livestock by a single agency, and access to large areas of land. These were key features of the collectives that were more or less successfully established in the 1950s, but they were also accompanied by the high levels of investment required to establish motor pools and mechanized hay production facilities. Equivalent investment in the present-day pastoral sector would have to be financed on much more favourable terms than those offered by commercial banks, and the success of any new enterprises of this sort would depend upon relatively secure markets for pastoral products. It may be that a more productive pastoral sector will require major investment, not only in infrastructure such as road and rail links, but in institutions capable of organizing specialized pastoral production on a sufficiently large-scale. This may be as essential as the large-scale investments that are needed in marketing if the pastoral sector is to be restored to anything like its previous role.

9

The Hidden Side of Group Behaviour: A Gender Analysis of Community Forestry in South Asia

BINA AGARWAL

9.1. INTRODUCTION

Community forestry groups, managing State or community-owned forest resources, represent one of the most rapidly growing forms of collective action in the developing world. They thus provide an especially useful study in how groups function. This chapter focuses on South Asian experience to illuminate how such groups, ostensibly set-up to operate on principles of cooperation, and meant to involve and benefit all members of the rural community, often effectively exclude significant sections, such as women. While seemingly participatory, equitable and efficient, they cloak substantial gender-related inequities and inefficiencies. The chapter also analyses what underlies such unfavourable outcomes and how the outcomes could be improved.

The interactive effect of one outcome on another is examined as well. For instance, excluding women (often the principal users of community forests) from a group's decision-making bodies could have a range of negative efficiency fallouts, such as the framing of inappropriate or inequitable rules that are difficult to enforce. I analyse these issues (which typically cut across class/caste divisions) mainly from a gender perspective. Where relevant, the interplay of class/caste with gender, in defining outcomes for different categories of women, is also outlined.

The chapter argues that the outcomes of group functioning are determined especially by rules, norms, and perceptions, in addition to the household and personal endowments and attributes of those affected. All of these factors can work to the disadvantage of women, both separately and interactively. To what extent they can be changed in women's favour will depend on women's bargaining power *vis-a-vis* the State, the community, and the family. The factors that are likely to affect women's bargaining power in these three arenas are spelt out as well. While the context here

This is a shorter, updated, and somewhat different version of a paper presented at the Conference on Group Behaviour and Development, held at UNU/WIDER, Helsinki, September 1999. The longer version has appeared as an UNU/WIDER working paper (Agarwal 2000*a*). I am most grateful to the conference participants for their responses, and especially to Judith Heyer for her comments on an earlier draft.

is community forestry, the conceptual framework would also be relevant to understanding the gendered dimensions of group functioning in a number of other contexts, including water user's associations.

The chapter is based largely on the fieldvisits and interviews I undertook during 1998–99 in eighty-seven community forestry sites across five states of India (Gujarat, Karnataka, Madhya Pradesh, Orissa, and the Uttar Pradesh hills) and two districts (Kaski and Dang) of Nepal.[1] These are supplemented by existing case studies and some earlier visits to selected sites. Information was obtained mostly through unstructured interviews with villagers, at times with women and men in separate groups, at other times with both sexes jointly, in addition to individual interviews with key informants, especially office bearers in the community forestry groups.

9.2. BACKGROUND

In rural South Asia, forests and village commons have always been important sources of basic necessities and supplementary livelihoods, providing villagers with firewood, fodder, small timber, and various non-timber products. Especially for the poor and women who own little private land, they have been a critical element in survival. In India's semi-arid regions in the 1980s, for instance, the landless and landpoor procured over 90 per cent of their firewood and satisfied 69–89 per cent of their grazing needs from common pool resources (Jodha 1986). At that time, firewood alone provided 65–67 per cent of total domestic energy in the hills and desert areas of India and over 90 per cent in Nepal as a whole (Agarwal 1987). This situation remained largely unchanged even in the early 1990s when community forestry programmes were formally launched in both countries. Firewood was then still the single most important source (and for many the only source) of rural domestic energy in South Asia, and was still largely gathered, not bought. In 1992–93, for instance, 62 per cent of rural India's domestic energy came from firewood. In most Indian states over 80 per cent of rural households used some firewood as domestic fuel; and, taking an all-India average, only about 15 per cent of the firewood so used was purchased (Natrajan 1995).

Over time, however, people's ability to fulfil their needs had been eroding with the decline in communal resources, due both to degradation and to shifts in property rights away from communities to the State and to individuals. The push toward community forest management represented a small but notable reversal in these processes of statization and privatization, toward a re-establishment of greater community control over forests and village commons. Indeed there is now a mushrooming of community forestry groups (CFGs) in South Asia.[2]

In India, these CFGs include: (i) State-initiated groups formed under the Joint Forest Management (JFM) programme launched in 1990, in which village communities and the government share the responsibilities and benefits of regenerating degraded

[1] In India, the term 'state' relates to the biggest administrative divisions within the country and is not to be confused with 'State', used throughout in the political economy sense of the word. In Nepal the biggest administrative divisions are 'districts'. In India, districts are smaller divisions within states.

[2] I will be using CFG as a general term to cover all types of community forestry groups.

local forests; (ii) self-initiated groups, started autonomously by a village council, youth club or village elder and concentrated mainly in Bihar and Orissa; and (iii) groups with a mixed history, such as the *van panchayats* or forest councils in the hills of Uttar Pradesh (UP) initiated by the British in the 1930s. Some of these have survived or been revived by NGOs. JFM groups are the most widespread, both geographically and in terms of forest area. To date, virtually all Indian states have passed JFM resolutions. These allow participating villagers access to most non-timber forest products and to 25–50 per cent (varying by state) of any mature timber harvested. There were approximately 63,000 JFM groups in 2001, covering 14.2 million hectares (mha) or 18.6 per cent of the 76.5 mha administered as forest land (Sehgal 2001). In addition, there are a few thousand groups of the other types.

Nepal's community forestry programme launched in 1993 is largely State-initiated. Here the State transfers even good forest to a set of identified users who form a forest user group (FUG) and are entitled to all of the benefits.[3] In 2000, there were 9100 FUGs involving one million households and covering 0.66 mha or 11.4 per cent (the target being 61 per cent) of the country's 5.8 mha of total forest land (Government of Nepal 2000). In both India and Nepal, NGOs can act as catalysts or intermediaries in group formation and functioning.

Unlike the old systems of communal resource management which typically recognized the usufruct rights of all village residents, the new CFGs represent a more formalized system of rights. Typically these rights are based either on membership (as in the State-initiated groups), or on rules specified by selected (often self-selected) community members (as in the self-initiated groups). In other words, membership, or some other formal system, is replacing village citizenship as the defining criterion for establishing rights in the commons.

This raises some critical questions, such as: how are the CFGs performing in terms of participation, equity, and efficiency from the perspective of women, especially the poor? Are the emerging systems of rights in communal property inclusive and equitable, or are they replicating the patterns of élite and male centredness that characterize rights in private land? The section below focuses on these concerns.

9.3. GENDERED OUTCOMES: PARTICIPATION, EQUITY, AND EFFICIENCY

In terms of forest regeneration, many CFGs have had notable success. Typically what is involved is restriction of entry and protection, although in some cases replanting is also done. Even with simple protection, natural revival is often rapid if the rootstock is intact. Within five to seven years, many of the severely degraded tracts in semi-arid India have been covered with young trees; and areas with some vegetation, but notably declining, show encouraging signs of regeneration. Hence in most ecological zones, as a result of the CFG initiatives, beneficial results are noted, and in a number of cases it has been reported that incomes and employment have increased,[4] seasonal

[3] The government, however, retains the right to reclaim any forests seen to be mismanaged by the FUGs.
[4] See, e.g., Raju *et al.* (1993); Kant *et al.* (1991); and SPWD (1994).

outmigration has fallen,[5] the land's carrying capacity has improved, and biodiversity has been enhanced.[6] Some villages have even received awards for conservation (Shah and Shah 1995; my fieldvisits during 1998–99).

Viewed from a gender perspective (and especially the perspective of poor women), however, these results look less impressive on several important counts: effective participation; equity in the sharing of costs and benefits; and efficiency in functioning.

9.3.1. *Participation*

In both India and Nepal, the State-initiated groups generally have a two-tier organizational structure, consisting of a general body with members drawn from the whole village and an executive committee (EC) of some 9–15 persons. Typically the general body meets once or twice a year and the EC meets about once a month. Both bodies, interactively, define the rules for forest use and benefit sharing, the structure of fines for rule violation, the method of protection (e.g. guards, patrol groups, etc.), and so on. Which category of persons has a voice in the general body and the EC bears critically on how well these organizations function, and who gains or loses from them.

Women's effective participation in CFG decision-making would require not only that they become members of the group (the general body, the EC), but that they attend and speak up at group meetings, and (at least some of the time) can ensure that decisions are in their interest. Such participation is important both in itself, as an indicator of democratic institutional functioning, and for its effects on cost and benefit sharing and on efficiency. To what extent do women in general, and poor women in particular, so participate?

Participation in Management

Women usually constitute less than 10 per cent of the general bodies in most JFM groups;[7] they are typically absent in the self-initiated groups;[8] and are few or none in the *van panchayats*.[9] Their presence in Nepal's FUGs is similarly sparse. A study of seven FUGs in eastern Nepal found that only 3.5 per cent of those recorded as users in the FUGs were women (Dahal 1994: 78).

In India, the eligibility criteria for membership in the JFM general body and the EC vary by state. Eight of the twenty-two states for which information is so far available restrict general body membership to only one person per household. This is almost always the male household head. In eight other states, due to amendments in the initial Orders, both spouses, or one man and one woman, can now be members, but this still excludes other household adults. Only three states have opened membership to all village adults. In the self-initiated autonomous CFGs, the customary exclusion of

[5] See, Viegas and Menon (1993) and Chopra and Gulati (1997).
[6] Raju *et al.* (1993); Arul and Poffenberger (1990); also my fieldvisits in 1995 and 1998–99.
[7] Roy *et al.* (1992); Guhathakurta and Bhatia (1992); and Narain (1994); also my fieldvisits 1998–99.
[8] Kant *et al.* (1991); Singh and Kumar (1993); and my fieldwork in 1998–99.
[9] Sharma and Sinha (1993); Tata Energy Research Unit (TERI 1995); also my fieldwork in 1998–99. In the TERI study, out of the fifty *van panchayats* examined, only nine had any women members.

women from village decision-making bodies has been replicated. In Nepal's FUGs, again, the household is the unit of membership, and in male-headed households it is the man's name that is entered in the membership list (Seeley 1996).

Without being general body members, women usually hear little about what transpires at meetings. Many women complain:

Our husbands don't tell us about meetings. They simply say they have a meeting and go, when the watchman brings around the notice for the meeting (woman to author, Five village mouza, Orissa, 1998).

When we ask them what happened at the meeting, they say: what will you gain by knowing? (women to author, Five village mouza, Orissa, 1998).

Typically men don't tell their wives what happens in meetings. Even if there is a dispute about something, they don't tell us; nor do they volunteer information about other matters (women to author, Khedipada village, Gujarat, 1999).

Women's representation in the ECs is also typically low, although there is some variation by region and context. In a study of twenty JFM groups in West Bengal (east India) 60 per cent had no women EC members, and only 8 per cent of the 180 EC members were women. Landless families, similarly, are little represented in the ECs (Sarin 1998). In many states, recent JFM resolutions require the inclusion of women in the EC, ranging from a minimum of two or three to one-third, but I found that the women so included were rarely chosen by other women as their representatives. Sometimes, to fill the mandatory slots, male EC members chose the women even without consulting them. Such women are seldom active or effective. In Nepal again, women have only a nominal presence in the ECs. Those who join are usually poorly informed about the activities of their FUG, and some are even unaware that they are EC members (Upadhyay and Jeddere-Fisher 1998; Moffatt 1998).

Whether from a lack of awareness, or the constraints discussed later, only a small percentage of the women who are general body or EC members usually attend the meetings. Those who attend rarely speak up, and if they do speak they say their opinions are given little weight.

Men don't listen, except perhaps one or two. Men feel they should be the spokespersons (woman to author, Garbe Kuna village, Kaski district, Nepal, 1998).

What is the point of going to meetings. We would only sit silently (women to author, Panasa Diha village, Orissa, 1998).

I attend *van panchayat* meetings, but I only sign, I don't say much. Or I say I agree (woman *van panchayat* member to author, Sallarautela village, UP hills).

Having a voice in the EC is important since this is the site for discussions and decisions on many critical aspects of CFG functioning. As matters stand, women are not party to many crucial decisions. An analysis of JFM decision-making in five Gujarat villages revealed that all major decisions on forest protection, use, distribution of wood and grass, and future planning, were taken by men. The only joint decisions with women were those concerning tree nurseries (Joshi 1998). Women are also often left out of the CFG teams that go on 'exposure' visits to other sites, or that receive technical training in new silviculture practices.

Although there are some contrasting examples of all-women CFGs and mixed CFGs with a high female presence, these remain atypical. All-women CFGs, for instance, are found especially in the UP hills and parts of Nepal where there is high male outmigration; and a scattering of them have also emerged in other regions, catalysed by a local NGO, a forest official, or an international donor.[10] Occasionally women initiate one themselves. There are no consolidated figures for India, but in Nepal, in 2000, all-women FUGs constituted less than 3.8 per cent of all FUGs, controlling 1.1 per cent of all FUG land. Half of the all-women FUGs have 10 ha or less, and virtually none have over 50 ha. Typically this is degraded land needing tree planting, while mixed FUGs commonly control a few hundred hectares and usually this is natural forest.[11] Similarly, mixed groups with a high female presence (say 30 per cent or even 50 per cent women in the general body) are found only in selected pockets, as in parts of Gujarat and West Bengal.[12]

Participation in Protection

Despite their limited presence as formal members, many women play an active role in protection. In formal terms, the bounded forest area is usually protected either by employing a guard, with CFG members contributing the wage, or by forming a patrol group from among member households. A male guard or an all-male patrol characterized 45 and 18 per cent respectively of the eighty-seven sites I visited. Only a small percentage of patrols were constituted by both sexes, or by women alone, and there was a rare female guard. Occasionally, there are shifts from all-women to all-men patrols, and vice versa. More commonly, women patrol informally. In some villages of Gujarat and the UP hills, they have formed separate informal protection groups parallel to men's because they feel men's formal patrolling is ineffective.

Women's informal vigilance improves protection in important ways. In most villages I visited, women told me that they had apprehended intruders both from other villages and from their own, and that when they caught women intruders they sought to dissuade them from breaking the rules. In fire fighting, likewise, women join in enthusiastically; and in several instances women's alertness alone has saved the forest.

On the one hand, therefore, most women are excluded from CFG membership and management; on the other hand, many women contribute notably to protection efforts, indicating their stake in forest regeneration. However, women's limited involvement in the decision-making process has implications for both equity and efficiency.

9.3.2. *Equity*

How equitable are the CFGs in the sharing of costs and benefits?

---

[10] e.g. Mukerjee and Roy (1993); Correa (1997); Adhikari *et al.* (1991); Mansingh (1991); Regmi (1989); Singh and Burra (1993) and Raju (1997); also my fieldwork in 1998–99.

[11] Calculated from figures given in Government of Nepal (2000).

[12] Narain (1994); Viegas and Menon (1993); also my fieldvisits in 1998–99.

Cost Bearing

The costs of forest closure are broadly of two types: those associated with protection and management and those associated with forgoing forest use (see Table 9.1). The former usually includes costs such as membership fees, the forest guard's pay, the opportunity cost of patrolling time, and so on. These types of costs are borne largely by men. The costs of forgoing forest use include the opportunity cost of time spent in finding alternative sites for essential items such as firewood and fodder, other costs (identified below) associated with firewood shortages, the loss of livelihoods based on non-timber forest products, and so on. These types of costs fall largely on women.

Consider the firewood-related effects in more detail. Firewood is an everyday need, obtaining which is mainly women's responsibility (compared with, say, small timber that is needed occasionally for agricultural implements, etc., and is mainly men's responsibility). Typically when protection begins, all human and animal entry is banned, especially in the semi-arid regions. Where the land was barren anyway this caused no extra hardship. But where earlier women could fulfill at least part of their firewood needs from the protected area, after closure they were forced to travel to neighbouring sites, involving additional time, energy, and (where those sites were also

Table 9.1. *Main potential costs and benefits of forest closure by gender*

Mainly affecting women	Mainly affecting men
Costs	
Firewood shortages (more time and energy expended in collection and/or cooking; and adverse health effects)	Membership fee
	Patrolling time/guard's pay
	Fodder shortages (purchase)
Fodder shortages (more time and energy expended in collection)	Loss of source for small timber
	Erosion of some livelihoods: for example, blacksmiths using woodfuel in furnaces
Increased time in stallfeeding animals	
Informal patrolling time	
Erosion of some livelihoods: for example, firewood sellers, NTFP collectors	
Fines if caught stealing firewood	
Enhanced (late entry) membership fee	
Benefits	
Firewood supply (a few weeks, if forest is opened)	Small timber (if allowed)
	Housebuilding timber (if allowed)
Fodder supply (a few weeks, if forest is opened)	Cash (if distributed) from sale of forest products
NTFP (seasonal)	Use of collective fund

Note: This is a broad outline of the main *direct* costs and benefits. Not each of these need apply to every CFG. There may also be some *indirect* costs and benefits. For instance, a greater supply of firewood indirectly benefits the whole family.

NTFP = Non-timber forest products. These are largely collected by women.

being protected) the risk of being caught and fined.[13] As a result, in the early years of JFM, Sarin (1995) noted that in some protected sites in Gujarat and West Bengal, women's collection time for a headload of firewood had increased from 1–2 hours to 4–5 hours or more, and journeys of half a kilometre had lengthened to 8–9. In many households, women were also compelled to take their daughters along, spending over six hours a day to walk five times farther, for the same quantity of fuelwood (Shah and Shah 1995). Over time this could negatively affect the girls' education. When neighbouring villages too started protecting, many women faced severe shortages. Most sought to make do with the limited firewood available from trees on their home fields, supplemented by inferior fuels which have other negative consequences (described below). But even with such shifts, some (especially the landless) were compelled to continue collecting clandestinely, risking fines and abuse if caught.

Such gendered consequences were widespread, causing considerable resentment among the women. For example, in Pingot village (Gujarat), women, when asked about the award for environmental conservation conferred on the village, responded with bitterness: 'What forest? We used to go [there] to pick fuelwood, but ever since the men have started protecting it they don't even allow us to look at it!' (Shah and Shah 1995: 80).

In most places, this picture has remained largely unchanged even after several years of protection. Of the eighty-seven CFGs I visited in 1998–99, firewood was available in eighty. Of these forty-five (60 per cent) still had a ban on firewood collection, with twenty-one not opening the forest at all and twenty-four opening it for a few days annually for drywood collection and/or cutback and cleaning operations. The remaining CFGs allowed some collection, usually only of fallen twigs and branches. Even after years of protection, women thus reported a persistence of firewood shortages in most of the villages I visited in Gujarat, the UP hills, Karnataka, parts of Madhya Pradesh bordering Gujarat, and in the Kaski and Dang districts of Nepal. The exceptions were some parts of Orissa, Karnataka and Madhya Pradesh with older forests, where collection was allowed on a regular basis from the start.

Some common responses by women are given below:

We go in the morning and only return in the evening. Since the end of the rainy season, we have been going every day. I go myself and so does my daughter. Earlier too there was a shortage but not as acute (woman EC member to author, Kangod village, Karnataka, 1998).

It is women who need the forest, they need firewood to cook. . . . Men preach to women about not cutting trees, but what can women do? They cannot cook food without firewood and they cannot collect firewood from other places (group discussion with women in Kabhre Palanchok, Nepal, cited in Hobley 1996: 147).

Where possible, women have tried to substitute other fuels. A few are able to switch to biogas (usually where there is an effective NGO programme), but most turn to twigs, dung cakes, agricultural waste, or even dry leaves. Fire from these latter fuels needs careful tending which increases cooking time and prevents women from simultaneously attending to other work. Moreover, these fuels cause more fumes, with

---

[13] Sarin (1995); Agarwal (1997a); also my fieldwork in 1998–99.

negative health effects in poorly ventilated conditions. In several villages women also report economizing on fuel by forgoing a winter fire for space heating (even in the sub-zero temperatures of the Nepal hills), giving the animals cold feed, not heating winter bath water or heating it only for husbands, and so on.

Usually women from both middle and poor peasant households report such domestic energy problems, since even in the better-off homes firewood is typically gathered and not purchased. Most do not have many trees on their private land. Women of landless or landpoor households are, however, the worst off, since without private land they also have no crop waste or trees of their own, and few cattle for dung.[14] In fact, forest closure has forced many to sell-off parts of their animal stock. As a poor woman in Khut village (UP hills) told me: 'We don't know in the morning if we will be able to cook at night'. Another added: 'Our bahus (daughters-in-law) have to undertake a full day's journey to get a basket of grass and some firewood from the Reserve Forest.' Her daughter-in-law pitched in: 'But even in the Reserve Forest you can be caught by the forest guard. I paid Rs 20 as a fine to retrieve my axe, and all I was doing was cutting a fallen log.' Again in Nepal, in Tallo Goungonda village (Kaski district), a group of poor women told me: 'We go at night . . . Other women have gas and stoves, but we are poor, so we have to steal.'

Similarly, since grazing is usually banned, households with cattle have to procure fodder in other ways. Since cattle care is usually women's responsibility, if the household cannot afford to buy fodder women have to spend additional time looking for other sites to procure some. Moreover, animals now have to be stall-fed. In parts of Gujarat many women report an extra workload of 2–3 hours due to stall-feeding alone. Where some of the better-off households have replaced their goats with stall-fed milch cattle, it has further increased women's labour.

As the forests have regenerated, at best these hardships have been alleviated; they have not disappeared. Firewood shortages, for instance, continue to be reported even 8–10 years after protection in many regions, despite the quite large areas being protected. By one estimate, about 0.2 ha of forest is needed per household for meeting firewood and other subsistence needs, and many Gujarat villages have several times this area (Shah 1997). Certainly, in fifteen of my nineteen Gujarat fieldwork sites, the protected area per capita exceeded this norm (and nine of the nineteen villages were each protecting over 100 ha). Although specific estimates (such as 0.2 ha per household) might be contested by some, many agree that both in Gujarat and elsewhere more could be extracted sustainably than is currently being allowed. This could be supplemented by other measures, such as planning fuelwood plantations in a part of the forest, promoting and maintaining workable biogas plants, and so on. In many places, therefore, the scarcities that women are experiencing appear to have less to do with aggregate availability or a lack of potential solutions than with women's limited bargaining power, whereby their problems are seen as individual/private rather than as warranting community attention.

---

[14] See also Jodha (1986) on differences between landed and landpoor rural households in India, in their relative dependence on the commons for firewood and fodder.

Benefit Sharing

There are also gender inequities in benefit sharing. In some cases the benefits are not distributed at all. Among Orissa's self-initiated groups, for example, a number of all-male youth clubs have completely banned forest entry and have been selling the wood (obtained from thinning and cleaning operations), as well as other forest produce. In many cases, the quite substantial funds so obtained have been spent on an annual religious festival (my fieldvisits, 1998), or on a clubhouse or club functions (Singh and Kumar 1993).

In other types of CFGs, the money is normally put in a collective fund to be used as the group deems fit. Women typically have little say in how it is used:

The money obtained from grass and firewood is kept by them in their fund. We have not seen one penny of it. We buy grass, which is auctioned by bundles (women to author, Ghusra village, Dang district, Nepal, 1998).

Where the CFGs distribute the benefits, say in the form of firewood or grass, as in some of the JFM groups, women of non-member households usually receive none, since entitlements are typically linked to membership. Often these are poor households whose members have to migrate for work, or are out all day on wage labour and cannot easily contribute to patrolling or to the guard's wages.

Even in member households usually men alone can claim the benefits directly, either because only they are members, or because entitlements are on a household basis, so that even if both spouses are members they get only one share. Of course women can benefit indirectly in some degree, say if the benefits are in kind (such as firewood); or where member households continue to enjoy the right to collect dry wood or leaves from the protected area.[15] But where the CFGs distribute cash benefits, money given to men does not guarantee equal sharing, or even any sharing, within the family. In fact, outside the context of forest management there is substantial evidence of men in poor households spending a significant part of their incomes on personal items (tobacco, liquor, etc.), while women spend almost all of their incomes on basic household needs.[16] This pattern is found repeated in the context of CFGs. In many cases, men are found to spend the money on gambling, liquor, or personal items.[17]

Many women are aware that unless they receive a share *directly* (rather than through male members), they may get nothing. When asked their views on this at a meeting of three JFM villages in West Bengal, in which both women and men were present, all the women wanted equal and separate shares for husbands and wives (Sarin 1995). Being members in their own right would be one way in which women could benefit directly, provided that the individual and not the household was the unit of entitlement.

Inequities also arise because people differ in their needs, or in their ability to contribute or to pay. Broadly, three types of principles/norms can underlie the distribution of forest products: market-determined, contribution, and need. While seemingly neutral,

---

[15] Kant *et al.* (1991); ISO/Swedforest (1993); and Arul and Poffenberger (1990); also my fieldwork in 1998–99.   [16] See, Mencher (1988), and Noponen (1991) for India.
[17] Guhathakurta and Bhatia (1992), and my fieldwork in 1998–99.

these distributive principles have notable gender and class implications. The market principle (or willingness to pay) embodied in practices such as the auctioning of grass to the highest bidder, tends to be both unequal *and* inequitable, since those who cannot afford to pay have to do without. Given that rural women, even in rich households, tend to have less access to financial resources than men, auctions tend to be both anti-poor and anti-women. Distribution according to contribution, say by giving each household that contributes to protection an equal number of grass bundles, would be equal but inequitable for those more dependent on the commons for grass, such as the poorer households, and women in general. Moreover, women's ability to contribute may be circumscribed: for instance, even if they wanted to join patrol duty, they may be socially prevented from doing so by norms of seclusion. Only where distribution embodies some concept of economic need, such as where poor women are given rights to an additional grass patch, would the distribution be relatively more equitable, in that those most in need would get more.

In my fieldwork I found that contribution (in terms of membership fees, protection, etc.) was the most common criterion underlying distribution, with all contributing households having equal claims to the fuelwood or grass cut during the forest opening days. However, there were also occasional cases of auctioning, such as the auctioning of grass in the UP hills and Nepal, and of other forest produce by many of Orissa's self-initiated groups. Economic need seldom guided distribution. Hence for poor women in particular, the outcome tended to prove inequitable.

In recent collective action literature, questions of equity have been raised largely in terms of whether existing economic and social inequality affects the possibility of collective action and efficient institutional functioning.[18] There has been a relative neglect of whether or not the *outcomes* of collective action (in terms of, say, cost and benefit sharing) are equitable, and how those outcomes impinge on the sustainability of collective action. As argued above, equity of outcome is important, in itself, for evaluating institutions governing the commons, quite apart from the links between equity and efficiency (as between participation and efficiency) that are elaborated below.

9.3.3. *Efficiency*

Women's lack of participation in CFG decision-making, and gender inequities in the sharing of costs and benefits from protection, can have a range of efficiency implications. Some initiatives, for example, may fail to take-off at all; others may not sustain the gains, or there may be a notable gap between the gains realized and those realizable (in terms of resource productivity and diversity, satisfying household needs, enhancing incomes, etc.). Inefficiencies can stem from one or more of the following problems (see also, Agarwal 2000*b*).

First, there are rule violations. In almost all the villages I visited there were at least some cases of rule violation, and at times this was a frequent occurrence. Violations by

---

[18] See e.g. Ostrom (1990); Bardhan (1993); and Baland and Platteau (1996, 1999).

men usually involve timber for self-use or sale (the latter in areas with commercially valuable trees). Violations by women typically involve firewood. Where a CFG bans collection without consulting women or addressing their difficulties, many women are under great pressure to break the rules, given their daily need for fuelwood. Sometimes, in situations of acute need, women enter into persistent altercations with the guards.[19] In one Gujarat village the guard threatened to resign as a result. Only then did the EC address the issue and agree to open the forest for a few days annually. In Agarwal's study (1999) of a *van panchayat* village, women constituted 70–80 per cent of reported offenders between 1951 and 1991, many of them belonging to poor and low caste households.

A second source of inefficiency lies in inadequate information sharing with women. Information about the rules (especially membership rules), conflicts encountered, or other aspects of forest management, does not always reach women (my fieldvisits, 1998–99). Similarly, male forest officials seldom consult women or seek their feedback when preparing micro-plans for forest development. Some women hear about the plans through their husbands, others not at all (Guhathakurta and Bhatia 1992). Such communication problems can prove particularly acute in regions of high male outmigration.

Third, inefficiencies can arise if the male guard or patrol fails to notice resource depletion. During my 1995 fieldvisit to Gujarat, a women's informal patrol in Machipada village took me to the protected site, and, pointing out the illegal cuttings which the men had missed, noted: 'Men don't check carefully for illegal cuttings. Women keep a more careful lookout'. My subsequent fieldwork in 1998–99 revealed similar differences in several other field sites. This gender difference, at least in part, arises because women, as the main and most frequent collectors of forest products, are more familiar with the forest than men.

Fourth, and relatedly, there are problems in catching transgressors. In virtually all the regions I visited, all-male patrols or male guards were unable to deal effectively with women intruders because they risked being charged with sexual harassment or molestation. Threats to this effect were not uncommon when non-member women, or women from neighbouring villages, were caught. In some incidents, women and their families had even registered false police cases against patrol members, or beaten them up. Equally, however, women on their own find it difficult to do night patrolling or to confront aggressive male intruders. By all accounts, the most efficient solution appears to be a patrol team consisting of both sexes. Recognizing this, in some regions male patrollers have included some village women in their patrol, but this is atypical.

When women voluntarily set up informal patrols, even where there is a male guard or patrol, the efficiency of protection can improve notably. In their study of twelve *van panchayats*, Sharma and Sinha (1993) found that the four which could be deemed 'robust' all had active women's associations. However, in so far as women's groups

---

[19] E.g. Shah and Shah (1995); Singh and Kumar (1993); and Agarwal (1997*a*); also my field interviews during 1998–99.

are typically informal, they lack the authority to punish offenders who still have to be reported to the formal (typically all-male) committees. This separation of authority and responsibility introduces inefficiencies in functioning. For instance, sometimes male EC members fail to mete out punishments to the culprits women catch, causing women to abandon their efforts. I found several such cases in Karnataka, Gujarat and the UP hills. Also, when women catch intruders, they are seldom party to discussions or decisions on appropriate sanctions.

Fifth, and relatedly, efficient functioning requires effective methods of conflict resolution. This is made difficult with women's virtual exclusion from the formal committees, especially where the conflict involves women, as is not infrequently the case with firewood-related intrusions.

A sixth form of inefficiency stems from taking little account of women's knowledge of plants and species when preparing plans for forest regeneration. Women and men are often privy to different types of knowledge due to differences in the tasks they perform, and in their spatial domains. Women as the main fuel and fodder collectors can often better explain the attributes of trees than men (Pandey 1990); and can identify a large number of trees, shrubs, and grasses in the vicinity of fields and pastures (Chen 1993). In general, women are better informed about the local environment in which they gather and collect, and men about species found in distant areas (Gaul 1994). Women's systematic exclusion from decision-making and management of new planting programmes is thus likely to have negative efficiency implications, by failing to tap women's knowledge of diverse species for enhancing biodiversity.

A seventh form of inefficiency can arise from ignoring possible gender differences in preferences, say regarding when grass should be cut or which trees should be planted. I found that in the rare cases when women were consulted, they often came up with alternative, more suitable suggestions on when the forest should be opened for forest produce collection. Women are also known to usually prefer trees which have more domestic use value, as for fuel and fodder, while men more typically opt for trees that bring in cash[20] (the exceptions being cases where fuel and fodder are ample, in which case women too might prefer commercial species: Chen 1993). Women's greater involvement in forest planning would thus better fulfil household needs and increase commitment to the initiative.

Basically, when examined from a gender perspective, it is clear that the CFGs are violating many of the conditions deemed by several scholars to be necessary for building enduring institutions for managing common pool resources. This includes conditions such as ensuring that those affected by the rules participate in framing and modifying the rules; that the rules are simple and fair; that there are effective mechanisms for monitoring the resource and resolving conflicts; and so on.[21]

Despite women's low involvement, forests might regenerate, but some of the initiatives might not sustain, and others might produce less than the full potential benefits.

[20] See, e.g. Brara (1987) and Hobley (1996).
[21] See, especially, Ostrom (1990) and Baland and Platteau (1996).

9.4. WHAT DETERMINES GENDERED OUTCOMES?

The gender-related efficiency outcomes discussed above are in large part *secondary* outcomes, stemming from women's low participation in the CFGs and from inequities in the rules of forest use, benefit sharing, etc. Efficiency outcomes are therefore not discussed separately below. Rather, I focus on what underlies women's low participation and the inequities in cost and benefit sharing.

In broad terms, the degree of participation and the distribution of costs and benefits can be seen to depend especially on the following factors: rules, norms, perceptions, the person's individual endowments and attributes, and their household endowments and attributes (which define where they fall within the structural hierarchies of class, caste, etc).

9.4.1. *Factors Affecting Women's Participation*

Rules

In formal CFGs, such as the JFM groups in India or the FUGs in Nepal, rules determine membership in the general body or the EC. As noted earlier, where the rule restricts membership to only one person per household, the male household head tends to join. The rule that allows one man and one woman per household is somewhat more inclusive; but full inclusiveness would require all adults to be allowed to join. This is rare.

In addition to the rules themselves, a lack of awareness of the rules, or of changes therein, can also constrain women's participation. In West Bengal, for instance, a study of nineteen CFGs showed that even four years after the state order was amended to allow women's inclusion, barely two-fifths of the members knew of the change (Raju 1997).

Among the self-initiated groups (that lack formal membership rules), long-standing conventions, which traditionally excluded women from public decision-making forums, also deny women entry into the CFGs.

Social Norms

Even when membership rules are favourable and women join, they seldom attend or speak up at meetings because social norms place strictures on their visibility, mobility, and behaviour. These norms, whether internalized by women or imposed on them by threat of gossip, reprimand, or even violence, impinge directly on women's autonomy and ability to participate effectively in CFGs dominated by men.[22]

Some communities have quite strict female seclusion norms. But more pervasive is the subtle gendering of physical space and social behaviour. For instance, norms often dictate a gender segregation of public space. Women of 'good character' are expected to avoid village spaces where men congregate, such as tea stalls and the market place (Agarwal 1994). For older women, the restriction is generally less, but never fully

---

[22] See also Stewart's (1996) more general discussion on the function of norms in hierarchical contexts.

absent. As a result, many women feel uncomfortable going to CFG meetings, unless explicitly invited by the men:

The meetings are considered for men only. Women are never called. The men attend and their opinions or consent are taken as representative of the whole family—it's understood (woman in a *van panchayat* village, UP hills, cited in Britt 1993: 148).

Rural women and men can't sit together. But we convey our decisions to them (man to author, Chattipur village, Orissa, 1998).

The gender division of labour is another pernicious norm. The fact that women bear the main responsibility of childcare and housework, in addition to the load of agricultural work, cattle care, etc., makes for high work burdens and logistical constraints. This seriously restricts women's ability to attend lengthy meetings held at inconvenient times. As some women in Barde village (Karnataka, south India) told me in 1998: 'There are problems in attending meetings since we need to cook and serve the evening meal. The meeting is long. We also have to feed the cattle'. Men are usually reluctant to share not just domestic tasks and childcare, but even cattle care. Most women in the *van panchayat* villages she studied told Mansingh (1991) that they did not have time to 'sit around for [the] four hours that it took to have a meeting in the middle of the day'. As a result women's attendance thinned out over time.

Norms also reduce women's participation by creating subtle gender hierarchies, such as by requiring women to sit on the floor while husbands and older men sit at a higher level on cots, or requiring women to sit at the back of the meeting space where they are less visible and less able to raise a point effectively. Moreover, where senior male family members are present, women either do not attend meetings, or do not oppose men publicly. The hierarchy that marks 'respectful' behaviour in the family also marks community gatherings.[23]

Social Perceptions

Incorrect perceptions regarding women's abilities impinge on men's willingness to include women in the CFGs. Men often view women's involvement in CFGs as serving no useful purpose and tend to downplay their potential contributions. Some men's direct responses to my questions are indicative:

There is no advantage in having women in the EC. We have been told by the forest officials that we must have two women in the committee, that is why we have included them (male to author, Pathari village, Karnataka).

Women can't make any helpful suggestions (man to author, Arjunpur village, Orissa, 1998).

Women are illiterate. If they come to meetings, we men might as well stay at home (EC chairman to author, Ghusra village, Dang district, Nepal, 1998).

In some cases, I found that the men who were decrying my interviewing the women on the grounds that they were illiterate, were themselves illiterate!

[23] See also, Raju (1997).

Entrenched Territorial Claims

Men oppose women's inclusion much more strongly once their own claims are entrenched. For instance, where CFGs start out with only male members, or where men feel they have a prior claim to the land, they resist new claimants. Some young men in Basapur village (Karnataka) reacted to the idea of including women in CFGs as follows: 'Women have DWACRA,[24] they have savings groups, why don't you leave the CFGs to us men?' (author's fieldwork, 1998). Men in Asundriya village, Gujarat, strongly opposed NGO attempts to increase women's CFG membership arguing: 'Why do we need women? What we are doing is ok' (author's fieldwork, 1999). In Kudamunda village, Orissa, when I asked the women who wanted their own separate patch for protection why they needed one, they responded:

If we have our own forest, we would not need to ask the men each time for a bit of wood.

They are not willing to give us even a patch to protect. Why would they be willing to give us a whole tree if we asked?

Personal Endowments and Attributes

Women's lesser access to personal property or political connections reduces the weight of their opinions. In addition, limited experience in public interaction undermines their effectiveness in public forums. Some of these disadvantages can partly be overcome if the women are older, married, have leadership qualities, and the self-confidence to speak up. In many CFGs, the few women members are widows, or older married women living in their parental homes who often tend to be less socially constrained (Narain 1994; Britt 1997).

Household Endowments and Attributes

Finally, factors such as the class and caste position of the woman's household are likely to matter where the village is multi-caste and dominated by the upper-caste, or where the CFG is constituted of several villages that are caste/class homogeneous in themselves, but that differ hierarchically in this respect from other villages in the CFG.[25] But the caste factor works in complex ways. On the one hand, being low-caste and poor can adversely affect a person's ability to bargain for a better deal within a predominantly upper-caste community; and even low-caste men (like women in general) often hesitate to speak up at meetings in such contexts. On the other hand, low-caste women are less subject than upper-caste women to norms of seclusion, restricted mobility, and soft speech.

9.4.2. *Factors Affecting Distributional Equity*

Similar (*but not identical*) factors affect gender inequitable outcomes in terms of costs and benefits. The principal factor underlying gender differences in cost sharing appears

---

[24] DWACRA: Development of Women and Children in Rural Areas. This is an anti-poverty programme of the Indian government under which, among other things, women's groups are given subsidized loans for income-generating activities.   [25] My fieldwork in 1998–99. See also, Sarin (1998) and Hobley (1996).

to be social norms governing the gender division of labour. As already discussed, women's primary responsibility for firewood and fodder means that women bear the bulk of the costs of forgoing forest use.

Benefit sharing is likely to be affected especially by five types of factors. One, there are the rules regarding entitlements to benefits. Here both entry rules and distribution rules matter. As noted earlier, access to some types of benefits is linked to membership. However, even if both spouses are members, the woman may not get a separate or additional share if the CFG has decided that the household rather than the individual will be the unit of distribution. In recent years, this has in fact proved to be a bottleneck in inducting women members in parts of Gujarat, where women are demanding shares on an individual basis as a condition for their joining. Hence while women's low participation in CFG decision-making affects equity of outcome through the distribution rules, inequitable distribution rules can, in turn, restrict women's participation.

Two, the norms/principles (willingness to pay, contribution, or need) underlying distribution affect equity of benefit sharing. At present (as noted earlier), contribution is the dominant criterion underlying distribution rules in most CFGs. Under this, all those contributing get equal access to the resource or equal amounts of firewood/fodder when distributed. Auctions are undertaken in some cases, and distribution by economic need is rare.

Three, perceptions about need, contribution, and deservedness matter. Even if there were to be a shift from contribution to need as the defining principle, whether or not women get a better deal can still depend on whether they were *perceived* as deserving more (Agarwal 1997*b*; Sen 1990). There can be and often is a divergence between what a person actually contributes, needs, or is able to do, and perceptions about her/his contributions, needs, and abilities. Hence, for instance, women's contribution to household income is often undervalued, both by family members and by those implementing development programmes, because of the 'invisible' nature of many household tasks that rural women perform. These tasks (such as collecting firewood and fodder, stall-feeding animals, storing and processing grain, etc.) are often economically invisible since they usually do not bring in cash returns; and those done within the home compound are also rendered physically invisible. Hence, women *seen* to be participating in forest management would be better placed to claim equal benefits with men in that their contributions would be better recognized.

Four, whether or not the outcome is equitable depends on pre-existing personal endowments and attributes. Since women as a gender (even if not all women as individuals) have fewer private economic endowments, CFG shares given only to male members typically result in inequitable outcomes for women in both rich and poor households. Again, women's personal attributes such as age and marital status can affect intra-household distribution by influencing perceptions about deservedness.

Five, as we have noted, how acutely women are affected by forest closure or shortages is influenced by their household's economic endowments and social attributes, in particular by their household's class, caste, ethnicity, etc. However, in some respects, this can work in both directions. For instance, while women in upper-caste households that own land and animals can get some fuel and fodder from private assets, they are also likely to face greater social strictures on their mobility, which would limit their options with respect to alternative collection sites. Moreover, for fuelwood, except those able to afford cooking gas, the class difference may not be substantial, since many women even of middle peasant households have to depend mostly on what they themselves can gather.

9.5. IMPROVING OUTCOMES FOR WOMEN: THE BARGAINING FRAMEWORK

In what ways can the factors noted above be acted upon to improve outcomes? Some factors predate the forestry programmes and have deep economic and social roots. The programmes could, however, either entrench them further or provide an opportunity for weakening them. Other factors, such as CFG rules, are part of institutional functioning. Both types of factors are constituted at several levels. Rules, for instance, are broadly made at two levels: the State and the community. Membership criteria under JFM are determined at the State level, but whether forest closure should be total or partial, or how different forest products should be distributed, is determined largely by the community. And social norms, social perceptions, and endowments, are constituted and contested at all levels—within the State, the community, the family, and various institutions of civil governance (including NGOs).

A promising analytical framework for examining the possibilities for change on all these counts is that of bargaining. Women's ability to change rules, norms, perceptions, and endowments in a gender-progressive direction would depend on their bargaining power—with the State, the community, and the family, as the case may be. What would affect women's ability to bargain effectively in these three arenas?

9.5.1. *Bargaining: Some Conceptual Issues*[26]

The State
First, consider bargaining with the State. To begin with, the State too can be seen as an arena of bargaining at multiple levels. For instance, the State may formulate gender-progressive laws at the highest level, but it could face resistance in implementation from the local bureaucracy. Or some departments or ministries may pursue gender-progressive policies within an overall gender-retrogressive State structure (women's ministries are cases in point). Likewise, there are often some gender-progressive individuals within State departments who play key positive roles, typically but not only in response to demands made by interest groups.[27] In other words, the State is an arena of contestation between parties (such as policy-making and policy-implementing bodies), and/or between different regional elements of the State structure with varying commitments to gender equality.

The State might respond positively to demands by gender-progressive groups/NGOs because such groups could build up political pressure, say with the support of opposition parties and/or the media, with implications for voting patterns; or

---

[26] For elaboration, see Agarwal (1997*b*).   [27] See also, Sanyal (1991) and Agarwal (1994).

because of pressure from international aid agencies; or because the State recognizes the inefficacy both of market mechanisms and of its own machinery in implementing essential development programmes. In India, the State's attempts since the mid-1980s to enlist NGO support for various developmental projects, including that of community forestry, reflects this recognition.

We would expect women's bargaining strength with the State to depend on a complex set of factors, such as, whether they function as a group or as individuals; and the cohesiveness and strength of the group. The bargaining power of such a group is likely to be higher the larger and more unified it is; the greater the political weight carried by the castes/classes of which it is composed; the greater its command over economic resources; the more the support it gets from NGOs, the media, academics, and international donors; and the more State officials are influenced by gender-progressive norms and perceptions.

The Community

The second important arena of bargaining is the community. Implicit or explicit bargaining can occur between an individual (or a subset of individuals) and the community over the rules and norms governing, say, economic resource use, and social behaviour, and over the enforcement of those rules and norms. Non-compliance with CFG rules could be seen as a form of implicit bargaining.

As with the State, women's bargaining power within the community would be enhanced if they had support from external agents such as NGOs and the State. Group cohesiveness and strength is also important. For instance, an individual woman breaking seclusion norms could easily be penalized, say by casting aspersions on her character. Such reprisals are less possible if a group of women decide to transgress the norms.[28]

In addition, in a multi-caste/class-heterogeneous village, we would expect women's bargaining power to depend on the socio-economic composition of their group and their ability to command funds. In the sharing of communal resources, for instance, the negotiating strength of low-caste or poor peasant women, even if they formed a group, is likely to be weaker than that of high-caste or rich peasant women whose caste or class as a whole commands greater power in the village.

The Family

The third major arena of bargaining is the family. Intra-family bargaining for a more equitable sharing of benefits or tasks, or for greater freedom to participate publicly, is perhaps the most complex aspect of bargaining. This complexity is spelt out in Agarwal (1994, 1997*b*), but broadly four types of factors are likely to impinge on a woman's bargaining power in the home: her personal endowments and attributes (educational level, whether or not she earns an income, property ownership, age, marital status, etc.); her ability to draw upon extra-household support from friends, relatives, women's groups in the village, gender-progressive NGOs outside the village, and the State; social

---

[28] For elaboration and illustrative examples, see Agarwal (1994).

norms (which might define who gets what, or who does what within the household); and social perceptions (say about deservedness).

Some of the common determinants of bargaining power in all three arenas discussed above are support from external agents, social norms and perceptions, and group strength. Norms, perceptions, and group strength require some elaboration.

Social norms can affect bargaining power in both direct and indirect ways. For instance, norms that restrict women's presence in public spaces directly reduce women's ability to bargain for rule changes within CFGs. In addition, they do so indirectly by reducing women's ability to build contacts with NGOs or State officials. Social norms can also influence how bargaining is conducted: for example, covertly or overtly; aggressively or quietly. In cultures or contexts where social norms stifle explicit voice, women may be pushed into using covert forms of contestation within the family, such as persistent complaining or withdrawing into silence (Agarwal 1994). Moreover, attempts to change social norms can themselves constitute a bargaining process.

Social perceptions can affect women's bargaining power in so far as women's contributions and abilities diverge from perceptions about their contributions and abilities. As noted earlier, much of what women do is rendered invisible and therefore undervalued by both families and communities. To the extent that women internalize these perceptions, they can self-restrict their range of options or what they seek to change and bargain over. To enhance women's bargaining power, a necessary step would thus be to change women's own perceptions about their potential options and abilities, as well as the perceptions of their families, the community and the State regarding their abilities and the legitimacy of their claims.

Group strength can prove to be a critical factor at all levels of bargaining and in all forms of bargaining (including over social norms and perceptions). Here village women's group strength derives not merely from the number of women who would like, say, a change in rules and norms, but also from their willingness to act collectively in their common interest, an interest predicated on gender. In other words, it depends on whether gender is a basis of group identity, over and above the possible divisiveness of caste or class. The creation of such group identity will thus need to be part of the process of improving outcomes for women.

Let us now consider ground experience in attempts to improve women's participation and distributional equity in CFGs. These experiences do not illustrate all elements of the bargaining framework spelt out above, but they reveal some key elements.

9.5.2. *Bargaining: Ground Experience*

The State

JFM experience indicates that successfully bargaining with the State for changing the initial rules of entry is not very difficult. Pressure from external agents such as gender-progressive NGOs and key individuals, for instance, has led a number of Indian states to make JFM membership rules more women-inclusive. Here village women did not have to explicitly bargain for changes, but the women's movement in South Asia has brought about a sufficient shift in perceptions regarding gender inequalities to make such issues easier to resolve with the State, through outside intervention. Village women, on this count, thus start from a position of some bargaining strength.

The Community
Bargaining with the community to ensure that more women-inclusive membership rules are implemented, and to increase women's effective voice in CFGs, has proved more difficult. On the positive side, some of the gender-progressive NGOs, forest officials, and donors have used their bargaining power with the community to bring about changes in women's favour, sometimes on their own initiative, at other times when village women approached them.

For instance, some Indian NGOs have made high female membership in mixed groups a condition for forming the groups. In Gujarat, one NGO insists on 50 per cent women when starting new CFGs. Similarly, some state-level officials in India have increased women's membership in mixed groups, by stipulating that there should be at least 30 per cent women in the general body, or by refusing to start meetings unless the men also invite the women (Viegas and Menon 1993; Sarin 1998). For distributional equity, likewise, when the staff of a Gujarat-based NGO took up women's complaints about firewood shortages at a CFG meeting, it resulted in a shift from total closure of the forest to its opening for a few days annually. However, for a larger and sustained impact, an active input is required from women themselves.

Left to themselves, women have typically relied on covert forms of bargaining to change distributional rules, such as simply ignoring closure rules, challenging the authority of the patrol group or guard who catches them, persistently complaining, and so on. In some instances, this had led village committees to open the forest for short spells. However, complaining or breaking rules (with the risk of being caught and fined) are seldom the most effective ways of changing the rules. For effective change, women are likely to need more formal involvement in rule making and the bargaining power to ensure changes in their favour.

Ground experience suggests that to bring this about, for a start, a critical mass of vocal women is necessary. This can give women more voice in mixed forums, and help them challenge restrictive social norms and perceptions. As some women interviewed by Britt (1993: 146) in the UP hills stressed: 'without a good majority of women present it is impossible to express opinions.' There is a growing consensus among gender-progressive NGOs and elements of the State apparatus that to build a critical mass of vocal women within CFGs will need, as a first step, the formation of separate women's groups. Maya Devi (a Nepalese grass roots activist with long experience in group organizing) put it to me emphatically:

In mixed groups when women speak men make fun of them, so women need to learn to deal with this . . . . When women join a [separate] group they gradually lose their fear of making fools of themselves when speaking up . . . . Women need their own small groups. This is what I know from my 22 years of experience working with the government and NGOs.

There is less consensus, however, on what type of group this should be. Where all-women CFGs have been formed, many have done well in terms of protection and increasing women's self-confidence. However, so far, all-women CFGs (as noted earlier), have usually arisen in special circumstances, and are still marginal in terms of numbers and area protected. Also, they cannot solve the problem of women's low presence and lack of effective voice in the more typical all-male or mixed CFGs. For this, other kinds of efforts are needed. Toward this end, some rural NGOs have been forming all-women savings-and-credit groups, which, unlike CFGs, do not involve a resource over which there is a generalized community claim. In some regions, more multi-functional women's groups, such as *mahila mangal dals* in the UP hills, or *amma samuhs* in Nepal, are also doing well.

Such separate women's groups (organized around savings or some other issue) have helped build women's self-confidence and experience in collective functioning and promoted a sense of collective identity. They have also increased women's ability to deal with government agencies, improved male perceptions about women's capabilities, and brought about some change in social norms which earlier confined women to the domestic space. The response below is fairly typical:

Men used to shut us up and say we shouldn't speak. Women learned to speak up in a *sangathan* (group). Earlier we couldn't speak up even at home. Now we can be more assertive and also go out. I am able to help other women gain confidence as well (woman leader to author, Vejpur village, Gujarat, 1999).

These experiences are not dissimilar to those of many other rural women's groups across South Asia, which too indicate that group strength, external agency support, and activities that enable women to make a visible contribution (especially in monetary terms) can alter social norms and perceptions, and increase the social acceptance of women in public roles. But in many villages, separate women's groups have also sharpened gender segregation in collective functioning. Often women's savings groups are seen as 'women's groups' and the CFGs as 'men's groups'. Basically, working collectively in separate groups does not adequately challenge unequal gender relations or noticeably change the dynamics of *mixed* group functioning. In other words, forming separate women's groups appears to be a necessary condition but not a sufficient one for women's effective participation in the CFGs.

For effective integration, more concerted efforts appear necessary. In a few cases, NGOs working with both women and men have sought to integrate all-women groups with the CFG. An NGO in rural Karnataka, for instance, encourages women's savings groups to discuss CFG functioning, collect CFG membership dues, and persuade women to join the CFG. As a result, in several of its villages, some 80–90 per cent of the women in the savings groups are now in the CFG general body.[29] To bring this about, however, has taken many years of persistent effort and trust building between the NGO, the women, and the villagers.

An alternative approach (to my knowledge yet to be tried) could be to form a women's subgroup within each mixed CFG. Such a subgroup could first meet separately to discuss women's specific forest-related concerns, and then strategically place these

---

[29] Personal communication in 1998 from Pratibha Mundergee, former worker in this NGO.

concerns in the full CFG meeting. This could also enable female EC members to better represent women's interests within the CFG.

The Family

Bargaining within the family, as noted, is one of the most complex issues to tackle and few rural NGOs directly intervene in intra-household relations. Forming all-women groups can, however, have indirect positive effects. For instance, during my fieldvisits I found several cases where a women's group had supported individual women in their negotiations with husbands, or where joining a group had improved women's situation at home.

There are one or two men who objected to their wives attending our meetings, and said you can't go. But when our women's association came to their aid, the men let their wives go (women to author in Almavadi village, Gujarat, 1998).

My husband feels I contribute financially, take up employment, obtain credit for the home. This increases his respect for me (woman to author, Almavadi village, Gujarat, 1998).

In other words, group strength and women's visible contributions can help weaken restrictive social norms, and improve a man's view of his wife's deservedness. However, some norms, such as the gender division of domestic work, are particularly rigid. Also gender inequalities in economic endowments remain entrenched, putting women in a considerably weaker bargaining position in the family, relative to men (Agarwal 1994, 1997*b*).

Finally, any group, including a CFG, is likely to be affected not only by its immediate locale, but also by the wider context of structural and cultural inequalities within which it is located. For instance, both participation and distributional equity are affected by the pre-existing inequalities predicated on the caste and class of women's households, as well as on gender. These inequalities are unlikely to decline substantially within the parameters of CFG functioning. For instance, greater participation in CFGs alone is unlikely to notably improve the economic endowment position of women *vis-a-vis* men or of the poor *vis-a-vis* the rich. To change this would need more wide-ranging measures to enhance the access of women, and of poor and low-caste households in general, to land and other assets.

9.6. CONCLUSION

CFGs are a significant example of group functioning. While many have done quite well in regenerating the environment (at least in an immediate sense), they have been less successful in bringing about women's participation in CFG decision-making, or in ensuring gender equity in the sharing of costs and benefits from forest protection. As a result, they have also failed to tap the full potential of the collective effort. Improving participation and equity is thus important both in itself and because it can prove complementary to (rather than, as usually assumed, in conflict with) efficiency.

This analysis shows that for more participatory, equitable, and efficient outcomes, it appears necessary that there are changes in factors such as rules, norms, and perceptions, and the pre-existing structural inequalities in endowments and attributes of women's households and of women themselves.

As argued here, it is useful to conceptualize such change within a bargaining framework, and to act on the factors that will strengthen women's bargaining power with the State, the community and the family. This has been achieved to some degree through the intervention of external agents, such as NGOs, forest officials and donors, who in some cases have acted both directly and indirectly, the latter especially by forming separate women's groups at the village level to enhance women's self-confidence and collective strength. At the same time, the analysis cautions that such separate women's groups can also lead to greater gender segregation, unless conscious steps are taken to integrate these women's groups with mixed CFGs. An alternative approach, which might work better, is to form women's subgroups within each CFG. In either case, these are only a few steps among the many that will be needed to transform mixed CFGs into more gender egalitarian institutions.

10

Informal Women's Groups in Rural Bangladesh: Operation and Outcomes

SIMEEN MAHMUD

10.1. INTRODUCTION

Bangladesh is well known for the success of its small-scale, village level groups of rural poor, and of women. The fact that these are so widespread, and so long-standing, is in strong contrast to many other groups discussed in this volume. Their particular combinations of methods and activities also make them unusual. What has made it possible to get these groups together, on a continuing basis, to strengthen the position of the poor, and in particular poor women? This chapter looks at some of the aspects of group operation that help to explain this success. It also looks at links between group operation and outcomes.

Bangladesh is unusual for the extent of the direct poverty alleviation programmes of government and non-governmental organizations (NGOs). The major goal of these programmes has been to promote self-employment among the poor through a number of development interventions. An added objective, particularly articulated by NGOs, is that of improving the position of women. To achieve these broad development goals, government and NGOs organize the poor and women at the village level. At present, the village-based 'informal' group is believed to be the most effective instrument for the delivery of both financial (micro-credit) and human resource (awareness raising, health, literacy, skills training) inputs to participating women and households.

Despite the fact that the 'informal' group forms the crucial link between the programme and its beneficiaries, the role of the group in influencing outcomes has not been sufficiently acknowledged. The nature of group formation and operation has not featured in the discussion of the institutional aspects of such development efforts.[1] This is partly because of inadequate empirical attention to the group as an entity, which can operate in the market and the society more effectively than individuals, and partly because of a lack of formal recognition of the potential of groups to influence collective

---

[1] This discussion has been dominated by the organizational aspects of programme performance including the approaches to input delivery in terms of the minimalist versus the credit-plus approach, the exclusion phenomenon, administrative efficiency of input delivery, targetting participants, and programme sustainability.

and individual behaviour. The role of the group in influencing behaviour achieves particular significance for poor women since, given their low bargaining position in society, the group acts as an important non-kin source of support for women.

An obvious example of the effectiveness of group operation in influencing individual behaviour is the consistently high repayment rates of borrowers in micro-credit programmes that operate through groups. In an otherwise low-savings, subsistence environment, such behaviour is achieved through group discipline and peer monitoring. Grass roots workers also frequently cite instances of public protest against oppressive practices and social injustices like low and tied wages, inequitable distribution of *khas* (government owned) land and water, and the poor quality of public services, by organized groups of the rural poor in a context where class hierarchies are strong. Similarly, women's joint economic ventures for income earning, particularly in non-traditional activities, represent a collective effort to participate in the market, something which is relatively restricted for individual women. Some groups perform better than others. There is evidence from informal women's groups that the dynamics of group formation and operation influence financial and social outcomes (van Koppen and Mahmud 1994; Mahmud and Huda 1998). Group characteristics also significantly affect the risk-pooling benefits of groups and consequently their loan repayment performance (Sharma and Zeller 1998).

This chapter discusses the operation of informal women's groups organized by NGOs for the achievement of poverty alleviation and other objectives. It will attempt to link group operation to the outcomes of collective action. The next section reviews the general findings of the existing literature. Section 10.3 discusses case studies of informal group operation. The conclusions of the paper are in Section 10.4.

10.2. GENERAL FINDINGS OF THE EXISTING LITERATURE

Despite strong theoretical underpinnings for a causal relationship between the inputs provided by programmes and the attainment of programme objectives, this link has been difficult to establish empirically. Explanations of why some persons and households derive greater benefit from participation in government and NGO programmes compared to others have not been very satisfactory.[2] The role of group formation and operation in influencing the outcomes of development programmes in Bangladesh at the household and individual levels is not well understood.

The existing literature consists of in-depth case studies that document the process of group mobilization and operation, and studies based on survey data that have

---

[2] Assessing the impact of participation in a NGO programme has featured prominently in the research agenda in Bangladesh (Rahman 1986; Hossain 1988; BIDS 1990; Mustafa *et al.* 1995; Rahman and Khandker 1994; Khandker and Chowdhury 1996; Pitt and Khandker 1996; Hashemi, Schuler and Riley 1996; Mahmud 1994; Amin and Pebley 1994; Mahmud and Huda 1998; Steele *et al.* 1998; Zohir 2001; Sen 2001; Mahmud 2001). The general framework for predicting programme effects has been the neoclassical model of maximizing household utility under initial household socio-economic and human resource constraints. The problem of explaining the reasons for differential programme impact remains even after controlling for the effects of non-random programme placement, whereby programmes systematically select villages according to criteria that influence the uptake of programme inputs.

attempted to link group characteristics to outcomes. The in-depth case studies use qualitative information to describe the process of group formation and to describe how participation in group-based activities have changed women's lives in terms of their unity and solidarity, their productivity and incomes, and their intra-household relationships (Huq undated; Howes 1996; Casper undated; Mannan *et al.* 1995; Todd 1996). The effect on gender relationships and women's empowerment has also featured in several studies, with conflicting conclusions, but always in relation to women's access to micro-credit rather than in relation to women's group membership (Goetz and Sengupta 1996; Kabeer 1998; Mahmud 1999). Studies based on survey data test hypotheses about the effects of group characteristics and group operations on collective outcomes and individual behaviours (van Koppen and Mahmud 1996; Sharma and Zeller 1998; Mahmud and Huda 1998). There are also several evaluation reports that discuss the process of group formation, issues of sustainability of groups and group performance (Yunus 1983; Gibbons 1990; BRDB 1998).

10.2.1. *The Process of Group Formation*

In rural areas of Bangladesh, women live in isolation from the public sphere, subordinated by gender and class relationships. Mobilizing women at the village level starts with a process of increasing women's 'awareness of a whole series of common interests which might give them the strength and the opportunity to organise' (quoted in Huq undated). Outsiders can initiate this process by stimulating awareness and creating a social 'space' for women to organize themselves for collective action. Group formation in rural Bangladesh is not spontaneous but induced from outside. The process of mobilization can be a long one in which the identification of a group of women with shared interests is only the beginning. Rural society is a complex structure rooted in the institutions of religion, patriarchy, and kinship, all of which affect the formation and operation of women's groups.

The strategy for mobilizing informal groups is very similar across programmes. The general pattern is as follows. The local or area office of the programme decides to take the programme to a particular village. This decision is based on initial visits to the village to identify prospective beneficiaries of the programme or target households[3] and on interviews with key informants to assess the local demand for the type of inputs provided by the programme. In the second phase, field workers make direct contacts with women belonging to target households through a series of home visits.[4] At these visits the field worker encourages women to articulate their common problems and discusses the possibility of organizing to undertake collective action. Through these conversations the field worker identifies a woman who can play a role in mobilizing

---

[3] Most programmes have specific criteria for identifying target or potential beneficiary households. Examples of these criteria are ownership of land not more than fifty decimals and/or labour selling by the household head for 100 days or more during the year.

[4] At these visits the field worker makes herself acceptable by creating fictive kinship relations, answering personal questions, sitting with the women on the ground, and so on, and engages women in conversations around their work, family life, domestic problems, health, children, etc.

other village women to form a group. This woman usually has leadership qualities defined in terms of a strong and dominating personality, is more vocal, and may be slightly more educated than the others.

The decision whether a woman should join a group or not is usually a household decision that is strongly influenced by the opinions of the husband, the extended family, neighbours, and other women who have formed groups. Husbands' support is often secured by the fact that most programmes provide collateral free loans that benefit husbands. Group formation is facilitated by the 'demonstration effect' provided by the existence of well-performing groups. There can be some opposition from the village elite to the idea of poor women organizing into groups. This is expressed as being on such grounds as that 'women behave as men', which is equated with the violation of norms of women's seclusion or *purdah*, but it is actually a symptom of weakening class-based relationships. Localized opposition expressed as vague threats is diminishing over time partly because women themselves realize that the threats are not a real barrier.

10.2.2. *Group Functions*

Groups mobilize around a number of functions that may be described as 'efficiency' or 'claims' functions. In the subsistence and credit-constrained economy of rural Bangladesh the *efficiency function* of informal women's groups is to create an economic base for women. This is usually achieved by generating a cash fund on which members can draw and by creating opportunities for members to engage in relatively remunerative income earning work. The group fund is generated by the process of members saving small amounts of cash every week to put into a common pool,[5] which represents a source of both capital for investment and security for crises and emergencies. Evaluations of women's groups organized under a government programme showed that the savings function of the group is perceived by group members as more important than the credit function (BRDB 1998).

The group fund is used for investment in individual or joint income earning activities either as equity for obtaining a loan from a micro-credit programme or on its own. Individual income earning activities are usually confined to women's traditional activities like livestock rearing, cow fattening, poultry raising, paddy husking, money lending, and produce trading,[6] in most cases jointly with husbands or male relatives. Joint income earning activities are more ambitious and include such non-traditional activities as land leasing for crop production, pond fisheries, water selling for irrigation, chick hatcheries, plant nurseries, earthworks for roads and embankments, and construction work. The group fund can increase women's bargaining power in the market place allowing them to engage in profitable investment.[7] Collective income earning

---

[5] Although cash savings were rare traditionally, the habit of saving 'a fistful of rice each day' has been converted into the group practice of weekly cash savings.

[6] The purchase of paddy and other crops at harvest time and resale for a profit several months later.

[7] For example, mature women's groups that have accumulated sizeable savings can compete effectively with other land mortgage holders since they offer lower mortgage rates and the assurance that the land will be returned when the loan is repaid.

is usually undertaken after group members have acquired some skills in running a business venture individually. Collective income earning ventures usually require assistance from a government or NGO programme in the early stages in terms of acquiring resources, planning, account maintenance, and so on.

The group fund is also used to provide individual loans to members. One of the purposes of these loans is to prevent borrowing from money-lenders at high interest rates during times of crises, although there is no evidence that money-lender borrowing decreases in practice when such individual loans are given.[8] Group funds are also used to bail out members who have lost their capital investment, such as a cow bought with a Grameen Bank loan for example. The group fund is seen as an insurance against individual crises and provides a sense of economic security to group members, as well as a source of credit for undertaking activities for which credit might otherwise be unavailable.

The *claims function* of informal groups consists of creating a political base for women within the context of their subordinate position with respect to gender and class. The group provides a support base which gives women a sense of solidarity against different kinds of class and gender-based oppression. This solidarity is consolidated through regular meetings of group members, consciousness raising, and the process of pooling weekly savings. As a result 'women become more aware that it lies within their power to question, and begin to change, what previously appeared as the natural and unalterable state of affairs' (Howes 1996). Having attained a basic level of awareness and cohesion, groups, encouraged by NGO field workers, begin to engage in various types of *andolan* (social action or protest) against injustices like illegal divorce, second marriage, and domestic violence. Later they engage in collective action to recover loans or press for higher wages too (Huq undated).

In some cases the claims function is the dominant function and the uniting force within the group. In others the efficiency function, as embodied in the group fund and collective income earning activity, becomes the dominant reason for staying together. In most cases both claims and efficiency functions are pursued. The role of the NGO or government programme is important here. Not all programmes have components that explicitly support the claims functions of informal groups, in which case social action assumes a secondary role in group performance.

10.2.3. *Group Operation*

The achievement of group objectives depends at least partly upon how the group operates. Group operation can be assessed through a number of functional indicators. These include the behavioural norms that shape the internal relationships of group members, the rules for inclusion in and exclusion from the group, selection of the leadership, mechanisms for monitoring and supervision, and mechanisms for conflict resolution. The following assessment of group operation is based on information reported in existing literature cited at the beginning of Section 10.2.

---

[8] Results from an on-going study of micro-credit programmes in Bangladesh reveal that informal borrowing is just as common among members of such programmes as non-members (BIDS 1997).

Group operation is based on internal relations of cooperation, mutual trust, and reciprocity (COOP), combined with some power and control (P/C) and some elements of material incentives (M). Members appear to be willing to conform to group discipline[9] for the achievement of long-term individual objectives of economic and political emancipation. Reports that group meetings are conducted regularly and group decisions are reached collectively can be taken as indications that members subscribe to group objectives. Groups also take responsibility for supporting members who face individual difficulties that may lead to inconsistent behaviour, and often act so that members *can* conform with group interests. Members generally appear to display trust and confidence in group leaders to conduct group affairs efficiently and equitably. In most groups leadership positions are on a long-term basis, and only change in the event of unavoidable circumstances like ill health, family responsibility, or migration, and rarely due to a lack of confidence (although groups may dissolve or disintegrate due to lack of confidence in leaders).

The primary responsibility for screening potential members lies with group leaders. To ensure shared objectives and minimal conflict of interest women have to belong to the same social class. Members have to live in close proximity to facilitate the exchange of information and reduce the cost of peer supervision. Members have to agree to abide by the disciplinary rules set out by the government or NGO programme.[10] Rules are strictly enforced since experience suggests that digressing from them can be costly in terms of group cohesion and, ultimately, in terms of group performance and outcomes. Exclusion rules are less explicit. Direct expulsions are seen only in the case of strong conflict of interest, and even then groups may disintegrate and re-form rather than resorting to direct expulsions that are difficult to achieve without acrimony.

Group *leadership* is generally vested in a few members. The group selects a chairperson, secretary, and treasurer usually from among those who played active roles in the mobilization of the group. The process of selection is often influenced by the field worker, who identifies some women to mobilize others for group formation. The benefits of leadership are not very tangible and leaders normally have to put in relatively large amounts of time and effort[11] which suggests the presence of altruistic motives on the part of the leaders. The behaviour of individual members towards leaders suggests that group leaders are treated as 'first among equals'. For example, although group leaders are respected for their greater knowledge and capability in decision making it is also stressed that leaders are from the same social class as the general members.

Group *cohesion*, which depends upon all members behaving according to group interests, is valued highly. All members including leaders are expected to behave in a 'consistent' fashion. When this does not happen, as when leadership positions

[9] These include attending regular group meetings, contributing to the group fund, participating in collective activities, participating in group protests, and so on.

[10] Like reciting openly the sixteen rules of the Grameen Bank or making the public commitment that members will protest against injustice by others and will not engage in any unfair actions themselves.

[11] The responsibilities of group leaders include calling and conducting weekly or monthly meetings, collecting and keeping savings, initiating collective actions like income earning work, resolving conflicts within the group, ensuring regular repayment of loan instalments on individual loans, and so on.

are dominated by women from the upper classes, members rarely articulate their dissatisfaction since it is against the norms of behaviour to vocalize opposition against someone with a higher social status. The group simply disintegrates and re-forms with a more homogeneous membership. In this way women are able to by-pass the strong influence of prevailing norms to secure their group objectives.

Monitoring and supervision is not very visible. Strict inclusion rules mean that 'deviant' elements are eliminated from the beginning. Because members are neighbours and many are kin-related monitoring information is easily available. The pressure to conform is strong since neighbours and relatives can exert pressure on potentially deviant members and their households through existing relationships.

In groups that get credit from government organizations or NGOs loan default is minimized by group-based lending whereby borrowers assume the tasks of monitoring and supervision. The incentives for monitoring the action of peers comes from the fact that members are jointly liable for loan repayment and lose access to further loans unless the debts of the group are discharged.[12] Small groups are believed to provide better incentives for peer monitoring. There is also some evidence to suggest that diversity of risk among the membership reduces the propensity to default and increases the returns from risk pooling (Sharma and Zeller 1998).

There is not much information on *conflict resolution* within groups. However, the incidence of internal conflicts appears to be positively related to the size of the group and negatively to the homogeneity of membership. This is suggested by evidence associated with the commonly reported practice of dissolving groups in the face of persistent conflicts of interest, groups re-emerging later without the deviant members or leaders. The irrigation groups studied by van Koppen and Mahmud are a good example (van Koppen and Mahmud 1996). In this case, conflicts of interest arise from the inclusion in groups of both water sellers and water buyers. These conflicts are difficult to resolve and significantly increase the probability that the group will ultimately lose ownership of its capital investment, namely its pump (van Koppen and Mahmud 1996). A strong and cohesive[13] group is able to retain control over its investment better than a weak group by being active in resource mobilization, operational decisions, and the distribution of outputs. The field worker is often reported as playing a role in conflict resolution, especially in the case of conflicts with outsiders such as land disputes or conflicts over the designation of command areas for irrigation purposes.

10.2.4. *Group Outcomes*

Women who are members of groups usually report that the group becomes the nucleus of their livelihood activities and that they experience varied benefits of being organized

---

[12] Stiglitz (1990) has shown that 'The gains from peer monitoring more than offset the loss in expected utility from the increased risk-bearing' in such circumstances.

[13] Group cohesion was defined by van Koppen and Mahmud as a composite of four elements of group operation. These were internal solidarity or 'consistency', external relations, knowledge and skills, and group activity.

or of being 'united'. These benefits, the outcomes of group operation, can be assessed both on the grounds of efficiency and on the grounds of equity.

Women report material benefits from most collective income earning work but the magnitude of such gains is difficult to assess given that women discount their labour inputs and accurate records of costs are rarely available. In the study of water selling irrigation groups, participation provided negligible direct gains to women in terms of profits, and some limited gains in terms of wages. These gains were dependent upon external factors like the degree of domination by male relatives in the group's operations and on internal factors like group cohesion (van Koppen and Mahmud 1996). However, although financial returns from women's-group-based economic activities are relatively small, they are important, representing as they do an independent source of income for women.

Women also report that they gain in confidence and self esteem as a result of attending regular meetings and undertaking income earning economic activity. Group members are more likely to visit places outside the home, on their own, or accompanied by other women rather than by their husbands. They are shown more respect within the community and by their clients. There have also been changes in intra-household gender relations in terms of a more influential role in household decisions and greater control over their own incomes (Huq undated; Gibbons 1990; van Koppen and Mahmud 1996). However, the fact that loans to women are frequently used by their male relatives has been seen as 'women's loss of direct control over their loans' and been interpreted as an adverse effect of women's membership in micro-credit programmes on gender relations (Goetz and Sengupta 1996). Such an argument is weak since 'loan control' has been equated with who uses the loan rather than with who decides how the loan is to be used. With women's restricted access to markets it is quite usual that loans are 'used by' male relatives, but this does not necessariliy imply anything about loan control. In general the opportunity cost of group membership often appears to be outweighed by the gains in women's social status and improved gender relationships.

The *within-group equity* aspects of group operation are evident from the nature of internal resource allocation patterns. The privileges associated with leadership positions are not very great. Access to skills training has a tendency to favour members who have relatively less domestic work (small household or older children), and perhaps more schooling. This is accepted by members as being in the interests of the group. The distribution of personal loans from the group fund or the sharing of group-based programme credit among members is in theory based on need and capability as assessed by the entire group. Paid labour required for collective economic ventures is hired from among group members or their male relatives, also according to need and ability. Although these decisions are reported as being group decisions, they may not always be very equitable in practice—members usually accept decisions as being in the best interest of the group (van Koppen and Mahmud 1996). All members are equally responsible for unpaid labour contributions in joint economic activities, like water selling or crop cultivation on leased land, and outputs are distributed in accordance with individual contributions. On the whole, therefore, the pattern of intra-group cost and benefit allocation as evidenced by labour contributions and distribution of outputs, suggests that within-group operations are fairly equitable.

Women link the poor performance of some groups in achieving objectives to the lack of homogeneity of group membership. In one study that explored the impact of group dynamics on outcomes, the homogeneity index (calculated as a composite score based on members' age, years of schooling, and whether belonging to a household with a labour selling head) was found to be the most significant predictor of individual members' behaviour, after controlling for household and individual effects (Mahmud and Huda 1998). There was also a very strong correlation between the index of homogeneity and the index of group activity (calculated as a composite score based on members' average loan amount, average savings, average days of training, whether able to sign her name, and the age of the group). In this case, group homogeneity, or members' sharing of common problems and interests, appeared to increase the likelihood of members behaving in conformity with group objectives.

The question of *between-group equity* is not directly discussed in the literature, but may be an issue since many NGOs support the formation of federations of groups at different administrative levels. Representation on higher bodies is quite prestigious and sought after, but depends very much upon success at the group level. The selection process for representation may impinge upon between-group equity. Additionally, the need to be successful may cause groups to be stricter about inclusion rules, leading to the systematic exclusion of people like the extreme poor and female headed households.

10.2.5. *The Context for Group Formation*

There is some evidence that the socio-economic background of the community, which shapes the norms of behaviour in social relationships, is important for group mobilization strategies and the functioning of the informal group. The context for group formation and operation may be either favourable or hostile to the process of mobilization of poor women depending upon the interests of 'significant' others within the community. This may influence to a large extent the functions (and objectives) of the group and later the actual outcomes. The approach of the supporting government or NGO programme mobilizing the poor for poverty alleviation is also an important factor in determining group composition, group dynamics, and the distribution of the benefits of collective action.

The approaches of government and NGO programmes to poverty alleviation range from the community approach to the women's empowerment approach. In the *community approach*, where the poor are mobilized around the need to acquire a community-based resource like a deep tubewell or *khas* land, women are not organized into separate groups, and the broader male-dominated relationships re-emerge within the group. In the *household approach* women are seen as the most cost-effective conduits through which inputs reach households, and women are mobilized into separate groups around the needs of their households. In these cases intra-household relationships are reflected in the internal operations of the group. In the *women's empowerment approach* women are mobilized around their specific need to attain both gender equity and economic efficiency in their collective actions. In this case the position of women is more likely to be strengthened, although even these groups can be used to serve male interests, for example, by creating opportunities for men's access to valuable resources like an irrigation pump.

In the study of women's irrigation groups (van Koppen and Mahmud 1996) the mobilization strategy of the NGO determined the dynamics within the group, and the outcomes. Groups that were organized to serve the interests of the water buyers, or the water users (husbands' of group members), were less likely to produce outcomes that led to women's financial or other benefits compared to groups that were organized explicitly to serve the interests of the women water sellers themselves. The former groups were likely to be 'weak' since in practice they represented husbands rather than women themselves. They also tended to have less cohesion among members and leaders, and be more conflictual. The 'strong' groups were more likely to be supported by NGOs which had a women's empowerment approach to poverty alleviation and group mobilization rather than other approaches.

10.3. CASE STUDIES

This section will examine four women's groups in rural Bangladesh involved in joint income earning activities. The purpose of the section will be to identify the dominant mode of operation of the group, analyse group performance, and attempt to establish links between performance and outcomes from the perspectives of efficiency and equity.

The case studies were chosen from groups covered by two NGOs that had been working in rural areas in Bangladesh since the mid-1970s. Both of these NGOs maintain an empowerment (of women and of the poor generally) approach to group mobilization for poverty alleviation. Two groups were selected from each NGO's list on the recommendation of the NGO. The pairs were selected from the same area to control for differences in the socio-economic context as far as possible. In each case, one of the groups was deemed relatively more successful, one relatively less successful, by the NGO.[14] The groups are designated A and B from one NGO and C and D from the other, A and C being deemed the relatively more successful group in each pair.

The case studies were done by a research assistant trained by the author during March 1999, with a week of field work for each case study group. A semi-structured questionnaire was used to obtain information on group mobilization and operation. Information was collected on the initial conditions of group formation, group motivation and objectives, and group functions and operational procedures. Information was also obtained on individual members' socio-economic status, their relationship with group members and neighbours, and on intra-household behaviour such as the decision to join the group, credit use, and spousal relationship.

---

[14] The NGOs had distinct criteria for grading groups. These were based mainly on the NGO's perception of the ability of the group to operate independently to achieve its objectives. The objectives varied for the two NGOs.

10.3.1. *The Case Study Groups*

The main characteristics of the case study groups are summarized in Table 10.1.

Groups A and B are in a very poor rural area. There are several NGOs active in the area, including the Grameen Bank, which provides loans to group members in their capacity as members of Grameen Bank groups. The poor in the area are mobilized quite visibly and systematically, though NGO activity is not as great as it is in the area in which Groups C and D are located. Groups A and B were formed with the explicit objective of fighting social oppression. Members' husbands are labourers, transport workers and small businessmen (Group A), labourers, sharecroppers, and cobblers (Group B). The impetus for forming Group A, in 1988, came from members and members' wives in a male group that had been started by the NGO. The initiative for forming Group B, in 1995, came directly from the NGO. There was some opposition from the village elite to the formation of Group A. Group B faced a positive or indifferent village elite. By the time it was formed, Group A had paved the way.

The activities of Groups A and B include protest against class oppression, illegal occupation of land, low wages, and employers' sexual harassment of employees. These groups also set up courts (*shalish*) for resolving conflicts among the poor. Group members share work and child care, make *kathas*(cotton quilts made from old clothes), make small consumption loans to each other, and help each other when they have difficulty contributing the weekly Tk. 2 to the group fund.

Both groups cultivate crops on leased land as a joint activity. In Group B the work is done by husbands because women in this group do not work in the fields. Crop cultivation makes very small profits for both groups. Group A also has a pond fishery which has not yet become fully operational. Group A started providing individual loans for paddy trading early in 1999. It was too early at the time of the study to know how profitable these loans would be.

Group A had a balance of Tk. 10,000 (about $200) in its group fund at the time of the survey; Group B had Tk. 6450 (about $130).[15] These group funds have been accumulated almost entirely through individual members' contributions of Tk. 2 per week. Small amounts are used to finance crop cultivation. Group A's 1999 paddy trading loans also came from its group fund. Group B says that 'profits on group savings will be distributed after 5 years.'

All but one of the twenty-five members in Group A have been members since the start. Group B's twenty-five members include two who replaced members who migrated out of the area. Stability of group membership is encouraged by the rules of operation of the group fund. Group savings cannot be withdrawn if members wish to leave. Moreover, new members can only join by contributing a full individual share of the savings accumulated by the group.[16] This makes it virtually impossible for new members from poor social groups to join except in the very early years of a group's life.

---

[15] $1 = Tk. 50.

[16] The one member of Group A who had joined after the start was the Chairperson's married daughter. She joined sufficiently early on to be able to contribute a savings share that had not yet become very large.

Table 10.1. *Summary of case study groups*

	Group A	Group B	Group C	Group D
Date of formation	1988	1995	1984	1989
No. of members	25	25	14	17
No. of widows	5	2	4	3
Av. age of members	38	29	33	36
Av. age at formation	23	26	18	26
Husbands' occupations	Labourers; transporters; businessmen	Labourers; sharecroppers; cobblers	Businessmen; traders; rickshaw drivers; van drivers	Businessmen; labourers
Initiative for group formation	Local	NGO	NGO	NGO
NGO role	advisory	advisory	strong control	consid. control
Group activities				
a) Social action	protest, courts	protest, courts	?	?
b) Mutual support	share work; child care; small loans	share work; child care; small loans	share work; child care; small loans	share work; child care; small loans
c) Economic	crop cultivation; pond fishery; paddy loans ('99) to individuals	crop cultivation (husbands' labour)	social forestry; pond fishery ('96); NGO loans to individuals	Reinforced concrete pipe & latrine construction; NGO loans to individuals
Group fund				
a) weekly contribution	Tk. 2	Tk. 2	Tk. 10	Tk. 5
b) accumulated total	Tk. 10,000	Tk. 6450	Tk. 18,350	?
c) use	small amounts for group activities; paddy loans (from '99)	small amounts for group activities; 'profits will be distributed after five years'	small amounts for group activities; 'keeping in bank account for ten years'	small amounts for group activities; individual loans (from '99)

Groups C and D are located in a somewhat better off area than Groups A and B. There is greater NGO activity in this area than in the area of Groups A and B. The goals of Groups C and D are poverty alleviation and women's empowerment, and there is more emphasis on economic activities than on fighting social oppression. Members' husbands are small businessmen, traders, rickshaw and van drivers (Group C), small businessmen and labourers (Group D). The initiative for forming Groups C and D came from the NGO, which provides loans and maintains a continuing involvement. The NGO is particularly strongly involved in Group C, in which it approves new members, and plays a substantial part in decision-making. The initial attitude of the village elite was quite hostile to Group C when it was formed in 1984, but more favourable to Group D, formed in 1989. The hostility to Group C arose from its claims on resources for collective income earning activity.

Members of these two groups help each other with child care, small rice loans, and contributions to the group fund when individuals have difficulty with this. In Group D they also help each other to make visits outside the village. Direct protest against class oppression is not mentioned in relation to either of these groups, however.

Group C's main joint activity is a social forestry project, started in 1984 when the group was formed. The savings of five members, including three leaders, are invested in the project. All of these members provided labour for guarding plants. Group C also started a pond fishery in 1996. At first there was strong external opposition to the leasing of the pond. The dispute lasted over a year and was ultimately resolved through the active participation of the NGO field worker and the federation of the groups. All members now contribute labour to the pond fishery, as well as cash. There is also an NGO loan, repaid from fish sales. The fishery has made small profits and losses. The profits are reinvested in the hope of earning more substantial profits in future.

Group D's main joint activity is the construction of reinforced concrete pipes and water sealed latrines for sale. Five members (three leaders and two widows who were deemed 'needy') contribute paid labour financed out of sale proceeds. The enterprise is managed by the three leaders together with active NGO involvement and an NGO loan to the group. One quarter of the net proceeds goes to the group fund as compensation to the group for allowing these members to use the loan. The project appears viable but profits are not known 'because the records are only verbal'. (Although accounts are only kept verbally, since dues are settled after each transaction, payments to the group fund and individual group members can be made fairly accurately.)

Groups C and D both channel NGO loans to individuals, the groups accepting joint liability for the loans. Group D has also been providing individual loans from its group fund, since January 1999.[17] Group C's loans finance individual trading and small business; Group D's loans house building, poultry keeping, and small business. The individual loans are used by husbands and families of group members in both groups. They appear to be profitable.

Group C had a balance of Tk. 18,350 (about $567) in its group fund at the time of the survey. Members contribute Tk. 10 weekly. This is invested in a bank account and

---

[17] The group cashier got the largest loan, Tk. 3000, from the group fund.

will not be withdrawn for ten years. There is no information on the balance in Group D's group fund. Members of Group D contribute Tk. 5 weekly.

Group D's 17 members have been members from the start. Members were expelled from Group C on two separate occasions, however, reducing the membership from 17 initially to 14 at the time of the survey. The expulsions were connected with controversy regarding labour inputs for guarding plants in the social forestry project, and a lack of confidence in the Chairperson's ability to manage that project.

10.3.2. *General Discussion*

The difference between the 'more successful' and 'less successful' groups does not appear to be very great. Group A has done more than Group B but this could simply be because Group A has been in existence for much longer than Group B. There is little difference in observed outcomes between Groups C and D.

The groups all have small, relatively homogeneous memberships, and strict inclusion/exclusion criteria. All groups operate in very similar ways, within a movement that has established patterns of operation or rules, made them generally acceptable, and demonstrated their effectiveness. The rules of operation of the case study groups are very similar to those set out in the general discussion in Section 10.2. Members have to attend weekly meetings, contribute to weekly savings, participate in protests when these are organized, and contribute labour when called upon to do so. There are fines for failure to attend meetings (specifically mentioned in relation to Group D which was also the only group in which meetings were said to be irregular), for late or defaulted weekly savings contributions (Groups C, D), and for failure to provide labour contributions (Groups A, B). Members make very substantial commitments of time and effort, and very substantial savings contributions, over long periods of time. Sustained and continued operation implies that members have been willing to continue to make such contributions over considerable periods of time. There are strong pressures to conform, and strong sanctions, including the ultimate sanction of expulsion at considerable cost to members concerned. These are not sufficient to explain all of the support, however.

The pre-existing reciprocal relationships between members are formalized in the COOP process of group operation. The process of COOP itself clearly produces results/outcomes that are valued in their own right. Meeting regularly, making regular contributions, giving each other mutual support in everyday life, etc. is valued in itself, as are the solidarity and empowerment that it creates.

The case studies suggest that the operational role of pooling individual savings into a group fund has been underestimated. The group fund provides an economic base that holds the group together. The group fund acts as a monitoring device which promotes internal 'consistency' of action. The fund is also a catalyst for democratic decision-making since the use of group funds has to be decided collectively. It promotes cooperation and reciprocity because group funds may be used to advance personal loans for family enterprises. The group fund also fosters a sense of unity and solidarity since it represents a source of collective bargaining power for women in the market place.

In other words, the savings generation function of the group has a number of positive externalities that may be just as important for group operation as peer monitoring.

The direct concrete results of group action appear to be modest but significant. The groups have been relatively cautious, not over-extending themselves, particularly in relation to their use of group funds. They have had conservative financial management, not taking on too much (indeed they could be accused of taking on too little). This may be an important part of the reason for their success. The retention of large sums in the group fund strengthens bargaining power and helps them to retain stable memberships as noted above.

All four groups have elements of P/C and M as well as COOP, COOP clearly dominating. Internal relations are based on mutual trust and reciprocity (COOP), combined with a slight hierarchy between leaders and the other members, reflecting the hierarchies in their external kin relationships (P/C). The leaders are endowed with certain altruistic motivations towards the group. There are also elements of M in all the case study groups.

There are questions concerning the relationship between leaders and members: the extent to which leaders operate through P/C, and the extent to which members have democratic control over leaders, etc. NGO field workers identified 'mobilizers' to start all but one of the case study groups, and these became the chairpersons. Chairpersons had a major role in selecting members, and other leaders. Chairpersons clearly gained acceptance, and then maintained it. They were said to rule by consent; they were said to prove themselves. They did this partly through their socially dominant positions reinforced by external relationships, partly through their behaviour, and partly through the support of the NGOs.

There were no instances of changes in leadership in the case study groups, but groups in which there are problems tend to disintegrate so they would not be part of the sample. In Group C, the group in which members did disagree seriously with the leadership, the problem was resolved by expelling members rather than by changing leaders. There were power struggles which the Chairperson won in that case.

The role of the NGOs has been to act as catalysts for the formation of groups which may end up having a good deal of autonomy. Only some NGOs have resisted the temptation to provide the groups with too many resources. Some NGOs provide groups only sufficient resources so that they can operate independently; others try to maintain a more dependent relationship. The NGOs are described as creating space, creating awareness, mobilizing and selecting leaders, and helping groups to get off the ground. They are also described as setting out criteria for membership, and for leadership, and setting out procedures. In Groups C and D they provide loans and strong continuing support and control. Groups A and B have no NGO loans, and there is less close NGO involvement and control. The NGOs are concerned about sustainability, and whether the groups can continue if they withdraw, as evidenced by the emphasis on questions about this in the survey.

The role of men is a difficult and less understood issue. There is evidence in the literature of tensions, if not outright opposition, between members of women's groups and men mainly portrayed as situations in which men benefit from loans which women have to repay, with a possible increase in domestic violence, etc. (Goetz and Sengupta 1995). In the case studies discussed here, men clearly benefited considerably from the formation of the groups. It was said that 'Husbands see groups as beneficial to them—and were in all cases positive, and positively involved, in their formation and continuation.' One could see the whole exercise as a good strategy for the men, men getting women to obtain loans, attend meetings, contribute savings, and provide labour contributions, in return for a little recognition and some increase in social status. Although such questions need to be raised, the reality is rarely a situation in which women and men within households have distinct and diverse goals. More often, the reality is a situation in which women and men have different livelihood strategies but shared goals. Within those strategies women may include group membership and men may include a loan financed activity, the shared goal being to obtain a collateral-free NGO loan.

Finally, the case studies raise questions about the role of non-economic outcomes, and the interaction between economic and non-economic outcomes. In Groups A and B non-economic outcomes dominate; in Groups C and D economic. It is clear that Groups C and D, in promoting economic outcomes, are promoting non-economic outcomes too. It is not as obvious that Groups A and B, in promoting non-economic outcomes, are doing the reverse. Direct economic results in Groups A and B appear rather limited. However, non-economic results of Groups A and B and the indirect economic results associated with those, appear strong.

Members seem to think that they benefit enough to continue making contributions. However, it is not clear that the rather limited economic benefits justify the costs when member contributions are properly valued and all the NGO and other costs are factored in. Benefits appear rather insubstantial in economic terms, at least in the short term: joint activities are barely making profits; non-economic benefits are intangible; it is only loans for individual activities that make profits that are more than marginal. However, without a better understanding of how these apparently small or negligible benefits are judged by the women themselves in comparison with the costs of their contributions to group membership, the short-term benefits are difficult to assess. These groups may be much more efficient in the long term, if one takes into account all the benefits to growth and development that increased self-esteem, self-confidence, empowerment, and mutual support, might bring.

The case study groups appear to be stronger on equity and claims functions than on efficiency functions, at least in the short term. Equity and claims functions are clearly being performed with some success, though the extent of the success is difficult to evaluate.

10.4. CONCLUSION

The case study results confirm many of the findings of the general literature reported in Section 10.2. They also bring out a number of features of particular interest to us that are not brought out in the discussion of the general literature. The discussion of the case studies has stressed interactions between economic and non-economic outcomes, the details of group operation and functioning, the role of leaders, and the role of savings, for example.

The fact that these groups operate in COOP mode is clearly linked with the effectiveness of social action, mutual support, and solidarity. Other aspects of their success are less clearly linked with their COOP mode of operation. The relatively conservative operation of group funds may be the result of the way the groups operate and may be important for their success. The membership implications of the way in which group funds are managed clearly make an important contribution to their success. Individual loans benefiting husbands and families may also be an important part of their success in reducing or eliminating resistance, or positively eliciting men's support.

The link between group functioning and outcomes, especially the non–economic ones, appears to be fairly predictable, almost tempting the conclusion of a blueprint for group mobilization and operation. The non-economic gains, such as increased self esteem, enhanced agency, mutual support, etc. can create the social environment for other development interventions to work better. In fact, group members in micro-credit programmes are known to be more likely to send children, particularly girls, to school, use family planning methods, and be more mobile compared to other similar non-member women. Even if the short-term positive effects on women's social status are discounted, the long-term efficiency of these groups lies in these growth and positive development related externalities.

11

Sex Workers in Calcutta and the Dynamics of Collective Action: Political Activism, Community Identity, and Group Behaviour

11.1. INTRODUCTION

This chapter examines how vulnerable and marginalized sections of society come to form groups and engage in collective action, despite the fact that there is often little social cohesion or cooperation among them and they are weighed down by multiple forms of exploitation. The key questions posed in this chapter are:

- Why and how is it possible to form an organization, and to forge a common identity, in the face of social constraints and internal fragmentation among members of the group?
- How is a group formally constituted and how is the group identity constructed?
- How is a group sustained by generating significant changes in the perceptions, attitudes, and behaviour of members of the group?
- How far and in what ways can such a group achieve success in terms of claims, equity, and the reconfiguration of political power?

The analytical focus of this chapter is the role of collective identity, conceptions of unity, mutual support, and reciprocity in the formation of groups. The chapter investigates collective self-representation and expression of community identity as the motors of group activity, rather than the gratification of individual, material needs, or subjective personal satisfaction. The attempt here is to go beyond an understanding of group

The research for this paper was done in March 1999 in Calcutta with members of SHIP and the DMSC. I conducted group discussions and personal interviews, and also attended several meetings of SHIP and the DMSC as an observer. I perused the printed material produced by SHIP and the DMSC, as well as press reports and articles on them. For their help with this research, I am deeply indebted to: Nandinee Bandyopadhyay, Dr Smarajit Jana, Sadhana Mukherjee, Amitrajit Saha, Rekha Choudhuri, Mitra Routh, Debashish Mukherjee, Mrinal Kanti (Bacchu) Datta, Ishika Basu, Rita (Laji) Datta, Saraswati Sarkar, Reba Mitra, Putul Singh, Kabita Ray, Sudipta Biswas, Kohinoor Begum, and all the sex workers/peer educators who participated with enthusiasm and excitement in group discussions and interviews.

behaviour based on methodological individualism, which seeks to explain the operation of groups in terms of the benefits that individuals within the group derive *as individuals* from their participation in a collective. The aim here is to understand how individuals may become part of a group, not in their own personal interest, however defined, but in the general interest of the group as a collective entity—the 'we' being the more important determinant than the 'I'. Is it possible that individuals cohere in a group from a genuine belief in the normative superiority of the collective?

In recent analytical literature, especially in writing inspired by the concepts of 'social capital' and 'trust', key assumptions about the necessary pre-conditions for a COOP mode of group action include a history of cooperative action, a lack of internal conflict among members of the group, the presence of a set of well-defined societal and cultural norms, and the impetus of powerful institutional incentives. But, can successful groups be formed in the absence of these enabling factors? This opens up the question of whether cooperation can be forged through action, rather than being inherited historically, or bequeathed culturally, or derived from favourable social conditions. This requires that we conceptualize social capital and trust, not as a given stock which can be readily drawn upon, but in terms of a dynamic process of crafting through power struggles and political conflict. This chapter analyses how a process of social and political activism might help to generate cooperation, surmounting both societal and historical impediments. The analytical emphasis is then on collective action itself as a dynamic force in generating and consolidating cooperative group behaviour. Such an analysis also helps us to grasp how engagement in group action transforms individual motivation and behaviour, rather than the opposite. This kind of understanding of the process of forging COOP behaviour within a collective is important for developmental initiatives. Otherwise, we would be in danger of assuming that those without a history of cooperation would be forever doomed to non-cooperative interaction, and, thus, fail to seize the initiative to improve their own condition.

To illustrate the above themes, this essay analyses the experience of sex workers of Calcutta. In November 1997, the First National Conference of Sex Workers in India was held in Calcutta, with 3500 participants, for over three days. They claimed their rights as workers and citizens, and marked their presence in the public arena in order to protest against their social exclusion and stigmatization by 'respectable' society. Prostitutes, as they are usually called, had never before asserted themselves politically. The driving force behind this conference was the DMSC—*Durbar Mahila Samanwaya Committee* (Durbar Women's Collaborative Committee). Formed in July 1995, the DMSC is the organization of poorer sex workers who operate in and around Calcutta. Sex workers are a socially marginalized and stigmatized group, forbidden from expressing themselves in public, often by the law, which criminalizes them. They lack a history of political activism or collective mobilization. Moreover, individual sex workers usually suffer from intense poverty and frequently lack literacy, and are, therefore, believed to be ignorant and incapable of developing political consciousness. The formation and consolidation of a powerful political organization of sex workers is widely seen to be an unusual development. The sex trade is highly competitive, with much secrecy and suspicion among the workers. The population of sex workers is stratified, socially heterogeneous and mobile. These factors tend to preclude the possibility of sex workers developing a sense of shared identity and interest, or group cohesion. Yet, the DMSC is not only a highly active political organization, but is also based on a sense of collective identity, group rights, and solidarity in action of a large number of sex workers from Calcutta who have succeeded in surmounting their personal and commercial rivalries to present themselves as a united group. The sex trade continues to be conflict-ridden and fraught with animosities and distrust. For their political organization, however, sex workers highlight their unity and mutual support, and place the collective over the individual. Most remarkably, 'prostitutes' who tend to conceal their identity in public, now identify themselves unequivocally as 'sex workers' ('*jouno kormi*' in the Bengali language), under the organizational canopy of the DMSC.

In analysing the formation of a group by sex workers, this chapter examines the key role of political action in shaping group dynamics, and, in particular, highlights two points bearing on this issue. First, it explores how political activism enables the reconstitution of the 'self' and the redefinition of subjectivity. It investigates how political actors come to reconceptualize their own potential as humans which in turn helps them to sustain collective action and enlarge its scope. Second, this chapter underscores how collective action is propelled by struggles against extant forms of domination and subordination, and by questioning or challenging accepted norms of social hierarchy and distribution. The focus here is on 'politics' defined as action undertaken to reconfigure power relations. This is a largely under-emphasized theme in the literature and practice of development, where politics is usually seen in terms of making claims or understanding 'advocacy' in the interest of disadvantaged groups. This chapter hopes to show that the success of the DMSC as a dynamic group lies in surpassing precisely such a limited conception of politics.

The DMSC, as we shall see, was formed in the context of an internationally funded development intervention, implemented locally by a government medical institute and NGOs, for the promotion of sexual health among sex workers. An analysis of the emergence of the DMSC enables us to gain insight into the ways in which successful collective action can be generated by development initiatives, and can, in turn, contribute to equity, well being, and empowerment.

The following section sets out the context within which the DMSC emerged, by describing the social environment associated with the sex trade in Calcutta and the forms of exploitation experienced by sex workers. Section 11.3 discusses the salient features of development intervention among sex workers that facilitated the emergence of the DMSC. Section 11.4 examines the early stages of crystallization of group unity, and the development of a sense of community among sex workers, in the course of their involvement in the health intervention programme as Peer Educators. Sections 11.5 analyses the role of political mobilization and struggle for empowerment in the success and sustainability of the DMSC. The concluding section identifies the key features and the causes of the sex workers' collective mobilization.

11.2. THE DMSC AND ITS SOCIAL SETTING

The DMSC, with fifty-four branches in early 1999, draws its formal fee-paying membership of about 2000, as well as its wider constituency of support of 40,000 (as claimed by the DMSC members), from the sex workers of Calcutta and several of the districts of West Bengal. The core of the organization and its activities are based in the various 'red light' areas of Calcutta and its vicinity, which together have an estimated population of 18,000 sex workers, who are from different parts of India, Bangladesh, and Nepal. This chapter concentrates on the red light areas of Calcutta.

The DMSC is an organization of brothel-based sex workers usually resident in known 'red light' areas or working there regularly. Most of them come from economically poor backgrounds. They operate at the least lucrative end of the sex trade, with a clientele drawn from the middle classes and poorer sections of society. The market for sex work is a stratified one, depending on the social and economic status of the clientele. This stratification is reflected in social and economic differentiation among sex workers themselves, as well as in patterns of neighbourhood diversification, with women in some 'red light' localities entertaining more affluent men than others. While some sex workers commute daily from outside, those involved in the DMSC live and work in the 'red light' districts. Some of them operate on their own, renting rooms directly from local landlords or brothel-keepers. A handful of such independent sex workers also act as madams (*malkins*) and employ others. A large number of sex workers, however, remain under the tutelage of madams or pimps, to whom they surrender either all or a fixed portion of their income. In return, they get a living-cum-working space, the approval of the madam to work in the brothel, and sometimes they get food. While working conditions and social relations within the sex trade remain oppressive for almost all sex workers, the situation is particularly dire for those who find themselves in relationships of virtual bondage to the madams. Cases of physical and mental abuse of the sex workers by madams and pimps are not unknown. Yet, they have little choice but to remain in this position in the social and commercial hierarchy of the sex trade. Social constraints, frequently coupled with economic compulsions, almost invariably prevent sex workers from returning to their homes, or from starting their own families and finding employment other than sex work. Sex workers find themselves exposed to extortion and violence from the police as well as from local toughs, some of whom are pimps. These *'goondas'* or *'mastaans'* are bullies who exact money from local populations under threat of violence. The more menacing among the *goondas*, from the sex workers' perspective, are those embroiled in theft, drugs, and other 'criminal' activities. Refusal to yield to the demands of these *goondas* frequently elicits the responses of rape, torture, knifing, and arson.

The sex workers' experience is marked by social marginalization and exclusion—this is no less relevant to their lives than the structures of power within the sex trade and its local environment. Sex work is treated as an immoral activity of deviant or duped and poverty stricken women who pose a threat, variously, to 'public health, civic order, social stability and sexual morality'.[1] Sex workers often find themselves targets of law and order drives or of civic regeneration and urban improvement initiatives, when occupants of brothels face eviction from their areas of work and habitation. When treated with a less punitive and more benevolent orientation, they are made the objects of moral upliftment, improvement, and rehabilitation with a view to 'rescuing' them from their 'fallen' condition.[2] Even in these cases, sex workers are treated with pity and disdain, and remain outside the pale of society. When rehabilitated, they are seldom completely accepted in society unless their identity as erstwhile prostitutes is concealed. From the sex workers' perspective, once a woman is *identified* as a 'fallen' person, she is doomed forever to what is perceived as a life of gloom, secrecy, and private misery. Madhavi Jaiswal and Gita De are not un-typical in visualizing their lives as confined to 'dark alleys', 'imprisoned in the darkness ... [of] a closed room'.[3]

Sex workers do not dislike their work *per se* or consider it sinful. They do, however, feel oppressed by the social and personal misery that sex work brings, not least because of the social discrimination and rejection that they face—an environment which they refer to as their claustrophobic world of darkness. To describe their own plight, sex workers frequently employ the metaphors of dark blind alleys; of the prison, cage, and fetters, and of lower depths or the underground.[4] The social condemnation and dehumanization that sex workers face taint their offspring too. For them, there is little hope of a 'normal' life, as they are denied access to decent education and employment opportunities.

No one individual sex worker can act alone to surmount these problems, even to achieve minimal material redress, let alone address the problem of social exclusion. Collective action is the only solution, but this is usually impossible in the lonely and stratified world of sex workers. Brothel keepers and madams prevent social mingling among sex workers and help breed an intense sense of rivalry. Sex workers themselves are fragmented by a stratified market and they are highly competitive in their own interactions as they vie for clients. Often they are geographically dispersed in various neighbourhoods. They move frequently from one 'red light' area to another in search of work or to flee local violence and oppression. This is a bitterly divided and conflict-ridden milieu. How did the DMSC come into being in the face of such seemingly insurmountable impediments to collective action? Is it because sex workers came to realize that the pursuit of their individual interests would be best advanced through the formation of a trade union type of organization? Is it because they felt that defining

---

[1] Jana, S., Bandyopadhyay, N., Mukherjee, S., Datta, N., and Saha, A., 'STD/HIV intervention with sex workers in West Bengal', mimeo, undated, pp. 2–3. [This paper is available at the SHIP office. A version of this paper has been published as follows, but it was not available to me: Jana, S., Bandyopadhyay, N., Mukherjee, S., Datta, N., and Saha, A. 'STD/HIV intervention with sex workers in West Bengal, India'. *AIDS 1998*, 12(Suppl. B), S101–8.]   [2] *Ibid.*, pp. 2–3.

[3] Durbar Mahila Samanwaya Committee (1998). *The 'Fallen' Learn to Rise: The Social Impact of STD-HIV Intervention Programme* 2nd edn. Calcutta: pp. 32, 34.

[4] Group discussion among sex workers on violence in their lives, conducted by the staff of SHIP, 19 March 1999.

a new community identity through social action and political struggle would help in reversing their collective marginalization and powerlessness?

11.3. DEVELOPMENT INTERVENTION AND THE EMERGENCE OF THE DMSC

For an organized group or self-defined collective to emerge and then to sustain itself successfully, it is necessary for some significant changes to occur which act as the catalyst or trigger. This section discusses how, for sex workers in Calcutta in the 1990s, this catalyst came in the form of initiatives to combat AIDS. The scene for mobilization of the sex workers was set by the opening up of new discursive and political spaces by global flows of aid for AIDS containment. With the outbreak of the HIV/AIDS epidemic in the early 1980s, sex workers everywhere soon found themselves identified as a high-risk group and open to increasing public scrutiny. This was especially the case in the Third World, where the use of condoms by sex workers is believed to be low. Moreover, many of those involved in development policy and practice often believe that 'the more extreme conditions of poverty, deprivation and disadvantage that characterize sex work in developing countries' make these sex workers especially prone to HIV/AIDS.[5] They are supposed to have low levels of health and hygiene awareness, as well as an inability to practise safe sex arising from the economic compulsion to secure clients, including those who demand unprotected sex. International donor agencies have, from the 1980s, increasingly directed funds towards HIV/AIDS interventions among Third World sex workers.

A health intervention programme of this kind provided the context for collective mobilization of sex workers in Calcutta. Following a WHO-sponsored pilot survey into the incidence of HIV/AIDS and STD among sex workers in some areas of Calcutta in 1992,[6] an intervention programme was launched under the auspices of the All India Institute of Hygiene and Public Health, with government support. The programme was run by a consortium of NGOs and community-based organizations, initially funded by NORAD from December 1992 to September 1994, and then by the ODA (latterly DFID) from October 1994. This STD–HIV Intervention Programme (SHIP) involved the establishment of health clinics for sex workers, distribution of condoms, and a sexual health awareness campaign.[7] From the outset, SHIP espoused a community-based approach and brought local sex workers into the programme to act as 'peer educators'.

---

[5] Evans, C. (1999). 'An international review of the rationale, role and evaluation of community development approaches in interventions to reduce HIV transmission in sex work', mimeo. Horizons Project, Population Council, Regional Office for South & East Asia, New Delhi, India), p. 6.

[6] The survey was organized by the WHO(GPA) funded National AIDS Control Organisation (NACO) in India, and conducted by the All India Institute of Hygiene & Public Health, Calcutta (AIIH&PH).

[7] For the early history of SHIP, see Dr Kevin R. O'Reilly, Dr Thierry Mertens, Ms Geeta Sethi, Dr Lalith Bhutani, Ms Nandinee Bandyopadhyay, 'Evaluation of the Sonagachi Project, Calcutta: 31 October–14 November 1995, (15 March 1996). (Sonagachi is the main red-light area in Calcutta where SHIP was first launched in 1992). [Note: This evaluation of SHIP, at the time funded by the ODA, was organized by the British Council, Calcutta, at the request of the Minister of Health and Welfare, Government of West Bengal.]

'Peers' as they came to be called, were provided with six weeks of training. This was designed to enable peers to disseminate information and raise consciousness about the epidemiology and pathology of STD and HIV infections and about the practice of safe sex using condoms, with the ultimate aim of improving general health conditions and minimizing exposure to HIV infection. Peers, initially half a dozen, but numbering 125 in early 1999 in Calcutta (and 180 if the districts of West Bengal are included), were partly based at clinics, where they explained the problems of STD and HIV to other sex workers. More importantly, they visited brothels for 'door to door campaigns' to persuade sex workers to visit the clinics for health checks, immunization, or treatment.[8]

From the public health point of view, SHIP has been a significant success,[9] with a notable decline in the incidence of STD,[10] a major increase in condom use (2.2 per cent in 1992 to 81.7 per cent in 1995),[11] and the achievement of a progressively lower rate of HIV prevalence among sex workers in Calcutta compared to all other metropolitan towns of Asia.[12] However, for the purpose of this discussion, and indeed for the sex workers themselves, the most important impact of SHIP has been on the formation of their own organization and the resulting political mobilization. The specific form and the nature of the intervention adopted by SHIP played an instrumental role in this.

The brochure published by SHIP explains that its approach was to give due respect to sex workers, recognize their profession, and rely on their opinions.[13] So, responding to sex workers' understanding of their own needs, SHIP undertook 'a number of varied activities unrelated to AIDS'.[14] The feedback from early peers made SHIP realize that an 'integrated approach' was necessary, for sexual behaviour cannot be changed in isolation from other aspects of sex workers' lives. As a result, 'the project concentrated on the broader and more fundamental issue of social power relations which shape people's "behaviour"' and adopted strategies for the empowerment of sex workers'.[15] In order to enable sex workers to deal with their social rejection, their lack of bargaining power, and their exposure to 'local mafias' and the 'nexus of landlords, politicians, policemen',[16] SHIP identified the following clusters of problems that required attention:[17]

1. 'Lack of social acceptance of sex work as a profession. . . . Judgmental approach towards sex trade and profession. . . . Socially imposed insecurity.'[18]
2. The perpetuation of gender inequality in society and the sexual division of labour as well as the exercise of control over women's reproductive behaviour in the interest

---

[8] All India Institute of Hygiene and Public Health, Calcutta, *A Dream, A Pledge, A Fulfilment: Five Years' Stint at Sonagachi* (AIIH&PH, Calcutta, November 1997), p. 6.

[9] 'Evaluation of Sonagachi Project', pp. 16–22.

[10] *A Dream, A Pledge*, p. 17, table 12; *Fallen*, p. 19. [For example, between 1992 and 1995, decline of 70.1% in N. gonorrhoea Smear/culture; reduction of 11.7% in T. Vaginalis (wet mouth); reduction of 72.4% in C.albicans (culture); reduction of 15.6% in Syphilis (VDRL).]

[11] *A Dream, A Pledge*, p. 15; *Fallen*, pp. 16–19.

[12] *Fallen*, p. 21, cites *The Telegraph*, 18 September 1995: Sonagachi was hailed as the biggest brothel in Asia with a record negative growth rate of AIDS; *Newsweek*, 15 February 1999: A report on DMSC, entitled 'India: Red-light revolution', mentions that HIV incidence among sex workers in Sonagachi is 5% as compared to over 45% in Bombay brothels.   [13] *A Dream, A Pledge*, p. 7.

[14] *Ibid.*, p. 6.   [15] Jana *et al.*, 'STD/HIV Intervention', p. 6.   [16] *A Dream, A Pledge*, p. 9.

[17] *Ibid.*; Jana *et al.*, 'STD/HIV Intervention', pp. 4–6.   [18] *A Dream, A Pledge*, p. 9.

of maintenance of private property and patriarchy, all of which have implications for branding as immoral or deviant any sexual intercourse outside 'legitimate' heterosexual, monogamous, matrimonial alliances.[19]

3. 'Low socio-economic status of SWs—not the economic poverty but the poverty which consists in the lack of power to resist oppression, inability to understand the rights, and the lack of opportunity to organise themselves to overcome the inhuman and exploitative conditions'.[20]

4. 'Legal ambiguity of sex work',[21] which makes sex workers prone to police oppression.

SHIP gradually came to adopt an approach that emphasized 'the empowerment of SWs both at community and societal level[s]'. SHIP did not attempt to involve itself directly in the everyday struggles of sex workers, but sought to create conditions which would enable sex workers to gain confidence, skills, and social power, thus equipping them to initiate their own struggles. SHIP's approach covered three broad areas.

First, the problem of legal ambiguity of sex work was addressed by demanding recognition under the law and the abolition of the *Prevention of Immoral Trafficking in Women Act, 1986* (PITA) which effectively criminalizes sex workers. Under PITA, sexual intercourse for monetary considerations is defined as 'illicit' and soliciting in public is outlawed. Although the rationale behind this act was to protect young women from pimps and others who 'traffic' in women, in practice, the emphasis on 'immorality' focuses police and legal attention on sex workers themselves.[22] SHIP argued that sex workers should have the same status as any other self-employed professional group with their own institutional mechanisms (such as an autonomous board) for internal regulation of the sex trade. Further, they argued that sex workers should have similar rights as other workers to engage in industrial action to achieve better working conditions and remuneration.[23] All of this would ensure that sex workers had greater rights and bargaining power within the trade and would thus bring about significant, beneficial changes both in their sexual behaviour and in their lives, in general. Above all, SHIP urged that PITA should be abolished. Sex workers should come under the purview of general civil, criminal, and labour laws of the land, and should not be legally stigmatized and denied the rights of full citizens, for example, by coming under special prostitution laws.[24]

Second, SHIP took practical measures to deal with the broader question of empowerment. This meant that the education programme for peers not only dealt with STD issues, but it was also designed 'for attainment of self reliance, confidence and dignity, and transfer that image to influence other members of the community' (sic), with the ultimate aim of undertaking effective collective bargaining. A peer's role was envisaged

[19] *A Dream, A Pledge* p. 9; *Sex Workers' Manifesto: The First National Conference of Sex Workers Organised by Durbar Mahila Samanwaya Committee, Calcutta, November 1997* (DMSC, Calcutta, 1997).

[20] *A Dream, A Pledge*, p. 9.   [21] *Ibid.*; *The Telegraph*, 16 March 1998.

[22] 'Memorandum on Reform of Laws relating to Prostitution in India'. Prepared by the Centre for Feminist Legal Research, January 1999.

[23] *Gatar Khatiye Khai, Shramiker Adhikar Chai* [Sex work is legitimate work: We want workers' rights] (Press Release for the First National Conference of Sex Workers, November 1997).   [24] *Ibid.*

not simply as a health educator, but as a 'community leader, community mobiliser and an agent of social change'.[25] In order to fortify their more encompassing role, non-formal classes were organized for peers by SHIP, which the peers themselves demanded. The classes did not only deal with basic literacy, arithmetic and health education, but also with a wide variety of issues that impinge upon sex workers' lives, including medicine, science, history, politics, gender and patriarchy, civics, and human rights.[26]

Third, an important element in SHIP's strategy of empowerment of sex workers was the forging of a positive identity for sex workers in defiance of their socially constructed image. SHIP realized early on that peers needed 'to ensure that the entire body of sex workers in the locality developed a positive self-image, had self-esteem and confidence'.[27] SHIP was also unequivocal that 'the success of any intervention programme working with sex workers depends on the possibilities the Project can create for the sex workers to negotiate and re-interpret the dominant discourses that frame them'.[28] Discussions among sex workers that SHIP facilitated in order to achieve this objective, soon prompted sex workers to see themselves as akin to all workers who hire out their bodies and sell manual skills.[29] Indeed, the key slogan at the First National Conference of Sex Workers, coined by the DMSC, was: 'We labour with our bodies; we demand the rights of labourers' or 'Sex work is legitimate work: we want workers' rights'.

Neither the integrated, community-based approach of involving the active participation of the target development group, nor the idea of achieving empowerment through development initiatives were radically new concepts in the 1990s.[30] However, as applied to sex workers, this form of development intervention was rare, even though it was advocated by WHO.[31] Most interventions, including other contemporary interventions in Calcutta, have been rehabilitation oriented. From the sex worker's perspective, the SHIP approach was more meaningful, not least because peers played a very significant role in enabling SHIP to realize that an 'integrated approach' was necessary, and it is to SHIP's credit that it acknowledged this need and acted upon it.[32] SHIP enabled sex workers to develop their collective interests within the trade, and also provided them with the opportunity to define their identity as a community, enunciate their rights as workers and citizens, express themselves creatively, and articulate their needs, feelings, and emotions.

Here, it is worth noting how SHIP contained potential opposition, particularly from 'power brokers' within the sex trade. SHIP was careful from the outset to ensure that any destabilizing tendencies were diffused. SHIP personnel involved madams and

[25] *A Dream, A Pledge,* p. 9; *Fallen,* pp. 28, 41.

[26] Sandip Bandyopadhyay, *They Speak their Word: A Note on the Education Programme for the Calcutta Sex Workers* (AIIH&PH, Calcutta, not dated). A leaflet produced by SHIP to explicate the creation of a 'background primer' for the non-formal education of the peers acknowledges the intellectual influence of Paulo Freire: Sandip Bandyopadhyay, *Amader A-Aa-Ka-Kha* [Our ABC]: *Learning to Read, Write and Rise* (AIIH&PH, Calcutta, not dated). [27] Jana *et al.,* 'STD/HIV Intervention', p. 6.

[28] *Ibid.,* p. 10.

[29] Interview with Putul Singh, sex worker and member of DMSC, 25 March 1999.

[30] Evans, 'International review of . . . community based approaches', *passim.* [31] *Ibid.,* pp. 10–12.

[32] Jana *et al.,* 'STD/HIV Intervention', p. 4.

pimps in some of their activities, emphasizing the common benefits that would accrue to the sex trade if public health conditions were augmented—it could be argued that the control of STD and HIV would help boost the sex trade by allaying clients' fears of disease transmission. Moreover, SHIP dampened the potential wrath of 'power brokers' by avoiding a rehabilitation approach, thus signalling that it did not intend to introduce major structural changes in the sex industry.[33]

11.4. FROM PEER EDUCATORS TO DMSC ACTIVISTS: COMMUNITY AND IDENTITY

In this section we see why sex workers initially volunteered to become peers, what it meant to them to act as peers and why they then came to form the DMSC. While SHIP expected elderly, retired, and under-employed sex workers to offer themselves as peers as a source of livelihood,[34] in practice younger women with children, those who had already been locally active in organizing collectively, and many others, joined as peers. Anima Banerjee was urged by her local school teacher son to become a peer, as this would be a socially meaningful activity.[35] Mala Singh, another former sex worker who now lives with a partner in a 'red-light' area and runs an illicit liquor shop, joined at the behest of her partner, who had been active locally in combating incidents of violence against women. She felt that her illegal trade in alcohol was ethically counteracted by the socially useful work of SHIP, and then DMSC.[36] Kohinoor Begum joined because she felt that working as a peer was an acceptable form of occupation—she could see herself as any other worker in society.[37] Munni Singh too emphasized the importance of the 'job': 'I had been so engrossed in the last twenty-three years of my life in providing pleasure to innumerable men-folk that I had forgotten my own happiness. I came to know the thrills of a job after joining the project'.[38] In Madhavi Jaiswal's view, being a peer 'enabled her to face society with confidence . . . . [and] to emerge out of the dark alleys and venture into light'. She saw the Project as a means of improving herself and as a form of self-expression.[39] Mamata Ghosh expressed similar sentiments: 'Earlier I could not speak to anyone—but now I speak to all people'.[40] Gita De felt that it was not the money that made her eager to join SHIP as a peer. '[E]ven [if] I did not get much money, I would get a job at least. I would be able to interact with many people. . . . I felt I had been imprisoned in the darkness before I had joined the Project and that I had gained a new life. I felt I was released from a closed room and could see the sunlight'.[41] Chobi celebrated a similar sense of liberation: 'We were in a *jailkhana* [prison]. It is the Project that has taken us out into the outer world'.[42] For Uma Mondal, the use of the term 'sex worker' by SHIP was a revelation. This term was very different from the insulting and abusive words with which sex workers were usually addressed. Equally importantly, though, she valued the opportunity she got as a peer, and later through

---

[33] Jana *et al.*, 'STD/HIV Intervention', p. 9.   [34] *Ibid.*, p. 5.
[35] Group discussion among sex workers conducted by the author, 17 March 1999.   [36] *Ibid.*
[37] Personal interview, 18 March 1999.   [38] *Fallen*, p. 20.   [39] *Ibid.*, p. 32.
[40] *Ibid.*, p. 20.   [41] *Ibid.*, p. 34.   [42] *Ibid.*, p. 15.

the DMSC to undertake socially relevant activities in unison with other sex workers through a legitimate channel.[43]

A few of the women who came to SHIP as peers had a history of local self-assertion, both individual and collective. For them SHIP could be the refuge of rebels. Sadhana Mukherjee, the first secretary of the DMSC, tried to resist the oppression of *goondas* in her neighbourhood, and had been frustrated in her efforts. SHIP provided her with the hope of launching a collective offensive against them and of strengthening sex workers in general.[44] When Putul Singh and others from the Sethbagan 'red light' area joined SHIP, they had already been engaged in collective local activism. Women in Sethbagan had formed a neighbourhood vigilance organization in 1984–85 called the *Shramajibi Mahila Sangha* (the Association of Labouring Women), and had defined themselves as working women. The main impetus behind the formation of the *Mahila Sangha* had been to tackle the menace of local *goondas*. In addition, the group used voluntary contributions by sex workers and their clients to introduce free health-care for sex workers and literacy classes for their children.[45] They did not, however, find it easy to sustain their activities. Internal squabbles, especially over money, undermined their unity and effectiveness.[46] When SHIP emerged, some members amalgamated the *Mahila Sangha* with SHIP, and subsequently with the DMSC, and most of them started working as peers. Putul Singh says, 'We joined the Programme [SHIP], because in it we found an opportunity to continue with our struggle'.[47] She also claims that although women in Sethbagan still have their personal disagreements and animosities, they now sink their differences and unite over the work of the DMSC.[48]

The various reasons the sex workers give for joining SHIP suggests that a large number of peers did so less for money than for self expression, self esteem, social recognition, and a sense of social responsibility and involvement. SHIP provided them the space to redefine their identity, both individually and collectively. There is, however, an interesting paradox here. It appears that a number of sex workers left the sex trade and came to devote their time to SHIP as paid employees (peers), and to the DMSC as unpaid volunteers.[49] These women are the most vocal in the DMSC in proclaiming the rights and identities of sex workers. They have taken the opportunity provided by SHIP to escape the everyday material oppression of the sex trade. Yet, they have not used the opportunity to deny or conceal their identity as sex workers. Indeed, they now appear to be far more confident about expressing and projecting this identity. This paradox of highly mobilized sex workers leaving the profession while at the same time publicly identifying themselves as sex workers reinforces the point that their reason for joining SHIP had a great deal to do with questions of identity and self-expression.

---

[43] Group discussion, 17 March 1999.   [44] *Ibid.*

[45] *Fallen*, pp. 10–11; Putul Singh (in association with Mamata Das), '*Sethbagane Mahila Sangha gorey othar suchana*' [The Origin and Development of the Mahila Sangha in Sethbagan], *Souvenir of the First National Conference of Sex Workers, 14–16 November 1997, Calcutta* (DMSC, Calcutta, 1997), pages not numbered.

[46] Personal interview with Putul Singh, 17 March 1999 and 25 March 1999.

[47] *Fallen*, pp. 10–11.

[48] Personal interview with Putul Singh, 17 March 1999 and 25 March 1999.   [49] *Fallen*, p. 20.

Once they became peers, this issue of identity, especially collective identity, became of increasing importance to them. If, initially, they had joined SHIP as peers out of individual motivation to redefine their identity and gain personal respectability, thereafter it became a matter of forging a new collective identity, eventually leading to the formation of the DMSC, in which the collective would come to assume primacy over the individual. This transition can be best understood by exploring some salient features of the sex workers' experience as peer educators. An important identity symbol for peers is the uniform worn at clinics and during 'door to door' brothel visits. The uniform consists of a green apron coat with a red-cross printed on it, and an identity card. In the sex worker's eyes, this is almost a sacred vestment that endows them with a special status and enables them to transcend their daily grind. Pushpa, a sex worker, says: 'This apron has changed my life, my identity. Now I can tell others that I am a social worker, a health worker'.[50] A SHIP report comments, 'the uniform . . . stand[s] for self esteem. They prefer it to costly sarees because they knew [sic] that a uniform is a symbol of social recognition'.[51] Of course, a uniform is also a symbol of being part of a group or institution. This in itself is highly valued by those who are treated as outcasts and marginalized. Uma Mondal says that the apron bestows special responsibilities and public authority upon peers, and they have to conduct themselves accordingly. Peers feel obliged to act in the common interest of all sex workers: 'we think of others first before we think of ourselves'.[52] Bonani, another sex worker, was quoted in a Calcutta newspaper as saying: 'All my life I lived a wretched life. It is entirely a different feeling to share other's worries and help people get out of their problems'.[53] Uma Mondal feels that it is this altruistic, public role that inspires and animates peers, and enables them to identity themselves publicly as socially responsible sex workers with confidence and without shame.[54]

In a similar fashion, the experience of being identified by the epithet 'peer' soon came to assume distinctive significance. It would not be an exaggeration to view the term 'peer' as a poignant polysemic neologism in the vernacular of the sex workers, laden with multiple connotations. At one level, it marks social distinction and personal achievement. This is evident from sex workers' testimonies, documented in a SHIP publication, in which they express an obvious pride in what they see as the honour of being appointed peers by SHIP.[55] The term peer, thus, is a symbol of social worth and standing. Introducing themselves as peers of SHIP seems almost like identifying themselves as doctors or lawyers—professions which are highly respected by society. At another level, the term peer has assumed cognate status with 'comrade' or 'mate', signifying equality and community. Of course, in the English language, the term 'peer' does mean equal, but this is not known to sex workers. To them, the sense of equality contained in the term is socially and experientially constructed. It also seems to have assumed the status of a fictive kinship term, denoting sorority and solidarity. Doing collective work for ones 'sisters' and acting in unison as peers gradually seems to have

---

[50] *Fallen*, p. 15.   [51] *Ibid.*   [52] Group discussion and personal interview, 17 March 1999.
[53] *The Telegraph*, 9 May 1998.   [54] Group discussion and personal interview, 17 March 1999.
[55] *Fallen*, pp. 32–4.

acquired superior normative power among sex workers. This element of acting in concert played a central role in the genesis of the DMSC.

Through the collective experience of being peers, sex workers soon felt that the self was important only within the broader framework of the collective. The focus, then, inevitably shifted towards political activism, and social movement type initiatives to redefine their collective identity as socially acceptable and to further their shared goals. As some of the major functionaries of SHIP point out, and as the ODA Evaluation Report of SHIP reiterates, peers realized that 'given the asymmetrical power relations within the sex industry and their social exclusion, the only way the sex workers could gain greater control over their own bodies, sexuality, income, health or life was through mutual support, collective bargaining and united action'.[56] Sex workers almost invariably stress that they are now fighting as a group and for future generations, not for themselves personally.[57] Pushpo Sarkar says: 'Now we all stand together and for each other. . . . We may die [fighting], but our work must go on, our organisation [DMSC] must forge ahead, we will never look back'.[58] Uma Mondal says: '[In the struggle], I may die personally, a few more of us may die, even a 100 or a 1000, but we are not afraid to die, for there are 40,000 behind us. Those who kill us will not be spared by anybody, they will be pickled by the others. This is why we do not fear to embrace death. We *are* surging forward apace and we *will* surge forward even further; we do not have the time to look back'.[59]

The confidence that sex workers gained from their experience of being peers and part of an institution,[60] as well as their valorization of collective action, laid the foundation upon which the edifice of the DMSC was built.[61] While engaged in clinical work with SHIP from 1992, some early peers soon envisaged the need to enlarge the ambit of their activities. Moreover, peers began to feel emboldened to act collectively against their local oppressors. They also realized that such activities could not be undertaken directly as part of the health intervention project. In 1993, with the support of SHIP, sex workers formed the nucleus of an organization with thirteen members or 'convenors'. This informal core group, called the 'Interlink Committee', with representatives from twelve 'red light' districts in Calcutta, assumed a more formal character in 1995, when it was registered as the DMSC. Under this new formal structure, branch committees of the DMSC were formed in various neighbourhoods (fifty-four such branches existed in West Bengal in early 1999), with a central executive committee consisting of representatives from the branch committees. Officers of the committees were appointed through internal elections from 1997. The branches and the central committee hold regular meetings which are open not only to formal fee-paying members, but to all interested sex workers, although voting rights are restricted according to stipulations in the constitution.

---

[56] Jana *et al.*, 'STD/HIV Intervention', p. 6; 'Evaluation of the Sonagachi project', p. 29.

[57] Personal interview with Putul Singh, 25 March 1999.   [58] Group discussion, 17 March 1999.

[59] *Ibid.*

[60] For the impact of SHIP on peer educators, see 'Evaluation of the Sonagachi project', pp. 27–30.

[61] The following account is based on *Fallen*, pp. 21–2; Jana *et al.*, 'STD/HIV Intervention', p. 7; Group discussion, 17 March 1999.

From 1993, and even more so after its formal registration in 1995, the DMSC has undertaken campaigns in the 'red light' areas against perceived acts of oppression or injustice, which have both demonstrated its power to dominant groups and drawn in the support of an increasing number of sex workers. While the fee-paying membership of the DMSC was about 2000 in early 1999, many hundreds more are associated with the organization. DMSC activists claim that they have the state-wide support of 40,000 sex workers—an estimate arrived at from the number of people who have attended meetings, processions, and demonstrations.

Interestingly, in the sex workers' own version of the genesis of the DMSC, they claim a significant role and agency for themselves, while not denying the contribution of SHIP and their indebtedness to Dr Jana, the director of SHIP. SHIP, however, seems to present the DMSC as a product of the intervention programme. SHIP's fifty-page 1997 publication about the mobilization of sex workers and the DMSC, entitled *The 'Fallen' Learn to Rise*, is subtitled *The Social Impact of STD-HIV Intervention*. The booklet was published soon after the 1995 ODA evaluation of SHIP (reported in March 1996) and coincided with the publication of a SHIP-AIIH&PH brochure in 1997, entitled *A Dream, A Pledge, A Fulfilment: Five years' Stint at Sonagachi*. In all these publications, the pivotal role of SHIP in the creation of the DMSC is emphasized.

It does seem that the DMSC is very much a creature of SHIP and fully backed by it. SHIP has assisted the DMSC in attracting funding, and provides it with logistical support, advisory personnel, strategic planning, and office infrastructure, as well as masterminding much of the DMSC's activities, at least until recently. For an outsider, it is often difficult to distinguish between SHIP and the DMSC, in practice, despite formal, constitutional distinction. However, despite the singular importance of SHIP, the sex workers did provide the woman power and commitment behind the DMSC. Most importantly, sex workers see the DMSC as their own creation and appropriate it for themselves. In the group discussion that I conducted, some sex workers declared at the very outset that they were going to recount the 'true' history of the DMSC rather than the version usually related for the benefit of 'visitors'—donor agencies and the press. I was granted this privileged treatment because I was introduced to the sex workers as an interested and sympathetic 'friend', seeking to help and understand the DMSC, and not as a project evaluator, or a journalist. In this 'truthful' narrative, while they repeatedly acknowledged the undeniable value of the 'canopy' provided by SHIP and the paternal authority of Dr Jana, they stressed their own struggles and action, and expressed a keen sense of their own agency and initiative. They presented themselves as the subjects of their own autonomous action and political struggle. Anima Banerjee pointed out that when they were simply peers of SHIP, outsiders who showed an interest in their work were only concerned with AIDS, not with the sex workers themselves. However, with the growing strength of their 'own' organization, extensive interest has been generated about sex workers themselves, their problems, and their struggle.[62] The appropriation of the DMSC, by the sex workers, as their own creation

---

[62] Group discussion, 17 March 1999.

reveals the centrality of the issues of identity, belonging, ownership, sense of agency, and power.

An instance of the sex workers' quest to register their ownership of the DMSC comes from the First National Conference of Sex Workers in November 1997, convened by the DMSC.[63] This conference was organized by SHIP personnel, with the help of the top leadership of the DMSC and a number of prominent peers. On the first day of the three-day meeting, the usual format of a large national conference was adhered to, with an inaugural ceremony consisting of speeches by government ministers, important officials, and administrators, and the director of SHIP. During a lull in the proceedings on the first day of the conference, one of the organizers decided to invite participation from the audience. Sex workers were asked to mount the stage to sing, dance, or recite verses as they wished, or to ascend the official podium to speak their minds. This invitation elicited an unexpected response, and soon the entire formal, stilted tenor of the proceedings changed. During the following two days, sex workers seized the initiative and set the agenda for the remainder of the conference. They took the leading role in the workshops organized to discuss the various issues associated with sex work. The personnel of SHIP became increasingly marginal in the face of the animated and passionate participation of sex workers. The general atmosphere at the conference venue, a large sports stadium, also changed. Sex workers arrived at the conference from the second day with their children, families, and partners, and the site assumed the atmosphere of a festive street-carnival rather than that of a formal political conference. No longer was this a solemn political meeting, but an ebullient self-expression of hitherto repressed and secluded women in the public arena, a joyous celebration of their ability and potential. This event achieved the conquest of public space by sex workers much more effectively than the inaugural parade of dignitaries on the proscenium. The personnel of SHIP acknowledge this event as a defining, symbolic moment in the history of the DMSC, not so much because a national conference had been successfully staged, but because the sex workers who were present there had proved themselves to be the agents of their own struggle and articulated their identity as a community with aplomb in public.[64] They were well on their way to outgrowing SHIP and spearheading their own politics through the DMSC.

11.5. THE DMSC IN ACTION: COLLECTIVE STRUGGLE, POWER, AND POLITICS

The issues of identity, agency, and political struggle recurred throughout the entire gamut of the multi-pronged activities of the DMSC, to which we now turn in this section, for these are the elements that contributed to group crystallization, cohesion, and sustainability. The DMSC has undertaken various social and political initiatives since its inception in 1993. One of its early activities was to challenge the violence and extortion resorted to by *goondas*. Under the leadership of the DMSC, local women in

[63] Personal interview with Nandinee Bandyopadhyay, Gender Consultant to SHIP and DMSC, 26 March 1999.   [64] *Ibid.*

a number of 'red light' districts organized themselves, confronted *goondas*, captured them, and then turned them over to the police. These women now refuse to yield to the oppression of *goondas* in silence, and retaliate whenever necessary. Sex workers have found the courage, with SHIP support, to stage rallies and demonstrations against *goondas*, and to approach politicians, councillors, and other locally influential people and professionals. By building up public opinion against the *goondas*, they have been able to pressurize the police to take effective action, while previously their complaints had gone completely unheeded. Sex workers now claim that the regime of *goondas* has been virtually abolished, and relate stories about erstwhile fearsome *goondas* who now not only apologize for their earlier behaviour but also provide monetary help to the DMSC.[65] Sex workers also report triumphantly that *goondas* now address them reverentially as '*didi*' or elder sister.[66] They have also organized public meetings, processions, and rallies against police harassment, extortion, and raids in brothels. They have surrounded police stations and sat in vigil until assurance was given to stop unlawful and coercive police action.[67] They now derive immense satisfaction from the fact that the police no longer dare to treat them publicly as criminals, but rather interact with them with politeness and even respect. At police stations, instead of being kept waiting for hours for a hearing and then refused the right to even lodge 'first information reports' on cases of assault and violence, they are now readily attended to, offered a seat, and addressed as '*didi*'.[68] Sex workers have also mounted successful protests against local authorities to prevent their eviction from brothels or from 'red light' areas.[69] In all these endeavours, the DMSC has been able to rally the mass of sex workers. The DMSC activists argue that they have successfully curbed the arbitrary power of *goondas*, police, and local administrators: first, because they have demonstrated in practice the strength of unity and the power of organization; second, because they are no longer scared to protest; and third, above all, because they have become fully aware of their rights as citizens and are unflinching in ensuring that their rights are recognized.[70] This transformation of mute suffering to effective collective resistance is considered a major achievement by all sex workers. Moreover, in sharp contrast to their traditional image they have projected themselves as upright, moral, and law-abiding citizens, acting in the interest of the law and public order.

The DMSC has also taken the initiative to organize local women against madams and pimps when terms of exchange were unequal and working conditions exploitative within the sex trade. The DMSC activists have regularly intervened in cases of physical abuse or financial extortion by madams or pimps and acted as negotiators or arranged demonstrations and police action against offending parties, who have usually capitulated for fear of the law or disruption of their business.[71]

---

[65] Group discussion, 17 March 1999; *Fallen*, p. 22; Jana *et al.*, 'STD/HIV Intervention', p. 7.
[66] *Newsweek*, 15 February 1999.
[67] Group discussion, 17 March 1999; *Fallen*, p. 22; Jana *et al.*, 'STD/HIV Intervention', p. 7.
[68] Group discussion, 17 March 1999, especially comments by Mala Singh.
[69] Group discussion, 17 March 1999; *Fallen*, p. 22; Jana *et al.*, 'STD/HIV Intervention', p. 7.
[70] Group discussion, 17 March 1999.
[71] *Ibid.*; *Fallen*, p. 22; Jana *et al.*, 'STD/HIV Intervention', p. 7.

In addition to engaging in agitation against injustice and oppression in 'red light' areas, the DMSC has intervened decisively on a number of occasions to terminate or draw attention to illegal, unethical, and unauthorized immunization or drug trials for HIV infection on sex workers and forcibly testing them for AIDS.[72] AIDS monitoring of sex workers is conducted either without their knowledge or their informed consent and so is seen as an act of violence.[73] Uma Mondal recalls that during one of the early protests, she delivered a speech at a public meeting in which she vehemently condemned the doctors who dared to 'experiment' on sex workers. For, she argued, the doctors display even greater contempt and lack of respect towards sex workers than towards chimpanzees, monkeys, and other animals who have to be purchased at a price for experiments. She was outraged that no value was attached to sex workers as human beings.[74] Such expressions of protest, which may or may not be effective in preventing AIDS screening or drug trials, have nonetheless enabled sex workers to proclaim their own self-worth and rights as human beings.

A major initiative of the DMSC, with advice from SHIP, was to launch, in June 1995, the sex workers' own savings, credit, and consumer cooperative society—the Usha Multipurpose Cooperative. At its inception, the Cooperative received the personal support of the Minister for Cooperatives, who agreed to provide it with Rs One Lakh from his departmental funds. In early 1999 the Cooperative had six governing body members, all of whom were sex workers. The original aim of the Society was to achieve self-reliance for sex workers in securing loans to meet unforeseen expenses or to sustain them when they were unable to work due to ill health or family problems. Sex workers usually obtained loans from local usurers at exorbitant rates of interest, frequently forcing them into long periods of indebtedness and adding to their financial insecurity and poverty. The Usha Cooperative aims to surmount this problem by accepting regular deposits from sex workers from which loans are advanced to those in need. The Cooperative also seeks to address issues like old-age security and also makes products like condoms available at affordable prices. While the savings and credit aspects of the Cooperative's work, as well as the marketing of condoms, are now well established, other projects are gradually being explored. In particular, a 'home' for elderly or 'retired' sex workers is being planned, where vocational training and self-employment schemes will be introduced. Future plans include the provision of evening or night-time nursery or crèche facilities for the children of practising sex workers.[75]

While self-reliance and economic security are central to the establishment of the Cooperative, issues of identity and social recognition are also integral to its formation and operation. At the time of its registration, official objection was raised to 'prostitutes' forming such a cooperative, as it violated a clause in the regulations which stipulated that only persons 'of high moral character' were eligible. After much negotiation, and direct appeals to the government, the Minister for Cooperatives agreed to omit the

---

[72] *Ibid.*

[73] Group discussion on violence, 19 March 1999.   [74] Group discussion, 17 March 1999.

[75] *Fallen*, pp. 39–40; Personal interview with Saraswati Sarkar, sex worker and secretary of Usha Cooperative, 19 March 1999; Some information was also gleaned from my attendance at the Annual General Meeting of the Usha Cooperative on 15 March 1999.

requirement 'of high moral character' from the relevant clause.[76] Sex workers had been advised by the officials concerned to register their Cooperative under the category of 'housewives', but they refused to hide behind this euphemism, insisting that they be called sex workers.[77] This victory was no less significant to them than the achievement of organizing and successfully running the Cooperative. The Usha Cooperative is an interesting example of the inextricable interplay of practical, material concerns with the sex workers' urge to express their identity and rights. It is the latter that prompts sex workers to be totally committed to the Society, depositing their money with regularity and rarely defaulting on repayment of loan interests.[78] It is also worth noting that several sex workers mentioned that initially they had been wary of the Cooperative, expecting it to be yet another organization aiming to rob them of their money. However, they soon came to realize that the distinguishing feature of this Cooperative was that it was their 'own' and run by themselves.[79] It was evidently this sense of ownership that gave them the confidence to commit their hard-earned money to the Cooperative and to comply scrupulously with its savings and credit rules.

It is obvious from all these activities that sex workers have gained important material and practical advantages as a result of the formation of the DMSC. Above all, they have built up a sense of solidarity and experienced the exhilaration of collective action. The DMSC's activities have gathered increasing momentum, fuelled by the heady brew of standing together publicly and challenging powerful groups with success. One sex worker asserted during a group discussion, and many of the others concurred, that the most poignant moment in the DMSC's career was a midnight procession of sex workers with flaming torches on 1 May 1998.[80] Not only did they seek to establish their identity as workers by celebrating Labour Day in this way, but they dared to transgress the spatial and symbolic boundaries etched out for them by society. In this procession, those who work furtively in the dark, in the back lanes of the city, burst forth triumphantly on to the main streets, without shame or fear, illuminated with their own light. This was an exuberant event, expressing the sex workers' new found power, inner strength, and confidence. Instances like these suggest that political activism and social mobilization have themselves acted as the main motor, driving group action forward, generating a strong belief in and commitment to the unity of the community and collective political assertion. If the DMSC's activities had been confined to practical achievements alone, then the organization would most likely have been a transient one, in which women participated spasmodically over specific issues at particular times. Moreover, instead of being based on cooperation, the organization would have become the focus of conflict and competition of rival sections of sex workers, each seeking to gain control over material and practical benefits. In contrast, the DMSC has been able to sustain itself as a united entity, with a continuing organizational presence. This has been possible because all the activities of the DMSC described so far have implicitly

---

[76] Information supplied by Dr Jana director of SHIP.

[77] Jana *et al.*, 'STD/HIV Intervention', p. 8.

[78] Personal interview with Saraswati Sarkar, 19 March 1999.   [79] Group discussion, 17 March 1999.

[80] *Ibid.* (statement of Anima Banerjee).

or explicitly encompassed elements of collective mobilization, political struggle, and community identity. As we shall now see, all these elements were far more overtly expressed in other activities of the DMSC.

One of the key initiatives of the DMSC, frequently and usually with advice and assistance from SHIP, has been to enhance the profile of sex workers as a socially responsible community in the public sphere. In a group discussion, a majority of sex workers stated that as a result of the activities of the DMSC in this particular respect, they have been able to meet people from all walks of life with confidence, to present themselves in society with dignity, and to 'stand up in society' on equal terms with other citizens.[81] In this regard, the DMSC's initiatives are many and varied.[82] From 1993 onwards, the DMSC (or its precursor, the Interlink Committee) has participated every year in the Calcutta Book Fair, the single most important, annual, intellectual and cultural event in the city of Calcutta. They have sold and distributed published material explaining their problems, needs, and struggle. The DMSC has also convened regular national and state level meetings and conferences to register its presence in public politics, and the organization has sought to ensure that such occasions are graced by the presence of influential public personalities, including government ministers and politicians, who now covet the electoral support of this highly mobilized constituency. The association of prominent figures with the DMSC has earned the organization much needed public attention and recognition. This has also permitted the DMSC to locate itself in the mainstream of institutional political life. On the one hand, this has greatly boosted the power they can now exercise in their locality. On the other hand, it has given the sex workers a collective sense of authority and confidence. An international news magazine quoted a sex worker who revelled in the fact that: 'Now we sit across from public officials and discuss our health and welfare.'[83] In addition, a number of discussion sessions have been hosted by the DMSC with members of the Calcutta intelligentsia who have historically played a key role in moulding dominant social discourses in the city. The DMSC, with advice from SHIP, was shrewd enough to realize that in order to define a new and socially acceptable collective identity for themselves, they would need to convince the opinion moulders.

It is not simply through words, but through deeds too, that the sex workers of the DMSC have sought to make themselves socially acceptable as a community. As seen earlier, sex workers have consistently sought to present themselves as morally upright and law-abiding, with a sense of civic duty. Two areas in which sex workers can make a significant contribution, have been particularly emphasized as socially useful— the prevention of AIDS and child prostitution. Sex workers have launched AIDS awareness campaigns in the city, organized candle-light vigils in memory of AIDS vic-tims, attended international conferences on AIDS control, and introduced a telephone advisory and counselling service on AIDS—the 'Positive Hotline'—'womanned' by sex workers themselves. Although the problem of AIDS is not one that 'respectable'

---

[81] Group discussion, 17 March 1999.

[82] An exhaustive list of DMSC's activities until 1997 can be found in *Fallen*, pp. 35–40, 42–3.

[83] *Newsweek*, 15 February 1999.

society in Calcutta is overly concerned about, these initiatives have gained the DMSC international acclaim, which has, in turn, augmented the social standing of sex workers in Calcutta. The DMSC has also attempted to prevent the entry of minors into the profession, and 'rescued' young girls and sent them back to their families. The much publicized success of the DMSC in containing under-aged prostitution[84] has enhanced the image of sex workers as 'responsible' citizens.

It is worth bearing in mind here that, at the international level, in the 1980s and 1990s, considerable value was attached to these two areas of work—AIDS and child labour. Sex workers of the DMSC have been able to locate their work successfully in the interstices of these global trends to define themselves as a community of virtue. While being fully alive to the propaganda benefits, sex workers themselves have also evidently taken their role in 'social work' very seriously, and internalized the self-image of being responsible, socially aware citizens. Sex workers pointed out that in the past, because of lack of confidence and low self-esteem, they had been unable to act as socially responsible people. Now with their experience as peers in the SHIP project, they feel confident about their ability to do 'social work'. One sex worker explained the significance of this transformation saying that if in the past, she had seen an injured person in a road accident, she would simply have walked away feeling that she was a lowly social outcast, who had neither the right nor the skills to step in and help. However, now she feels that just like any other citizen she too could help such a person.[85] It is indeed with this spirit of duty and newly acquired capability that they attempt to carve out a role for themselves in what they describe as 'social work'.

This new identity defined through conceptions of civic awareness and social duty, and a right to intervene in public issues, has been fleshed out in some other initiatives of the DMSC. The DMSC has taken part in Women's Day celebrations, and attended meetings in 1998 to protest against nuclear detonation by the Indian government. Similarly, in one of their meetings with intellectuals in March 1999, sex workers set the agenda to discuss the plight of oppressed minorities in India. By aligning and identifying themselves with such deprived groups, sex workers are seeking to root their community identity in a wider history of social oppression and exclusion. In all these initiatives, we repeatedly come back to the central issue of community identity in the politics of the DMSC.

In the cultural initiatives undertaken by the DMSC, with the help and advice of SHIP, we find again the central issue of community identity. The DMSC has formed a cultural front, *Komal Gandhar*, 'to express ourselves through music, dance, plays, painting and writing'.[86] Sex workers have staged cultural performances and undertaken creative writing, some of which has been published in the regular journal of SHIP. Art competitions and cultural programmes have also been organized for the children of the sex workers. All of this is intended to give sex workers and their children 'an opportunity

---

[84] According to SHIP surveys, in 1995, one in five sex workers was of age 19 or less, while in 1998, one in thirty falls in that age group.

[85] Group discussion, 17 March 1999, and personal interviews with Putul Singh and Kohinoor Begum, 18 March 1999.   [86] Leaflet of *Komal Gandhar*, available from DMSC/SHIP office.

to claim the right to enjoy ourselves through cultural expression'.[87] However, cultural pursuits are also about the right to free, open and public self-expression for those who are denied such rights. Moreover, sex workers expect that cultural activities will help in 'neutralising some of the brutalising experiences' that they and their children face.[88] Sex workers feel that expressions of their cultural talent earn them the right to mingle with 'respectable' society by virtue of their cultural achievements.

Guria, an organization based in Delhi, sought to provide a public forum for the 'art' of courtesans and 'public' or 'fallen' women by organizing a national cultural festival in 1998.[89] Members of *Komal Gandhar* seized the opportunity provided by *Guria*. They staged a musical play, entitled *'Amader Katha'* (Our Story), which was not merely intended as an aesthetic production, but aimed to outline the plight of sex workers. *'Amader Katha'* depicted the story of young women driven by poverty to 'red light' districts, being exploited by the police, madams, and *goondas*, and forced to have unprotected sex.[90] The play poignantly portrayed the anger and pain of sex workers, and won the highest award at the festival. More recent productions of *Komal Gandhar* tell of the historical development of prostitution, and relate this to the present predicament of sex workers and the genesis of their united protest marked by the formation of the DMSC.[91] In this way, the sex workers are actively constructing a history for themselves as an oppressed community, while at the same time attempting to root their experience in the general history of humankind.

Following their spectacular success in the *Guria* festival, performers of *Komal Gandhar* have participated in a number of national and international cultural festivals, and have been much feted. Most notably, they performed at the 12th World AIDS Conference in Geneva, where, after an initial audition, they were invited to stage their performance at the inaugural session.[92] This great accolade, as they see it, has entrenched the Geneva event in the collective memory of sex workers with great symbolic significance. The achievement was recounted to me by a large number of sex workers as if it was a personal experience, although only a handful of them actually travelled to Geneva. The winning of cultural recognition has been a source of extraordinary confidence and pride, and has exploded the myth that sex workers are 'uncultured', unrefined, vulgar or coarse.[93] The struggle of the sex workers is, thus, not only about the tangible exercise of power, but also about challenging their exclusion from symbolic and cultural forms of power.

Lest all of what has been said so far has portrayed an idealized image of the sex workers' political mobilization as moving and romantic, beckoning us to celebrate

---

[87] *Ibid.* [88] *Ibid.*

[89] *Nav Bharat Times*, 29 March 1998; *The Pioneer*, (Lucknow), 27 March 1998.

[90] Personal interview with Mala Singh, 17 March 1999; Undated press-cuttings from *Nai Duniya* and *Dainik Jagaran*, held at DMSC office.

[91] Personal interview with Sudipta Biswas, sex worker and performer with *Komal Gandhar*, 18 March 1999.

[92] *The Telegraph*, 28 July 1998; Personal interviews with a number of sex workers.

[93] Group discussion, 17 March 1999; Personal interviews with Mala Singh and Putul Singh, 17 March 1999 and 18 March 1999.

the 'true' struggles of particularly wretched people, let me hasten to disabuse this impression. It needs to be reiterated that we are talking about hard political strife and a messy, bitter struggle. Sex workers have had to rock the edifice of historically inherited and socially reproduced prejudices, as well as uproot entrenched structures of power. Their political activity is not about pretty cultural programmes and high-spirited symbolic gestures. Their political struggle is also far from the anodyne 'social impact' of SHIP. With a keen sense of political realities, sex workers have sought legitimacy and endorsement from abroad and from the development community. They are aware of 'visitors' and are always ready to present a positive and development-friendly public face—a combination of exploited innocence, confidence, and achievement. However, under the garb of a development intervention, what is unfolding here is a serious and bitter struggle. It is indeed this struggle for rights and power that makes the DMSC, as a group, effective, dynamic, and successful in achieving equity and well-being from their own perspective. As the DMSC activists emphasize, sex workers are now proud, confident, in control of their lives and destinies, socially and politically assertive, and able to fight to defend their rights as workers and citizens in an environment in which they are themselves redefining the extant relations of power. Their capacity to elicit practical benefits has been greatly augmented by their ability to present themselves publicly as a cohesive group, based in turn on their successful definition of collective self-identity. Even the spectacular public health successes of SHIP are ultimately based on the interplay of SHIP and the DMSC.

11.6. CONCLUSION

What conclusions can we draw from this experience about motivation for group formation and group mobilization, and about the nature of group activity? In other words, what stimulated participation in group action, promoted individual commitment to the group, and engendered cooperative action and group cohesion? What contributed to its success in achieving well-being and equity, and in making itself dynamic and sustainable? Three main points can be highlighted:

- recasting of identity, reconceptualization of capabilities, and redefinition of subjectivity;
- construction of community;
- political action to challenge extant forms of power, and the role of political struggle in impelling the sustained and committed involvement of sex workers in the politics of the DMSC.

Undeniably, the practical benefits that the sex workers hoped to gain, initially from joining the SHIP project, and then by forming the DMSC, played an important role in motivating them to engage in collective action. However, the attraction of these practical incentives alone may well have confined their engagement in group activity to self-interested *quid pro quo* transactions. Moreover, group activity based entirely on the tangible, material benefits reaped by members can easily cause a group to become riven by internal conflict. It is also unlikely to inspire consensual collective action or enduring participation. However, the case of the sex workers shows that the issues of community, identity, and struggle for power have engendered both cooperation and continued participation. These points will be elaborated below, underscoring arguments presented in the course of this chapter.

(1) *The role of SHIP, community construction, and the political conception of empowerment*

SHIP emphasized a community-based approach to empowerment.[94] What is interesting and important about SHIP is its specific interpretation of this aim, and the ways in which it sought to realize this aim in practice. Community-based approaches often assume that there is a community already in existence, which can be made the target of development interventions. SHIP realized that sex workers were not a community in any sense, a point that is now well recognized in the development literature on HIV/AIDS interventions.[95] Sex workers lack the usual community attributes of a shared sense of belonging, experience, history, memory, origin or abode as well as common social codes and ideas. The important issue then is to facilitate the ideological definition and discursive construction of a community, which can animate a newly constructed group and generate a common purpose over specific goals. SHIP and the DMSC succeed because a community identity has been defined on which consensus over group action is based. Sex workers see themselves as a community *within the context of their group action and their political struggle*, and project themselves as such.

The second important dimension of SHIP's intervention relates to empowerment. Empowerment, unusually, in the history of development interventions, has been interpreted not simply to mean better economic conditions or bargaining power, but to encompass a struggle through which extant social perceptions are challenged and through which alterations are sought in power relations. This is an overtly political conception of empowerment, which has to be operationalized through political mobilization and action. In development literature and practice, even when empowerment is seen in its broader sense, the need for political action is seldom, if ever, acknowledged. The underlying aim of development interventions is rarely to reconfigure power relations through wholesale structural changes in society and politics. Instead, advocacy for better policy regimes or redirection of resources in favour of the disadvantaged are the preferred modes of action, and political initiatives are framed in this limited sense.[96] Interestingly, SHIP does not seem to have escaped the problems inherent in political mobilization within a developmental context. While SHIP seems to have unleashed what are in essence serious political struggles, these are categorized under the acceptable terminology of an 'integrated' approach to managed change that goes beyond public health interventions and incorporates some wider aspects of the problems faced by the target group of sex workers. Moreover, the problem of political resistance to

---

[94] For community development approaches to HIV/AIDS intervention, see Evans, 'International review of . . . community development approaches', *passim*, and especially, pp. 12–13, 15, 33–4.

[95] *Ibid.*, pp. 12–13.

[96] Joan Mencher (1999). 'NGOs: Are they a force for change?'. *Economic and Political Weekly*, 34 (30): 2083.

the DMSC by powerful groups was, to some extent, diffused by emphasizing that the DMSC's aim was not to disrupt political order and help mobilize sex workers to be socially responsible citizens engaged in 'social work'. Now that a certain degree of mobilization has been achieved, and this has served the purpose of advancing the public health cause, SHIP appears to be favouring a more limited approach. Concerns over the institutionalization of the DMSC and its organizational sustainability seem to be taking precedence over activist political struggles and mounting radical ideological or social challenges. Despite these ambiguities, however, SHIP's interpretation of empowerment has gone a long way in enabling group activity to succeed by allowing the political activism of the DMSC.

(2) *The DMSC and collective identity*

It is obvious from the case of the sex workers in Calcutta that, for such a group to emerge, to function effectively, and remain dynamic, the definition of collective identity is paramount. From the perspective of sex workers, as we have seen, the urgent need is to redefine who they are and what they are capable of contributing, in order to live in a society where they have equal rights. The sex workers' statements and actions are a constant reminder of the fact that without the re-definition of identity, most activities would be meaningless to them, and only partially relevant to their needs. As we have seen, this definition of identity is about belonging, and thus about the primacy of the collective or the group. Had the issue of collective, as opposed to individual, identity not been at the centre of the activities of the DMSC, the group might never have coalesced, let alone achieved success. The centrality of collective identity in the case of sex workers, clearly underpinned the individuals' commitment to the group and encouraged altruism, COOP, and cohesion among its members. Here we see how individuals find meaning in and identify themselves with the group, and how the group defines their identity, and shapes their goals and patterns of behaviour.

(3) *Political struggle as the motor of group action and cohesion*

We have seen that the exhilaration and excitement generated by agitational politics and activism played a crucial role in propelling the sex workers forward as a group. The successes achieved through political struggles, as well as the spectacular and symbolic elements of political mobilization, bred ever greater conviction and enthusiasm among sex workers and gave a major boost to group activity. Individual commitment to group activity was thus, to a large extent, predicated on successful political activism. Most importantly, it would not be an exaggeration to argue that sex workers view their political struggles as the most important *raison d'être* of the DMSC. This was brought out at a meeting of the central executive committee of the DMSC on 26 March 1999. In early 1999 it was planned that the DMSC would gradually take over the actual running of the STD/HIV intervention programme. In this context, the meeting explored the questions of organizational enlargement, sustainability, and capacity building of the DMSC. Gradually, the concerns of the meeting shifted away from themes of organizational continuity and resilience, as DMSC activists began to express their need to expand the range of their political struggles. They felt that the organization would begin to stagnate and ossify if they ceased to support sex workers in challenging the powerful. They argued that even if it meant an increase in formal membership figures, it would not be possible to maintain the commitment and involvement of the constituency of support unless the DMSC stayed in the forefront of the struggles of sex workers. Sadhana Mukherjee, former Secretary of the DMSC, stated that their next task, after having successfully tamed *goondas*, the police, and power brokers within the sex industry, should be to take on the powerful political parties in an attempt to further the wider political goals of sex workers. Many hurdles and foes had been overcome, she argued, but many more still remained, including some formidable ones. Moreover, the fruits of the battles already won had to be protected through continued political activism. The future development of the DMSC depended on the the sex workers' ability to face these challenges. In her view, fortifying the organization, in the sense of routinized bureaucratic institutionalization, would not help the cause. Although no very clear plan emerged at this meeting about the path for progress, it was evident that the sex workers keenly appreciated the importance of political action in maintaining group activity.

Finally, it should be noted that group cohesion in the case of the sex workers in Calcutta did not derive from a historically inherited stock of 'social capital', but through the construction of community identity and an activist political struggle. This realization helps us to broaden the discussion about the nature and significance of 'social capital' taken loosely to mean a set of shared ideas that promote COOP. The sex workers' case provides evidence that those who are not fortunate enough to be able to draw upon a pool of 'social capital' can forge such 'capital' through collective political struggle. Moreover, dynamic group action can arise in a situation of social tension and political conflict, rather than being nurtured and facilitated by pre-existing, apparently consensual, 'social capital' within a context of social cohesion.

12

Non-market Relationships in Health Care

MAUREEN MACKINTOSH AND LUCY GILSON

12.1. INTRODUCTION

Do collaborative or co-operative (COOP) non-market relationships within groups generate more equitable outcomes than hierarchical or quasi-market (M) modes of organization? That was one of the questions that motivated the WIDER workshop for which an earlier draft of this paper was prepared. This paper seeks to answer that question, in a reworked form, for the case of health care systems in low and middle income countries. The answer, we argue, is no. COOP is not in itself a force for equity. COOP and hierarchical (P/C) modes of non-market behaviour within and between groups can each be associated with redistributive or regressive health care systems.

However, the nature of non-market working relationships in health care facilities, health care systems, and government ministries *is* an important determinant of equitable or inequitable access to care. Moves towards greater equity in health care require the difficult process of redistribution of resources from the better off to the poor in unequal societies. We argue here that redistributive health care works best when embedded in intra-group and inter-group non-market relationships that can sustain it over time. Health policy, we therefore argue, needs to take non-market behaviour seriously.

We make this argument in three stages. First we develop a typology of non-market behaviour appropriate to the health care context, drawing on a literature review[1] of health care provision in lower income countries that concentrates particularly on the government sector. This involves 'unpacking' the concept of COOP, as used in this book, to distinguish the 'free gift' process that forms an inevitable element of

Lucy Gilson is a part-time member of the Health Economics and Financing Programme of the London School of Hygiene and Tropical Medicine which receives financial support from the UK's Department for International Development (DFID). Maureen Mackintosh worked on this paper in the context of a research project with Paula Tibandebage, also supported by the DFID. The contents of this paper are the sole responsibility of the authors, and do not reflect the policies and practices of the DFID. The authors would like to thank participants at the WIDER workshop on Group Behaviour and Development in Helsinki, September 1999, especially the book editors, and also Paul Anand, for comments on an earlier draft.

[1] A longer draft of the review, summarized here, was presented to the Helsinki workshop (Mackintosh and Gilson 2000).

redistribution from non-market reciprocity (reciprocated gifts). It also involves attention to inter-group relationships, since the relationship between patients and would-be patients and health facilities' staff is a core element of health care equity and access. Hence our discussion treats patients who share norms of health-seeking behaviour as an informal group.[2]

Using our typology and a range of examples from the literature, we show that health policy makers in low and middle income countries make assumptions about non-market behaviour that are frequently incorrect, and we argue that this is a cause of health policy failure. The final section draws out implications for an approach to health policy that treats non-market relationships, not as infinitely malleable, but as having, like market processes, a 'life' and logic of their own.

12.2. NORMS AND MEANINGS: CONCEPTUALIZING NON-MARKET RELATIONSHIPS IN HEALTH CARE

We begin by defining our field of study negatively: those relationships relevant to health care equity and access that are not relations of market exchange, that is, that do not consist in the exchange of goods and services for cash. We then create positive classifications of the non-market relationships examined in the health care literature, and the behaviour they shape, employing two sources of evidence: what people say about their understanding of their behaviour, and the observed behaviour and its outcomes.

Our analytical approach to the evidence draws on institutional economics and anthropology. Within each of these literatures there is an analytical divide. On one side are conceptual approaches rooted in methodological individualism, typically employing a transactional metaphor for analysing relationships. On the other are forms of analysis that treat, for example, norms and patterns of behaviour as having explanatory power in their own right rather than necessarily requiring explanation from individualist premises.

Much economic analysis of non-market institutional relationships rewrites all relationships among professional colleagues, or between employer and employee, or between nurse and patient, as either monetary or 'gift' exchange. Such work treats the metaphor of exchange[3] as its core explanation of behaviour. Offer (1997) for example, puts forward a broad concept of an 'economy of regard' that would explain behaviour such as ethical professional resistance to perverse material incentives by the need of professionals to sustain the regard of peers.

Almost any of the human behaviour patterns examined in this chapter *can* be studied through a transactional lens. But to do so has costs: notably, it tends to elide transactions and non-transactional behaviour as empirical categories. We have chosen not to analyse all behaviour of interest to health policy makers as transactional. Instead, we treat non-market exchange as one among several empirical categories for investigation, rather than the fundamental analytical category driving the argument.

---

[2] See also Tibandebage and Mackintosh in this volume.

[3] The concept of the 'metaphor of exchange' and its appropriateness as a framework of analysis in the health and social care fields is discussed further in Mackintosh (2000a).

In addition to explanations rooted in individual incentives, we therefore also treat norms and established patterns of behaviour as having explanatory power,[4] not as themselves necessarily requiring explanation from individualist premises. Hilary Standing (1992: 476) argues that the particular value of anthropological accounts in health care lies in their stress on 'understanding the meanings attached to behaviour', and 'the importance of contextualising social practices as part of the wider ... environment'. We draw on anthropological literature in seeking to understand the role of culture and meanings in the social construction of norms of behaviour within health care systems.[5]

By 'meanings' we refer to the social understandings that shape health care behaviour and experience: examples in the paper are the competing meanings given to certain forms of treatment—such as vaccinations—and shared understandings of the legitimacy of certain forms of power, such as that emanating from political position or caste. 'Meanings' is thus a concept at the discursive level, a discursive building block of all our conceptual categories of non-market behaviour. We do not define our conceptual categories on discursive evidence alone (that is, on what people think or say they are doing), but we do regard discursive constructions as highly relevant to the analysis.

By contrast, we understand 'norms', not simply as shared ideas of what 'should' happen, but as institutions in Mary Douglas' sense (Douglas 1987): taken-for-granted patterns of thought and activity, shaped by feedback between ideas and experience. We analyse health care systems as composed of institutions in this sense: of forms of taken-for-granted behaviour understood by the participants in context.

12.2.1. *Categories of Non-market Behaviour*

Non-market Exchange

The context of this study of non-market relationships is extensive marketization of health care, through health sector reform and liberalization. Non-market exchange, that is,[6] reciprocity not taking the form of exchanges of goods and services for cash, both shapes and is shaped by marketization. Examples of non-market exchange in health care include trading of votes for non-monetary favours; participation in reciprocal savings schemes to pay health care fees; and participation in reciprocal kin-based networks of home care for those who fall ill.

Our three categories of non-market exchange are illustrated by the examples just given: individualized something-for-something barter; contributions to the creation

---

[4] In the health policy literature we are in good company: Titmuss, for example, in his much-cited study of blood donating, treats altruistic behaviour not as simply an individual choice but as a norm that can be fostered, an aspect of social integration, arguing that health care systems can allow, 'the "theme of the gift"— of generosity towards strangers—to spread among social groups and generations.' (Titmuss 1970: 225)

[5] The paper thus takes a social constructionist approach to health care systems, since it treats discursive understandings and social relationships as actively creating the system. There is a growing literature on European health care and social policy written from this perspective (e.g. Hughes and Lewis 1998; Williams 1989); an example of field research on the discursive aspects of social (re)construction in health and social care is Mackintosh (2000*b*).

[6] We are aware that some monetized exchange may not be categorizable as 'market' exchange; we have not examined 'quasi-market' (M) relationships, which are not widespread in health care outside the industrialized countries.

of a common pool resource in return for access to it; and contributions to looser networks of reciprocity. Part of the definition of 'gift' exchange in the anthropology literature since Mauss (1924) is the close association of the nature of the gift with the giver's and receiver's social locations: gifts, in one strand of thought, are inalienable—they remain also with the giver, and create social relations of dependence and obligation—in contrast to alienable commodities (Gregory 1982). Anthropologists have been moving away from this sharp distinction between 'gifts' and 'commodities' towards more complex categories of non-monetized exchange, but they retain the emphasis on non-market exchange as shaping social relations among transactors (Humphrey and Hugh-Jones 1992).

These forms of non-market exchange—with the possible exception of individualized barter—fall within COOP, since reciprocity is part of the definition of the COOP mode of operation as defined in Chapter 1 in this book.

The Exercise of Unequal Power

Our second broad category is behaviour classifiable as the exercise of unequal power. This category fits well with the P/C mode of operation defined in Chapter 1, and is crucial to any analysis of redistribution of resources in unequal societies. Examples thus include the allocation of tax revenues to health care by a hierarchically organized bureaucracy.

The category also includes the exercise of power within narrower institutional settings: for example, imbalances of power and standing between professional groups, between health care facilities, or between staff and patients, and their consequences for resource allocation. Attempts to construct countervailing power, for example, on behalf of patients, or to undermine existing patterns of unequal allocation on the basis of privilege, require attention to these types of allocative behaviour and the unequal relationships that shape them. We argue that in the health care policy literature the focus on equity as an objective can obscure the exercise of power as a practice.

Duty, Commitment, and 'Free Gifts'

The sociological literature contains a second concept of the 'gift': the common parlance idea of the 'free gift'. Carrier (1995) calls this concept of gifts, 'gratuitous favours': formal expressions of love and thanks, and acknowledgement of relationships, but socially framed as not reciprocated. There are analogous forms of behaviour understood by health care participants and recipients as motivated by duty or ethical commitment outside of any process of reciprocity. Ethical resistance to material incentives to cheat falls within this category, as does the following of professional rules of conduct for their own sake, and behaviour based on political and ideological commitment.

This category captures the construction of redistribution, in much health policy debate, as a duty of health care systems' participants. The policy literature criticizes redistributive failure while paying too little attention to designing relationships that can sustain redistributive commitment. This category of behaviour includes unreciprocated contributions to health care outcomes whether they take the form of 'free gifts' from the rich to the poor or vice versa. We argue that ethical commitments to others are both important and fragile. 'Free gifts' are hard to sustain on the basis of ethical commitment alone, and are robust only when embedded in other non-market relationships.

The separation of this category from reciprocity unpacks the COOP mode of operation, since voluntary commitment appears in the COOP definition. However, some activities socially construed as voluntary contributions may from another perspective appear as forced: conflicting meanings of this kind are, for example, given by different participants to some 'participatory' health care activities. We do not treat our three categories as non-intersecting modes of operation, but rather as a typology of behaviour to which competing meanings may be attached in unequal societies.

Finally, these types of behaviour can operate both within and between groups. By 'group' in this statement, we refer both to groups as defined in the Introduction to this book, such as the staff of a facility, and also to what we term (see Section 12.1) informal groups, for example, of patients, defined by shared norms of behaviour. The norms in question may concern behaviour towards outsiders as well as behaviour towards other group members. Health care access is importantly shaped, for example, by the behaviour of facility staff towards patients. Our objective is to analyse the implications of norms of behaviour for redistributive outcomes.

12.3. NON-MARKET BEHAVIOUR IN HEALTH CARE: ASSUMPTIONS AND EVIDENCE

Non-market behaviour is an important determinant of the quality of health care and the distribution of health care access. This section illustrates that proposition by reviewing evidence from low and middle income countries concerning five topics linked to the financing and delivery of care. The evidence is drawn mainly from the government sector, since the health policy literature on these topics focuses mainly on this sector, and more importantly, since government action is central to the redistributive process. The topics are: exemption of the poor from health care fees; allocation of tax funding within health care systems; mutual insurance and mutual self-help, including social health insurance; community participation and community management; and health workers' professional behaviour. These topics were selected for consideration because they involve, or are assumed to involve, non-market behaviour; because they cover important policy issues in health care that are relevant to the achievement of greater equity and inclusion; and because relevant evidence was available.

Health policy makers frequently make strong but incorrect assumptions about non-market behaviour. Table 12.1 summarizes the divergence between the assumptions found in the policy literature and the research evidence. The table uses the categories of non-market behaviour outlined in Section 12.2, separating non-market exchange from dutiful and committed behaviour and free gifts; it also divides the benevolent from the self-serving exercise of power.[7]

---

[7] We have labelled our categories of non-market behaviour in relation to COOP and P/C modes of operation, but note that our categories refer to behaviour between as well as within groups.

Table 12.1. *Assumptions and evidence on non-market behaviour*

Topic investigated	Categories of expected/observed behaviour			
	Reciprocity/ non-market exchange (COOP1)	Duty, commitment, free gifts (COOP2)	Benevolent exercise of unequal power (P/C1)	Self-serving exercise of unequal power (P/C2)
1. Institution-level exemptions				
Policy assumptions		✓ (gifts downward)	✓	
Observed behaviour				✓
2. Tax funding allocation				
Policy assumptions			✓	
Observed behaviour	✓		✓	✓
3. Mutual insurance and self-help				
Policy assumptions	✓	✓ (gifts downward)	✓	
Observed behaviour	✓			✓
4. Community participation and management				
Policy assumptions	✓			
Observed behaviour		✓ (gifts upward)		✓
5. Health worker professional behaviour				
Policy assumptions			✓	
Observed behaviour	✓		✓	✓

Table 12.1 highlights the weight given in policy assumptions of non-market behaviour to free gifts 'downwards' (from the better off to the poor) as well as to the benevolent exercise of unequal power and reciprocity. These forms of behaviour are expected to deliver the policy objectives of increasing equity and inclusion. Such expectations are belied however, as the table shows, by observations of behaviour in practice as dominated (though not completely characterized) by gifts 'upwards' from poor to the better off, and by the self-serving uses of unequal power as well as forms of reciprocity that are different from those assumed.

The expectations of benevolent behaviour can be illustrated for each topic. As fees are introduced or increased at government health care facilities as part of health sector reforms, those institutions are often required by higher administrative levels to offer some free or reduced price care to certain pre-identified categories of people, usually including very poor would-be patients (Gilson *et al.* 1995; Russell and Gilson 1997). These exemptions are thus construed in the health policy literature as unreciprocated local 'free gifts' from those who can pay to those who cannot.

The health policy literature on tax funding allocation considers efficient allocation and redistribution to be a matter of political will and benevolent administrative action

(World Bank 1995, 1996, 1997; Gertler 1998). The growing literature on social and mutual insurance in health care similarly assumes that redistributive 'gifts' and allocations can be grafted onto reciprocity-based insurance systems. People are assumed to pay most readily into voluntary mutual risk-pooling schemes with fixed contributions, but to increase inclusiveness such schemes are urged to support some who are unable to pay (Normand 1999). At the same time, although often established initially for the better off, national social insurance schemes are encouraged to relate payment to income and to subsidize access by the poor.

The literature on community participation and management in health care also often draws on a policy model of reciprocity: community members are expected to participate in decision-making in return for service improvements that benefit the community served by the local health facility. This literature sees reciprocity as socially inclusive: a 'strategy that provides people with the sense that they can solve their problems through careful reflection and collective action' (Zakus and Lysack 1998: 2).

Finally, policy generally assumes that the interaction between provider and patient reflects the benevolent use of unequal power: health workers are assumed to use their superior knowledge in patients' interests, and professional ethics to prevent abuse of power derived from that knowledge.

The evidence available in the health care literature, however, casts doubt on *all* of these general expectations about non-market behaviour.

Studies on the effectiveness of exemption schemes show that the poorest rarely benefit, and that some exemptions, sometimes a quite large proportion, are directed to the non-poor (Gilson *et al.* 1999; Newbrander *et al.* 1997; Tibandebage and Mackintosh, this volume). There is also clear evidence that the better off benefit disproportionately from the allocation of tax funding to health care, notably because of over-allocation to secondary and curative health care (World Bank 1993, 1995, 1996, 1997; Barnum and Kutzin 1993; Gertler 1998).

Social and mutual insurance schemes in lower income countries are not particularly redistributive. The most inclusive were the communal health care systems in China and Vietnam, but these collapsed along with the collective agricultural production relations in which they were embedded (Liu *et al.* 1996; Bloom 1998). Indian evidence suggests that voluntary mutual insurance is hard to establish or sustain in contexts of acute social and income inequality (Giridhar 1993). African mutual insurance schemes, while displaying successful risk-pooling on a reciprocal basis, tend to exclude the very poor (Atim 1999; Criel *et al.* 1999). Compulsory, employer-based 'social insurance' schemes in lower income countries often display well documented problems of corruption and inefficiency. Giridhar (1993) gives examples from Asia. In Africa, the schemes that exist have been heavily tax-subsidized. There is no evidence that contributions to such schemes have, as some commentators expected, 'released' tax funding to be reallocated to the poor in either Africa or transitional Asia (Abel-Smith and Rawal 1994; Ensor 1999; Vogel 1990).

The community health worker (CHW) programmes seen by some as a mechanism of community empowerment (Werner 1981) have often, in practice, operated as a cheap extension of the formal primary care network, 'bridging gaps between fixed health facilities and local communities' (Walt 1990: 168) through volunteer labour and local fund-raising. CHWs' work has thus frequently been locally construed as an unreciprocated gift from poor people to the *state*—rather than a reciprocated gift to the community. Some schemes involving voluntary participation have, therefore, been opposed by communities fearing that they will result in the withdrawal of formal facilities (Zakus and Lysack 1998).

Finally, although many health workers try to behave professionally, a common deterrent to using public health services is perceived poor quality, particularly poor provider attitudes. Rudeness and even cruelty towards patients (Bassett *et al.* 1997; Gilson *et al.* 1994; Jewkes *et al.* 1998) clearly represent a breakdown of the non-market behaviour expected of health workers. Demanding and accepting 'informal payments' represents a shift to a particularly abusive form of market exchange (McPake *et al.* 1999; Tibandebage and Mackintosh, this volume). Jewkes *et al.* (1998) found that patients in low income areas, and those most likely to be perceived as inferior and reprehensible such as teenagers, were most likely to face abuse.

Such evidence suggests that two common policy assumptions about non-market behaviour in health care—that the benevolent exercise of unequal power can be mandated, and that reciprocity can be administratively created and then enjoined to operate redistributively—are particularly problematic. Section 12.4 examines further research evidence on non-market behaviour in practice and its determinants.

12.4. EXPLAINING NON-MARKET BEHAVIOUR

Although the health policy literature assumes certain types of non-market behaviour, the linear policy-to-implementation framework of health care research frequently blocks investigation of the nature and determinants of such behaviour. This policy mindset treats non-market behaviour as if it followed no logic, or had no dynamics of its own. (By contrast, the importance of proper incentive design in promoting market behaviour is well recognized.) Non-market responses are thus expected to be malleable: prescriptive policies—such as exemption rules or redistribution of tax funding away from the middle classes—are regarded as, in principle, unproblematic, their implementation a matter of political or institutional will. The result is a shortage of research on non-market behaviour in practice.

The logic of non-market behaviour as analysed below is understood (see Section 12.2) as shaped by interacting sets of shared understandings and norms of behaviour, responding to experiences of health care within highly unequal social structures. This perspective implies that non-market behaviour—like market exchange—responds to both cultural understandings and individual incentives.

12.4.1. *Exemptions Practice: Conflicts of Norms and Incentives*

Research suggests that two main conflicts of norms and incentive structures underlie the failure of existing exemption systems to protect the poor. Financial sustainability is frequently established, in both national and local understanding, as the primary goal of user fee systems and community financing schemes. This understanding turns exemptions into a 'free gift' that health workers are deterred from giving since the gift will reduce revenue relative to costs, possibly reduce perceived quality of service, and even limit personal gains (Gilson *et al.* 1999; Newbrander *et al.* 1997; Russell and Gilson 1997). The competing goal of revenue generation has thus shifted these facilities towards more market-driven behaviour. In this context, the frequent vagueness of the guidance given to decision-makers on who should receive protection only further undermines the weight given to equity considerations (Gilson *et al.* 1999; Newbrander *et al.* 1997).

Redistributive commitment is often further undermined by conflict with local social hierarchy and the exercise of unequal social and administrative power. Those with status, prestige, and power within communities frequently obtain free treatment because of who they are, or because they can exercise power over local decision-makers (Gilson *et al.* 1995, 1998, 1999; Russell and Gilson 1997). Less frequently, the hierarchical decision-making practices that persist in the health sector have deterred exemptions: strict guidelines on price levels, for example, leave little room for local decision-makers to adapt them in ways that may better protect vulnerable groups. The social marginalization of the poorest also influences exemption practice, and sustains 'accepted wisdom' such as the misperception by local decision-makers that prices are affordable for the poorest (Gilson *et al.* 1999).

12.4.2. *Tax Funding Allocation: Contestation, Barter Trading, and the Exercise of Power*

Behavioural processes of allocation of tax funding in health care appear to be poorly researched except in the Indian literature. Indian studies document a contrast between closed, elite-centred allocation processes and political barter systems with regressive outcomes on the one hand, and more open national or local political processes, focused around social demands backed by political organizing, with more progressive outcomes on the other hand.

Thus Jeffrey (1998) examines the extent to which doctors in India, perceiving incentives to pursue urban specialist medical careers, have been able to shape public spending priorities, including training staff for the private sector (see also Duggal and Antia 1993). The exercise of power for elite group interests is also displayed in substantial allocations for civil servants' and parliamentary members' health care, in India as in much of Africa (World Bank 1995; Huff-Rouselle and Akuamoah-Boateng 1998). Conversely, Jeffrey (1988: 236) argues that the tendency for nurses to be recruited from the disadvantaged classes in India, together with the 'polluting' connotations of their work, have undermined the profession's ability to lobby for pay and status, with adverse consequences for the funding of maternal and child health services.

Jeffrey also reports that the state-level allocation of public health care resources responds strongly to the ability of individual politicians to exert pressure over detailed decisions, such as the siting of a primary health care centre, or access by particular individuals to hospital treatment, medical training or jobs. Such non-market allocative relations are explicitly reciprocal: 'barter' relations of a personal kind between politicians and others. The currency of exchange may be political allegiance, return favours or cash; it may be immediate reciprocity or a debt returned as a later favour (Jeffrey 1988: 173). Such non-market individual exchange is likely to be regressive, since those endowed with more resources command more favours in return.

Yet the Indian studies also show that political commitment and ideology in favour of redistribution can influence health care tax allocation behaviour, especially when associated with active political pressure. In Kerala, for example, collective political organizing to keep health care facilities open is long standing (Sen 1992), and the high proportion of state public spending devoted to social sectors (40 per cent in Kerala, 1974–90 as compared to the Indian average of 32 per cent) is rooted in open elections won on support for social provision including health care (Narayana 1999). In contrast, in the large northern states with the worst health care record, these issues do not figure in party programmes and electoral politics are overwhelmingly dominated by elite concerns (Drèze and Sen 1995: 103).

12.4.3. *Mutual Insurance and Mutual Self-help: Reciprocity versus Redistribution?*

European social insurance systems grew out of long experience of mutual societies including trade-union schemes (de Swaan 1988). We found frustratingly little literature about non-market behaviour within formal 'social insurance' schemes for health care in lower income countries, but much more on mutuals. Health care draws on (at least) four kinds of formal or informal mutuality: voluntary mutual health care insurance; mutual savings and insurance schemes that include support for health care fees; informal mutual support within communities to help people to use formal health care; and mutual support within communities for caring for the sick at home. Some relevant generalizations about non-market behaviour can be drawn from this case-study literature.

All mutuals are processes of non-market reciprocity. The most informal take the form of 'generalized reciprocity' as this concept is used in the anthropology literature, where contributions to the care of others are made in the expectation of a return of care when in need. Formal mutual savings schemes are more like collective 'contracts' (Van den Brink and Chavas 1997) providing lump sums for ceremonies and crises (including health care fees) in return for regular contributions, but in those too, the 'sanctioning mechanisms' lie in kinship and neighbourhood and the consequences of social ostracism. The norms on which mutuals are based—socially understood mutual gift giving—thus exclude those who cannot contribute.

There are exceptions within informal home care to this exclusion, as when the long-term sick are cared for by drawing upon competing norms of duty or commitment (unreciprocated gifts). Caring of this type is not only structured by kinship ties but also by unequal power relations between men and women and by moral norms. For example, a Mexican case study of care for gay men suffering from AIDS (Castro *et al.* 1998) showed women doing the physical caring, while men might provide material resources. It also showed that support was influenced by material interests—such as inheritance—and by moral judgements: support was often greater for those judged infected 'accidentally' rather than as a result of 'immoral' behaviour (*ibid.* 1479). Finally, lack of support also resulted from lack of resources and resultant physical and emotional exhaustion.

Norms of informal mutual resource support for health care costs in poor communities include the sharing of information and medicines; networks of personalized contacts with health workers; sharing domestic work to allow others to work for cash to pay fees; and mutual loans and gifts of cash for fees (Booth *et al.* 1995; MacCormack and Lwihula 1983; Gilson *et al.* 1994; Moser 1998; Sauerborn *et al.* 1996; Whyte 1992). These forms of mutuality are equally vulnerable to poverty and economic crisis. Sauerborn *et al.* (1996) found that such networks in Burkina Faso excluded the poorer households. Moser (1998) found dense networks of mutual support among women in poor urban communities in Lusaka, Manila, and Guayaquil (Ecuador) that were severely undermined by falling incomes, thus worsening further the health impact of economic crisis.

A growing literature on more formal savings schemes including health care—notably in Africa—argues that these are strongest when they are both embedded in, and operate to strengthen, wider social ties (Atim 1999). In urban areas one scheme was based in a single ethnic group; another involved social obligations such as funeral attendance. In African rural areas there are also 'a myriad of associations and social groups' of this kind but, curiously, the increasing numbers of health care mutual insurance schemes encouraged by donors are never linked to them 'in such a way as to enhance solidarity' within them (Atim 1999: 887). The health care schemes, where successful, do increase use of the formal health care system by the seriously ill (Criel *et al.* 1999). However, both the health care and the broader schemes again exclude the poorest, who cannot pay the fixed contributions. We found no documented case of more formal mutual schemes with contributions related to ability to pay.

12.4.4. *Community Participation: Unequal Power and Free Gifts Upwards*

The failures of community participation and management highlighted in Section 12.3 appear to be rooted in the exercise of unequal power: by local elites and by national administrative structures. This behaviour contrasts sharply with the policy presentation of participation as joint action for common benefit. This gap may in part arise because 'community' is often used very loosely in this literature (Jewkes and Murcott 1996): community participation often 'elicits powerful images of a harmonious and equitable place where reciprocity and mutual concern prevail' (Zakus and Lysack 1998: 4). The great diversity of interests and concerns within communities is rarely investigated, and the voices of community members rarely heard in this literature.

Participatory structures are frequently imposed by administrative authorities on communities in a disempowering manner, undermining the voluntarism that effective community participation requires (McPake *et al.* 1992; Zakus and Lysack 1998). Administrative practice allows the elite to select community representatives rather than developing processes to attract those who might wish to serve their communities (Gilson *et al.* 1999; McPake *et al.* 1992; Sauerborn *et al.* 1989; Walt 1990). The sharp constraints imposed by administrative rules on effective devolution of power shift *local* understandings of participation from collective action to expand a pool of resources for mutual local benefit, towards enforced, unreciprocated resource contributions to an externally managed system. This leads, in turn, to demands that CHWs be paid, thus shifting their allegiance more firmly to the state (Walt 1990; McPake *et al.* 1992).

The policy literature on participation displays an acceptance of unequal returns by social class and 'free gifts' from the poorest. For example, Zakus and Lysack (1998: 6) state that the 'rewards for community participants are largely philosophical, emotional, and symbolic as compared to health professionals and managers for whom participation offers tangible and career advantages'. The literature says little on the expressed motivations of community members who become involved in health care, and hence does not analyse the sustainability of this type of regressive 'free gift'.

Despite the failure of policy to engage with the consequences of social inequality for participatory processes, the objectives of the schemes are generally cast in terms of democracy, equity, and the inclusion of the disadvantaged (Jarrett and Ofusu-Amaah 1992; Werner 1981). Health 'empowerment' through advocacy and social activism, challenging traditional social relationships, conflicts however with co-operative notions of 'community' action (Zakus and Lysack 1998). The confusion can be dangerous. Where the interests of the poor have indeed been promoted, the consequence has often been forceful opposition, including documented cases of the killing or 'disappearance' of CHWs (Walt 1990).

Representatives of the most disadvantaged within communities are very rarely brought into formal decision-making, and their voice and needs rarely heard (Gilson *et al.* 1999). The lack, or limited role, of women in such structures is just one example of the broader problem (McPake *et al.* 1992; Gilson *et al.* 1999). The poorest and the disadvantaged may, therefore, be least supportive of participatory processes, preferring external agents (such as health care providers/managers) to be in charge of community health activities (Stone 1992).

12.4.5. *Health Care Workers: The Limits of Benevolence*

The problems patients experience with health care worker behaviour have severe implications for trust and communication, and hence for access and quality of care.

The explanations of such experiences offered by researchers suggest that poor provider behaviour is driven by an interacting set of norms and experiences. These include: the pursuit of professional and social status by nurses who feel threatened by worsening working conditions and by medical and social hierarchies; habitual dismissal by professionals of patients' knowledge and understanding; and patients' informal resistance tactics, such as 'cheeky' behaviour. One study found deliberate misinformation by clinicians to, especially, women patients with sexually transmitted diseases; some doctors failed to provide useful advice, and colluded with a social norm of allocating blame for the illnesses to women. Managers and professional bodies may implicitly sanction such behaviour towards patients by failing to resist it (Jewkes *et al.* 1998; Griffin and Lownes 1999; Tibandebage and Mackintosh, this volume).

Economic crisis has also undermined professional ethics, promoting the self-serving exercise of unequal power in pursuit of financial gain: thus, in Uganda in the early 1980s 'one of the most significant micro changes [resulting from broader economic crisis] was that professionals could only survive by ignoring their standard ethics' (Birungi 1998: 1456). Bassett *et al.* (1997), and McPake *et al.* (1999) make similar arguments. A Ugandan case study concentrating on injections traces the implications of the resultant collapse of trust in public health care (Birungi 1998). It shows that people have tried to re-establish safety by owning their own needles and syringes, and having them used by friends, kin, and known professionals, however poorly sterilized; in other words by 'domesticating' injections within local social relationships.

This kind of divergence of meanings and loss of trust works to undermine provider/patient relationships in other contexts. A study of vaccinations in Karnataka and Sri Lanka showed that suspicion and reasoned distrust of vaccinators undermined acceptance (Nichter 1990). Recipients perceived (rightly) that vaccinators were not clinically well informed; patients reworked the information they received in terms of local illness categories and developed false expectations of protection. Patients also saw the process as a transaction—not a gift—with nurses who would expect assistance with childbirth, for example, to be reciprocated by acceptance of vaccinations or family planning to fulfil their quotas.

12.5. NON-MARKET BEHAVIOUR: IMPLICATIONS FOR HEALTH POLICY

Our review of health policy literature highlights the gap between the (usually implicit) assumptions about non-market behaviour that frame health care policy and the (patchy) evidence. Although non-market behaviour in health care has an important influence over policy outcomes it is very poorly researched. Policy failure is, therefore, almost inevitable since policy neither recognizes nor seeks to shape non-market behaviour.

We have argued that non-market behaviour in practice is shaped by the norms, objectives, and frames of reference of different groups: communities sharing experiences and networks of reciprocity; health care professionals in different facilities; members of mutual schemes; elite civil servants; health care campaigners; politicians. The types of non-market behaviour analysed in Sections 12.3 and 12.4 operate both within and between these groups.

Lasting change in health care systems to support redistribution, therefore, implies sustainable change in the norms and relationships shaping non-market behaviour. Policy makers thus have to understand the frames of reference of others as well as their own. This section briefly outlines some of the implications in terms of reframing— changing the mindset—of health care policy, drawing on the examples in Sections 12.3 and 12.4.

12.5.1. *Resisting Market Pressures and Shaping Sustainable Redistributive Behaviour*

Health care reform, as part of broader economic liberalization, has contributed to widening power and income differentials, strengthened monetary incentives, and, in many parts of the world, has contributed to an economic crisis that has undermined the capacity of the poor to contribute to reciprocal networks of support. This is the context within which health care policy has imposed new (non-market) redistributive duties on low income communities.

We have traced conflicts between new community fee-based health care financing mechanisms and exemptions policies, and between local hierarchies of power and privilege and community management policies with (externally imposed) redistributive intent. In communities where poverty is focused and persistent—rather than a widely experienced intermittent risk—redistributive 'free gifts' from the better off in a local community to the poor are hard for institutions and communities to legitimate and sustain.[8] Our survey suggests ways in which the commitment of socially divided communities and health care institutions to sustain their poorest members and patients could be strengthened.

First, minimize conflict of incentives. The deliberate creation of financing norms and rules that undermine exemption mechanisms puts an enormous strain on institutions' and communities' commitment to redistribute. Creating funds to support exemptions that are separate from the revenue generated by a fee system may enable the giving of exemptions by allowing two separate norms to be established and supported: one, a commitment to revenue generation and institutional sustainability, and the other a commitment to protection of the poorest.

Second, research on an exemption mechanism in Thailand, the low income card scheme (Gilson *et al.* 1998), suggests other ways of strengthening a local norm of protection for the poorest within local understandings and procedures. Coverage of those below this scheme's income threshold is good by international standards and has been improving. Eligibility is determined by a panel of community representatives and health workers independently of health facility decision-making. Frameworks guiding decision-making are regularly revised in response to experience of success in protecting the poorest. Information campaigns targetted at beneficiaries to promote and aid their use of exemptions, as well as to promote their use of public health care, appear also to generate broader shared understanding and commitment to exemptions as a proper use of funds.

Finally, giving the poorest a voice in divided communities is hard and may even be dangerous (see Section 12.4). The way may be eased if the meaning of the redistributive 'gift' can also be understood in more reciprocal terms. Local cultural norms may allow space for reworking the understanding of exemption mechanisms in terms of the duties of the better off, and may also allow some scope for material or symbolic reciprocity

---

[8] The theoretical economic literature concerned with equity also stresses the need for policy to economize on 'benevolence', as being a scarce and easily depleted resource. This concept of the unreciprocated gift as 'benevolence' is from James Meade, see several papers in Atkinson (1993).

upwards. For example, in Thai communities, the observed 'leakage' of exemptions to some non-poor with close connections to village leaders and those held in high regard within the community is socially construed as 'a helping each other way'. As one person explained, 'This is a way to express our gratitude to them. Without their support, our centre would be in problems . . . . Don't you know that granting a card to those people would mean to make them proud and honoured?' (Gilson *et al.* 1998: 41–2). This type of reciprocity may help to give the schemes legitimacy and sustainability.

12.5.2. *Shaping Commitment in Low Income Communities and Making it Sustainable*

One benefit of treating duty or commitment—'free gifts'—as a separate analytical category from exchange is that it brings to the foreground the importance for health care policy of attention to supporting and encouraging the development of ethical norms. The last example included ways of supporting an ethic of commitment 'downwards'. But, as Section 12.4 argued, some recent health policies have been framed as a demand for free gifts 'upwards': from poor or relatively poor people to 'communities' that may be socially very unequal, or even to the state. As a result, CHW programmes have tended to be unsustainable, their aspirations unfulfilled.

A case study of a successful CHW programme implemented in Ceara state in Brazil (Tendler 1997) suggests, however, that recognizing the power and conflict involved in specific contexts, as well as the needs and motivations of the CHWs, may allow participation to be designed in ways that lessen the burden on low income participants. Tendler identifies five critical elements of the programme that promoted good morale among its CHWs (known as health agents):

- a transparent hiring process based on merit which accorded newly hired workers considerable prestige;
- a public information and education campaign which emphasized the 'noble mission' of the programme to reduce infant mortality and disease;
- encouragement to those who were not appointed as health agents to work as informal monitors of the programme as a whole;
- opportunities for appointees for further training which could be transported to other jobs;
- promoting job satisfaction by allowing health agents to take on extra tasks as they saw necessary (e.g. some basic curative tasks or general chores to help mothers, rather than limiting their services only to preventive care, so gaining the trust and support of the community being served).

This successful Brazilian experience marries material incentives (financial reward, or access to opportunities for such rewards) to non-material rewards (such as job satisfaction, scope for innovation, and personal standing) and associates the mix with the promotion of ethical motivations and commitment. If a context is created where commitment is protected and can flourish, and individuals can build the pursuit of other rewards upon it, then programmes can lose their construction as an externally demanded free gift from the poor.

12.5.3. *Embedding Health Care Initiatives in Existing Mutual Support Networks*

Section 12.4 argued that mutual insurance in health care is a valuable form of solidarity, but needs to be rooted in—as well as contribute to—supportive social relationships. Commentators in Africa are now suggesting that mutual health insurance schemes would be greatly strengthened if they were more closely integrated with existing mutual savings and assistance schemes, that draw in their turn sources of solidarity from ethnicity, neighbourhood, and workplace.

However, Van den Brink and Chavas (1997) warn that governments should not try to incorporate local savings schemes into formal structures, since governments are not part of the local 'moral economy' and will almost inevitably undermine the schemes. Rather they should create enabling legal frameworks. This shift of mind-set from setting up structures to encouraging independent institutional development illustrates the kind of revised policy approach proposed, that takes non-market relationships seriously, as having a life of their own not easily amenable to being reorganized by policy makers.

Health care reforms that cut back services during recession undermine, in the process, communities' scope for reciprocal health care support (Section 12.4). The exclusive policy focus, in resource use decisions, on health gain for the population needs to be qualified by a concern to support informal reciprocity and home care as important aspects of the health care process as a whole.

12.5.4. *Attention to Meanings: Rebuilding Trust and Communication*

Longstanding problems in health care systems (in high and low income countries) include professionals' assumptions of monopoly of knowledge; contempt for patients' experience when it does not fit predetermined models; failure to communicate and listen, tipping over into misinformation and abuse; and the privileging of treatment over care. Section 12.4 gave examples of different meanings constructed around particular forms of treatment by patients and health care staff, and their consequences for risk and loss of trust, demonstrating our general point about the role of discursive construction of actions in shaping non-market behaviour.

Responses to such situations involve both altering health care provider behaviour and also changing the terms of communication. Birungi (1998), for example, having documented the 'domestication' of injections and its dangers, argues that needles and syringes can only be drawn out of the home through opening up the sterilization process and its rationale to public scrutiny and participation: '. . . trust relations seem to be built on personal relations and confidence tends to be influenced by what people get exposed to, see, and hear about institutions'. (*ibid.* 1458)

12.5.5. *Tackling Power and Hierarchy, Legitimating Claims*

We have argued that the prescriptive emphasis on equity in health policy tends to obscure the exercise of power and the operation of hierarchy. The literature on non-market behaviour in tax allocation suggests a range of policies that can help to push allocation mechanisms in more redistributive directions, by identifying and strengthening mechanisms that constrain self-allocation by the elite.

Greater public information, including information campaigns and media access to health care system information, can enhance understanding of practice and strengthen the capacity of disadvantaged groups to make claims through both the political and the health care system. Establishing legal rights and norms, and working with groups who can challenge the elite, can also contain their influence.

Decentralization may support redistributive policy ends, but only if shaped by an appropriate combination of clear central guidelines, genuine audited central government commitment to redistributive allocation, and openness to local adaptation and review, including review of central practice (Gilson and Travis 1998). Allocation criteria based on formulae assist public scrutiny. To achieve this, non-market behaviour needs to be addressed explicitly. For example, personalized barter relationships have developed between officials and the members of the public in some governmental organizations (Section 12.4),[9] and these need to be explicitly fought.

Social inequality within the state is compatible, in principle and practice, with redistributive behaviour in social sectors, but can be sustained only where ideology, political legitimacy, and appropriate non-market behaviour by politicians and civil servants is sustained. External organizing, by trade unions and communities, is a force sustaining governmental redistributive commitment where it exists.

Shared meanings between government and population are also important for the legitimacy of health care redistribution through the tax system. For example, Chiang (1995: 228) recounts how in Taiwan national health insurance was politically constructed by the Kuomintang as 'a critical indicator of "good" government in a modernising nation', accelerating the acceptance of universalization of access through tax subsidy. The Korean national health insurance system, in principle universal, is characterized in practice by high costs and high co-payments, resulting in limited coverage. Yang (1996) argues that resolving exclusion involves constructing 'shared understandings' and positive public meanings around the concept of social insurance perhaps through a 'citizen's movement backed by formal consumers' organisations' (*ibid.* 251). Londoño and Frenk (1997) argue that overcoming the blockage on health care redistribution in Latin American countries represented by institutionally polarized health care systems

---

[9] This also occurs in health facilities and is likely to be associated with a culture of informal monetary payments (Tibandebage and Mackintosh, this volume).

involves governments' taking responsibility for 'social mobilisation' and 'advocacy' to create the social basis for universalization.

12.6. CONCLUSION

Policy makers' stated objectives are typically redistributive; their behavioural assumptions a mix of reciprocity (COOP1) and the benevolent use of power (P/C1). However, while there are many desirable networks of reciprocity in health care, they cannot be created by administrative fiat. Institutions built upon reciprocity do not easily incorporate the 'free gifts' required in redistributive behaviour (part of what we have called COOP2). The operation of unequal power and privilege (P/C2), and the process of non-market and market exchange in unequal societies, will always tend to pull against these forms of non-market behaviour, moving health care systems in unequalizing directions.

Reciprocity of a non-individualized sort, such as risk-pooling and informal reciprocal support (a large part of COOP1) is not in itself highly redistributive. It can, however, increase inclusiveness in at least two ways. By pooling risks, it makes protection available to higher risk as well as low risk people, at a common fee. Since the poor are more likely to be ill than the better off, and less likely to be able to afford unplanned out-of-pocket payments, this increases inclusiveness. Second, and perhaps as important, these kinds of reciprocity spread understanding of and experience of solidarity within the health care system, and help to legitimize inclusive institutions. So, policy needs to nurture beneficial reciprocity, but reciprocity alone excludes the very poor.

Our evidence suggests rather that redistribution is most sustainable when it is socially construed simultaneously in terms of both free gifts (from the better off to the poor), and reciprocity (the recognition of mutual dependence between the elite and the poor within communities). Legitimizing redistributive behaviour in this way must involve both governments and citizens. The East Asian examples, already cited, are reinforced by European experience. This suggests that national compulsory social insurance for health care, once established, is socially and politically stable because, by embedding redistribution within reciprocal insurance relationships, it reinforces the norms and values within which it is based (Barr 1993; Besley and Gouveia 1994).

At present the opposite frequently occurs in many lower income countries. Failures of the public health care system interact with the vulnerability of the poor to worsen their access to care. A presentational and policy emphasis on equity, often reinforced by donors' requirements, disguises regressive and exclusionary behaviour. Health care policy and research need to move away from linear prescription–outcome models, and to investigate, recognize, respect and then seek to shape the logic of non-market behaviour. Close attention to non-market behaviour and a realistic assessment of the problems and possibilities of how to sustain institutional commitment to redistribution might in the medium term produce more equitable institutional design.

13

Institutional Cultures and Regulatory Relationships in a Liberalizing Health Care System: A Tanzanian Case Study

PAULA TIBANDEBAGE AND MAUREEN MACKINTOSH

13.1. INTRODUCTION: INSTITUTIONAL CULTURES AND REGULATORY RELATIONSHIPS IN HEALTH CARE

This paper draws on a study of the formal and informal regulatory relationships that shape the Tanzanian health care system. Liberalization of private for-profit health care practice in Tanzania, and the introduction of officially set fees in government health care facilities, date from the early 1990s; before that, only government facilities and those owned by religious bodies were allowed to operate. The fieldwork on which this paper is based, undertaken in 1998, provides a set of observations, from staff, patients, and household members,[1] of one moment in an emerging mixed (public/private/religious and non-governmental) health care system that is still changing rapidly.

This paper employs two concepts to analyse the behaviour of this mixed health care system: institutional culture and informal regulatory relationships. By the 'institutional culture' of health care facilities, we mean the norms of behaviour within facilities and in particular of facility staff towards patients and would-be patients. And by 'norms' of behaviour, we mean patterns of behaviour that are widespread, are generally tolerated

This study, entitled 'Managing and regulating mixed health care systems, a Tanzanian case study in comparative perspective', was financed by the ESCOR Committee of the Department for International Development (DFID), UK, whose support is gratefully acknowledged. The content of this chapter is the sole responsibility of the authors and does not represent the official policies or practices of the DFID. The field research referred to was mainly undertaken during August–October 1998. The study and the writing of this paper has also benefitted from the support of the Open University, UK and the Oxford University Rhodes Race Relations Fund. The authors would like to thank participants in the WIDER workshop on Group Behaviour and Development, Helsinki September 1999, especially the book editors, and also Paul Anand, for comments on an earlier draft.

[1] Owners, managers and/or staff were interviewed in 10 hospitals and 36 lower level health facilities (health centres and dispensaries) in three regions of Tanzania; in addition there were 108 interviews in households within the facilities' catchment areas (49 in Mbeya, 37 in Dar es Salaam and 22 in Coast Region), plus 272 exit interviews with patients at facilities.

or accepted as proper, are reinforced by responses of others, and are quite hard for individuals to resist even if they run against what is felt to be right.

This concept of facilities' institutional culture as defined by empirically researchable norms of behaviour relates quite closely to the general concept of 'modes of operation' of groups put forward in Chapter 1 of this volume. Facilities can be understood as formally constituted 'groups'. We identify patterns of market transactional behaviour between facilities and patients (but not 'quasi'-market transactions,[2] which do not appear to exist in the context studied), and seek to relate these to patterns of non-market hierarchical control (P/C), and non-market ethical and socially inclusive behaviour (both included here in COOP), observed within facilities and between facilities' staff and the patients.[3]

We argue that the institutional cultures observed in facilities are shaped by informal regulatory relationships that cross facilities' boundaries. We are here using 'regulation' in the broadest sense of the socio-legal and political economy literature (Baldwin *et al.* 1998*a*: 4), to include not only the legal framework of rules and formal decision-making procedures, but also informal working relationships between facilities and 'customary assumptions, often barely articulated, about the substantive purpose of the activities that are being pursued' (Hancher and Moran 1989). It is a particular theme of the paper that these regulatory relationships involve patients and would-be patients, who are thus also active participants in shaping institutional cultures. We are therefore considering as 'informal groups' (see Mackintosh and Gilson in this volume), both professional networks, and also groups of patients and members of the public who share assumptions and norms of behaviour.

The main focus of the paper is on the implications of observed institutional cultures for inequity and exclusion. We consider how particular patterns of institutional behaviour in a low income context can shape a health care system to be actively complicit in the creation and reproduction of poverty and inequality. We compare institutional cultures in government and non-government facilities to show how charging mechanisms and an associated culture of abuse and lack of care can impoverish and exclude, and how these effects can also be mitigated and resisted. The paper thus addresses the concern of this volume with the equity outcomes of group behaviour.

The argument proceeds as follows. Section 13.2 sets out some evidence from the study that the health care system in the late 1990s was characterized by quite widespread exclusion and neglect. Sections 13.3–5 build up an analysis of facilities' institutional cultures and some of the regulatory relationships shaping them: first through patients' eyes, then from facility interviews. Section 13.6 draws some brief conclusions for health care regulation.

---

[2] By 'quasi-market' here we are referring to the explicit use of exchange mechanisms to manage internal relationships within health care facilities or within the government health care sector (Le Grand 1991).

[3] The problem of finding theoretical categories for reciprocated and non-reciprocated 'gift' relationships across group boundaries in health care (included here in COOP) is explored further in the paper by Mackintosh and Gilson in this volume.

13.2. LIBERALIZATION AND IMPOVERISHMENT

13.2.1. *Exclusion and the Nature of the Health Care Transaction*

Impoverishment and exclusion are processes that operate through institutional change, and it has long been argued that liberalization in social sectors can exacerbate them (Cornia *et al.* 1987). Tanzania is one of the poorest countries in the world, with an estimated GDP per head of US$120. Economic liberalization in Tanzania in the 1980s and 1990s followed a period of severe economic crisis, and has included the promotion of private sector participation in health care and education alongside the introduction of user fees in the government sector. Private for-profit medical practice, abolished in 1977, was reintroduced in 1991; user fees were introduced, in public hospitals in 1993, and subsequently in some health centres and dispensaries.

In the 1980s, only government facilities and those owned by religious organizations provided formal sector health care.[4] The religious facilities charged fees; government facilities officially did not, but there was patchy and largely undocumented informal charging. In such a context, once user fees are officially introduced these interact with other types of charges in ways relevant for policy (Tibandebage 1999). Studies in Tanzania and in comparable contexts show that the introduction of official user fees has reduced the utilization of public health facilities (Mwabu *et al.* 1995; Anyimawi 1989; De Bethune 1989; Msamanga *et al.* 1996; Walraven 1996), with the poor most strongly affected (Gertler and Van der Gaag 1990; Sauerborn *et al.* 1994; Karanja *et al.* 1995; Booth *et al.* 1995; Gilson 1997). The predicament of the poor is worsened by the positive correlation between poverty and ill health: it is those who most need health care who are particularly excluded.

Patients' experience of access to, or exclusion from, health care facilities is shaped both by the level of payment demanded in relation to their ability to pay, and by the relationships that frame the transaction: the availability of waivers and deferral of payment, and the perceived quality of the resultant service including the warmth of the reception or conversely the abuse and neglect they may face even after payment. The nature of the transaction with the patient in this broad sense is a key element of a facility's institutional culture.

13.2.2. *Evidence of Exclusion from Health Care*

Accounts of exclusion and neglect resulting from inability to pay for health care are drawn here from interviews in four districts in Tanzania: a diverse urban district of the capital, Dar es Salaam; a low income rural district in Coast region close to the capital; and two districts, one urban, one rural in Mbeya region in the south-western highlands. The two urban areas had a private for-profit health care sector. There were few such providers outside the towns.

We aimed to understand exclusion and its consequences from the point of view of would-be patients. In 108 household interviews we asked: 'Have you or anyone you

---

[4] There are also large numbers of traditional healers and birth attendants, not included in this study.

know ever been excluded from treatment because of inability to pay?' Open-ended follow-up questions asked for details, and forty-four incidents were recounted. Some people had been refused treatment for inability to pay amounts as tiny as Tsh 100 (US$0.14). Exclusion from government facilities resulted from inability to pay not only formal charges, but also informal charges (bribes) demanded by staff. Using examples, we summarize the main outcomes of exclusion.

Some people who are excluded from treatment die. Here is one of several accounts of children dying because of inability to bribe medical personnel:

I went to seek treatment for my child. I knew that there is no service charge for children at the [government hospital], but the child was not attended to. Then came the nurse who examined the child and said, 'Lady, your child has caught fever'. 'Indeed, a high fever', I replied. Then the nurse asked, 'But do you have some money? No service is available without money here.' I told her that I did not have any money. The nurse left and never returned. I stayed at the hospital until 4.00 o'clock when I decided to go back home. During the same night, the fever persisted and the child passed away. The following day I was awoken to bury my late child.

Other accounts concerned a woman in Mbeya who died because she was unable to pay for an emergency caesarean; a patient who was refused treatment at a religious facility in Dar es Salaam and was then neglected at a government health centre until he died; and an anaemic child who died untreated at a public hospital in Coast, while his mother had gone back home to borrow some money.

When refused treatment, some people went home to sell possessions or borrow from relatives and friends. Incidents recounted included an accident victim who waited a week untreated in a government hospital until relatives assembled the Tsh 40,000 (US$55) for the operation, and several similar cases of in-patient treatment withheld.

Furthermore, exclusion often occurred before diagnosis, with particularly serious implications in cases of infectious and contagious diseases. Here is an example from Mbeya; the charge demanded is a bribe.

My young brother was attending TB treatment and was asked by a doctor to pay a monthly charge of Tsh 5000 which he was unable to pay. So he was denied not only the drugs but also registration.

13.2.3. *Access to Free Treatment*

Interviewees' accounts of exclusion chiefly concerned government facilities, particularly hospitals, suggesting that people went to them as the last resort. Looking for contrasting experience, we also asked household interviewees whether they had ever received, or knew someone who had received, free treatment from local health facilities.

Some government dispensaries and health centres, mainly in rural areas, still did not charge official fees; some provided free treatment if drugs happened to be available and some staff did not ask for bribes. So their role as safety net had not been completely eroded in Mbeya and Coast region. However in Dar es Salaam, 80 per cent of respondents had never so much as heard of a case of free treatment.

Patients said that it was very difficult to get exemption from fees on the basis of inability to pay in any type of facility: private, religious, or government, despite the

Table 13.1. *Result for the patient of inability to pay all the charges requested, by sector, Mbeya, Dar es Salaam and Coast (number of patients)*

Consequence	Sector			Total patients
	Government	Religious/NGO	Private	
Excluded	6	1	1	8
Defer all or part	2	11	11	24
(of which, part treatment)		(9)	(3)	(12)
Exempted part	3	4	1	8
Total	11	16	13	40
(Total as % of all interviewees asked for personal payment)	(24)	(22)	(21)	(22)

existence of a formal system of such exemptions in government facilities. Accounts of exemption were generally about belonging to particular categories of patients—not necessarily poor—such as staff members. At one voluntary hospital in Dar es Salaam, a religious community, which owned the facility, ran their own welfare scheme for community members. One government hospital, in Coast region, appeared—unusually in this study—to be applying official criteria of exemption on grounds of age:

My 70-year old father went to [a government hospital] for his leg and stomach problems. He was told that because of his age, he was entitled to get free treatment and his registration card was marked 'exempted'.

The religious and NGO facilities and the private sector were more willing than the government sector to defer fees or partially waive them for those who could not pay. Exit patients were asked whether they had been able to pay all the money asked; 22 per cent of patients asked to pay something said no. Table 13.1 shows what happened next.

As Table 13.1 shows, deferring payment quite often meant partial treatment, especially in the religious sector. At one religious dispensary in Dar es Salaam, an interviewee said the doctor:

decided that since I cannot pay all the Tsh 2500 at once, I should pay Tsh 500 every time I come for each of the five injections until all five are administered.

If patients cannot find the money, or if they forego the remaining treatment to meet some more urgent need, then they may develop resistance or recover poorly.

13.2.4. *Can the Poor Afford to Pay?*

To a large extent, patients needed money in their pocket to get treatment when ill, implying exclusion (including self-exclusion) for those without cash. Poverty in

Table 13.2. *Mean[5] payment by patients interviewed on
exit from dispensaries and health centres, by sector,
Mbeya, Dar es Salaam (DSM) and Coast 1998 (Tsh)*

Ownership	Mbeya	DSM	Coast
Government	224	970	*
Religious/NGO	4301	2720	1400
Private	4931	2013	1500

Note: *No government dispensary charges recorded.

Tanzania is extreme, and there is active debate about the extent to which people are able to pay for health care.

Incomes are very unequally distributed, with 6.9 per cent of GDP estimated to go to the poorest 20 per cent, compared to 45.4 per cent to the best-off 20 per cent (World Bank 1998/99). A 1998 rural household budget survey[6] estimated that 65 per cent of the rural population had incomes below a rural poverty line of Tsh 138,831 (US$198, per adult equivalent per year, for basic food and non-food expenditures). Combining rural and peri-urban data gave a poverty line of Tsh 145,232 (US$207), with 56.4 per cent of the population estimated to be living below it. About half the population have been estimated to live below the national poverty line (World Bank 1998/99; UNDP 1998).

The official minimum wage was Tsh 35,000 (US$50) per month in 1998. Jobs were few, and many people worked for less. The minimum wage would not support three adults at the rural and peri-urban poverty line of Tsh 12,103 per month; however, the average poor household had 6.44 members (adults plus children) (Semboja and Rutasitara 1999). We can compare these income data to 1998 health care charges.

Table 13.2 shows mean payments recorded by those patients who were asked to pay at lower level health facilities visited: all those interviewed at Dar es Salaam facilities; all those visiting non-government facilities in Mbeya and Coast; and a minority of patients met at government facilities in Mbeya. The mean payment for a single visit to a non-government facility in Mbeya was 12–14 per cent of the minimum wage. In Dar es Salaam it was 6–7 per cent (but in Dar es Salaam there were no free options). The government facilities were cheaper than the non-government facilities, but drugs were often unavailable and so had in addition to be bought at pharmacies. Furthermore, the household survey cited above showed that in rural Tanzania in 1998 about 75 per cent of the budget was on average spent on food, leaving about 25 per cent for all non-food essentials. Twenty five per cent of the adult-equivalent monthly rural poverty line was less than Tsh 3000, and most households lived below this poverty line, suggesting again how hard the above charges were to pay.

This comparison between charges, minimum wages and poverty incomes helps to explain how interviewees in our study could be excluded from treatment in a

[5] Median payments are very similar to the means: the data are not very skewed. Data are from interviews with patients on exit from facilities.
[6] Results of the 1998 REPOA survey are drawn from Semboja and Rutasitara 1999.

government facility for inability to pay an informal charge of Tsh 100. Incomes in the rural areas especially are frequently irregular as well as low. And once people have sold possessions and borrowed, they are, as a mission doctor emphasized, impoverished for the future. Our evidence supports the few previous studies examining the impoverishing consequences for the poor of struggling to mobilize resources for treatment through the sale of land, animals, farm produce and other possessions and valuables, and through borrowing from relatives (Abel-Smith 1987; Abel-Smith and Rawal 1982).

13.3. EMERGING INSTITUTIONAL CULTURES THROUGH PATIENTS' EYES

The transaction that provides access or excludes a poor person from treatment is not a one-off market event. Rather, it is shaped by the expectations of staff and patients, by the culture of the facility's handling of patients, especially those with little money, and by often painful personalized negotiation around the consequences of non-payment.

This study found that patients were quite well informed about health care facilities' characteristics, and that they drew rather consistent distinctions between perceived quality of care in different sectors: government facilities, those owned by private individuals, and those owned by religious or other non-governmental non-profit organizations. A question asking which sector offered best value for money was found clear and relevant by household respondents; those who did not answer it (26 out of 108 interviewees) generally lacked experience of different sectors, rather than not understanding the question. Information and experience circulate in this health care market, and facilities develop reputations that influence behaviour.

13.3.1. *The Government Sector*

There is much evidence in the study of a widespread culture in government facilities—especially hospitals—of demanding informal payments (bribes) in exchange for service, and of associated neglect of patients. Household interviewees described numerous such incidents. Patients interviewed on exit were asked for reasons for choosing the particular facility. If good or reasonable quality of care was mentioned, there was a follow up question asking for more detail. Over sixty interviewees found some good to be said of the government facility visited, but rather few mentioned the aspects listed in Table 13.3. The zero against 'do not have to bribe', and the affirmative answers on that point in other sectors, support the household interviewees' accounts.

Bribery, neglect, and abusive language had caused people to lose trust in some government facilities and to fear going to them. One interviewee said he would rather stay at home and die than go to a particular government hospital. People were angry and frustrated, since they saw government facilities as important not only for those with little money, but also because they were thought to have the best qualified personnel and diagnostic equipment (especially important for referrals), or because they might well be the only facilities within walking distance.

Table 13.3. *Number of affirmative responses on specified aspects of good quality, by ownership of facility (patients in Dar es Salaam, Mbeya and Coast hospitals, dispensaries, and health centres)*

Response item	Government	Private	Religious
Staff more polite	10	21	30
Waiting time short	10	28	15
There is little hassle	9	30	20
Do not have to bribe	0	12	7
Total patients responding to question	52	65	63
(% of interviewees)	(54)	(72)	(74)

Note: Interviewees may have mentioned more than one aspect of quality.

People saw limited prospects for reversing the problems:

I do not see any viable solution to this because even if one complains, nothing is done about it.

Another interviewee argued that it was difficult to correct the situation because the whole system was corrupt, from the Ministry level right down to health facilities. Another pointed out, however, that bribery was hard to stop because it was two-way traffic:

Patients do make their contribution to this habit, because they tend to influence staff to accept bribes, even before the staff demand them.

However, as Table 13.3 also suggests, some government facilities—particularly some rural dispensaries—seemed to be handling patients well. For example, asked whether government, private or religious facilities gave best value for money, most household respondents in Coast region chose government facilities, citing free treatment and good patient care especially at the government health centre. In Mbeya there were positive comments, and few complaints of bribes, from patients at some government dispensaries. The contrast in perceived quality of government facilities between rural and urban areas was striking.

13.3.2. *Private Facilities*

In contrast to long waiting times in government facilities, private facilities had a reputation for promptness of response. The private sector gained the largest number of affirmative responses on 'shorter waiting time' and 'little hassle' in Table 13.3. Interviewees were well able to explain the nature, benefits, and risks of the transaction with private profit-seeking facilities. One interviewee in Dar es Salaam said:

Private facilities give the best value for money because once the money is paid a patient gets all the required treatment. Staff tend to treat a patient as 'king'.

Several interviewees explained that private providers are in business and have to try very hard to please their customers in order to survive.

On the negative side, interviewees complained about high charges. Other complaints displayed understanding of the market incentives facing private practitioners. Interviewees pointed to the use of unqualified staff such as 'Red Cross medical aides', and explained that businesses tended towards unethical medical practices such as prescribing expired drugs and unwillingness to refer complicated cases. Such behaviour has been documented elsewhere (Kumaranayake 1997; Bennett 1991), and was exacerbated here by the financial fragility and high bankruptcy rate of private facilities (see also Tibandebage *et al.* 2001). Incidents recounted included two children paralysed by improperly administered injections by unqualified staff, and a death because a private facility referred too late. A village leader had intervened to try to stop a private facility selling expired drugs.

13.3.3. *Religious Facilities*

The religious sector had by far the best general reputation of the three sectors. Respondents' perceptions of religious facilities associated their mode of operation with norms of kindness, caring, and concern for others' well-being. Respondents consistently argued that religious facilities' staff were more polite and attentive than staff in the other sectors (Table 13.3). Nearly 70 per cent of household respondents thought religious and NGO facilities gave the best value for money, some specifying that it was 'especially religious' or 'especially missionary' facilities that cared well for patients and charged lower fees than private facilities.

Asked to explain these norms, that seemed to guide behaviour and modes of operation in religious facilities, an interviewee in Dar es Salaam said:

Voluntary facilities, especially the religious ones give the best value for money because they are committed to humanitarian motives rather than profit making. Also staff's attitude is based on religious teachings.

Another interviewee mentioned more specific management and staff qualities:

Facilities owned by religious organizations offer services worth the money paid because they are committed to their religious course to offer services rather than make profits. Management make close follow-up of the facilities' activities and the staff are trustworthy.

Many other respondents expressed similar views. Some interviewees explained how people walk long distances, sometimes to a different region, to seek treatment in religious facilities.

One can see how the strength of this reputation for quality in the minds of vulnerable patients could be traded upon by the less scrupulous. Some religious facilities studied were charging low fees and apparently operating on a charitable basis; however other religious facilities were the most expensive in the whole study.

13.4. INSTITUTIONAL CULTURES IN THREE SECTORS

How does the nature of the transaction between patient and facility interact with facilities' internal institutional culture? This section seeks to answer this question for each sector, drawing on facility interviews and data.

13.4.1. *The Government Sector: Individualized Appropriation* Versus *Ethical Norms*

The variation in behaviour of government facilities, described by patients, is important, given the extent to which the sector is still seen by patients as a last resort, and given the ineffectiveness of the worst institutions in this respect. Our data suggest that, for government facilities, a number of indicators of probity and ethical behaviour tend to move together. The indicators are: the extent of exemption from fees on grounds other than inability to pay; the level and form of bribery; the distancing from and even abuse of patients; and the effectiveness of financial control. Facilities with the more embedded bribery cultures, and with the most distorted exemption mechanisms, were also seen by patients as more abusive and neglectful than other facilities; and appear to have lower levels of probity in managing public funds.

Table 13.4. *Two government hospitals: financial and activity indicators*

Indicator	Hospital A	Hospital B
Number of beds	419	201
Inpatients/bed 1997/8	32.5	71.1
Outpatients 1997/8	57,111	122,137
Salary exp./patient 1997/8	6505	1608
Drugs exp./patient 1997/8	5586	169
Fee income/patient 1997/8	1188	190
Total income/patient 1997/8	11,629	2758

These connections are sharpest at hospital level, as will be illustrated here.[7] Table 13.4 contrasts two government hospitals: a referral hospital also serving as a district hospital in Mbeya (Hospital A), and a district hospital in Coast region that also had a few specialist functions such as training and accident trauma treatment (Hospital B).

Hospital A had twice the number of beds, less than half the number of inpatients per bed, and less than half the outpatients. Its total income was over twice that of Hospital B, and its expenditure per patient, on both salaries and drugs, was much higher. Hospital A was also charging its patients more, on average, officially—bribes

---

[7] Similar connections can be drawn at health centre and dispensary level; space prevents further presentation of evidence here.

aside—than Hospital B. Its total income was twice that of Hospital B, and its income per patient was over four times as high as Hospital B's.

However, there is really no doubt that the better hospital was Hospital B. Everything—patients' views, observation, household interviews, staff interviews, patient numbers, views of staff in other facilities—confirms this. Hospital B was doing better, with fewer resources, on all the dimensions listed above.[8]

In both hospitals, household interviews report demands for bribes by both doctors and nurses, and delay or refusal of treatment without bribes. However the extent, consistency, and severity of the demands and of the associated abuse and neglect of patients was far worse in Hospital A. In Hospital A, patients complained that bribery might still elicit no service, while in Hospital B interviewees complained that those who bribed received better treatment. There were far more complaints about doctors neglecting patients to pursue private practice at Hospital A than at Hospital B. This may be in part because Hospital B is in a rural area. In urban areas doctors have more opportunities for private earnings. Tibandebage *et al.* (2001) found that the predominant source of part time doctors for private hospitals in Dar es Salaam was the government referral hospital in the city.

Both hospitals claimed to have a formal exemption system for the indigent, involving a social worker. However we met no patient or household interviewee who had ever used such a system. Hospitals have official instructions to exempt certain *categories* of patients, for example by type of illness or by age, and the two hospitals differed sharply in their behaviour. Both hospitals exempted their own staff from fees, but only in Hospital A did managers accept that staff might present non-family members as eligible without sanction. Patients reported that in Hospital B small children and elderly people, who were supposed to be treated free, often did in fact obtain free treatment, while such patients were likely to be faced with demands for bribes in Hospital A. Bribery and exemptions are intertwined in Hospital A; for example a patient recounted:

The urine test required Tsh 2500 but I had only Tsh 2000. The laboratory technician accepted this and exempted me from paying Tsh 500.

This bill however should have been Tsh 450; the technician had inflated it, then kindly reduced it a little.

Both hospitals were struggling with inadequate government funding. However, a number of indicators suggest much better financial control in Hospital B. In Hospital A, the hospital pharmacy contained when visited not so much as an aspirin from our checklist of standard drugs, was poorly supervised, and patients confirmed that they frequently received prescriptions to buy drugs and supplies from private pharmacies. In Hospital B the pharmacy store was found to be reasonably stocked, was better managed, and patients made comments such as, 'drugs shortage is only occasional'.

---

[8] There are reasons, including larger numbers of specialists and more complex case mix in Hospital A, why the contrast may be overstated by the data, but no plausible adjustments alter the conclusion, given the scale of the differences observed.

Methods of financial control were more convincing in Hospital B, which had a functioning system of pre-audited expenditure, and a history of financial autonomy unusual for the government sector. Hospital A had less autonomy, and poor control, and senior staff accepted that theft was going on. A good contrast is provided by the user fee funds. Hospital B valued them; allowed doctors to draw on them instantly in emergencies; and could account for them precisely. Hospital A could not give precise totals, but thought only around 50 per cent of fees due were collected. Perhaps most tellingly, the fees, representing close to 20 per cent of their recorded spending on drugs and medical supplies, were described in Hospital A as 'negligible' in relation to their problems.

These differences come together in institutional attitudes to bribery and mismanagement of patients. No senior staff member in Hospital B tried to justify such behaviour. One said, 'No one takes money from patients, despite the shortage of doctors and nurses we face . . . . If it ever happens, it is unethical.' In Hospital A a manager, rightly very angry at the nurses' wages and working conditions and the lack of support to nurses from doctors, came close to defending abuse on those grounds. A senior staff member at Hospital A accepted that most of the exemptions given by the hospital were going to the wrong people; Hospital B's managers accepted no such thing. In Hospital A, a manager argued that hospital fee exemptions for the indigent 'can never work'; in Hospital B we were told the hospital allowed any of its senior management to give an exemption in an emergency to someone unable to pay.

What can be admitted, what is tolerated, does not tell us what happens; what people claim happens will differ from the events. However, the evidence consistently suggests that one can trace two different trajectories for institutional culture in these two hospitals. Hospital B had built up and sustained a mixture of strong financial and managerial control (a P/C mode of operation) and considerable individual commitment by staff to ethical service provision despite low salaries.[9] Hospital A's culture was characterized by a loss of central financial control in favour of widespread (not universal) individualized appropriation for private gain. This is the least desirable type of market transactional relationship from the patients' point of view because it is abusive and unpredictable. In the face of it, patients with money sought to spend it in other sectors.

13.4.2. *Religious Facilities: Charitable Cultures* Versus *Provision for the Better Off*

If the government sector failed as a last resort, patients with little money might turn to the religious sector. Here too they faced a cultural divide. Most of the facilities in the 'religious and NGO' group were facilities with a religious mission or label.[10] Among both Christian and Muslim facilities there were some whose charging policy, relations with patients and development plans for the facility could together be characterized as

---

[9] Such individual commitment is included in the COOP category in Chapter 1; in Mackintosh and Gilson in this volume it would fall into the 'duty, commitment, and free gifts' category of non-market behaviour.

[10] Just two were owned by non-religious NGOs, one local, one international.

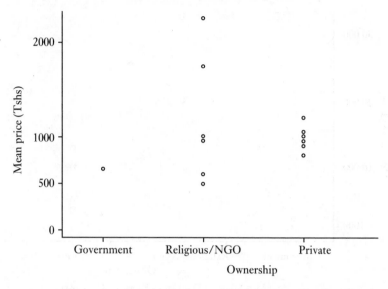

Figure 13.1. *Mbeya dispensaries and health centres: dotplot, robust mean of stated prices for a common set of services and treatments provided by all facilities imposing official charges*

'charitable' and others whose institutional culture focused, with similar consistency, on the better off.

The implications of these two cultures for patients show up in the price data, and we illustrate the point here from the Mbeya data for dispensaries and health centres, and for the three regions for hospitals. We have two sources of information on pricing: what patients say they paid, and what facilities say they charged. Similarity between the two is an indicator of institutional probity and financial control in the non-government as well as the public sector. As Fig. 13.1 shows, the two most expensive and two least expensive dispensaries and health centres studied in Mbeya, on the basis of a robust mean[11] of stated prices for a bundle of services and treatments all facilities provided, were religious or NGO facilities. Figure 13.2 illustrates the same divide at hospital level:[12] in the independent sectors, the cheapest and the two dearest hospitals were religious-owned; the private hospitals all fall in between.

The facilities in Mbeya falling into the 'charitable' category—two religious dispensaries and a religious hospital—all received donations and applied them to reducing prices, specifying affordability as a central concern in setting prices. They were the

---

[11] Data are from interviews with facilities staff; a 'robust mean' provides a measure of central tendency of data of this type, it is calculated as twice the median plus the quartiles, divided by four. The set of services including consultation fees, treatments (for example wound dressing) and specific drugs treatments, supplied by every facility in the sample. A great deal of effort was put into ensuring comparability of price data between facilities, and the conclusion in the text is not sensitive to the exact mix of services chosen.

[12] Based on a different set of services and treatments, not including drugs since one hospital refused data on drug prices.

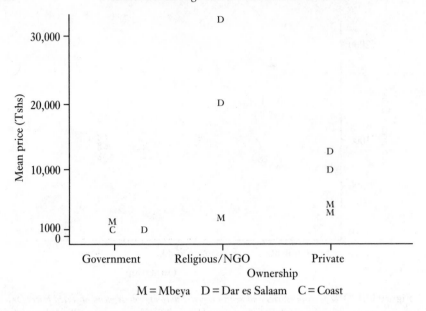

Figure 13.2. *Mbeya, Dar es Salaam and Coast, dotplot, robust mean of stated prices for a common set of services provided by all hospitals*

cheapest non-government facilities at their level; one charitable dispensary was indeed as cheap as a fee-charging government health centre (and better at allowing deferral of fees for those unable to pay in emergencies); the hospital could be as cheap as the government hospital for some types of cases, allowing for informal charges and pre-scription costs at the government hospital. All provided preventative services, which they regarded as central to their activity, and were well regarded by patients for the attitude of the staff. There were comparable charitable dispensaries in Dar es Salaam and Coast districts. It was these charitable facilities, many of which are finding it hard to maintain access to donations, that particularly gave the religious sector its reputation for value for money.

In sharp contrast, two types of religious facilities were charging much higher prices. Some facilities were trading on the general reputation of religious facilities to charge a socially wide range of patients substantially more than they seemed likely to be able to afford in the medium term. Others were pursuing deliberate market segmentation: charging higher prices to a clientele composed almost entirely of the better off and those being paid for by employers.

Both categories can be illustrated from Mbeya. One religious dispensary, receiving donations, was doing only curative care and was charging more than any privately owned dispensary studied in Mbeya. Furthermore, it had poor internal financial con-trol and incentives: the clinical officers both prescribed and took money. Probably as a result, many of our interviewees had been charged more than the facility's stated prices. The doctor in charge maintained that most families could afford these charges;

however almost all the patients interviewed had difficulties paying. This facility was making a surplus and reinvesting it, along with donations, in the construction of a small hospital.

The other high charging religious facility in Fig. 13.1 fell into the second category. It had long served a predominantly better off clientele in Mbeya, and among household interviewees it was the better off who knew and used it. The facility did very little preventative care, and was expanding by developing specialist clinics and the ability to manage chronic illness.

At the hospital level, it was strikingly the religious hospitals in Dar es Salaam that were pursuing this market segmentation strategy. Two religious hospitals in Dar es Salaam charged the highest prices in the whole set of facilities interviewed. One was losing patients as a result; the other was chiefly used by patients paid for by employers. One summarized its strategy as aiming to be 'the best private hospital' in the city.

The religious facilities also had some cultural features in common, notably the emphasis on good attitudes of staff towards patients. The charitable facilities were more willing to defer or partially waive payment than were the fee-charging government facilities. The charitable hospital discussed above claimed—and the patients independently confirmed—that they would admit someone who urgently required inpatient treatment even if they arrived without money, although they told relatives they must pay later and many did. Finally, the viable religious facilities in both categories displayed strong financial control. Both institutional cultures in this sector thus displayed a mix of P/C management and of COOP in the broad sense of good general behaviour by staff towards patients. However the two cultures had very different implications for equity and accessibility, one being quite accessible and inclusive, the other charging high prices and serving mainly the better off.

13.4.3. *The Private Sector: Two Types of Competitive Strategy*

The health care private sector was a recent creation, and changing rapidly. With a couple of Dar es Salaam exceptions, private facilities studied were small compared to long established government and religious facilities, and most private providers were struggling to survive. Market pricing was competitive: Figure 13.1 above shows that in Mbeya private sector charges were rather compressed, and facility interviews confirmed close attention to each others' pricing. In this context, the private sector tended to focus on competing for patients, and this focus in turn shaped responses to poverty. As Table 13.1 showed, private facilities rarely waived but did defer payment, and some dispensaries had large bad debts. The sector's institutional culture was also coloured by market incentives, some perverse.

In Mbeya, for example, the standard market strategy among the private dispensaries interviewed was to try to make a living doing a limited range of curative care. Two however were approaching the problem differently. Both were owned by MDs and run by their wives who were nurses. These two were seeking to expand numbers of patients, first by keeping charges slightly below—but close to—going rates, and second, by offering free or nearly free mother and child health (MCH) services of the type also provided by the public sector. Both were given vaccines by the government for this service, but were cross-subsidizing the labour involved from curative care, and one was planning to add free post-natal care. Both saw these services as part of their effort to increase patient numbers: it 'draws people in', and then they might come back when they were ill. These two facilities seemed viable; they had sufficient patients and were making a profit. They were charging less than a number of the religious facilities in town, and patients confirmed their stated prices.

In Dar es Salaam, a similar approach to market strategy could be found in the private hospital sector. At hospital level Dar es Salaam residents' options were all very problematic. One private hospital in Dar es Salaam, while charging higher prices than the Mbeya private hospitals (Fig. 13.2), charged lower prices than the religious hospitals in the city centre and appeared to have a socially more mixed clientele. It offered MCH services free, and compared to other inner city hospitals had a relatively small proportion of company-funded patients.

The private sector was thus diverse, displaying a range of approaches to shaping market transactions with patients. While it was possible to shape a strategy based on competent, moderately priced provision, there were strong market incentives to weaken safety and probity. Dispensaries, since they sold drugs, had incentives to over-prescribe, and the staff had strong incentives to cheat owners. One owner recounted recurrent problems with her clinical officers over-prescribing and pocketing the profits in her absence. One owner lost financial control and went bankrupt during the study. It was particularly in this sector that low prices could reflect very poor quality, and high charges per patient could reflect dangerous clinical practices such as misdiagnosis to sell expensive drugs and pretence at diagnostic testing. The problem is a familiar one throughout the world: perverse market incentives in private health care constantly tend to undermine even determined efforts to combine P/C management control with motivated staff to produce decent and moderately priced health care; the problem is particularly severe in low income markets.

13.5. INTER-GROUP REGULATORY RELATIONSHIPS: REFERRAL

Regulatory relationships were defined in Section 13.1 as interactions across facility and sectoral boundaries that influence facilities' culture and behaviour. Such relationships include relations between staff and patients, and working relationships within professional groups such as doctors which operate across facility boundaries. Referral, and its problems, illustrates both types of relationship.

By 'referral relationships' we mean the willingness to send patients on to other providers when necessary; decision-making about to whom to refer; and the consequences for patients of these processes. Health care staff understand 'referral' as mainly a relationship between professionals. However, referral emerged in this study as a process largely managed, with difficulty if at all, by the patients themselves. Most referral was 'self-referral', a phrase implying that the primary responsibility was the patient's or their relatives'. Dispensaries 'just tell patients to go' to hospital, and on arrival patients waited in a hospital queue to be diagnosed from scratch. One dispensary doctor therefore expressed the view that to avoid delay patients should be educated to go direct to hospitals with serious illness. Since most patients had to pay at each facility, moving between facilities put a considerable further burden on vulnerable patients.

Patients sent on by dispensaries to government hospitals frequently returned untreated, having waited long periods or been faced with demands for payments they could not afford. Increasingly, patients were refusing to be sent to certain government hospitals. The worst problems were faced by the patients of non-government, and especially private, practitioners. In Mbeya, an MD running a private dispensary said his patients asked him *not* to write referral letters to the government hospital, because if he did, 'they may die there': they would be ill treated and asked for large bribes. In Dar es Salaam, private practitioners said their patients were harassed and neglected at the district hospital. In Mbeya and Coast, the government hospitals imposed higher official charges when they knew the patient came from the private sector.

Some dispensaries in all sectors tried to use personal networks to improve referral experience. Some government dispensaries would send a nurse with severely ill patients, but patients generally had to pay for their transport. One NGO dispensary had part time doctors who also worked at the government referral hospital and assisted their dispensary patients there. Government hospital queue-jumping and direct access to specialists through professional networks was one of the services for which better-off and company-subsidized patients paid private doctors.

The result of these pressures—and of the market opportunities opened up by liberalization—was the growth of referral to non-government facilities. In Mbeya there were religious health centres and dispensaries that could do a wide range of diagnostic tests, or had reputations for treating particular problems such as children's illnesses. Private dispensaries sent cases on to them. Charitable religious hospitals were increasingly seen by government dispensaries and health centres, and by patients, as an alternative to government hospitals. In Dar es Salaam, the private hospitals also got self-referrals by people frustrated by government hospitals, and new out-patients sent by private and religious dispensaries. Referral patterns were thus changing with liberalization.

Religious and NGO organizations were also setting up their own referral networks. One NGO organization had a hospital and several dispensaries, and referred patients paid no additional fee for the hospital consultation. In Mbeya, one mission dispensary had ambitious plans for a mission referral network.

Private for-profit providers were however reluctant to refer to each other. One private dispensary owner said that to refer to a local private hospital would be regarded as 'a failure'. A dispensary owner in Mbeya said, 'referral from private to private will never work'. A director of a small private hospital in Dar es Salaam said he would not refer to another private hospital, since it would take advantage of the opportunity (that is, to steal his patient). Hospital doctors in all sectors complained that private primary practitioners tended to overcharge, sometimes manage illness very badly, and to refer too late. As a result patients tended to arrive seriously ill, requiring emergency intervention, and with no money left.

13.6. POLICY IMPLICATIONS: REGULATORY INTERVENTION FOR EQUITY OBJECTIVES

The concept of informal regulatory relationships defined in Section 13.1 implies that government as policy maker and rule-setter operates as just one among a number of health care stakeholders—which also include government health care providers—in seeking to shape the system. The problems of exclusion outlined in Section 13.2 imply that a liberalizing health care system such as this requires regulatory relationships that mitigate impoverishing processes and encourage the system to move in a more inclusive direction over time. Governments can influence these relationships, a process sometimes called in the literature 'informal institutional design' (Dryzek 1996). Furthermore, governments can shape the 'regulatory arena' (Hancher and Moran 1989: 153): the issues open to public debate and pressure, and the range of people and organizations who have a say.

This view of regulatory intervention is distinct from the more formal concept of regulation common in the economic literature and in utility regulation, and frequently transferred from there to health care thinking (Mackintosh 1999). The approach we are outlining here concentrates on influencing working relationships and processes, rather than on rules and monitoring.[13] While utility regulation, furthermore, tends to emphasize the promotion of competition, health care policy makers face the problem that the perverse incentives characteristic of health care markets limit the usefulness of this approach. We are suggesting a regulatory style that gives more weight to the encouragement of inclusiveness and ethical behaviour at facility level.

Patients participate in shaping institutional cultures, through shared expectations, the creation of reputations and choice of facility, although they have very little leverage and are often mistreated. Regulatory intervention to improve access and responsiveness can therefore build on shared information among patients, including price levels, access, exemptions, and quality of care. Patients and the community can be given more leverage over the health care system through forms of community representation on boards of health facilities, or community health councils with rights to pursue complaints. Publicity and education could also strengthen patient organizing and involvement: for example, publication of local ranges of prices and expected maximum prices for types of treatment.

A second general finding on regulatory relationships was the continuing existence of accessibility, probity and professional behaviour in parts of the government sector. We have argued that different aspects of institutional cultures interact. Hence, intervention to reconstruct the worst government facilities needs to build on and learn from the better cases, and to tackle simultaneously the improvement of top-down control and the encouragement of self-motivated ethical behaviour.

Third, we found that the private sector included some facilities with moderate prices and a willingness to do preventative work, with whom the government could

---

[13] In the socio-legal literature on industrial regulation, Ayres and Braithwaite's (1992) concept of 'tripartism' is a similarly collaborative concept.

collaborate in improving access to health care. Some experiments in this regard are currently underway in Tanzania. In more detailed regulatory proposals from this research (Tibandebage and Mackintosh, forthcoming) we suggest strengthening self-regulation through, for example, a collaboratively managed system of 'kite marking' private providers who offer acceptable quality at moderate prices; this could be a marketing tool and a basis for self-organization and lobbying, and might be associated with some government support in return for commitments to negotiated standards.

Fourth, regulation could recognize religious sector diversity and make appropriate distinctions for policy purposes between the motivations and behaviour of charitable facilities and those serving the middle classes. Privileges for the charitable facilities—such as cheaper wholesale sources of drugs, access to official donations, and tax relief not available to others—and could be associated with obligations such as ethical referral behaviour and collaboration in improving access to primary and preventative care.

Fifth, regulatory intervention could build selectively on informal inter-group working relationships that are in the interests of patients, rather than leaving referral, for example, to be managed and struggled with by patients themselves. All such regulatory interventions need to be locally adapted, and to build on networks and relationships already developing in specific areas.

Finally, formal rules and regulations can be flouted; they are most likely to be observed when they are legitimate, that is, accepted by the people and institutions to whom they apply. Regulatory intervention can include the shaping of informal working relations in such a way that formal rules can be negotiated and sustained. Formal rules should where possible be rooted in and compatible with informal regulatory relationships.

One way to summarize this approach to regulation would be to understand the setting of formal regulatory rules, and formal inspection, as a P/C approach to regulation. As within facilities, so in inter-group regulation in health care, central rule setting and control is an essential framework for collaboration, but one that can only work if rooted in collaborative cultures. This paper also makes the point however[14] that there is nothing in collaborative self-regulation—or more generally in collaborative cultures—that guarantees an equitable approach to access for patients. Institutional cultures of the COOP variety can quite easily be focused on provision for the better off, as they are in some religious facilities analysed above. To improve equity, regulatory intervention has—among other things—to seek to support and sustain the existing facilities that provide cheap or free access to care of acceptable quality, and to reform the government facilities that have become exclusionary.

[14] This is the central theme of Mackintosh and Gilson in this volume.

14

The Case of Indigenous NGOs in Uganda's Health Sector

CHRISTY CANNON LORGEN

14.1. INTRODUCTION

This chapter argues that Ugandan NGOs operating in the health sector are experiencing contradictions between two modes of operation, M and COOP modes, which are shaped both by the external and internal environment for NGOs.[1] The internal environment refers to the NGO's own ways of working, relationships within the NGO, and the techniques and language used by the staff. The external environment for NGOs indicates the influence of other actors, particularly the donors which fund NGOs and the governments which regulate them. Changes in these environments have tended to highlight the contradictions between M and COOP modes; these contradictions create tensions within the NGOs. The chapter explores the effects of these tensions on group behaviour and on the nature of outcomes.[2]

The tensions between M and COOP cultures for NGOs are heightened by a worldwide shift to a more market-oriented approach to development. Structural adjustment programmes in Uganda and elsewhere have emphasized privatization and the 'rolling back of the state'. As the government and donors search for alternative providers of social services, NGOs have gained a higher profile than ever before. Although NGOs are also frequently credited with the ability to promote democracy and strengthen civil society, the chapter's focus on NGOs in the health sector places greater importance on their role in service provision. Health care, never provided wholly by government, is increasingly privatized in Uganda, and NGOs are an important part of this trend. This chapter focuses mainly on the changing financial environment for Ugandan NGOs: the

I greatly appreciate the support of Nuffield College, Oxford, and the Marshall Scholarship Commission in funding the field research for this paper, and the support of the WIDER Project on Group Behaviour and Development. I am particularly grateful to Megan Vaughan and Ines Smyth for their guidance and support during the research and to Judith Heyer and Rosemary Thorp for their very helpful assistance with the paper.
All interviews were conducted by the author in Uganda in 1995 and 1996.

[1] This paper draws on doctoral research conducted in Uganda in 1995 and 1996.

[2] 'Outcomes', for NGOs involved in the health sector, are *broadly* defined here as the activities of an NGO and the impact and distributional reach of these activities.

increase in the volume of funds going to the NGO sector as a whole; the greater proportion of these funds coming from official sources; and the consequent changes in funder/NGO relationships.[3]

The increase in donor[4] funding to NGOs has given rise to several consequences, which reflect a move towards an M mode of operation. Internally, there has been an increase in the use of management/private sector language and techniques, a push for growth and expansion, and more competition for jobs within the NGO. Externally, the quasi-market mode is reflected in increased competition with other NGOs for funding, territory, reputation, and influence; in a perceived need to be more 'business-like' in terms of planning, accounting, evaluating, and in their relationships with governments and donors; in a tendency to pursue contracts or competitive tenders with donors, in which funding is seen as a commercial exchange rather than a gift;[5] and in greater demands for 'upward' accountability to donors or government. Many membership organizations have begun to emphasize income-generation and the collection of dues, sometimes at the expense of their less affluent members, which then affects their outcomes as far as equity is concerned. As NGOs attract more funding from donors, many new NGOs have formed which some observers feel are motivated more by profit than by service. NGOs searching for their niche in the market often adjust their approach to become eligible for funding. Donors, reacting to the dominant market paradigm, are asking for 'value for money'.

The M mode of operation can be contrasted with a more traditional understanding of NGOs, which corresponds with the COOP mode of operation. The following values are traditionally associated with NGOs: altruism, voluntarism, compassion, charity, and participation. Internally, NGOs have sought to encourage the sharing of responsibility. External to the NGO, the COOP mode manifests itself through the traditional NGO emphasis on working with communities, often in an informal way through personal relationships based on trust. Many NGOs and community-based organizations are 'membership organizations', with membership reflecting cooperative ties. NGOs often claim to have 'downward' accountability to their beneficiaries or members. These characteristics are not features of every NGO, and it has been argued that they can be seen as NGO folklore or NGO myth as much as NGO reality. Yet the folklore remains compelling.

This chapter asks the following questions: What has been the historical balance between M and COOP modes? How has the shift in the NGO environment affected this balance? What are the effects on outcomes? And, in a look to the future, might it be possible to incorporate the positive elements of the newer M into the more traditional COOP mode without sacrificing the positive elements of COOP?

---

[3] Other factors in the changing external environment for NGOs include changes in government policy, such as decentralization and new regulations for NGOs, changes in the general economic situation, and shifting areas of instability within the country. Although these are significant, the paper concentrates on the consequences of increased funding for NGOs.

[4] 'Donor' is used here as a generic term for 'funder'. For Ugandan NGOs, donors are most often Northern NGOs, although increasingly bilateral donors are channeling some funding directly to Ugandan NGOs, rather than using a Northern NGO as an intermediary.   [5] Davies (1997).

To address these questions, the chapter focuses on a specific kind of group: indigenous NGOs in Uganda's health sector. These groups have an efficiency function in that their activities are a response to market and state failures in the provision of health care, yet many groups combine this role with a claims function in that they advance the claims of their members or beneficiaries to power and/or resources. Ideally the outcomes of NGO activities, in terms of efficiency and equity, should be measured in terms of the impact on the ultimate beneficiaries: Do services reach the beneficiaries more efficiently? Are resources better distributed? Are beneficiaries better able to claim their rights to health care, as a result of an NGO's work? Although this chapter does not discuss beneficiaries, since it is based on research which focused solely on institutional actors, it is important to note that NGOs which claim to work on behalf of the poor must ultimately be judged by their impact on the poor. Indeed the extent of this impact is often questioned. This chapter, however, looks at outcomes in terms of how NGOs decide to use their time and resources in light of the growing tension between M and COOP modes and particularly how these decisions are influenced by their environment; looking beyond this to impact on beneficiaries is a matter for further research.

Section 14.2 gives a brief background to the NGO sector in Uganda. Section 14.3 presents two detailed case studies of NGOs in the health sector. Section 14.4 analyses how the contradictions between the two modes are working out in practice among health sector NGOs, and Section 14.5 concludes.

14.2. BACKGROUND: THE NGO SECTOR IN UGANDA

This section will look briefly at the historical background of NGOs, in the context of Uganda's political economy. Although our focus is on Ugandan NGOs, Northern NGOs are relevant both as their counterparts in the wider NGO sector and as the most significant source of funding for Ugandan NGOs.

The formal voluntary, non-profit, or non-governmental sector (versus informal community groups) began in Uganda with the arrival of Christian missionaries in the late 1800s. The churches became involved in health care and education long before the state began to provide services, and this tradition now represents the most enduring element of the NGO sector in the country.

After independence from Britain in 1962 and during Obote's first regime, the NGO sector expanded rapidly, as the missions continued to provide services and several Northern NGOs came to Uganda. Many of the first Northern NGOs in Uganda, such as Oxfam and CAFOD, channelled their support through the churches. However, like many other post-independence African rulers, Obote enlarged the role of the state in service provision, and the government took control of some mission schools. While NGOs remained free to operate in more remote areas, mainly in the traditional fields of health and welfare, the role of NGOs was perceived, at least by the government, to be transitional. When resources became available, the state intended to take over the services of the NGOs (Therkildsen and Semboja 1995). Yet after the overthrow of Obote's government through a military coup in 1971, developments under Idi Amin greatly reduced the likelihood of the state taking over NGO services. Although Amin's government initially increased the role of the state in service provision, state provision of these activities quickly broke down. In the face of serious human rights abuses, most Northern NGOs left Uganda.

The Ugandan historical context has led to a strong use of the COOP mode amongst NGOs. During the years of violence and unrest in Uganda, NGOs served largely as a survival mechanism, in part stimulated by the collapse of public services (Brett 1992: 31). The organizations performed an 'efficiency' function in the face of complete market, and state, failure. The churches in Uganda became, almost by default, the only significant providers of services, especially in the health sector. Parent–teacher associations (PTAs) raised fees and organized community labour to construct and maintain schools (Brett 1992: 31). Local NGOs and various cooperative groups formed to pursue development activities. Cooperatives for marketing such goods as coffee and cotton were particularly important in rural areas, and trade unions continued to develop. At community level, people relied on helping each other. A tradition of community labour had existed in Uganda since pre-colonial times, serving to promote the common good, to provide mutual support, or to help weaker members of the community (World Bank 1993: 116–117). Often known as *rwot keri* in the North, for 'groups of farmers', or *munno mukabi* in other parts of Uganda, for 'friend in need', community efforts may include hoeing fields, weeding, providing assistance to a widow, or forming a savings club. *Engozi* groups, or stretcher societies, assist community members with transport to health facilities. Although 'spontaneous community organizations often lack skills and resources' (Barton and Wamai 1994: 94), in Uganda these groups have flourished and adapted to change (Riddell and Robinson 1995: 191).

After Amin was overthrown in 1979, many Northern NGOs returned or came for the first time to Uganda. As Obote's second regime proved to be as violent as Amin's, relief activities came to dominate the work of the voluntary sector, especially in Karamoja during the famine from 1979–81, in West Nile, and later in the Luwero Triangle near Kampala where tens of thousands of civilians were killed. NGOs also increased their role in service provision. The early 1980s were 'trying times' for NGOs in Uganda (Riddell and Robinson 1995: 193); working in a politically unstable country with a collapsing infrastructure was difficult and very expensive. Northern NGOs found that it often made sense to work with and through Ugandan NGOs, especially the churches.

The origins and motivations of Ugandan NGOs are important. As in other African countries, many NGOs have developed in Uganda which resemble their Northern counterparts and funders in their stated values, norms, and conventions; some have been virtually created by Northern NGOs. However, many Ugandan grass roots organizations have formed independently from any Northern impetus, having some of their origins in pre-colonial forms of social organization, as described above. Yet both avenues for the development of Ugandan NGOs tended to use a COOP model. The COOP mode that existed among Northern NGOs, albeit for different reasons and with different origins than in their Ugandan counterparts, provided a further impetus for this mode among Ugandan NGOs.

With the advent of the National Resistance Movement government under President Museveni in 1986 and greater stability in the country since then, NGOs have been functioning in a much less hostile environment. The increased openness in Uganda's current political economy means that some groups have been able to take on a 'claims' function in addition to the more typical 'efficiency' function which prevailed in light of state and market failure under Amin and Obote. The government has sought to create an 'enabling environment' for NGOs.

The NGO sector has grown in numbers and resources. More Northern NGOs are establishing a presence, and Ugandan NGOs have proliferated. It is estimated that there are now around 2000–3000 NGOs in the country, if the many small local NGOs are included. Although the exact figure of aid from Northern NGOs is not known, some estimates put the amount at $125 million a year (World Bank 1995: 18; Bigsten 1995). The worldwide trend of donors channeling support through NGOs has certainly reached Uganda, and this support has enhanced the growth of the NGO sector—and equally has brought the M mode of operations to Uganda vigorously.

This is illuminated by case studies (see next section), although it is difficult to generalize because NGOs in Uganda differ in their structure, activities, origins, motivations, geographical coverage, the amount and nature of resources available to them, the sources of their funding, and the extent of their interaction or collaboration with the government, donors, and other NGOs. The distinction between Northern and Southern/Ugandan NGOs is particularly significant.

14.3. CASE STUDIES

This section of the chapter looks at two specific cases of Ugandan NGOs and the tensions influencing their within-group behaviour as a result of the contradictions described above. These are the Uganda Community-Based Health Care Association (UCBHCA) and the AIDS Support Organization (TASO).

14.3.1. *The Uganda Community-Based Health Care Association*

The UCBHCA is an interesting organization to consider in a study of groups because it is actually a group of groups, specifically a group of community-based health care (CBHC) organizations. The entire concept of CBHC as well as the behaviour of the groups involved in it is historically based on the COOP mode, as the case study will illustrate. The evolution of new financial arrangements with the UCBHCA's principal donor, UNICEF, reflects the shift in development paradigms towards more of an M model. The tensions and pressures experienced by the UCBHCA as a result of this new emphasis are affecting its outcomes, particularly for its member organizations.

When the present Ugandan government came to power in 1986, CBHC was not a priority in the health sector. Although President Museveni expressed concern for the improvement of primary health care, the bias towards curative care, originating in the colonial period and prevalent in much of Africa, continued. At this time, UNICEF was arguably the most influential and generous donor involved with the health sector in Uganda. Government officials and UNICEF representatives in Uganda agreed to make an effort to raise the profile of CBHC in the country and to coordinate the many NGOs which were becoming involved in CBHC. The UCBHCA was created in 1986, mostly with UNICEF funding, 'to try to fill some of the gaps in primary health care and coordinate the local work of national and international NGOs working in health' and to attempt to balance the focus on tertiary medicine (Barton and Wamai 1994: 95).

The UCBHCA, comprised of a Secretariat,[6] Executive Board, and its member CBHC organizations, constitutes an umbrella body which plays a coordinating role for its members and provides training, information, evaluation, and support. Thus the UCBHCA is a formal group, in that it is an organized collection of people who act and take decisions together. Its member groups are often organized along more informal lines than is the umbrella group. The Association has become well known for its role in developing training packages for CBHC facilitators and trainers, community health workers, traditional birth attendants, and health committees. The membership has grown considerably from around 100 CBHC programmes at its inception to almost 400 programmes in 1997. Members include church-based CBHC programmes as well as secular ones, and this mix is reflected in the make-up of the Board. Although the UCBHCA itself can be considered a Ugandan NGO, both Northern and Ugandan NGOs are members of the Association, which has been called 'the most promising collaborative venture' among NGOs in the country (de Coninck 1992: 17). UNICEF and Oxfam have been the most significant supporters of the Association; the UCBHCA also receives funding from several other Northern NGOs and from its membership fees. For several years, Oxfam provided a Technical Adviser to the UCBHCA, who was considered an Oxfam employee, on secondment to the UCBHCA. His role was to strengthen the capacity of the UCBHCA by overseeing the programmes, giving technical support, and providing training in several areas.

The UCBHCA has encouraged and facilitated the formation of district CBHCAs. Twenty-five of the country's thirty-nine districts now have district CBHCAs, with eight considered active and effective. A debate continues around how to organize the DCBHCAs, given the current government policy of decentralization, and around the relationship between the central UCBHCA and its district counterparts. This debate reflects the constant need for NGOs to evolve, depending on their circumstances and changes in the external environment. For the UCBHCA, there has been concern that the focus on decentralization reduces the importance of the central organization, such that tensions exist around how much energy should be devoted to the central UCBHCA and how much to the district bodies, particularly in light of serious resource constraints. Some observers have argued that decentralization makes the central body unnecessary and irrelevant. Others counter that while decentralization gives more authority and discretion to the districts, important policy decisions are still made at national/central level and that if CBHC is truly valued, there must be an overarching association at this

---

[6] The Secretariat consists of the Executive Secretary, the Technical Advisor, between three and five CBHC Trainers, and around three support staff. Resource limitations mean that this is effectively a skeleton staff.

level.[7] An element of self-preservation is strong in the debate, as the UCBHCA staff seek to protect their positions, that is, their livelihoods.

An important outcome of the work of the UCBHCA has been to influence the government to adopt a community-based approach in its own policies and activities. It can be argued that the government's official adoption of a CBHC approach shows that the work of the UCBHCA and other NGOs can influence government policy. Although it is difficult to determine the exact causes of a shift in the government's approach, the many NGOs supporting CBHC have provided an example of what can be achieved at community level. However, the work of NGOs in the area of lobbying and advocacy can be more complex than it first appears: this effort on the part of the UCBHCA was funded and driven by donors, and from a more cynical perspective, it can be argued that the adoption of CBHC as official government policy reflects the tendency for donors to prevail in policy debates. The UCBHCA has been powerfully shaped by the agenda of its donors, the most important factor in its external environment. Yet even though the donor community may have found advocacy activities to be effective in changing government attitudes, these activities are difficult to measure. Moreover, donors, though they still want to prevail in policy debates, may consider that there are more straightforward ways of doing this than funding NGO advocacy work. Lobbying and advocacy work may suffer as the quasi-market for development funds makes it easier for NGOs, like the UCBHCA, to obtain funding for more measurable activities.

Recently, financial worries have deeply shaken the Association. In 1995, UNICEF decided to reduce its funding of the UCBHCA drastically, by ceasing payment of salaries and administrative costs and paying the Association only for specific work performed, thus moving to a contractual relationship. According to the UCBHCA's Technical Adviser, 'UNICEF dropped us' (interview 1995). In the short term, this generated a funding crisis. The UCBHCA has since been faced with the dilemma of covering its administrative and overhead costs while redefining its role in this new context. Adjustment to this change has been very difficult for some members of the Secretariat. Many observers note the different personalities of the two key actors in the UCBHCA, portraying the Oxfam-seconded Technical Adviser, as a 'careerist' who represents a new generation of NGO staff, and the Executive Secretary, as a member of the 'old school' who finds it harder to accept new ways of working/behaviour.

Of interest is the language used by the actors involved to discuss the change in UNICEF's support, which captures the tension between the COOP and M modes of operation. Reflecting on the role of the Executive Board in the past (known then as the Steering Committee), the Executive Secretary recalls: 'They were steering the Association in a family-like context. It was not an NGO with a bureaucracy, not seen as a growing organization, but as a small unit to coordinate and strengthen and train in CBHC' (interview 1995). He adds, 'We are like a child abandoned by its mother or weaned suddenly. We are supposed to become independent now, like a company'.

---

[7] The physical location of the UCBHCA secretariat on the grounds of the Ministry of Health offices in Entebbe is also seen as an important factor in the efforts to lobby—and enjoy informal rapport with—central government officials, who ultimately still exercise a great deal of influence over what happens in the districts.

An official of UNICEF expresses the desire for the UCBHCA to grow up and become less dependent: 'The UCBHCA is our baby . . . . We won't be giving the same money to the UCBHCA; they have to sell their services. They say like a child: you're abandoning us! It's time for them to grow and be more alone' (interview 1995). In response to this pressure, the Association's Executive Secretary quotes a Ugandan proverb, 'That which grows too fast dies too soon' (interview 1995).

This change in donor support is not unique to the UCBHCA. Pressure on NGOs to be more business-like and competitive has become increasingly common. In the case of the UCBHCA, this pressure conflicts with its origin and early nature which correspond closely with the COOP mode. UNICEF virtually gave birth to the UCBHCA, creating the Association according to its own strategy and nurturing it until the recent change in policy. The relatively informal nature of the group, based on a 'family' of its members, was eventually seen as a shortcoming, in the sense that the casual and cooperative nature of the group meant that there was little pressure to achieve higher performance standards or to compete more effectively. The Government of Uganda–UNICEF 1995–2000 Country Programme is now using the services of the UCBHCA in the area of community capacity-building. The terms of reference note that the UCBHCA is 'contracting out its services' and that this contract will 'contribute in building the Association's capacity to manage and market its services' (UNICEF 1995). This language of 'contracting' and 'marketing' is unfamiliar to the UCBHCA and implies a mode of operation with which its staff are not entirely comfortable. The UNICEF official most closely involved with the UCBHCA understands that the move to a contractual relationship may feel unnatural to the Association:

There is an in-built attitude of the members of the Association of managing their affairs not like a business but like a family affair, day-to-day. They are not conceived as a company, able to market their service. They should look at the resources available and use them to produce and be more fruitful. There are many church-related programmes which came out of generosity and voluntarism, so they do not have the logic of marketing. It is not their background. (interview 1996)

When asked if the UCBHCA now risks losing these qualities of generosity and voluntarism, the UNICEF representative answers, 'They can design themselves to protect voluntarism. It should not be abandoned' (interview 1996). Yet despite this caveat, the expectations of—and pressure on—the UCBHCA are that it must alter its functions and mode of operation to generate more income and be more self-sufficient and proactive, in short, to become more of a market actor.

In particular, these changes affect the functions of training and support of members as, in many cases, the UCBHCA costs itself out of the range affordable by its members. The UCBHCA's Executive Secretary laments: 'As a company, we must be paid for services, but members can't pay. They are poor, except for the big NGOs. So how do we relate to them if we can't give them free services?' (interview 1995). Officials of several member programmes express regret at their inability to afford the services of the 'new' UCBHCA for training (interviews 1995).[8] In addition, since support and

---

[8] UNICEF officials hoped that other sources of funding would become available for UCBHCA training, particularly from the World Bank.

coordination of members is a more qualitative and less tangible activity in terms of outcomes, many worry that this role of the UCBHCA will suffer. An official of a Northern NGO notes, 'Now the UCBHCA depends on doing training for UNICEF to stay alive. The end point is training instead of being an association of its members' (interview 1995). The accountability of the UCBHCA to its members is weakened. The funding pressures mean that the UCBHCA is pushed towards being a service organization and away from its 'claims' function, towards an M role and away from a COOP mode.

The UCBHCA is thus experiencing contradictory pressures. UNICEF officials value the participatory, member-oriented, COOP approach of the UCBHCA. Yet at the same time, they want the UCBHCA to be more like a private for-profit company. The encouragement of competition is a symbol of the M mode of operation for NGOs. It may be true that the UCBHCA in its earlier form was not sustainable, due to its extreme dependency on one donor. Although the new opportunities for contracts may keep the Association alive, its supporters remain concerned about the outcomes or consequences for its members. It is not clear how the UCBHCA will manage and reconcile the tensions and inherent contradictions between the COOP and M models.

14.3.2. *The AIDS Support Organization*

TASO was founded in 1986 as an organization to counsel and care for AIDS patients. TASO now works in the areas of counselling, education and nursing, as well as the provision of some material assistance to people with AIDS and their families. TASO's theme is 'living positively with AIDS', and the NGO has been called 'the most important grassroots response to AIDS in Uganda outside the official medical and research services' (Barnett and Blaikie 1992: 158). Rapid growth has led to TASO clinics in several districts, usually attached to government hospitals and staffed mainly by volunteers. The care and counselling provided by TASO and other NGOs active in the area of HIV/AIDS have been particularly crucial because the public health sector has focused more on AIDS prevention and has lacked capacity in these other areas (Iliffe 1998). Thus this group has played an important efficiency function, in that the state has not been able to cope with the burden of HIV/AIDS and the market has little interest.

The efficiency function of non-governmental groups can, in a sense, become a self-fulfilling prophecy, contributing to the shortcomings of public services. There is a saying in Uganda: 'If it's AIDS, it's TASO'. While this attitude frustrates government officials trying to cope with the AIDS epidemic, it reflects the perception of the wider aid community and can result in a higher profile for NGO interventions and a tendency to overlook the value of government inputs.

Like the UCBHCA, TASO is experiencing pressure from its donors to incorporate market-oriented ways of working into its approach. In contrast to the UCBHCA, however, TASO's financial backing has not become less flexible; it has simply grown. TASO expanded very quickly, from two to ten districts, after donors noticed the success of its efforts (in an environment in which donors are primed to note and support successful NGOs). Its growth thus far puts TASO under pressure to expand to more districts. Donors who are interested in supporting AIDS efforts frequently want to contract their projects to TASO. Although this has increased TASO's funding and workload, it has not enhanced its internal capacity or financial security, and it has left little space for COOP modes of operation, particularly at management level.

The expansion of an NGO, often due to donor support, can lead to a diminution of its COOP aspects, a tendency which is shown in the case of TASO. TASO, like many other NGOs, originated in a 'family' model. Its founder formed TASO in 1986, as an informal support group, when her husband became ill with AIDS. Of the 16 original members, 12 have died of AIDS. TASO thus began from the concept of a family or community of sufferers and supporters. Now, an official of TASO explains:

We want to be a family, and we should not ignore that element. But we can't afford to be unprofessional. Now expectations have grown. Before, we could say: We are learning. There was no one to learn from. After nine years in the field, we can't use this excuse. Professionalism and efficiency are expected. We can't have both very comfortably. It's a compromise. So now we can be less family-based. (interview 1996)

The growth of TASO means that it is expected to behave more like a company, much like the case of the UCBHCA. It is now a very big Ugandan NGO, with a large office, a public relations team, and a very sizeable annual budget.

Although the pressure on NGOs to move towards the M mode of operation often comes from donors, it can be argued that donors continue to seek the input of NGOs in part because of their unique, more COOP-oriented characteristics. In this way, the desires of donors influence an NGO and can lead to contradictions which are felt within the group. Two examples of donor interaction with TASO reflect these contradictions. First, TASO's participation in the quasi-market for donor funds has forced a change in its mode of operation. Recently, a consortium of donors pressured TASO to add family planning services, especially condom distribution and birth control pills, to its counselling and care of AIDS patients. TASO staff would prefer to refer patients to family planning clinics, but the donors have persisted. A TASO official comments, 'We are happy to have the money, but we don't know. We might bite off more than we can chew' (interview 1996). A donor official reassures: 'TASO is very insecure about family planning. It is new and seems more technical. It's just a matter of time. They'll get more comfortable with it' (interview 1996). This example reflects the donor view of TASO as a market actor: if the donors pay for family planning, then TASO must provide family planning.

The second example, however, suggests that donors value those characteristics of TASO which are distinct from those of the private sector, as indicated by the comments of an official from a bilateral donor:

We have given $2.5 million to TASO over five years. They can handle it. With this amount of money, a contracts consultant comes to Kampala from Nairobi. So this guy came and asked TASO: What's your negotiated overhead rate? They had no idea! They're not a firm. They work with communities. We fund them *because* they don't know what this is. (interview 1996)

This comment takes us directly to our next section, as it reveals how donors may want COOP and M behaviour from NGOs, simultaneously, and how they may be difficult to combine.

14.4. THE EVOLVING CONTRADICTIONS BETWEEN MODES

This section draws on the case studies of the UCBHCA and TASO to analyse further the contradictions between the COOP and M modes of operation, which have arisen from the changing international context, and the effects of these contradictions on NGO operations and outcomes.

We see two strands to the analysis. First, there is an *inherent* contradiction between the two modes, which becomes more evident as the role of M increases. Second, there are diverse forces at work increasing the role of M and thus the potential for contradiction. On the basic contradiction, the COOP mode of operation gives NGOs their competitive edge with donors. Historically, donors have valued the COOP way of working, in particular the closeness of NGOs to the poor. The community base of NGOs makes them, some argue, more accountable to the poor, since they are intimately involved with the poor with whom they work. The supposed efficiency of the NGOs derives in part from paying 'altruistic' people less than they might earn elsewhere, but also in part from the relationship which NGOs are able to form with the community at the grassroots. NGOs are often seen to have a comparative advantage not as market providers, but in terms of the nature of the relationships they form and maintain. This comparative advantage can potentially be undermined by the emphasis on M group behaviour, as shown in the cases of the UCBHCA and TASO. The message came through vividly in the case of TASO, described above, where the donor actually says that it funds TASO *because* the NGO does not know its overhead rate. However, TASO's ability to handle large sums of money was still important. Ideally, donors would like NGOs to combine both modes; '[NGOs'] relationship with the "people" is seen as giving them greater public legitimacy than government while their managerial features are seen as permitting private sector levels of cost control and efficiency' (Hulme and Edwards 1997: 6). Along these lines, while donors often require strict 'upward' accountability of the NGOs which they fund, they usually also require that NGOs demonstrate some level of 'downward' accountability to the communities with which they work, again valuing NGOs for their COOP orientation. In an ideal world, NGOs could try to use the positive elements of these two modes; however, in reality, working in both modes requires energy and effort, and work in one mode may contradict work in the other. For example, in terms of how TASO staff allocate their time and effort, managing the two modes can be very complicated. We can develop our understanding of this complexity as we analyse the consequences of the increase in the role of M.

The source of the increased emphasis on M comes, as we have seen, from the increasing dependency on donor funding. This dependency is a consequence of the changing environment. In general, 'dependency' refers to reliance on another actor for support. Dependency, whether financial or otherwise, can affect the power relations between actors and can undermine the possibility of meaningful partnership. The dependency of NGOs on donor funding may make jobs less secure within an NGO and may increase competition between NGOs. NGO staff themselves are concerned to maintain the activities and income of their group, in part because the NGO is their livelihood. The macro-environment has also led to an increased desire, in Uganda and other African countries, for employment with an NGO. Policy measures linked to structural adjustment have meant a decline in wages or the loss of jobs for the middle class Africans, especially civil servants. A job with an NGO has come to be seen as a positive career move, paying more and offering better benefits than a similar job with a government agency if one is even available. The voluntary service becomes a sort of privatized version of the civil service. An example from Oxfam in Uganda is that its Kampala office had two senior employees who had joined Oxfam from previous jobs at the Ministry of Finance; despite the prestige associated with their government jobs, the sense of stability and future prospects that they associated with a job at Oxfam meant that the switch was viewed as a positive career move. NGOs are thus increasingly perceived as channels for promoting one's own interests, rather than for realizing the voluntarism traditionally associated with the non-profit sector. The new cadre of NGO managers often have professional loyalty, rather than emotional loyalty, to the NGO's objectives.[9] The constant stream of new Ugandan NGOs provides middle-class employment which is otherwise in short supply. This trend influences group behaviour in these NGOs.

Crucially, this increased dependency means, above all increased weight to the agenda of the donor. As donors—and in particular Northern NGOs—themselves come under pressure to be more businesslike, this translates into pressure on those they fund. The pressure is the more effective, because NGOs themselves have become important sources of employment. Ugandan NGOs have powerfully expressed their survival instincts, or the need to bring in enough money to remain viable.[10] NGO staff are worried, like most Ugandans, about supporting their families, and it is hardly surprising if they adjust their approach and behaviour to coincide with the criteria of funders, as in the case of TASO taking on family planning provision.

The increased weight given to the donors' agenda implies, first, increased emphasis on sustainability, in the sense of financial viability after the withdrawal of donor finance. The desire of donors to achieve sustainability means that they are usually unwilling to commit resources to a programme, whether governmental or non-governmental, for more than three to five years (Desai and Howes 1995: 92). This affects internal

---

[9] Although professional loyalty may become more important than emotional loyalty, it is important to distinguish between pressures on NGOs to behave more like market actors and pressures on NGOs to become more 'professional'. Professionalism can mean many different things and can be expected to take many different forms. If professionalism means the right to be autonomous on their own ground, the effort to achieve higher performance standards, or simply to be good at what they do, these remain more traditional goals for NGOs and are not necessarily incompatible with the COOP mode of operation.

[10] Although more donor funds are going through the NGO sector, the increase in the number of Ugandan NGOs has heightened the competition for these funds to the extent that funding can actually be more difficult to obtain now than in the past.

behaviour of NGOs by making them insecure as well as preoccupied with the quest for funding. A study of NGOs in the area of micro-finance argues that NGOs react defensively to the donor demand for sustainability (Dichter 1997: 130). It concludes that 'international NGOs, for whom sustainability was never before a value (charity and compassion were after all never meant to be subject to bottom-line business values) are now often afraid to admit openly that they would still like to accomplish some things that cannot by definition pay for themselves' (Dichter 1997: 132). These things that cannot pay for themselves are again traditional NGO activities, such as health education or immunization, that do not generate income but achieve a public good. Yet 'sustainability', in the sense of financial self-sufficiency, is valued as a comparative advantage in the competitive NGO market. The potential for contradictions between the COOP and M modes is effectively highlighted in the warning that 'NGOs will continue to try to refine and test their micro-finance techniques in the crucible of self-sustainability. In so doing, it is quite possible that they will get farther and farther away from what they may do best, social intermediation at the grassroots' (Dichter 1997: 137).

In this context, competition for funding can mean that NGOs will choose areas in which it is easier to show results, often quantitative such as numbers of latrines built or community health workers trained, and will avoid more difficult activities, such as malaria control, or less tangible activities, such as support to membership or training of other NGOs in the case of the UCBHCA; these choices greatly affect outcomes.

Second, the increased weight of donor agendas leads to pressure for more ser-vice contracting, with consequences for behaviour and change in practices. NGOs already surrender some autonomy when they engage in coordinated programmes with governments (Bebbington and Farrington 1993: 49). Contracting with donors can fur-ther 'deviate NGOs from their primary objectives and compromise their autonomy' (Robinson 1997: 76). Thus when NGOs accept some elements of the M mode of operation, especially when they enter the market for their services, they may forfeit some of the autonomy traditionally, if not entirely accurately, associated with the NGO sector. We note that the UCBHCA, founded, in effect, by UNICEF, was never really autonomous, while TASO was.

Contractual arrangements affect outcomes because with them NGOs only do what they are contracted to do, as shown in the two case studies. Bilateral donors may contract NGOs to implement programmes; while this is still considered bilateral aid and is often targeted at the government, the government does not receive the funding directly. The role of contractor is familiar to some NGOs, such as CARE, and relatively foreign to others, such as the Save the Children Fund-UK. Contracting can shape an NGO's activities. An official of a bilateral donor says of an American NGO, 'The NGO is flexible and behaves like a contracting agency. With this one and a few others, they'll take on what you pay for' (interview 1995). Here, 'flexibility' is considered a 'quasi-market' characteristic because the NGO is willing to carry out a wide range of work for which there is a buyer.

Third, increased dependency allows the donor's agenda to influence autonomy in what NGOs say, as well as what they choose to do. In the present context in

Uganda, NGOs might be less likely to speak out concerning donor and government policy (i.e. 'don't bite the hand that feeds you'). Many NGOs have traditionally campaigned, sometimes successfully, against the policies of large donors, especially regarding structural adjustment and debt. Lobbying of the government is often considered an important role of NGOs, such as the case of the UCBHCA lobbying for greater budgetary allocations to community-based health care at national and district level. Closer relationships with donors and with the government, particularly when an NGO is supported by bilateral funds, may inhibit such lobbying, especially lobbying which involves criticism. This may take some 'voice' from the NGO sector.

In addition to the impact of the donor's agenda, increased competition for funds affects NGOs. This implies changed priorities in allocation of time, and an increased tension for Ugandan NGOs, between devoting group energy to competition or to coordination with other NGOs. A competitive atmosphere, over funds, territory, image, visibility, message, or the ability to influence the government, may make coordination of NGO activities, and the formation of a collective NGO voice, more difficult. Moreover, as the NGO sector becomes more competitive and arguably donor-driven in Uganda, many have argued that the need for coordination becomes greater, so that NGOs can maintain a strong voice. This is exemplified in Uganda's Rakai District, which is crowded with over sixty NGOs in the field of HIV/AIDS, often duplicating each other's services while other areas remain neglected. As NGOs take on a greater role in the health sector, for example, the coordination of activities becomes more important, to ensure appropriate coverage and quality of services, that is, efficient and equitable outcomes.

Dependency influences the allocation of time and energy within NGOs. It creates extra work for NGOs because of donor demands for reports, accounts, and other information.[11] The rules and bureaucratic procedures (M mode) associated with donor funding may prove incompatible with the desire of NGOs to be flexible and quick to act (COOP mode). In one large World Bank programme in Uganda which funded several NGOs, the NGOs found fault with the frequent delays in the delivery of funding and materials as well as the complicated reporting requirements. Complex and clumsy procurement and funding procedures threatened the efficacy of NGOs at the grassroots level. Such delays may weaken the community basis of the NGO 'way of working'; they reduce the NGO's 'downward' accountability to its beneficiaries and its legitimacy in the eyes of the community or in the eyes of its members, as in the case of the UCBHCA. However, it should be noted that NGOs can learn from such experiences and manage more effectively in the future, for example, through the arrangement of donor consortia

---

[11] An article about informational demands on NGOs from donors (Davies 1997) is relevant here. If the transaction that takes place when a donor funds an NGO is seen as a gift, this tends to correspond to a more *laissez-faire* attitude of donors concerning information, in which the NGO is trusted, not harassed. If this transaction is seen as a commercial exchange, the attitude of the donor tends to be more 'hard-line': this is a contract, and NGOs are under an obligation to produce the goods (information about developments that took place as a result of the granted resources) (Davies 1997: 616). The more 'hard-line' demands for information correspond to the 'quasi-market' mode of operation for NGOs and also reflect the growing emphasis on upward accountability for NGOs.

and the development of skills in such areas as reporting and accounting. The World Bank can also learn and try to avoid practices that undermine NGO operations.

The increase in competition in Uganda's non-governmental sector strongly reflects the M mode of operations for NGOs. For example, UNICEF has exerted pressure on the UCBHCA to be more competitive and has contracted some of its CBHC work to other NGOs to show the UCBHCA that its threats are serious. In the private sector, successful competition is the way to increase one's market share and win more contracts. Yet, competition makes the uniqueness of NGOs even more important, for as 'competition for the donor dollar is stronger than ever and is not likely to lessen, the need to appear different, and especially to appear effective, drives NGOs' (Dichter 1997: 137). The tensions between competition and coordination within the NGO sector in Uganda thus relate to the wider pressures to behave in contradictory ways.

In the competition for funding among Ugandan NGOs, resemblance between a Ugandan NGO and Northern NGOs in structure and style can constitute a comparative advantage. As an Oxfam official admits, 'international NGOs fail to recognise the legitimacy of traditional forms of organization. We need a structure where we see ourselves. We are drawn to Western-educated, articulate people. We are readier to respond' (interview, 1996). Such similarity can be enhanced by the presence in the Ugandan NGO of a highly educated Ugandan (the UCBHCA's technical advisor was a very gifted Kenyan) or an expatriate who is usually fluent in English and in the jargon of NGO proposals. Without such staff, smaller Ugandan NGOs may be at a disadvantage in the market for funds. Efforts to resemble Northern organizations clearly affect group behaviour, not necessarily in a negative way; if these efforts attract funds, they can improve the group's outcomes.

Ideally, the relationship between Northern and Ugandan NGOs is one of reciprocity where Northern NGOs give support, both financial and otherwise, as well as a voice when it may be difficult for Ugandan NGOs to speak out on an issue, while partnership with Ugandan NGOs gives legitimacy to Northern NGOs. However, the reality is that the relationship has become increasingly unbalanced. Closer ties with bilateral donors on the part of some Northern NGOs may weaken these COOP-based 'partnerships' even more as accountability to the donor becomes more important than accountability to the recipient Ugandan partner. Likewise, the support of bilateral donors to Ugandan NGOs was at first mainly channelled through Northern NGOs. The more recent phenomenon of direct donor support to Ugandan NGOs has worried Northern NGOs in terms of its implications for their own funding; this sense of threat can further weaken partnerships and can divide the NGO community. Accountability of the Northern donor NGO to the Ugandan recipient NGO is also extremely difficult to implement, which prevents the relationship from being truly reciprocal.

14.5. CONCLUSION

The above analysis suggests that the combination of the increase in funds going to NGOs and a more general move to the market in countries like Uganda and to the market paradigm internationally poses a serious challenge to the traditional ideals of NGOs, such as cooperation and trust.

NGOs need to find ways to reconcile the tensions they are experiencing between the COOP and M modes of operation and to draw on both modes to maximize the positive outcomes of their work. As we have seen, this includes internal elements, that is, policies *within* NGOs, as they make decisions about the ways to balance conflicting pressures, and external elements, that is, policies *towards* NGOs, of both governments and donors, to the extent that these influence within-group behaviour.

Circumstances differ greatly for individual NGOs, such that it is difficult to make generalizations about ways to mitigate the tensions between the COOP and M modes of operation. However, efforts to define a mandate and goals clearly, to reduce dependency on a single donor, to refuse to engage in activities that fall outside their goals and mandate, to point out to donors any destructive effects of their actions, and to keep capacity in line with activities, are of primary importance. Furthermore, as NGOs attempt to draw on both modes of operation, their efforts will be greatly enhanced by the development of a businesslike approach and measures of achievement in relation to non-market costs and benefits.

In their relationships with Ugandan NGOs, donors need to be much more aware of the effects of their demands and funding practices on NGOs. Donors, whether Northern NGOs or official aid donors, do not always realize that their emphasis on an M mode of operation may undermine the within-group COOP mode that drew them to the NGO in the first place. Yet the time spent on such activities as, for example, accounting to donors may have a positive impact on NGO performance and capacity; thus NGO advocates must be wary of over-simplifying the effects of donor funding on NGO behaviour.

In conclusion, the ways in which the wider aid community works with NGOs, and why it does so, lead to changes within NGOs and affect their outcomes. The changing external environment in Uganda tends to encourage an M mode of operation. As NGO staff embrace this mode, it appears to contradict the aspects of their behaviour which are more cooperative. The resulting tension can affect NGO outcomes, in terms of the activities they choose to pursue and the impact of those activities. The tension can affect equity and claims functions, particularly for member organizations, if the needs of members take second place to a donor-led agenda. Although it may not be possible to avoid the tensions arising from the clash between the two modes, it may be possible to mitigate these tensions and take the best from both modes.

15

Conclusions

JUDITH HEYER, FRANCES STEWART, AND
ROSEMARY THORP

15.1. INTRODUCTION

This book has explored how a focus on group rather than individual behaviour enriches our understanding of development outcomes and policies. We started with the recognition that the magnitude of activities within groups greatly outweighs that of interactions between groups, yet most economists' models treat groups as quasi-individuals. This book aimed to challenge this by using different theoretical perspectives to explore within-group behaviour, focusing principally on economic activity. A driving motivation behind the study is the need to deepen our insight into the consequences of the shift to the market-dominant development paradigm affecting the majority of developing countries today, since this appears to be a major influence on group functioning and development outcomes. To investigate this relationship we studied both how macro-paradigms affect the mode of group behaviour at the micro-level, and how the modes of functioning (P/C, COOP, or M) relate to efficiency and equity outcomes.

Chapter 1 presented our framework, and posed the main questions we wanted to answer, coming to some preliminary conclusions drawing on some of the material presented in the main body of this book, especially the two general chapters by Alkire and Deneulin, and Stewart. In the body of the book we have presented case studies of groups and their functioning and outcomes. What we seek to do here is to set out our conclusions and to review in detail how they are supported by the case studies. The cases fall into three groups, shown schematically in Table 15.1, which analyses them in terms of our typologies, on the one hand of group functions, on the other of mode of operation. The next section provides brief summaries of the case studies. Following this we use the case studies to explore the relationship between their findings and the two levels of causation identified as fundamental to understanding the developmental significance of groups—the impact of macro-norms on group behaviour, and in particular on the mode of behaviour a group adopted, that is, whether it was P/C, COOP, or M; and the impact of the modes of behaviour adopted on outcomes, defined in terms of efficiency, equity, and well-being. We conclude with theoretical and policy implications.

Table 15.1. *Schematic overview of case studies*

Type of group	Problems addressed	Mechanisms adopted	Other functions	Mode of operation	Outcome		
					Efficiency	Equity	Empowerment of poor
Market failure							
Fishing, Senegal	Externalities	Limit output	Claims: raise prices	COOP & P/C	Varied, some positive	Increased share of poor fishermen; excluded some	None
Producer Assoc., NE Brazil and southern Italy	Indivisibilities, externalities	Quality control, marketing	Claims: raise prices and incomes	COOP & P/C & M	Positive	Positive though benefits unequally shared	Positive
Farmer Assoc., Korea and Taiwan	Information, indivisibilities	Technical assistance, marketing, credit	Claims: improve terms via pressure on government	COOP & P/C (more COOP in Taiwan)	Positive	Positive	Positive
Coffee Federation, Colombia	Indivisibilities, information	Quality control, marketing, information	Claims: bargain with government on prices and resources	P/C & COOP & M	Positive	Positive, though benefits unequally shared, and some regions excluded	?
Mongolian collectives	Indivisibilities, information	Marketing, infrastructure	None	P/C & COOP	Positive	Positive	Positive
Community Forestry, South Asia	Externalities	Limit offtake, patrols	None	COOP & P/C	Positive	Positive for men; negative for women	?
Claims							
Women's groups, Bangladesh	Empowerment	Savings funds, group action	Some efficiency: credit	COOP & P/C	Positive, small	Positive	Strong
Sex workers, Calcutta	Empowerment, work conditions	Campaigns, members' education	Some efficiency	COOP & P/C	Positive, small	Positive	Very strong
Pro bono							
Health sector, Tanzania	Inequity	Provide services to poor	Some efficiency	P/C, COOP & M	Some, varied	Varied	None
NGOs, Uganda	Externalities	Provide services to poor	Some efficiency	P/C, COOP & M	Some	Some	None

15.2. AN OVERVIEW OF THE CASE STUDIES

15.2.1. *Groups with a Primary Market Failure Function*

Groups in which this function dominates are analysed in Chapters 4–9. These chapters shed light on the characteristics of groups that take collective action to overcome market failures, on the outcomes achieved, and on the relation between their *modus operandi* and these outcomes. The literature has long suggested that problems of fragmentation and individual self-interest make collective action difficult. However, collective action does emerge in many situations. In Chapter 4, Gaspart and Platteau analyse group action aimed at limiting the catch by fishermen of the Senegalese coast. This poses a particular challenge because of the unpredictability of fish catches, the variety of fishing technologies, and the geographical spread of the harvest zone. Yet some groups in Senegal, as elsewhere, get established, survive, and succeed in regulating the catch. The authors emphasize the role of technology and market conditions, as well as social relations, in effective group action. The most basic requirement for success is shown to be a clear economic gain, in this case the result of a sufficiently inelastic demand which means that higher prices are associated with restrictions in the catch.

A particularly interesting finding is the role of technology in explaining both the choice of method to limit fishing, and the overall likelihood of success. The scope for cheating is in part a function of technology. It is easier to monitor the number of trips than it is to regulate the size of the catch (boxes can be hidden, sold at sea or discreetly in a crowd at the point of landing). Further, net fishing makes catch quotas difficult, since so many fish may be caught with one sweep that controlling quantity means requiring fishermen to throw back a catch, which is psychologically unacceptable. However, limiting the number of trips may also fail, particularly where the restriction takes the form of a trip every other day. The unpredictability of the catch day by day makes people resent alternate day systems. In addition, alternate day fishing may interfere with traditional methods of redistribution, in which the better-off lend their equipment to less well-off group members, but become disinclined to do this when boats may only go out every other day. In general, schemes to limit fishing succeed where technology and social relations are favourable, in a context in which all individual members are similarly placed with respect to market and environmental conditions.

The importance of a clear economic gain from group activity is emphasized likewise by Bianchi who in Chapter 5 looks at producer associations in southern Italy and NE Brazil. There was a clear economic advantage to be had from collective action in all Bianchi's cases. What he emphasizes is that in each case the potential was harnessed by effective leadership.

In NE Brazil, groups producing and marketing sisal and cashew nuts, respectively, increased income, employment and productivity, performing efficiency and claims functions. In southern Italy, buffalo milk producer groups had a distinct impact by exerting controls over the quality of their product, thereby increasing their market, and by learning to spread buffalo pregnancies through the year to bring seasonal fluctuations in production closer to seasonal fluctuations in demand. The catalyst in all cases was access to a market niche, obtained with external support. In all three cases, the focus on a particular product was crucial, both as the source of a marketing opportunity and also to eliminate potential conflict between producers with different product interests. A common ideology, liberation theology preached by the radical arm of the Catholic Church, unified the groups in NE Brazil. Group members shared a recognition of the urgency of making common cause against the rich and powerful.

In Bianchi's cases, the internal differentiation of each group, and elements of P/C at the local level, allowed leadership to emerge in the context of mainly COOP relationships. Yet P/C at the local level in contexts such as those of NE Brazil and southern Italy often leads to abuse. The secret lies, Bianchi argues, in learning what fosters the kind of group that attracts socially conscious and effective local leaders. It is also important to understand what permits members to delegate a degree of autonomy to these leaders. It may be the homogeneity of values that allows clarification of and agreement on group goals. Some form of democratic control by members is clearly important here. Alternatively, it may be a hierarchical local social structure that makes some form of leadership acceptable, as in the southern Italy case. High quality leaders in turn were clearly attracted by having enough autonomy of decision-making to be able to achieve their goals.

In Chapter 6, Burmeister *et al.* look at producer associations in a very different context: Korea and Taiwan during the period of strong agricultural growth from 1960 to 1980. As with most producer associations covered in this book, efficiency goals are peculiarly effectively achieved through informal cooperation, in which trust and group identity are used to sustain cooperation. In this case the groups are concerned with the supply of inputs, the marketing of the crop (rice), and the provision of extension services. The feedback, informal collaboration, and close interest of farmers allowed the provision of services—especially the supply of fertilizer—to be well tailored to local conditions. The voice given to farmers helped to ensure that the detail of policies, and even their overall shape, were well matched to local needs.

The source of success in both Korea and Taiwan came from a blend of P/C and COOP. The origins and context of the groups are clearly P/C: these were state initiatives in a top-down context, embedded in an authoritarian culture. The state origin resulted in a structure within the producer association that mirrored that of the state and facilitated coordination. Yet cleverly, they were able to benefit from the egalitarian structure and COOP traditions of the countryside, the result of early land reform and cooperative labour traditions evolved to manage rice irrigation and seasonal labour needs.

The chapter allows us to flesh out the elements that foster a COOP mode that successfully modifies the inherent rigidity of P/C. The authors draw attention to the fact that in Taiwan, in contrast to Korea, officials of the association are farmers themselves, with levels of education and income similar to those of the members, and there is much movement of staff between levels, increasing information flows, and the impact of farmer-members' preferences. In Taiwan, extension agents go to village meetings, whereas in Korea the local leaders are more typically summoned to the regional office. Local activity is fostered and strengthened by funding arrangements that increase dependence on local sources in Taiwan: rural industrialization makes this possible.

In Chapter 7, Thorp discusses a large and successful producer association, the Coffee Federation of Colombia, that has been in existence for over seventy years. She analyses the factors contributing to success, and asks how far that success is put in jeopardy by the recent shift in paradigm, and with what consequences. She demonstrates how collective action, facilitated over time by groups, and by the complex culture and institutions which come to underpin them, may be threatened by market reforms which fail to recognize the importance of collective action and the conditions underpinning it, especially in a market-dominated world. She shows the importance of collective action in a situation where high quality coffee has been produced by thousands of small producers for well over fifty years. The coffee must be carefully monitored, warehoused, and marketed internationally. All of this required group action over time. Tiny family farms based on family labour provide a successful solution to the principal agent challenge of careful and selective picking that is essential to the quality of the coffee. The elite that formed and have always run the Federation have had a strong understanding of both micro- and macro-political and economic considerations. The result is a mix of P/C and COOP which facilitates M, resonating with the Taiwanese and Korean stories, despite the fact that Colombia lacks their relative rural equity.

Thorp argues that the macro-role of the Coffee Federation has depended crucially on its micro-role, and vice versa. Sufficient numbers of small producers believed in 'their' organization that they could constitute a tax base, and provide important political support, for the Federation. The macro-international bargaining role and the internal finessing of diversification out of coffee gave the coffee sector a longer and more stable life over time than would have been likely had the Federation not existed in its elitist-yet-mass form.

However, the Federation intervenes in coffee marketing in ways unacceptable to free marketeers. External advisers such as the World Bank have recommended modifying the Federation, or even abolishing it. The chapter suggests that this would deprive Colombian policy makers of important mechanisms for delivering rural services and productivity improvements in the countryside.

Sneath (Chapter 8) has a parallel interest in recent market reforms. He focuses on the decollectivization of the Mongolian pastoral economy. He argues that the reformers' inadequate understanding of the role of groups and what was necessary to sustain them in the collectivist era is at least in part responsible for the very poor performance of pastoral production since the reforms of the early 1990s. Among other factors contributing to the poor performance were the removal of subsidies and decline in prices and market opportunities associated with the separation of the Mongolian livestock economy from the former Soviet Union.

Economies of scale have always been an essential feature of Mongolia's pastoral economy, since animals have to be pastured over huge arid and semi-arid areas, with careful attention to seasonality to avoid livestock loss. Sneath recounts a fascinating history, wherein first the vast monastic estates and then collective farms provided a solid institutional foundation within which traditional encampments, or groups of nomadic households, could exist, on a basis of COOP within a P/C structure. The latter included command over labour and regulation of access to pasture. Special teams were organized to take stock to distant pastures at times of fodder shortage.

In 1991, all state and collective enterprises were privatized, some initially in the form of cooperatives. Much of the infrastructure vanished. Officials of the former collectives no longer regulated access to pasture, and families became reluctant to move between different pastures, at least partly 'for fear that their best pastures may be used by others if they vacate them' (p. 169).

By the second half of the 1990s, most of the cooperatives had gone bankrupt or ceased trading. As the lack of infrastructure and poor market conditions took their toll, and prices fell, members preferred to resort to family networks to procure and sell goods. The result was a catastrophic fall in production and increased inequality. Sneath concludes that the reformers failed to understand the role of non-market relations in sustaining collective action and economies of scale in the previous system. Important infrastructure is no longer available, and there is no longer that degree of trust that allows people to know, for example, that they can safely engage in seasonal patterns of movement, and commit their assets to joint trading arrangements.

As in the studies by Thorp and Burmeister *et al.*, Agarwal in Chapter 9 has focused on groups which have a clear efficiency function recognized by the authorities. She looks at community forest groups in India and Nepal. The Indian government has recognized that the task of regenerating and protecting the forest can only be done with the participation of the community. Agarwal finds convincing evidence of the beneficial effect of the groups she studies, on income, employment, and regeneration. But the equity outcomes of these groups' activities are not favourable for women. Agarwal focuses on groups where the male members operate in COOP mode. She argues that many women have low participation in formal structures, and when they are present, little voice. (The few all-women groups have small areas of poor quality forest land.) Yet women sometimes do the work of patrolling—even setting up their own patrol to parallel the men's, on the grounds that the men's patrol is ineffective. Moreover, they bear the heaviest costs of forest closure—for example, it is they who have to go further afield to find firewood—while they get a disproportionately low share of the benefits. The result of female exclusion is to reduce the efficiency as well as the equity of the groups, forcing women into rule violations, depriving the organization of women's detailed knowledge of the forest and of women's ability to patrol, and of their role in conflict resolution.

This exclusion is shown to proceed from rules, norms, and perceptions in the wider society, as well as the attributes and endowments of households and of women themselves, a theme further developed in relation to our second and third types of groups. Agarwal describes the disabling dark side of many social norms. The hierarchy that marks what is 'respectful' behaviour in the family gets carried over into community space—women sitting on the floor at the back, for example, while men sit at the front on chairs or cots. Perceptions are readily internalized too—'women can't make any helpful suggestions' (p. 199). Levels of education and limited experience create vicious circles.

However, norms, rules, and even perceptions can be changed—and this can be in part the work of groups as well. In the final section, Agarwal develops a bargaining model to elucidate processes that can help to generate change, *vis-à-vis* the state, the community, and the family. The role of other groups such as NGOs, and the role of group solidarity and support, are given prominence here.

15.2.2. *Groups with a Primary Claims Function*

In Chapter 10, Mahmud looks at groups which have a primary claims function and also an efficiency function: women's groups in rural Bangladesh. She reviews the general literature on women's groups in rural Bangladesh and then summarizes the results of a study of four poor rural women's groups that function as COOP groups with elements of P/C. Contrary to what one might expect in a traditional, patriarchal environment, claims groups which also have efficiency functions have worked rather well. Their success is closely related to homogeneity of membership, clear rules on exclusion and inclusion, and the specific activities of the group. In the cases studied by Mahmud the key activity is the creation of a savings fund, which promotes a sense of unity and solidarity, as well as bargaining power; it furthers a healthy democratic decision-making process concerning its development and use; and it holds the group together. The most important effects of these groups overall appear to be the 'self esteem, self-confidence, empowerment [and] mutual support' that might bring 'benefits to growth and development' in the longer run (p. 224). Mahmud finds evidence that COOP is valued for itself, for creating solidarity and empowerment. Male family members support these groups, benefiting from the loans and other gains that women bring to their households. The groups have had strong political and NGO backing.

The efficiency outcomes of these groups are generally assessed as positive, but rather limited, particularly considering the relatively long time some of the groups have been in existence. The women's own perceptions of the gains may have been exaggerated by their tendency to undervalue their time. The success of the groups in creating a political base for women, and important elements of support and solidarity, the claims function, is clearer.

In Chapter 11, Gooptu's analysis of sex workers in Calcutta takes further some of the issues raised by Mahmud. She shows that one of the most diverse, fragmented, internally competitive, and conflictual sets of individuals can become an effective claims group. She emphasizes the role of opposition to oppression, as do Mahmud and Bianchi. As did the oppressed and impoverished small farmers of NE Brazil, so the 'socially marginalized and stigmatized' sex workers of Calcutta created a positive identity. Gooptu also confirms one of the insights of Mahmud's study: the valuing of COOP for itself, as a force for empowerment.

Gooptu's case study traces the formation of an organization of poorer sex workers, the DMSC. Beginning in 1995, and arising out of NGO and public sector concern for health in the face of the AIDS epidemic, the DMSC found a way to create a group from unlikely candidates. The DMSC started with collective action for sex workers to achieve legal recognition and to defend themselves against abuse and violence. The secret of the DMSC's success was a growing capacity to create a positive identity that was enabling, leading for example to social responsibility being manifested where previously it was immobilized, in action against child prostitution and AIDS prevention. The results reinforced self-esteem and capacity, vividly expressed throughout the interviews in metaphors of liberation, dark and light: 'I felt I was released from a closed room and could see the sunlight' (p. 236).

Among Gooptu's conclusions are that the NGO behind the initiative recognized the need to construct community, where most development interventions presume it already exists. The NGO was also prepared to support initiatives which led to empowerment, and the creation of the DMSC which engaged directly in political action.

15.2.3. *Groups with a Primary* pro bono *Function*

Each of the studies here takes up the theme that Thorp and Sneath develop: the importance of understanding modes of operation as paradigms shift. They all also give pride of place to the role of norms conditioning how groups function and how effective they are in meeting their *pro bono* objectives.

In Chapter 12, Mackintosh and Gilson synthesize a wide sweep of empirical literature on non-market relationships in health care, and echo Gooptu and Agarwal in emphasizing the role of norms in explaining behaviour. The chapter focuses on the importance of understanding the logic of non-market behaviour and the ways in which it changes as paradigms shift. The policy areas which Mackintosh and Gilson review are central to the move to more market-oriented health care systems. Much of their analysis is aimed at illuminating the difference between assumptions and actuality, cautioning policy makers about the dangers of making false assumptions about behaviour, whether of groups or of individuals. Their aim is also to demonstrate the importance of understanding the logic of non-market behaviour in order to formulate policies that are useful.

In a rich analysis of five policy areas, the authors discuss non-market behaviour and why it is important for policy makers to understand it. For example, they show that in prescribing exemption from newly introduced fees for health care, the authorities *assume* a mode of behaviour that amounts to unreciprocated free gifts from those who can pay to those who cannot, leading to successful free or reduced price care to pre-identified groups. At the same time, authorities often establish principles of financial sustainability at the health facility level which create incentives that conflict with these exemption policies. Moreover, 'redistributive commitment is often further undermined by conflict with local social hierarchy .... Those with status, prestige, and power within communities frequently obtain free treatment because of who they are ...' (p. 261). An important conclusion is that effective redistribution may require (well-motivated) P/C. Another example discussed is the assumption that mutual health care insurance associations can achieve substantial redistribution to the

poor through intra-group transfers. This assumes that such associations are inclusive, whereas in reality they are not; in particular, they are likely to exclude the poor.
A third example is the discussion of community participation in which Mackintosh
and Gilson point out that 'participation' involves free gifts of time for purposes which
may not be seen as rewarding or even legitimate for the communities or individuals
concerned.

The next chapter, by Tibandebage and Mackintosh explores these insights further in
a detailed study of the health care sector in Tanzania. This is a clear case of a paradigm
shift affecting group behaviour at grass roots levels. Health care is vulnerable during
liberalization, as a result of perverse incentives which encourage health personnel to
provide services to rich patients rather than general services to the poor, and to minimize their efforts unless carefully monitored. Tibandebage and Mackintosh's study
of government and private health facilities provides many examples. At the same time
many instances of good practices are found in all three types of health facility studied
(government, religious, and private sector non-religious), with dedicated health care
personnel doing their best to provide services to those in need.

Tibandebage and Mackintosh's study compares groups which are principally
pro bono (state and charitable health facilities with proclaimed redistributive objectives) with groups which are self-interested (private for-profit health care facilities).
The authors compared two government hospitals, and found, paradoxically, that the
better resourced produced far less efficient and equitable health care, pointing to the
importance of mode of behaviour in determining outcomes. They surveyed a large
number of facilities in the government, religious, and private sector, and found again
that the outcomes varied significantly *within* each category.

The key characteristics that shape access and exclusion vary across types of health
care facilities, and lead the authors to a concept of 'institutional culture', which moder-
ates P/C and makes COOP behaviour work *for* or *against* patients' interests. Hospitals
within the government sector were found to have wide differences in bribery cultures;
practices of abuse of, and distance from, patients; and effectiveness of financial control;
the three elements tending to move together.

The findings lead the authors to focus on the role of 'informal institutional
design': building up and sustaining appropriate informal cultures, through encouraging patients' information and networking, community representation on health care
boards, the rewarding of institutions which reveal ethical behaviour and willingness to
do preventative work, and community negotiation of formal rules to give them legitimacy. As the previous chapter argues, whether COOP behaviour is conducive to equity
depends on the norms, attitudes, and practices behind it.

The final study is our only case explicitly focusing on NGOs. Lorgen's chapter is a
study of indigenous NGOs in Uganda's health sector, which is undergoing a process
of privatization. Lorgen traces the way in which the new emphasis of international
donors on accountability *to them*, and on business-like behaviour, may conflict with
COOP practices. Yet those same COOP practices may sustain NGOs' own type of
accountability to their partners, beneficiaries or members, and may also be a prime
reason why the donors wish to work with NGOs in the first place.

Lorgen looks at two case studies in detail. The first is a community-based health care group, the UCBHCA principally funded by UNICEF, training health workers, traditional birth attendants, and health committees. It operates at the critical point identified by Mackintosh and Gilson, the shaping of 'institutional culture'. The shift in paradigm and the new emphases of donors are creating a change in culture in a direction that undermines the organization's ability to support equity and claims objectives. The UCBHCA is required by funders to move to contracting out its services, but the executive secretary laments: 'As a company, we must be paid for services, but members can't pay. They are poor . . . . So how do we relate to them if we can't give them free services?' (p. 298). The same NGO also has an important lobbying function, but 'is pushed towards being a service organization and away from its "claims" function' (p. 299).

The second study is of an NGO working with AIDS patients, TASO. The group has experienced a huge increase in funding and with that has come 'pressure from its donors to incorporate market-oriented ways of working' (p. 299). What began as a community of sufferers and supporters (of the original sixteen members, twelve have died of AIDS) has had to become a large 'company'. As one donor says, '. . . this guy came and asked TASO: What's your negotiated overhead rate? They had no idea! They're not a firm. They work with communities. We fund them *because* they don't know what this is' (p. 300).

As external funding increases, the donors' agenda acquires more weight and activities that cannot be justified in the language of the market risk being marginalized. The claims function may be particularly compromised by this new dependency as local NGOs that can learn the donors' language and style acquire comparative advantage.

15.3. GENERAL FINDINGS FROM THE CASE STUDIES

15.3.1. *The Impact of Macro-norms on Group Behaviour*

We found evidence of a strong impact of macro-norms on group behaviour, for example, in the shifting behaviour of health sector groups noted by Mackintosh and Gilson, Tibandebage and Mackintosh, and Stewart, as well as in the Coffee Federation in Colombia analysed by Thorp, and in NGO behaviour described by Lorgen. The impact of macro-norms on group behaviour was also a central feature in Agarwal's discussion of gender discrimination in forest groups, and in Sneath's discussion of the collapse of the pastoral economy in Mongolia. In Agarwal's case, societal norms worked against women in what were essentially COOP groups.

The shift in societal norms over the past two decades—from a statist perspective with a restricted role for the market (i.e. predominantly P/C and to some extent COOP), towards strong market orientation—has exerted powerful and effective pressures for micro-institutions to move in a similar direction, in many cases working against COOP. For many groups, especially market failure and *pro bono* groups, it seems to be difficult to avoid these pressures. Moreover, once a group changes its mode of behaviour it too contributes to changing macro-norms. However, we should not assume that such changes are necessarily purely destructive, or that in the presence of predominantly market-oriented macro-norms all groups will invariably shift their mode of operation from P/C and COOP to M. Some groups will do so. But new groups will be formed in reaction to the new circumstances. This has happened in developed countries over time with the weakening of traditional and customary groups: in the nineteenth century, workers' organizations developed in reaction to the *laissez-faire* market; and in the twentieth century, citizens' associations developed in abundance. In Kenya today, customary cooperation among pastoralists has been weakened, but a rich variety of solidarity groups have developed in the urban informal sector.[1] Some groups in our sample challenged the prevailing macro-norms, in particular, the two sets of claims groups (the sex workers associations in India; and the women's groups in Bangladesh). However, the groups challenging the norms are greatly outnumbered by the groups which do not. Macro-norms appear to have a powerful, if not all encompassing, influence on group behaviour.

We should note that a number of the case studies have shown that macro- and societal norms do not always affect outcomes through modes of operation. They also affect outcomes directly, and sometimes independently of modes of operation. Agarwal shows how macro- and societal norms relating to gender affect the outcomes of forest groups regardless of mode of operation. Thus, COOP groups may have very different outcomes in different contexts as the way they operate reflects local norms and social structures. For example, in a strongly market-oriented economy, COOP groups may more often result in forms of rent-seeking than in a P/C or COOP environment.

15.3.2. *Modes of Operation and Outcomes*

An important preliminary consideration here is that our groups were pre-selected to represent success in some degree—that is, we only looked at groups that had survived and were thought to have made a positive contribution to development objectives. We also chose our groups because they had worked with or for poor people. Any conclusions about the impact on efficiency and equity are heavily coloured by this selection bias. Our conclusions must, therefore, be interpreted as showing what groups *can* achieve, not what *all* groups *do*.

The case studies showed clearly that all groups combine modes of behaviour. There is some COOP in every group—groups could not function without it. Some element of P/C also seems unavoidable, and indeed may be desirable or even necessary for group efficiency as we argue below. Groups can, however, function without M—for example, it played a negligible role in the claims groups, and also in some of the market failure groups (e.g. the fishermen), while in the health sector in the strictly P/C era, medical personnel were paid, but the role of financial incentives was subordinate (Stewart). Where M does dominate, elements of P/C and COOP continue. Thus, when we speak of the impact of a particular mode of behaviour, this means a dominant, not an exclusive, mode of behaviour.

[1] These are documented by Baland and Platteau (1998).

While each type of group (market failure, claims, and *pro bono*) contained elements of each of the modes of behaviour, the claims groups tended to be the most COOP. In these cases, COOP was particularly important in fostering empowerment and self-esteem. It was also important in eliciting participation. The *pro bono* groups were frequently strongly P/C, while the market failure groups adopted a combination of the three modes, some being mainly COOP (e.g. the forestry groups, the fishermen), and some mainly P/C (the Coffee Federation and the Korean Farmers' Associations), and some a combination of P/C and COOP (the producer groups discussed by Bianchi and the Taiwan Farmers' Associations).

We note that the functions of groups evolve over time, as do their modes of behaviour. Moreover, groups frequently perform more than one function. The groups primarily aimed at overcoming market failures invariably also made some contribution to claims, many improving the bargaining position of their members *vis-a-vis* other parts of society, especially the government. The claims groups had or acquired some market failure functions, also, for example, providing services for their members. The *pro bono* groups were invariably concerned with both market failure (e.g. overcoming health externalities) and redistribution.

15.3.3. *Modes of Operation and Market Failure Outcomes*

All of our groups whose primary function was to address market failure did indeed do so. These positive efficiency achievements were secured by groups which were predominantly P/C with elements of COOP and M (e.g. farmers' associations in Korea, collectives in Mongolia, the Coffee Federation in Colombia), and also by groups which were predominantly COOP with elements of P/C (the forestry and fishing groups, and the producer associations of NE Brazil).

Some elements of both P/C and COOP seem to be essential for efficiency. COOP reduces monitoring costs, and also achieves efficiency benefits through more effective utilization of local knowledge and better service delivery (the Coffee Federation of Colombia, producers' associations in Korea and Taiwan). Some types of activities by their very nature lend themselves to greater efficiency gains associated with COOP (family monitoring of coffee picking, access to small farmers' expertise in Taiwan and Korea). Not only may there be less need to monitor and enforce with a COOP mode, but also there may be additional positive contributions over and above those that can be elicited through monitoring and enforcement. These contributions include the intrinsic value of the process of cooperation (Mahmud, Gooptu), and things that people do out of goodwill that is inextricably linked with operating in COOP mode (e.g. informal consultation among medical personnel).

The introduction of a strong element of M did not seem to increase the efficiency of the outcome, and indeed may have weakened it, by reducing people's motivation and requiring more transactions workers relative to production workers. In the most extreme case, in Mongolia, the groups were dissolved altogether, replacing them by the market, and this had, at least over the short to medium term, highly adverse effects on efficiency. In the health sector cases, including the NGOs in Uganda, the adoption of a more market-oriented approach has involved charges to the poor who have, therefore, reduced their participation, while more generally financial incentives have tended to reduce people's motivation particularly in relation to important unremunerated tasks. Increasingly, however, in the health sector cases, M (or quasi-markets) are being introduced into group activities supposedly on efficiency grounds, as a means of securing action in line with group objectives. Because these are within-group transactions, a quasi-market has to be introduced and this involves transactions costs which can be heavy, including considerable monitoring. Moreover, quite often, it is difficult to measure and give a monetary valuation to within-group activities (NGOs in Uganda); not only is it costly to do so, but it may distort the operations of the group, as they seek to maximize their contribution to the activities which are measured and rewarded and reduce their contribution elsewhere, especially since some activities are easy to measure or quantify and others are not. The non-measured activities may include activities that are very valuable.

It seems that COOP is an essential element in efficient outcomes, and this can be undermined by too strong an element of M (Lorgen, Sneath). It can also be weakened by conflict within the group. For example, where fishermen came from different places, Gaspart and Platteau report reduced COOP and collective action.

Technical factors may also make collective action solutions non-viable because monitoring requirements are excessive or the gains are insufficient (cf. Gaspart and Platteau). It also appeared that a leader or outside agent was required in many of the successful COOP groups, to take the initiative (Thorp, Bianchi, Mahmud). COOP may also fail because the general political, ideological, and institutional climate is hostile (Sneath, and Lorgen), an example of the influence of the macro-environment over particular groups' behaviour.

In general, however, because COOP is difficult to sustain in pure form, and because it may not be efficient when activities become large and complex, it usually needs to be backed up by some P/C or M. In associations of buffalo mozarella producers in southern Italy, for example, (democratic) COOP decision-making in relation to rules, fines, and penalties, is combined with the strict imposition of fines and penalties on members who do not obey the rules (Bianchi); and Indian forest groups organize themselves cooperatively to monitor, and impose sanctions on, transgressors of their rules (Agarwal).

There is a strong suggestion by Mackintosh and Gilson that in *pro bono* groups, P/C is more effective than COOP in 'delivering the goods', because with too much COOP group members try to garner the benefits for themselves. Tibandebage and Mackintosh argue powerfully from health sector experiences in Tanzania that COOP embedded in certain types of norms may lead to very inequitable results in *pro bono* groups, for example, through bribery, overcharging, and exclusion from care of those least equipped to defend themselves (i.e. lacking resources and education).

Further, P/C may be needed to provide leadership, even in groups that are predominantly COOP, as, for example, in Bianchi's groups. Accountability and democracy can reconcile leadership with COOP, keeping P/C within limits (as in Bianchi's Brazilian cases).

15.3.4. *Modes of Operation and Equity Outcomes*

In analysing the impact on equity, it is necessary to differentiate within group equity from equity relating to those outside the group; and to consider whether the distribution in either respect meets an ideal of reaching the poorest. One also needs to differentiate between the three types of group, market failure, claims, and *pro bono*.

The objective of our groups with primary market failure functions was to improve efficiency, not equity. However, as the groups were formed among poor people, their success in remedying market failure meant that they usually contributed to the equity objective as well. The extent to which they did so evidently varied according to who were members of the group (i.e. whether the group included rich as well as poor producers) and the distribution of benefits within the group. For example, the Coffee Federation included large as well as small producers and the poor certainly benefited, but the rich benefited more. This was a predominantly P/C organization, and the distribution of benefits reflected the internal distribution of power. Both the P/C mode and the unequal sharing of benefits reflected the inequality of power and resources among members of the group, independently of its formation. The benefits of the farmer associations of Taiwan and Korea appear to have been shared more equally, even though these had strong P/C elements. What was important was that the groups were formed among rather homogeneous sets of farmers (Burmeister *et al.*).

Market failure groups adopting COOP as a way of solving a collective action problem, tend to be associated with relatively equal shares of the benefits among participants. The benefits were broadly equally shared within the group among the fishermen (whose groups were largely COOP organizations) and among the (male) members of the forestry groups (COOP organizations), as well as members of the producer groups in NE Brazil (P/C and COOP). Sometimes, however, considerable within-group inequity is tolerated, because it is perceived that the leaders contribute to the achievement of the goals of the group and societal norms sanction such inequality. Thorp argues this for the Colombian Coffee Federation. Bianchi maintains that leadership is the key to the successful formation and continuation of his COOP groups. His groups *required* some inequality, leaders standing out from the rest of the membership. There were elements of this among Mahmud's rural women's groups in Bangladesh too.

The claims groups tended to exhibit relatively equitable within-group distribution and generally increased the share of societal resources secured by their members. Since the ones we studied were formed among the relatively poor, they contributed to a more egalitarian society.

The *pro bono* groups aim at improving the well-being of people outside the group itself, the 'target' groups being the relatively poor. Where effective, they, therefore, improve societal distribution. But as noted earlier, Mackintosh and Gilson suggest that they are not always effective in this regard: in COOP groups rent-seeking results in the group itself taking many of the benefits, while with M the poor tend to be excluded. A P/C mode may be more effective in reaching the target group, although within-group equity may be less.

The adoption of an M mode tends to be unequalizing within the group relative to COOP, as people are rewarded according to their skills and productivity, but this can lead to more equality than P/C. The distributional impact of M outside the group also tends to be unequalizing, as only those who can pay receive the benefits. Tibandebage and Mackintosh show this happening as user charges were introduced in the health sector in Tanzania. Lorgen shows how pressures towards more M make it more difficult to reach the poor in the case of Ugandan NGOs for other reasons as well. However, the other modes of operation don't always reach the poor either.

In each of our cases, poor members of the groups achieved some gain, the gains generally being more equally shared among the more COOP groups. However, many of the groups *excluded* some poorer sections of the community—women, in the case of the forestry groups, some very poor and itinerant fishermen in the case of Senegal, poor farmers not producing coffee in Colombia. Those who were excluded not only did not benefit, but in some cases actually lost, as resources were diverted away from them to the group concerned. Thus, we can conclude that on balance, the poorer sections of society gained by the activities of the groups we observed, but the very poorest did not, and some of the excluded lost. The problem is that groups generally need to be exclusive to function, to sustain loyalty and commitment, and to keep conflict to a manageable level (see Mahmud). The distributional impact then depends on who is included, and who is excluded. Some of the groups deliberately excluded wealthier people (e.g. the women's groups in Bangladesh, even though they excluded some of the very poor too); others included richer members (the Coffee Federation in Colombia). The former had a more egalitarian impact than the latter.

Our general conclusions on outcomes are that groups formed among the poor can contribute to enhanced efficiency, equity, *and* empowerment. They require some COOP to achieve the efficiency objective, combined with P/C, and efficiency may be raised with some M. But if either P/C or M is carried to the point that it undermines COOP, the efficiency function may be impaired. As far as equity is concerned, the impact is likely to vary according to the type of group and its mode of behaviour. COOP is more likely to be consistent with within-group equity than P/C, although the fact of a dominant P/C mode often reflects unequal power among members, and it is this as well as P/C as such which delivers inequality. For both market failure and claims groups, whether the overall societal impact is equitable depends above all on whether the groups include the poorer members of society or exclude them. Rich men's clubs obviously do not improve distribution; poor people's generally do. *Pro bono* groups are in a different position: if they succeed in their aims, they do, by definition, improve societal equity, but their success can be diluted or even nullified by rent-seeking. P/C may be better at reaching the poor outside the group than COOP to the extent that it is better at preventing diversion of resources through rent-seeking. But M, which is designed to counter rent-seeking, often legalizes it, strengthening discrimination against the poor. A dominant M mode is unlikely to produce either within-group equity, or societal equity. Where M becomes too dominant it can threaten both efficiency and equity, although in a subordinate role it can contribute to both.

The discussion above has demonstrated the importance of the distinction between the three types of group functions. In general, claims groups are more likely to be COOP, and more likely to have outcomes that are within-group equitable. Market failure groups are often less equitable—both within and between groups. When formed among the poor, however, such groups increase societal equity. *Pro bono* groups are paternalistic (P/C) by their nature, but may also have elements of COOP since the philosophy of many NGOs performing such functions is COOP, and this will tend to have some impact on group mode. They are intended to provide benefits to people who are less well off than the group members, that is, broadly to improve societal equity. However, as noted earlier, whatever the primary function of a particular group, most groups have other functions as a secondary aspect. The overlap in functions again emphasizes the fact that groups formed among poor people are likely to improve societal equity, not only by improving incomes but also by increasing political and bargaining power.

15.3.5. *The Implications of the Current Market Reforms*

If we put these conclusions on modes and outcomes together with our findings on the impact of macro-norms on group modes of behaviour, then the present situation appears alarming. The market paradigm has become dominant at a macro level, and is visibly pushing groups in this direction, threatening the very existence of some (e.g. the Colombian Coffee Federation and collectives in Mongolia), and transforming the behaviour of many others (health and education services the world over, NGOs, and so on). The new thinking undervalues COOP, tending to identify it with its most negative manifestations of rent-seeking and mutual back-scratching in the state-led industrialization period, thereby risking undermining the valuable aspects of COOP. COOP by developing trust can give people confidence in norms and rules, allow information to circulate, reduce uncertainty and thereby assist investment and growth. It can also increase commitment and reduce alienation. The new market-oriented paradigm also typically fails to understand the prevalence of self-serving P/C and how it tends to subvert the outcomes of M, particularly with regard to equity (Sneath's study of Mongolia is a graphic illustration). Moreover, the introduction of more M aimed at stimulating competitive behaviour may change the way people act more generally, with seriously damaging results particularly to COOP. The tension is most explicitly discussed in Lorgen's case study, in which it is argued that M and COOP are in direct conflict in the case of Ugandan NGOs in the health sector, as the role of M increases. As donors' agendas shift in the direction of market criteria, the conflict worsens. The current orthodoxy, Stewart argues, adopts an inconsistent and unsatisfactory solution to these tensions, in advocating, on the one hand, more M, and on the other, the construction of social capital. 'There is an inherent inconsistency between giving an overriding role to a market model of development, based on individual maximizing behaviour, and the adoption of more socially oriented norms' (p. 49). The universal presumption in favour of M in every arena needs to be abandoned. Non-market behaviour needs to be valued and protected as well.

15.3.6. *Theoretical Implications*

We have shown groups to be pervasive, and we have shown that their behaviour has a significant impact on development outcomes. The increasing prominence given to 'social capital' and to micro-institutional incentives and outcomes by those working in the neoclassical tradition represents a partial recognition of this. But we conclude that it is necessary to go beyond such analysis in important respects:

(1) recognizing that mode of behaviour and outcomes are heavily influenced by the prevalent macro-norms, to which they also contribute;
(2) recognizing the important role of a social perspective in understanding groups that is not based on individual maximizing behaviour and is non-transactional;
(3) recognizing the importance of groups that perform claims and *pro bono* functions as well as those performing market failure functions, whereas current economic analysis of institutions focuses heavily on groups performing market failure functions;
(4) recognizing the pervasive role of COOP and P/C as well as M, in contrast to the neoclassical analysis of institutions which essentially assumes that M is dominant, and that other modes (P/C or COOP) generally represent an inefficient deviation from this.

A broad theoretical conclusion which stands out from our studies is the poverty of a framework asserting the primacy of material advancement as the sole criterion for action, and evaluation of that action. Some of the most effective cases among those examined give primacy to self-fulfilment, identity, and empowerment which are promoted by (and also contribute to) group formation (Gooptu, Agarwal, Bianchi, Mahmud, Lorgen). This conclusion is reinforced by the theoretical analysis of Alkire and Deneulin. Identity and empowerment are valuable in themselves: this is difficult to deny after reading the account of the sex workers of Calcutta. But identity and empowerment also have instrumental value. For Bianchi, for example, identity constructed around opposition to oppression allows the group to hold together through bad times and achieve market failure and claims functions in the longer run.

The poverty of a framework that focuses primarily on the individual is also demonstrated in this book. It is not sufficient to adopt an individual maximizing framework and only to take norms and perceptions into account in the formation of individual preferences. This would lose the insights of, for example, the work on the health sector reported here, which shows how by *starting* from the role of norms and beliefs, it is possible to predict and interpret failures and perverse policy outcomes. Gooptu's account of sex workers in Calcutta can only be interpreted within a framework that recognizes that collective interest may override individual interest. She gives us the important insight that identity forged through political action can be powerful in its own right. This is also demonstrated by Bianchi's account of the small producers of NE Brazil. These conclusions are reinforced by the observation that groups may evolve, so that a group which can initially be well analysed from the perspective of the individual maximizing economist's paradigm, may become one where the real gains have to do, say, with changing identity (and vice versa). These points lead us to stress the value of using multiple frameworks to achieve a full understanding of the role of groups in the development process.

15.3.7. *Policy Implications*

Our intention in this study was to open up debate on issues which are vital for patterns of development today, and which get missed in much of the general discussion of development issues. While there are policy implications, this was not the main point of the study. Nevertheless, important policy conclusions follow.

Our findings suggest that the recent paradigm shift towards enhancing the market is undervaluing COOP and placing excessive emphasis on M for efficient and equitable group functioning. If this were widely accepted it would modify policies influencing macro-norms in important directions, although norms are the outcome of a myriad of influences and the direct influence may be limited. Our findings also suggest concrete policies directed towards groups at the micro-level. Moreover, as societal norms at a macro-level are constituted by individuals' and groups' beliefs and behaviour, changing micro-behaviour will also contribute to macro-change. However, many of our cases demonstrate how history can surprise us—groups evolve with unforeseen consequences. For this reason, heavy-handed overly precise policy recommendations could be counterproductive. Moreover, given the overwhelming importance of macro-influences, the contribution of micro-changes is likely to be secondary.

At the macro-level, we are calling for a change in philosophy, towards more recognition of the value of collective action and of COOP, and more support for values, actions, general policies, and projects which support them. This support should recognize the potential negative aspects of COOP (rent-seeking, back-scratching) and seek institutional innovations and improvements to monitor and control them. Institutional frameworks should, in general, support a modified evolution of the market model with a greater role for group action, in both market failure and claims roles. Policy makers, NGOs, and educators, all need to be made more aware that M measures that may appear desirable for efficiency reasons when viewed in isolation, may form part of a cumulative erosion of values and norms that underpin both equity and efficiency. They also need to understand that such measures may fail if they falsely assume the presence of the values and norms presupposed by the market.

Governments have direct influence or control over large areas of activity: for example, direct control over systems of health care and education in many countries; considerable influence over credit allocation; power to determine property rights; and so on. In each of these (and many other) areas, the current trend is towards a reduced role for the state and an increased role for the private sector, and within state-supported areas more use of financial incentives, less use of COOP. We have suggested that these changes in mode of behaviour are threatening not only equity but also efficiency. Our study suggests that in each area, the costs of excessive marketization need to be recognized, COOP needs to be sustained, and the role of financial incentives needs to be limited. This is not to support a rent-seeking structure: monitoring and penalties are needed to prevent this. But legitimizing rent-seeking via marketization does not eliminate its ill-effects.

Groups formed among the poor empower them and increase their control over resources. The poor achieve far more working together than operating individually. Hence, policies need to support the formation of groups among the poor. Ways in which this can be achieved include:

(1) increased backing and support for departments or ministries of cooperatives with explicit briefs to include the poor;
(2) credit systems which favour groups of poor people. This can be achieved by regulations of the banking system that demand a certain proportion of loans to low-income activities (as in India).[2] Strong government and international support for particular institutions can also work in this direction, as in the case, for example, of the development of the Grameen Bank and other institutions in Bangladesh. While these were mainly the results of the initiatives of a few individuals who formed powerful NGOs, their widespread effects stem from the strong support they gained from the government and the international community;
(3) legal, financial, and technical support for groups formed to enhance the claims of the poor. This would include legal systems which make it straightforward to form small-scale collectives; and the legal recognition of group ownership of assets;
(4) policies to promote work on the valuation of non-market returns to be included in any evaluation of group activities. Valuation of these returns can be a means of protecting groups such as NGOs and communities against the pressures of shifting paradigms (cf. chapter by Lorgen);
(5) work in the area of 'informal institutional design' to identify ways of fostering information flows, trust, and voice so that the balance of norms and attitudes within groups favours equity. NGOs can play a useful role in this regard, as indicated by the study of Bangladesh women's groups;
(6) development of appropriate training for people to initiate and develop group formation among the poor;
(7) policies to contribute to the institutional needs of macroeconomic restructuring: these should pay attention to the role of groups as facilitators, and to the possible vulnerability of groups which become exposed to competition too abruptly.

On the negative side, it is important to try to ensure that the poor do not get excluded by the development of groups, and that abuse of power within and by groups is controlled and regulated. Fostering democratic institutions and safeguards in the society at large may be helpful; so may strengthening institutions that support enforcement, conflict resolution, etc. Competition laws can reduce monopolies, and abuse of power.

Specific policy suggestions will differ from country to country and must depend on the context. But since the broad sweep of changing paradigms in the world today is

[2] This regulation accounts for the development of the successful Self-Employed Women's Association in India (SEWA) for example.

almost universal, the direction of change, if not the specific changes, is also likely to be so. In this book, we have tried to open up the area of group activity for research, discussion, and policy, and to do so by widening the theoretical perspective taken beyond an individual maximizing approach. In the light of this work, we are convinced that there is an urgent need to question and modify the prevailing analytic and policy paradigm, and much that can be done to do so.

References

Abel-Smith, B. (1987). 'Review of 'Financing health services in developing countries: An agenda for reform''. *Health Policy and Planning*, 2(4): 355–6.

—— and Rawal, P. (1982). 'Can the poor afford "free" health services? A case study of Tanzania'. *Health Policy and Planning*, 7(4): 329–41.

—— —— (1994). 'Employers' willingness to pay: The case for compulsory health insurance in Tanzania'. *Health Policy and Planning*, 9(4): 409–18.

Adhikari, N., Yadav, G., Ray, S. B., and Kumar, S. (1991). 'Process documentation of women's involvement in forest management at Maheshpur, Ranchi,' in R. Singh (ed.), *Managing the Village Commons, Proceedings of the National Workshop*, 15–16 Dec. 1991, Indian Institute of Forest Management, Bhopal, pp. 118–23.

Agarwal, A. (1999). 'State formation in community spaces: Control over forests in the Kumaon Himalaya, India'. Paper prepared for presentation at the University of California, Berkeley. Workshop on Environmental Politics, 30 April 1999.

Agarwal, B. (1987). 'Under the cooking pot: The political economy of the domestic fuel crisis in rural South Asia', *IDS Bulletin*, 18(1): 11–22.

—— (1994). *A Field of One's Own: Gender and Land Rights in South Asia*. Cambridge: Cambridge University Press.

—— (1997a). 'Environmental action, gender equity and women's participation'. *Development and Change*, 28(1): 1–44.

—— (1997b). ' "Bargaining" and gender relations: Within and beyond the household'. *Feminist Economics*, 3(1): 1–51.

—— (2000a). 'Group functioning and community forestry: A gender perspective'. Helsinki: WIDER, Working Paper No. 172.

—— (2000b). 'Conceptualizing environmental collective action: Why gender matters'. *Cambridge Journal of Economics*, 24(3): 283–310.

—— (2001). 'Gender inequaltiy, cooperation and environmental sustainability'. Paper presented at the conference on inequality, collective action and environmental sustainability, Santa Fe Institute, Santa Fe, New Mexico, 21–23 September.

Ahn, K. (1997). 'Trends in and determinants of income distribution in Korea'. *Journal of Economic Development*, 22: 27–56.

Akerlof, G. (1997). 'Social distance and social decisions'. *Econometrica*, 65(5): 1005–27.

Akerlof, G. A. (1983). 'Loyalty filters'. *American Economic Review*, 73(1): 54–63.

—— and Kranton, R. E. (1998). 'Economics and identity'. Russell Sage Foundation Working Paper 136. New York: Russell Sage Foundation.

—— —— (2000). 'Economics and identity'. *Quarterly Journal of Economics*, 115(3): 715–53.

All India Institute of Hygiene and Public Health (1997). *A Dream, A Pledge, A Fulfilment: Five Years' Stint at Sonagachi*, Calcutta, AIIH&PH, November.

Almy, S. (1998). 'Vertical societies and co-operative structures: Problems of fit in Northeastern Brazil', in D. W. Attwood and B. S. Baviskar (eds), *Who Shares: Co-operatives and Rural Development*. Oxford: Oxford University Press, pp. 46–68.

Amin, S. (1974). *Accumulation on a World Scale: A Critique of the Theory of Underdevelopment*. New York: Monthly Review Press.

Amin, S. and Pebley A. R. (1994). 'Gender inequality within households: The impact of a women's development programme in 36 Bangladeshi villages', *Bangladesh Development Studies*, 22 (2–3), 121–54.

Amsden, A. (1989). *Asia's Next Giant: South Korea and Late Industrialisation*. New York: Oxford University Press.

Anyimawi, C. A. (1989). 'The social cost of the International Monetary Fund's adjustment programs for poverty: The case of health care development in Ghana'. *International Journal of Health Services*, 19(3): 531–47.

Aoki, M. (2001). 'Community norms and embeddedness: A game theoretic approach', in Aoki and Hayami (eds), *Communities and Markets in Economic Development*. Oxford: Oxford University Press, pp. 97–125.

APAEB (various years) 'Relatorio Anual', Valente, Feira de Santana, Bahia: Grafica Modelo.

Apthorpe, R. (1974). 'The burden of land reform in Taiwan: An Asian model land reform re-analyzed'. *World Development*, 7: 519–30.

Aqua, R. (1974). *Local Government and Rural Development in South Korea*. Ithaca: Rural Development Committee, Center for International Studies, Cornell University.

Ardyn Erh, No. 193 (1411). 27 Sept. 1996.

Aristotle (1994). *Ethique à Nicomaque*, J. Tricot (trans.), librairie Vrin: Paris.

Arrow, K. J. (1963). *Social Choice and Individual Values*. New York: John Wiley & Sons, Cowles Foundation for Research in Economics at Yale University.

—— Sen, A. K., and Suzumara, K. (1997). *Social Choice Re-Examined*, vols 1&2. Basingstoke: MacMillan.

Arul, N. J. and Poffenburger, M. (1990). 'FPC Case Studies', in R. S. Pathan, N. J. Arul, and M. Poffenburger (eds), *Forest Protection Committees in Gujarat: Joint Management Initiative*. Ford Foundation, New Delhi, Working Paper No. 7, pp. 13–25.

Ashana, S. (1994). 'Economic crisis, adjustment and the impact on health', in D. R. Phillips and Y. Verhasselt (eds), *Health and Development*. Routledge: London and New York, pp. 50–64.

Asian Development Bank (1992). *Mongolia: A Centrally Planned Economy in Transition*. Oxford, Oxford University Press.

—— (1994). 'Agricultural sector study of Mongolia'. Division 1, Agricultural Department, Feb. 1994.

Atim, C. (1999). 'Social movements and health insurance: A critical evaluation of voluntary, non-profit insurance schemes with case studies from Ghana and Cameroons'. *Social Science and Medicine*, 48: 881–96.

Atkinson, A. B. (ed.) (1993). *Alternatives to Capitalism: The Economics of Partnership*. Basingstoke: MacMillan.

Attwood, D. W. and Baviskar, B. S. (1987). 'Why do some co-operatives work but not others? A comparative analysis of sugar co-operatives in India'. *Economic and Political Weekly*, 22(26): A38–45.

—— and Baviskar, G. (1985). 'Co-operatives in anthropological perspective. Report of a symposium on co-operatives and rural development'. *Economic and Political Weekly*, 20(1): 18–19.

Avineri, S. and De-Shalit, A. (1992). *Communitarianism and Individualism*. Oxford: Oxford University Press.

Axelrod, R. A. (1984). *The Evolution of Cooperation*. New York: Basic Books.

Ayres, I. and Braithwaite, J. (1992). *Responsive Regulation: Transcending the Deregulation Debate*. Oxford: Oxford University Press.

Badhwar, N. K. (1996). 'Moral agency, commitment and impartiality'. *Social Philosophy and Policy*, 13(1): pp. 1–26.

Bain, I. (1993). *Agricultural Reform in Taiwan: From Here to Modernity?* Hong Kong: The Chinese University Press.

Baland, J.-M. and Platteau, J.-P. (1995). 'Does heterogeneity hinder collective action?' *Cahiers de la Faculte Economique et Sociales*, 146. Namur: Centre de Recherche en Economie du Developpement.

——— (1996). *Halting Degradation of Natural Resources—Is There a Role for Rural Communities?* Oxford: Clarendon Press.

——— (1998). 'Participation in informal solidarity groups in a poor urban environment: The case of Kibera, Nairobi'. Namur: Centre de Recherche en Economie du Developpement.

——— (1999). 'The ambiguous impact of inequality on local resource management'. *World Development*, 27(5): 773–88.

Balassa, B. (1971). *The Structure of Protection in Developing Countries*. Baltimore: John Hopkins Press.

Baldwin, R., Scott, C., and Hood, C. (1998a). 'Introduction', in Baldwin, Scott, and Hood (eds), *A Reader on Regulation*. Oxford: Oxford University Press, pp. 1–55.

——— ——— (eds) (1998b). *A Reader on Regulation*. Oxford: Oxford University Press.

Ban, S. H. (1979). 'Agricultural growth in Korea, 1918–1971', in Y. Hayami *et al.* (eds), *Agricultural Growth in Japan, Taiwan, Korea and the Philippines*. Honolulu: University of Hawaii, pp. 90–116.

——— (1982). 'The growth of agricultural output and productivity in Korea, 1918–1978', in C.-M. Hon and T.-S. Yu (eds), *Agricultural Development in China, Japan and Korea*. Taipei: Academia Sinica.

——— Moon, P. Y., and Perkins, D. H. (1980). *Rural Development*. Cambridge, MA: Harvard University Press.

Bandyopadhyay, S. (not dated). *They Speak Their Word: A Note on the Education Programme for the Calcutta Sex Workers*. Calcutta: All India Institute for Health and Public Health.

——— (not dated). *Amader A -Aa-Ka-Kha [Our ABC]: Learning to Read, Write and Rise*. Calcutta: All India Institute of Health and Public Health.

Banerjee, S. (1998). *Dangerous Outcast: The Prostitutes in Nineteenth Century Bengal*. Calcutta: Seagull.

Bank of Korea (various issues). *Economic Statistics Yearbook*. Seoul: Bank of Korea.

Bardhan, P. (1989). 'The new institutional economics and development theory: A brief critical assessment'. *World Development*, 17(9): 1389–95.

——— (1993). 'Analytics of the institutions of informal cooperation in rural development'. *World Development*, 21(4): 633–9.

Barker, R. and Herdt, R. W. (1985). *The Rice Economy of Asia*. Baltimore, MD: Johns Hopkins University Press.

Barnett, T. and Blaikie, P. (1992). *AIDS in Africa: Its Present and Future Impact*. London: Belhaven Press.

Barnum, H. and Kutzin, J. (1993). *Public Hospitals in Developing Countries: Resource Use, Cost, Financing*. Baltimore: Johns Hopkins University Press.

Barr, A. (2000). *Collective Action and Bilateral Interaction in Ghanaian Entrepreneurial Networks*, Working Papers No. 182, May. Helsinki: WIDER.

——— (2000). 'Social capital and technical information flows in the Ghanaian manufacturing sector'. *Oxford Economic Papers*, 52(3): 539–59.

Barr, N. (1993). *The Economics of the Welfare State*, 2nd edn. London: Wiedenfeld and Nicholson.

Barry-Gérard, M., Fonteneau, A., and Diouf, T. (1992*a*). *Evaluation des ressources exploitables par la pêche artisanale*. Rapport d'une séminaire tenu au CRODT (Dakar), 2 tomes, Paris: Editions de l'Orstom.

Barry-Gérard, M., Kebe, M., and Thiam, M. (1992*b*). 'Exploitation des ressources halieutiques côtières dans les eaux sous juridiction sénégalaise', in A. T. Diaw, A. Ba, P. Bouland, P. S. Diouf, L. A. Lake, M. A. Mbow, P. Ndiaye, and M. D. Thiam (eds), *Programmes zones humides de l'UICN. Actes de l'atelier de Gorée*. 27–29 juillet 1992, pp. 291–310.

Barth, F. (1964). 'Capital, investment and the social structure of a pastoral nomad group in south Persia,' in R. Firth, and B. S. Yamey (eds), *Capital, Saving and Credit in Peasant Societies: Studies from Asia, Oceania, the Caribbean and middle America*. London: Allen and Unwin, pp. 69–81.

Barton, T. and Wamai, G. (1994). *Equity and Vulnerability: A Situation Analysis of Women, Adolescents and Children in Uganda*. Kampala: The Government of Uganda and the Uganda National Council for Children.

Bassett, M. T., Bijlmakers, L., and Sanders, D. M. (1997). 'Professionalism, patient satisfaction and quality of health care: Experience during Zimbabwe's structural adjustment programme'. *Social Science and Medicine*, 45(12): 1845–52.

Bates, R. (1997). *Open Economy Politics*. Princeton: Princeton University Press.

Bates, R. H. (1981). *Markets and States in Tropical Africa: The Political Basis of Agricultural Policies*. Berkeley: University of California Press.

Bawden, C. R. (1968). *The Modern History of Mongolia*. London: Weidenfield and Nicolson.

Bebbington, A. and Farrington, J. (1993). *Reluctant Partners? Non-governmental Organisations, the State and Sustainable Agricultural Development*. London: Routledge.

Becker, G. (1981). *A Treatise on the Family*. Boston: Harvard University Press.

——(1993). 'Nobel lecture: The economic way of looking at behavior'. *Journal of Political Economy*, 101: 385–409.

Becker, G. S. (1976). *The Economic Approach to Human Behaviour*. Chicago: University of Chicago Press.

——(1996). *Accounting for Tastes*. Cambridge, MA: Harvard University Press.

Bennett, S. (1991). 'The mystique of markets: Public and private health care in developing countries'. *Public Health and Policy departmental publication No. 4*. London: London School of Hygiene and Tropical Medicine.

Bennett, J. W. (1983). 'Agricultural co-operatives in the development process: Perspectives from social science'. *Studies in Comparative International Development*, 18(1–2): 3–68.

Berman, P. and Khan, M. E. (eds) (1993). *Paying for India's Health Care*. New Delhi: Sage.

Berry, A. (1997). 'The income distribution threat in Latin America'. *Latin American Research Review*, 32(2): 3–40.

Besley, T. and Gouveia, M. (1994). 'Health care'. *Economic Policy*, 19: 200–60.

Bhagwati, J. N. (1982). 'Directly unproductive, profit-seeking activities'. *Journal of Political Economy*, 90: 988–1002.

Bhargava, R. (1992). *Individualism in Social Science*. Oxford: Clarendon Press.

Bianchi, T. (1998). 'The complex task of surviving: Lessons for policy-makers from Northeast Brazilian Co-operatives'. *Report to the Bank of the Northeast on the Strategy of Assisting Small-Scale Producers Organized in Associations and Co-operatives*, 14 October.

—— (1999*a*). 'With and without co-operation: Two alternative development strategies in the food processing industry in the Italian South'. Paper presented at the American Political Science Association Meeting, 2–5 September.

—— (1999*b*). 'APAEB's Natural Fiber'. *Grassroots Development: Journal of the Inter-American Foundation*, 22(1): 38–45.

BIDS (Bangladesh Institute of Development studies) (1990). 'Evaluation of poverty alleviation programs in Bangladesh', (mimeo). Dhaka: Bangladesh Institute of Development Studies.

Bigsten, A. (1995). *Boom and Poverty in Uganda*. Swedish International Development Authority.

Birungi, H. (1998). 'Injections and self-help: Risk and trust in Ugandan health care'. *Social Science and Medicine*, 47(10): 1455–62.

Bisin, A. and Verdier, T. (1998). 'On the cultural transmission of preferences for social status'. *Journal of Public Economics*, 70: 75–97.

Bloom, G. (1998). 'Primary health care meets the market in China and Vietnam'. *Health Policy*, 44: 233–52.

Bohnet, I. and Frey, B. S. (1994). 'Direct democratic rules: The role of discussion'. *Kyklos*, 47: 341–54.

Bojö, J. (1990). *Environment and Development: An Economic Approach*. Dordrecht: Kluwer.

Booth, D., Milimo, J., Bond, G., Chimuka, S., *et al.* (1995). 'Coping with cost recovery'. Report to SIDA, commissioned through the Development Studies Unit, Department of Social Anthropology, Stockholm University.

Bourdieu, P. (1977). *An Outline of a Theory of Practice*. Cambridge: Cambridge University Press.

Bowles, S. and Gintis, H. (1993). 'The revenge of Homo Economicus: Contested exchange and the revival of political economy'. *Journal of Economic Perspectives*, 7: 83–102.

—— —— (1995). 'Productivity-enhancing egalitarian policies'. *International Labor Review*, 134(4–5): 559–85.

—— —— (1996). 'Efficient re-distribution: New rules for markets, states and communities'. *Politics and Society*, 24(4).

—— —— (1998*a*). 'The moral economy of communities: Structured populations and the evolution of pro-social norms'. *Ethnology and Sociobiology*, 19(1).

—— —— (1998*b*). *Recasting Egalitarianism: New Rules for Communities, States and Markets*. London: Verso.

Brake, J., *et al.* (undated). *The National Agricultural Cooperative Federation: An Appraisal* (Special Report No. 1, Korean Agricultural Sector Study). East Lansing, MI: Department of Agricultural Economics, Michigan State University and Seoul, Korea: Agricultural Economics Research Institute, Ministry of Agriculture and Forestry.

Brandt, V. (1971). *Korean Village Between Farm and Sea*. Cambridge, MA: Harvard University Press.

—— and Lee, M. (1979). 'Community development in the Republic of Korea', in R. Dore and Z. Mars (eds), *Community Development: Comparative Case Studies in India, the Republic of Korea, Mexico and Tanzania*. London: Croom Helm, pp. 49–135.

Brara, R. (1987). 'Shifting sands: A study of rights in common pastures', mimeo. Jaipur: Institute of Development Studies.

Braverman, A. and Guasch, J. L. (1987). 'Rural credit reforms in LDCs: Issues and evidence'. *Journal of Economic Development*, 14: 7–34.

—— Luis Guash, J., Huppi, M., and Pohlmeier, L. (1991). 'Promoting rural co-operatives in developing countries: The case of sub-saharan Africa'. *World Bank Discussion Papers*, No. 121, Washington DC: World Bank.

Bray, F. (1986). *The Rice Economies: Technology and Development in Asian Societies*. Berkeley, CA: University of California Press.

BRDB (1998). 'Study on group sustainability'. BRDB Institutional Support Project, Report No. 27, Bangladesh Rural Development Board, Dhaka.

Brett, E. A. (1992). *Providing for the Rural Poor: Institutional Decay and Transformation in Uganda*. Sussex: IDS Research Reports.

Britt, C. (1993). 'Out of the wood? Local institutions and community forest management in two central Himalayan villages', draft monograph. Ithaca: Cornell University.

Britt, C (1997). 'Federation-building and networking: FECOFUN and experiences from user groups Nepal', Discussion Paper. New Delhi: Ford Foundation.

Bruun, O. and Odgaard, O. (1996). 'A society and economy in transition', in O. Bruun and O. Odgaard (eds), *Mongolia in Transition: Old Patterns, New Challenges*. Nordic Institute of Asian Studies, Studies in Asian Topics, No. 22. Richmond, Surrey: Curzon Press, pp. 23–41.

Buchanan, J. M., Tollison, R. D., and Tullock, G. (eds) (1980). *Toward a Theory of the Rent-seeking Society*. College Station: Texas University Press.

Burmeister, L. (1988). *Research, Realpolitik and Development in Korea: The State and the Green Revolution*. Boulder, CO: Westview Press.

—— (1990). 'State, industrialisation and agricultural policy in Korea'. *Development and Change*, 21: 197–223.

—— (1992). 'Korean minifarm agriculture: From articulation to disarticulation'. *The Journal of Developing Areas*, 26(2): 145–67.

—— (1999). 'From parastatal control to corporatist intermediation: The Korean agriculture cooperation in transition', in D. McNamara (ed.), *Corporatism and Korean Capitalism*. London: Routledge, pp. 110–38.

Burns, T. R. (1994). 'Two conceptions of human agency: Rational choice theory and the social theory of action', in Sztompka Piotr (ed.), *Agency and Structure: Reorienting Social Theory*. Yverdon; Reading: Gordon and Breach, pp. 197–249.

Cahiers de la Faculte Economique et Sociales, 146. Namur: Centre de Recherche en Economie du Developpement.

Campi, A. J. (1994). 'The special cultural and social challenges involved in modernizing Mongolia's nomadic socialist economy', in E. H. Kaplan and D. W. Whisenhunt (eds), *Opus-cula Altaica: Essays Presented in Honour of Henry Schwarz*. Washington: Centre for East Asian Studies, Western Washington University, pp. 212–49.

Carrier, J. G. (1995). *Gifts and Commodities: Exchange and Western Capitalism since 1700*. London: Routledge.

Caspar, K. (undated). 'A case study on the impact of group formation and credit on traditional *society security* networks and exchange relations of women', Visiting Research Scholar, Research and Evaluation Division, BRAC, Dhaka.

Castro, R., Orozco, E., Aggleton, P., Eroza, E., and Hernandez, J. J. (1998). 'Family responses to HIV/AIDS in Mexico'. *Social Science and Medicine*, 47(10): 1473–84.

Central Bank of China (various issues). *Financial Statistics Monthly*. Taipei: Central Bank of China.

Centre for Feminist Legal Research (1999). *Memorandum on Reform of Laws Relating to Prostitution in India*, January.

Chambers, R. (1994). 'Participatory Rural Appraisal (PRA): Challenges, potentials and paradigms'. *World Development*, 22(10): 1437–54.

Chang, C.-C. and Hsieh, T.-C. (1998). 'The economic efficiency of the Credit Department of Farmers' Associations in Taiwan'. *Applied Financial Economics*, 8: 409–18.

Che, Y.-K. and Yoo, S.-W. (2001). 'Optimal incentives for teams'. *American Economic Review*, 91(3): 525–41.

Chen, M. (1993). 'Women and wasteland development in India: An issue paper', in A. Singh and N. Burra (eds), *Women and Wasteland Development in India*. Delhi: Sage Publishers, pp. 21–90.

Chenery, H., *et al.* (1974). *Redistribution with Growth*. Oxford: Oxford University Press.

Cheng, T. J., Haggard, S., and Kang, D. (1996). 'Institutions and growth in Korea and Taiwan: The bureaucracy'. *Journal of Development Studies*, 34: 87–111.

Chiang, T. (1995). 'Taiwan's 1995 health care reform'. *Health Policy*, 39: 225–39.

Chopra, K. and Gulati, S. C. (1997). 'Environmental degradation and population movements: The role of property rights'. *Environment and Resource Economics*, 9: 383–408.

CIA World Factbook 1998 entry on Mongolia. (http://www.odci.gov/cia/publications/factbook/mg.html).

Clark, A. and Oswald, A. (1998). 'Comparison-concave utility and following behavior in social and economic settings'. *Journal of Public Economics*, 70: 133–55.

Coase, R. H. (1937). 'The nature of the firm', *Economica*, New Series, Vol. 4, pp. 386–405.

—— (1937). 'The nature of the firm'. Reprinted in O. Williamson (ed.) (1990) *Industrial Organization*. Aldershot, UK: Elgar, pp. 3–22.

—— (1960). 'The problem of social cost'. *Journal of Law and Economics*, 3: 1–44.

Coffee Federation (various years). *Informes del Gerente*. Annual reports to the Coffee Congress.

Cole, H., Mailath, G., and Postlewaite, A. (1998). 'Class systems and the enforcement of social norms'. *Journal of Public Economics*, 70: 5–35.

Coleman, J. (1990). *Foundations of Social Theory*. Cambridge: Harvard University Press.

Conybeare, J. (1982). 'The rent-seeking state and revenue diversification'. *World Politics*, 35: 25–42.

Copans, J. (1980). *Les Marabouts et l'arachide: la Confrèrie Mouride et les Paysans au Sénégal*. Paris: Editions le Sycamore.

Cornia, E. G. A., Jolly, R., and Stewart, F. (1987). *Adjustment with a Human Face: Protecting the Vulnerable and Promoting Growth*. Oxford: Clarendon Press.

Cornia, G. A. (1999). 'Liberalisation, globalisation and income distribution'. WIDER Working Paper No. 157. Helsinki: WIDER.

—— Jolly, R., and Stewart, F. (1987). *Adjustment with a Human Face*. Oxford: Oxford University Press.

Correa, M. (1997). *Gender and Joint Forest Planning and Management: A Research Study in Uttara Kannada District, Karnataka*. Dharwad: India Development Service.

Coughlin, R. E. (1991). 'The economic person in a sociological context', in A. Etzioni and P. Lawrence (eds), *Socio-economics: Towards a New Synthesis*. Armonk, New York: M.E. Sharpe, pp. 35–57.

Cowen, M. P. and Shenton, R. W. (1996) *Doctrines of Development*. London: Routledge.

CRECE (1997). *Programa de reestructuración y desarrollo de las regiones cafeteras*. Manizales: CRECE.

Creese, A. (1991). 'User charges for health care: A review of recent experience'. *Health Policy and Planning*, 6(4): 309–19.

Criel, B., Van der Stuyft, P., and Van Lerberghe, W. (1999). 'The Bwamanda hospital insurance scheme: Effective for whom? A study of its impact on hospital utilization patterns'. *Social Science and Medicine*, 48: 897–911.

CRODT (Centre de Recherches Océanographiques de Dakar-Thiaroye) (1998). *Archives scientifiques*, N° 205, February.

—— and DOPM (Direction de l'Océanographie et de la Pêche Maritime) (1998). *Recensement national du parc piroguier et des infrastructures liées à la pêche*, Ministère de la Pêche et des Transports Maritimes, Observatoire Economique de la Pêche au Sénégal, Dakar.

Crook, R. and Manor, J. (1998). *Democracy and Decentralisation in South Asia and West Africa: Participation, Accountability and Performance*. Cambridge: Cambridge University Press.

Csikszentmihalyi, M. (1997). 'Happiness and creativity: Going with the flow'. *Futurist*, Sept.–Oct., 8–12.

Cumings, B. (1981). *The Origins of the Korean War*. Princeton, NJ: Princeton University Press.

Curto de Casa, S. I. (1994).'Health care in Latin America', in D. Phillips and Y. Verhasselt (eds), *Health and Development*, London: Routledge, pp. 234–48.

Dahal, D. R. (1994). *A Review of Forest User Groups: Case Studies from Eastern Nepal*. Kathmandu: ICIMOD.

Dahl, G. (1979). 'Ecology and equality: The Boran case', in L' Equipe Ecologie at Anthropologie des Sociétés Pastorales (eds), *Pastoral Production and Society (Production Pastorale et Société)*. Cambridge: Cambridge University Press, pp. 261–82.

Dalziel, P. and Lattimore, R. (1996). *The New Zealand Macro-economy: A Briefing on the Reforms*. Melbourne: Oxford University Press.

Davies, R. (1997). 'Donor information demands and NGO institutional development'. *Journal of International Development*, 9(4): 613–20.

Davis, J. (1996). 'An anthropologist's view of exchange'. *Oxford Development Studies*, 24(1): 47–60.

Davison, G. M. (1993). *Agricultural Development and the Fate of Farmers in Taiwan*, Unpublished PhD thesis, University of Minnesota.

De Bethune, X., Alfani, S., and Lahaye, J. P. (1989). 'The influence of an abrupt price increase in health service utilisation: Evidence from Zaire'. *Health Policy and Planning*, 4(1): 76–81.

de Coninck, J. (1992). *Evaluating the Impact of NGOs in Rural Poverty Alleviation: Uganda Country Study*. Overseas Development Institute (ODI) Working Paper 51. London: ODI.

de Janvry, A., Sadoulet, E., and Thorbecke, E. (1993). 'Introduction'. *World Development*, 21(4): 565–75.

de Lasson, A. (1976). 'The Farmers' Association approach to rural development: The case of Taiwan'. No. 19, *Socio-economic studies on rural development*, Institute for Rural Development, Goettingen: University of Goettingen.

De Renzio, P. (1997). 'Social capital and good government: A discussion of theoretical issues with reference to the Bolivian case'. London School of Economics and Political Science, Development Studies Institute, *unpublished*.

—— (1999). 'Bigmen and Wantoks: Social capital and group behaviour in Papua New Guinea'. Working Paper No. 27. Oxford: Queen Elizabeth House.

de Swaan, A. (1988). *In Care of the State*. Cambridge: Polity Press.

Dean, J., Desai, S., and Reidel, J. (1994). *Trade Policy Reform in Developing Countries Since 1985: A Review of the Evidence*. World Bank Discussion Papers No. 267. Washington, DC: World Bank.

Deci, E. L. and Ryan, R. M. (1985). *Intrinsic Motivation and Self-Determination in Human Behavior*. New York: Plenum Press.

—— (1971). 'Effect of externally mediated rewards on intrinsic motivation'. *Journal of Personality and Social Psychology*, 18: 113–20.

Dembinski, P. (1998). 'Le Piège de l'Economisme: Quand l'Arithmétique Remplace l'Ethique', in B. SitterLiver and P. Caroni (eds), *Der Mensch, ein Egoist?* Freiburg: Universitätsverlage, pp. 227–45.

Demeulenaere, P. (1996). *Homo Œconomicus: Enquête sur la Constitution d'un Paradigme*. Paris: Presses Universitaires de France.

Deneulin, S. (1999). 'Affiliation and the political nature of economic man'. Queen Elizabeth House, processed, University of Oxford.

Denison, D. (1990). *Corporate Culture and Organisational Effectiveness*. New York: J. Wiley.

——(1991). 'Organisational culture and "collective" human capital', in Etzioni and Lawrence (eds), *op. cit.*, pp. 263–73.

Desai, B. M. and Mellor, J. W. (1993). *Institutional Finance for Agricultural Development*. Washington, DC: International Food Policy Research Institute.

Desai, V. and Howes, M. (1995). 'Accountability and participation: A case study from Bombay'. In M. Edwards and D. Hulme (eds.), *Non-Governmental Organisations—Performance and Accountability: Beyond the Magic Bullet*. London: Earthscan Publications Ltd, pp. 83–94.

Devine, J. (1996). *NGOs: Changing Fashion or Fashioning Change?* Centre for Development Studies Occasional Paper 02/96. Bath: Centre for Development Studies, University of Bath.

Di Maggio, P. (1991). 'Social structure, institutions and cultural goods: The case of the United States', in P. Bourdieu and J. Coleman (eds), *Social Theory for a Changing Society*. Boulder, CO: Westview Press, pp. 133–55.

——(1994). 'Culture and economy', in N. Smelser and R. Svedberg (eds), *The Handbook of Economic Sociology*. Princeton: Princeton University Press, pp. 27–57.

Dichter, T. (1997). 'Appeasing the gods of sustainability: The future of international NGOs in microfinance'. In D. Hulme and M. Edwards (eds.), *NGOs, States, and Donors: Too Close for Comfort?* London: Macmillan Press Ltd, pp. 128–39.

Donham, D. (1981). 'Beyond the domestic mode of production'. *Man*, 16: 515–41.

Douglas, M. (1987). *How Institutions Think*. London: Routledge & Kegan Paul.

Drèze, J. and Sen, A. K. (1995). *India: Economic Development and Social Opportunity*. Delhi: Oxford University Press.

Dryzek, J. (1996). 'The informal logic of institutional design', in R. Goodin, (ed.), *The Theory of Institutional Design*. Cambridge: Cambridge University Press, pp. 103–25.

Duggal, R. and Antia, N. H. (1993). 'Health financing in India: A review and agenda', in Berman and Khan (eds), *Paying for India's Health Care*. New Delhi: Sage, pp. 53–71.

Dugger, W. (1994). 'Methodological differences between institutional and neo-classical economics', in D. Hausman (ed.), *The Philosophy of Economics: An Anthology*. Cambridge: Cambridge University Press, pp. 336–45.

Durbar Mahila Samanwaya Committee (1997). *Sex Workers' Manifesto: The First National Conference of Sex Workers Organised by Durbar Mahila Samanwaya Committee. Calcutta, November 1997*. Calcutta: DMSC.

——(1998). *The 'Fallen' Learn to Rise: The Social Impact of STD-HIV Intervention Programme*, 2nd edn. Calcutta: DMSC.

Durkheim, E. (1893). *De la Division du Travail Social*. Paris: F. Alcan.

——(1976). *The Elementary Forms of Religious Life*. London: Allen & Unwin.

——(1978). *Emile Durkheim of Institutional Analysis*, Mark Traugott (ed. and trans.). Chicago and London: University of Chicago Press.

Easterly, W. R. (2001). 'The effect of IMF and World Bank programs on poverty'. Policy Research Working Paper 2517, (Washington DC: World Bank).

Economist, 8 May 1999.

Elbadawi, L. A. (1992). 'Why structural adjustment has not succeeded in sub-Saharan Africa'. World Bank Working Paper Series, WPS 1000. Washington DC: World Bank.

Elster, J. (1989a). *The Cement of Society, A Study of Social Order*. Cambridge: Cambridge University Press.

——(1989b). 'Social norms and economic theory'. *Journal of Economic Perspectives*, 3(4): 99–117.

Ensminger, J. (1992). *Making the Market: The Institutional Transformation of an African Society*. Cambridge: Cambridge University Press.

Ensor, T. (1999). 'Developing health insurance in transitional Asia'. *Social Science and Medicine*, 48: 871–9.

Enzle, M. E. *et al.* (1991). 'Self-versus other-reward administration and intrinsic motivation'. *Journal of Experimental Psychology*, 27(5): 468–79.

Esman, M. and Uphoff, N. (1984). *Local Organisations: Intermediaries in Rural Development*. Ithaca: Cornell University Press.

Etzioni, A. and Lawrence, P. (eds) (1991). *Socio-economics: Towards a New Synthesis*. Armonk, New York: M.E. Sharpe.

——(1991). 'Contemporary liberals, communitarians and individual choices', in A. Etzioni and P. Lawrence (eds), *Socio-economics: Towards a New Synthesis*. Armonk, New York: M.E. Sharpe, pp. 59–73.

Evans, C. (1999). 'An international review of the rationale, role and evaluation of community development approaches in interventions to reduce HIV transmission in sex work', mimeo. *Horizons Project*, Population Council, Regional Office for South and East Asia, New Delhi, India, January.

Evans, P. (1996). 'Government action, social capital and development: Reviewing the evidence on synergy'. *World Development*, 24: 1119–32.

Fals-Borda, O. *et al.* (1976). 'The crisis of rural co-operatives: Problems in Africa, Asia and Latin America', in J. Nash, J. Dandler, and N. S. Hopkins (eds), *Popular Participation in Social Change*. The Hague: Mouton Publishers, pp. 439–56.

Fehr, E. and Gachter, S. (1998). 'Reciprocity and economics: The economic implications of Homo Reciprocans'. *European Economic Review*, 42(3–5): 845–59.

Fei, J. and Ranis, G. (1964). *Development of the Labor Surplus Economy*. New York: Richard Irwin.

Fei, J. C. H. and Ranis, G. (1975). 'A model of growth and employment in the open dualistic economy: The cases of Korea and Taiwan'. *Journal of Development Studies*, 11(2): 32–63.

——————and Kuo, S. W. Y. (1979). *Growth with Equity, The Taiwan Case*. Oxford: Oxford University Press.

Feierman, S. (1985). 'Struggles for control: The social roots of health and healing in modern Africa'. *African Studies Review*, 28: 73–145.

Fershtman, C. and Weiss, Y. (1998). 'Social rewards, externalities and stable preferences'. *Journal of Public Economics*, 70: 53–73.

Fine, B. (1999*a*). 'From Bourdieu to Becker: Economics confronts the social sciences'. *Working Draft*, School of Oriental and African Studies, LSE, London.

——(1999*b*). 'The World Bank and social capital: A critical skinning'. *First and Provisional Draft*, SOAS, LSE, London.

Flanagan, O. and Rorty, A. O. (1990). *Identity, Character and Morality: Essays in Moral Psychology*. Cambridge, MA: MIT Press.

Folbre, N. (1986). 'Hearts and spades: Paradigms of household economics', *World Development*, 14, pp. 245–55.

Folbre, N. (1994). *Who Pays for the Kids: Gender and the Structures of Constraint*. London: Routledge.

Food and Agriculture Organisation of the United Nations (FAO) (1991). 'Proceedings of the international workshop on pastoralism and socio-economic development: Mongolia, 4–12 September 1990'. Rome, M/U5300E/1/11.91/500.

Fowler, A. (1997). *Striking a Balance: A Guide to Enhancing the Effectiveness of Non-governmental Organisations in International Development.* London: Earthscan Publications Ltd.

Fox, J. (1992). 'Democratic rural development: Leadership accountability in regional peasant organizations'. *Development and Change*, 23: 209–44.

Frank, A. G. (1969). *Capitalism and Underdevelopment in Latin America: Historical Studies of Chile and Brazil.* New York: Monthly Review Press.

Frank, R. H. (1991). *Microeconomic Theory and Behavior.* New York; London: McGraw-Hill.

—— *et al.* (1993). 'Does studying economics inhibit co-operation'. *Journal of Economic Perspectives*, 7: 159–71.

Frey, B. (1997). *Not Just for Money: An Economic Theory of Personal Motivation.* Aldershot: Edwar Elgar.

—— and Oberholzer-Gee, F. (1997). 'The cost of price incentives: An empirical analysis of motivation crowding-out'. *American Economic Review*, 87(4): 746–55.

—— and Stutzer, A. (1999). 'Happiness, economy and institutions'. *Preliminary Version.*

Friedman, M. (1994). 'The methodology of positive economics', in D. Hausman (ed.), see below, pp. 180–213.

Fugelstad, F. (1983). *A History of Niger, 1850–1960.* Cambridge: Cambridge University Press.

Fukuyama, F. (1999). *The Great Disruption.* New York: The Free Press.

Funk, C. L. (1998). 'Practising what we preach? The influence of a societal interest on civic engagement'. *Political Psychology*, 19(3): 601–14.

Furnivall, J. (1948). *Colonial Policy and Practice.* Cambridge: Cambridge University Press.

Furtado, C. (1967). *Development and Underdevelopment.* Berkeley: University of California Press.

Gaul, K. K. (1994). 'Negotiated positions and shifting terrains: Apprehension of forest resources in the Western Himalaya'. PhD dissertation, Department of Anthropology, University of Massachusetts, Amherst.

Gellner, E. (1988). *State and Society in Soviet Thought.* Oxford: Oxford University Press.

Gerrard, B. (ed.) (1993). *The Economics of Rationality.* London: Routledge.

Gertler, P. (1998). 'On the road to social health insurance: The Asian experience'. *World Development*, 26(4): 717–32.

—— and Van der Gaag, J. (1990). *The Willingness to Pay for Medical Care: Evidence from the Developing Countries.* Washington: World Bank.

Gibbons, I. (1990). 'The mobilisation of women in rural Bangladesh'. Paper prepared for the Swedish Embassy Development Cooperation Office, Bangladesh, Dhaka.

Giddens, A. (1984). *The Constitution of Society.* Oxford: Blackwell.

—— (1992). *Sociology.* London: Polity Press.

Gilson, L., Russell, S., and Buse, K. (1995). 'The political economy of cost recovery: Towards equitable health financing policy'. *Journal of International Development*, 7(3): 369–401.

—— Heggenhougen, K., and Alilio, M. (1994). 'A Tanzanian evaluation of community satisfaction with primary care'. *Social Science and Medicine*, 39(6): 767–80.

—— Kalyalya, D., Kuchler, F., Oranga, H. M., and Ouendo, M. (1999). 'Promoting equity within community financing schemes: Experiences from three African countries'. *Public Health and Policy Departmental Publication 31.* London: London School of Hygiene and Tropical Medicine.

—— Russell, S., Rauyajin, O. *et al.* (1998). 'Exempting the poor: A review and evaluation of the Low Income Card Scheme in Thailand'. *Public Health and Policy Departmental Publication 30.* London: London School of Hygiene and Tropical Medicine.

—— (1997). 'The lessons of user fee experience in Africa'. *Health Policy and Planning*, 12(4): 273–85.

—— and Travis, P. (1998). 'Health system decentralisation in Africa: An overview of experiences in eight countries'. Mimeo, Johannesburg, January.

Gintis, H. (1993). 'The revenge of Homo Economicus: Contested exchange and the revival of political economy'. *Journal of Economic Perspectives*, 7: 83–102.

Gintis, H. (1998). *The Individual in Economic Theory: A Research Agenda*, processed. MA: University of Massuchusetts.

Giridhar, G. (1993). 'Concepts and practice in health care insurance schemes', in Berman and Khan (eds), *Paying for India's Health Care*. New Delhi: Sage, pp. 261–79.

Glennerster, H. (1995). *British Social Policy Since 1945*. Oxford: Blackwell.

Goetz, A. M. and Sengupta, R. (1996). 'Who takes the credit? Gender, power, and control over loan use in rural Bangladesh'. *World Development*, 24(1): 45–63.

Gold, T. (1986). *State and Society in the Taiwan Miracle*. Armonk, NY: M.E. Sharpe, Inc.

Goldstein, W. and Hogarth, R. (eds) (1997). *Research on Judgment and Decision-Making: Currents, Connections, and Controversies*. Cambridge Series on Judgment and Decision Making. Cambridge: Cambridge University Press.

Good, C. (1991). 'Pioneer medical missions in Colonial Africa'. *Social Science and Medicine*, 32(1): 1–10.

Gooptu, N. (2000). 'Sex workers in Calcutta and the dynamics of collective action: Political activism, community identity and group behaviour'. Working Paper No. 185. Helsinki: WIDER.

Government of Nepal (2000). *Forest User Group Statistics*. Community and Private Forestry Division, Department of Forests, Kathmandu.

Graham, C. (1994). *Safety Nets, Politics and the Poor*. Washington DC: Brookings.

Granovetter, M. (1985). 'Economic action, social structure and embeddedness'. *American Journal of Sociology*, 91: 481–510.

—— (1991). 'The social construction of economic institutions', in A. Etzioni and P. Lawrence (eds), *Socio-economics: Towards a New Synthesis*. Armonk, New York: M.E. Sharpe, pp. 75–81.

Gregory, C. (1982). *Gifts and Commodities*. London: Academic Press.

Griffin, K. (1995). 'Economic strategy during the transition', in K. Griffin (ed.), *Poverty and the Transition to a Market Economy in Mongolia*. New York: St Martin's Press, pp. 1–26.

—— and Lowndes, C. (1999). 'Gender, sexuality and the prevention of sexually transmitted diseases: A Brazilian study of clinical practice'. *Social Science and Medicine*. 48: 283–92.

Grindle, M. S. (1991). 'The new political economy: Positive economics and negative politics', in G. M. Meier (ed.), *Politics and Policy Making in Developing Countries*. San Francisco: International Center for Economic Growth, pp. 41–67.

Grootaert, C. (1997).'Social capital: The missing link?', in World Bank. *Expanding the Measure of Wealth: Indicators of Environmentally Sustainable Development*. Washington, DC: World Bank, pp. 77–93.

Guhathakurta, P. and Bhatia, K. S. (1992). *A Case Study on Gender and Forest Resources in West Bengal*. Delhi: World Bank, 16 June.

Haggard, S. (1995). *'Japanese colonialism and Korean development: A critique'*. La Jolla, California, Graduate School of International Relations and Pacific Studies, University of California, Research Report, 95-04.

Hancher, L. and Moran, M. (1989). 'Organising regulatory space', in L. Haucher and M. Moran (eds) *Capitalism, Culture and Economic Regulation*. Oxford: Oxford University Press, pp. 271–99.

Hans, S. *et al.* (undated). *Organisation and Performance of the Agricultural Marketing System in South Korea*. Special Report No. 7, Korean Agricultural Sector Study. East Lansing,

MI: Department of Agricultural Economics, Michigan State University and Seoul, Korea: Agricultural Economics Research Institute, Ministry of Agriculture and Forestry.

Hargreaves-Heap, S. (1989). *Rationality in Economics*. Oxford: Basil Blackwell.

Harris, J. and De Renzio, P. (1997). 'Missing link or analytically missing: The concept of social capital'. *Journal of International Development*, 9(7): 919–37.

Harvey, G. E. (1925). *Burma, 1782–1852. Cambridge History of India*, vol. 5, Cambridge.

Hashemi, S. M., Schuler S. R. and Riley A. P. (1996). 'Rural credit programs and women's empowerment in Bangladesh' *World Development*, 24(4), 635–53.

Hausman, D. (ed) (1994). *The Philosophy of Economics: An Anthology*. Cambridge: Cambridge University Press, 2nd edition.

——and McPherson, M. (1994). 'Economics, rationality and ethics', in D. Hausman (ed.), *op.cit.*, pp. 252–77.

Hazledine, T. (1998). *Taking New Zealand Seriously: The Economics of Decency*. Auckland: Harper Collins.

Hechter, M. (1987). *Principles of Group Solidarity*. Berkeley, London: University of California Press.

Heilbronner, R. (1993). *21st Century Capitalism*. New York: Norton and Co.

Heyer, J., Stewart, F., and Thorp, R. (1999). 'Group behaviour and development', Working Paper No. 161. Helsinki: WIDER

Hirsch, F. (1976). *Social Limits to Growth*. Cambridge, MA: Harvard University Press.

——(1959). *Getting Ahead Collectively*. Oxford: Pergamon Press.

Hirschman, A. O. (1977). *The Passions and the Interests: Political Arguments for Capitalism Before its Triumph*. Princeton: Princeton University Press.

——(1982). 'Rival interpretations of market society: Civilising, destructive or feeble?' *Journal of Economic Literature*, XX: 1463–84.

——(1984). *Getting Ahead Collectively*. Oxford: Pergamon Press.

Ho, S. P. S. (1978). *Economic Development of Taiwan, 1860–1970*. New Haven: Yale University Press.

——(1982). 'Economic development and rural industry in South Korea and Taiwan'. *World Development*, 10: 973–90.

Hobley, M. (1996). *Participatory Forestry: The Process of Change in India and Nepal*. London: Overseas Development Institute.

Hogarth, R. and Reder, M. (1987). *Rational Choice: The Contrast between Economics and Psychology*. Chicago; London: University of Chicago Press.

Holmquist, (1979). 'Class structure, peasant participation and rural self-help', in J. Barkan and J. Okumu (eds), *Politics and Public Policy in Kenya and Tanzania*, New York: Praeger, pp. 171–94.

Hom, H. *et al.* (1994). 'The effects of co-operative and individualistic reward on intrinsic motivation'. *Journal of Genetic Psychology*, 155(1): 87–97.

Hossain, M. (1988). 'Credit for alleviation of rural poverty: The Grameen Bank in Bangladesh', Research Report 65. Washington DC: International Food Policy Research Institute, in collaboration with the Bangladesh Institute of Development Studies.

Hou, C.-M. and Yu, T.-S. (eds) (1982). *Agricultural Development in China, Japan and Korea*. Taipei: Academia Sinica.

House, J. S. *et al.* (1998). 'Social relationship and health'. *Sciences*, 37: 11–28.

Houthakker, H. (1961). 'The present state of consumption theory'. *Econometrica*, 29(4): 704–40.

Howes, M. (1996). 'NGOs and the development of membership organizations: The case of Saptagram', mimeo, Institute of Development Studies, Sussex.

Huff-Rousselle, M. and Akuamoah-Boateng, J. (1998). 'The first private sector health insurance company in Ghana'. *International Journal of Health Planning and Management*, 13: 165–75.

Hughes, G. and Lewis, G. A. (eds) (1998). *Unsettling Welfare: The Reconstruction of Social Policy*. London: Routledge with the Open University.

Hulme, D. and Montgomery, R. (1994). 'Cooperatives, credit and the poor: Private interest, public choice and collective action in Sri Lanka'. *Savings and Development*, 3/XVIII: 359–82.

Hulme, D. and Edwards, M. (1997). 'NGOs, states, and donors: An overview', in D. Hulme and M. Edwards (eds), *NGOs, States, and Donors: Too Close for Comfort?* London: Macmillan Press Ltd, pp. 3–22.

Humphrey, C. (1978). 'Pastoral nomadism in Mongolia: The role of herdsmen's cooperatives in the national economy'. *Development and Change*, 9: 133–60.

—— and Hugh-Jones, S. (1992). 'Introduction: Barter, exchange and value', in C. Humphrey and S. Hugh-Jones (eds), *Barter, Exchange and Value: An Anthropological Approach*. Cambridge: Cambridge University Press, pp. 1–20.

—— and Sneath, D. (1999). 'Pastoralism and institutional change in Inner Asia: Comparative perspectives from the MECCIA reasearch project', in C. Humphrey and D. Sneath (eds), *The End of Nomadism? Society, State and the Environment in Inner Asia*, Central Asia Book Series. Durham, NC: Duke University Press.

Huq, T. (undated). 'Mobilising rural poor women: Case from Bangladesh', Paper submitted in partial fulfillment of the requirements for the degree in M.A. in Development Studies, The Institute of Social Studies, The Hague.

Hussi, P., Murphy, J., Lindberg, O., and Brenneman, L. (1993). 'The development of co-operatives and other rural organizations: The role of the World Bank'. *World Bank Technical Papers, Africa Technical Department Series*, No. 199, World Bank, Washington DC.

Hyer, P. and Jagchid, S. (1983). *A Mongolian Living Buddha: Biography of the Kanjurwa Khutughtu*. Albany: State University of New York Press.

IDRC (1995). 'Power and inequality inside the Favela', *Reports* 23: 18–19, 1 April.

Iliffe, J. (1998). *East African Doctors, A History of the Modern Profession*. Cambridge: Cambridge University Press.

Illy, H. F. (1983). 'How to build in the germs of failure: Credit cooperatives in French Cameroon', in J. D. von Pischke, *et al.* (eds), *Rural Financial Markets in Developing Countries*. Baltimore: Johns Hopkins University Press, pp. 269–301.

ILO (1972). *Employment, Incomes and Equality, A Strategy for Increasing Productive Employment in Kenya*. Geneva: ILO.

—— (1976). *Employment, Growth and Basic Needs: A One-World Problem*. Geneva: ILO.

IMAR Editorial Group (1986). Mengguzu Shehui Lishi Diaocha (The Social History Investigation of the Mongolian Nationality), Hohhot, Inner Mongolian People's Press.

ISO/Swedforest (1993). *Forests, People and Protection: Case Studies of Voluntary Forest Protection by Communities in Orissa*. New Delhi: Swedish International Development Agency (SIDA).

James, M. J. (1989). *'The Technological Behaviour of Public Enterprises in Developing Countries'*. London: Routledge.

Jana, S., Bandyopadhyay, N., Mukherjee, S., Datta, N., and Saha, A. (1998). 'STD/HIV intervention with sex workers in West Bengal, India'. *AIDS*, 12(Suppl. B).

Jarrett, S. and Ofosu-Amaah, S. (1992). 'Strengthening health services for MCH in Africa: The first four years of the "Bamako Initiative"'. *Health Policy and Planning*, 7(2): 164–76.

Jeffery, R. (1988). *The Politics of Health in India*. Berkeley: The University of California Press.

Jewkes, R. and Murcott, A. (1996). 'Meaning of community'. *Social Science and Medicine*, 43(4): 555–63.

—— Abrahams, N. and Mvo, Z. (1998). 'Why do nurses abuse patients? Reflections from South African obstetric services'. *Social Science and Medicine*, 47(11): 1781–95.

Jodha, N. S. (1986). 'Common property resources and the rural poor'. *Economic and Political Weekly*, 21(27): 1169–81.

Johnson, R. N. and Libecap, G. D. (1982). 'Contracting problems and regulation: The case of the fishery'. *American Economic Review*, 72: 1005–22.

Jones, T. J. (1971). 'Agricultural credit institutions', in M. B. Blase (ed.), *Institutions in Agricultural Development*. Ames, Iowa: Iowa State University, pp. 168–84.

Jong, P. C. (1991). 'Republic of Korea (1)', in Asian Productivity Organisation (ed.), *Agricultural Cooperatives in Asia and the Pacific*. Tokyo: Asian Productivity Organisation, pp. 241–52.

Joshi, S. (1998). 'Report of the workshop on JFM and Women'. Agha Khan Rural Support Programme, Netrang, Gujarat, 14 Sept.

Junguito, R. and Pizano, D. (1991). *Produccion de Café en Colombia*. Bogota: Fondo Cultural Cafetero y Fedesarrollo.

—— —— (1997). *Instituciones e Instrumentos de la Política Cafetera en Colombia*. Bogota: Fondo Cultural Cafetero y Fedesarrollo.

Ka, Chih-ming (1995). *Japanese Colonialism in Taiwan: Land Tenure, Development, and Dependency, 1895–1945*. Boulder, CO: Westview.

Kabeer, N. (1998). ' "Money can't buy me love"? Re-evaluating gender, credit and empowerment in rural Bangladesh'. Discussion Paper 363, Institute of Development Studies, University of Sussex.

Kahneman, D. and Tversky, A. (1979). 'Prospect theory: An analysis of decision under risk'. *Econometrica*, 47(1): 263–91.

Kakwani, N. (1995). 'Structural adjustment and performance in living standards in developing countries'. *Development and Change*, 26(3): 469–502.

Kameda, T. *et al.* (1992). 'Social dilemmas, subgroups and motivation loss in task'. *Social Psychology Quarterly*, 55(1): 47–56.

Kandiyoti, D. (1988). 'Bargaining with patriarchy'. *Gender and Society*, 2: 274–90.

Kant, S., Singh, N. M., and Singh, K. K. (1991). *Community-based Forest Management Systems* (*Case Studies from Orissa*. New Delhi: SIDA; Bhopal: Indian Institute of Forest Management; and New Delhi: ISO/Swedforest).

Karanja, M., Bloom, G. H., and Segall, M. (1995). 'Impact of user charges on vulnerable groups: The case of Kibwezi in rural Kenya'. *Social Science and Medicine*, 41: 829–35.

Kaufman, B. E. (1999). 'Expanding the behavioral foundations of labor economics'. *Industrial and Labor Relations Review*, 52(3): 361–92.

Kay, J. (1988). *The Role of Business in Society*. Said Business School, Oxford: University of Oxford.

—— (1998). *The Role of Business in Society*, processed. Said Business School, University of Oxford.

Kenworthy, L. (1997). 'Civic engagement, social capital, and economic co-operation'. *American Behavioral Scientist*, 40(5): 645–56.

Kerven, C. (ed.) (1999). 'Impacts of privatisation on range and livestock management in semi-arid Central Asia: Workshop results. Summary of papers presented at a workshop from 18–21 November 1998, at the Macaulay Land Use Research Institute, Aberdeen, Scotland'. Unpublished report, Overseas Development Institute, London.

Kervyn, B. (1989). 'Campesinos y Acción Collectiva: La Organización del Espacio en Communidades de la Sierra del Perú'. *Revista Andina*, 13(1): 7–81.

Khan, M. and Knight, M. (1985). 'Fund-supported adjustment progams and economic growth'. IMF Occasional Paper 41. Washington, DC: IMF.

Khan, M. (1990). 'The macro-economic effects of fund-supported adjustment programs'. *IMF Staff Papers*, 37.

Khandker, S. R. and Chowdhury O. H. (1996). 'Targeted credit programs and rural poverty in Bangladesh', Discussion Papers, 336. Washington DC: World Bank.

Killick, T. (1976). 'The possibilities of development planning'. *Oxford Economic Papers*, 41: 161–84.

—— (1988). 'A reaction too far: Contemporary thinking about the role of the state with special reference to developing countries'. London: ODI.

Killick, T., Malik, M., and Manuel, M. (1991). 'What can we know about the effects of the IMF Programmes?. ODI Working Paper 47. London: ODI.

Knight, F. (1944). 'Realism and relevance in the theory of demand'. *Journal of Political Economy*, 52(4): 289–318.

Kohn, A. (1998). 'Why incentives plans cannot work'. *Harvard Business Review*, 71(5): 54–60.

Korten, D. (1990). *Getting to the 21st Century: Voluntary Action and the Global Agenda*. West Hartford: Kumarian Press.

Kreps, D. M. (1997). 'The interaction between norms and economic incentives: Intrinsic motivation and extrinsic incentives'. *American Economic Review*, 87(2): 59–64.

Krueger, A. (1974). 'The political economy of the rent-seeking society'. *American Economic Review*, 64: 291–303.

Krugman, P. (1990). *Rethinking International Trade*. Cambridge, MA: MIT Press.

Kumaranayake, L. (1997). 'The role of regulation: Influencing private sector activity within health sector reform'. *Journal of International Development*, 9(4): 641–9.

Kuo, S. W. Y. (1983). *The Taiwan Economy in Transition*. Boulder, CO: Westview Press.

Kuo, Y. C. and Lee, C. Y. (1982). 'Farmers' organisations and agricultural development in Taiwan', in C. M. Hou and T. S. Yu (eds), *Agricultural Development in China, Japan and Korea*. Taipei: Academica Sinica, pp. 759–80.

Kurien, P. A. (1994). 'Non-economic bases of economic behavior: The consumption, investment and exchange patterns of three emigrant communities in Kerala, India'. *Development and Change*, 25: 757–83.

Kwoh, M. H. (1966). *Farmers Associations and Their Contributions Toward Agricultural and Rural Development in Taiwan*. Rome: FAO.

Lal, D. (1984). 'The political economy of the predatory state'. Development Research Department. Discussion Paper DRD 105 (Washington DC: World Bank).

Lane, R. (1991). *The Market Experience*. Cambridge: Cambridge University Press.

Larson, A. and Hulbert, H. (1966). *Study of Agricultural Cooperatives in Korea (National Agricultural Cooperative Federation)*. Seoul, Korea: US Operation Mission to Korea and Madison; WI: International Cooperative Training Center, University of Wisconsin.

Lattimore, O. (1940). *Inner Asian Frontiers of China American Geographical Society*. Research Series No. 21. London, New York: Oxford University Press.

Lawson, T. (1997). *Economics and Reality*. London: Routledge.

Le Grand, J. (1991). 'Quasi-markers and social policy'. *Economic Journal*, 101: 1256–67.

—— (1997). 'Knights, knaves or pawns? Human behaviour and social policy'. *Journal of Social Policy*, 37(2): 149–69.

Lee, C. and Culver, D. W. (1985). 'Agricultural development in three Asian countries: A comparative analysis'. *Agricultural Economics Research*, 37: 8–13.

Lee, C. W. (1991). 'Republic of Korea (1)', in Asian Productivity Organisation (ed.), *Agricultural Cooperatives in Asia and the Pacific*. Tokyo: Asian Productivity Organisation, pp. 253–69.

Lee, T. H. and Chen, Y. E. (1979). 'Agricultural growth in Taiwan, 1911–72', in Y. Hayami, *et al.* (eds), *Agricultural Growth in Japan, Taiwan, Korea and the Philippines*. Honolulu: University of Hawaii Press, pp. 59–89.

Lee, T. Y., Kim, D. H., and Adams, D. W. (1977). 'Savings deposits and credit activities in South Korean agricultural cooperatives: 1961–75'. *Asian Survey*, 17: 1182–94.

Legrand, J. (1997). 'Knights, knaves or pawns? Human behavior and social policy', *Journal of Social Policy*, 26: 149–69.

Lele, U. (1981). 'Cooperatives and the poor: A comparative perspective'. *World Development*, 9: 55–72.

Lepper, M. R. and Greene, D. (1978). *The Hidden Costs of Reward: New Perspectives on the Psychology of Human Motivation*. New York: Erlbaum.

Lewin, S. B. (1996). 'Economics and psychology: Lessons for our own day from the early twentieth century'. *Journal of Economic Literature*, 34: 1293–323.

Lewis, W. A. (1950). 'The industrialisation of the British West Indies'. *Caribbean Economic Review*, II: 1.

——(1954). 'Economic development with unlimited supplies of labour'. *Manchester School*, 22(2): 139–91.

Leys, C. (1975). *Underdevelopment in Kenya: The Political Economy of Neo-Colonialism*. London: Hienemann.

Libecap, G. D. (1990). *Contracting for Property Rights*. New York: Cambridge University Press.

—— and Wiggins, S. N. (1984). 'Contracting responses to the common pool: Prorationing of crude oil production'. *American Economic Review*, 74(1): 87–98.

Lindbeck, A. (1997). 'Incentives and social norms in household behavior'. *American Economic Review*, 87(2): 370–7.

Little, I. M. D. (1982). *Economic Development: Theory, Policy and International Relations*. New York: Basic Books.

—— Scott, M. Fg., and Scitovsky, T. (1970). *Industry and Trade in Some Developing Countries: A Comparative Study*. Oxford: Oxford University Press.

Liu, Yuanli, Hu, Shanlian, Fu, Wei, and Hsaio, William (1996). 'Is community financing necessary and feasible in rural China?'. *Health Policy*, 38: 155–71.

Lomnitz, L. A. (1977). *Networks and Marginality: Life in a Mexican Shantytown*. New York: Academic Press.

Londoño, J.-L. and Frenk, J. (1997). 'Structured pluralism: Towards an innovative model for health system reform in Latin America'. *Health Policy*, 41: 1–36.

Lucas, R. E. (1988). 'On the mechanics of economic development'. *Journal of Monetary Economics*, 22.

Lundberg, M. (1999). 'Land distribution Gini-coefficient', processed. Washington DC: World Bank.

Lyons, M. L. (1994). 'Public health in Colonial Africa: The Belgian Congo', in D. Porter (ed.), *The History of Public Health and the Modern State*. Atlanta and Amsterdam: Rodopi B.V., pp. 356–84.

MacCormack, C. and Lwihula, G. (1983). 'Failure to participate in malaria chemo-suppression programme: North Mara, Tanzania'. *Journal of Tropical Medicine and Hygiene*, 86(3): 99–107.

Mackintosh, M. (1997). 'Informal regulation: A conceptual framework and application to decentralised mixed finance in health care'. Paper Prepared for Conference on 'Public Sector Management for the Next Century'. Manchester: IDPM, 29 June–2 July.

Mackintosh, M. (1999). 'Informal regulation: A conceptual framework and application to decentralised mixed finance in health care', in M. Mackintosh and R. Roy (eds), *Economic Decentralization and Public Management Reform*. Cheltenham: Edward Elgar.

—— (2000*a*). 'Exchange and the metaphor of exchange: Economic cultures in social care', in G. Lewis, J. Clarke, and S. Gurwitz (eds), *Rethinking Social Policy*. London: Sage.

—— (2000*b*). 'Flexible contracting? Economic cultures and implicit contracts in social care'. *Journal of Social Policy*, 29(1): 1–19.

—— and Gilson, L. (2000). *Non-market Relationships in Health Care*. Open Discussion Papers in Economics No. 19. The Open University, Milton Keynes.

Mackintosh, M. and Roy, R. (eds) (1999). *Economic Decentralization and Public Management Reform*. Aldershot: Edward Elgar.

Mahalanobis, P. C. (1953). 'Some observations on the process of growth in national income'. *Sankhya*, 14: 4.

Mahmud, S. (1994). 'The role of women's employment programmes in influencing fertility regulation in rural Bangladesh'. *Bangladesh Development Studies*, 22(2–3), 93–120.

—— and S. Huda (1998). 'Participation in BRAC's Rural Development Programme and the impact of group dynamics on individual outcomes', Working Paper No. 24. Dhaka: BRAC-ICDDRB Joint Research Project at Matlab.

—— and Huda, S. (1998). 'Participation in BRAC's rural development programme and the impact of group dynamics on individual outcomes'. Working Paper 24, BRAC-ICDDR, B Joint Research Project, Dhaka.

—— (1999). 'Micro-credit and women's empowerment: Exploring the linkages', (draft). Bangladesh Institute of Development Studies, Dhaka.

—— (2001). 'Participation in micro-credit programmes and impact on social well-being and women's empowerment', in *Monitoring and Evaluation of Micro-finance Institutions*, (mimeo). Dhaka: Bangladesh Institute of Development Studies.

Maki, U., Gustafsson, B., and Knuden, Ch. (1993). *Rationality, Institutions and Economic Methodology*. London: Routledge.

Mamdani, M. (1996). *Citizen and Subject: Contemporary Africa and the Legacy of Late Colonialism*. Princeton: James Currey.

Manderson, L. (1999). 'Public health then and now'. *American Journal of Public Health*, 89(1): 102–7.

Mannan, M. *et al.* (1995). 'Formation of village organizations: The first three months'. Working Paper 4, BRAC-ICDDR, B Joint Research Project, Dhaka.

Mansingh, O. (1991). 'Community organization and ecological restoration: An analysis of strategic options for NGOs in central Himalaya, with particular reference to the Community Forestry Programme of the NGO Chirag'. MA dissertation in Rural Development, AFRAS, University of Sussex.

Mao, Y. K. and Schive, C. (1995). 'Agricultural and industrial development in Taiwan', in J. W. Mellor (ed.), *Agriculture on the Road to Industrialisation*. Baltimore: Johns Hopkins University, pp. 23–66.

Marx, K. (1886). *Das Kapital*. London: Glaisher.

Marx, K. and Engels, F. (1968) [1948]. *The Communist Manifesto*. New York: The Washington Square Press.

Mason, E. S., Je Kim, M., Perkins, D. H., Suk Kim, K., and Cole, D. C. (1980). *The Economic and Social Modernization of the Republic of Korea*. Cambridge, MA: Harvard University Press.

Mauss, M. (1924). *The Gift: Forms and Functions of Exchange in Archaic Societies*, I. Cunnison (trans.). Washington: Smithsonian Institute.

Mbembe, A. (1988). *Afrique Indociles: Christianisme, Pouvoir at Etat en Société Postcoloniale*. Paris: Karthala.

Mboya, T. (1963). 'African Socialism', *Transition*, 7 (Kampala), reprinted in W. H. Friedland and C. G. Rosberg (eds), *African Socialism* (1964). Stanford: Stanford University Press, pp. 250–58.

McElroy, M. and Horney, M. J. (1981). 'Nash-bargained household decisions: Toward a generalization of the theory of demand'. *International Economic Review*, 22: 333–50.

McPake, B., Asiimwe, D., Mwesigye, F., Ofumbi, M., Ortenblad, L., Streefland, P., and Turinde, A. (1999). 'Informal economic activities of public health workers in Uganda: Implications for quality and accessibility of care'. *Social Science and Medicine*, 49(7): 849–66.

—— Hanson, K., and Mills, A. (1992). 'Implementing the Bamako initiative in Africa: A review and five case studies'. PHP Departmental Publication No. 8. London: London School of Hygiene and Tropical Medicine.

Mencher, J. P. (1988). 'Women's work and poverty': Contributions to Household Maintenance in Two Regions of South India', in D. Dwyer and J. Bruce (eds), *A Home Divided: Women and Income in the Third World*. Stanford: Stanford University Press, pp. 99–119.

—— (1999). 'NGOs: Are they a force for change?'. *Economic and Political Weekly*, 34(30): 24 July.

Mengistu, B. (1993). 'Parastatals', in J. Krieger (ed.), *The Oxford Companion to Politics of the World*. New York: Oxford University Press, pp. 682–5.

Mill, J. S. (1967). *Essays on Economics and Society: Volumes IV and V of the Collected Work of John Stuart Mill*. Toronto: University of Toronto Press.

Ministry of Agriculture and Fisheries (MAFF) (1964). *Farm Household Economic Survey*. Seoul, Korea: MAFF.

Ministry of Agriculture and Industry of Mongolia (1998). 'Mongolian agriculture and agro-industry'. Report published on the worldwide web (http://www.agriculture.mn/agroindustry.htm#2).

Moffatt, M. (1998). 'A gender analysis of community forestry and community leasehold forestry in Nepal with a macro-meso-micro framework'. MA Dissertation in Development Policy Analysis, Department of Economics and Social Studies, University of Manchester.

Mongolian Academy of Sciences (1990). B g d Nairamdah Mongol Ard Uls: šndesnii Atlas (Mongolian Peoples Republic: Basic Atlas), Ulaanbaatar, Mongolian Academy of Sciences publications.

Monroe, K. (1996). *The Heart of Altruism: Perception of a Common Humanity*. Princeton, NJ: Princeton University Press.

Montenegro, S. (1996). 'El papel de las regiones para la estabilidad macroeconómica de Colombia', in *Desarrollo y Sociedad* No. 38, CEDE, Facultad de Economia, Universidad de los Andes.

—— (1999). 'Estabilidad macroeconómica y el sistema político en Colombia', in M. Cardenas and S. Montenegro (eds), *Economia Política de las Finanzas Publicas en América Latina*. Bogota: Tercer Mundo-Fedesarrollo, pp. 171–86.

Montesquieu, C. L. (1748). *De L'esprit des Lois*. Paris: Garnier.

Montgomery, J. D. (1988). *Bureaucrats and People: Grassroots Participation in Third World Development*. Baltimore: Johns Hopkins.

Montoya-Aquilar, C. and Marchant-Cavieres, L. (1994). 'The effect of economic changes in health care and health in Chile'. *International Journal of Health Planning and Management*, 9: 279–94.

Moon, P. Y. (1984). 'Agricultural modernization and rural development'. *Rural Review*, 11(4): 59–60.

Moore, M. (1988). 'Economic growth and the rise of civil society: Agriculture in Taiwan and South Korea', in G. White (ed.), *Developmental States in East Asia*. New York: St. Martin's Press, pp. 113–52.

Morell, D. and Samudavinja, C. (1981). *Political Conflict in Thailand*. Cambridge, MA: Oelgeschlager, Gunn and Hain.

Morley, S. A. (1995). *Poverty and Inequality in Latin America: The Impact of Adjustment and Recovery in the 1980s*. Baltimore: Johns Hopkins University Press.

Morris and Adelman (1989). 'Nineteenth-century development experience and lessons for today'. *World Development*, 17(9): 1317–432.

Moser, C. (1996). *Confronting Crisis: A Comparative Study of Household Responses to Poverty and Vulnerability in Four Poor Urban Communities*. Washington DC: World Bank.

——(1998) 'The asset vulnerability framework: Re-assessing urban poverty reduction strategies'. *World Development*, 26(1): 1–19.

Mosley, P., Harrigan, J., and Toye, J. (1991). *Aid and Power*. London: Routledge.

Msamanga O. I., Urasa, D., and Mujinja, P. (1996). 'Equity of access to public, private not-for-profit and private for-profit health facilities in two regions in Tanzania'. Final Research Paper Submitted to UNICEF, mimeo. New York.

Mukerjee, R. and Roy, S. B. (1993). 'Influence of social institutions on women's participation in JFM: A case study from Sargarh, North Bengal'. Working Paper No. 17. Calcutta: IBRAD.

Mulhall, S. and Swift, A. (1992). *Liberals and Communitarians*. Oxford: Blackwell.

Mustafa, S. *et al.* (1995). 'Impact assessment study of BRAC's Rural Development programme, Final Report'. Dhaka: BRAC, Research and Evaluation Division.

Mwabu G. S., Mwanzia, J., and Liambila, W. (1995). 'User charges in government health facilities in Kenya: Effects on attendance and revenue'. *Health Policy and Planning*, 10(2): 164–70.

Nabli and Nugent (1989). 'The new institutional economics and its applicability to development'. *World Development*, 17(9): 1333–47.

Narain, U. (1994). 'Women's involvement in joint forest management: Analyzing the issues', draft paper, 6 May.

Narayan, D. and Pritchett, L. (1996). 'Cents and sociability: Household income and social capital in rural Tanzania'. *Environment Department and Policy Research Department*. Washington DC: World Bank.

Narayan, P. (1999). 'Bonds and bridges: Social capital and poverty'. *Poverty Group, PREM*, Washington DC: World Bank.

Narayana, D. (1999). 'Public expenditure reform without policy change: Infrastructure investment and health care service provision under fiscal squeeze in Kerala', in Mackintosh and Roy (eds), *Economic Decentralization and Public Management Reform*. Aldershot: Edward Elgar, pp. 106–21.

National Statistical Office of Mongolia, Mongol šlsyn Statistikiin Emhtgel, (Mongolian Statistical Yearbook) (1998). Ulaanbaatar, 1999.

Natrajan, I. (1995). 'Trends in firewood consumption in rural India'. *Margin*, 28(1): 41–5.

Newbrander, W., Collins, D., and Gilson, L. (1997). 'Equity in the provision of health care: Ensuring access of the poor to services under user fee systems'. Paper Presented at the Conference on Strengthening Health Care Financing: Recent developments and innovations, Harare, Zimbabwe.

Nichter, M. (1990). 'Vaccinations in South Asia: False expectations and commanding metaphors', in J. Coreil and J. D. Mull (eds), *Anthropology and Primary Health Care*. Boulder, CO: Westview Press, pp. 196–221.

Nolan, P. (1995). *China's Rise, Russia's Fall: Politics, Economics and Planning in the Transition from Stalinism*. Basingstoke and London: MacMillan.

Noponen, H. (1991). 'The dynamics of work and survival for urban poor: A gender analysis of panel data from Madras'. *Development and Change*, 22(2): 233–60.

Normand, C. (1999). 'Using social insurance to meet policy goals'. *Social Science and Medicine*, 48: 865–9.

North, D. (1989). 'Institutions and economic growth: An historical introduction'. *World Development*, 17(9): 1319–32.

—— (1990). *Institutions, Institutional Change and Economic Performance*. New York: Cambridge University Press.

Nugent, J. E. (1986). 'Applications of the theory of transactions costs and collective action to development problems and policy'. Paper for Cornell Conference on 'The Role of Institutions in Economic Development'. Ithaca: Cornell.

Nussbaum, M. C. (1997). 'Flawed foundations: The philosophical critique of a (particular) type of economics'. *University of Chicago Law Review*, 34(4): 1197–214.

Nyonator, F. and Kutzin, J. (1999). 'Health for some? The effects of user fees in the Volta region of Ghana'. *Health Policy and Planning*, 14(4): 329–41.

Oakley, A. (1994). *Classical Economic Man: Human Agency and Methodology in the Political Economy of Adam Smith and JS. Mill*. Aldershot: Edward Elgar.

Ocampo, J. A. (1989). 'La consolidación de la industria cafetera, 1930–1958', in A. Tirado Mejía (ed.), *Nueva Historia de Colombia*, vol 5. Bogota: Planeta, pp. 213–32.

Odgaard, O. (1996). 'Living standards and poverty', in O. Bruun and O. Odgaard (eds), *Mongolia in Transition: Old patterns, new challenges*. Nordic Institute of Asian Studies, Studies in Asian Topics, No. 22. Richmond, Surrey: Curzon Press pp. 103–34.

Offer, A. (1997). 'Between the gift and the market: The economy of regard'. *Economic History Review*, L(3): 450–76.

Olson, M. (1965). *The Logic of Collective Action*. Cambridge, MA: Harvard University Press.

—— (1997). 'La explotación de la agricultura'. Lecture given at the 70th Anniversary of the Colombian Coffee Federation, Medellin, July.

Oman, C. and Wigneraja, G. (1991). *The Postwar Evolution of Development Thinking*. London: Macmillan.

Oostendorp, R. (1995). *Adam Smith, Social Norm and Economic Behavior*. Harvard Doctoral Thesis.

O'Reilly, K. R., Mertens, T., Sethi, G., Bhutani, L., and Bandopadhyay, N. (1996). '*Evaluation of the Sonagachi Project, Calcutta: October 31st–November 14th, 1995*. Calcutta: British Council, 15 March.

Oshima, H. T. (1986). 'The transition from an agricultural to an industrial economy in East Asia'. *Economic Development and Cultural Change*, 34: 783–809.

—— (1987). *Economic Growth in Monsoon Asia: A Comparative Survey*. Tokyo: University of Tokyo Press.

Osorio, C. (1996). 'Cooperaçao Entre Pequenos Produtores: Casos do Nordeste Brasileiro'. Portuguese translation of unpublished PhD thesis, University College London, September 1990.

Ostrom, E. (1990). *Governing the Commons: The Evolution of Institutions for Collective Action*. New York: Cambridge University Press.

——(1996). 'Crossing the great divide: Coproduction, Synergy and Development'. *World Development*, 24: 1073–87.

——(1998). 'A behavioral approach to the rational choice theory of collective action'. *American Political Science Review*, 92(1): 1–22.

—— Gardner, R., and Walker, J. (1990). *Rules, Games, and Common-pool Resources*. Ann Arbor: University of Michigan Press.

Owen, R. (1817). *A New View of Society*. Reprinted 1963. London: Dent.

Palacios, M. (1980). *Coffee in Colombia, 1850–1970: An Economic, Social, and Political History*. Cambridge: Cambridge University Press.

Palma, G. (1978). 'Dependency: A formal theory of underdevelopment or a methodology for the analysis of concrete situations of underdevelopment?'. *World Development*, 6.

Pandey, S. (1990). 'Women in Hattidunde forest management in Dhading district, Nepal'. MPE Series No. 9, International Center for Integrated Mountain Development (ICIMOD), Kathmandu, Nepal.

Park, S. (1993). *A Study of the Banking Production Efficiency of the Primary Agricultural Cooperatives in Korea: A Cost Function Approach*. Unpublished PhD Dissertation. Columbus, OH: The Ohio State University.

Parlement Européen (1996). *Document de travail sur les accords internationaux de pêche*. Commission de pêche (written by P. Crampton), Brussels.

Patrick, H. (1994). 'Comparisons, contrasts and implications', in H. Patrick (ed.), *The Financial Development of Japan, Korea and Taiwan*. Oxford: Oxford University Press, pp. 325–71.

Patton, A. (1996). *Physicians, Colonial Raciosm and Diaspora in West Africa*. Miami: University Press of Florida.

Pearce, D. (1990). *Economics of Natural Resources and the Environment*. London: Harvester Wheatsheaf.

Peters, M. and Marshall, G. (1996). *Individualism and Community: Education and Social Policy in the Post-Modern Condition*. London: Falmer Press.

Peters, P. E. (ed), (2000) *Development Encounters: Sites of participation and Knowledge*. Cambridge MA: Harvard Institute for International Development.

Pettit, P. (1996). 'Institutional design and rational choice', in R. Goodin (ed.), *The Theory of Institutional Design*. Cambridge: Cambridge University Press, pp. 54–89.

Picciotto, R. (1992). *Participatory Development: Myths and Dilemmas*. World Bank Policy Research Working Papers, WPS 930. Washington, DC: World Bank.

Piketty, T. (1998). 'Self-fulfilling beliefs about social status'. *Journal of Public Economics*, 70: 115–32.

Platteau, J.-P. (1994). 'Behind the market stage where real societies exist: Part II, The role of moral norms'. *Journal of Development Studies*, 30: 3.

—— and Seki, E. (2001). 'Community arrangements to overcome market failures: Pooling groups in Japanese fisheries', in M. Aoki and Y. Hayami (eds), *Communities and Markets in Economic Development*. Oxford and New York: Oxford University Press, pp. 344–402.

Pitt, M. and Khandker S. R. (1996). 'Household and intrahousehold impact of the Grameen Bank and similar targeted credit programs in Bangladesh', Discussion Papers, 320. Washington DC: World Bank.

Polanyi, K. (1957). *The Great Transformation*. Boston: Beacon Press.

Prebisch, R. (1950). *The Economic Development of Latin America and its Principal Problems*. New York: United Nations.

——(1964). *Towards a New Trade Policy for Development*. Report by the Secretary General of UNCTAD. New York: United Nations.

Putnam, R. (1993*a*). *Making Democracy Work: Civic Traditions in Modern Italy*. Princeton: Princeton University Press.

——(1993*b*). 'The prosperous community: Social capital and public life'. *The American Prospect*, 13.

Putnam, R. D. (1995). 'Bowling alone: America's declining social capital'. *Journal of Democracy*, 6: 65–78.

——(2000). *Bowling Alone*. New York: Simon Schuster.

Rahman, R. I. (1986). 'Impact of Grameen Bank on the situation of poor rural women', Working Paper No 1, Grameen Bank Evaluation Project. Dhaka: Bangladesh Institute of Development Studies.

—— and Khandker S. R. (1994). 'Role of targeted credit programmes in promoting employment and productivity of the poor in Bangladesh', *Bangladesh Development Studies*, 22 (2–3), 49–92.

Raju, G., Vaghela, R., and Raju, M. S. (1993). *Development of People's Institutions for Management of Forests*. Ahmedabad: VIKSAT.

Raju, M. (1997). 'Seeking niches in forest canopy: An enquiry into women's participation', mimeographed report. Delhi: Ford Foundation.

Ranis, G. (1989). 'Macro policies, the terms of trade and the spatial dimension of balanced growth', in Nurul Islam (ed.), *The Balance Between Industry and Agriculture in Economic Development*. Hong Kong: MacMillan Press.

——(1993). 'Labor markets, human capital and development performance in East Asia'. Economic Growth Center Discussion Paper #697, Yale University.

——(1995). 'Another look at the East Asian miracle'. *World Bank Economic Review*, 9: 509–34.

—— and Stewart, F. (1993). 'Rural nonagricultural activities in development: Theory and application'. *Journal of Development Economics*, 40(1): 75–101.

Reed, E. (1979). *Group Farming in Smallholder Agriculture: Experience and Potential in South Korea*. Unpublished PhD dissertation. Madison, WI: University of Wisconsin.

Regmi, S. C. (1989). 'Female participation in forest resource management. A case study of a women's forest committee in a Nepalese village'. MSc dissertation in Social Development, Graduate School of the Ateneo de Manila University.

Republic of Korea (various issues). *Korea Statistical Yearbook*. Seoul: National Statistical Office.

Ricard, S. (1781). *Traité Général du Commerce*. Amsterdam: Chez E. van Harrevelt et Soeters.

Riddell, R. and Robinson, M. (1995). *Non-governmental Organisations and Rural Poverty Alleviation*. Oxford: Clarendon Press.

Robinson, M. (1997) 'Privatising the voluntary sector: NGOs as public service contractors?' in D. Hulme and M. Edwards (eds), *NGOs, States, and Donors: Too Close for Comfort?*. London: MacMillan Press, pp. 59–78.

Roemer, P. M. (1986). 'Increasing returns and long run growth'. *Journal of Political Economy*, 99.

Roy, S. B., Mukerjee, R., and Chatterjee, M. (*c*.1992). 'Endogenous development, gender role in participatory forest management'. Calcutta: IBRAD.

Russell, S. and Gilson, L. (1997). 'User fee policies to promote health service access for the poor: A wolf in sheep's clothing'. *International Journal of Health Services*, 27(2): 359–79.

Ruttan, V. W. (1989). 'Institutional innovation and agricultural development'. *World Development*, 17(9): 1375–87.

Sah, R. J. and Stiglitz, J. E. (1985). 'The social cost of labor and project evaluation: A general approach'. *Journal of Public Economics*, 28: 135–63.

Sahlins, M. D. (1972). *Stone Age Economics*. Chicago: Aldine Atherton.

Samuelson, P. (1938). 'A note on the pure theory of consumers behavior'. *Economica*, 5.

Sanjdorj, M. (1980). *Manchu Chinese Colonial Rule in Northern Mongolia*. London: C. Hurst and Co.

Sanyal, B. (1991). 'Antagonistic cooperation: A case study of non-governmental organizations, government, and donors relationships in income-generating projects in Bangladesh'. *World Development*, 19(10): 1367–79.

Sarin, M. (1995). 'Regenerating India's forest: Reconciling gender equity and joint forest management'. *IDS Bulletin*, 26(1): 83–91.

—— (1998). Who is gaining? Who is losing? Gender and equality concerns in joint forest management. New Delhi: Society for Promotion of Wasteland Development.

Sauerborn, R., Nougtara, A., and Latimer, E. (1994). 'The elasticity of demand for health care in Burkina Faso: Differences across age and income groups'. *Health Policy and Planning*, 9(2): 185–92.

—— Adams, A., and Hien, M. (1996). 'Household strategies to cope with the economic costs of illness'. *Social Science and Medicine*, 43(3): 291–301.

—— Nougtara, A., and Diesfeld, H. J. (1989), 'Low utilisation of community health workers: Results from a household interview survey in Burkina Faso'. *Social Science and Medicine*, 29(10): 1163–74.

Schotter, A. (1981). *Economic Theory and Social Institutions*. Cambridge: Cambridge University Press.

Scitovsky, T. (1985). 'Economic development in Taiwan and South Korea: 1965–81'. *Food Research Institute Studies*, 19: 214–64.

Seabright, P. (1993). 'Managing local commons: Theoretical issues in incentive design'. *Journal of Economic Perspectives*, 17: 4.

—— (1997). 'Is co-operation habit-forming', in P. Dasgupta and K.-G. Mäler (eds), *The Environment and Emerging Development Issues*, vol. 2. Oxford: Clarendon Press, pp. 283–307.

Seeley, J. (1996). 'Who benefits from participatory forest management'. *Banko Janakari*, 6(1): 38–9.

Seers, D. (1971). 'Employment mission to Colombia', in R. Robinson and O. Johnston (eds), *Prospects for Employment in the Nineteen Seventies*. London: HMSO, pp. 28–31.

Sehgal, S. (2001). *Joint Forest Management: A Decade and Beyond*. Paper Presented at the Workshop on Policy Implications of Knowledge with Respect to Common Pool Resources in India. The Institute of Economic Growth, Delhi, 14 September.

Semboja, J. and Rutasitara, L. (1999). 'Poverty, growth, inequality and the role of government in poverty alleviation in Tanzania'. Report Presented at a Workshop on Poverty, Income Distribution and Labour Market Issues in Sub-Saharan Africa, Accra, Ghana.

Sen, A. (1973). 'Behaviour and the Concept of Preference'. *Economica*, 40: 241–59.

—— (1977). 'Rational fools: A critique of the behavioural foundations of economic theory'. *Philosophy and Public Affairs*, 6: 317–44.

—— (1982). *Choice, Welfare and Measurement*. Oxford: Blackwell.

—— (1982). 'Rational fools: A critique of the behavioral foundations of economic theory', in A. Sen, *Choice, Welfare and Measurement*. Oxford: Basil Blackwell, pp. 84–106.

—— (1985). *Commodities and Capabilities*. Amsterdam: Elsevier Science Publishing.

—— (1985). 'Goals, commitment and identity'. *Journal of Law, Economics and Organisation*, 1–2: 341–55.

—— (1987). *On Ethics and Economics*. New York: Basil Blackwell.

—— (1990). 'Gender and cooperative conflicts', in I. Tinker (ed.), *Persistent Inequalities*. Oxford and New York: Oxford University Press, pp. 123–49.

—— (1992). 'Social need and public accountability: The case of Kerala', in M. Wuyts, M. Mackintosh, and T. Hewitt (eds), *Development Policy and Public Action*. Oxford: Oxford University Press with the Open University, pp. 253–77.

—— (1993). 'Internal consistency of choice', *Econometrica*, 61(3), pp. 495–521.

—— (1994*a*). *Economic Wealth and Moral Sentiments*. Lecture held for Bank Hofmann AG, Zurich, April.

—— (1994*b*). 'The formulation of rational choice'. *American Economic Review, AEA Papers and Proceedings*, 84(2): 385–90.

—— (1995). 'Is the idea of purely internal consistency of choice bizarre?', in J. Altham and R. Harrison (eds), *World, Mind and Ethics: Essays on the Ethical Philosophy of Bernard Williams*. Cambridge: Cambridge University Press, pp. 19–31.

—— (1997*a*). 'Economics, business principles and moral sentiments'. *Business Ethics Quarterly*, 7(3): 5–15.

—— (1997*b*). 'Maximisation and the act of choice'. *Econometrica*, 65(4): 745–79.

—— (1999), *Reason before Identity*. Romanes Lecture for 1998. Oxford: Oxford University Press.

—— (1999). *Development as Freedom*. Oxford: Oxford University Press.

Sen, B. (2001). 'Poverty reduction and graduation: Emerging trends from PKSF-supported MFIs', in *Monitoring and Evaluation of Micro-finance Institutions*, (mimeo). Dhaka: Bangladesh Institute of Development Studies.

Shah, A. (1997). 'Jurisdiction versus equity: Tale of two villages'. *Wastelands News*, Feb.–April, 1997, 5863.

Shah, M. K. and Shah, P. (1995). 'Gender, environment and livelihood security: An alternative viewpoint from India'. *IDS Bulletin*, 26(1): 75–82.

Sharma, A. and Sinha, A. (1993). 'A study of the common property resources in the project area of the Central Himalaya rural action group', mimeo. Indian Institute of Forest Management, Bhopal, Madhya Pradesh.

Sharma, M. and Zeller, M. (1998). 'Repayment performance in group-based credit programs in Bangladesh: An empirical analysis', mimeo. Food Consumption and Nutrition Division, IFPRI, Washington.

Sheehy, D. (1996). 'Sustainable livestock use of pastoral resources', in Bruun and Odgaard (eds), *Mongolia in Transition: Old Pattern and New Challenges*. Richmond, Surrey: Curzon.

Shen, T. (1970). *The Sino-American Joint Commission on Rural Development: Twenty Years of Cooperation for Agricultural Development*. Ithaca, NY: Cornell University Press.

Shin, G. (1996). 'The history making of collective action: The Korean peasant uprisings of 1946'. *American Journal of Sociology*, 99(6): 1596–625.

Sikkink, K. (1991). *Ideas and Institutions: Developmentalism in Brazil and Argentina*. Ithaca: Cornell University Press.

Simon, H. (1982). *Models of Bounded Rationality*. Cambridge, MA: MIT Press.

Simukov, A. D. (1933). ' 'Hotoni' (Hotons) in Sovrennaya Mongoliya'. *Contemporary Mongolia*, 3: 19–32).

Singh, A. and Burra, N. (eds) (1993). *Women and Wasteland Development in India*. New Delhi: Sage Publications.

Singh, N. and Kumar, K. (1993). 'Community initiatives to protect and manage forests in Balangir and Sambalpur districts', mimeo. New Delhi: SIDA.

Singh, P. (1997). *'Sethbagane Mahila Sangha gorey othar suchana [The origin and development of the Mahila Sangha in Sethbagan]*, Souvenir of the First National Conference of Sex Workers, 14–16 November, 1997, Calcutta*. Calcutta: DMSC.

Smillie, I. (1995). *The Alms Bazaar: Altruism under Fire—Non-Profit Organizations and International Development*. London: Intermediate Technology Publications.

Smith, A. (1759). *The Theory of Moral Sentiments*, London: printed for A. Miller in the Strand, and A. Kincard and J. Bell in Edinburgh.

Smith, A. (1776). *An Inquiry into the Nature and Causes of The Wealth of Nations*. London: W. Strathan and T. Caldwell.

—— (1880). *The Wealth of Nations*, 2nd edn. Oxford: Clarendon Press.

—— (1937). *Wealth of Nations*. New York: Modern Library.

Sneath, D. (1999). 'Spatial mobility and Inner Asian pastoralism', chapter 6 of C. Humphrey and D. Sneath, *The End of Nomadism? Society, State and the Environment in Inner Asia*, Durham NC: Duke University Press.

Sneath, D. (2000). *Changing Inner Mongolia: Pastoral Mongolian Society and the Chinese State*. Oxford: Oxford University Press.

Sorensen, C. (1988). *Over the Mountains are Mountains: Korean Peasant Households and Their Adaptations to Rapid Industrialisation*. Seattle, WA: University of Washington Press.

SPWD (1994). *Joint Forest Management Update, 1993*. New Delhi: Society for Promotion of Wastelands Development.

Standing, H. (1992). 'Aids: Conceptual and methodological issues in researching sexual behaviour in Sub-Saharan Africa'. *Social Science and Medicine*, 34(5): 475–83.

Statistical Office of Mongolia (1993). Mongolyn Ediin Zasag, Niigem 1992 (Mongolian Economy and Society in 1992). Ulaanbaatar: J. L. D. Gurval.

Stavis, B. (1974). *Rural Local Governance and Agricultural Development in Taiwan*. Special Series on Rural Local Government, RLG No. 15. Ithaca, NY: Rural Development Committee, Cornell University.

—— (1982). 'Rural local governance and agricultural development in Taiwan', in N. T. Uphoff (ed.), *Rural Development and Local Organisation in Asia*. Delhi: Macmillan.

Steele, F., S. Amin and R. T. Naved (1998). 'The impact of an integrated micro-credit program on women's empowerment and fertility behaviour in rural Bangladesh', Working Paper no. 115. New York: Population Council, Policy Research Division.

Stewart, F. (1996). 'Groups for good or ill'. *Oxford Development Studies*, 24(1): 9–25.

—— and Berry, A. (1999). 'Globalisation, liberalisation and inequality: Expectations and experience', in A. Hurrell and N. Woods (eds), *Inequality, Globalization and World Politics*. Oxford: Oxford University Press, pp. 150–86.

Stiglitz, J. E. (1990). 'Peer monitoring and credit markets'. *The World Bank Economic Review*, 4(3): 351–66.

Stiglitz, J. E. and Weiss, A. (1981).'Credit rationing in markets with imperfect information'. *American Economic Review*, 71: 393–410.

—— (1989). 'Markets, market failures and development'. *American Economic Review*, 79(2)

—— (1991). 'The invisible hand and modern welfare economics'. *NBER Working Paper Series*, 3641.

Stone, L. (1992). 'Cultural influences in community participation in health'. *Social Science and Medicine*, 35(4): 409–17.

Streeten, P. and Associates (1981). *First Things First, Meeting Basic Human Needs in Developing Countries*. New York: Oxford University Press.

Sugden, R. (1986). *The Economics of Rights, Cooperation and Welfare*. Oxford: Blackwell.

Swedberg, R. and Granovetter, M. (1992). *The Sociology of Economic Life*. Oxford: Westview Press.

Tata Energy Research Institute (TERI) (1995). 'Community participation in van panchayats of Kumaon region of Uttar Pradesh'. Paper No. 1, Part I. Delhi: TERI.

Taylor, C. and Hudson, M. C. (1972). *World Handbook of Political and Social Indicators*. New Haven, CT: Yale University Press.

Taylor, M. (1987). *The Possibility of Cooperation*. Cambridge: Cambridge University Press.

Tendler, J. (1983). 'What to think about co-operatives: A guide from Bolivia', in Peter Hakim (ed.), *Direct to the Poor: Grassroots Development in Latin America*. Boulder, CO and London: Rienner, pp. 85–116.

—— (1997). *Good Government in the Tropics*. Baltimore: Johns Hopkins Press.

Thaler, R. (1980). 'Towards a positive theory of consumer choice'. *Journal of Economic Behaviour and Organisation*, 1.

Therkildsen, O. and Semboja, J. (1995). 'A new look at service provision in East Africa', in O. Therkildsen and J. Semboja (eds), *Service Provision Under Stress in East Africa*. London: James Currey, pp. 1–34.

Thill, E. E. *et al.* (1998). 'On how task-contingent rewards, individual differences in causality orientations, and imagery abilities are related to intrinsic motivation and performance'. *European Journal of Social Psychology*, 28(4): 483–507.

Thorp, R. (1998). *Progress, Poverty and Exclusion: An Economic History of Latin America in the 20th Century*. Washington, DC: Interamerican Development Bank and Baltimore: Johns Hopkins Press.

—— (1991). *Economic Management and Economic Development in Peru and Colombia*. Basingstoke: Macmillan.

Tibandebage, P. (1999). 'Charging for health care in Tanzania: Official pricing in a liberalized environment', in Mackintosh and Roy (eds), *Decentralization and Public Management Reform*. Aldershot: Edward Elgar, pp. 176–201.

—— and Mackintosh, M. (forthcoming). 'Inclusion by design? Rethinking health care market regulation in the Tanzanian context'. *Journal of Development Studies*.

—— Semboja, H., Mujinja, P., and Ngonyani, H. (2001). 'Private sector development: A case of private health facilities'. *ESRF Discussion Paper Series* No. 26, Dar es Salaam, April.

Tirole, J. (1996). 'A theory of collective reputations with applications to the persistence of corruption and to firm quality'. *The Review of Economic Studies*, 63(214): 1–22.

Titmuss, R. (1970). *The Gift Relationship*. London: Allen and Unwin.

Todd, H. (1996). *Women at the Centre: Grameen Bank Borrowers After One Decade*. Boulder, CO: Westview Press.

Toye, J. (1992). 'Interest group politics and the implementation of adjustment policies in Sub-Saharan Africa'. *Journal of International Development*, 4: 183–98.

Trumper, R. and Phillips, L. (1996). 'Give me discipline and give me death: Neoliberalism and health in Chile'. *Race and Class*, 37(3): 19–34.

Tserendash, S. and Erdenebaatar, B. (1993). 'Performance and management of natural pasture in Mongolia'. *Nomadic Peoples*, 33: 9–15.

Turner, J. C. (1987). *Rediscovering the Social Group: A Self-Categorization Theory*. Oxford: Basil Blackwell.

Tversky, A. and Kahneman, D. (1981). 'The framing of decisions and the psychology of choices'. *Science*, 211: 453–8.

UNDP (United Nations Development Programme) (1995). *Human Development Report 1995*. New York: United Nations.

—— (1997). *Human Development Report, Mongolia 1997*. Ulaanbaatar.

—— (1990). *Human Development Report 1990*. New York: Oxford University Press.

—— (1998). *Human Development Report 1998*. New York: Oxford University Press.

—— (1999). *Human Development Report 1999*. New York: Oxford University Press.

UNICEF (1995). *Terms of Reference for the UCBHCA to Implement the Community Capacity Building Process*, mimeo.

United Nations (1992). *World Investment Report 1992: Transnational Corporations as Engines of Growth*. New York: United Nations.

United Nations Systems in Mongolia (1999). Annual Report 1998, Report published on the internet (http://www.un-mongolia.mn/publications/anrep98.pdf).

United States Embassy (1999). 'Embassy cable, Subject: IMI: Mongolia shows signs of economic growth: 1998 statistics compiled'. Report published on the internet (http://us-mongolia.com/general/economy.html).

Upadhyay, S. and Jeddere-Fisher, K. (1998). 'An analysis of community forestry characteristics in the Dhaulagiri hills'. Nepal–UK Community Forestry Project, Report N/NUKCFP/09, Kathmandu.

Uphoff, N. (1993). 'Grassroots organisations and NGOs in rural development: Opportunities with diminishing states and expanded markets'. *World Development*, 21: 607–22.

Van den Brink, R. and Chavas, J.-P. (1997). 'The microeconomics of an indigenous African institution: The rotating savings and credit association'. *Economic Development and Cultural Change*, 45(4): 743–72.

Van Koppen, B. and Mahmud, S. (1996). *Women and Water-pumps in Bangladesh: The Impact of Participation in Irrigation Groups on Women's Status*. London: Intermediate Technology Publications.

Vanberg, V. (1994). *Rules and Choice in Economics*. London: Routledge.

Vaughan, M. (1991). *Curing their Ills: Colonial Power and African Illness*. Cambridge: Polity Press.

—— (1994). 'Healing and curing: Issues in the social history and anthropology of medicine in Africa'. *The Society for the Social History of Medicine*, 7(2): 283–95.

Viegas, P. and Menon, G. (1993). 'Bringing government and people together: Forest protection committees of West Bengal—Role and Participation of Women', in A. Singh and N. Burra (eds), *Women and Wasteland Development in India*. New Delhi: Sage Publications, pp. 171–210.

Vogel, R. J. (1990). 'An analysis of three national health insurance proposals in sub-Saharan Africa'. *International Journal of Health Planning and Management*, 5: 271–85.

von Ginneken, W. (1995). 'Employment promotion and the social safety-net', in K. Griffin (ed.), *Poverty and the Transition to a Market Economy in Mongolia*. New York: St Martin's Press, pp. 45–62.

Von Hippel, E. (1987). 'Co-operation between rivals: Informal know-how trading'. *Research Policy*, 16(6): 291–302.

Wade, R. Personal communication (fall 1993).

—— (1982). *Irrigation and Agricultural Politics in South Korea*. Boulder, CO: Westview Press.

—— (1985). 'Common property resource management in South Indian villages', ch. 13 of the *Proceedings of the Conference on Common Property Resource Management*, 21–26 April.

—— (1988). *Village Republics: Economic Conditions for Collective Action in South India*. Cambridge: Cambridge University Press.

—— (1990). *Governing the Market*. Princeton: Princeton University Press.

Walraven, G. (1996). 'Willingness to pay for district hospital services in rural Tanzania'. *Health Policy and Planning*, 11(4): 428–37.

Walt, G. (ed.) (1990). *Community Health Workers in National Programmes: Just Another Pair of Hands?* Milton Keynes: Open University Press.

Warren, B. (1980). *Imperialism: Pioneer of Capitalism*. London: New Left Books.

Wells, M. (1981). 'Success in whose terms? Evaluation of a co-operative farm'. *Human Organization*, 40(3): 239–46.

Werhane, P. (1991). *Adam Smith and His Legacy: Modern Capitalism*. Oxford: Oxford University Press.

Werner, D. (1981). 'The village health worker: Lackey or liberator?' *World Health Forum*, 2(1): 46–54.

White, G. and Robinson, M. (1998). 'Towards synergy in social provision: Civic organisations and the state', in M. Minogue, C. Polidano, and D. Hulme (eds), *Beyond the New Public Management, Changing Ideas and Practice in Governance*. Cheltenham: Edward Elgar.

Whyte, S. R. (1992). 'Pharmaceuticals as folk medicine: Transformations in social relations of health care in Uganda'. *Culture, Medicine and Psychiatry*, 16: 163–86.

Wiggins, D. (1980). 'Weakness of will, commensurability and the objects of deliberation and desire', in A. Rorty (ed.), *Essays on Aristotle's Ethics*. Berkeley; London: University of California Press, pp. 241–66.

Wilkins, A. and Ouchi, W. (1983). 'Efficient cultures: Exploring the relationship between culture and organisational performance'. *Administrative Science Quarterly*, 28: 468–81.

Williams, D. M. (1996). 'Grassland enclosures: Catalyst of land degradation in Inner Mongolia'. *Human Organisation*, 55(3): 307–13.

Williams, F. (1989). 'Social policy'. *A Critical Introduction: Issues of Race, Gender and Class*. Cambridge: Polity Press.

Williamson, J. (ed.) (1990). *Latin American Adjustment: How much has Happened*. Washington DC: Institute for International Economics.

—— (1990). 'What Washington means by policy reform', in Williamson (ed.). *op. cit.*

Williamson, O. (1975). *Markets and Hierarchies: Analysis and Antitrust Implications: A Study in the Economics of Internal Organisation*. New York: The Free Press.

Williamson O. E. (1985). *The Economic Institutions of Capitalism: Firms, Markets, Relational Contracting*, New York: Free Press; London: Collier MacMillan.

Wilson, H. (1977). *The Imperial Experience in SubSaharan Africa Since 1870*. Minneapolis: University of Minneapolis Press.

World Bank (1990). *Report on Adjustment Lending II: Policies for the Recovery of Growth*. Washington DC: World Bank.

—— (1993). *World Development Report*. Washington: World Bank.

—— (1993). *The East Asian Miracle: Economic Growth and Public Policy*. New York: Oxford University Press.

—— (1993). *Uganda: Growing out of Poverty*. Washington DC: World Bank.

World Bank (1994) *Mongolia: Country Economic Memorandum; Priorities in Macroeconomic Management.* Report No. 13612-MOG. Country Operations Division, China and Mongolia Department, Asia and Pacific Regional Office.

——(1995). *Uganda: The Challenge of Growth and Poverty Reduction.* Washington DC: World Bank.

——(1995). *India: Policy and Finance Strategies for Strengthening Primary Health Care Services.* Report No. 13042-IN. World Bank Population and Human Resources Division, South Asia Country Department II (Bhutan, India, Nepal).

——(1996). *Health Policy in Eastern Africa: A Structural Approach to Resource Allocation,* vols. I–IV. Nairobi, East Africa Department, Africa Region, World Bank.

——(1997). *World Development Report. The State in a Changing World.* Washington: World Bank.

——(1997). 'Social capital: The missing link', in *Monitoring Environmental Progress: Expanding the Measure of Wealth,* Environment Department, Washington DC: World Bank.

——(1997). *Chile: Poverty and Income Distribution in a High-Growth Economy 1987–1995.* Washington DC: World Bank.

——(1998/9). *World Development Report: Knowledge for Development.* Washington: World Bank and Oxford University Press.

——(1999). *World Development Report 1998/99: Knowledge for Development.* New York and Oxford: Oxford University Press.

——and UNDP (1989). *Africa's Adjustment and Growth in the 1980s.* Washington DC: World Bank.

Yager, J. A. (1988). *Transforming Agriculture in Taiwan: The Experience of the Joint Commission on Rural Reconstruction.* Ithaca: Cornell University Press.

Yang, B.-M. (1996). 'The role of health insurance in the growth of the private health sector in Korea'. *International Journal of Health Planning and Management,* 11: 321–252.

Yang, C. K. (1979). 'Republic of Korea', in Asian Productivity Organisation (ed.), *Fertiliser Distribution in Selected Asian Countries.* Tokyo: Asian Productivity Organisation, pp. 104–16.

Young, C. (1994). *The African Colonial State in Comparative Perspective.* New Haven: Yale.

Yunus, M. (1983). 'Group-based savings and credit for the rural poor', Paper presented at the Inter-Country Workshop on Group-Based Savings and Credit for the Rural Poor. Bogra, November 1983.

Zakus, J. D. L. and Lysack, C. L. (1998). 'Review article: Revisiting community Participation'. *Health Policy and Planning,* 13(1): 1–12.

Zasagyn Gazar Medeel (Official Mongolian Government Newspaper). Various issues. Ulaanbaatar: State Publishing House.

Zohir, S. (2001). 'Impact of micro-finance on rural employment' in *Monitoring and Evaluation of Micro-finance Institutions,* (mimeo). Dhaka: Bangladesh Institute of Development Studies.

Index